Currents in Communication

Textbook ⟩ Reader ⟩ Notebook

Elliot King ⟩ Russell Cook ⟩ Mitchell Tropin

Loyola University Maryland

Kendall Hunt
publishing company

Cover image credits:
Front cover: © Shutterstock, Inc.
Back cover:
      Top image: © Shutterstock, Inc.
      Middle image: clock, silhouette, leaves, and hammer photos—Russell J. Cook
              Obama and map photos—© Shutterstock, Inc.
      Bottom image: Russell J. Cook

Kendall Hunt

publishing company

www.kendallhunt.com
Send all inquiries to:
4050 Westmark Drive
Dubuque, IA 52004-1840

Copyright © 2010 by Kendall Hunt Publishing Company

ISBN 978-0-7575-7699-7

Printed in the United States of America
10 9 8 7 6 5 4 3 2 1

Contents

Preface

The vast proliferation of the media—communications technologies and the meaningful content they transmit—are the defining characteristics of our lives today. If people tried to note every time they encounter some content distributed over any communication medium, the task would be virtually impossible. We are enveloped in a mediated environment that shapes every part of our lives.

This book is intended to serve as a foundational text for students who plan to major in communication for their undergraduate education. It has five primary educational objectives that correspond with the five major elements of the book. The goals of the text are to

- motivate to think deeply and broadly about the study of communication,

- introduce students to ideas about the impact of communication on society,

- explore the basic concepts associated with media production,

- describe the opportunities associated with a career in media, and

- help students become more aggressive readers.

Required Reading: In "Reading as an Act of Creation," one of the authors of this book, Elliot King, makes a compelling case that engaging with what you are reading as if you are in a dialogue with the author is a way to make reading more informative, and more enjoyable by giving the readership a sense of ownership of the work. He also explains how highlighting the text and making notes in the margins, in essence, creates a whole new document with the reader as co-author. To illustrate this approach, the pages of the Required Reading are marked and annotated in the manner he recommends.

Media convergence has been one of the most significant developments of modern communications. As the world moves towards computer-based communication networks—in the guise of computers themselves, smart phones such as Apple's iPhone and Research in Motion's Blackberry smart phones and cell phones using Google's Android mobile operating system, or tablet computers such as the iPad—the lines between different channels of communication are blurring. Journalism no longer is confined to print or broadcast. Advertising and public relations increasingly are concerned with the use of social media. All sorts of content can be mediated in all sorts of different ways.

To address this profound change, **Currents in Communication** is not arranged in the typical fashion used by most introductory textbooks. Instead of organizing each chapter around a medium—newspapers, broadcasting, movies, etc.—or a professional activity—journalism, public relations, advertising, music, etc.—the book is organized topically and focused on key knowledge that all communication students should know, regardless of the specific media industry they might want to enter or even if they don't wish ultimately to become communication professionals. The siloed approach to media industries is fading rapidly in the real world. As a result, for example, the field of public relations is addressed in this book in the opening chapter about prominent people in communication industries, in the chapter on communication and the marketplace, in the chapter on media industries, in the chapter on media careers, and in the chapter about new opportunities in the media.

To achieve its learning aims, the book is divided into four major sections with each section having three or four chapters. Each major section addresses one of the learning aims. The first section, for example, called "Thinking about Communication" is designed to introduce students to the academic study of communication. In the second section, "The Impact of Communication" looks at the role the media played in politics, the marketplace, entertainment and building community. The third section, "Producing and Consuming Media," examines general and theoretical issues associated with creating and understanding media content; chapters cover topics such as media aesthetics and media literacy. The final section explores the characteristics of different media industries and career opportunities those industries offer.

To achieve the last learning aim—to teach students to be more aggressive readers—each chapter is paired with a related reading. The readings are drawn either from the academic literature on the subject of the chapter or from some other outside source. On the bottom of the pages of the required readings are blank lines for notes made by the reader. The use of the notes area is demonstrated on the required reading for this preface. The reading discusses how to be a more active and aggressive reader. Reading, in our view, should not be a passive activity. When students read, they should enter into a dialogue with the author.

Each chapter is organized in the same way that this preface is organized. The subject of the chapter is introduced and then the chapter's learning aims are listed. The learning aims are immediately followed by a description of the required reading for the chapter. The idea is that students should read the chapter text first. The knowledge and insight gained from that effort should deepen their understanding of the required reading, which immediately follows.

Currents in Communication will provide students with a strong base from which they can further pursue the study of communication, giving them the knowledge they need to better understand the media both as consumers and producers of mediated content. To that end, we feel that engagement with this material will play an important role in students' educational experience whether or not they ultimately become media professionals.

The media define the environment in which we live. To engage in the world means to engage, in large part, with the media. **Currents in Communication** represents a first step in enabling students to pursue that engagement in a richer and more informed way.

Reading as an Act of Creation

[margin note: ???]

By Elliot King

In the wake of the explosive growth in the popularity of video games and the World Wide Web, interactive media has been touted as the way increase viewers interest in whatever is being presented. As opposed to television, movies, and reading—which are widely seen as passive activities in which viewers and readers sit back and absorb the content being provided—with interactive media, people must respond physically, usually by clicking a game controller or a mouse, to engage in the experience. The combination of "viewing and doing, clicking and scrolling" is thought to make the material more compelling and better able to hold the player's or user's attention. Since people must respond to keep the experience moving forward, they also must play closer attention to what they are doing. And for anyone who has ever tried to make a 13-year-old boy stop playing a video game and start reading a book, the argument seems to have a lot of merit. *[margin note: like my father]*

With that in mind, the television industry and movie producers have tried to make their content more interactive too, providing viewers with the possibility to make choices. In television, those efforts have taken on several forms ranging from texting in votes on different reality contest shows such as *American Idol* to allowing viewers to buy items they see in a television show immediately. With movies, the efforts have come largely when they are distributed on DVDs, although in the summer of 2010, the movie musical *Grease* was released along with a campaign to get the audience to sing along with the movie. The thought was to make the show more interactive. On *[margin note: literal def.]* balance, to a large extent, the experiments with interactivity have done little to enhance the television- or movie-watching experience. *[margin note: IMAX interactive?]*

*[margin notes: !!! / #1 / *]* Reading is a different story. The idea that reading should be a passive experience is wrong. Good reading should be an active experience and, in most cases, it should be an interactive experience. The best readers, and the readers who ultimately learn and

NOTES

Context for reading: the latest electronic media

graphs 1&2 = intro = media context

Perhaps understating how people can respond strongly emotionally or intellectually to movies or TV, even if no specific action.

Main Thesis? Throwback?

retain the most from what they read, often see themselves in a dialogue with the author of whatever it is that they are reading. Interacting with what you are reading leads to better understanding, insight, and a sense of "ownership" of the material.

The idea that printed text is "passive" material comes, at least in part, from the way we are taught to read. An important pre-step in teaching young children to read is reading to them. Reading to young children is critical in building in them a love of books. But being read to is the ultimate in passive experiences. The young child is expected to sit quietly and listen. Most readers do not ask children questions mid-story, if at all. Interestingly, many children have the ability to sustain interest and to listen to someone reading to them. Many, however, love to turn the page, or otherwise interact with the book itself.

The next step in the process of learning to read comes in the early grades in school. The emphasis at this stage is learning how to decode words (either through phonetics or whole words, it makes no difference), to understand the words associated with the letters and how those words form sentences. Once again, this is largely a passive activity. From time to time, young students will be asked to read out loud either to the teacher or to a whole class. This is not interactivity; this is performance. Many readers, both young and old, uncomfortable with either their reading or performance skills feel very uncomfortable reading aloud.

Too often, the final step in learning to read is comprehension. Once a student can decode words and sentences, the primary challenge is to understand the material. For most students, by the time they reach middle school, the entire focus of reading is comprehension—what have you learned from what you have read? In literature classes, teaching comprehension consists of breaking texts down into their constituent parts—plot, characters, tone, style, mood, word choice, etc. The thought is that through an analysis of the parts, an understanding of the whole, along with a more fundamental understanding of the story, will emerge.

Many commonly used active reading strategies revolve around understanding literature. One widely circulated approach calls for students to visualize, clarify, question, predict, connect, and evaluate. That can be a good approach for fiction and even poetry. But does visualizing what the author of an academic article is trying to say help? Can it even be done?

Instruction in the reading and comprehension of nonfiction is often minimal. The techniques used for improving the understanding of fiction are generally not entirely relevant. Instead, students are given an article or a book and instructed to extract the most important information from it. The expectation seems to be that since they can decode words and sentences, they should be able to understand the meaning of an entire article or book.

#2 PASSIVE

#3

NONE !!!

!!!

NOTES

"Steps" uses here like an outline

Academic/nonfiction ≠ lit. class

MAIN POINT #3: H.S. English didn't prepare me for college reading.

The problem is that, taken as a whole, except for works written by the most entertaining authors, much of the material we have to read in school and in life is pretty boring. Not infrequently, it takes a lot of effort just to read the words, and, because of the way we are taught to read—which primarily focuses on decoding—if those words don't trigger our imaginations in some profound way the process becomes very tedious very quickly. For many, even the great works of literature are pretty dull to read. Have you ever tried to read *Moby Dick* by Herman Melville or *Ulysses* by James Joyce? If you have, you know what I mean. *Ulysses* was named the most important novel of the 20th Century in a poll conducted by the Modern Library publishing company but I doubt that one person in 10,000 can read it outside the context of an English seminar. For many people, classic literature serves best as a fast-acting sedative. Most academic writing and writing on specialized topics is even worse.

Reading, however, should not be conceptualized as simply trying to extract information or to comprehend what has been read. The reading experience is richer, fuller and more engrossing when the reader enters into a dialogue with the author through the words on the page. Reading is not a one-way process in which the reader tries to absorb content. Reading should be a two-way process in which a deeper understanding of the text is developed though responding, questioning, and challenging the text, as well as associating the material with other aspects of your experiences.

The first step in turning the reading process into a dialogue is identifying what the whole book or article generally is about. Whenever you enter into a conversation, you have a general idea about the subject or topic of the conversation. When reading non-fiction, you can usually get a sense of the article or book by reading the abstract, preface, prologue or introduction as well as the section headings, if there are section headings, or the table of contents. If a piece lacks these signals concerning its content, skimming the book or article first is usually helpful. This is sometimes called inspectional reading.

Margin annotations:

*

actually liked hat book! Call me ishmael.

AMEN !!!

*

#4 –

would be easier

Not cheating?!

Tile ought to be hint.

!!! test term

NOTES

Evidence:

—School reading boring.

—They do ask us our opinion.

What's the link between boring to read and difficult to read?

We see how this book measures up!

don't be boring.***

MAIN PT. #4—talk to author as you read. Sounds nice but difficult.

What if I don't know as much as the author?

HOW TO DO IT STEP 1 – Scope out the reading.

other hints: pictures, blurbs, as a friend, Google search

#4–2

The second step is reading closely in order to target the writer's main points. As you are reading, you want to locate the main arguments in the text and the evidence that supports those points. Underlining or highlighting the main points and the supporting detail or evidence can be helpful for retention.

#5

＊

Unfortunately, for many students, if they underline key points at all, they stop at that step. Their articles and books are filled with underlined or highlighted passages. In my own experience, when I reread the passages I have underlined or highlighted, I frequently find that I have marked the same idea over and over again or I have forgotten why I marked those passages in the first place.

That's me!

While underlining is useful, there are other ways to mark passages of interest in a text. Some people use double lines in the margin. Others use asterisks marks, with a greater number of asterisks noting a great interest in the passage.

Underlining or the other markings you might use should serve as the launching point for the next step in turning reading

#4–3

into a dialogue, which is determining the structure of the argument and being able to summarize it. It can be helpful to number each major point the writer makes as well as the evidence the author uses to support those points. In essence, you are superimposing an outline onto the article or book chapter. At the end of each section of the "outline," you should try to summarize the arguments as you understand them.

!!!

The process to this point can be compared to listening closely to the text. What is the text telling you? But when all you do is listen, it is like hearing a lecture, not engaging in a dialogue. And it is often hard to give your complete attention to a long and complicated lecture. In addition to listening to the text, you must talk back to it to be really engaged. In "talking" back to the text, you can ask yourself a series of questions. The first question is what passages do you find confusing or do you simply don't understand? Are those passages critical to understanding the overall argument or content of the book? If they are, what do you need to learn or do to understand them?

＊   #6

#6–1

NOTES

HOW TO DO IT STEP 2 – Underline main points.

HELPFUL:

1) Marking on page is active.

2) Remember faster when rereading because of marks.

MAIN PT. #5: Most students simply underline and forget it.

Texting shorthand?

HOW TO DO IT STEP 3: Outline & summarize

Show's structure of author's arguments.

MAIN PT. #6 Have to talk back.

But let's assume you can efficiently decode the material—you do understand it a basic level. The next question is: do you agree with the arguments? Do you think the author is right or wrong? Do you think the evidence the author provides, in fact, supports the point being made? In other words, you must evaluate the material.

#6–2

Evaluation is a natural element in any conversation. Let's say you are talking about movies with a friend and the friend says, "I think Meryl Streep is the greatest actress in history." You might respond, "I totally agree." Or you might say, "I completely disagree." If you disagree, the friend might respond, "But look how she has played so many different roles. She was completely different in *Julie/Julia* than she was in *It's Complicated*." You might answer, "Yeah, but she doesn't have the glamour of a Katherine Hepburn, who also played a lot of different roles." You are both presenting evidence to support your positions.

good movie

But the key point is that the back and forth between you keeps the conversation going and makes it interesting. If your friend said, "I think Meryl Streep is the greatest actress in history," and you didn't respond at all, your friend would probably follow up by saying, "Are you listening to me?" With reading, so many people never respond. The question is—are they really listening? In the same vein, if you

don't respond, and your friend keeps droning on about Meryl Streep, you are going lose interest in that conversation very quickly. If somebody asks you what you talked about with the person, your reply might be: "You know, blah, blah, blah." If you don't respond to what you read, it can quickly turn into a bunch of blah, blah, blah. No wonder too many people find reading boring.

But anybody who has ever engaged in an interesting conversation knows that agreeing or disagreeing with what your conversational partner says is only part of the formula for success. As important is situating what the other speaker says within the context of your own experience. For example, your friend might say (generically), "And then this happened to me and I reacted in this way." Your response might be, "I totally understand. That reminds me of a time when a similar thing happened to me." Once again, this kind of interaction keeps the conversation moving forward.

Talking with the text

With reading, you want to figure out how the passage you are reading matches with other things you have read—either in the same work, or in other works with which you are familiar. Let's say you are reading an article in the third week of a semester. Do the author's arguments line up with what you read in the second week of the semester? Does what you are reading in

#6–3

Another comparison: other readings.

NOTES

Question to ask myself:

1) What don't understand? Defended? Skip?

2) Do I agree? *** Evaluate – give my arguments

3) What do I need to learn?

Conversation = give & take

This author is conversational, but what about hard-to-read authors or stuff?

Comparisons from own life – being more involved in conversation.

the fourth chapter of the book support or contradict what you have read in the third chapter? As importantly—or perhaps more importantly—how does what you are reading match your own, personal experience. Have you seen in the world what the author suggests that you should see? "Opera is the grandest of all the performing arts," an author might write. "I don't think so," you might respond.

Will forget #7

*

The dialogue that I am suggesting cannot just take place in the reader's mind. A true dialogue requires physical activity. In this case, a critical aspect of talking to the text is making marginal notes. You should mark in the text your summaries of the author's arguments and the evidence you find compelling or unpersuasive; your points of agreement and disagreement and why; the outside associations you make as your read certain passages. Many people hesitate to write in books (trained perhaps in elementary school, when textbooks had to be returned at the end of the school year.) But when you buy a book, you have the right of ownership.

Yes, and for selling college textbooks back to bookstore for $$$!

More importantly, adding marginal notes is a creative process. You transform a text from just what the author has written to a record of your interaction with the text. In the long run, what you have written might be just as important as, or more important than, what the author has written. As an added benefit, when you return to a text after a period of time, your marginal notes will remind you of what you found important and unimportant in the text (and why) in a much more complete way than a series of static underlined passages.

memory

Notes + underlin-inggo together.

But there is even a bigger pay off than that. Turning reading into a dialogue guides readers into playing a much more active role in the process of making meaning and incorporating what has been read into their personal experience. And by adding a record of our interactions with a text itself, it transforms the text into something new and original— the article or book is no longer just the author's words lying fallow, waiting to be decoded. You have created a unique record of a dialogue between you and the author.

* #8 **

Most people find conversation and dialogue interesting and engaging and almost nobody falls asleep in the process.

NOTES

3 comparisions to make:

1) other readings 2) personal exp.

MAIN PT.: Margin notes make the ideas stick.

Where the creativity comes from in the article title: Writing on it makes it your own.

Might be overall thesis – interacting with text transforms it into a new, two-way conversation.

MAINT PTS. OF ARTICLE:

#1 – Thesis: Good reading = interactive exp.

#2 – Reading education teaches passivity.

#3 – Nonfiction different from English lit.

With reading, it is true that in many cases, simply decoding the words and understanding the simple meaning of articles and books can be challenging. The decoding process can be incredibly tedious if you see reading as a passive activity. But by understanding reading as a dialogue and marking your texts to record that dialogue, you turn reading from a passive activity into an act of creation. And what can be more interesting than that?

dirty word?

Author's main goal: don't be boring. ***

NOTES

#4 – HOW TO: (1) overview (2) mark main pts. (3) outline structure

#5 – Most students only underline – forget.

#6 – HOW TALK BACK? (1) Which parts confusing? (2) Do I agree? (3) Compare with other readings, own exp.

#7 – Must record conversation with notes.

#8 – Active reading creates new writing.

Section

1

THE COMMUNICATION EXPERIENCE

Chapter

①

Media Matters

"Speak clearly, if you speak at all; carve every word before you let it fall."

—Justice Oliver Wendell Holmes

"Words are, of course, the most powerful drug used by mankind."

—Rudyard Kipling

Consider the professional lives of journalists working for printed publications, broadcast news, and Web sites; of public relations consultants communicating their messages to a broad range of communities of interests; and of the professionals who create and distribute advertising messages that may influence millions of people. Nearly every day, they sit at computers, putting together facts, background information, and analysis. Perhaps illustrations or video will be added. The material may be prepared for print, the Internet, radio, or television—maybe for multiple outlets.

These professionals agonize over word selections and other choices regarding voice, tone, and structure. They struggle to select just the right graphics and to make sure that sound and images complement each other. And their completed work may be read or viewed by audiences ranging from several hundred to tens of millions of people.

What these professionals and others are communicating is material that matters in our lives. The mass media, which includes books, newspapers, magazines, television, radio, film and video, and the Internet, as well as the content they transmit, have alerted the public to issues that affect our world, such as the deadly spread of DDT and the danger of global warming. The mass media have challenged the actions of the largest companies in the world, exposing the dangers of unsafe automobiles and the failings of presidents. The mass media absorb the attention of millions of viewers, entertaining and informing them at the same time.

The mass media can play destructive roles as well. They can bully and intimidate people. They can deceive. A skillful use of the media has led to the rise of some the world's worst tyrants. On perhaps a less monumental scale, the mass media can misdirect people to inconsequential things while masking or ignoring events that have a real impact on people's lives. In short, the media fill the everyday needs of audiences, whether it is the latest news about a celebrity, a football score, how Wall Street is performing, medical developments, or a new local law that affects a neighborhood.

The media are often controlled by large and complex organizations that wield an extraordinary degree of power. But at the bottom line, those organizations fundamentally are controlled and managed by individuals. And it is individuals who create the content that audiences see. People report the news, create the television shows, build the Web sites, compose the music, craft the advertising, and devise the advertising strategies that influence the way the world works and the way people see themselves.

This chapter examines the lives of some of the media professionals who have had a major impact on the way the media work and on society itself. It also describes some of the episodes in which the role of the media has had a major impact on society.

In this chapter, you will

- be introduced to several major media figures and

- learn about major events with which these individuals were involved.

Paraphrasing Sir Isaac Newton, we see more clearly when we stand on the shoulders of giants. Communication is no exception. Understanding how communications matters includes learning about the pioneers, innovators and leaders who drove the development of the media and used it to help shape the world.

Required Reading: "The Pirate," is a profile of Rupert Murdoch, perhaps the most powerful person in mass communications in the first decade of the 21st century. Murdoch's media conglomerate, News Corp., owns the newspaper the *Wall Street Journal*, the Fox Channel, Fox News, MySpace, Twentieth Century Fox movie and

television studios, *American Idol*, the *New York Post*, *Times of London*, the Sky Channel, and much more.

Here are some of the leading figures who helped shape the major communications industries and the way the world is viewed.

TELEVISION

When television was first created, many people felt it was merely radio with pictures, and few saw its tremendous potential for becoming a major part of our daily lives. As the technology improved, pioneers took advantage of the possibilities to make television the dominant medium and a dominant institution in our society. Roone Arledge, Edward R. Murrow, and Oprah Winfrey helped shape television and give it its character.

Roone Arledge (1931–2002)

As president of ABC Sports from 1968 until 1990 and then president of ABC News from 1977 until his death in 2002, Roone Arledge had a far-reaching impact on the presentation of both news and sports on television. *Life* magazine called him one of the top 100 most important Americans in the 20th century.

Among his many accomplishments, Arledge created the longest-running regular broadcast in television history—*Monday Night Football*. He developed the groundbreaking show the *Wide World of Sports*, whose catch phrase, "the thrill of victory; the agony of defeat," entered the popular lexicon. He was one of the first to truly apply new production techniques available in television to sports, making sports programming more entertaining for the viewers. With his success in making sports more engrossing, and with a proven ability to attract large audiences to his shows, Arledge then turned his talents to the news, working to make news stories more vivid to audiences.

Arledge's primary insight was recognizing the need for a more personal touch in sports broadcasting. He started what has become known as "up close and personal" coverage of sports figures that brought viewers into their lives and allowed them to see sports figures as real people. He showed the courage of athletes through grueling months of training and preparation, and how the athlete had to deal with off-the-field issues. Arledge rejected simply "boosting" the athletes or a team. Instead, he revealed to viewers all sides of competition.

When Arledge took over ABC Sports, he envisioned how technology could greatly improve the fan's enjoyment of events. He encouraged technicians to create new products specifically for sports coverage. For example, he introduced "instant replay," using innovative technology that was faster than videotape. Instant replay is now an integral part of coverage of any sports event. With *Wide World of Sports* and *Monday Night Football*, ABC became a dominant force in sports broadcasting.

Not satisfied with dominating television sports, Arledge took a big risk by agreeing to be president of ABC News. Once again, Arledge made ABC competitive with the other major networks by creating innovative programming. He saw that there could be a large nighttime audience that did not want to watch Johnny Carson or other entertainment-oriented shows and responded with a revolutionary news program, *Nightline*, which devoted an entire 90-minute show or even several shows to fully examining one issue. Under the direction of news anchor Ted Koppel, the show became one of television's most distinguished programs.

Nightline became a widely watched program in 1979, when Iran went through its revolution, in which the monarchy under the Shah was replaced by a revolutionary Islamic Republic. During the fall of the Shah's government, Iranian students and militants seized the U.S. embassy in Tehran, taking 53 Americans hostage. The Americans were held captive from November 4, 1979, to January 20, 1981—444 days. Each night, Koppel would remind viewers of how long the hostages were being held—keeping vigil for the captives.

Arledge saw that sports and news had something in common—drama. "Creating an artificial situation (or re-creation) fraught with incredible tension, and then seeing how people perform. It's exciting, it's exhilarating," he said in a 1976 interview. "You must use the camera and the microphone to broadcast an image that approximates what the brain perceives, not merely what the eye sees," Arledge said. "Only then can you create the illusion of reality … making pictures and words that move people."

Of the ten Olympic Games that Arledge produced, the most eventful was the 1972 Olympics in Munich. "It was supposed to be Germany's step back into acceptance after World War II," Arledge noted. Toward the end of the event, Arab commandos invaded the Olympic Village and took Israeli athletes hostage. ABC became the world's link to Munich, because the authorities had cut off German television. ABC's cameras could continue coverage because they were not broadcasting in Munich, but rather were using a satellite feed. ABC broadcaster Jim McKay was told by Arledge to report the news "straight" without any of the flair usually associated with sports—demonstrating that sportscasters could deliver the most important news of the day.

Edward R. Murrow (1908–1965)

While television carried live reports of many important news events, its role in the rise and fall of Senator Joe McCarthy of Wisconsin was one of the pivotal moments in demonstrating the impact television would have on politics. Legendary CBS newsman Edward R. Murrow played a central role in that drama.

Joseph McCarthy, a Republican senator from Wisconsin, was elected to Congress as a war hero. In the period following the end of World War II, an international competition known as the "Cold War" arose between the Soviet Union, which was a totalitarian Communist country, and the United States, which championed capitalism and democracy. The Soviet Union had developed its own atomic bomb, and alarm was rampant over possible Communist infiltration of the Federal government, the military, and other American institutions. McCarthy used his prominence in the U.S. Senate to make everyone fear that their neighbors or work colleagues were Communist agents, becoming a leading voice in the anti-Communist camp.

Television and newspapers were unwilling to stand up to McCarthy, giving him a free hand to make outrageous and unfounded charges against leading politicians and ordinary citizens alike. People were labeled "Communist sympathizers" or "fellow travelers" based simply by associating with liberal-thinking individuals. Hollywood and television engaged in witch-hunts against actors, writers, and producers, who were banned from working. Many prominent writers and entertainers could not find work after being added to the "Blacklist."

Two men decided to confront the senator: CBS's top journalist, Edward R. Murrow, and his producer, Fred Friendly. Murrow had been a long-time member of CBS's news team, joining the company in 1935. In 1937, he headed CBS's operations in Europe and began to build a team of correspondents for what was then solely a radio network. In 1938, CBS created the *World News Roundup*, providing coverage from throughout Europe, and Murrow achieved celebrity status for his reporting from London during World War II.

In the early 1950s, as television became more prominent, Murrow played a leading role in the development of CBS television news. Among other projects, Murrow and Friendly created a weekly news show titled *See It Now*. Based on an earlier radio program, *See It Now* was one of the pioneering television news shows in the documentary tradition.

In 1954, Murrow and Friendly made Senator McCarthy the subject of a *See It Now* broadcast. They decided the best way to challenge McCarthy was by using his own words, rather than making a personal attack. Murrow started collecting material about McCarthy, which he assembled into a now-famous broadcast on March 9 of that year. The program was composed almost entirely of McCarthy's own speeches, exposing the politician as an irresponsible opportunist who destroyed people's lives through reckless allegations.

At the end of the broadcast, Murrow also noted that McCarthy was not solely responsible for the harm caused by "McCarthyism." In words that became famous, Murrow said, "The actions of the junior senator from Wisconsin have caused alarm and dismay amongst our allies abroad, and given considerable comfort to our enemies. And whose fault is that? Not really his. He didn't create this situation of fear; he merely exploited it—and rather successfully. Cassius was right. 'The fault, dear Brutus, is not in our stars, but in ourselves.'"

Murrow and Friendly's confrontation with McCarthy showed that television could be a major force in national politics and the issues confronting the United States. The importance of television's exposure of McCarthy's excesses was not lost on the press. *New York Times* television critic Jack Gould wrote: "Last week may be remembered as the week that broadcasting recaptured its soul."

Oprah Winfrey (1954–)

From very humble roots, Oprah Winfrey emerged as one of the most influential people in the United States and a one-woman media conglomerate. Her empire includes a widely watched television show, a magazine titled *O* that features her on the cover, roles in movies, books, radio, a cable network, and an Internet presence. She is among the most influential and richest women in the world.

Born into poverty in Mississippi and raised in inner city Milwaukee, Winfrey moved to Nashville, Tennessee as a young teenager. While still in high school, she got a job in radio and before she was 20 years old was the news anchor at WLAC-TV in Nashville. In 1976, she moved to Baltimore's WJZ-TV, where she was co-anchor of the local news broadcast, and two years later was recruited to host a talk show, *People Are Talking*, which debuted in 1978. Her success on that show led to her being recruited to host *AM Chicago*, a low-rated morning talk show. Within months, the show was number one in the Chicago market, displacing *Donahue*, Phil Donahue's talk show, which had pioneered the more confessional talk show format. Based on that success, *AM Chicago* was renamed *The Oprah Winfrey Show*. It was expanded to a full hour and began broadcasting nationally in 1986, quickly climbed past *Donahue* in the national ratings.

After her Chicago-based television talk show achieved great success, Winfrey showed tremendous business talent by syndicating her show and owning the syndication company. That meant she retained a larger share of the revenues and profits the show generated. In July 2007, *TV Guide* reported that Winfrey was the highest-paid television entertainer in the United States during the past year. She earned an estimated $260 million during the year. This amount was more than five times the earnings of the person in second place, *American Idol's* Simon Cowell. By 2008, her income had increased to $275 million.

Not satisfied to be solely in television, Winfrey won acclaim for her performance in such movies as *The Color Purple* and *Beloved*. She followed her movie success by launching her own monthly magazine, *O*, and Web sites related to the magazine.

Kitty Kelley, known for her tell-all books about Jackie Kennedy and Princess Diana, described Winfrey in these words: "As a woman, she has wielded an unprecedented amount of influence over the American culture and psyche ... There has been no other person in the 20th century whose convictions and values have impacted the American public in such a significant way. ... I see her as probably the most powerful woman in our society. I think Oprah has influenced every medium that she's touched."

The strongest indicator of Winfrey's influence is "Oprah's Book Club," which she introduced to her daily show in 1996. Whether Winfrey discussed a classic book, an obscure one, or something from an unknown author, the books became best sellers almost instantly after being mentioned by her. In the process, she revived interest in such classics as John Steinbeck's 1952 *East of Eden* and Alan Paton's *Cry, the Beloved Nation*.

Winfrey continues to be a powerful figure in communications. Her influence extends even to the U.S. Congress. Haunted by her own childhood experience with rape, Winfrey convinced lawmakers to pass legislation that established a national database of convicted child abusers. The "Oprah" bill was signed into law in 1993.

Meanwhile, Winfrey's media empire has continued to grow. In 1998, along with Geraldine Laybourne, the founder of the children's cable network Nickelodeon, and the production company Carsey-Werner-Mandabach, Winfrey set up Oxygen Media, a cable network and related Web sites aimed specifically at women. The initiative had grown out of Winfrey's Web site, Oprah.com, which she had established earlier in conjunction with the Internet service provider AOL. In 2007, NBC acquired Oxygen Media for $925 million. Winfrey announced in 2009 that she was joining with Discovery Communications to create OWN, the Oprah Winfrey Network, a cable television channel.

RADIO

The age of broadcasting began in November 1920, when thousands of people in Pittsburgh learned through the new medium of radio that Warren G. Harding had defeated James M. Cox in the race for the presidency of the United States. Radio became a mass medium largely through the efforts of David Sarnoff, chairman of the Radio Corporation of America. While radio allowed for the transmission of sound to anybody who had a receiver, the question was what should fill the airways. Radio broadcasters responded with a variety of news, drama, interactive talk, and sports. However, the content that commanded most airtime was music.

As an audio form, music is ideally suited for radio. With the invention of the transistor radio and the car radio, radio became mobile and music became the backdrop for activities ranging from driving to jogging. In the 1950s, radio announcers on stations that played popular music played a large role in determining which recording artists got airtime necessary to build their followings.

In the 1980s, talk radio hosts such as Rush Limbaugh responded to a growing conservative listening audience in the United States, demonstrating that radio could have a significant influence in politics as well as entertainment.

Alan Freed (1921–1965)

Born in 1921, Alan Freed got his first job in radio at WKST in New Castle, Pennsylvania. After stops in Youngstown, Ohio, and Akron, Ohio, he began to host a radio show at WJW in Cleveland, that played "rhythm and blues" music, which was the music recorded by black artists, also called "race music" in the popular media of the time, such as *Billboard*, the main magazine of the music industry.

Freed organized a concert in Cleveland, where the arena was overrun by enthusiastic fans, both white and black. Afterward, Freed began describing the music as "rock and roll." He is widely credited with creating that term and opening the doors to whites accepting black music. During the 1950s, if a black musician wrote and recorded a popular song, white artists would record their own version of it—"cover" it.

Black artists such as Little Richard and Fats Domino would hear their songs recorded by white artists such as Pat Boone, who had big hits with Little Richard's song "Tutti Frutti" and Domino's "Ain't That a Shame." According to legend, Boone wanted to record the song as "Isn't It a Shame." Freed would not go along with the industry's racist practices and played the original versions of many legendary rock and roll songs, introducing many black artists, to wider audiences.

Freed also held concerts so young fans could see white and black recording artists in person. After moving to WINS in New York in 1954, Freed held a landmark concert featuring both black and white performers. Shortly thereafter, the term *rock and roll* began to be used as a distinct musical category. Rock and roll stars such as Buddy Holly and Elvis Presley became national icons.

In addition to his role in popularizing rock and roll, Freed established the practice of the disc jockey, or "deejay," as a personality who was much more than an announcer who read commercials and gave information on the last song played. Calling himself "Moondog," Freed would bang on a telephone book while a song was playing to emphasize the beat. He became a national personality and produced the first rock-and-roll show on television in 1957.

Caught up in a corruption scandal in 1959, in which he was charged with demanding bribes to give specific records airtime, Freed was fired but then rehired by KDAY in Los Angeles in 1960. In 1962, he was convicted of commercial bribery and fined $300.

Freed was among the original inductees to the Rock and Roll Hall of Fame in Cleveland in 1986. His antics and connection to his listening audience would become the model used by deejays over the years, such as Casey Kasem, Wolfman Jack, Cousin Bruce Morrow, Murray the K, and Howard Stern.

Rush Limbaugh (1951–)

Rush Limbaugh has been widely considered to be the most influential talk radio personality and conservative political commentator in the country almost from the time he launched his politically oriented talk show in the late 1980s. He is among the first of many conservative commentators hosting talk radio shows. Taken as a group, these commentators have influenced the political views of millions of Americans.

Born in Cape Girardeau, Missouri, in 1951 to a family with deep ties to the Republican Party,

Limbaugh dropped out of college after a year. In the early 1970s, he moved to Pennsylvania, where he found a job as a disc jockey for a Top 40 music radio station near Pittsburgh. For the rest of the decade, he moved from station to station and then served a stint as the director of promotions for the Kansas City Royals baseball team. He returned to radio in 1984, when he took a position with a Sacramento radio station as a talk-show host, replacing Morton Downey, Jr. Downey had created a genre called "trash television," in which his guests would yell at each other, going head to head on issues under discussion. His fans were called "loudmouths."

In 1987, the Federal Communications Commission (FCC) repealed what was known as the Fairness Doctrine, which required radio and television stations to give time to both sides of political issues. That meant that radio hosts such as Limbaugh were free to air their views without giving time to the other side. Limbaugh took advantage of the new environment. As his show gained popularity, he came to the attention of the former president of ABC Radio, who wanted to syndicate the show. Limbaugh moved to WABC and launched a national show in 1989.

By the early 1990s, Limbaugh was the most widely listened-to person on radio. His show was heard on 650 radio stations across the country, and his legions of followers called themselves "dittoheads." In 2006, his average daily listening audience was around 13.5 million.

Limbaugh's success led to several other conservative radio hosts for call-in shows, including Michael Savage, Sean Hannity, and Glenn Beck. In 2009, Rahm Emanuel, the chief of staff to President Barack Obama, expressed his opinion that Rush Limbaugh was effectively the most powerful voice in the Republican Party.

NEWSPAPERS

Since the 1700s, newspapers have been the primary source of local, national, and international news for most people. Over the decades, newspaper publishers, editors, and reporters have shown the power of print to provide a strong voice in politics and American culture. Indeed, Thomas Jefferson, the third president of the United States, opined that, given the choice between having a government without newspapers or newspapers without a government, he would choose newspapers without a government. He also said that no government should be without censors, and where there is a free press, none ever will be.

Legendary publisher Joseph Pulitzer contended that the role of the press is to afflict the comfortable and comfort the afflicted. And over the years, newspapers have done just that—exposing corruption, crime, malfeasance, and atrocities. But newspapers cover more than just politics. For nearly 200 years, they have been the primary source of business, cultural, and sports news as well.

Ida B. Wells-Barnett (1862–1931)

Ida B. Wells-Barnett crusaded against the lynching of blacks and advocated for the rights of African Americans and women. She was born in 1862 to parents who were enslaved prior to the Civil War but able to support themselves because her mother was well known for her culinary skills and her father was an outstanding carpenter. Her parents died in a yellow fever epidemic when she was 14 years old. She was able to keep her family together by securing a teaching job and continued her education at Rust College. She eventually moved to Memphis to live with an aunt.

A turning point in Wells-Barnett's life was an incident in 1884, before the days when the segregation of the races had been given the constitutional stamp of approval by the U.S. Supreme Court decision of *Plessy v. Ferguson*. She was asked by a train conductor to give up her seat to a white man. The conductor told her that she belonged in the rail car reserved for blacks, but that car was already crowded with passengers. In her autobiography, Wells-Barnett described how she responded to the conductor's orders: "I refused, saying that the forward car [closest to the locomotive] was a smoker, and as I was in the ladies' car, I proposed to stay ... [The conductor] tried to drag me out of the seat, but the moment he caught hold of my arm I fastened my teeth in the back of his hand. I had braced my feet against the seat in front and was holding to the back, and as he had already been badly bitten, he didn't try it again by himself. He went forward and got the baggage man and another man to help him and of course they succeeded in dragging me out." Wells-Barnett later sued the railroad, but more importantly, the incident convinced her that she needed to speak out. Thus began her career as a journalist.

In 1889, Wells-Barnett became a partner in a black-owned newspaper based in Memphis called *The Free Speech and Headlight*. Three years later, an angry mob of white men attacked the three black owners of a grocery store that was successfully competing with a white-owned establishment. When the black men defended their store, a white man was shot. The grocery store owners were arrested but then taken from the jail by a white mob and lynched. In response, Wells-Barnett called on blacks to leave town and to use their economic power to fight against discrimination. African Americans heeded her pleas and began leaving Memphis by the hundreds. Those who stayed behind boycotted white businesses, creating financial hardships for commercial establishments as well as for the public transportation system.

Wells-Barnett's protests hit a nerve in the white community of Memphis, who destroyed the offices where she worked, while Wells-Barnett was in Philadelphia. She felt that she could not return to Memphis and joined the staff of the *New York Age*.

After relocating, Wells-Barnett became the head of an anti-lynching organization and began to investigate and publicize lynching throughout the South. She published her findings in *Southern Horrors: Lynch Law in All Its Phases*. In 1893, she undertook a speaking tour of Great Britain to raise awareness of lynching and to raise money to

combat it. Two years later, Wells-Barnett moved to Chicago, where she married Ferdinand Barnett, a lawyer, activist, and newspaper editor.

The Barnetts had three children, but Wells-Barnett continued to crusade on behalf of both African Americans and women. In 1909, she became a founding member of the National Association for the Advancement of Colored People (NAACP), which became the preeminent civil rights organization for most of the 20th century. She also worked for urban reform in Chicago and became one of the first black women to run for public office in the United States when she ran for the Illinois state legislature in 1930.

William Randolph Hearst (1863–1951)

William Randolph Hearst was one of the first great American media moguls. He used his empire of newspapers, magazines, and radio stations to influence American public opinion. His newspapers reflected the best and worst of American journalism. He could direct his editors to launch investigative projects that led to much-needed reforms, but he also engaged in sordid and lurid sensationalism. He could ignore the facts when they interfered with a good story and occasionally invented facts to create a sensational story. His larger-than-life persona was parodied in Orson Welles' groundbreaking movie *Citizen Kane* in 1941, which infuriated Hearst. The movie flopped at the box office because of negative publicity from Hearst newspapers but later was recognized as a classic film.

Hearst's entry into journalism in 1887 was largely by accident. His father, a U.S. senator and millionaire mining executive, was given a small newspaper, the *San Francisco Examiner*, as payment for a debt. Hearst's father turned it over to his son. Successful in San Francisco, Hearst purchased the *New York Morning Journal* in 1896 and launched a circulation war against the *New York World*, owned by Joseph Pulitzer. Pulitzer had created a new kind of mass newspaper, with a circulation ten times greater than most of its competitors. The *World* targeted the emerging working class, including new immigrants streaming to the United States from all parts of Europe. Hearst set off to capture the same market.

The tactics both Hearst and Pulitzer used consisted of flamboyant headlines, human-interest stories, and crusades for political causes close to their hearts. Hearst is perhaps best known for his campaign to get the United States into a war with Spain in 1898. Hearst papers started running stories about Cuba's uprising against Spain. But the papers soon began exaggerating their claims to make the stories more sensational. Cubans were shown being tortured and abused. Many of the stories were simply not true.

The excessive nature of Hearst's stories gave rise to several pejorative terms for journalism, including sensationalism—or "overhyping" a story— and the *Yellow Press*, after "The Yellow Kid," a comic strip in Hearst's newspaper. These terms are still used today to identify biased, sensationalized reporting.

As circulation climbed, Hearst continued to push the boundaries, publishing more outrageous stories about Spain's treatment of Cubans. In his book, *The Brass Check: A Study of American Journalism*, Upton Sinclair charged that Hearst reporters were "willing by deliberate and shameful lies, made out of whole cloth, to stir nations to enmity and drive them to murderous war." Sinclair also asserted that Hearst's newspapers lied "remorselessly about radicals," noting that Hearst reporters excluded "the word Socialist from their columns" and obeyed "a standing order in all Hearst offices that American socialism shall never be mentioned favorably."

One of the darkest examples of Hearst's misuse of his media power involved his campaign to ruin Roscoe "Fatty" Arbuckle, one of Hollywood's biggest silent movie stars, who made comedies with Charlie Chaplin and Buster Keaton. Following completion of a movie, Arbuckle went to San Francisco to celebrate. Hollywood prohibited the sale of liquor, but San Francisco was wide open. At a party held in Arbuckle's hotel suite, a young actress, Virginia Rappe, became ill and was hospitalized for peritonitis caused by a ruptured bladder. Rumors spread that Arbuckle, who weighed more than 300 pounds, had crushed Rappe when he raped her.

Arbuckle was charged with murder even though there was no evidence that he had had sexual contact with Rappe. Hearst used his nationwide chain of newspapers to vilify Arbuckle, publishing sensationalized stories that made Arbuckle seem like a sexual monster. The first two trials ended in mistrials. After the third trial, Arbuckle was found innocent by a jury, which also apologized to Arbuckle for the mistreatment he had received from many quarters, especially the press. Nonetheless, Arbuckle's career was destroyed in the process.

Despite these excesses, Hearst went on to build a chain of newspapers. By the mid-1920s, he owned 28 newspapers, including the *Los Angeles Examiner*, the *Boston American*, and the *Chicago Examiner*. He also built a stable of magazines such as *Cosmopolitan*, *Redbook*, *Seventeen*, and *Popular Mechanics*.

Hearst's power faded during the Great Depression. He opposed Franklin D. Roosevelt, who was a popular president. During the Great Depression, financial setbacks forced him to give up control of his media empire. After World War II, Hearst's company added radio and television stations to its stable of media properties, and the company still functions today as a privately held media company.

Katherine Graham (1917–2001)

Katherine Graham, the publisher of the *Washington Post* for two decades, was more than just one of the most powerful women in the mass media. On two occasions, she stood up for freedom of the press, showing that a powerful media outlet could be a force for tremendous good. Graham was the daughter of Eugene Meyer, who purchased the *Post* in 1933. At the time, the *Post* was one of Washington's lesser-read papers. She later married Philip Graham, who became the paper's publisher. Katherine Graham worked as a newspaper reporter herself, first for a newspaper in San Francisco and then for the *Post*. But she decided to leave the work environment to raise her family.

Philip Graham had a history of depression and committed suicide in 1963. At first unsure of what to do, Katherine Graham decided to assume the role of publisher of the newspaper and president of the company. Under her leadership, the *Post* became the most-read paper in Washington and developed a reputation for outstanding journalism.

Graham faced her first test of leadership with the fight over the publication of the "Pentagon Papers," which were a classified history of the United States' involvement in Vietnam, going back to 1945, when Vietnam was a French colony. The history revealed U.S. government secrets about the war that, though not a threat to the security of the United States, would have been highly embarrassing to then-President Richard Nixon. The study was classified top-secret, but one of its authors, Daniel Ellsberg, decided that the government's war policy was wrong and gave a copy to *New York Times* reporter Neil Sheehan and later, to *Washington Post* editor, Ben Bagdikian.

After the Nixon administration succeeded in getting a court order to stop the *Times'* publication of the Pentagon Papers, Graham had to decide whether the *Post* should publish the document. Since the documents did not involve an immediate threat to the country, how could she justify violating federal law by publishing top-secret documents? The papers had several explosive pieces of information, including the fact that Nixon had ordered the secret bombing of two neutral countries, Cambodia and Laos. The information showed that Nixon was withholding critical information from the American public. Graham realized that the *Post* had a public obligation to publish the Pentagon Papers—even though it created huge risks for her newspaper.

The Nixon Administration applied tremendous pressure on Graham, warning that they would shut down the *Post* if necessary, but Graham refused to knuckle under. The U.S. Supreme Court decided in June 1971 that the Nixon White House had failed to prove that publishing the Pentagon Papers would harm national security and lifted any restraints on the *Post* and *Times*. The decision was a resounding affirmation that the First Amendment prohibits the government from blocking the publication of information—a doctrine known as "prior restraint."

The next occasion on which the *Post* and Graham would stand up to the Nixon administration came during the Watergate scandal. *Post* reporters Bob Woodward and Carl Bernstein uncovered information that showed that President Nixon was involved in a cover-up of illegal activities undertaken on behalf of his reelection campaign, including multiple break-ins at the Democratic National Committee's offices in the Watergate building.

After the *Washington Post* started publishing stories indicating Nixon's ties to the Watergate burglars, the White House started threatening Graham, who recounted the intimidation she experienced. On one occasion, Nixon warned her that he would block the license renewal of the *Post's* television station. "The *Post* is going to have damnable, damnable problems out of this one. They have a television station ... and they're going to have to get it renewed. ... The game has to be played awfully rough," Nixon warned.

Two weeks later, a pivotal Bernstein and Woodward article appeared on the *Post's* front page. The reporters had dug up information that Nixon reelection officials had a secret fund that was controlled by five people, one of whom was Attorney General John Mitchell.

As Woodward and Bernstein got closer to the truth, Nixon's campaign to undermine public confidence in the *Post* intensified. Graham did not waver despite the pressure. After Nixon was overwhelmingly reelected in 1972, the White House turned up the heat against Graham and her paper. The White House started blocking *Post* reporters from covering government events—even social events. Government officials refused to answer phone calls from *Post* reporters. Still Graham would not give in. She repeatedly assured Woodward and Bernstein that she would continue to support them. Slowly, with each Watergate story, a picture was presented to the public of a president intent on circumventing the U.S. Constitution.

Just when it seemed darkest for Graham, there came the announcement: The *Post* won the Pulitzer Prize for meritorious service for its Watergate reporting. After months of seeing little support from other news organizations, other papers and network news programs started investigating the White House's illegal and questionable actions. In the following months, the Nixon White House tapes were revealed. As the tapes revealed more of the inner workings of the White House, President Nixon was forced to resign on August 9, 1974.

Graham continued to oversee the *Post* and made it one of the greatest newspapers in the United States. Her autobiography, *Personal History*, an honest and even painful account of her life, received the Pulitzer Prize in 1998.

MAGAZINES

The magazine was one of the earliest forms of mass communication. Before newspapers were published regularly, magazines containing essays and other creative material were being published in England. Some of the earlier novelists and raconteurs, such as Daniel Defoe and Jonathan Swift, edited and published magazines in the early 1700s.

Over the next three centuries, magazines evolved through many different forms. In the early 1900s, some magazines were known for their investigative articles into corruption in business and government. In the middle of the century, magazines such as *Life* and *Look* reached huge national audiences. Their reliance on the use of color photography helped pave the way for a more visual culture. And, when competitive pressure from television made it hard to sustain many mass-circulation magazines, magazines continued to thrive when they were targeted at specific audiences. Targeting is still essential to the vitality of magazines, many of which have developed vital presences on the World Wide Web.

Ida Tarbell (1857–1944)

Ida Tarbell was a pioneer in investigative journalism. Her tireless research would result in the breakup of the Standard Oil Company, the most powerful company in the United States at the beginning of the 20th century. Born in the Pennsylvania oil fields in 1857, she was the daughter of a small-time oil producer and supplier of barrels for oil production. Her family experienced firsthand the pressure put on smaller producers by larger companies such as Standard Oil.

After graduating from high school at the top of her class, Tarbell attended Allegheny College, where she majored in biology. Upon graduation, she took a position as a school teacher, but when she realized that she liked writing more than teaching, she found a position writing for *The Chautauquan* magazine, a teaching supplement for home study courses, becoming its managing editor in 1886. In 1890, Tarbell moved to Paris to study and write the biography of the leader of an influential salon during the French Revolution. There, she came to the attention of Samuel McClure, the proprietor of *McClure's Magazine*, who eventually brought her onto his staff and commissioned her to write a popular series about the lives of Napoleon Bonaparte and Abraham Lincoln. Her series on Lincoln, which contained new information about his early years that Tarbell uncovered through painstaking research, dramatically increased the circulation of the magazine.

McClure then agreed to let Tarbell look into the life of John D. Rockefeller, the owner of Standard Oil Company, the most powerful company in the growing oil business. Rockefeller was the richest man in the United States, and the Standard Oil Trust almost completely controlled the oil industry. Through an elaborate national distribution system, Standard served the oil needs of 80 percent of all American towns—from the largest city to the smallest town. Rockefeller's personal fortune peaked in 1912 at almost $900 million. Challenging such a powerful figure required extraordinary research and care in her reporting. Tarbell could not afford a single misstep. Her writing also had to be compelling to convince her audiences that Rockefeller's oil monopoly harmed American businesses and homes.

After nearly two years of research, Tarbell's prose in a series of groundbreaking articles in *McClure's* powerfully indicted John D. Rockefeller's business practices. The articles later were collected and published in a single volume, *The History of the Standard Oil Company*.

In this excerpt from one of her *McClure's* articles, Tarbell explains why Rockefeller had to be closely scrutinized: "John D. Rockefeller exercises a powerful control over the very sources of American intellectual and religious inspiration. Now a man who possesses this kind of influence cannot be allowed to live in the dark. The public not only has the right to know what sort of a man he is; it is the duty of the public to know. How else can the public discharge the most solemn obligation it owes to itself and to the future, to keep the springs of its higher life clean? ... From time immemorial men who have risen to power have had to face this question. Kings, tyrants, chieftains, since the world began have stood or have fallen as they have convinced the public that they were giving or not giving a just return for the power allowed them. The time is here when Mr. Rockefeller must face the verdict of the public by which he lives."

Oil industry historian Daniel Yergin would call Tarbell's book the "most important business book ever written." Tarbell's articles would eventually lead, in 1911, to the U.S. Supreme Court's order of the breakup of Standard Oil, the world's first multinational corporation, into a group of smaller companies, many which ultimately re-merged with one another into the oil giants in business now, including Chevron and ExxonMobil. Tarbell also set the standard for research-based investigative reporting.

Henry Luce (1898–1967)

In the years after World War I, the pace of American life picked up. As cities grew and communications networks expanded, people did not have much time to consider the events of the day. Or so it seemed to Henry Luce, the son of Christian missionaries. Two years after Luce graduated from Yale University, he and a partner, Brit Hadden, decided to launch a new magazine, a magazine that would cover events briefly and succinctly—a kind of weekly news roundup. He called the magazine *Time*.

Luce's magazine took a distinct approach to news coverage. Reporters submitted memos to a group of editors, who would write the stories that would eventually appear on *Time's* pages. Luce used this approach to ensure that all stories in his magazine reflected the same authoritative tone and that there was uniformity in the voice of the magazine. *Time* employed an energized writing style to make the news more appealing to readers. He coined new words, such as "tycoon," to create a distinct voice for his magazine. He invented the concept of the "cover story." There were no bylines in *Time* until editorial policy was changed the late 20th century.

Time magazine carried tremendous influence, which Luce used to pursue his public policy agenda, particularly concerning the Far East. For example, after World War II, Luce, a staunch anti-Communist helped convince U.S. political leaders to recognize Chinese warlord Chiang Kai-shek as the true leader of China and to oppose the Communist leader Mao Zedong. Later Luce directed his editors to print news stories and editorials supporting U.S. involvement in Vietnam and to suppress reporters' dispatches that were critical of government policy.

Luce went on to create a stable of other magazines. In 1930, he established *Fortune* magazine, devoted to the coverage of business and aimed at what Luce called the "aristocracy of our business civilization." In 1936, Luce launched *Life*, the first all-photographic U.S. news magazine and one of the more successful photojournalism publications ever. By the 1950s *Life* sold more than 13.5 million copies per week. In 1954, Luce debuted *Sports Illustrated*, which brought sophistication to sports journalism. The quality of *Sports Illustrated's* articles was new to sports journalism, and it was rewarded with a high circulation. *Sport Illustrated* became the first magazine with a circulation over one million to win the National Magazine Award for General Excellence twice.

Luce hired many top writers and photographers to work for his magazines, such as writers Archibald MacLeish and Ernest Hemingway and photographers Margaret Bourke-White and Robert Capa. Luce's journalists were always the best paid and commanded the greatest respect of news sources and fellow journalists.

John H. Johnson (1918–2005)

John Harold Johnson, the grandson of slaves, built a large media empire targeted to the African-American community. He was the first African American to be listed on the Forbes 400 list of richest people in the United States.

Born in rural Arkansas, Johnson's family moved to Chicago in 1933. Johnson edited his high school newspaper and upon graduation went to work as an office boy at an insurance company; within two years, he was the assistant to the president. One of his assignments was to prepare a monthly digest of news articles. As he prepared the newsletter, he wondered if the African-American community might like to have a similar publication. In his autobiography, Johnson says that his idea was a "Negro Digest" that would be patterned after the highly popular *Reader's Digest*. After years of struggling to get the necessary funding, Johnson launched the *Negro Digest* in 1942.

Johnson's publication would tap a market long overlooked. For the first time, black readers could find articles on African-American history, literature, arts, and cultural issues. Within six months, the *Digest's* circulation reached 50,000. After several decades of publication, its name was changed to *Black World*.

Negro Digest was only the beginning for Johnson. Johnson's next success was *Ebony*, a photo magazine that would be a black version of *Life* magazine. Johnson emphasized positive aspects of black life, celebrating black musicians, athletes, and movie stars. Johnson would later write that his goal with *Ebony* was to "show not only the Negroes but also white people that Negroes got married, had beauty contests, gave parties, ran successful businesses, and did all the other normal things of life."

Johnson did not avoid controversy, expanding *Ebony's* content to address race relations, black militancy, and crimes by African Americans against African Americans. Everything in the magazine was addressed to the black consumer.

Johnson's stable of publications would grow to include *Tan* magazine, a true-confessions-type publication; *Jet*, a weekly news digest; and *Ebony Jr.*, a children's magazine. Johnson also expanded into radio, television production, and book publishing.

In 1996, President Bill Clinton bestowed the Presidential Medal of Freedom on Johnson. Johnson will be remembered as "a pioneer in black journalism when a large part of America lived in the shadow of segregation and open racism," according to Rupert Cornwell of London's *Independent* newspaper.

Gloria Steinem (1934–)

Gloria Steinem blazed a trail for other woman writers and journalists. She shattered notions of traditional reporting beats for female reporters, such as supermarket openings or fashion shows. Her journalistic innovations showed that women were interested in well-crafted articles about issues that matter to their gender. A vigorous political activist, Steinem helped create the Women's Action Alliance, the National Women's Political Caucus, and Choice USA. She was the founding president of the *Ms.* Foundation for Women and helped create Take Our Daughters to Work Day.

Born in Toledo, Ohio, Steinem was the granddaughter of a noted suffragette. She attended Smith College and upon graduation took an extended internship in India. She returned to the United States determined to fight against social injustice and the growing income gaps between the wealthy and poor and between men and women.

Steinem's first job in journalism was with a humor publication, *Help!* In the early 1960s, she received what she called her first serious assignment from Clay Felker, then an editor at *Esquire* magazine. In 1963, she wrote an attention-getting article for *Show* magazine in the muckraking tradition of the pioneering female journalist Nelly Bly. To research her topic, Steinem got a job as a "bunny" at a Playboy Club and then wrote a two-part series about the way women were being mistreated at the club.

In 1968, Steinem took a job at *New York* magazine, which was being run by Clay Felker. She wrote about politics and later immersed herself in feminist causes. This combination of interests propelled Steinem into the limelight as a feminist leader. In 1971, she joined Bella Abzug, Shirley Chisholm, and Betty Friedan to form the National Women's Political Caucus, encouraging women's participation in the 1972 election. The caucus publicized such women's issues as underrepresentation of women in politics.

The following year, 1972, would be a pivotal time for women's journalism. *New York* magazine publisher Clay Felker gave Steinem the go-ahead to create the first mass-circulation feminist magazine, *Ms.* The first issue was tucked inside the weekly issue of *New York*. After a positive response, *Ms.* was formally launched and quickly gained a circulation of 500,000. *Ms.* was a brazen

act of independence in the 1970s, according to the magazine's Web site. "At the time, the fledgling feminist movement was either denigrated or dismissed in the mainstream media—if it was mentioned at all. Most magazines for women were limited to advice about saving marriages, raising babies, or using the right cosmetics."

The list of firsts pioneered by *Ms.* is long. It was the first to feature prominent U.S. women demanding the repeal of laws that criminalized abortion. It was the first to explain and advocate for the Equal Rights Amendment. *Ms.* was the first to

> rate presidential candidates on women's issues. It was the first to

> feature domestic violence and sexual harassment on the cover of a women's magazine. It was the first to report on feminist protests of pornography.

> focus attention on and expose the undue influence of advertising on magazine journalism.

As *Ms.* editor, Steinem gained became an influential spokesperson for women's rights issues. Besides her work with *Ms.*, Steinem became a highly regarded author with publication of her first book, *Outrageous Acts and Everyday Rebellions*. The book included her recollections of the past, such as her experience as a Playboy bunny, and also highlighted the lives of other notable 20th century women. Steinem wrote about issues that mattered to women, such as disparities in pay and sexual exploitation. Steinem was inducted into the Women's Hall of Fame in 1993 and the American Society of Magazine Editors Hall of Fame in 1998.

NONFICTION BOOKS

Nonfiction books can be written within many different contexts. Some are based on long years of archival research. They can be memoirs, biographies, or autobiographies. They can be spiritual books, how-to books, and advice treatises. In this section, however, the authors of nonfiction books that have had significant social impact are profiled. Interestingly, though their authors are not included here, several works of fiction, including *Uncle Tom's Cabin* by Harriet Beecher Stowe and *The Jungle* by Upton Sinclair, have also exerted tremendous influence on public opinion.

Truman Capote (1924–1984)

Published in 1966, Truman Capote's *In Cold Blood* was the first in a new genre of writing that Capote would describe as "the nonfiction novel." *In Cold Blood* stood apart from other nonfiction books of its time by combining techniques usually associated with creative fiction, such as the extensive use of dialogue and description to create psychological drama with the meticulous reporting associated with journalism. Even though *In Cold Blood* read like a novel, Capote claimed that everything in it from beginning to end was true, a claim that was challenged by many critics.

By the 1960s, Capote was already one of the most notorious writers of his time. His first book, *Other Voices, Other Rooms*, published in 1948, dealt frankly with gay themes and made Capote an instant celebrity. Capote's novella, *Breakfast at Tiffany's*, had become a widely successful movie. Capote loved his celebrity, using his vicious wit and overt homosexuality to keep him in the public's eye. A unique character, he was a frequent television guest and was well known for his distinctive, high-pitched voice, odd vocal mannerisms, and offbeat manner of dress.

In 1959, Capote noticed a small newspaper item that described the murder of a rural Kansas family of four. A frequent contributor to *The New Yorker* magazine, Capote saw the incident as the vehicle for a new writing genre that would combine fiction-writing techniques with nonfiction reality. With support from *The New Yorker's* editor-in-chief, William Shawn, Capote left New York City for a small town in Kansas, where he would spend six years researching his book, spending many hours interviewing the two apprehended murderers.

Working as a team with his childhood friend Harper Lee, who would later have her own literary success with the novel *To Kill a Mockingbird*, Capote talked to the local townspeople, local police, and FBI agents involved in the murder case. During the same time, Richard Eugene Hickock and Perry Edward Smith were appealing their death sentence. During interviews, he never took notes or used a tape recorder; afterward, he would dictate his notes from memory to Lee.

During his interviews with the two murderers, Hickock and Smith, Capote became infatuated with Smith and wanted to save him from a death sentence. Capote faced a terrible dilemma, however, for sparing Perry from the gallows would reduce the commercial value of his book. Years of hard work, research, and writing would be worthless. Ultimately, Capote paid for excellent lawyers to appeal Perry's and Hickock's death sentences, but never mounted a campaign to draw attention to their situation. Capote would later attend Perry's execution.

In Cold Blood was serialized in *The New Yorker* in 1965 and published in hardcover by Random House in 1966. It became a milestone in a new approach to journalism that appeared in the 1960s dubbed the "New Journalism." Other writers—including Tom Wolfe, Joan Didion, and Norman Mailer—embraced Capote's model of factual journalistic writing with colorful prose intended to help readers understand the emotional and psychological essence of events. Capote enjoyed enormous critical and financial success from *In Cold Blood*, but he would never write another major novel or nonfiction book.

Rachel Carson (1907–1964)

Rachel Carson was a writer, scientist, and ecologist. She grew up in the rural town of Springdale, Pennsylvania. She was taught a love of nature by her mother and eventually received an M.A. in zoology from the Johns Hopkins University in 1932. She went on to write radio scripts for the U.S. Department of Fisheries and eventually became editor-in-chief for the U.S. Fish and Wildlife Service. Carson's book *The Sea Around Us*, published in 1952, established her reputation as a major nature writer.

While still working at the U.S. Fish and Wildlife Service, Carson had become concerned about the damage being done to the environment by the widespread and indiscriminant use of pesticides, particularly *dichlorodiphenyltrichloroethane* or DDT, which was introduced during World War II to control diseases spread by mosquitoes. After the war, agricultural use of DDT skyrocketed around the world, despite scientists' warnings of possible health hazards of the chemical.

In 1958, Carson received a letter from a friend in Massachusetts bemoaning the deaths of large birds on Cape Cod caused by the use of DDT. Having already accumulated a large amount of information about the dangers of DDT, but unable to obtain a magazine assignment to write about the topic, she decided to write a book. *Silent Spring* took four years to complete. She concluded that DDT had harmed birds and other wildlife and had contaminated the world's food supply.

Silent Spring was serialized in *The New Yorker* in 1962. The public reaction was immediate. The chemical industry struck back vigorously, but *Silent Spring* soon changed the public debate from whether pesticides were unsafe to which pesticides were unsafe. Within a year of the book's publication, the Federal government enacted much stricter regulations on DDT and eventually banned it.

Rachel Carson is widely credited with launching the modern environmental movement and with reshaping public attitudes both about nature and about technological advances in general. Interestingly, the most compelling chapter in *Silent Spring* is "A Fable for Tomorrow," in which Carson imagines a town where all life, including wildlife, vegetation, and humanity, has been "silenced" by DDT.

MOVIES

Films do more than simply provide a compelling entertainment experience and gather huge audiences. Movies create celebrities and have a huge impact on popular culture. While the collaborative art of filmmaking can cost tens or even hundreds of millions of dollars and require the talents of hundreds of people, the director is generally viewed as the guiding creator of the final cinematic product. Top directors have their own way of making the audience see the world.

Orson Welles (1915–1985)

Orson Welles's movie *Citizen Kane* is regarded by some critics as the greatest film ever made. Welles was only 25 years old when he directed *Citizen Kane*. Three years earlier he had shaken up the country when he produced a radio play, *War of the Worlds,* that convinced thousands of listeners that Martians had landed in New Jersey. Welles also was a brilliant actor and theatrical producer.

Born in Kenosha, Wisconsin, as a young man Welles started out in theatre in New York, picking up extra work as a radio actor. This would lead to the formation of the Mercury Theatre, where he formed lifelong friendships with such actors as Joseph Cotton, Agnes Morehead, Everett Sloane, and John Houseman. Members of the Mercury Theatre would be involved in all of Welles's greatest productions. Initially successful in radio and on the stage, Welles would have his greatest impact in the movies.

Initially, Welles wanted to adapt Joseph Conrad's classic novella *Heart of Darkness*. Instead, he turned to a project conceived by screenwriter Herman J. Mankiewicz that would be based on the life of William Randolph Hearst, one of the most powerful men in the United States at the time. The project presented several challenges. Foremost was that Hearst was not a man to be trifled with and was likely to use his powerful media empire to squash any film that showed him in an unflattering light.

Welles knew his studio, RKO, would shut down production if Hearst got wind of the film, so to protect his project, Welles told studio executives throughout production that he was only filming scenes as tests. The ruse worked, and Welles was able to finish his ambitious picture. In it, he made groundbreaking use of dramatic new film techniques such flashbacks, use of fake documentary film, and innovative lighting and deep focus by cinematographer Gregg Toland.

When *Citizen Kane* was released, it provoked an uproar. The similarities between the fictitious Charles Foster Kane and William Randolph Hearst were undeniable. Never before had a film so brazenly parodied a major political and social figure. Hearst's media outlets boycotted the film, and at one point, Hearst tried to frame Welles by putting a prostitute in Welles's hotel room when the director was away. A policeman who saw the scam alerted Welles before Hearst's henchmen could trap him. The film's box office receipts were disappointing, and it was overlooked for Academy Awards. Welles went on to direct other films, such as *The Magnificent Ambersons, The Stranger, Lady from Shanghai,* and *Touch of Evil,* but never again would Welles enjoy the creative freedom he enjoyed with *Citizen Kane.*

Years after its release, *Citizen Kane* would be revived at film festivals and would influence young filmmakers around the world, especially in France, where directors such as Francois Truffaut acknowledged how Welles changed the way feature films were created. In 2002, he was voted the greatest film director of all time in the British Film Institute's poll of Top Ten Directors.

Steven Spielberg (1946–)

Steven Spielberg is one of the most influential director/producers in the history of cinema. He has created movies on a variety of themes ranging from horror to adventure to science fiction to the Holocaust to World War II. Spielberg's list of hit movies includes *Raiders of the Lost Ark, E.T.: The Extra-Terrestrial, Jurassic Park, Saving Private Ryan,* and *Schindler's List.*

Born in Cincinnati, Ohio, Spielberg grew up in New Jersey and Arizona. After his parents divorced, Spielberg lived with his father in Sarasota, California. He attended California State University, Long Beach, but he dropped out to try to break into Hollywood. His entry into the business was as an assistant editor for the classic television show *Wagon Train,* a production role for which he apparently received no credit. Spielberg produced and directed a series of short films and worked in television on such shows as *Rod Sterling's Night Gallery, Marcus Welby, M.D.,* and *Columbo,* in which Peter Falk starred as a disheveled detective who irritated his high-powered suspects as he gathered the evidence to arrest them.

In 1974 Spielberg directed his first full-length feature film, *The Sugarland Express,* starring Goldie Hawn. Based on a true story, the movie portrays a woman who convinces her husband to break out of prison and then joins him to kidnap their child from the child's foster home.

The Sugarland Express marked Spielberg as a rising star. The release of his next movie, *Jaws,* in 1975 made him an international sensation. Based on Peter Benchley's novel about a shark attack, *Jaws* is credited with creating the concept of the summer blockbuster movie. Over the next ten years, Spielberg directed or produced a series of megahits, including *Close Encounters of the Third Kind,* which was a UFO film with a twist at the ending; *Raiders of the Lost Ark; Poltergeist;* and *E.T.: The Extra-Terrestrial,* which was the highest-grossing film of all time when it was released. Spielberg's production company also had a string of blockbusters with *Back to the Future, An American Tail,* and others.

Over time, Spielberg chafed at being labeled a director of only crowd-pleasing, light entertainment. In the late 1980s and 1990s, he directed a series of the powerful dramas for adults, including *The Color Purple* starring Whoopi Goldberg and Oprah Winfrey, *Schindler's List* starring Liam Neeson and Ben Kingsley, and *Saving Private Ryan* starring Tom Hanks and Matt Damon.

Saving Private Ryan revised the way Hollywood presented World War II to audiences. Earlier films on the conflict would largely glorify combat. Directors were reluctant to say anything negative about World War II since it was a "just" war. *Ryan* showed that even a good war could be brutal.

In *Schindler's List*, Spielberg raised the question of what one man can do against an enormous evil—the Nazis. Based on a true story, *Schindler's List* is considered one of the most compelling movies ever made, as it shows the complete insanity of the Nazi Holocaust and the heroic efforts of those who opposed it. Spielberg won Academy Awards for Best Director for *Saving Private Ryan* and *Schindler's List*. Both movies won the Oscar for Best Picture.

In 1994, Spielberg founded the company Dreamworks with partners Jeffrey Katzenberg, the former president of the Walt Disney Company, and David Geffen, a major record producer. In that capacity, Spielberg continued to produce and direct a steady stream of commercially successful movies. He also became involved in other projects, perhaps most notably funding The Shoah Project, which recorded the oral histories of survivors of the Nazi Holocaust. In 2006, *Premiere* magazine named Spielberg the most influential and powerful person in the motion picture industry, and *Time* magazine named him one of the most important people of the 20th century.

Spike Lee (1957–)

Spike Lee is a pioneering African-American film director. His movies reflect his personal vision and a compelling look at American society. Before he was 30, Lee created the groundbreaking film on contemporary black life, *She's Gotta Have It*. The film took a critical look at sexual relations between black men and women. Made for $175,000, the film grossed more than $7 million in revenue, a number that immediately caught the attention of powerful figures in Hollywood.

Born in Atlanta, Georgia, in 1957, Lee moved to Brooklyn, New York, at an early age. His father was a jazz musician and his mother was a teacher.

Lee attended Morehouse College in Atlanta and studied film at Clark Atlanta University. Both are historically black colleges. He then attended the New York University film directing program and earned his graduate degree.

After *She's Gotta Have It*, Lee directed *School Daze*, starring Laurence Fishburne, a musical drama set in a historically black college in which members of a sorority and a fraternity clash with students who reject traditional black college lifestyles. In 1989, Lee directed *Do the Right Thing*, which many people consider his signature movie. In it, he turns his camera eye on the Bedford-Stuyvesant neighborhood in Brooklyn. Lee plays the character of a pizza delivery man. The pizza shop where he works becomes a flashpoint for racial tension. Lee's 1992 biopic *Malcolm X* starred Denzel Washington as the revered African American activist. When the film ran into budget troubles, prominent fellow entertainers contributed financially to Lee's project, including Bill Cosby, Oprah Winfrey, Michael Jordan, Magic Johnson, Janet Jackson, and Prince.

Lee's films examine black life in a way other directors had not approached. Over the years, Lee has moved from close examination of black life to scrutinizing social and political issues, such as his film *4 Little Girls*, which is about the bombing of a black church in Alabama during the height of the civil-rights movement, and *A Requiem in Four Acts*, a documentary on life in New Orleans in the aftermath of Hurricane Katrina. His *Miracle at St. Anna's* was probably the first film to look at the experience of black soldiers during World War II—a period when the U.S. armed forces were still segregated.

Throughout his career, Lee has fought to open doors for black filmmakers, saying the film industry still does not respect the achievements of African-American directors, such as Lee, John Singleton, and Lee Daniels. "The studio system is rigged against people of color," Lee has said, arguing that regardless of how gifted black directors may be, they still struggle to get studio executives to "green-light" their proposals. The African-American experience is relegated to three Hollywood ghettos, he has argued: lowbrow comedy, romantic comedy, and hip-hop gangsta shoot-'em-ups. African-American films outside those categories have trouble getting made.

In a 1996 speech in San Francisco, Lee talked about his relationship with Hollywood and how he has achieved a somewhat unique position in the film industry—that of a black director who has maintained his independence while making great movies. When he entered New York University, Lee said that he did nothing but make films. "We spent very little time in the classroom, without making films. If you're not working on your films, you're working on your classmates' films. And that's where I became a filmmaker—by just actually doing stuff. I really believe that; if you want to do something, if you want to be a writer, you got to write; if you want to be a filmmaker, you have to make films. Luckily, my thesis film was a film called *Joe's Bed-Stuy Barbershop* and it won a student Academy Award. With that acclaim, with the little acclaim that that award brought, I got an agent, from William Morris. I was very new to the game."

When an agent failed to get him any assignments, he produced his first film independently, which meant he retained creative control. When the film turned out to earn a great deal of money, a precedent was set that the studios would always give him creative control of his film projects.

Lee also has a clear vision for what he wants to achieve as a filmmaker. "Growing up in this country, the rich culture I saw in my neighborhood, in my family—I didn't see that on television or on the movie screen. It was always my ambition that if I was successful, I would try to portray a truthful portrait of African Americans in this country, negative and positive."

THE INTERNET

As the newest communication platform and one that is used for a broad range of purposes, the Internet has not yet had the time to be the platform for many noteworthy practitioners who work will survive over time in the same way other types of media have. Most of the most famous people associated with the Internet are those who have invented the most popular services and Web sites, including Tim Berners-Lee, who invented the World Wide Web; Jeff Bezos, who created Amazon.com; Pierre Omidyar, who founded eBay; Larry Page and Sergey Brin, who founded Google; and Mark Zuckerberg, who founded Facebook.

People have been able to attract attention to themselves via the Web, but that attention, though widespread, is often short-lived. Nevertheless, a new generation of media entrepreneurs is emerging. For example, Arianna Huffington, who was once best known for being the wife of a losing candidate for the U.S. Senate, founded *The Huffington Post,* a combination news and blogging Web site that has gained enormous popularity. Other prominent figures are sure to emerge as the Internet continues to become embedded as a very significant communications platform.

Matt Drudge (1966–)

Matt Drudge was an unlikely candidate to demonstrate the Internet's potential for breaking news stories. Nonetheless, a story he published ultimately led to the impeachment of President Bill Clinton. Born in 1966 in Takoma Park, Maryland, Drudge was a self-described C-minus student who said he hated living with his "hippie parents." He worked as a convenience-store clerk for a time and then at the gift shop at CBS Studios in Los Angeles.

Drudge was also a news junkie. In 1994, he began posting news tidbits to a Usenet listserv, a way to distribute information online to subscribers. The following year, in 1995, he began producing *The Drudge Report*, basically a listing of rumors, gossip, and other items that he found by incessantly trolling the Internet and the World Wide Web. Ironically, the first scoop for which he gained attention came in a more prosaic fashion—it was an advance copy of television ratings he found in the trash while working at the CBS gift shop. Web surfers and some journalists began to visit his site to learn the CBS gossip he overheard behind the gift shop counter.

As the popularity of Drudge's site grew, he widened his scope and began to report widely on politics and other items. Viewing himself as a tipster and his site as a tip sheet, he never verified his items and seemed unconcerned about their accuracy. For example, Drudge posted a link to a totally untrue story about a romantic extramarital affair of Senator John Kerry, Democrat from Massachusetts, and another story that President Bill Clinton had fathered a child with an African-American woman.

When confronted with a false story, Drudge would publish a retraction and an apology, but then he would publish the next outrageous account. In 1997, he became one of the first online news producers involved in a libel suit brought by White House aide Sidney Blumenthal, whom Drudge accused of being a wife beater. Drudge eventually settled the $30 million lawsuit out of court.

Nevertheless, Drudge had a talent for being the first to publicize hot news. For example, he was the first to report Princess Diana's death and the departure of Connie Chung from CBS Television. In 1998, he achieved instant fame when he reported that *Newsweek* was holding back a story about "a White House intern" (Monica Lewinsky) who was having an affair with President Bill Clinton. That affair would ultimately lead to the impeachment of President Clinton, although the U.S. Senate voted not to remove him from office.

Based on his celebrity from the Lewinsky affair, Drudge received a television contract with Fox News Channel, hosted a Sunday radio show, and wrote a book called *Drudge Manifesto*. By 2003, he was making about $1.2 million a year through the advertising on his Web site—working from his condo in Miami, where he monitors television stations, wire feeds, and thousands of e-mails. In 2004, the NBC political drama *The West Wing* spotlighted *The Drudge Report* in a plot about a Web-rumored sex scandal.

In many ways, Matt Drudge represents both the best and the worst of the potential for Internet journalism. As a lone individual without the backing of a major corporation, he is able to provide millions of people with information they want to read. On the other hand, he seems totally unburdened by concepts such as truth, accuracy, and social responsibility.

PUBLIC RELATIONS

The concept of public relations is as old or older than the mass media themselves. The notion that communication with others is vital to accomplish goals is very basic. With the invention of the mass media in the 19th century, the idea of public relations became intertwined with stunts, promotions, and, on occasion, exaggeration or deception. P.T. Barnum's dictum that "there's a sucker born every minute" seemed to be the animating spirit of what was then called "publicity."

In the early part of the 20th century, a more professional and scientific approach to public relations began to emerge. The new conception of the public relations saw it as a profession incorporating scientific research and standards of conduct. Public relations is a tool to help companies and organizations of all kinds to interact with targeted communities of interest and sought to shape public opinion in a meaningful way for the long term, not merely the one-shot publicity stunt.

Edward Bernays (1891–1995)

As a profession, public relations came of age in the 20th century. Edward Bernays often is credited as the "father of public relations" for his role in defining the industry's philosophy and methods, building on Ivy Lee's *Declaration of Principles* of 1906, which proposed that public-relations practitioners have a public responsibility beyond their obligations to their clients. Bernays viewed public relations as a science, contending that mass persuasion required the involvement of the social sciences. He characterized the scientific approach to molding public opinion as the "engineering of consent."

Born in 1891, Bernays was the nephew of Sigmund Freud, who founded the field of psychoanalysis. Educated at Cornell University, Bernays drew on the ideas of his uncle as well as those of Gustav LeBon and Wilfred Trotter, both of whom wanted to understand the psychology of crowds, to develop a new approach to public relations. Bernays wanted public relations to separate itself from the ballyhoo of press agentry common at the time. As he explained it, the evolution from press agent to public relations counsel "was no mere difference in nomenclature, no euphemistic changeover. It was a different activity, in approach and execution ... [We were now] dealing with the interaction between client and public."

One of Bernays' major contributions to public relations was his development of the two-way symmetric approach model for public relations. This approach uses feedback as a way to improve the effectiveness of an organization's message. Evaluative research is conducted, but the results are used strictly to alter public attitudes in favor of the organization's objectives.

Bernays applied his approach in a wide range of public-relations campaigns that ranged from encouraging people to eat more bananas to trying to convince people to bathe more often. On behalf of a client who wanted to sell more bacon, he promoted the notion of a big breakfast. One of his early achievements was convincing the public that it was acceptable for young women to smoke. For this public relations campaign, he photographed debutants smoking cigarettes during Easter parades in major cities. Smoking became a symbol of women's liberation and freedom. Ironically, Bernays later worked on campaigns to discourage smoking.

Bernays drew a sharp distinction between advertising and public relations. While advertising professionals were paid to get people to accept new products and ideas, "public relations counsels," as he liked to call himself, were integral players in the distribution of ideas. In his 1928 book,

Manipulating Public Opinion, he wrote, "This is an age of mass production. In the mass production of materials, a broad technique has been developed and applied to their distribution. In this age, too, there must be a technique for the mass distribution of ideas."

ADVERTISING

Advertising is one of the first and most powerful communications industries. The earliest printed publications in England—posters and handbills—carried advertising announcements. With innovations of mass production, mass media, and high-speed transportation, advertising assumed an increasingly important role in business. Since manufacturers could make goods in quantity and sell them efficiently in distant markets, they needed a way to communicate their messages to their potential customers. Advertising was that vehicle.

New media technologies have repeatedly transformed advertising throughout its history. During the 1950s, and the growth of broadcast television provided a major boost to advertising and spurred scientific measurement of advertising effectiveness. In fact, for its first four decades, U.S. television was supported almost entirely by advertising revenues. Competition from television for advertising dollars eventually forced out of business the large circulation weekly photomagazines such as *Life* and *Look*.

Commercial media content on the Internet has emerged as largely an advertising-supported activity. Internet advertising is increasingly seen as an essential strategy for promoting products and services.

In 2006, Microsoft spend 20 percent of its revenues, $11.5 billion, on advertising. Microsoft was not alone. Coca-Cola spent $2.5 billion and Yahoo! spent $1.3 billion. In the 2008 presidential election race, the campaigns of Barack Obama and John McCain raised huge amounts of donations via their Web sites and together spent $450 million on television advertising alone from April to November, according to the Campaign Media Analysis Group.

Mary Wells Lawrence (1928–)

Mary Wells Lawrence helped usher in a new, creative era in advertising. She injected advertising with humor, pizzazz, and originality. Many of her ad campaigns are still remembered today. Advertising's first international superstar, Lawrence was the founding president of the advertising agency Wells Rich Green, at one point the world's highest-paid woman executive, and the first female chief executive officer of a company listed on the New York Stock Exchange.

Born in 1928 in Youngstown, Ohio, Lawrence studied for two years in the late 1940s at the Carnegie Institute of Technology and then went to New York City to study drama. After a stint as the fashion advertising manager for Macy's department stores, she became a copywriter and copy group head for the advertising agency McCann Erickson in 1953. In 1957, she joined the agency Doyle Dane Bernbach as vice president and chief copywriter. She has credited the partners of this agency as having had a significant influence on her career.

In 1967, she joined the ad firm of Jack Tinker & Partners, a prestigious agency noted for its creativity, and began her partnership with Richard Rich and the art director Stewart Green. The trio created many of the most memorable campaigns in advertising. The first was a novel ad campaign for Braniff International Airways. The campaign, "End of the Plain Plane," built an entirely new image for the airline. Instead of focusing on a single product, Lawrence developed a total approach that included changing the uniforms of Braniff flight attendants and painting the airplanes themselves.

In 1966, the trio formed Wells Rich Green. The firm won the Braniff account and quickly expanded their client roster. Three of Lawrence's campaigns for the cold relief medicine Alka Seltzer are considered iconic, including the campaign that used the jingle, "plop, plop, fizz, fizz, oh, what a relief it is." Two of her taglines for Alka Seltzer campaigns, "Try it, you'll like it," and "I can't believe I ate the whole thing," entered the popular lexicon.

Lawrence also crafted Ford Motor Company's "Quality is Job One" campaign as well as the long-running "I ♥ New York" campaign to promote tourism in New York. Lawrence's ads were effective because they were humorous and did not insult the audience's intelligence. The "I ♥ New York" graphic was created by the famous graphic artist Milton Glaser.

In 1971, Lawrence was named Advertising Woman of the Year by the American Advertising Federation, and in 1999, she was inducted into the American Advertising Hall of Fame. According to Charlie Moss, who served as creative director for Lawrence's agency, "Mary was to Madison Avenue what Muhammad Ali was to boxing."

MEDIA THEORISTS

Communication researchers and theorists have developed many of the key ways that people think about communication and understand the role of mass communications in social life. The scientific study of the mass media is relatively new, dating back to the advent of the broadcasting media in the 1920s and 30s, but media theorists can trace their roots back to the Greek philosopher Aristotle. Ironically, few people who study how the media create celebrities become celebrities themselves. However, one mid-century scholar's theories about the effects of the media were so startlingly new and his manner of expression so intriguing that he himself rose to celebrity status.

Marshall McLuhan (1911–1980)

Marshall McLuhan studied the impact of television on society by placing television within a context of evolving media systems. He hypothesized that how we communicate helps to shape how we think and that media systems have an impact on human evolution. He predicted sweeping changes to society as a result of the emerging medium of television. He coined catch phrases to capture the public's imagination and is perhaps best known for his slogans "the medium is the message" and "the global village," which predicted a worldwide electronic communication network decades before the advent of the Internet.

Born in 1911 in Edmonton, Alberta, McLuhan grew up in Winnipeg, Manitoba, where he attended the University of Manitoba. After a long and circuitous route, he received a Ph.D. in literature from the University of Cambridge in England. In the early 1950s, he joined the faculty of St. Michael's College, a Catholic college associated with the University of Toronto. He won a grant from the Ford Foundation to conduct seminars on communication and culture, and he ultimately established the Center for Communication and Technology.

In 1951 McLuhan published a pioneering book, *Mechanical Bride: Folklore of Industrial Man*, which examined the role of media in popular culture. The book looked at a variety of newspaper and magazine articles and advertisements, analyzing them for their use of symbolism, their aesthetics, and the implications between the images and text. *The Mechanical Bride* also analyzed examples of persuasion in contemporary culture.

Following the success of *The Mechanical Bride*, McLuhan turned to studying the influence of communications. His next major publication was his 1962 book *The Gutenberg Galaxy*, a pioneering study in the fields of oral culture, print culture, and the media. McLuhan's view was that communication technology, starting from the first press with movable type to electronic media, had a profound effect on social organization.

McLuhan's best-known book was *Understanding Media: The Extensions of Man* (1964), which suggested that scholars studying communication should shift the focus of their study from the content transmitted by the mass media to the media themselves. He claimed that the media powerfully determine the messages, or, as he put it, the medium *is* the message. He contended that certain media by their nature are "hot," which means the viewer does not have to do much to determine the meaning. However, some media are "cool," which means the viewer must work, must interact, to understand the message. Movies are hot, for example, while comics are cool.

McLuhan appeared on numerous television programs in Canada and the United States and was featured in popular magazines such as *Newsweek, Life, Esquire, Fortune,* and *The New Yorker.* In 1991 *Wired* magazine claimed McLuhan as its patron saint. He even had a humorous cameo appearance in Woody Allen's 1977 film *Annie Hall*, supposedly to debunk a pompous college professor arguing with Woody while they stood in line for movie tickets.

McLuhan's ideas have been modified and extended by many researchers, including Neil Postman and Joshua Meyrowitz. While it is no longer thought that the medium entirely determines the message, the idea that different media facilitate or constrain certain types of content and meaning has been a fruitful area for researchers to explore. Moreover, McLuhan's vision of a global village with an electronic nervous system is seen as prescient with the rise of the Internet.

CONCLUSION

Though the communications media are large, complex, global institutions dependent on advanced technologies and employing hundreds of thousands of workers, all media communication is basically a process of people creating and sharing meaningful content. Within every media industry, individuals can make a big impact on this communication process. They can change the way different media operate; the way people relate to one another, and the way people see the world. Several people who have a huge impact in the media world are profiled in this chapter. Because media matters, there will be more big impact players in the future. In the final analysis, communication is about individual people and their relationships to others and to the world.

THE PIRATE

by Ken Auletta

When Rupert Murdoch arrives at his office on the Twentieth Century Fox lot, in Los Angeles, the single television is set to CNN, and the sound is off. At about eight-thirty, Dot Wyndoe, Murdoch's assistant of thirty-three years, spreads newspapers out on a shelf across from his desk: "TOP COP NICKED MY WIFE," blares one of his London tabloids, the *Sun*; "LOVE JUDGE COMES HOME," screams the New York *Post*. These are the only noisy elements in the office. Even the phones are quiet. Numerous calls stack up and are announced on an electronic monitor at his right elbow. Pastel paintings by Australian artists hang on snow-white walls over white couches and armchairs.

Murdoch's hair is turning white. He is sixty-four, and his shoulders stoop slightly. His voice is soft, and his manner is unfailingly courteous, as he sits with one leg tucked under the other. Only the hard brown eyes suggest that he is a predator.

He spends most of his time on the phone. He phones while driving his BMW to work, and he starts phoning from his desk as soon as he arrives, about 7 A.M. He always apologizes for disturbing an employee at an odd hour or on vacation, but the apology is more a ritual than a sign of genuine contrition. He hardly ever says hello or goodbye.

Murdoch lives in Beverly Hills, in a Spanish-style house, on six acres, formerly owned by Jules Stein, the founder of MCA. He's often away, doing business out of a Gulfstream jet he owns, or from one or another of the offices he keeps in several cities, including New York, where he works from a high-rise on Sixth Avenue near Times Square. This office is also white, and it has seven silent TV sets.

"Eric, sorry to wake you," Murdoch was saying from the New York office one recent afternoon. It was before dawn in Australia, and he had reached Eric Walsh, a lobbyist based in Canberra, who has been advising him on how to get the Chinese government to sanction his Star TV satellite system. "I was going to go to Hong Kong for a week, but I've been invited for a one-day conference in Beijing," he told Walsh. Murdoch wanted to know if he should reach out to the Chinese. And, if so, when? "Do I need an alibi?" he asked Walsh. "Or can I just write and say, 'I need a half hour of your time'?"

READING NOTES

Walsh cautioned Murdoch to stay in the background. "Nobody understands what's going on in there," Murdoch mused in response, slipping down further in his soft leather chair, until his head was not much higher than his desk. "Everyone has different readings. You just never bloody know."

Without the support of the Chinese government, Star TV can have no paid subscribers, and advertisers stay away. That situation translates into big losses projected at eighty million dollars in the current fiscal year, Murdoch says. He owns a satellite service that can potentially reach two-thirds of the world's population, yet, because of widespread concern in Asia about "cultural imperialism" and the impact of uncensored images and information, he has had to curb his aggressive tendencies. "My Chinese friends tell me, 'Just go there every month,'" he says. "'Knock on doors. It may take ten years.'" This is not the message that Murdoch wants to hear.

> *Murdoch is the chairman, C.E.O., and principal shareholder of a company, the News Corporation, that produced nearly nine billion dollars in revenue this year and more than a billion in profits, but he feels frustrated. He is frustrated by China. He is frustrated because he has no international news network to supply his Fox network here, or his Sky or Star satellite services in Europe and Asia, while Ted Turner has CNN. And until last month he was frustrated because he owned the rights to televise sporting events all over the world but didn't own a sports network, like ESPN.*

Over all, however, these frustrations present mere skirmishes in a global war that Murdoch is winning. All the media deals and maneuvers of the past few months have come about, in part, because Disney and Time Warner felt that they had to catch up to Murdoch. "He basically wants to conquer the world," says Sumner Redstone, the chairman of Viacom. "And

he seems to be doing it." Former press lords, like Lord Beaverbrook, William Randolph Hearst, and Henry Luce, were dominant figures in a single medium on a single continent. Rupert Murdoch's empire spreads across six continents and nine different media: newspapers (his company owns or has an interest in a hundred and thirty-two); magazines (he owns or has an interest in twenty-five, including *TV Guide*, which has the largest circulation of any weekly magazine in the United States); books (HarperCollins and Zondervan, the dominant publisher of religious books); broadcasting (the Fox network, twelve TV stations in the United States; fifteen per cent of the Seven network, in Australia; and Sky Radio, in Britain); direct-broadcast satellite television (Star TV, in Asia; forty per cent of BSkyB, in Europe; half ownership of Vox, in Germany; and a yet to be named joint venture with Globo, in South America); cable (the fX network, in the United States; Canal Fox, in Latin America; and half ownership of Foxtel, in Australia); a movie studio (Twentieth Century Fox); home video (Fox Video); and online access to the worldwide Internet (Delphi). Murdoch not only reaches readers; he also holds the electronic keys to their homes.

Murdoch moves more swiftly than most rivals, takes bigger risks, and never gives up. In fact, despite public denials he has made, in late October he was still contemplating ways to reverse the deal that Time Warner announced in September to buy Turner Broadcasting System—a deal that blocked some of Murdoch's own expansionist plans. One scheme that he discussed internally and ordered his bankers and lawyers to dissect carefully was to attempt a takeover of Time Warner valued at more than forty billion dollars. "We're working hard at it," a central figure in the News Corporation said in late October, days before Murdoch became convinced that the effort would fail. The impediment, two participants say, was not finding partners but figuring out how to avoid the steep capital-gains taxes on the sale of Time Warner's

READING NOTES

_____

_____

_____

_____

_____

various pieces to eager buyers. The idea was to make a bid for Time Warner in the next few months, before the merger with Turner was consummated. There were internal discussions about such potential partners as the Bronfmans, whose Seagram already owns just under fifteen per cent of Time Warner; US West, which owns twenty-five per cent of Time Warner's entertainment assets and opposes the terms of the Turner merger, and John Malone, the president and C.E.O. of Tele-Communications, Inc., the world's largest cable company.

Murdoch created the first global media network by investing in both software (movies, TV shows, sports franchises, publishing) and the distribution platforms (the Fox network, cable, and TV satellite systems) that disseminate the software. Within the next few years, the News Corporation's satellite system will blanket South America, in addition to Asia and Europe and parts of the Middle East and Africa. "Basically, we want to establish satellite platforms in major parts of the world," Murdoch explains. "And that gives us leverage here." If a cable-box owner or a programmer—John Malone or Time Warner, for instance—wants to reach a foreign market covered by one of Murdoch's satellite systems, Murdoch can extract favors from the programmer in the markets it controls in the United States. "What we're trying to do is put ourselves in a position in other countries that some of these cable companies are in in this country," he says. He wants to be the gatekeeper.

To advance his grand plan, Murdoch arranged a summit meeting in suburban Denver on August 10th with John Malone, of TCI. Murdoch called the meeting because he believed that Malone was necessary for capturing two of the missing pieces in his empire—the sports network and the news network. Malone owns fifteen regional cable sports channels and is a partner with Charles Dolan's Cablevision Systems in other regional sports channels around the country; these,

when joined with Murdoch's and Malone's overseas sports holdings, could become the foundation for an international sports network. In addition, Malone was Ted Turner's most influential shareholder and could link Murdoch with CNN. Murdoch was assuming that Turner was a possible partner, and Malone was openly dismissive of Time Warner's management.

The day before the meeting, Murdoch summoned to his California office Chase Carey, the chairman and C.E.O. of Fox Television, and Preston Padden, the president of network distribution for Fox and the president of telecommunications and television for the News Corporation. Murdoch, from behind the oak table he uses as a desk, began by noting that at that moment Malone was trying to help Turner finance a bid to acquire CBS, which would compete with Fox. "I think he intends to screw us," Murdoch said.

The three men held another caucus the next day, huddling in green upholstered armchairs on Murdoch's Gulfstream as it headed toward Denver for the meeting, at 2 P.M. They knew that Malone and Turner needed cash to take over CBS, and they talked about how Turner might be encouraged to sell something.

"The only asset we'd be interested in is CNN," Carey said.

Padden asked what might happen if Fox became a one-third owner in CNN.

"You don't want to hand over all your news efforts to Ted," said Murdoch, who is as wary of Turner's being too liberal as Turner is of Murdoch's being too conservative.

A car waited at the Denver airport to take Murdoch, Carey, and Padden to TCI headquarters. The meeting was held in a stark, glass-walled conference room dominated by a black granite oval table. The only refreshments were a few cans of diet soda and a thermos of coffee on a granite sideboard; each corner of the room was occupied by a rubber plant.

READING NOTES

_____

_____

_____

_____

_____

Malone, attired in a red-and-white checked short-sleeved button-down shirt and chinos, was careful not to sit at the head of the table. Flanked by two TCI executives, he took a seat across from the Murdoch trio. The table was bare except for a single folded sheet of paper in front of Malone.

The six men, who did not rise from their seats for the next four hours, began with industry gossip, which soon bored Murdoch. He changed the subject: "Are you getting it together for Ted and CBS?"

"We know where the money will come from," Malone answered. "The question is Time Warner. I think their strategy is to drive Ted nuts." Time Warner, which, like TCI, then owned about twenty per cent of Turner Broadcasting, had the right to veto all acquisitions, and it was thwarting the takeover of CBS. Malone said, contemptuously, that he thought Gerald Levin, the Time Warner chairman and president, was seesawing, because his management was engaged in an internal war.

Rather offhandedly, Murdoch asked, "Does Ted want to sell any assets?"

"No," Malone replied, with equal aplomb. "I don't know of any asset Ted wants to part with." He knew that Murdoch was fishing, hoping he could hook CNN.

Privately, Murdoch describes Malone as "the most brilliant strategist" he knows. Malone says the same thing about Murdoch, and over the years they have been both adversaries and allies, depending on the venture. It's difficult to keep track of partnerships in the communications business these days, because the players change sides depending on the country or on the deal.

Malone had several goals in this meeting. He wanted to see if there were areas where he and Murdoch could do business together, and he wanted to avoid conflicts. Both were interested in creating a sports network that could compete with ESPN, and he thought he could get Murdoch to invest in the regional sports channels that TCI shared with Charles Dolan's Cablevision.

"The fact is," Malone told Murdoch during their summit, "we tried to merge our sports with Chuck's maybe fifty times." Each time, the plan unravelled because Malone and Dolan could never agree on who would run the partnership. But Malone was convinced that if a third party came in—someone "who may be more objective than we can be with each other," perhaps Murdoch—a successful merger could be achieved. "Between us, we have all the regional sports networks in the country controlled—except Minneapolis," he said, and that came to thirty-three million subscribers. "The real value for us," he went on, "is putting these together," thereby creating a powerful entity for buying worldwide sports rights, as ESPN does.

Malone and Murdoch then began a *tour d'horizon*, starting with a review of what each of them was doing to reach the estimated seventy million television households in Central and South America, and how each was faring in Europe. Malone did most of the talking. "I guess at this point Europe is pretty stable," he said. A short time later, he said, "The thing we haven't talked about is Japan." He barely moved as he spoke, keeping two fingers pressed to his temples. "We have a deal there in sports, and we have to discuss how that relates to Star."

"Star isn't there at the moment," Murdoch said. "But we are pretty far down the road." He asked how Time Warner was doing in Japan.

"They're running way behind us," Malone said. "They came to us and asked, 'Why don't we do a joint venture?'" He went on to say that he had rejected this for two reasons: first, it was dumb politics, since most nations carefully limit foreign ownership; second, "Time Warner is brain-damaged in terms of making decisions. You've got to move fast." Malone then returned to sports: "All these pieces fit, Rupert. We

READING NOTES

_____

_____

_____

_____

_____

ought to be able to arrive at this"—a sports merger—"in painless fashion." He added, "We think Asia will take awhile."

"Japan is now," Murdoch said.

"Either you guys get in or ESPN will own sports," Malone warned.

"We got to go in and kick ass," Murdoch agreed.

Dolan was difficult to negotiate with, Malone warned.

"If we have to go without him, well go without him," Murdoch said. They could always fold in Cablevision later. What Murdoch needed was some numbers from Malone.

The single sheet of paper slid across the table. It contained, Malone explained, what TCI thought each of its fifteen regional sports channels was worth.

Afterward, I asked Murdoch and Malone separately if there was anything they had discussed alone. Only one thing, Murdoch replied: in a private moment, Malone had "tried to talk me into buying five per cent of Time Warner to put it in play." Malone also conceded that they had talked about Time Warner.

Murdoch thought that he had accomplished half his mission. He was confident that he and Malone would make a sports deal, but he felt that CNN was slipping away, not least because Turner would probably spurn him. A fair number of communications-company C.E.O.s think that Murdoch is a pirate.

CNN became even further out of reach the following month, when Time Warner announced a merger with Turner. This was a real blow. Murdoch and Malone had been outmaneuvered. Malone no longer sat in the cockpit with Turner. His role had been reduced to that of a passenger and an investor. "The picture is confusing," a subdued Murdoch told me in late September. "Strategies are changing day to day." He partly blamed Jane Fonda, who is Turner's wife. "I surmise Jane had

a great hand in it," he said. "'We can change the world together.'"

Despite the setback, Murdoch and Malone's meeting did produce some concrete results. Murdoch chased Charles Dolan, and when, as Malone had anticipated, they could not reach an agreement the News Corporation and TCI negotiated, and on October 31st announced that they had agreed to become partners in a new, worldwide Fox sports network to compete with ESPN. They also have tentatively agreed to become partners in a direct satellite system in South America.

Malone sees Murdoch's strategy as much broader than that of his foes. He is not just trying to "get big," Malone observes. "He sees the nexus between programming and platform." Unlike Disney and Viacom, which have both concentrated on programming, Murdoch owns satellite distribution systems that span the globe. And, unlike his competitors in the satellite business, he owns a programming factory—Twentieth Century Fox. Competitors like NBC own neither. And TCI, Malone admits, has cable platforms but is "too weak in programming." Furthermore, unlike Time Warner and Viacom, Murdoch doesn't have a lot of debt: he has several billion dollars of investment capital available. And, unlike any other communications giants except perhaps Sumner Redstone and Bill Gates, he has a controlling interest in his company. "Rupert is a bit like a painter with a canvas, but in his mind the canvas has no perimeters," Arthur Siskind, the general counsel for the News Corporation, observes. "He's going to keep painting and painting."

Murdoch is a pirate; he will cunningly circumvent rules, and sometimes principles, to get his way, as his recent adventures in China demonstrate.

Sometime in 1992, Murdoch took his initial look at Star TV, which was then a five-channel satellite service operating out of Hong Kong and reaching fifty-three countries. He wanted to enter into a partnership with the owner—Li Ka-shing, a Hong Kong billionaire, who was on good terms with the Chinese government, and with Li's son, Richard, who ran the company on behalf of his father—but only if the News Corporation could manage Star. In July of 1993, Murdoch offered five hundred and twenty-five million dollars for sixty-four per cent of Star, and that led to an agreement.

Murdoch was confident that Li and his son could run political interference from China. Others were less certain. Robert Wright, the president of NBC, recalls that one reason NBC had not pursued a deal with Star was the fear of opposition from the Chinese government. Perhaps Murdoch, too, should have worried more about this. The Chinese were still smarting from an abortive attempt he had made earlier that year to buy thirty per cent of Hong Kong's largest broadcaster, TVB, despite a law stipulating that no foreign entity could own more than twenty per cent of a communications company if it also owned another media outlet, and Murdoch did—the *South China Morning Post* (which he subsequently sold).

Murdoch seems to have thought that he could get around the Chinese authorities' hostility towards his ownership of Star, because technically he did not need the sanction of *any* government to deliver pictures from space. Besides, Murdoch is supremely confident—to the point of arrogance, perhaps—that he can get what he wants. "Rupert figured he could find a way to deal with China," George Vradenburg, who was then an executive vice-president of Fox, recalls.

If it had not been for the Speech, Murdoch might have found a way. On September 1, 1993, he invited hundreds of advertisers to Whitehall Palace, in London, and gave a speech explaining why the News Corporation was at the cutting edge of the communications revolution. He declared that George Orwell was wrong. "Advances in the technology of telecommunications have proved an unambiguous threat to totalitarian regimes everywhere," he said. "Fax machines enable dissidents to bypass state-controlled print media; direct-dial telephony makes it difficult for a state to control interpersonal voice communications. And satellite broadcasting makes it possible for information-hungry residents of many closed societies to bypass state-controlled television channels."

A month after the Whitehall speech, the Chinese Prime Minister signed into law a virtual ban on individual ownership of satellite dishes, and a suddenly chastened Murdoch was forced to show solicitude toward a totalitarian regime. He consulted many experts. He moved to Hong Kong for six weeks, and he reached out to Chinese officials. "He analyzed the problem objectively," his public-relations adviser, Howard Rubenstein, recalls. "He didn't make any excuses. It was an error that he made."

Murdoch had spoken like the libertarian he has professed to be, but now he chose to be reëducated, and among the lessons he learned was how deeply the Chinese government detested the BBC, whose World Service news was carried on a Star channel. The regime was especially angered by a BBC documentary that investigated Chairman Mao's unorthodox sexual habits. And, since the BBC was British, it was seen as the ally of forces that sought to keep Hong Kong independent of the mainland.

In April of 1994, Murdoch removed the BBC from the Star network in China and replaced it with Chinese-language films. "The BBC was driving them nuts," Murdoch says. "It's not worth it." The Chinese government is "scared to death of what happened in Tiananmen Square," he says. "The truth is—and we Americans don't like to admit it—that authoritarian countries can work. There may have been human-rights abuses in Chile. But that country under Pinochet raised living standards. And now it has a democracy. The best thing you can do in China is engage the Chinese and wait."

READING NOTES

How does Murdoch explain his new tolerance for dictatorships? "I'm not saying they're right," he replies. "You don't go in there and run a controlled press. You just stay out of the press."

As he did with the BBC?

"Yes," he replies. "We're not proud of that decision. It was the only way."

Murdoch was not the only media potentate to grovel to a repressive regime. In Asia at about this time, Ted Turner, after meeting with Chinese broadcasting officials, criticized the United States for trying to "tell so many other countries in the world what to do" about human rights. And, when the former Prime Minister of Singapore and his son, the deputy prime minister, threatened to sue for libel because of an article in the *International Herald Tribune* suggesting that the deputy prime minister had been appointed to his post in an act of nepotism, the paper, which is owned by the New York *Times* and the Washington *Post*, issued an abject public apology.

Murdoch's campaign to win over the Chinese authorities was multifaceted. It included replacing Star's English-only format with programming in Chinese; buying sports rights to badminton and other sports popular with the Chinese; joining with four international music companies to create a music channel for local Chinese talent; becoming a partner with the Tianjin Sports Development Company in the construction of four television studios and post-production centers; starting a pay-TV channel in Mandarin; and putting up five million four hundred thousand dollars for a joint investment with the Communist Party organ, *People's Daily*, to provide, among other things, an on-line version of the kind of dull newspaper that he would never publish in the West.

Last winter, Basic Books, a division of the News Corporation's HarperCollins, brought out a hagiography of Deng Xiaoping by his youngest daughter,

Deng Rong, who wrote under her nickname, Deng Maomao. Ms. Deng has long served as her father's personal secretary, and is married to He Ping, the head of Poly Technologies, one of the country's largest military conglomerates. The HarperCollins catalogue announced that the book by Ms. Deng, who Murdoch said received an advance of ten or twenty thousand dollars, would benefit from promotional efforts that would be coördinated with News Corporation media outlets. Despite the meagre advance, Murdoch feted Ms. Deng as if she were Tom Clancy. Last February, he attended a book party on the top floor of the Waldorf-Astoria sponsored by HarperCollins. He gave a private lunch for her at his ranch in Carmel. And he and his wife were hosts at a dinner for her in a private dining room at Le Cirque. There were six tables of eight, and among those who attended were Cyrus Vance and the Chinese Ambassadors to Washington and the United Nations. After a four-course meal, Murdoch rose and, a guest recalls, toasted Deng Xiaoping as "a man who had brought China into the modern world." This summer, Murdoch was confident enough of victory in China to have the News Corporation invest three hundred million dollars more to buy the thirty-six per cent of Star TV that it did not already own. In a further development that perhaps reflects Murdoch's solicitousness toward the Chinese government, in September HarperCollins dropped out of the bidding for a book by the Chinese-American human-rights activist Harry Wu, who is despised by the Chinese government.

Murdoch's decision to boot the BBC out of China was condemned as "the most seedy of betrayals" by Christopher Patten, the governor of Hong Kong. To espouse freedom of speech at home "but to curtail it elsewhere for reasons of inevitably short-term commercial expediency" was, he implied, immoral—or, at least, amoral. Some businessmen have defended Murdoch. "Being tough is sometimes confused with being amoral," Sumner Redstone says. "They are not

READING NOTES

_____

_____

_____

_____

_____

the same thing. He's doing what he has to do to solve his problems with the Chinese government. He's being smart to do that." It's just business, in other words.

But some of Murdoch's colleagues demur. "When matters of principle and expediency clash with Rupert, expediency wins every time," says Frank Barlow, who, as the managing director of the London-based media conglomerate Pearson, is chairman of the *Financial Times* and oversees the Penguin publishing group. "I don't think we would have dumped the BBC. From time to time, the *Financial Times* gets banned in some countries. But that doesn't alter our approach. We published the Salman Rushdie book. And stood behind Salman Rushdie." Joe Roth, who successfully ran the Fox studio for Murdoch and has called him a "visionary," nevertheless suggests that he can be coldly amoral. "I think of him in business as a guy who will do whatever he needs to do to get it done."

Murdoch's detachment can be traced to his childhood, in Australia. Sir Keith and Lady Elisabeth Murdoch, his parents, sent young Rupert to a boarding school, Geelong Grammar, near Melbourne, which featured military discipline, cadet parades, and occasional canings, and he rebelled against all of them. He was teased a lot at school, he recalls. "I was always a bit of an outsider. That undoubtedly came from my father and his position." Sir Keith ran a chain of newspapers, and the sons of the landed gentry at Geelong considered journalism a low-rent business. Asa Briggs, a social historian who was Murdoch's "moral tutor" at Oxford, recalls that Rupert "always had to have an enemy." Another strong emotion that goes back to his boyhood is a disdain for intimacy. "I learned early that getting very close to people can be dangerous if you're going to be in a position of public responsibility," Murdoch told me.

The lonely young rebel grew up to be a rebel capitalist. Murdoch's News Corporation is a large company run like a small one. A single individual makes big decisions, quickly, and for reasons he sometimes does not explain. For example, members of Murdoch's board have wondered about the dollar drain imposed by a favorite Murdoch toy, the New York *Post*. Murdoch himself says that this year the *Post* will lose "close to twenty million dollars"—a figure that will raise the net total losses Murdoch has endured in the thirteen years he has owned the paper to more than a hundred million dollars. Yet he wouldn't think of closing it. It offers a powerful political platform. And, besides, at heart he thinks of himself as a newspaperman.

As a manager, Murdoch employs an instinctual and hands-on style. He will plunge into one of his businesses for a week or two, focussing all his attention on it until he masters it. He has a minimal staff of experts and shuns formal meetings, preferring the telephone or one-on-one encounters. In most cases, all that Murdoch requires from those who run his various properties is a one-page weekly financial report containing no narrative—just a recitation of expenditures and revenues, budgeted versus actual totals, and this year's revenues versus last year's.

There is no chief operating officer at the News Corporation. The board is composed of thirteen people, only three of whom are non-employees, non-consultants, or non-family members. George Vradenburg says, "He operates the company as a private, independent family company. And it has the strengths and the weaknesses of that. The strength is quick decisions. The weakness is that no one else has independent knowledge of what is going on in all of the company. Everyone is vulnerable to his health."

Murdoch delegates—except when he doesn't want to. He is clearly not as deeply engaged in the movies as he is in, say, *Post* headlines. "The long lead times frustrate him," says Peter Chernin, the chairman of Twentieth Century Fox. "It's hard to get him involved." Joe Roth, who preceded Chernin as the studio's chief, guesses that Murdoch reads maybe one script a year.

READING NOTES

_____

_____

_____

_____

_____

Murdoch's fabled do-it-alone impatience was one of several things that led the News Corporation to the precipice of bankruptcy in 1990. For example, Murdoch negotiated the nearly three-billion-dollar purchase of *TV Guide* from Walter Annenberg without calling on his lawyer, Howard Squadron, or his investment banker, Stanley Shuman.

Murdoch has had only one chief operating officer, Gus Fischer, and Fischer lasted only four years in that position. "He never told people in New York, 'You are now reporting to Gus.' It was difficult," recalls Fischer, who left the News Corporation in March and is now an independent entrepreneur. "I think he feels much more comfortable having someone who calls him if he wants to go to the bathroom. Don't get me wrong. I'm not saying this in a negative way, against Rupert. I'm just saying it's his style." While many executives have been with Murdoch for decades, there has been carnage near the top of the company. Murdoch, observes Joe Roth, who now runs the Disney studios, "makes you feel fungible." Even Barry Diller, whom Murdoch himself has credited with building the Fox network, was pushed out—despite denials at the time—when he asked for a larger slice of the company. Other Fox executives who "were feeling too proprietary," as Howard Squadron phrases it, also have gone.

Personally, Murdoch is a gentleman. He treats executives as part of his extended family: he invited them to his son Lachlan's engagement party, he remembers spouses' names, he rarely raises his voice. "He's not abusive," a senior News Corporation executive says. "But when he turns on you, it's"—he snaps a finger—"like that." In the past decade, Murdoch has had four deputies who appeared to be his No. 2—Donald Kummerfeld, Gus Fischer, Andrew Knight, and Richard Searby, the chairman of the board for ten years and a friend of fifty years.

When Sir Keith died, in 1952, the twenty-one-year-old Murdoch prepared to take over his father's business.

The son had always thought of his father as a press lord, but in fact he had been employed by a newspaper chain; Sir Keith had owned only two newspapers, the Adelaide *News* and the Brisbane *Courier-Mail*, and the Brisbane paper was sold to pay taxes. So in 1953, when Rupert returned home from Oxford and a stint at a London paper, his empire consisted of a single newspaper with a daily circulation of under a hundred thousand. But before Murdoch was thirty he had acquired a number of newspapers and a TV station. He became a British press lord in early 1969, when he bested Robert Maxwell for the *News of the World*, a London Sunday tabloid with a circulation of approximately six million. Murdoch employed his charm to induce the Carr family, which had controlled the paper for nearly eighty years, to spurn a richer offer from Maxwell, whom the Carrs, like others, thought an odious man. Murdoch was seen as the safe choice, and he pledged to run the paper in partnership with the Carrs. But, as with so much of Murdoch's life, his acts are open to multiple interpretations. He argues that his pledge to the Carrs conflicted with his responsibility to shareholders. "It didn't take me long to realize that it was a total wreck of a company," he explains.

His treatment of the Carr family intensified an impression that would grow and forever shadow Murdoch: that his word is counterfeit, and he can't be trusted. The impression is widespread that people in journalism and business help him at a critical point and are then discarded. Eight years after he bought the *News of the World*, he started courting Dorothy Schiff, the owner of the *Post*. They had been brought together by Murdoch's friend Clay Felker, the editor and founder of *New York*. Murdoch induced her to sell the *Post* to him, and he transformed it from a dull liberal paper into a racy conservative one. Around that time, Felker confided to Murdoch that he was having difficulties with his board. Weeks later, Murdoch betrayed Felker by going behind his back and acquiring *New York*. Murdoch said at the time that the board wanted to sell

READING NOTES

_____

_____

_____

_____

_____

the company, because it thought that Felker was profligate. Most of the editorial staff—including this writer—sided with Felker and quit.

The feeling that Murdoch is a betrayer has been heightened by shifts in his political position. The purchase of the London *Sun*, in 1969, for instance, roughly coincided with Murdoch's transformation from an Oxford leftist who had kept a bust of Lenin in his room into a passionate capitalist. The political epiphany came, he recalls, when he grappled with England's trade unions. "This sounds very subjective and selfish," he told me, "but living in Britain and having to handle fifteen print unions every night and wondering if your papers were going to come out—if anything could make you conservative, it was handling the British print unions as they were in those days." Not long after Murdoch bought the *Sun* and tarted it up with topless women and gossip posing as news, compelling the other tabloids to follow his lead, the editorial voice of the paper veered to the right, and by the end of the decade it had become a fight-to-the-death defender of Margaret Thatcher.

A Conservative had rarely had the editorial backing of a working-class English newspaper before the *Sun* supported Thatcher in the 1979 elections. "I believe we were right to support Thatcher in critical times when she had no other supporters," Murdoch says now. "I think what people don't understand about me is that I'm not just a businessman working in a very interesting industry. I am someone who's interested in ideas." Throughout the eighties Murdoch was protected by the Thatcher government in ways that were crucial to his business, most notably in the broadening of his base as a newspaper owner.

Despite his disdain for the establishment, Murdoch always wanted to own an influential newspaper—one read by the establishment. First, in 1976, he tried to buy the London *Observer*, but was rebuffed by journalists

fearful of his reputation for political interference. Then, in 1981, he pulled off a spectacular coup, gaining control of the biggest quality weekly, the profitable *Sunday Times*, and also of the loss-making daily *Times*. Since he already owned the *Sun* and the weekly *News of the World*, it was expected that his bid would get mired in a protracted review by the Monopolies and Mergers Commission, but a recommendation of a referral to the commission was overruled by the government on the ground that the papers would die if Murdoch wasn't allowed to save them.

The staffs of both the *Times* papers were seduced by a pledge that an independent board would approve the hiring and firing of editors and that Murdoch would not interfere in the editorial operations of the papers. In a year, however, the editor of the *Times*, Harold Evans (the husband of the editor of this magazine), was ousted by Murdoch. The paper became an editorial partisan for Thatcher.

Encouraged by the political climate that Thatcher had created, Murdoch audaciously schemed to break the stranglehold of the newspaper unions—whose contracts called for eighteen men on a printing press when only five or six were needed—by secretly building what came to be called Fortress Wapping, a modern printing plant and headquarters surrounded by tall fences topped with coils of razor wire. He carried out the Wapping gamble with military precision. While he was negotiating, he ordered computers and new printing presses to be installed and tested in an abandoned warehouse on the Thames, and when negotiations collapsed he stunned the unions by transporting this equipment to Wapping, along with non-union workers to operate it. When mayhem threatened and thousands of angry workers paraded outside, more than a thousand police were on hand to preserve law and order. Murdoch concedes that he could not have succeeded if Labour had been in power.

READING NOTES

_____

_____

_____

_____

_____

Although the Conservatives remain in power in England, Murdoch worries that the government will "screw" him—an expression he often uses.

Might his papers support the British Labour leader, Tony Blair?

Murdoch laughs. "We're not tied to any party," he says. "The big question with Tony Blair, who's very impressive, is what he will be allowed to do by his own party if he ever achieves power." In July, Murdoch flew Blair to Australia to speak at the News Corporation's week-long management retreat, on Hayman Island. Unlike previous Labour leaders, Blair is prepared to entertain the deregulation of much of the communications business. Over cappuccino a few blocks from Parliament, one of Blair's associates said to me that although many Labour backbenchers had made a commitment to limit the percentage of broadcast outlets and newspapers that Murdoch could own, "I would be extremely surprised if that commitment was honored." What the Party is trying to do, the associate admits, is fudge the issue. Though this associate is privately critical of Murdoch's power, he says, "It would be absolutely mad for me to talk about Murdoch publicly." Blair's goal, he admits, is to get Murdoch's support, but the Party would be happy just to keep him neutral. Rupert Murdoch is a bit of a prude. "I guess it's my Scottish blood," he says—and a conventional family man. The only photographs in his New York and California offices are of his family. He has four children: a daughter, Prudence, from his first marriage, and two sons and a daughter with his second wife, the former Anna Tory. Elisabeth, twenty-seven, is married to Elkin Pianim, a Ghanaian whom she met in college. Until recently, the couple owned two TV stations in northern California. Lachlan, twenty-four, joined the News Corporation last year and is based in Australia. And James, twenty-two, has completed his junior year at Harvard and has dropped out to start a record company with two friends. Anna Murdoch is thirteen years younger than Rupert. They met when she was a cub reporter on Murdoch's *Daily Mirror* in Australia. Today, she is a novelist, and serves on the News Corporation board. Their son James says, "I don't know of any confidant other than my mother. I couldn't imagine him going to anyone but my mother. She's as tough as nails." She is also more conservative than her husband. A devout Catholic, she is implacably opposed to abortion and thinks it should be illegal; he does not (though he would eliminate federal funding). "She doesn't like 'The Simpsons,'" Murdoch says. "I think it's brilliant." She voted for George Bush in 1992, he recalls, while he voted for Ross Perot, as a protest. Today, she favors Bob Dole for President, while Murdoch likes Colin Powell. "He appears to be a man of very fine character," Murdoch says. "I agree with a lot of what he says."

Murdoch's family values and taste have rarely interfered with what goes on in the pages of his papers or in his television programming. The sexually raunchy shows are manufactured rather cynically. "I wouldn't let a thirteen-year-old watch 'Melrose Place,'" Murdoch admits. Yet Fox not only broadcasts "Melrose Place" but has shifted it from 9 P.M. to 8 P.M., the traditional children's hour. Murdoch introduced tabloid TV news magazines to America in 1986, with "A Current Affair," on Fox, encouraging others to follow him and to push the envelope, as they say, of bad taste. "He's confirmed the suspicion that shit sells," a former network president observes.

Prurience, whether manifested by the bare-breasted women who appear daily on page 3 of the *Sun*, and who are referred to as "*Sun* lovelies," or the sexual escapades of politicians or the Royal Family, is a staple of Murdoch's newspapers. This summer, for example, the New York *Post* got a lot of mileage out of pillorying Judge Kimba Wood for allegedly having a romance

READING NOTES

_____

_____

_____

_____

_____

with a married investment banker. The Kimba Wood story passed three Murdoch tabloid tests. First, he says, "it's a soap opera," an entertaining spectacle. Second, it fuels envy and resentment—and thus circulation—because it's about "high society," as he calls it. It tells the little people how the other half lives—repressed-schoolmarm judge likes sex! Third, it displays what Anthea Disney, who has worked on Murdoch's London tabloids and now serves as a top Murdoch executive, calls a "visceral" Fleet Street attitude of rebellion against social pretense. She also edited *TV Guide* for four years, and she recalls that Murdoch would always say to his editors, "Do you think this is too upmarket? Do you think it should be more mass?" Kimba Wood was "mass."

There was another reason the Kimba Wood tale pleased Murdoch, he confesses: "She put my friend in jail for ten years." Wood presided over the trial of the investment banker Michael Milken, sentencing him to a stiff ten years in jail for securities fraud (but allowing him to serve only two in return for coöperating with authorities). Murdoch has been loyal to Milken. Last spring, Milken was retained as a consultant in a deal in which MCI committed two billion dollars to the News Corporation; and "Payback: The Conspiracy to Destroy Michael Milken and His Financial Revolution," by Daniel Fischel, was published recently by HarperCollins and excerpted in the *Post*.

Murdoch's journalism follows a pattern. When he plunged into editing the *News of the World*, in 1969, he immediately applied lessons he had learned as a sub-editor at Lord Beaverbrook's *Daily Express* the year after he graduated from Oxford. Murdoch believes that a paper—particularly a working-class paper—has to be "fun," a form of entertainment. The true public trust is to give the public what it wants. "Populism" and commerce drove Murdoch's papers to invade the bedrooms of the Royal Family and to print jingoistic headlines, and populism combined with commerce accounts for the introduction of softer features in both the *Sunday Times* and the *Times* after he took them over.

But is what Murdoch's tabloids do so different from what tabloids have traditionally done in England? "I think it's fair to say that the British don't have the same sense of dignity about the press that Americans have," says Roger Laughton, who spent much of his career at the BBC and is today the C.E.O. of Meridian Broadcasting. "The British press is far more competitive, and very professional, but I wouldn't say it has a range of ethical considerations that it takes into account. That predates Murdoch. He didn't behave out of character with the way the press operated here, or in Australia. Others have tried to do the same many times in the past. That's what being a press baron implied."

Certainly Murdoch's products do not speak with one voice. The *Australian*—Australia's first national daily newspaper, which he launched, and, he told me, nurtured for twenty years, until it turned profitable—was used as a political weapon in the 1972 and 1975 national elections, but it is a respectable publication today. As are the daily and *Sunday Times*. Nor are Murdoch's politics as simple as the conventional view of him suggests. He is, for example, a fiery advocate of law and order, yet a quiet opponent of the death penalty. "It brutalizes society," he explains, echoing an objection often lodged against his newspapers.

Murdoch has not tried to insert his conservative views into his movies or television, according to Hollywood associates. This is not true of his approach to news. "He never called me and said, 'Don't do a story.' Or 'Do a story,'" recalls the former Fox News executive producer David Corvo, who is now a vice-president of NBC News. "But once, when I went over the list of network contracts coming up—Bryant Gumbel, Leslie Stahl, Steve Kroft, and so on—he just brushed them off. I felt that he wanted a conservative. I don't know how you build a credible news division with an agenda."

READING NOTES

_____

_____

_____

_____

_____

Murdoch believes that his critics do what he does, the difference being that they're hypocrites and he's not. He complains that reporters for the *Times* and the *Wall Street Journal*, for instance, "write more subjectively" than reporters do in England. He seems suspicious of anyone who proclaims journalism a calling. "Journalism has been mistaken over the past two decades for some kind of profession," says one of Murdoch's favorite journalists, Steve Dunleavy, who has worked for him on many continents since 1967. "We're not doctors. We're not lawyers. We're not architects. It's not a profession. It's a craft. We're the same as carpenters or mechanics."

But Murdoch is not a traditional press baron. Frank Barlow points out the difference: "I don't think there was ever any suggestion that the old press barons received any benefit for their businesses. Maybe because they weren't in any other businesses. Now it is not unusual to read that Murdoch gets benefits." This goes to the heart of the critique of Murdoch's journalism: too often, it becomes the servant of his political or commerical interests. What gives him the most pleasure in all his empire, Murdoch told me, is this: "Being involved with the editor of a paper in a day-to-day campaign. Trying to influence people." Barry Diller says, "Rupert is a pure conservative, except for purposes of manipulation."

Murdoch's papers do influence people, and he has used this influence to support political figures, who may then be in his debt. The *Sun* made Thatcher acceptable to its working-class readers. His Australian newspapers have influenced elections. Reporters on both the *Australian* and the New York *Post* protested in the seventies that Murdoch used their news pages to reward favored candidates and to savage those he disliked. The *Post* helped elect the current Republican mayor of New York City and governor of New York State, and the state's Republican and Democratic senators. When the new governor, George Pataki, wanted to meet with corporate leaders after his election last year, he asked Murdoch to act as host of the meeting. When Mayor Rudolph Giuliani's wife, Donna Hanover, was rehired as a TV reporter, it was Murdoch's Fox-owned station—WNYW—that recruited her. Murdoch nearly lost his empire in 1990, when he was on the edge of bankruptcy, and another threat surfaced in late 1993. The New York chapter of the N.A.A.C.P. filed a petition charging that Murdoch had misled the F.C.C. in 1985, when he was launching the Fox network. Federal law stipulates that a foreign citizen cannot own more than one quarter of a broadcast station's capital stock, and it was then that Murdoch changed his nationality, becoming an American citizen. But a tenacious volunteer lawyer for the N.A.A.C.P., David Honig, discovered while digging through Fox's applications for station licenses that although Murdoch himself had seventy-six-percent voting control over Fox, his Australian holding company, the News Corporation, indirectly owned more than ninety-nine per cent of the equity of its stations. Thus, the N.A.A.C.P. claimed, Fox had exceeded the foreign-ownership limit, thereby depriving minority Americans of an opportunity to bid for a broadcast license.

Murdoch viewed the N.A.A.C.P. allegations, Preston Padden notes, "as a minor irritation." It wasn't until the fall of 1994, when NBC filed a similar petition, that he began to fret that it was more than a nuisance. NBC charged that all of Murdoch's 1985 station-license applications were false. This was war. Murdoch directed strategy meetings, edited press releases, and camped with Padden in Washington and visited members of the key congressional committees. "We were not asking anybody to do anything," says Padden. "Our pitch was 'This outburst by NBC was because they didn't like competition in the marketplace.'" It was the O.J. defense: us versus them.

Although Murdoch has never been a major financial contributor to politicians, he bet heavily on a

READING NOTES

_____

_____

_____

_____

_____

Republican victory in 1994. In the months after the election, and so far without attracting much notice, a subsidiary of Murdoch's News Corporation—an entity that had never made a soft-money contribution—donated a total of two hundred thousand dollars to the Republican House and Senate Campaign Committees. According to Fred Wertheimer, the former president of Common Cause, this dwarfed contributions made previously by any of Murdoch's companies. "These guys haven't played the Washington game that much," Wertheimer says of Murdoch and his people. "But they know it's a candy store. There's an awful lot to be purchased." Immediately after the election, Padden arranged for Murdoch to visit a total of seventeen public officials, including eight Democrats. One of the first visits was with Speaker-elect Gingrich. "It was a ten-minute meeting—maximum," Murdoch says. "We met in the hall, because there were too many people in his office. It was just chitchat. We talked about the chances of his getting his Contract with America passed." Padden, who was also present, says, "None of their conversation had anything to do with this business." Then he adds, "I piped up at the end to say that NBC was going after us." However brief this part of the conversation was, it was initially denied by a Gingrich spokesman, who said that neither NBC nor any other matter before the F.C.C. or before Congress was discussed.

One month after this hallway encounter, it was revealed that Gingrich had signed a two-book contract with HarperCollins worth four and a half million dollars, likely the largest book advance ever received by an officeholder and the third-largest advance ever received by an American public figure. Murdoch denied that he knew anything about Gingrich's book contract. "I was telephoned in Beijing on Christmas Eve and told that it had happened," he says. "Howard Rubenstein called me. I went crazy. I knew critics would explode." Gingrich denied knowing that Murdoch was connected to HarperCollins. The

denials did not quiet the Democrats or the editorials. It was unseemly for a public official to take such an advance, and Gingrich implicitly acknowledged this when he belatedly announced that he would accept no advance and would take only royalties that the book actually earned. The most charitable interpretation is that there was an appearance of conflict for Gingrich to receive such a large amount of money from a company with business before Congress; the least charitable is that it was a bribe.

HarperCollins has a history of signing book deals with leaders of countries that the News Corporation has a commercial interest in—from Margaret Thatcher to Deng's daughter, from Mikhail and Raisa Gorbachev to Boris Yeltsin, from a Saudi prince to Dan Quayle. And in some cases (those of Thatcher and Gorbachev) Murdoch actually negotiated the deals. But it is possible that Murdoch was not told ahead of time of the Gingrich book deal. William Shinker, a former publisher of HarperCollins, says the C.E.O. of HarperCollins, George Craig, had the authority to approve payments of that size without clearing the decision with Murdoch. Murdoch says he has since amended the policy; now he must personally sign off on any advance above a million dollars.

Murdoch wrote a letter to the F.C.C. chairman, Reed Hundt, in December in which he expressed "personal anguish" about the storm surrounding his motives and declared that he was an American citizen and exercised "de facto control of the News Corporation and all its businesses." He felt mistreated by the establishment, and in his deposition to the F.C.C. he said he felt that the agency would be playing a game of "semantics" if it counted News Corporation equity as foreign ownership but did not count Murdoch's voting control of the stock as American ownership. It was, he said, "a witch hunt." Republicans agreed. Larry Pressler, the chairman of the Senate Commerce Committee, and Jack Fields, the chairman of the

READING NOTES

_____

_____

_____

_____

_____

House telecommunications subcommittee, began making calls to the F.C.C. lambasting the Democrats for picking on Murdoch and Fox. Fields threatened a "top to bottom" review of the F.C.C. if Murdoch was persecuted further. The conservative Heritage Foundation issued a paper on rolling back regulations in which it urged the abolition of the F.C.C.

Murdoch was crafty, but he may have been lucky as well. In January, Apstar-2, the satellite that NBC had counted on to distribute its programs in Asia, blew up shortly after liftoff. A month later, NBC, which had accused Murdoch of making craven deals to advance his interests, made a craven deal with Murdoch: NBC withdrew its F.C.C. petition in return for a lease of two channels on Murdoch's Star satellite system.

By spring, the tide had turned in Murdoch's favor, and he knew it. On the morning, in May, when the F.C.C. was to rule, he arrived forty minutes early at the hearing room where the decision was to be announced, flanked by his photogenic wife, Anna, and his daughter Elisabeth and her husband. Murdoch had in his hand a statement thanking the commissioners for exonerating him and Fox from the charge that they had "lacked candor." When the Murdochs took seats in the second row, Preston Padden leaned over to them. "The commissioner has arranged for you to sit in the first row," he whispered. A phalanx of photographers snapped pictures of Anna Murdoch patting the shoulder of her husband's navy-blue double-breasted suit and straightening his red-and-blue polka-dot tie. The five commission members filed in and listened as the F.C.C. general counsel, William Kennard, announced that although the foreign ownership of Fox did exceed twenty-five per cent, the evidence did not support a conclusion that Fox misled the F.C.C., and that an American citizen—Rupert Murdoch—did indeed control the parent News Corporation. Moreover, Murdoch was invited to apply for a "public interest" exemption from the regulations requiring Fox to restructure its equity, and he promptly did so.

Murdoch was jubilant. David Honig, of the N.A.A.C.P., was not. His view of the ruling was this: "The process was tainted. I think they threw the Communications Act in the garbage. Murdoch's Republican cohorts blackmailed the F.C.C. by threatening its existence." Others marvelled at Murdoch's political dexterity. "I wish we could be as successful as he's been," Sumner Redstone says.

A few days after the F.C.C. ruling, MCI announced that it was investing two billion dollars in a thirteen-per-cent stake in the News Corporation, and not long before Murdoch had revealed that he would finance a new conservative magazine, the *Weekly Standard*, based in Washington and edited by William Kristol. He acquired a hundred-per-cent ownership of Star TV, and he anointed his son Lachlan its deputy chairman. In August, he combined Delphi, his Internet operation, with MCI's Internet operation. The same month, he raised fifty thousand dollars at a "21" fund-raising lunch for the Senate Commerce Committee chairman, Larry Pressler. Last week, in addition to concluding a sports link with Malone, Fox launched a children's-television venture with Saban Entertainment. This week, Fox and NBC expect to announce that they have acquired the rights to televise major-league baseball.

In recent days, Murdoch has concluded that he could probably not bring off a takeover of Time Warner at this point, but the mere fact that he contemplated it is testimony to his extraordinary bravado. He would enjoy claiming Warner Bros., with its huge film library, and HBO, and Time's various magazines.

The Time Warner-Turner merger—like Murdoch's expansion—has fuelled the debate over whether media behemoths like the News Corporation and Time Warner will monopolize the production and distribution of information and entertainment. Murdoch would argue that, in the long run, no one will be able to monopolize information. Eventually, even in China,

READING NOTES

---

customers will be able to bypass middlemen like Murdoch or the government and summon to their TVs, computers, or telephone screens any news source, any channel, any desired program. It would be difficult for any entity to screen E-mail or books or newspapers downloaded from one computer to another. Technology makes it possible for every citizen (who can afford a computer and a high-speed modem) to become a publisher. Those who fret about monopolies are seen as being trapped in a time warp, railing against past dangers. If government regulators try to impose new anti-monopoly rules, they risk suffocating the world's fastest-growing industry.

On the other side of the argument are arrayed those who believe that Murdoch approaches a monopoly, certainly in Australia and in England. News Corporation newspapers control more than fifty per cent of the daily and Sunday circulation in Australia and a third of the United Kingdom's national newspaper circulation. As part of a deal with Murdoch's BSkyB, TCI entered into a partnership with US West to carry Murdoch's programming on cable in the U.K. By making long-term deals with all the major Hollywood studios for movies, and by using Fox programming, BSkyB dominates most of the product and the chief means of reaching pay-TV customers in the U.K.

A traditional objection to a monopoly is that it restrains trade in order to control markets. When the distributor also owns the product distributed, conflicts arise. For example, it has been charged that before American cable companies like TCI and Time Warner would give channel space to CNBC, they insisted that it provide only business news, so as not to compete directly with CNN. Media companies, which are becoming entangled in local politics and multiple partnerships, are heading inexorably toward their own version of global *keiretsu*, the informal back-scratching system used by Japanese companies.

The issue of monopolies and what to do about telecommunications legislation will be discussed this week in Washington as nine House and eleven Senate members confer on how to reconcile bills passed in each chamber. On the agenda are matters of momentous significance for communication companies like Murdoch's News Corporation. Among them: Should broadcasters like Murdoch be allowed to own stations reaching thirty-five per cent of American viewers, or should the limit stay at twenty-five per cent? Should broadcasters like Murdoch have to bid on extra channels that technology will make available, or should this extra spectrum space be a gift to existing broadcasters? Should cross-ownership restrictions be lifted, allowing a broadcaster like Murdoch to own a newspaper in the same market where he owns a TV station?

Whether the News Corporation is a monoply or not, Murdoch wants to keep it a family company. "Lachlan is only twenty-four," Murdoch points out. "He's a young man. Certainly he is conducting himself well. His sister Lis is very keen on coming back into the company. Soon, I hope. I think James is undecided. He's determined to do his own thing. I took all three out to our management conference." To turn over the News Corporation to his young, untested children presupposes three things: that Murdoch will remain in charge perhaps another ten years, allowing them to gain valuable experience; that if he cannot stay another decade Anna Murdoch might be installed as C.E.O. for a period of time; and, finally, that a public company board would deem a family member a suitable replacement.

Murdoch believes he has built things that will endure. Still, while the Fox network and Sky and Star TV provide viewers with more choices, they are rarely better choices. Unlike the Sulzbergers or the Grahams, William Paley, or Henry Luce—no matter their many flaws and sometimes outrageous vices—Murdoch will

READING NOTES

_____

_____

_____

_____

_____

leave no monument except a successful corporation. He has boldly built a worldwide company, but he has rarely elevated taste or journalism. Competitors envy Murdoch's financial success and his bold vision, and politicians fear his power, but the News Corporation is a business that relies on a singular man who is now in his sixty-fifth year. Rupert Murdoch has created a much bigger empire than his father did, but his success may be just as fleeting. "I believe," Roger Laughton says, "that we're talking about Genghis Khan, not the Roman Empire."

READING NOTES

_____

_____

_____

_____

_____

Chapter ②

Thinking about Communication

"It is the theory that decides what can be observed."

—ALBERT EINSTEIN

The mass media have become a pervasive part of social life. In politics, in art, in culture, even in religious practice, the emergence of new communications technologies has had a profound impact on the structure of society and the way people understand their place in the world. As Natalie Davis has observed, when the printing press was introduced in France in the 16th century, new networks of communication were established, enabling new opportunities and options for people as well as providing new methods of social control. Even when literacy rates were still low, the publication of books exerted a profound influence on social relations and social structures.

For example, for centuries, it was forbidden to distribute copies of the Bible in the vernacular language of different countries in Europe, and only priests could interpret the meaning of the Bible and other religious texts for laypeople. But with printing, it became much easier to mass produce Bibles. Not only did versions of the Bible appear in the common languages people spoke, as a part of the Protestant Reformation, the laity were encouraged to learn how to read and to read the Bible directly. Rising literacy rates had a profound impact on social life.

In fact, some people argue that, with the introduction of the printing press and books, the common definition of who was "wise" shifted from who was "experienced" to who was "learned"—that is, who could read and access the knowledge archived in books. The basic findings that triggered the scientific revolution in the 1500s and 1600s—texts by Copernicus, Kepler, Galileo, and William Harvey, for example—were printed and circulated as books. In each, the author acknowledged the authority of the ancient thinker whose insights were considered critical in the area in which he was working, and then went on to contradict those insights. Since their books circulated relatively widely in Europe, though their ideas contradicted what was perceived at the time to be settled knowledge, their ideas could not be easily suppressed.

Consequently, the invention of movable type and the printing press enabled the scientific revolution in a significant way. Communications scholar Neil Postman, however, goes one step further in explaining how technology changes how people think. Because sentences are basically linear structures with beginnings, middles, and ends, as are most books, Postman argues that as a communications technology, printing fostered the human capacity for rational thought. On the other hand, television, which is nonlinear, destroys the capacity for rational thought, he contends.

But how can the role of communication in society, particularly mass communication, be identified and understood? This chapter will prove the basic building blocks students need to think broadly about communication processes. It will:

- explain the concepts involved in research in general

- explore the process of theory-building

- introduce key theories about selected communication processes

- sketch the history of the study of communication.

Required Reading: "Medium Theory," by Joshua Meyrowitz, lays out the theory that different kinds of communication technologies and infrastructures shape the way people think as well as shape social organizations. Perhaps the best-known medium theorist was Marshall McLuhan, whom Meyrowitz describes as a "second-generation" medium theorist. This article describes what he calls the three generations of medium theory.

WAYS OF KNOWING

How is it that people come to understand the world and the way it works? In other words, what are the ways of knowing? Perhaps the best way to understand the ways people come to know and to understand the world is to observe young children. While it is difficult to know exactly what children learn prior to acquiring language, it is very clear that even pre-verbal infants do learn. One method of learning is through imitation. A study conducted by Dahe Yang and Emily Bushnell presented at the *XVth Biennial International Conference on Infant Studies* found

that babies as young as 15 months can learn through imitation. Experimenters demonstrated specific toys to the toddlers and then presented them again with a similar toy. The babies were able to manipulate the new toy effectively along the lines that had been demonstrated earlier.

In a broader sense, from this experiment, it can be said that the babies learned through personal experience. And learning through personal experience takes place at ages even younger than 15 months. Young infants learn to recognize their mothers, other caregivers, and other objects in their environment. Personal experience is a very powerful form of learning and way of knowing. Personal experience plays a powerful role in shaping personality and each person's specific understanding of the world.

As children acquire language, a new avenue of learning and knowing becomes available—authority. Suddenly, parents can tell children what to do and expect children to obey them. The classic parental justification is "because I said so," which is also the classic call to authority. In the cliché scenario, a parent will instruct a child not to touch a stove because it is hot. The child can learn from authority and not touch the stove. Or, the child can opt to learn from personal experience and touch the stove. Presumably, the lesson is going to be the same.

Knowing by authority is deeply embedded in human society. The most obvious example of learning by deference to authority is in religious communities. For example, a member of the clergy will tell believers that they will go to heaven if they act in a certain way, and the people will act in the prescribed way because the authority the religious leader holds.

Parental control and religious practice are only two of the many areas of social life people learn and know through authority. People routinely defer to doctors and lawyers when it comes to medical or legal advice because doctors and lawyers, by definition, are the experts in medicine and law. Some people slavishly follow the recommendations of movie critics and book reviewers before choosing a movie to view or a book to read, and so on.

Knowing by authority is not always benign. Not infrequently, people yield to authority because if they do not, they will be sanctioned or punished in some way. Once again, this process is perhaps clearest in religious communities. If somebody does not yield to the way the religious authority understands and explains the world, the person could be expelled from the faith community.

Until the 16th century in Europe, authority was the predominant way of knowing. People adhered to specific customs and traditions. In many ways, a tradition is simply another form of authority. Prior to the 16th century, in much of Europe, it was thought that all knowledge had been discovered, and the primary responsibility of the educated elite was to conserve that knowledge. Greek thinkers such as Galen in medicine provided the foundational knowledge. If people disagreed with the foundational knowledge, they were seen to be challenging authority, and sanctions could be brought against them.

In the 1500s and 1600s in Europe, however, a new way of knowing began to emerge—knowing through observation, analysis, and generalization. Through a series of experiments, Harvey observed that blood circulated through the body, which contradicted what Galen had proposed. Copernicus, Kepler, and Galileo observed the stars and concluded that the universe did not revolve around the Earth but that the Earth revolved around the Sun. Their observations were a direct challenge to authority. Ironically enough, the turn toward observation also had a religious impulse to it. With the Protestant Reformation, the idea that God was present in all things was promulgated. If it were true that God was present in all things, the best way to understand God was to observe and understand God's creation—the world. This notion was embraced by many religious groups, including subgroups within the Roman Catholic Church, perhaps the primary social authority of the time.

All three ways of knowing—experience, observation, and authority—have their limitations. Learning from authority is risky because authority could be wrong. Moreover, authority is generally linked to power, and a challenge to authority is often perceived as a challenge to a group holding power. For example, the Catholic Church imprisoned Galileo not because educated people in the Church necessarily thought that his observations were wrong, but because he challenged the Church's power to control the diffusion of information. Personal experience and observation also have their limitations as ways of knowing as well. Most significantly, they are largely limited to the individual's perception, and consequently often subjective. Moreover, people's biographies and life courses, their education, and their social contexts shape and constrain what they observe and how they understand their experience. What people see, the axiom goes, depends on where they stand, so to speak.

THE SCIENTIFIC METHOD

As observation became a more dominant and accepted way of knowing, the question emerged as to how observations could be made that were not subjective, that is, not dependent on the vantage point or perspective of the observer. One response to that problem has come to be called the scientific method. The scientific method is a process of observation promulgated by Renaissance English scientist Francis Bacon, who proposed that knowledge should be acquired through the accumulation of data and inductive reasoning based on the data. Moreover, anybody who follows the same steps will observe the same phenomenon. Further, if a proper process is followed, the observations will not be tainted by perceptual bias or personal beliefs.

For example, many people believe that the news media are biased politically. Interestingly, people with conservative political views argue that the news media are biased toward the liberal perspective. Liberals argue that the media are biased toward the conservative perspective. The question is how to observe bias in the news media in a way that both liberals and conservatives can agree on the results, regardless of their own political leanings.

With its goal of generating what are called reproducible observations—if someone follows the prescribed steps, they will, within an acceptable range of variation, make the same observations and reach the same conclusions—the scientific method is systematic and generally applied to empirical observations. Empirical data are data that are observable and measurable. Systematic means that people using the scientific method follow specific steps in a specific order to make observations and to draw conclusions. The basic steps in the scientific method are:

1. Review the prior research on a specific topic and develop a research question.

2. Develop a hypothesis or preliminary answer to the research question.

3. Construct a method to collect data to test whether the hypothesis is true or false.

4. Collect the data.

5. Analyze the data.

6. Draw conclusions about the truth or falsity of the hypothesis.

7. Contextualize the finding within a larger understanding of the world.

The goal of the scientific method is to generate objective observations, evidence, and conclusions that explain the world as it is. Step by step, study by study, the world becomes better understood. Writing in the 19th century, social thinker Max Weber described this as a "demystification process." Events and phenomena that once looked mysterious and threatening to people are explained and in some cases controlled.

THE ROLE OF THEORY

Even as the world becomes better understood, however, many questions remain. The most general explanations of the way the world works—explanations from which researchers develop research questions and hypotheses to answer those questions and which are tested by gathering data—are called theories. A theory is an overarching framework that knits together existing evidence to provide a broader and more comprehensive understanding of the world. In scientific study, a theory is not a hunch or speculation. A theory is based on evidence already gathered that has supported or rejected a series of hypotheses.

One of the most well-known theories in science is the theory of evolution based on natural selection. From 1831 to 1836, Charles Darwin spent five years on the *HMS Beagle* traveling the world and making observations about the diversity of the biological world. To explain the evidence that he gathered, he proposed that certain species of plants and animals survive because they are more suited to a specific environment, and those who are less suited die out. As the natural environment changes, certain species will flourish and others will become extinct. The idea has come to be known popularly as "the survival of the fittest."

Based on Darwin's ideas, untold numbers of scientists have formulated hypotheses to see if the theory is correct. Often, the hypothesis takes the form of an if-then statement. If Darwin's theory of evolution is correct, then something specific should be observed. If the anticipated phenomenon is, in fact, observed, that provides more evidence that Darwin's theory of evolution is correct—that is, it provides the actual explanation of the way organisms on Earth have evolved. (An alternative explanation of the way organisms appeared on Earth is the creation story in the Bible. That explanation is accepted by millions of people because they accept the authority—the Bible—on which it is based.)

Theories are generated in two ways. One is a top-down method called deduction. Somebody will have an intuition or insight into the way a piece of the world works and will propose that explanation. The next step is to devise experiments whose results will help to validate or invalidate the theory. An alternative approach to developing theory is to gather the results of many related experiments and then develop an overarching explanation that can account for all of the results. This method of theorizing—called induction—produces what is sometimes called "grounded" theory because it starts with data and results rather than an overall story. Nonetheless, a grounded theory generates additional hypotheses that will support or refute the theory.

Once a theory has been proposed and is undergoing testing, in most cases, some experiments will produce results that will be consistent with the theory and some will not. In general, data that do not fit the expectations of a commonly accepted specific theory are labeled anomalous and disregarded. But over time, if enough so-called anomalous data are generated, the theory itself must be abandoned or reworked in a way to account for the data that did not meet what was expected from the theory. If the reworking of the theory is radical enough, it can be labeled a paradigm shift. A paradigm explains the vast majority of experimental results generated by researchers working in a specific area. If a significant amount of unexplained data and unanticipated results emerge, the paradigm must be reworked.

In the study of communication processes, all three ways of knowing are at work. Some of what is known about communication is based on authority, particularly authority reaching back to Aristotle and the teaching of rhetoric. Some of what is known about communication comes from personal experience. In fact, for many people, personal experience provides the baseline of what is known about communication. Some of what is known about communication processes comes from observation. That observation can come in two forms—the reporting often associated with journalism and observation more tightly tied to the scientific method.

In fact, applying the scientific method to the study of communication has proven to be very difficult to do. Many communication processes are hard to measure accurately, and measurement is an important element of standard empirical research. Moreover, since communication and human behavior are complex, it is very hard to isolate specific variables to understand which specific variable influences what specific outcome. In addition, though several compelling theories for both interpersonal and mass communication have been developed, in many cases, the anomalous data seems to be as significant as the results that support the theories. Finally, many people measure their own personal experience against theoretical predictions. If the predictions do not match their experience, they tend to disregard the theory.

SOURCES OF COMMUNICATION EDUCATION

One of the complexities associated with thinking about communication processes and their impact is that communication education has developed from three distinct sources—classical education in the form of rhetoric; professional education; and social science research. The questions asked by researchers working in each of those paradigms differ from one another, as does what is considered "significant" and what is considered "known."

Communication education stretches back at least to the ancient Greeks and is a central part of what is called classical education—the education that developed as Europe emerged from the Middle Ages, an education based on Greek tradition and focused on what were called the liberal arts. As the Greek system of governing evolved to include more people in the governing process, participation became paramount. Citizens had to engage in a public political process and put forth their positions effectively. During this time, it became apparent that some people were more persuasive than others. The study of rhetoric was an attempt to understand what the elements of effective speech were. For example, in the dialogue *Phaedrus*, Socrates helps Phaedrus understand the importance of having specific knowledge of a subject and understanding of one's audience to being persuasive.

The study of communication was codified in late antiquity in what were called the "seven liberal arts." The *trivium* (translated as "three roads") consisted of rhetoric, grammar, and logic. The *quadrivium* (translated as "four roads") consisted of arithmetic, geometry, music, and astronomy. The liberal arts became the basis of the curriculum at the early modern universities that emerged in Europe in the 11th and 12th centuries in Italy,

France, and England. Only after students mastered the liberal arts and received their bachelor of arts degrees could they continue to advanced learning in law, theology, or medicine. In his "Map of the System of Human Knowledge," French philosopher Denis Diderot, a major Enlightenment figure and a primary editor of the French *Encyclopédie* (*Encyclopedia*—an attempt to capture all knowledge at the time), placed the study of communication at the center of the science of man under the general heading of "Reason."

The classical curriculum dominated European higher education for several hundred years. In the mid- and late 19th century, higher education began to move in different directions, and the study of communications changed as well. The first major shift came in the early 19th century. In 1839, the first college geared toward the training of teachers was set up in Framingham, Massachusetts. Then, during the Civil War, the Morrill Land Grant Act of 1862 gave federal land to the various states for the establishment of colleges to educate students in the agricultural and mechanical arts as well as "to promote the liberal and practical education of the industrial classes in the several pursuits and professions in life." Over the decades that followed, professional education, as opposed to the classic study of the liberal arts, increasingly became a focal point in higher education in the United States.

The trend toward professional education reached communication education as well. In the late 1860s, Robert E. Lee, who had assumed the presidency of what was then called Washington College, launched the first program to train people to become journalists. In 1908, the school of journalism at the University of Missouri was established. Founded by Walter Williams, who thought journalism education should be professionalized, this was the first school of journalism in the United States.

Along the same lines, starting as early as 1885, advertising professionals wanted to improve the image of their industry and eliminate unprofessional behavior by establishing advertising degree programs at major universities. During the same period, several universities launched specialized programs aimed at preparing students for the business world. Professional advertising education was incorporated in that movement.

Higher education geared toward professional training was significantly different from the standard undergraduate curriculum at the time. Instead of focusing on liberal-arts education, it focused on the technical skills students needed to succeed in their chosen profession. In journalism, for example, while students were expected to take courses in other areas, the thrust of the program in journalism was on those skills needed to succeed in a newsroom.

The final stream of higher education that underscores communication education originated at the Johns Hopkins University, which calls itself the United States' "first research institution." Hopkins opened its doors in 1876 and was dedicated to the "encouragement of research ... and the advancement of individual scholars, who by their excellence will advance the sciences they pursue, and the society where they dwell." Hopkins adopted a German model of education in which students met in seminar instead of only attending lectures. Students also selected major areas of study rather than receiving a general liberal-arts education. Most important, in addition to teaching students, Hopkins was dedicated to the discovery of new knowledge through the use of scientific methods in both the physical world and the social world. Hopkins became the model of the modern research university, a model used by many of the largest and most prestigious universities in the United States and the world today.

The use of scientific methods to study communication processes began to gain traction after World War I and World War II. U.S. government officials wanted to understand better the impact of propaganda. The social scientific approach to communication education drew on concepts and techniques developed in other social sciences, including sociology, anthropology, and psychology. It focused on the way humans created, transmitted, and received messages, and then derived meaning from those messages.

All three approaches to higher education—the study of the liberal arts, professional education, and the research institution—are still in play at colleges and universities around the world. Communication is studied within the context of those three traditions. As a result, in many ways, the study of communication is not yet a unified discipline, but instead encompasses disparate approaches, issues, and concerns, depending on the tradition within which a person is working.

RHETORIC: THE FIRST STUDY OF COMMUNICATION

In ancient Greece, political and public life revolved, to a large part, around oratory—one person addressing many. Public speaking played an essential role in how political and judicial decisions were made. It was also the forum for the development and spread of philosophical ideas. Around twenty-five hundred years ago, itinerant teachers known collectively as the Sophists taught public speaking as a means of human improvement. The Sophists were professional, popular, and effective speakers. They were also criticized for their excesses, sometimes promising more than they could deliver.

The Greek philosopher Plato was appalled by the way skillful speakers could manipulate public audiences without regard for the truth of what they said. In several of his dialogues, he sought to distinguish between what he called "true" and "false" rhetoric. He disputed the idea that the art of persuasion as practiced by the Sophists, an art he called rhetoric after the Greek word for "speaker," could be separated from the art of dialectic, or examining arguments and opinions logically and critically, often through the question-and-answer method associated with Socrates. For example, in Plato's dialogue *Gorgias*, Socrates attempts to compel the Sophist Gorgias to precisely define rhetoric. Through questioning, Gorgias is forced to concede that rhetoric, whose goal is to instill beliefs in the listener, could be used unjustly. Later in the dialogue, the point is raised that rhetoricians do not know or impart truth, and the aim of rhetoric is gratification, and therefore is not ethical.

Plato's student Aristotle had a different view of rhetoric. In his work *The Art of Rhetoric*, which is still seen as a starting point for the study of communication, Aristotle proposed that rhetoric should be seen as a parallel skill to the art of dialectic. Rhetoric was the skill used for public persuasion and civic affairs, and the art of dialectic was integral to the development and clarification of ideas. Aristotle identified three categories of rhetoric used in civil affairs:

- judicial rhetoric to determine the truth or falsity of events that took place in the past,

- deliberative rhetoric to determine if a specific action should be taken in the future, and

- ceremonial rhetoric that was concerned with praise and blame in the present.

Good rhetoric is both persuasive and ethical, Aristotle argued. Persuasive speech is comprised of three elements, each of which can contribute to its effectiveness. The first is element is ethos, or the character of the speaker. The second element is pathos, or the emotional state of the listener. The third element is logos, or the argument itself. In a classic scenario, a speaker tries to persuade an audience to take a specific course of action by using all three elements. The audience must ultimately make a decision as to what to do.

The ideas of the Sophists, Plato, and Aristotle became the intellectual foundation for the great Roman rhetoricians such as Cicero. The study of rhetoric was also included in the *trivium*, the liberal arts associated with the use of language. As a part of the *trivium*, rhetoric was a key component of liberal-arts education for centuries.

THE MODERN STUDY OF COMMUNICATION

As classical education made room for professional education and research in colleges and universities, the study of communication expanded as well. In professional education, the apprenticeship model, a form of learning by authority, dominated even at the university level. People aspiring to enter a communications industry, such as journalism, were expected to study with experienced professionals. Faculties in these disciplines were filled by ex-journalists or advertising or public relations professionals. The approach in these programs often consisted of teaching students to replicate what was already in place.

The turn toward social science in higher education had a significant impact on the study of communication. Communication, of course, is a core human activity, so it was in some ways inevitable that the techniques used to study society scientifically would be used to try to understand communication processes better. Moreover, communication was no longer limited to speaking, either one person to one person or one person to many people, the context in which many of the ideas about rhetoric were developed. Starting with the advent of movable type in 1450, but truly accelerating with the invention of high-speed printing, the telegraph, and photography in the 19th century, mass media began to emerge. Suddenly, people could communicate with huge numbers of people with whom they had no personal contact and did not know, stretching the old formulation of logos, ethos, and pathos for analysis. Communication was no longer limited to interpersonal communication.

In fairly rapid succession, the phonograph, cinema, radio, and television were all created. In the process, the environment in which people lived changed radically. In the 1930s, for example, people could sit in their living rooms and hear the voice of the president of the United States directly. To many, that experience was astonishing. In the same decade, Adolf Hitler rose to power, in part by efficiently using the media to promulgate Nazi ideology. As the new media environment expanded and consumed more of people's attention and time, researchers began to wonder what was the role of communication, communications systems, the media, and the content and objects distributed through the media in the structure of society, culture, personal identity, and a host of other significant areas.

In 1927, in what is considered a classic work, the political scientist Harold Lasswell made the first attempt to understand propaganda from a social-scientific point of view. Over time, he came to define propaganda as a technique of influencing human action through the control of representations. In other words, governments and other entities could control human action through the use of symbols and the control of stories, news reports, pictures, and even music. Social control could be exerted through the social control of communication. The techniques used for propaganda described by Lasswell were consistent with the techniques used for persuasion. Some scholars argued that the difference between propaganda and persuasion lies mainly in the audience. Others point back to Plato's criticism of the risk inherent in severing persuasion from techniques of discerning the truth. Propaganda was persuasive speech that was also not completely truthful.

From this start, Lasswell began to think more broadly about communication. In 1948, he proposed a very simple model of communication. He posed the model in the form of a question: Who says what to whom through what medium? The model could be represented in this way: SPEAKER + MESSAGE + MEDIUM + RECEIVER = IMPACT. Though surprisingly simple, this model has provided a useful structure for social-scientific communications research. Researchers study who gets to speak; what messages are sent by whom; who has access to different channels of communication; what makes an audience responsive to one message and not another; and so on. In fact, the questions stimulated by this simple model are virtually endless.

The following year, telecommunications researchers Claude Shannon and Warren Weaver published *The Mathematical Theory of Communication*, which is considered the touchstone of information theory. Unlike Lasswell, Shannon and Weaver were not interested in the content of a message; information theory is actually a branch of applied mathematics. Shannon and Weaver were primarily interested in the quantification of information and the limits on compressing, storing, and reliably delivering that data, whatever its content, to the intended destination. To this end, Shannon and Weaver developed several additional key concepts for the study of communication, ideas such as noise and interference in the communication system, which has been used in social-scientific study of communication as well.

Lasswell, Shannon, and Weaver described communication within the context of other disciplines—Lasswell was interested in political science, Shannon and Weaver in telecommunications. In 1954, Wilbur Schramm established the study of communication as an academic discipline. Schramm had received a Ph.D. in English from the University of Iowa in 1932. When World War II broke out, he volunteered for government service and was assigned to what became the Office of War Information and then the U.S. Information Agency. There he worked with an interdisciplinary group of prominent social scientists including Lasswell, sociologist Paul Lazarsfeld, psychologists Kurt Lewin and Carl Hovland, and others to devise communication activities to support the war effort. Some might say that the Office of War Information and then the U.S. Information Agency served as the propaganda arm of the United States. The group also studied the impact of Allied and Nazi propaganda.

In 1943, Schramm left Washington to serve as the director of the school of journalism at the University of Iowa, where he established the Bureau of Communication Research and launched a doctoral program in communication. In 1947, he moved to the University of Illinois, where he became the first dean of the College of Communication and director of the Institute for Communication Research. Interestingly, in his capacity as editor of the University of Illinois Press, he was responsible for the publication of *The Mathematical Theory of Communication* by Shannon and Weaver. In 1954, Schramm published *The Process and Effects of Mass Communication*. Though Schramm was particularly influential in establishing an institutional basis for the study of communication, he also contributed some significant concepts, such as the idea of a field of experience. Senders encode messages within the context of their own experience, and receivers decode those messages according to their own experience. If there is no overlap in the senders' and the receivers' fields of experience, communication cannot take place. Clearly, as researchers think more deeply about communications processes, Lasswell's simple model becomes more complex.

THEORIES OF COMMUNICATION

Perhaps because communication plays such a huge role in social life, no grand, all-encompassing theory of communication has emerged. While the model of communication that Lasswell proposed and enhanced over the years has effectively helped to direct research activity, nobody has offered a global explanation about the relationship of communication, communication processes, and communication structures to social life. That communication has a relationship to community is clear. But the processes associated with communication and the impact of communication seem too complex and intertwined at this point to allow anybody to develop a sustained narrative that can synthesize data in an encompassing way.

Instead, communications researchers have proposed several of what sociologist Robert Merton called "middle-range theories." Middle-range theories do not try to explain everything about everything. Instead, they attempt to explain something about something. Middle-range theories usually start with a clearly defined aspect of social phenomena. Then, they are supported or disproved through the collection of data. Since the social scientific approach to communication research started with a concern with the impact of propaganda, the earliest theories in communication tried to explain the effect mass media have on the audience.

One of the earliest theories to try to explain how media affects people is called the "magic-bullet" theory or the "hypodermic-needle" theory. It is also sometimes called the "pessimistic mass society thesis." First proposed by Theodor Adorno, Max Horkheimer, and their colleagues at the Frankfurt School of Social Research in Germany in the 1930s, the idea is that media content is injected into viewers, who then respond to that content in either anticipated or unanticipated ways. Adorno and Horkheimer were witnessing the breakdown of democracy in Europe and the rise of Fascism and Nazism. The magic bullet theory seemed to explain the impact of propaganda very well. Mass media helped break social bonds among people, who would watch a charismatic political leader such as a Hitler and then blindly support that person, even if what the leader said was not true. If somebody asked, for example, "Why might somebody question a U.S. war effort?" The answer might be that they had succumbed to propaganda from the enemy, "infected" by the content injected into them by the media.

Propaganda is but one aspect of communication that seemed to be explained by the magic bullet or hypodermic needle theories of communication. The impact of advertising also seemed, at the time, as though it could be explained by these theories. After all, people watch advertisements on television or see an ad in a magazine and then go buy the product.

The first generation of scholars working within the media-effects paradigm found the potential of media effects very troubling. They equated the growth of mass media with the loss of interpersonal relationships and community. The audience, in this early paradigm, was conceived of as an amalgamation of individuals with little connection to one another. After all, of the hundred million or so people who watch football's Super Bowl each winter, how many does any individual actually know?

Because the media companies that controlled the channels of mass communication were mainly interested in making a profit, in this analysis, they catered to the lowest common denominator, providing material that was entertaining and easy to understand, and creating content that was most likely to attract the biggest audience. As a result, people were in danger of losing their ability to distinguish good work from bad and were cut off from the deeper realities of human existence, the realities explored through high culture. The hypodermic needle or magic bullet theory, described as a theory of strong media effects, led researchers to explore what kinds of messages were most effective.

While on the surface, the magic bullet theory seemed to provide an explanation for what was being observed by the first generation of researchers studying communication, there was much it did not explain as well. For example, why were some people influenced by advertising or propaganda, while others were not? Why did certain articles of clothing come to be seen as stylish and some not stylish? Why did the amount of money spent on political campaigning have so little effect for some candidates?

In an effort to resolve those questions, in 1955, communication researchers Elihu Katz and Paul Lazarsfeld published a landmark study called *Personal Influence*. Based on their research, they theorized that media do not affect everybody in the public directly. Instead, within different social groups, different people are looked at as the experts in a specific area. One person might be respected for having well-thought-out political opinions, while another might be seen as knowing a lot about fashion. People in those social circles turned to those "local" experts for advice and guidance in their areas of expertise. For their part, those experts, however, are very in tune with mediated content in their areas of expertise.

In fact, their familiarity with mediated content is a part of their claim to expertise and authority in a given realm. Simply put, people very interested in something pay a lot of attention to the media in those areas, and their friends seek their guidance. In short, Katz and Lazarsfeld proposed a two-step process for media effects. The media influence tastemakers and experts, who, in turn, influence their friends. This became known as the "weak media effects" theory and is one of the central theories underscoring the practice of public relations.

While the two-step process of media effects still provides a compelling explanation of how the impact of the media is diffused through society, it does not answer the question of why certain people pay attention to certain media products and other people do not. One theory, also proposed by Katz, this time in conjunction with researcher Jay Blumler, that addresses this issue is called "uses and gratifications." It is centered not on the messages, the intentions of the sender, or the specific impact of a message on an audience, but instead proposes that audiences seek out certain types of media because the mediated content fulfills a specific need or provides a specific gratification.

Specific social situations and psychological characteristics stimulate a need for media, and exposure to that media offers a particular gratification. As conceptualized by the uses-and-gratifications theory, the viewer plays a much more active role than the role envisioned in other media effects theories. In the magic bullet theory, for example, media content is injected into a powerless viewer. In the ``uses and gratifications'' theory, people instead seek out specific media content for specific reasons.

French sociologist Pierre Bourdieu built on the idea that people proactively seek out and use expressive objects, developing a theory of social stratification based on the idea of "taste." From his perspective, individuals occupy multidimensional social spaces defined by class, race, gender, social status, power, and other factors. In his 1984 book, *Distinctions: A Social Critique of the Judgment of Taste*, Bourdieu suggested that the way people present their social space to the world depicts and defines their status. In other words, people use and consume media to display to the world who they are and how they fit into society.

TEXTUAL ANALYSIS

Media effects and uses-and-gratification theories focus on the response of the audience to media content. But media analysis can focus on the content distributed through different channels of communication as well. The object of analysis is known generically as a "text," whether it be words, pictures, or sounds. The analysis of media texts has several different theoretical orientations.

Semiotics might be the most vigorous theoretical approach to the analysis of texts. Translated as the "science of signification," semiotics has its roots in the 19th century work of American pragmatist philosopher Charles Sanders Peirce and Swiss linguist Ferdinand de Saussure. Saussure saw language as a system of mutually defining entities, while Pierce's theory of meaning identified the content of a proposition with its truth or falsity, a difference that can be experienced. The key question asked in semiotics is how things become carriers of meanings, and semioticians have worked to develop a system of signification, or a determination of what various signs actually mean within specific contexts.

The idea of media literacy takes a different approach to textual analysis. In this approach, although the meaning of the content distributed through mass media might seem self-evident, in reality, content, particularly video and audio content, are created within the context of a complex set of rules, or "grammar," to use the terms of the paradigm. These rules can be used to express complex, multilayered concepts and ideas about the world. To understand fully the concepts and ideas contained in the multimedia world in which people live, they must be trained to "read" and "write" the language of images and sounds in the same way they learn to read and write the printed word. Historically, media literacy has been associated with teaching children to be able to discern the deeper messages embedded in media by enabling them to better "read" the media.

POLITICAL ECONOMY

Another theoretical framework for the study of communication orients researchers toward the study of who owns the media and how communications networks fit into the overall productive capacity of a society and the production of wealth. The great press critic A.J. Liebling once remarked that freedom of the press is reserved for people who own a press. Researchers working within a political economy framework take that quip very seriously.

The basic argument put forward by political economy theorists is that the press does not play an adversarial or watchdog role to government. Instead, because media companies either are organized as privately owned companies or operate under government control, the media serve to support the existing power structures in society. These theorists, however, do not propose that the media are involved in a grand conspiracy to somehow hoodwink the public in supporting the existing economic structures. Instead, the way media companies are owned and operated leads them to preselect people who will not challenge the status quo, but instead view the world in a way that is harmonious with the view of the political, economic, and social elite. In communicating that vision of the world, the media help reinforce it. As a result, far from being agents for social change, the media reinforce the status quo.

The most forceful application of this theoretical argument to the U.S. news media can be found in *Manufacturing Consent: The Political Economy of Mass Media*, written by Edward Hermann, a finance professor at the University of Pennsylvania, and Noam Chomsky, a world-renowned linguist at the Massachusetts Institute of Technology. Published in 1988, Hermann and Chomsky's book argues that the mass media serve as little more than propaganda arms of the political and economic elites. They put forth what they call the "propaganda model" of the mass media to account for the behavior of the corporate news media in the United States and contend that the mass media "serve to mobilize support for the special interests that dominate the state and private activity."

Controversy is reported in the press only when there is a division among the elites on certain issues. Those groups that hold radically alternative ideas about the way society and economy should be structured are shut out of the media, and consequently, it is difficult for their views and messages to reach great numbers of people.

The political economy approach to media analysis is rooted in a Marxist analysis of society. Marxism holds that the economic organization of society basically determines its social structure and cultural orientation. True social change can come only if the economy is restructured. In this view, the media help keep the existing power structure in place.

THE CRITICAL CULTURAL APPROACH

Many of the theoretical approaches to the study of mass communication focus on one aspect of the communication process, such as who owns the media, what messages are produced, and how they should be understood, or how the audience reacts to those messages. In the mid-1970s, a more holistic approach to media studies emerged, largely from the Center for Contemporary Cultural Studies in Birmingham, England. The cultural studies approach attempts to integrate aspects of the other theoretical approaches to communication.

One of the most prominent theorists to emerge from this orientation is Stuart Hall, who put forth the notion of encoding and decoding messages. Messages are encoded with an intended meaning. That encoding takes place within a specific cultural, political, and economic context, and that context has an impact on the encoding process. Those messages are then transmitted through a particular channel of communication, which also influences the meaning of the message. Moreover, different channels of communication can be controlled in different ways, which is also significant. Finally, the receiver decodes the messages. But the receiver is also embedded within a specific cultural, political, and economic context, which, once again, has an impact on the way a message is decoded.

Consequently, though messages may have intended meanings and even preferred meanings, those are not the only possible meanings. Communication consists of signs and symbols, and the meanings of those signs and symbols are determined by terms and references supplied by codes that exist both in their production, or encoding, and their reception, or decoding. The potential discontinuity between the production of meaning and the reception of meaning in communication is what has to be explored and investigated. Finally, communication is iterative, as receivers provide feedback to senders, who can then readjust their messages.

KEY TOPICS IN COMMUNICATION

Despite, or perhaps because of, the absence of a grand theory of communication and what some have seen as the inadequacy of the middle-range theories, as the media have played an increasingly important and pervasive role in social life, a series of practical or applied questions about the specific impact of media representations has emerged. These questions and issues are debated vigorously by large communities of people ranging from parents to politicians to other policymakers.

One of the most hotly contested issues has been the impact of violence in the media. Murder,

mayhem, and other forms of violence are a staple of many genres of television, including cartoons for children and prime-time series. Indeed, by the time children finish elementary school, if they have watched 25 hours of television a week, which is average, they will have witnessed around 8,000 murders and around 100,000 other acts of violence. The question is, does violence on television lead to violence in real life? The same question has been raised for video games. Many teenage boys and young men play violent "shoot-'em-up" video games. Does playing those games make them more prone to violent behavior?

The roots of this issue go back to the early days of television. As early as 1952, the U.S. House of Representatives held hearings about violence on television, and in 1972, the U.S. Surgeon General's Office reviewed all the studies about violence on television and concluded that violence on television did lead to a more violent society. In 2000, in a congressional hearing, six of the nation's top public health organizations, including the American Academy of Pediatrics, the American Psychological Association, and the American Medical Association, testified that based on 1,000 studies, a causal connection existed between media violence and aggressive behavior in some children.

Despite the evidence, the issue is not resolved and remains under study. Why does media violence affect some children and not others? If media violence leads to a rise in social violence, why has the level of violence in the United States diminished over the last decade? Even if there is a causal connection media violence and social violence, do we want the government to regulate media more closely? After all, violent shows such as *The Sopranos* have won critical acclaim and devoted fans.

Like violence in the media, sex in the media has been a subject of constant study. More than two-thirds of the shows on television have some sexual content. Does the representation of sex in the media, particularly in the movies and on television, lead to promiscuous behavior and the practice of unsafe sex? Does sex in the media hurt family values and show marriage in a bad light? Does sex in the media cheapen human relationships?

These issues are brought into sharper focus when the spotlight shifts to pornography. The graphic depiction of human sexual activity is extremely offensive to many people. Moreover, many observers believe that pornography objectifies the women involved—and the men as well—and can lead to violence against women and other undesirable social outcomes.

As with violence on television, there are many studies that indicate that sex in the media has troubling consequences. For example, children who watch a lot of television become sexually active at a younger age. Ironically, other studies have indicated that the most sexually experienced teens wish they had waited longer to begin to engage in sexual activity. A University of California study found that teenagers and pre-teens with televisions in their bedrooms are more likely to use drugs, smoke cigarettes, binge drink, and have sex. Nevertheless, the precise effect of sex in the media is still open for debate and additional study. Moreover, even if sex and violence in the media lead to undesirable outcomes, it is not clear what the public policy outcomes should be.

Related to sex and violence, the presentation of stereotypes in the media is of concern. If a specific community is portrayed in a poor or distasteful light, people who do not have much contact with people in that group might believe that the portrayal is accurate and be prejudiced against the group. For example, a gay person first began to appear regularly on television when Pedro Zamora was a member of the cast of *The Real World*, a reality television show, in 1993. In 1997, the comedian Ellen DeGeneres acknowledged that she was a lesbian on the television sitcom *Ellen*. In the long-running comedy television series *Will and Grace*, Will, a main character, was virtually the first gay man to be portrayed without stereotypical gay or effeminate characteristics. Prior to that, when gay people were shown on television, it was in a very exaggerated and stereotyped way.

And for several decades, gay people were not portrayed on television at all. It was as if they did not exist. The absence of media representations of gays and lesbians had an impact on the psychology of gay and lesbian teenagers. On the flip side, some people argue that the regular portrayal of gays and lesbians on television in some way encourages people to be gay and lesbian themselves, although there is no credible research data that supports that position.

While some media content clearly have a negative impact on social life, the media can also be used to achieve critical social aims. A considerable amount of research has been conducted to determine how to run effective public health campaigns on television. Public health campaigns address issues that have a significant public impact on different populations and can be defined both in terms of the methods they use and the goals of the campaign. One of the most effective public health campaigns has been the one to fight drunk driving, which has the tagline, "Friends don't let friends drive drunk." Motor-vehicle accidents are the number-one killer of children, teens, and adults aged two to 34 in the United States. Direct appeals to people not to drive after they have consumed alcohol did not seem to work. Research indicated, however, that the "friends" campaign seemed to empower people to prevent others from driving whom they could see were drunk.

Along the same lines, as part of a government suit settled in 1998 with the tobacco companies over false and misleading advertising, $246 billion was set aside to help people quit smoking. Making effective use of that money is an essential public-policy issue, as smoking is a leading cause of preventable deaths and imposes enormous health-care costs on society.

Another area of ongoing interest and concern for communications researchers is politics. Do the media report on politics in a fair and unbiased way? How do the media present or frame political issues? One of the most developed areas of study in the role of communication in politics is called "agenda setting." The question agenda setting raises is how issues make it onto the public agenda. For example, for decades after the Civil War, the lack of civil rights for African Americans was not considered a significant public issue and rarely was addressed by politicians, at least by white politicians. Starting in the late 1940s, however, civil rights slowly began to gain a spot on the public agenda. By the mid-1960s, it was one of the key issues under debate. The question is, what role did the media play (and do the media play today) in that process?

PROFESSIONAL PERFORMANCE

The relationship of communication to social life is complex and significant. In many instances, communication research is focused on very practical problems and issues related to routine business activity, measuring public opinion, and the effectiveness of other activities, such as advertising or public policies. Applied market research is perhaps the most common communication-research activity. Among other task, market research is geared to identifying:

- who might be interested in purchasing a specific product or why,

- how satisfied consumers are with a specific product and how the product might be enhanced, and

- how content consumers are with the supplier of a product or service.

In other words, market research attempts to identify and understand the market for a particular product and service. Market research often combines objective or quantitative data gathered via surveys with subjective or qualitative data gathered through interviews, observations, and focus groups.

Public opinion polling is a highly developed activity used to gauge what people think and feel about certain issues, goods, services, or people. If a poll is correctly structured and sample populations appropriated assembled, the opinion of the entire United States can be gauged with as few as 1,200 respondents. Polling has become an essential activity in political campaigns as candidates try to gauge their support as well as the effectiveness of their messages.

Many of the same techniques from market research and public opinion polling are used to evaluate the effectiveness of advertising, public relations, and various public policy initiatives and programs. Publically supported programs in drug prevention, sex education, general education, and other areas often must be able to demonstrate their effectiveness to continue to receive funding. In fact, the deployment of evaluation and outcomes research is increasingly common in many different areas of public life.

CONCLUSION

Communication is the central element of being human and social life. Communication is the way people make sense of the world around them and their place in the world. But communication processes are complex, constantly changing, and hard to understand.

Although there is no single grand or comprehensive theory of communication, starting with the Greeks and probably prior to that, people have thought about communication in many different ways and on many different levels. Several theories have emerged to try to understand the impact of the media on human behavior, on social organization, on politics, and on culture, or the way people make meaning in their lives.

Communication processes also have a profound impact on people's daily activities. Consequently, people have thought deeply about how to apply communication in a practical way to everyday life, including to business and other areas of living. Because it operates on so many levels, communication is a rich area to study and explore. As in most vibrant fields, the more questions are answered, the more questions arise.

MEDIUM THEORY

by Joshua Meyrowitz

FIRST-GENERATION MEDIUM THEORISTS

The best known and most controversial medium theorists are two Canadians, Harold Adams Innis and Herbert Marshall McLuhan. Trained as a political economist, Innis adapts the principles of economic monopolies to the study of information monopolies. He argues that one way in which social and political power is wielded is through control over communication media (such as a complex writing system controlled by a special class of priests). Information monopolies can be broken, however, by new media. Innis suggests that the medieval Church's monopoly over religious information, and thereby over salvation, was broken by the printing press. The printing press bypassed the Church's scribes and allowed for the wider availability of the Bible and other religious texts. The same content, the Bible, therefore, had different effects in different media.

Innis argues that elites can more easily control some media than others. A medium that is in short supply or that requires a special encoding or decoding skill has more potential to support the special interests of elite classes because they have more time and resources to exploit it. On the other hand, a medium that is easily accessible to the average person is more likely to help democratize a culture.

Innis also argues that most media of communication have a 'bias' either towards lasting a long time or towards being moved easily across great distances. He claims that the bias of a culture's dominant medium affects the degree of the culture's stability and conservatism as well as the culture's ability to take over and govern a large territory. 'Time biased' media such as stone hieroglyphics, he argues, lead to relatively small, stable societies because stone carvings last a long time and are rarely revised, and their limited mobility makes them poor means of keeping in touch with distant places. In contrast, messages on light, 'space-biased' papyrus allowed the Romans to maintain a large empire with a centralized government that delegated authority to distant provinces. But papyrus also led to more social change and greater instability. The Romans conquered and administered vast territories, but then their empire collapsed when they lost their supply of papyrus from Egypt.

READING NOTES

In his densely written *Empire and Communications* and *The Bias of Communication*, Innis rewrites human history as the history of communication technologies.[1] His overview begins with the cradle of civilization in Mesopotamia and Egypt and ends with the British empire and the Nazis.

Among the people Innis influenced was a literary scholar, Herbert Marshall McLuhan. Extending aspects of Innis's perspective, McLuhan's work adds the notion of 'sensory balance'. He analyses each medium as an extension of one or more of the human senses, limbs, or processes. McLuhan suggests that the use of different technologies affects the organization of the human senses and the structure of the culture. He divides history into three major periods: oral, writing/printing, and electronic. Each period, according to McLuhan, is characterized by its own interplay of the senses and therefore by its own forms of thinking and communicating. McLuhan also suggests that each medium requires its own style of behaviour, so that an intense performance that works well on the 'hot' medium of radio might seem very stiff and wooden on the 'cool' medium of television.[2]

Innis and McLuhan stand alone in terms of the breadth of history and culture they attempt to include within their frameworks. Other medium theorists, however, have looked at various segments of the spectrum of past and present media effects. Walter Ong, whose work influenced and was influenced by McLuhan's, has offered wonderfully rich studies of the shift from orality to literacy. Dimensions of this transition have also been explored by J. C. Carothers, Eric Havelock, Jack Goody and Ian Watt, and A. R. Luria.[3] All these scholars argue that literacy and orality foster very different modes of human consciousness. They describe how the spread of literacy affects social organization, the social definition of knowledge, the conception of the individual, and even types of mental illness.

The seemingly less dramatic shift from script to print has been explored in detail by H. L. Chaytor and Elizabeth Eisenstein.[4] Chaytor argues that print significantly changed the oral and scribal worlds by altering literary style, creating a new sense of 'authorship' and intellectual property, fostering the growth of nationalistic feelings, and modifying the psychological interaction of words and thought. Eisenstein echoes many of these themes and presents many cogent analyses and an enormous amount of evidence to support the argument (put forward by Innis and McLuhan) that the printing press revolutionized Western Europe by fostering the Reformation and the growth of modern science.

Walter Ong, Edmund Carpenter, Tony Schwartz, and Daniel Boorstin have looked at the ways in which electronic media have altered thinking patterns and social organization.[5] Carpenter and Schwartz are generally McLuhanesque in content, method, and style, but they add many fresh insights and examples. Ong and Boorstin present more traditional scholarly analyses that support McLuhan's basic arguments but also go beyond them. Ong describes the similarities and differences between the 'primary orality' of preliterate societies and the 'secondary orality' that results from the introduction of electronic media into literate societies. He looks at the spiritual, sensory, and psychological significance of the return of 'the word', as a spoken event, in an electronic form. Boorstin describes how new media 'mass-produce the moment', make experience 'repeatable', and join many other recent technological inventions in 'leveling times and places'. He also compares and contrasts political revolutions with technological revolutions and discusses the impact of new technologies, including electronic media, on our conceptions of history, nationality, and progress.

READING NOTES

THE HISTORY OF CIVILIZATION FROM A MEDIUM-THEORY PERSPECTIVE

Each of the medium theorists mentioned above covers different territory, takes a different approach, and reaches somewhat different conclusions. Yet when their arguments and analyses are taken together, a surprisingly consistent and clear image of the interaction of media and culture emerges. Broadly speaking, these theorists' works cohere into a shared image of three phases of civilization matched to three major forms of communicating: the move from traditional oral societies to modern print societies (via a transitional scribal phase), to an electronic global culture.

Traditional Oral Societies

In oral societies, the preservation of ideas and mores depends upon the living memory of people. A great deal of time and mental energy, therefore, must be spent in memorization and recitation. This form of 'living library' ties people closely to those who live around them. To make memorization possible, ideas are generally put in the form of rhythmic poetry and easily remembered mythic narrative. The oral culture's laws and traditions are conveyed through familiar stories filled with stock phrases and formulaic actions and events.

Oral cultures are 'closed' in two senses. First, since orality requires physical presence, oral cultures have few if any ways of interacting with the thinking of those who do not live with them physically. Second, 'individuality', in the modern sense, is limited. Individual expressions, novel ideas, and complex arguments can find little place in such cultures because they are difficult to remember (even by the persons who come up with them) and almost impossible to pass on to any significant number of others.

Such societies are 'traditional', not only in the sense of comparison with later ones, but also internally. That is, they tend to work hard to conserve what they already have and are. Change is slow because cultural and personal survival depend so heavily on memorizing what is already known and what has already been done and said. Creativity and newness are discouraged as potentially destructive forces.

The closed sphere of the oral community, however, also fosters dimensions of openness and fluidity in terms of social and sensory experience. There are relatively few distinctions in social status and perspective. And the oral world is one of rich involvement with and interplay of all the senses of hearing, sight, smell, taste, and touch.

The Transitional Scribal Phase

Writing begins to break down tribal cohesion and the oral mode of thinking because it offers a way to construct and preserve prose and to encode long strings of connected ideas that would be almost impossible for most people to memorize. The development of writing alters not only dissemination patterns but also the content of what is disseminated. Writing establishes the potential for true 'literature', 'science', and 'philosophy'.

With writing, symbolic communities begin to compete with practical communities. That is, writing allows literate people who live next to each other within the same physical environment to know and experience different things, to have different world views. At the same time, writing permits people who read the same material to feel connected to each other regardless of the physical distance between them. Writing, therefore, both splinters and unites people in new ways.

But, unlike speech and hearing, writing and reading are not 'natural' means of communicating. They require much learning and rote practice, and they have their full effect only when they are learned at a very young age, when the writing system used is easily mastered by large portions of the population, and when written materials are widely available. The impact of writing, therefore, is uneven until the development of the printing press in the fifteenth century, the spread of schooling, and the corresponding growth of literacy from the sixteenth to the nineteenth centuries. Further, the printing press has more impact on Western cultures than on Eastern cultures because many of the written symbol systems used in the East have too many signs to be learned by large portions of the population and are not easily adaptable to the technology of repeatable type.

The Rise of Modern Print Culture

The printing press and the relatively wide availability of printed materials further undermine the importance of the 'local community' in several ways. First, print divides people into separate communication systems. The poor and illiterate remain wholly dependent on oral communication, while the upper classes and growing middle class increasingly withdraw (both literally and metaphorically) to their libraries. For the literate, there is a retreat from the web of community life and extended kinship ties and a move toward greater isolation of the nuclear family.

While the wholly oral nature of community life once bound people into similar experiences and knowledge, reading and writing separate people into different informational worlds. The literate now read and write about things the illiterate cannot hear, speak, or remember, and different readers and writers develop different 'viewpoints' and 'perspectives'.

At the same time as printing creates smaller units of interaction at the expense of the oral community, it also bypasses the local community in the creation of *larger* political, spiritual, and intellectual units. The ability to 'see' on a printed page what were once only spoken folk languages, for example, fosters a sense of

unity among all those who use the same language (not just among those who speak it in the same time and place). Conceptions of 'them vs. us' change. Feudal societies based on face-to-face loyalties and oral oaths begin to give way to nation-states and to nationalism based on a shared printed language. Similarly, religious cohesion no longer depends exclusively on shared rituals with those one can see, hear, and touch. The potential for religious unity across great distances, along with disunity among those in the same place, is fostered by the patterns of sharing holy texts.

In oral societies, words are always *events*—as time-bound as thunder or a scream. Members of an oral culture are enmeshed in the ongoing texture of spoken communication. (Plato—an early booster for writing—wanted to ban the poets from his Republic in order to free citizens from the spell of oral recitation.) But in a print society the word becomes an *object* spatially fixed on a page—that one can state at and think about. Indeed, literate people often have difficulty thinking of a word without picturing it in written or printed form. Thus ideas move from the world of the aural and temporal to the world of the visual and spatial.

Print, even more than writing, undoes the tribal balance of the senses. The importance of the simultaneous aural surround yields to the dominance of the sequential sense of sight ('seeing it in black on white', 'following your line of thought', 'developing your point of view'). In the circular world of hearing, a person is always at the centre of whatever he or she is experiencing. But the visual, typographic person is, in a sense, always on the edge, an observer, who has time to think before reacting. A listener interrupts a speaker with a response, but a reader must let a writer have his or her 'say' before drafting a reply.

The break from intense, ongoing aural involvement distances people from sound, touch, and direct response and allows people to become more introspective and more individualistic. 'Rationality', which comes to be highly valued, resembles the form of printed type: step-by-step abstract reasoning along a continuous line of uninterrupted thought. From the simultaneous world of sound, literate cultures move toward a one-thing-at-a-time and a one-thing-after-another world. The isolation of stimuli fosters cause-and-effect thinking. Literate thinking diminishes the view of life as a repeating sequence of natural cycles and promotes the view of constant linear change and improvement.

Changes in thinking patterns are echoed by changes in physical settings: habitats evolve, over time, from villages and towns with winding paths to linear streets in grid-like cities. Production of goods moves to the assembly *line*. Modern classrooms are built with chairs bolted to the floors in rows just as letters are fixed on a page. The new physical settings generally discourage informal oral conversation. In short, the mental and physical worlds shift in structure from circles to lines, from the round world of sound to the linear form of typography.

The production of multiple copies of exactly the same text creates new conceptions of literary style, fame, authorship, and intellectual property. The ability to share the same knowledge across wide areas and the continual possibility of adding to, modifying, and correcting texts—without losing parts of them through mistakes in scribal copying—also fosters a new form of incremental growth of knowledge. In both oral and manuscript cultures, the key intellectual process was one of *preservation*. But with the printing of multiple copies of exactly the same text, there is a new 'safety in numbers' that allows the intellectual challenge to become one of *discovery* and change.

While scholars in a scribal culture spent much of their intellectual careers as in-depth commentators on the relatively few manuscripts available to them, scholars in a print culture shift to comparing and contrasting a wide spectrum of related literature and to contributing their own original work to the wide and rapidly widening stream of ideas.

In these ways, the printing press fosters the rapid growth of scientific inquiry and the rejection of traditional authority. In sixteenth-century Europe, for example, the ready availability of copies of holy texts in native tongues weakens the monopoly over salvation held by the Church and supports the Reformation, and the sudden spurt of cumulative knowledge fuels the Scientific Revolution and the spread of mechanical production.

Global Electronic Culture

Ironically, print culture comes to its full power just as the seeds of its destruction are planted. The late nineteenth century sees the drive toward universal literacy, but during the same years the first electronic media begin to be widely used: the telegraph and the telephone herald the future age of radio, television, and beyond. The use of electronic communication, like other media, takes time to develop and ripen before having dramatic, visible impact on social structure in the mid-twentieth century.

Electronic media bring back a key aspect of oral societies: simultaneity of action, perception, and reaction. Sensory experience again becomes a prime form of communicating. Yet the orality of electronic media is far different from the orality of the past. Unlike spoken communication, electronic communication is not subject to the physical limitations of time or space. Electronic messages can be preserved, and they can be experienced simultaneously by large numbers of people regardless of their physical locations.

Once again, the boundary line between 'them' and 'us' shifts, but the result is more diffuse and less predictable. The sense of 'us' is no longer formed solely by face-to-face oral solidarity or by the sharing of similar texts. Electronic media bypass traditional 'literary circles', group associations, and national boundaries and give us a new world view by thrusting us among people who have not read what we have read, have not shared our territory, and may not even speak our language.

While print allows for new ways of sharing knowledge, and industrialization enables the wide scale sharing of *products*, electronic media tend to foster new types of shared *experience*.

New forms of concrete sensory experience compete with abstract print knowledge. And the word returns in its old form—as an event rather than as an object. But the scale of sharing is far different. Electronic media are like extensions of our sensory apparatus that reach around the planet. Electronic sensors return us to seemingly 'direct' encounters, but on a global scale.

As a result of the widespread use of electronic media, there is a greater sense of personal involvement with those who would otherwise be strangers—or enemies. The seemingly direct experience of distant events by average citizens fosters a decline in print-supported notions of delegated authority, weakening the power of political parties, unions and government bureaucracies. The sharing of experience across nations dilutes the power of the nation state.

While written and printed words emphasize ideas, most electronic media emphasize feeling, appearance, mood. There is a decline in the salience of the straight line—in thinking, in literary narrative, in human-made spaces and organizations. There is a retreat from distant analysis and a dive into emotional and sensory involvement. The major questions are no longer 'Is it true?' 'Is it false?' Instead we more often ask, 'How does it look?' 'How does it feel?'

INFORMATION-SYSTEM THEORY: AN EXAMPLE OF SECOND-GENERATION MEDIUM THEORY

One dimension that is missing from the first generation of medium theory is a detailed attempt to link this theoretical perspective with analyses of everyday social interaction. My own medium-theory work involves a reformulation of role theory that can address the influence of media. There is room here only to sketch my model in its broadest outlines. Further, although the theory functions on both the micro and the macro level, I will focus here on the macro level in order to work towards a summary sketch of changes that can act as a sort of template to fit over the phases of civilization described above.

Roles as Information Networks

I argue that everyday behaviour is susceptible to change by new media of communication because social roles are inextricably tied into social communication. Social identity does not rest in people, but in a network of social relations. When social networks are altered, social identities will change. In any given social period, roles are shaped as much by *patterns* of access to social information as by the *content* of information. That is, different cultures and different historical periods are characterized by different role structures not only because of 'who knows what', but also because of 'who knows what about whom' and 'who knows what *compared* to whom'.

Patterns of access to social information are linked to patterns of access to social situations. People of the same status in society generally have access to the same or similar situations and information. People of different social status usually have access to different information and experience. Put differently, distinctions in behaviour, identity, and status are created and supported by separating people into different informational worlds. Patients are kept out of hospital staff meetings, customers stay out of restaurant kitchens, the officers' club is off limits to enlisted personnel, students are usually excluded from faculty meetings. If such distinctions could not be maintained, then the distinctions in identity and behaviour would also begin to blur. Of course, greater and lesser social differentiation is not brought about by a single act of inclusion or exclusion, but by the cumulative contribution of many prior different or similar experiences for different people.

In general, *the more situations and participants are segregated, the greater differentiation in status and behaviour.* Conversely, *the more situations and participants overlap, the less social differentiation in status and behaviour.* Situation segregation supports differences among people of different status by exposing different people to different experiences, by isolating the contexts for one social role from those of another, and by allowing for increased access to what Erving Goffman calls a 'back region': a private 'backstage area' for preparing for, and relaxing from, performances for 'the other'. The more backstage time and space social performers have, the more formal and distinct the onstage role performance can be.

Situations as Information-Systems

Although 'situations' are usually thought of in terms of physical locations, I argue that they are in fact 'information-systems'. That is, we often think of a social setting as being a *place* because the physical barriers of walls and distance once largely defined the boundaries of inclusion and exclusion in the communication processes occurring there. But *media* also play a role in defining the boundaries of social situations. In a literate culture, for example, an advice book for parents functions as an isolated 'place' for adult communication that cannot be 'overheard' by young,

illiterate children. Conversely, the presence of a television camera can transform a 'private' adult conversation into one that is accessible to children (as happens daily with TV talk shows).

Roles should therefore be thought of as fluid information-networks that are susceptible to restructuring through changes in information flow patterns, such as those brought on by changes in media use. Different media enhance and reduce the amount of shared experience for different people. Media also alter the extent to which we have a private, backstage area where we can relax from and rehearse for our onstage roles. In general, *media that segregate access to social situations will work to segregate roles; media that blur access to social situations will foster less distinct roles.*

The Role Triad

The impact of information access patterns becomes clearer when we look at how virtually all social roles can be described in terms of an information-network-sensitive triad of social roles:

Group Identity/Socialization/Hierarchy

Group Identity entails roles of affiliation or 'being' (such as male vs. female; professional vs. hard-hat; lawyer vs. doctor). Socialization involves roles of transition or 'becoming' (such as child to adult; medical student to doctor; immigrant to citizen; husband to father). Hierarchy describes roles of authority (such as political leader vs. voter; company president vs. company secretary; officers vs. enlisted personnel).

In everyday reality, the categories are not mutually exclusive. Most of us function in all three simultaneously: identified with a number of groups, at various stages of socialization into new roles, and at some particular rank or ranks within one or more hierarchies. Further, many roles have elements of more than one category. Being a child, for example, involves the issue of socialization, yet the relatively greater power and authority of adults make childhood an issue of hierarchy as well.

READING NOTES

_____

_____

_____

_____

_____

At the same time, each category has distinct elements: Group Identity allows for 'separate but equal' relationships, where members of different groups need not necessarily stand in any particular hierarchical or developmental relationship (doctors and lawyers, for example). Socialization is unlike group identity and hierarchy in that it involves expected development into the reference role (while doctors do not become lawyers, and men do not usually become women, all surviving children become adults). And roles of hierarchy depend on a 'separate but *unequal*' dimension that must appear to test on inherent superior qualities.

Each role category describes a myriad of roles, but is also represented by a quintessential example, a role that is shared by everyone in the society:

Group Identity—Male vs. Female.
We are each either male or female.

Socialization—Child to Adult.
We all move from childhood to adulthood.

Hierarchy—Political Leaders and Average Citizens.
We all participate in this relationship of political power.

Informational Characteristics of the Role Triad

Virtually every aspect of every social role can be described in terms of group identity, socialization, and/or hierarchy. Each of these role categories, in turn, can be described in terms of set patterns of access to social information.

Group identity depends upon *shared, but secret* information—that is, information and experience must be shared among group members but remain inaccessible to 'outsiders'. Traditional distinctions between social groups, therefore, are supported by separating people into different informational spheres where they have different experiences, develop different world views, become somewhat mysterious to each other, and where they can 'privately' rehearse for roles of interaction with members of other groups. Socialization involves *staggered access* to the situations and information of the new role or 'destination group'. Every stage of socialization into a new role involves both exposure to, and restriction from, social information. We tell sixth graders things we keep hidden from fifth graders, for example, and we continue to keep hidden from sixth graders things we will tell them as seventh graders.

Hierarchy rests upon *non-reciprocal* access to information, including tight control over performance, and mystification surrounding the need for control. Status is maintained by secrecy and by non-secret information going 'through channels', that is, passing from higher status to lower status individuals rather than the other way around or in no particular pattern.

Changes in the Role Triad

Changes in the number and type of social information-systems do not obliterate group identity, socialization, and hierarchy, but they change the specific form that each type of role takes in a given social period. The greater the number of distinct information-systems, the greater the number of distinct group identities, stages of socialization, and ranks of hierarchy. The more information-systems interlock, the more group identities, stages of socialization, and ranks of hierarchy blur. If, for example, we always taught fifth, sixth, and seventh graders in the same classroom, we would find it difficult to establish three distinct social identities for the children.

A medium-theory approach to role change suggests that different media are like different types of rooms—rooms that include and exclude people in different ways. The introduction of new media into a culture restructures the social world in the same way as building or removing walls may either isolate people into different groups or unite them into the same environment. Media that segregate situations will foster segregated behavioural patterns. Media that integrate situations will foster integrated behavioural patterns.

As I have detailed elsewhere, print media and electronic media differ along a number of dimensions that interact with the structure of social information networks.[6] In general, print media tend to segregate what people of different ages, sexes, and statuses know relative to each other and about each other, while electronic media, particularly television, tend to integrate the experience and knowledge of different people. Further, television's focus on personal appearance, gesture, and emotion demystifies many roles and emphasizes what is common to all humans. And television and other electronic media are especially potent transformers of roles since electronic media are especially potent transformers of roles since electronic media alter the once taken-for-granted relationship between physical place and social place, between *where* one is and what one experiences.

My medium-theory analysis of social roles yields a view of three phases of Group Identity, Socialization, and Hierarchy that is consistent with but adds another dimension to the three phases of culture outlined by the first-generation medium theorists.

THREE PHASES OF SOCIAL ROLES

Oral conceptions of Group Identity, Socialization, and Hierarchy

In oral societies, most of the distinctions that exist in group identities, socialization stages, and hierarchal roles are spatially rooted and supported.[7] Separate huts and activities support separate information-systems and therefore separate roles.

The importance of separate spheres in maintaining social differentiation is made more evident by the relative lack of role distinctions in nomadic oral societies. In nomadic hunter and gatherer societies, the difficulty of maintaining many separate places, or information-systems, for different people tends to involve everyone in everyone else's business. The lack of boundaries leads to relatively egalitarian male/female, child/adult, and leader/follower roles.[8]

Although men and women have some division of labour in hunter and gatherer societies, it is not as sharp as in agricultural and industrial societies, and doing the work of the opposite sex is not considered shameful or unusual. Because nomadic men cannot separate the public sphere from the domestic one, they cannot establish aura and distance. Women are involved in public decisions, and they play an important role in supporting the family. Men participate in childcare, and both men and women are expected to be gentle, mild-mannered, and non-competitive. The lack of a separate sphere for the nuclear family often leads to community involvement in family disputes.

Through the openness of nomadic life, children are included in most adult activities and are not sharply segregated by age or sex. Play and work often take place in the same sphere and involve similar activities. Sex play among children and adolescents is common. Obedience to adults is emphasized less than self-reliance, and physical punishment of children is rare.

Because leaders in nomadic societies cannot get away from those they lead, leaders cannot horde information or project a public image sharply different from their private behaviours. Leadership, therefore, is often more of a burden than a privilege. Leaders gain authority by setting the best example, by working harder than everyone else, by sharing more than others. Moreover, since there are no distinct spheres to which one can move as one changes status, nomads have few large-scale or long-term initiation rites.

But much of this changes when nomads settle down. Once they attach themselves to particular places, their social spheres begin to segregate. Household privacy leads to new forms of social differentiation. Women's responsibility for birth and lactation isolates them at home and starts to separate their everyday experience from that of men, who are more involved in a newly developed public sphere. Work becomes more clearly sex-typed and the socialization experiences of boys and girls become much more dissimilar. Spatial segregation also supports the development of a rudimentary hierarchy.

Even in sedentary agricultural societies, however, there is a limit to role segregation. The communication networks of the society remain oral; and, while some segregation is possible, separating what different members of the society know into *many* different oral networks is difficult. In oral societies, isolating children into year-by-year categories, for example, is generally impossible. The more typical distinctions are simply between children and adults, with a single significant rite of passage from childhood to adulthood (especially for boys). These rites are often called 'puberty rites', but they rarely coincide with individual physiological puberty.[9] They are, in fact, information-network rites, in which a whole group of children is given access to the locations and secrets of adults, whose dress and roles they then assume. Similarly, while separate spheres for men and women support some gender distinctions in knowledge, experience, behaviour, and dress, there is rarely a complex system of division of labour or a splintering of society into many different group identities. Unlike modern societies, there are not many stages or levels of differences among people, and rites of passage are significant but minimal in number.

Literate forms of Group Identity, Socialization, and Hierarchy

In the transitional scribal phase, society develops a split personality. In the Middle Ages, for example, the elites of the nobility and the Church use a monopoly on literacy to foster a starkly hierarchical system, marked by dramatic differences in dress, language, and activity between the literate elites and the illiterate masses. But within the continuing oral societies of village life far fewer distinctions exist.

In pre-print Western Europe, for example, children of illiterate families are treated as 'little adults'. Once past infancy, children dress like adults, work beside adults, go to war with adults, drink in taverns with adults, and sleep in the same beds as adults. What few schools exist (primarily to train clerics) are not segregated by ages. Children are not shielded from birth or death, and they often witness and engage in sex play. Conversely, adults are childlike by modern standards, enjoying games and stories that literate societies associate with children.[10]

Similarly, in pre-print Western Europe men and women share many rights and responsibilities. Women have the right to participate in municipal affairs; to sit on, and testify before, courts; to substitute for incapacitated husbands; and to inherit, as widows, the legal prerogatives of their dead husbands.[11] Peasant dress for men and women is very similar.

But the spread of print supports compartmentalization and specialization. The new emphasis on reading as a source of wisdom and religious salvation widens the gap between those who can read and those who cannot. Further, distinctions in reading abilities come to be seen as tied to 'natural' differences in rank and identity.

The young and illiterate are excluded from all printed communication, and come to seem very 'innocent'.

READING NOTES

Both 'childhood' and 'adulthood' are invented in Western culture in the sixteenth century, and their spread follows the spread of schooling.[12] All-age roles, behaviours, and dress begin to splinter into separate spheres for people of different ages and reading abilities. Children are increasingly isolated from adults and from children a year or two younger or older. Many topics come to seem unfit for children's ears and eyes.

Classrooms that mix the ages gradually fall into disfavour, and the age-graded school comes to be seen as the natural means of education. The schools develop a convenient monopoly. They depart from education in oral societies in that they control both knowledge and the skill (reading) that is required to attain it. Every grade of schooling involves revelation of some new information and continued secrecy surrounding other information.

The different levels of reading complexity offer a seemingly natural means of segmenting information— and people. All fields begin to develop 'introductory' texts that must be read before one can go on to 'advanced' texts. Identities splinter into a multitude of separate spheres based on distinct specialties and mastery of field-specific stages of literacy. The new grading of texts serves as barrier to straying from one field into another. Crossing into a new field demands that one must beat the embarrassment of starting again as a novice and slowly climbing a new ladder of printed knowledge. This contrasts markedly with the oral and scribal approach, which is inherently interdisciplinary and non-graded.

As printing spreads, women are told that only men need to become literate, and men use restricted literacy to enhance their positions relative to women. The earliest feminist movement in Western culture in the sixteenth and seventeenth centuries involves a failed attempt by women to maintain old rights.[13] Women come to be seen as part adult, part child. Elizabethan males express doubts over whether a woman could be considered as a reasoning creature and whether she has a soul.[14] Women are increasingly isolated in the domestic sphere and are increasingly thought to be too weak, irrational, and emotional to deal with activities in the male realm. As late as 1865, doctors warn officials of Vassar, a new college for women, that attempting to educate a woman as if she were a man is dangerous.[15] For many years, women are confined to a primarily oral subculture within a literate, male-dominated society. Moreover, minimally literate women are given the responsibility of caring for the increasingly dependent illiterate children.

Unlike oral societies with oral vows of allegiance, leadership in print societies is organized from a distance and is based on inaccessibility, delegated authority, and tight control over public image. Machiavelli's *The Prince*—written at the start of the print age—is an early 'political public-relations manual'. Training and etiquette manuals are published for people of both sexes different ages. Indeed, every category of age, sex, and class begins to be increasingly isolated from the information and experience of others.

The development of bounded nation-states with centralized leadership is paralleled on a lower level by the isolation of the nuclear family from the extended community of kin and neighbours. The spread of literacy, with its emphasis on hierarchy and sequence, supports a linear chain of command, from God-the-Father, through a strong national leader, to a father who is a god to his wife and children.

Separate information-systems foster distinct uses of separate places, with increasingly distinct rules of access to them and distinctions in appropriate behaviour within them. People pass from role to role many times a day and change status through various rites of passage (matriculation, graduation, promotion, marriage, etc.) dozens of times in a lifetime.

Birth, death, mental illness, and celebrations are increasingly removed from the home and put into isolated institutions. The membranes around the

READING NOTES

hospital, prison, military barracks, factory, and school thicken over several centuries.[16]

The unity and continuity of a print society is far different from the unity of an oral society. The oral society's unity is a 'homogeneous solidarity' that relies on people acting, thinking, and feeling in relatively similar ways. Unity in a print society, however, depends on heterogeneity. The whole world begins to be seen as a machine with distinct parts, distinct types of people, that fit together to make it work. Print society depends on division of labour, separation of social spheres, segmentation of identities by class, occupation, sex, and so forth. People are increasingly separated into distinct places in order to 'homogenize them into groups'—groups with single identities: 'students', 'workers', 'prisoners', 'mentally ill'. The people in these groups are each seen as interchangeable parts. And the distinct identities are subsumed under the larger system of internally consistent, linearly connected, and hierarchically arranged units.[17]

Print leads to an emphasis on stages, levels, and ranks. The world comes to seem naturally layered and segmented. There is a place for everything, and everything is to be in its place. Those who remain illiterate, however, remain at the bottom or outside of this system. They continue to maintain many of the features of oral societies. Ironically, as late as the nineteenth century, the labour of illiterate children helps to feed the growth of a special subculture for the innocent children of the literate classes: publishers hire lower-class children to hand-tint the engravings in the growing number of books for middle-class children.[18]

Electronic Conceptions of Group Identity, Socialization, and Hierarchy

Electronic media begin to be widely used even as the impact of print leads to heightened attempts to isolate social spheres. The 'child savers' of the late nineteenth century try to extend the isolation of the children's sphere to the lower classes. A woman's place is to be in the home. The isolation of rich from poor, men from women, young from old intensifies, and 'institutions' become more fully isolated spheres for handling each aspect of social life.

But electronic media begin to reverse the trend. The telephone, radio, and television make the boundaries of all social spheres more permeable. One can now 'witness' events without being physically present; one can communicate 'directly' with others without meeting in the same place. As a result, physical structures no longer fully mould social identity. The walls of the family home, for example, no longer wholly isolate the home from the outside community. Family members at home now have access to others and others have access to them. Now, *where* one is has less to do with who one is.

The social information available to the ghetto family now more closely resembles the information available to the middle-class family. Information available to women now more closely resembles information available to men. Formerly distinct groups share more information about society and about each other—information that once distinguished 'insiders' from 'outsiders'. As a result, traditional group bonds are weakened and traditional distinctions among groups become partially blurred. This leads to a pressure to integrate roles and rights even when no clear mechanisms for doing so exist.

The explosion of clashing cultures comes in the mid- to late 1960s, when the first generation to watch television before entering school (the temple of literacy) comes of age. This generation rejects traditional distinctions in roles for young and old, for men and women, and for authorities vs. average citizens. The integration of information networks leads to a demand to integrate physical locations through the civil rights movement, the women's movement, and the children's liberation movement. The tense confrontations of 'The Sixties' become more muted, not when the drive for such integration subsides, but as the 'revolutionary' values and behaviours of the 1960s spread throughout the culture.[19]

The membranes around institutions are thinning. Hospital and prison visiting hours and rights, for example, are expanding, and children are being allowed to visit institutions more freely. Fathers and children, once excluded from births of babies, are now included in what is called the 'family birthing process'. There is a decline in male-only clubs, adult-only restaurants, and dress-specific events and locations.[20]

We still live in and interact in segregated physical locales. But television and other electronic media have broken the age-old connection between *where* we are and what we know and experience. Children may still be sheltered at home, but television now takes them across the globe before parents give them permission to cross the street. Through television, women—once isolated in the domestic sphere—have been exposed to places and activities men used to tell them they should know nothing about. And while few of us actually travel to see our leaders in the flesh, television now shows us our politicians close up—stammering and stumbling in living colour. Television blurs the line between public and private by bringing the public sphere into the home, and by emphasizing the personal and emotional dimensions of public actions through its intimate close-ups of human faces.

Television has lifted many of the old veils of secrecy between children and adults, men and women, and politicians and average citizens. By blurring 'who knows what about whom' and 'who knows what compared to whom', television has fostered the blurring of social identities, socialization stages, and ranks of hierarchy. The electronic society is characterized by more adultlike children and more childlike adults; more career-oriented women and more family-oriented men; and by leaders who act more like the 'person next door', just as average citizens demand to have more of a say in local, national, and international affairs.

As we move forward, our society also spirals backwards. The middle and upper classes are moving towards the behaviours once associated with the illiterate lower classes. Premarital sex, high illegitimacy rates, 'shacking up', and drug use spread upward through all levels of society. As recently as the early 1970s, differences in teenage sexuality could still be predicted accurately on the basis of race, socio-economic status, religion, and residence. But many of these distinctions have largely disappeared.[21] These changes violate the print industrial society's belief in 'Progress'. Yet they support the view that we are retreating from 'literate forms' and returning to 'oral forms' of behaviour.

The relatively shared information environment fostered by electronic media does not lead to identical behaviours or attitudes. Far from it. While the world is more homogenized on the macro, societal level, the experience on the micro, personal level is the opposite: the individual's world becomes more heterogeneous, a world filled with more variety, more choices. Just as traditional differences among people of different ages, sexes, status, families, neighbourhoods, and nationalities are blurring, people of the same age, sex, status, families, neighbourhoods, and nationalities are becoming less similar to each other.

While the print social order segregated people in their 'special spheres' in order to homogenize individuals into interchangeable elements of a larger social machine, the electronic society integrates all groups into a common sphere with a new recognition of the special needs and idiosyncrasies of individuals. What people share is not identical behaviour, but a common set of options.

But sharing of options is too weak a bond to hold people together. Metaphors aside, one cannot consider the whole country or world as one's 'neighbourhood'

READING NOTES

or 'village'. Another outcome of the homogenization of information networks, therefore, is the development of many new, more superficial, more shifting groupings that form against the now relatively unified backdrop of common information. People traditionally united and divided into groups that corresponded primarily to social class, ethnicity, race, education type and level, religion, occupation, and neighbourhood. But current groupings also develop on the basis of wearing similar clothes, participating in similar sports, listening to the same type of music, or attending the same class.

Nations evolved from feudal systems of local alliances when local membranes and arteries of communication were superseded by national ones. Now, new arteries and membranes are bypassing nations and fostering the rise of a system of quickly changing, neo-feudal ties and alliances on a global scale. Here, too, there is both unification on the macro level and fragmentation on the micro level. Old boundary lines fade in significance as distinct European countries plan to join into a single economic unit and as once taken-for-granted differences between East and West blur. But new boundary lines are created as earlier unions—Soviet, Yugoslav, Czech/Slovak—splinter.

The above is merely a rough sketch of a medium-theory analysis of role changes. I have explored other aspects of this information-system approach to social behaviour elsewhere.[22] Moreover, this analysis of role change is only one example of second-generation medium theory. Other scholars have expanded this perspective in other ways. Susan Sontag has written about the pervasive role of photography in our culture. Edward Wachtel has explored the impact of technology on art and perception. Paul Levinson has written about technology as an agent of cognitive development and about the impact of computer networks and electronic text. Neil Postman has explored the epistemology of television compared with print. Sherry Turkle and Judith Perrolle have written about the ways in which computers affect what we know, how we behave, and the ways we think about ourselves. Susan Drucker has analysed how the televising of trials dramatically alters the way they are experienced by the culture. Shoshana Zuboff has studied the role of the 'smart machine' in redefining work and power. Ethan Katsh has written about the ways in which electronic media have transformed the legal system. Gary Gumpert and Susan Drucker have explored the ways in which communication technologies alter the nature and the use of public space. Roderick Hart has analysed how television has changed the way politics is conducted and perceived. Medium theory has also played a key role in Alvin Toffler's and James Burke's theories of social change.[23]

RELATIVE STRENGTHS AND LIMITS OF MEDIUM THEORY

Unlike content research, the 'effects' that medium theorists look for are generally difficult to demonstrate through 'social-scientific' methods. The recreation of a pre-electronic 'print culture' for observation or experimental manipulation, for example, is virtually impossible. And surveys are not particularly useful in medium theory since the point is often to examine types of structural changes and sources of influence that are out of the awareness of most people. There have been some significant attempts to test aspects of medium theory experimentally and descriptively.[24] For the most part, however, medium theory, especially macro-level medium theory, relies heavily on argument, historical analysis, and large-scale pattern identification. Although the best studies weigh evidence carefully and search for disconfirming as well as confirming examples, most medium theory is not supported by systematic quantitative analyses. For some people, this makes medium

READING NOTES

_____

_____

_____

_____

_____

theory much more exciting and interesting than traditional content analysis; to others, it makes medium theory frustrating and 'unscientific'.

Just as traditional content approaches tend to obscure important differences among media, medium approaches tend to overlook the significance of content. Generally, medium research is most helpful when looking at broad structural patterns over a long period of time. But medium theory is not terribly useful in short-term analysis of how to use a communication technology and whether and how to regulate it. A parent who is angry about the violent and advertising-saturated programmes his or her children see will find cold comfort in a medium perspective that argues that TV in general weakens the print-supported sphere of innocent childhood and returns us to a world where, to control what children know, parents must either censor their own experience or isolate themselves from their children. Similarly, a woman faced with a daily stream of often demeaning gender images on television may have difficulty focusing on the encouraging medium-theory argument that television, more than print, includes women in many all-male spheres of the culture. Rather than leaving such situations at the medium-theory level, we also need to look at the institutional and economic forces that shape media content. And, if we want to change the current media systems, we need to look at the available political options for doing so.

Medium theorists' focus on the characteristics of media has tended to lead to another weakness. Most medium theory begins with the invention and use of a medium and has tended to ignore the institutions that have important political and economic stakes in the development of some technologies over others. A political and economic system that is interested in stimulating consumption of goods and ideology, for example, is likely to foster the development of uni-directional mass communication technologies such as broadcast radio and television. Other technologies or similar technologies used differently—such as ham radio or interactive community television—may receive much less support and encouragement. Medium theory has also tended to ignore vast cultural differences that mute and alter the development, use, and perception of various communication technologies.

Although the response is inadequate, some medium theorists would probably counter that those who have focused on the roles of powerful political and economic institutions and on the influence of culture almost always ignore the ways in which the 'chosen' technologies have social consequences apart from those planned and often alter those very institutions and cultures that develop them.

Another common attack on medium theory is that, as a wholly 'deterministic' perspective, it ignores free will and is disproved by the many exceptions to its broad claims. Part of this critique may stem from the fact that medium theorists, in exploring a process that has been largely ignored, by mainstream media researchers, have tended to sketch very broad patterns of social change and have not been especially careful in stating qualifications. Certainly, the most useful way to look at medium theory is to think of it not as deterministic, but as a model that deals in general tendencies. Medium theorists suggest that each medium invites, allows, encourages, fosters some human actions while discouraging others. This perspective is no more deterministic than widely accepted analyses of how the paths of rivers and other geographical features have shaped general patterns of human settlement and exchange. Unlike medium theory, such analyses are rarely dismissed as deterministic and are not usually thought of as being disproved by exceptions to the general patterns Like medium theory, such analyses do not claim to predict precise outcomes (sharing a waterway may lead societies to peaceful trade or to war), but they do argue for a general structural prediction (sharing a waterway is more likely to lead to interaction than being on either side of an imposing mountain range). Indeed, since medium theory deals with human-made 'rivers' and 'mountains', it is inherently less deterministic than analyses of the impact of geographical features. Ultimately, the greatest loss of freedom and control results from ignoring the ways in which the communication pathways and barriers we shape tend to reshape us.

The relative strengths and weaknesses of content and medium perspectives are often most visible when we look to the past. Neither approach in isolation, for example, would have told us the full story of the impact of the spread of printing in the sixteenth and seventeenth centuries. A content/institutional approach probably would have led researchers to conclude that books had two major influences; (1) the fostering of religion (most early books were religious texts); and (2) the further empowering of central monarchical and religious authorities (who controlled most of what was printed). Yet most analysts would now agree that in the long term the printing press fostered the opposite: the weakening of religion with the growth of science and the decline of monarchs with the development of constitutional systems.

With respect to these long-term consequences, medium theory clearly wins. But one cannot discount the implications of content control over those people who actually lived through the initial years of printing. The medium-theory analysis of the long-term tendencies of printing would give little comfort to the family of William Carter who, after printing a pro-Catholic pamphlet in Protestant-dominated England in 1584, was promptly hanged. Similarly, our current information environment is choked by the way television content is controlled—regardless of the 'inherent characteristics' of the medium.

While examples from several centuries ago may be clearer and less controversial than those of the last few years, recent events such as 'People Power' in the Philippines, the Tienanmen Square protests in China, the revolutions in Eastern Europe, and the dissolution of the Soviet Union also offer insight into the relative strengths and weaknesses of content and medium approaches.

Conventional wisdom claims that most of these events were not predicted by 'the experts'. Yet, while it is certainly true that those who have focused on the traditional institutional/content approach could not anticipate such dramatic shifts within cultures where the media content was so tightly controlled, medium theorists have long predicted just such changes.[25]

Electronic media's inherent disregard for physical boundaries made it difficult for these countries to restrict their citizens' access to many aspects of Western culture. This gave these populations awareness of what they did not have, as well as awareness of global awareness. Television allowed them to protest not simply for the government forces that faced them in the streets but for the global television audience. And the rapid feedback of electronic technology allowed them to be encouraged by the ongoing global response (televised globally as well as transmitted through telephones and fax machines). The heightened global consciousness of heightened global consciousness encouraged each Eastern European country to wait its turn to enter the global television arena. These events were not simply reported on television; in many ways, they happened in, on, through, and because of television.[26]

Medium theory alone, however, cannot explain why the 'stories' we were told about the Philippines and Eastern Europe were still highly selective or why 'global television' does not look to all countries equally. The content of the US coverage of Philippine people power, for example, tended to embrace the century-old narrative of US 'benevolence' towards the Philippines, while largely ignoring the sordid aspects of the United States' 'pacification' of the islands and the backing of the Macros dictatorship.[27] Similarly, while massive TV news coverage was given to the overthrow of Soviet-backed regimes in Eastern Europe, almost no attention

READING NOTES

_____

_____

_____

_____

_____

was given to the simultaneous dramatic push for democracy in Latin America, where voters in Brazil and Chile—whose populations exceed that of all Eastern Europe—held their first free presidential elections since the United States encouraged brutal military coups in 1964 and 1973 respectively.[28]

The medium-theory view of the unique features of global electronic media gives us tremendous insight into the power and potential of our new technologies. But the content/institutional perspective allows us to observe how the selective use and foci of the global spotlight intersect with issues of power, ideology, economics, and journalistic conventions. We need to study all these things if we are to understand our media world.

Ultimately, medium theory is most helpful when it is used not to supplant content concerns but to add another dimension to our understanding of the media environment. What is needed is a better integration of medium theory with other perspectives.[29]

ENDNOTES

1. See Harold A. Innis, *The Bias of Communication* (Toronto: University of Toronto Press, 1964); and *Empire and Communications* (Toronto: University of Toronto Press, 1972).

2. See e.g. Marshall McLuhan, *The Gutenberg Galaxy: The Making of Typographic Man* (Toronto: University of Toronto Press, 1962), and *Understanding Media: The Extensions of Man* (New York: McGraw-Hill, 1964).

3. J. C. Carothers, 'Culture, psychiatry, and the written word', *Psychiatry*, 22 (1959), pp. 307–20; Jack Goody and Ian Watt, 'The consequences of literacy', *Comparative Studies in Society and History*, 5 (1963), pp. 304–45; Eric A. Havelock, *Preface to Plato* (Cambridge, Mass.: Harvard University Press, 1963); A. R. Luria, *Cognitive Development: Its Cultural and Social Foundations*, trans. Martin Lopez-Morillas and Lynn Solotaroff, ed. Michael Cole (Cambridge, Mass.: Harvard University Press, 1976); Walter J. Ong, *Ramus, Method, and the Decay of Dialogue* (Cambridge, Mass.: Harvard University Press, 1958); Walter J. Ong, *The Presence of the Word: Some Prolegomena for Cultural and Religious History* (New Haven, Conn. Yale University Press, 1967); Walter J. Ong, *Rhetoric, Romance and Culture* (Ithaca, NY Cornell University Press, 1971); Walter J. Ong, *Orality and Literacy The Technologizing of the Word* (Ithaca, NY: Cornell University Press, 1982). For a collection of case studies on the effects of literacy in traditional societies, see Jack Goody, (ed.), *Literacy in Traditional Societies* (Cambridge: Cambridge University Press, 1968).

4. H. J. Chaytor, *From Script to Print: An Introduction to Medieval Vernacular Literature* (1945; rpt. London: Sidgwick & Jackson, 1966); Elizabeth I,. Eisenstein, *The Printing Press as an Agent of Change: Communication and Cultural Transformations in Early-Modern Europe*, vols I and II (New York/Cambridge; Cambridge University Press, 1979).

5. Daniel J. Boorstin, *The Americans: The Democratic Experience* (New York; Random House, 1973), pp. 307–410; Daniel J. Boorstin, *The Republic of Technology: Reflections on our Future Community* (New York: Harper & Row, 1978); Edmund Carpenter. *Oh, What a Blow that Phantom Gave Me!* (New York: Holt, Rinehart & Winston, 1973); Edmund Carpenter and Ken Heyman, *They Became What They Beheld* (New York: Outerbridge & Dienstfrey/Ballantine, 1970); Tony Schwartz, *The Responsive Chord* (Garden City, NY: Anchor, 1974); Tony Schwartz, *Media: The Second God* (Garden City, NY: Anchor, 1983); Walter J. Ong, *The Presence of the Word*, pp. 17–110, 259–62, 287–324; Ong, *Interfaces of the Word: Studies in the Evolution of Consciousness and Culture* (Ithaca, NY: Cornell University Press, 1977), pp. 82–91, 305–41; Ong, *Orality and Literacy*, pp. 79–81, 135–8; Tony Schwartz, *The Responsive Chord* (Garden City, NY: Anchor, 1974).

6. Joshua Meyrowitz, *No Sense of Place: The Impact of Electronic Media on Social Behavior* (New York: Oxford University Press, 1985), pp. 69–125.

7. The references within this section are to anthropological and historical sources that document each particular role behaviour described. The overall argument presented in this section—that these behaviours fall into a pattern linked to different dominant forms of communication—is my own and is not necessarily one with which the cited authors would agree.

8. The claims about roles in hunter and gatherer societies in the next few paragraphs are culled from Charlotte G. O'Kelly, *Women and Men in Society* (New York: Van Nostrand, 1980); Patricia Draper, '!Kung Women: contrasts in sexual egalitarianism in foraging and sedentary contexts', in Rayna R. Reiter (ed.), *Toward an Anthropology of Women* (New York: Monthly Review Press, 1975), pp. 77–109; Jane C. Goodale, *Tiwi Wives: A Study of the Women of Melville Island, North Australia* (Seattle: University

of Washington Press, 1971); Lorna Marshall, *The !Kung of Nyae Nyae* (Cambridge, Mass.: Harvard University Press, 1976); Colin M. Turnbull, *The Forest People* (New York: Simon & Schuster), 1961; Ernestine Friedl, *Women and Men; An Anthropological View* (New York: Holt, Rinehart & Winston, 1975). For an analysis of how our own society now resembles some features of nomadic societies, see my *No Sense of Place*, pp. 315–17.

9. Arnold van Gennep, *The Rites of Passage*, trans. Monika B. Vizedom and Gabrielle L. Caffee (Chicago: University of Chicago Press, 1960).

10. Philippe Aries, *Centuries of Childhood: A Social History of Family Life*, trans. Robert Baldick (New York: Vintage, 1962).

11. David Hunt, *Parents and Children in History: The Psychology of Family Life in Early Modern France* (New York: Basic Books, 1970).

12. Aries, *Centuries of Childhood*; Lawrence Stone, *The Family, Sex, and Marriage* in England, 1500–1800 (New York: Harper & Row, 1977). See also, Meyrowitz, *No Sense of Place*, pp. 258–65, for an analysis of the many historical hints to the role of literacy in the development of 'childhood'.

13. Anne Oakley, *Sex, Gender and Society* (New York: Harper & Row, 1972).

14. Stone, *The Family, Sex, and Marriage in England*, 1500–1800, p. 196.

15. Sheila M. Rothman, *Women's Proper Place: A History of Changing Ideals and Practices, 1870 to the Present* (New York: Basic Books, 1978), pp. 26ff.

16. Michel Foucault, *Discipline and Punish: The Birth of the Prison*, trans. Alan Sheridan (New York: Pantheon, 1977).

17. Ibid.

18. John C. Sommerville, *The Rise and Fall of Childhood* (Beverly Hills, Calif.: Sage, 1982), pp. 145 and 160.

19. For documentation of this trend, see Meyrowitz, *No Sense of Place*, pp. 140–3.

20. For a detailing and analysis of all these trends, see Meyrowitz, *No Sense of Place*.

21. Alan Guttmacher Institute, *Teenage Pregnancy: The Problem that Hasn't Gone Away* (New York: Guttmacher Institute, 1981), p. 9.

22. Meyrowitz, *No Sense of Place*; Meyrowitz, 'Media as social contexts', in Ralph Rosnow and Marianthi Georgoudi (eds), *Contextualism and Understanding in Behavioral Science: Implications for Research and Theory*, (New York: Praeger, 1986), pp. 229–50; Meyrowitz, 'The generalized elsewhere', *Critical Studies in Mass Communication*, 6:3 (Sept. 1989), pp. 326–34; Meyrowitz, 'Using contextual analysis to bridge the study of mediated and unmediated behavior', in Brent D. Ruben and Leah A. Lievrouw (eds), *Mediation, Information, and Communication: Information and Behavior*, vol. 3, (New Brunswick, NJ: Transaction Press, 1990), pp. 67–94; Meyrowitz, 'Three worlds of strangers: boundary shifts and changes in "them" vs. "us"', *Annals of the Association of American Geographers*, 80:1 (Mar. 1990), pp. 129–31; Meyrowitz, 'Redefining the situation: extending dramaturgy into a theory of social change and media effects', in Stephen Riggins (ed.), *Beyond Goffman: Studies on Communication, Institution, and Social Interaction* (New York: Mouton de Gruyter, 1990), pp. 65–97.

23. Susan Sontag, *On Photography* (New York: Farrar, Straus & Giroux, 1977); Edward Wachtel, 'The influence of the window on Western art and vision', *The Structurist*, 17/18 (1977/1978), pp. 4–10; Edward Wachtel and Casey Man Kong Lum, 'The influence of Chinese script on painting and poetry', *Et cetera*, 48:3 (Fall 1991), pp. 275–91; Paul Levinson, *Mind at Large: Knowing in the Technological Age* (Greenwich, Conn.: JAI Press, 1988); Levinson, *Electronic Chronicles: Columns of the Changes in our Time* (Tallahassee, Fla.: Anamnesis Press, 1992); Neil Postman, *Amusing Ourselves to Death Public Discourse in the Age of Show Business* (New York: Penguin, 1985); Sherry Turkle, *The Second Self: Computers and the Human Spirit* (New York: Simon & Schuster, 1984), Judith A. Perrolle, *Computers and Social Change: Information Property, and Power* (Belmont, Calif.: Wadsworth Publishing, 1987); Susan J. Drucker, 'The televised mediated trial: formal and substantive characteristics', *Communication Quarterly*, 37:4 (Fall 1989), pp. 305–18; Shoshana Zuboff, *In the Age of the Smart Machine: The Future of Work and Power* (New York: Basic Books, 1984); M. Ethan Katsh, *The Electronic Media and the Transformation of Law* (New York: Oxford University Press, 1989); Gary Gumpert and Susan J. Drucker, 'From the Agora to the electronic shopping mall', *Critical Studies in Mass Communication*, 9:2 (1992) pp. 186–200; Roderick Hart, *Watching Politics, How Television Makes Us Feel* (New York: Oxford University Press, forthcoming); Alvin Toffler, *Future Shock* (New York: Random House, 1970); Alvin Toffler, *The Third Wave* (New York: Morrow, 1980); Toffler, *Powershift; Knowledge, Wealth, and Violence at the Edge of the 21st Century* (New York: Bantam Books, 1990); James Burke, *Connections* (Boston: Little, Brown, 1978).

24. See e.g. Stanley Milgram, 'The image freezing machine', in *The Individual in a Social World: Essays and Experiments* (Reading, Mass.: Addison-Wesley, 1977), pp. 339–50; Michael Pfau, 'A channel approach to television influence', *Journal of Broadcasting & Electronic Media*, 34:2 (Spring 1990),

READING NOTES

pp. 195–214; Michael Pfau and Jong Geun Kang, 'The relationship between media use patterns and the nature of media and message factors in the process of influence', *Southern Communication Journal* (forthcoming); Doris A. Graber, *Processing the News: How People Tame the Information Tide*, 2nd edn (New York: Longman, 1988), pp. 166–74. Turkle and Zuboff's work, cited in note 23, is rich in participant observation, but their real contributions are in their interpretation and analysis.

25. More than two decades before the 'surprise' fall of communism, for example, Marshall McLuhan and Quentin Fiore wrote in *War and Peace in the Global Village* (New York: Simon & Schuster, 1968), p. 5, that communism was a thing of the past and that electronic media would 'turn on' the Soviet Union. Here, as elsewhere, McLuhan also wrote of the splintering of nation states and of 'retribalization'. Similarly, in the mid-1980s, I described how electronic media were limiting the significance of the physical boundaries 'marked by walls, doors, and barbed wire, and enforced by laws, guards, and trained dogs' (*No Sense of Place*, p. 117).

26. For a further discussion of this issue see Joshua Meyrowitz, 'The power of television news', *The World & I, 7:6*, (June 1992), pp. 453–73, and Deirdre Boden, 'Reinventing the global village: communication and the revolutions of 1989', (unpublished paper).

27. For an excellent history of the US's early role in the Philippines and of the distortions in the US press concerning it, see Leon Wolff, *Little Brown Brother: How the United States Purchased and Pacified the Philippine Islands at the Century's Turn* (Garden City, NY: Doubleday, 1961). For an analysis of the US's 20-year alliance with the Marcos dictatorship, see Raymond Bonner, *Waltzing with a Dictator: The Marcoses and the Making of American Policy* (New York: Times Books, 1987).

28. For an analysis of this general, coverage pattern, but with a focus on print media, see Lawrence Wechsler, 'The media's one and only freedom story', *Columbia Journalism Review* (Mar./Apr. 1990), pp.25–31.

29. As I have argued elsewhere, content approaches and medium approaches should be combined with at least one other approach, media 'grammar' studies, in order to explore the media environment more fully. See Joshua Meyrowitz, 'The questionable reality of media', in John Brockman (ed.), *Ways of Knowing: The Reality Club* 3 (New York: Prentice-Hall, 1991), pp. 141–60; Meyrowitz, 'Images of media: hidden ferment—and harmony—in the field', *Journal of Communication*, 43:3 (Summer 1993), pp. 55–66.

READING NOTES

_____

_____

_____

_____

Chapter 3

Media Analysis

"Whoever controls the media—the images—controls the culture."

—ALLEN GINSBERG

Understanding how meaning is derived from media content is an important skill in understanding the world in which we live. Once applied mainly to literature, the notion of literacy, or decoding the multifaceted meanings of a work of art, also fits the process of understanding the meaning of photography, magazines, advertising, journalism, comic books, movies, radio, television, cable, video games, and the Web. These objects can be regarded as texts for study, description, analysis, and interpretation. Once disdained as low culture aimed at the mass audience's lowest common denominator, media now subsume the content considered to be "high culture"—or works intended to explore deeply the human condition—into a vibrant, global, cultural mash-up. Research shows that the media have considerable influence on the audience's beliefs tastes and understandings of the world. Therefore, media literacy skills are essential for people to think critically about the media messages they receive constantly.

Media literacy is like a detective's questioning of witnesses and gathering of physical evidence to get an overall picture of the "crime," or in this case, the "real" meaning or meanings of the text. To do so, one can apply analytical tools similar to those used for traditional literary analysis to the audiovisual texts of media arts. This chapter introduces three frameworks for analysis—semiotic, psychoanalytic, and Marxist—and concludes with an extended example of media analysis.

This chapter:

- introduces the idea of reading media as text,

- lay outs different levels of communication for analysis,

- explains three approaches to critical media analysis and interpretation—semiotic, psychoanalytic, and Marxist, and

- gives an extended example of critical media analysis.

Required Reading: Mitchell Stephens's book *the rise of the image, the fall of the word* traces the growing popularity of visual media, particularly television, and the corresponding decline in book reading in contemporary society. Stephens ponders the media's role in changing habits of the mind. Can a person who does not read books be considered literate? Does media literacy compensate for reduced reading literacy? Can books survive the media's audiovisual onslaught? Stephens's chapter considers these questions.

SOCIAL CONSTRUCTION OF REALITY AND CRITICAL CULTURAL STUDIES

Media literacy is founded on the idea that knowledge is socially constructed. In his 1922 book *Public Opinion*, newspaper columnist Walter Lippmann was perhaps among the first people to observe the media's power to influence, if not dictate, the way people understand the world, when he wrote that the mass media put "pictures in our heads." In other words, people learn how to think, feel, and act about the world and toward others in society primarily, or at least in large part, through media images. Individuals collaborate in the construction of their own "realities" by the media they choose. Peter Berger and Thomas Luckmann formalized these ideas about media formation of social roles in their book, *The Social Construction of Reality*. Recently, the new participatory culture of blogs, interactive games, social networks, and customizable media gives the media audience more say than ever before in social construction of knowledge.

The mass media can be criticized for spreading ideologies, or prevailing ways of thinking about the world. For example, advertising often is blamed for contributing to the U.S. culture of consumption in which buying and consuming things is portrayed as the only way to happiness. Advertisers, of course, do not see it that way. They believe that they are helping their clients to sell their products, which is advertising's primary goal.

But in an analysis of the ideology that sees advertising promoting a culture of consumption, the job of advertisers is to make people dissatisfied with what they have and to want more. U.S. capitalism seems to embrace this ideology as it calls on consumers to borrow and to spend in order to keep the economy "healthy," but at the cost of waste, pollution, and reduction of personal savings. In recent years, some advertisers have promoted products and services using an opposing ideology, sustainability or "going green," which celebrates resource conservation, recycling, and the general welfare over individual gratification.

The idea of studying the media for their impact on matters of ideology, cultural hegemony, nationality, ethnicity, race, class, or gender orientation date to the 1960s, when Richard Hogart, Stuart Hall, and others launched an innovative program of empirical research at the Centre for Contemporary Culture Studies at the University of Birmingham, England. Critical cultural studies is a catch-all for a variety of analytical approaches, including semiotics, psychoanalysis, Marxist criticism, feminist studies, comparative culture studies, and popular culture research. *The Nationwide Project* (1980) was an empirical study of the British television audience that brought much attention to the Centre. The project looked at how audience members of a particular BBC news program used dominant, oppositional, and negotiated readings of the television text. The project spawned imitators around the world.

Marxist criticism of popular culture was the focus of the Frankfurt School of Cultural Studies at the Institute for Social Research at the University of Frankfurt in Germany, including important thinkers such as Max Horkheimer, Theodor Adorno, and Jürgen Habermas. In their work, they consider how social elites use the mass media to shape the consciousness of the working class. For example, they accuse the media of acting in conjunction with the U.S. government to use the idea of a pure good, such as "spreading democracy," to rationalize its self-serving military, political, and economic aggression.

Not everyone accepts the validity of critical cultural studies and study of media texts. Yale

University literature professor Harold Bloom chastises the movement for polluting traditional literary studies, legitimizing the notion of political correctness, and turning young people away from reading.

LEVELS OF ANALYSIS

All media texts can be analyzed and interpreted as products of communication practices. This section introduces seven levels of human communication processes that can serve as starting points for analysis: verbal, nonverbal, intrapersonal, interpersonal, intercultural, small-group, and organizational communication (see Figure 3.1).

Verbal communication is using language to arouse meanings in people. Despite the growth of visual communication, the verbal still dominates meaning-formation in our culture. Because language requires interpretation, the audience actively collaborates in determining the mean-ings of verbal messages. According to linguistics, the meanings of words are conventional, or established arbitrarily and stabilized by community use. Language is a living thing—responsive to people's communicative needs. Linguists have noted that English, the multicultural language of the old British Empire, is the most pliant and adaptable among modern global languages, constantly taking on new words from the media world. For example, Merriam-Webster's recent "Words of the Year" include blog (2004), truthiness (2006, from Stephen Colbert of Comedy Central's *The Colbert Report*), and w00t (2007, the online gaming world's acronym for "we owned the other team").

Nonverbal communication—the use of objects, actions, sounds, time, or space to arouse meanings in other people—comes to the fore in the sights, sounds, and motions inherent in audiovisual media. Sometimes synonymous with visual, nonverbal includes a host of auditory (vocalics), moving (kinesics), tactile (haptics), gazing (oculesics), temporal (chronemics), and spatial (proxemics) gestures. An example of gestural communication is the emblem, which is a non-verbal gesture with a consistent verbal equivalent. For example, popular culture's embrace of

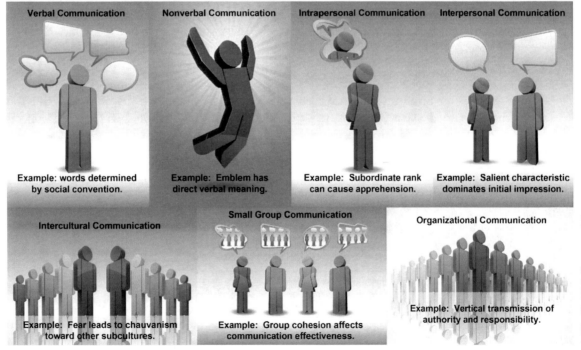

Figure 3.1—*Seven levels of human communication.*

sports has universalized the "high five" emblem. Another emblem is illustrated in the critical media analysis example at the end of this chapter.

Intrapersonal communication is using verbal and nonverbal means to convey meaning to the self. In this process, the self becomes a surrogate other. Talking to one's self to work out ideas is a normal phase of human intercourse. People embrace social roles intrapersonally by observing others' behaviors and deciding how to fit in. In this way, intrapersonal communication drives the social construction of reality. The critical media analysis example at the end of the chapter points out a movie character's intrapersonal moment.

Interpersonal communication is using verbal and nonverbal cues to arouse particular meanings in another person. It is perhaps the broadest category of human interaction. Small-group and large-group communication can be seen as special cases of the interpersonal category. All of these communication levels are part of the dialogic domain of human beings as gripped by the human need to relate to other people. In the dialogic mode, even a person marooned alone on a desert island will need to communicate to someone, which was the theme of the movie *Cast Away*, starring Tom Hanks, in which Hanks, marooned on a desert island, talks to a ball he names "Wilson." The example of critical media analysis at the end of this chapter illustrates a theory of interpersonal communication known as the salient characteristic, which is a feature or aspect of a person that stands out in an initial encounter and tends to dominate the initial impression that person makes in social relations.

Intercultural communication is an exchange of meanings between people who are influenced by their different cultures. Critical media analysis can show all sorts of intercultural differences—language, body language, proxemics, customs, dress, religion, rituals, holidays, and social institutions. U.S. mass media reflects the multiculturalism of centuries of immigration from all over the world.

The most rapidly growing U.S. subculture is Hispanic, representing Spanish-speaking immigrants from

Latin American and Caribbean nations, Europe, and even the Far East. Interestingly, although "Hispanic" looks like a large sub-community to English-speakers in the United States, each of the immigrant Hispanic subgroups, such as Cuban Americans or Mexican Americans, attempts to retain its own cultural heritage based on its country of origin, while assimilating into U.S. society.

Fear of the unknown causes some people to believe in their own subculture's superiority and to treat others with unfair stereotypes. The critical media analysis example at the end of this chapter illustrates a destructive response to this fear—chauvinism—which is boastful, exaggerated ethnocentrism. The mass media can be either a perpetuator of negative stereotypes or a positive vehicle for spreading knowledge of other cultures and promoting openness to diversity.

Small group communication is sharing meaning among two or more people with a common goal and shared rules. Small groups include families, co-workers, clubs, church or synagogue circles, neighborhood sports teams, regulars at the local pub, and friends on the social network Facebook. Members use one another to affirm personal choices, such as what politicians to vote for, what television shows to watch, or which brand of smart phone to buy. In addition to opinion leadership, another important internal variable affecting communication is group cohesion. The stronger the bond of membership, the more likely it is that members will pursue collective goals and ignore external messages.

Cohesion is illustrated in the critical media analysis example at the end of the chapter.

Organizational communication is sharing meaning through formal and informal channels in structured groups with defined boundaries that are too large for all members to know each other. Organizations include schools, universities, governments, sports leagues, corporations, worship communities, political-action committees, computer-game user groups, and celebrity fan clubs. Organizations' communication challenges include maintaining group cohesion and overcoming alienation. An effective strategy to address these challenges is to create small groups within the organization, in which members can more easily know one another. The critical media analysis example at the end of the chapter illustrates the concept of vertical transmission of organizational authority and responsibility.

Media literacy tools are useful for "reading" how the mass media inform, entertain, influence, and persuade. Sorting out the communication level of analysis is a useful first step for media literacy prior to semiotic, psychoanalytic, Marxist, or other analytical approaches. For example, analyzing newspapers as verbal versus nonverbal communication reveals the significance of the new national newspaper *USA Today* in 1982, with its innovative use of photos, information graphics, color, and indexing aimed at the busy business reader.

Relatively competitors that made little use of color on their pages such as *The New York Times* and the *Wall Street Journal* chided *USA Today* for being "McPaper," fast-food journalism. However, *USA Today's* new visual approach was popular with readers and within a decade the use of color was commonplace in the industry. Newspaper journalism morphed from being predominantly verbal to a verbal–nonverbal hybrid. Such classifications set the stage for reading media texts as systems of cultural signs (semiotics), expressions of the psyche (psychoanalysis), or outcomes of class struggle (Marxist analysis).

SEMIOTIC ANALYSIS OF THE MEDIA

One of the most compelling systems for analyzing media texts is called semiotics. Although the idea of semiotics has deep roots, its modern incarnation has its origin in the work of Swiss linguist Ferdinand de Saussure and the U.S. philosopher Charles Sanders Peirce. Saussure conceived a science that would investigate the nature of signs and what he believed would be the laws governing their use and meaning. A sign can be anything

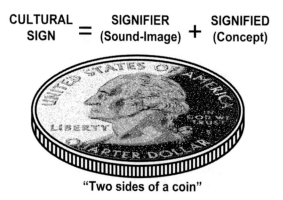

CULTURAL SIGN = SIGNIFIER (Sound-Image) + SIGNIFIED (Concept)

"Two sides of a coin"

qualities: ✓oppositions ✓arbitrary ✓in flux

Russell J. Cook

Figure 3.2—*Semiotics: Saussure's definition of a cultural sign.*

that has meaning—words, pictures, clothing styles, dance, music, sports, politics, movies, or television. Meaning is not in signs, but rather in people's relation to them. The process of sharing meaning is called signification.

Saussure applied the linguistic structure of words to all signs in his new science, semiology. Saussure said that a sign is the pairing of a signifier or "sound-image" with a signified or "concept," like two sides of a coin (see Figure 3.2). The meanings of all possible nonverbal sound-images are dependent on their paired word-based concepts. Saussure's idea was radically new. It meant that all human thought is both made possible by words and limited by them, a philosophy that became known as structuralism. Saussure's ideas were further developed by the French anthropologist Claude Levi-Strauss, who conceived of culture as similarly structured communication system and developed models based on linguistics, information theory, and cybernetics to interpret them. Semiology became a philosophical movement in Europe, spreading to France (Roland Barthes), Russia (Vladimir Propp), Italy (Umberto Eco), and England (John Fiske, John Hartley). The concepts associated with structuralism have been applied to other social and human sciences such as sociology, psychology, psychoanalysis, literary theory, and architecture.

Less theoretical and more pragmatic than Saussure, Peirce focused his semiotics (the term used in this book for both systems) on the iconic, indexical, and symbolic dimensions of signs (see Figure 3.3). Peirce's contributions to the new science of cultural signs were important, but little noticed at first. Americans were somewhat slower than their European counterparts to embrace the field.

Signs are inherently difficult to study. The first difficulty is that signs are a network of meaning oppositions. The same sign can have many such oppositions, creating a complicated web of meaning. For example, "red" can mean the opposite of "green," as in traffic signals. However, "red" also can oppose "black," as in life versus death (see Figure 3.4).

"Red" has many other meaning oppositions as well, most of which are too transitory to be dictionary definitions. One would expect red—the color of blood and fire—to have universal meaning around the world, but in fact, the meaning oppositions for red vary widely by culture: energy, life, heat, health, death, disease, sin, guilt, error, blushing, love, anger, courage, sacrifice, pain, pleasure, passion, beauty, adultery, Satan, aggression, wrath, war, triumph, Christmas, crucifixion, Pentecost, God, Valentine's Day, robustness, virility, boldness, enthusiasm, impetuousness, danger, the South, weddings, married women, and good luck. Red also is the most common color on national flags.

1. **Semiotics explores how things have meaning.**
2. **Semiotics says meaning is not _in_ things.**
3. **Semiotics says meaning is _between_ things.**

PEIRCE	ICON	INDEX	SYMBOL
signify by	resemblance	causal connection	convention
examples	pictures	smoke / fire	words flags numbers
process	See	Figure out	Learn

Figure 3.3—*Semiotics: Peirce's classification of cultural signs.*

mutation of signs = <u>floating signifiers</u>

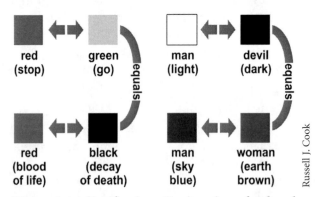

Figure 3.4—*Signification: Construction of cultural meaning through oppositional relations (signifiers) and meaning mutation (detached or "floating" signifiers).*

The second difficulty of signs is that they are made-up or arbitrary. For example, the fact that red stop signs are found around the world is a result of the conscious effort of many government authorities to make traffic signs universal, rather than a result of natural law. No color inherently means stop.

The color red undoubtedly catches people's attention, but its association with the negative idea of danger was an arbitrary choice. Another color could have been chosen, perhaps blue. Peirce's index category is the exception to the arbitrariness rule for signs: "where there's smoke, there's fire" is a learned connection.

A third difficulty of cultural signs is their impermanence. Signs are constantly changing. The signifier red is a good example of the impermanence of signs. The Red Scare refers to two historical periods, 1917 to 1920 and 1947 to 1957, when red was linked to fear of Communism's upsetting the capitalist social order. The U.S. government published propaganda maps showing Communism's "red menace" swallowing the world. Persons accused of being red were ostracized by society. Since 1991, with the collapse of Communist governments in the Soviet Union and Europe, the Communist meaning of red has dissipated into an historical oddity.

In U.S. political discourse in the early 21st century, the color red came to represent the Republican Party. The meaning emerged because red is the map color television broadcasters used to indicate which states won by Republicans in a political election. Blue was used to indicate states that the Democrats had won. Of course, 150 years earlier, the color blue was associated with those supporting the North in the Civil War and the color gray was associated with the South. Because signs continually take on new meanings, semiotic analysis is tied to time, place, and social and personal contexts.

If cultural signs were not so difficult to analyze, perhaps universal meanings for the media could be compiled, and semiotics would disappear. Media would be much easier to analyze in such a static semiotic world. But for many, the delight of media is precisely in its multilayered, indeterminate meanings. Because of signification's limitations of complexity, arbitrariness, and impermanence, semiotics will continue to be a valuable tool for media analysis.

The mass media's unstable cultural signs regularly mutate into new forms. Signifiers (sound-images) become detached from their signifieds (concepts), resulting in a mutation of cultural meanings called floating signifiers. It can be difficult or impossible to trace the pre-mutation meanings for floating signifiers, which appear strange, as if arising from nowhere. An entire system of floating signifiers is known as a semiosis (see Figure 3.4). The example of critical media analysis given at the end of this chapter shows how semioses of cultural signs in a film involving a fictional Middle Ages murder plot lead to misogyny.

PSYCHOANALYSIS OF THE MEDIA

Psychoanalysis is a therapy for tracing the motivations for conscious thoughts, words, and deeds to one's unconscious impulses and desires, in pursuit of mental health and a socially balanced and productive life. Because both conscious and unconscious human experience contributes to artistic expression in the mass media, psychoanalysis can be a useful tool for explaining a media audience's collective psyche based on the media texts attended. This section gives some of the basic ideas of Freudian and Jungian psychoanalysis and applies them to various media texts.

Many artists—including French and German surrealist poets, painters, and filmmakers of the 1920s—have found creative inspiration in Sigmund Freud's theories of the unconscious. Freud believed that the mind was basically divided into three parts. The "id" represents people's basic animal instincts. The superego is the part of the mind that represents what people understand as socially appropriate. The ego represents a person's sense of self; it negotiates between the id and the superego.

During the 1920s, the surrealists' self-proclaimed leader, André Breton, dedicated the movement to unleashing the creative impulses of the Freudian id, which he saw as repressed by the Freudian superego's societal rules, customs, and values. Breton said the purpose of surrealist art was to shock and disarm the superego, so that the "marvelous" images of unconscious life could be brought to consciousness. The surrealists especially admired the new medium of motion pictures for its ability to render super-realism—special effects such as magical appearances and disappearances, slow or fast motion, and superimposed images. The surrealists' creative impulse and delight in the "marvelous" are alive and well in today's movies, television, and video and computer games (see Figure 3.5).

Freud taught that neuroses come from repressed sexuality, which is disguised in social life as phallic symbols. Phalluses appear in advertising and entertainment media, such as guns, ballistic missiles, cigars, bottles, bananas, or even the Washington Monument (male), and flowers, cosmetics for lip decoration, breast cleavage, and high-heeled shoes (female).

According to Freud, infants have feelings of sexual love for the parent of the opposite sex, which violates the social taboo against incest. Accordingly, prepubescent boys desire to displace

Figure 3.5—*The surrealists' "marvelous" is alive and well in today's electronic media.*

Oedipus complex with his mother in Alfred Hitchcock's 1960 film *Psycho* has morbid aspects of necrophilia. Numerous scholars have recognized the Oedipal relationships of Luke Skywalker–Darth Vader and Luke–Leia in George Lucas' *Star Wars* saga, six-film project that launched with the release of *Star Wars: Episode 4—A New Hope* in 1977. Luke Skywalker, the hero, initially has a love interest in Princess Leia, who turns out to be his sister. The villain, Darth Vader, turns out to be Skywalker's father.

Carl Jung, a Swiss psychiatrist and Freud's colleague and associate, disagreed with Freud's interpretation of infantile sexuality. He saw the mind as made up of layers or strata. The first is the conscious mind—Freud's ego. The final layer is what he called the collective unconscious, a kind of universal mind similar in conception to Plato's ideas of ideal forms. The collective unconscious predates people's personal unconscious and is the repository for all religious, spiritual, and mythological symbols and experiences. For Jung, the collective unconscious was not metaphysical but psychobiological. Jung believed that archetypes, or conceptual constructs underlying religious and mythological constructs, were the building blocks of the unconscious mind as well as of a collective unconscious Archetypal characters abound in literature and the mass media, from the wise old man—Gandalf of *Lord of the Rings*—to the *femme fatale*—Æon Flux of the MTV animated series—to the brooding anti-hero Spiderman, to the trickster Bugs Bunny. *Star Wars'* "the Force" and *The Matrix* are two examples of contemporary media myths about Jung's collective unconscious.

Believing that dreams are wish fulfillment, Freud interpreted the content of some of his patients' dreams to treat their mental illnesses. According to Freud, bizarre images in dreams are the ego's defense mechanism to conceal repressed guilt. By contrast, Jung believed that dreams are not strictly personal but instead are manifestations of the collective unconscious, and therefore are populated by archetypes. According to Jung, dreams can contain symbols, fantasies, memories, plans, fears, and even visions into the future, all ruled by the logic of the dreamer's individual and collective

their fathers and to dominate their mothers' affections. Fear of being found out by their fathers—so-called castration anxiety—causes them to renounce their mothers' attentions and to direct their sexual interests toward other females, a defense mechanism known as displacement. Freud named this fundamental neurosis the Oedipus complex after the mythical king of ancient Thebes, who unknowingly killed his father and married his mother. In his irreconcilable guilt, he put out his own eyes, which created the mythological link between eyes and eroticism. Freud said that young girls experience similar Oedipal desires, which lead to jealousy of men and what he called "penis envy," now considered a laughably sexist concept.

Oedipal relationships crop up in media fairy tales. In *The Wizard of Oz*, Dorothy's odyssey through the magical Land of Oz can be interpreted as an orphan's search for her long-lost mother (Auntie Em is very nice, but not the real McCoy). Along the way, she encounters two incarnations of her mother, Glinda the Good Witch of the North and Miss Gulch, or the Wicked Witch of the West. Norman Bates' unconscious. Accordingly, dream images symbolize various aspects of the dreamer. Surrealists admired dreams and hallucinations for their glimpses into the unconscious, such as in Jean Cocteau's 1946 film *La Belle et la Bête* and Disney's 1991 animated version, *Beauty and the Beast.*

Hollywood is nicknamed the "Dream Factory" for good reason. The movies provide wish fulfillment of all sorts—vicarious flights of fancy, romantic encounters, dabblings in ultra-violence, gratifications of conspicuous consumption, and virtual self-actualization. A brief sampling follows of some notable cinematic dreams and hallucinations of films over the last three decades. Ken Russell's 1980 film *Altered States* is packed with intense dreams and hallucinations. Terry Gilliam's 1985 satire of technocracy, *Brazil,* is told through the main character's wish-fulfillment hallucinations. In 1991, two independent directors had successes with dream films: Steven Soderbergh captured the surreal world of *Kafka,* and David Cronenberg directed William S. Burroughs' famous drug-hallucination saga *Naked Lunch.* 1998 was a big year for hallucinations and dreams in the movies: Joel and Ethan Coen put "the Dude" through two hilarious acid flashbacks in their 1998 comedy *The Big Lebowski,* Gilliam directed the famous Hunter S. Thompson drug-trip saga *Fear and Loathing in Las Vegas.*

The Wichowski brothers, Andy and Larry, launched their virtual reality saga *The Matrix,* in 1999. Christopher Nolan's 2000 film *Memento* unraveled a mystery in a series of dreamlike flashbacks, the same year that Darren Aronofsky's tale of drug addiction, *Requiem for a Dream,* was released. James Cameron's high-tech epic *Avatar* (2009) depicts a virtual-reality dream world. It generated the highest gross revenues at the box office in history when it was released.

MARXIST ANALYSIS OF THE MEDIA

Karl Marx's theory of materialist production is one of history's most influential ideas, applicable not only to economics and politics, but also to the arts and media. Marx argued that culture—the way people see, understand, and make sense of the world—is based on the way the world is organized economically. Economic relationships are the most basic relationships. In fact, he argued, in the final analysis, all relationships are economic relationships.

In capitalism, the economic structure has two main parts—those who work, and those who own the tools and other necessary elements that enable work. In this analysis, the culture of capitalism preserves the economic structure of capitalism, which has led to vast inequalities of wealth between the workers and those who own the tools, which he calls the means of production.

Marxist critics claim that the wealthy ruling class in capitalist countries such as the United States controls the mass media in order to exploit the masses. The media spread false consciousnesses so that the masses do not realize they are being exploited. Such self-deception includes the myth of self-determination in reality television shows such as *American Idol* and *Survivor;* capitalist consumer values and conspicuous consumption in advertising and the movies; idolization of celebrities in fan magazines and on cable talk shows; female objectification in pornography, football cheerleaders, and beauty pageants; elevation of private business interests over public welfare in talk radio and business news; and the bandwagon effect in network news coverage of wars.

Another Marxist criticism of mass media is their manipulation of audiences to help workers to forget their feelings of alienation from being treated like commodities or replaceable cogs in production (see Figure 3.6). Movies and television often are accused of anaesthetizing the masses by promoting consumption, which in turn buoys the economy and increases corporate profits. From the Marxist perspective, advertising, including its product placements in the entertainment media, sows anxiety and dissatisfaction that only can be cured by spending more money.

Further, in this analysis, advertising will go to any length to achieve its goal of maintaining the class system, from debasing women to victimizing

© Michael D Brown, 2010. Shutterstock Inc.

Figure 3.6—*Marxist criticism: Media must anaesthetize workers from feeling alienation as cogs of materialist production.*

children, from reinforcing stereotypes to pretending to serve social welfare, from merchandizing dangerous products to exaggerating dangers. This school of media analysis is concerned with raising awareness to help individual audience members to resist the consumer culture, by understanding its sources, origins, and role in perpetuating the status quo.

George Orwell's 1949 novel *Nineteen Eighty-Four* painted a nightmarish scenario of "Big Brother," a totalitarian regime that ruled the world through its propaganda machine, the Ministry of Truth. To stave off the specter of Big Brother in the real world, the U.S. government made laws governing private media ownership to ensure competition, diversity of opinion, and accommodation of minority viewpoints. However, deregulation of the media and globalization of media corporations in the 1990s brought renewed worries about concentration of ownership and power of the mass media.

Most U.S. media industries have become oligopolies, with only a few companies controlling most of the business. A handful of global media conglomerates, or "mediagloms," control the majority of the world's print and electronic media, as well as nine-tenths of U.S. media companies. The largest media companies are Walt Disney Company, which ranked first globally in terms of revenue in 2009, followed by News Corporation, Time Warner, and Viacom.

Despite instrumental use of the media, British cultural scholar Raymond Williams says the Marxist critique of the media does not go far enough. Williams' cultural studies of television found that, by indoctrinating the masses with the ruling class's ideologies of democracy, capitalism, and consumer society, the media creates a hegemony or worldview that appears "natural" or the way the world "just is." The worldview supports the existing social structure and pervades beyond economics and politics to all conscious and unconscious life. While Williams gathered his ideas about the Western media's role in the Cold War and post–Cold War era, fundamentalist Islam rose as a new foe of Western capitalist hegemony and its pervasive media messengers. In fact, the clash between Western countries and fundamentalist Islamic extremists can be understood as a clash of competing hegemonic visions.

MEDIA ANALYSIS EXAMPLE

Following is a comprehensive analysis from several different analytical perspectives of the 1986 movie *The Name of the Rose*, starring Sean Connery, Christian Slater, and F. Murray Abraham, and directed by Jean-Jacques Annaud. The film is based on a novel by Umberto Eco, a world-renowned expert on semiotics. Eco's tale of medieval monastic intrigue uses multilayered communication modes that are rich for semiotic analysis. Eco was particularly fascinated with the stark, dramatic contrasts of medieval life. His main character's analysis of signs to solve a murder mystery was an extended metaphor for the reader's own experience of interpreting the text.

The plot of *The Name of the Rose* pits the Enlightenment and its embrace of reason against the religious superstition of the Dark Age. Reason is embodied by Franciscan scholar-monk William of Baskerville, played by Sean Connery, opposed by religious superstition as embodied by the Grand Inquisitor Bernardo Gui, played by F. Murray Abraham. Set in the year 1327, the story is narrated through the naive and idealistic eyes of William's young novice, Adso of Melk, played by Christian Slater.

Lighting and sets for the dank monastic chambers are especially effective in creating a world in which light metaphorically and literally struggles with darkness. The movie makes the most of the story's maze of dichotomous symbols: light/darkness, sight/blindness, good/evil, life/death, scientific deduction/superstition, individual/sect, truth/brainwashing, and Greek/Latin. Female viewers might be disgusted by the medieval attitude toward women depicted in the film.

The Name of the Rose depicts the era before Gutenberg's printing press, when monastic scribes wrote books out by hand. The key to solving the movie's mystery is an example of verbal communication: a manuscript written in the Greek language of Aristotle's *Second Book on Poetics*, which has been banned by the religious order for encouraging blasphemous levity in the abbey. Languages depend on shared meanings established by arbitrary convention and can be banned just as arbitrarily. Monk-sleuth William of Baskerville gradually unravels the murder mystery: Monks are dying after reading this forbidden book because the page corners have been treated with arsenic, which readers ingest when they lick their fingers to turn the manuscript's pages. Thus, verbal communication is literally killing the victims.

The Name of the Rose is packed with examples of nonverbal communication. A vivid example of body language in the film is the emblem of bowing before authority. William and his novice Adso of Melk bow repeatedly to their superiors to signal, "I honor you." However, as the plot thickens and William's unorthodox interpretation of clues brings him into conflict with abbey authorities,

he bows less deeply and adds upward glances as if to say, "You're the boss, but I'm right."

In *The Name of the Rose*, monastic novice Adso's internal struggle to talk about his sexual feelings with his master William amply illustrates the process of intrapersonal communication and communication apprehension. Adso hesitates to confess to his master that he has had sexual intercourse with a beggar woman. Young Adso feels nervous and self-conscious, but he eventually confides in his master, who already has guessed the truth. He tells his master that he loves the girl. William responds that Adso is confusing love with lust.

Interpersonal communication in one-on-one conversations drives the plots of most movies, and *The Name of the Rose* is no exception. Perhaps the most vividly strange character in the story is the evil monk Jorge de Burgos, played by Feodor Chaliapin, Jr. Jorge illustrates how a distinctive personal feature or salient characteristic can dominate initial impressions in interpersonal communication. Jorge's salient characteristic is severe cataracts that blind his eyes to light, a metaphor for his own religious superstition that blinds him to the truth. In a debate with the enlightened William, Jorge argues that comedy, represented by Aristotle's *Second Book on Poetics*, is contrary to God:

Jorge: Laughter is a devilish whim, which deforms, uh, the lineaments of the face and makes men look like monkeys.

William: Monkeys do not laugh. Laughter is particular to men.

Jorge: As is sin. Christ never laughed.

William: Can we be so sure?

Jorge: There is nothing in the Scriptures to say that he did.

William: And there's nothing in the Scriptures to say that he did not.

A clash of cultures between the Benedictine and Franciscan orders of the Roman Catholic Church provides a back-story for the plot of *The Name of* the Rose. William of Baskerville's archenemy and former tormentor, the Grand Inquisitor Bernardo Gui, demonstrates harmful intercultural communication known as chauvinism, or boastful ethnocentrism, toward the Franciscans and especially William. People can become ugly and dangerous when they believe their culture is superior. Gui is the epitome of such closed-mindedness.

The Franciscans employ small-group communication in *The Name of the Rose*. They fear reprisals from the Pope because their order emphasizes the poverty of Jesus Christ, in contrast to Papal wealth. When they learn that the Grand Inquisitor will arrive at the abbey, the Franciscans implore Brother William to repress his heretical views or risk bringing Gui's wrath onto their entire group. William's penchant for acting on his own instead of obeying his order threatens group cohesion.

The monastery's organizational communication provides the backdrop for the plot of *The Name of the Rose*. The film's many characters respond to both formal and informal channels of communication. The film's dark world is structured vertically, with God on top, peasants on the bottom, and the Church in between. All people have their place in this world and must not step out of their place, or they risk incurring the wrath of God through the Grand Inquisitor's charge of heresy. The punishment for heretics is burning at the stake. William's situation becomes untenable when his earthly solution to the abbey's diabolical murders threatened Gui's vertical authority.

The Name of the Rose depicts a strange, austere world in a fictional 14th century monastery far removed from modern life, yet through analysis of different levels of communication depicted the movie, we can empathize with its human situations and motivations. In terms of semiotics, the central conflict of *The Name of the Rose* is an overall semiosis of the Church (Gui, Jorge, knowledge is bad) versus Enlightenment (William, Adso, knowledge is good).

Umberto Eco modeled his main character on Arthur Conan Doyle's detective Sherlock Holmes, who epitomizes the pragmatic semiotician, deducing from seemingly insignificant, disconnected cultural details the solution to a mystery. Holmes's famous murder case The Hound of the Baskervilles marked the detective's return from Conan Doyle's eight-year writing hiatus. How fitting, then, that Eco should borrow the name Baskerville for his hero-sleuth in The Name of the Rose. Like Holmes, William of Baskerville returned from a mysterious hiatus, which is not explained until the end of the movie.

William has Holmes's powers of concentration, the same ability to see significance in the slightest details, the same passion for the quest of truth, and the same vanity. Eco even has his hero detective use experimental eyeglasses to search for clues, much as Conan Doyle's detective wielded his trademark magnifying glass. Like Conan Doyle's sidekick character Dr. Watson, Eco gave William an apprentice, Adso of Melk, as a foil to explain the abbey's strange characters and goings-on to the audience.

As enlightened as Sean Connery's character is in matters of crime detection and religious superstition, he is portrayed as typically backward in his attitude toward women. William counsels his novice, Adso, to repress his sexual thoughts about the peasant girl because woman is the Devil's device to tempt man away from God's ways. Historical drama aside, this is a startlingly sexist remark by a movie hero. Why would Eco burden his story with a side plot likely to remind the female half of his audience of the gender discrimination they suffer? Perhaps a semiotic analysis of *The Name of the Rose* can provide the answer.

The cosmic view of *The Name of the Rose* pitted earthbound man in eternal struggle between God in Heaven and the Devil in Hell (see Figure 3.7). Every member of society—the clergy, nobles, and serfs—had their roles in the static cosmic order for the generations. To persevere in their hopeless earthly existences and to earn heavenly rewards, the serfs looked heavenward to the goodness of God's light and shunned the Devil's darkness. This universe of starkly drawn oppositions—Man/God, Man/Devil, Light/Darkness, Good/

Bad, and so forth—offers a semiotic treasure trove of cultural signs.

In the medieval cosmic view depicted in *The Name of the Rose,* woman's gender opposition to man put her in a precarious position, in terms of semiotics. With the Christian focus on God the Father, the pagan celebration of the Earth Mother gave way to suspicion and fear of mysterious natural forces, including women's menstrual cycles and child-bearing. Consequently, woman became a floating signifier for opposition to God, hence William of Baskerville's sexist advice to Adso. As depicted in Figure 3.7, this semiosis of the medieval cosmic view aligned woman with the Devil. However, the plot twists of *The Name of the Rose* perform a final mutation of signification that redeems William and Adso, and gives female viewers something to cheer about at the end of the film.

In the film's dramatic conclusion, William's victory of enlightened knowledge, reason, and tolerance (light) over ignorance, superstition, and intolerance (darkness), followed by the deaths of Gui and Jorge, brings about a final mutation of signification (see Figure 3.8). The mutation inverts the man–woman relationship. Woman is lifted to communion with God–tolerance–knowledge–William–Adso, while man is forced to the nether region with the Devil–intolerance–ignorance–Jorge–Gui. At the end of the story, the peasant girl escapes death, William is forgiven his dogmatic sexism, and Adso overcomes his lustful feelings and commits his life to his master's search for truth.

The Name of the Rose is a strikingly noncommercial, idiosyncratic work of film art that nevertheless made money worldwide for its producers, earned British and French Academy Awards, and resurrected Sean Connery's film career. Analyzing the film's different levels of communication and semiotic structures applies new insights into the meaning of the film beyond its plot and market success.

Other analytical approaches might yield additional insights. For example, Marxist analysis might highlight the film's depiction of social

HEAVEN	God the Angels		Light of Day
EARTH	the Clergy Monks Nobles Serfs		Shadows of Earthly Existence
HELL	Evil Spirits Satan		Dark of Night

Russell J. Cook

Figure 3.7—*Semiotics of* The Name of the Rose: *Cosmic view in the Middle Ages.*

institutions and social class. Medieval serfs are suppressed by the Church in a pre-capitalist society. A Marxist analysis might reflect on the role of "reason" as the "hero" of the story and make the argument that reason is highly valued within capitalist societies. Consequently, the film reinforces capitalist values. Alternatively, a Marxist or political-economy analysis might look at who funded the production of the film, how it was distributed, and its critical reception.

Psychoanalysis might focus on Adso's struggles with sexuality and the need for the superego, in this case alternatively reason and religion, to control the id. At the end of the film, Adso leaves with the girl with whom he has fallen in love, demonstrating that neither faith nor reason is enough for fulfillment of every aspect of human life.

Semiosis = System of floating signifiers

Heaven-God-spirit-light-day-faith divinity-purity-mind-abstinence **MAN**

WOMAN evil-corruption-body-lust Hell-Satan-corpus-dark-night-doubt

Final Mutation of Semiosis

Heaven-God-spirit-light-day-faith divinity-purity-mind-abstinence William-Adso-knowledge-Greek tolerance-**WOMAN**

intolerance-**MAN** Jorge-Gui-ignorance-Latin evil-corruption-body-lust Hell-Satan-corpus-dark-night-doubt

Russell J. Cook

Figure 3.8—*Semiotics of* The Name of the Rose: *Semiosis and final mutation.*

Clearly, what a text "means" depends in large part on the kind of analysis that is applied to it. None of the meanings is necessarily more correct than any other. In fact, texts have multiple layers of meaning beyond the content on the surface. A systematic analysis of the content allows those layers of meaning to be peeled back and revealed.

CONCLUSION

As communications media have become more pervasive in society, the need to understand the meanings embedded in media content has become more acute. Even face-to-face oral communication is easily misinterpreted and misunderstood. For example, linguist Deborah Tannen has written several books, including *You Just Don't Understand: Men and Women in Conversation*, chronicling how words and nonverbal gestures have different meanings for men and women.

The product or content of different forms of communication generically have come to be called "texts," and all texts are open to analysis and interpretation. One level of analysis is the level of communication producing the texts. For example, Deborah Tannen is looking at interpersonal communication. A study of political conventions might rely on texts produced by group communication, while a researcher trying to understand the culture of a particular company would study organizational communication.

Many of the same tools used to analyze literary texts can be applied broadly to texts or narrative forms of all types, such as movies, television, and even video games. Using specific tools to read the embedded, often deep, meanings in a media text is known as media literacy.

But just as reading a book can lead to multiple interpretations, the analysis of most media content can lead to multiple meanings. The differences in the potential meanings of a given text become more apparent when observers apply systematic frameworks for interpretation.

Three of the most common frameworks for analysis are semiotics, psychoanalytic interpretation, and Marxist interpretation. Each of these frameworks emphasizes different elements and aspssssects of the text under study. Understanding the fuller meaning of a text through interpretation and analysis is critical in contemporary society. As content circulates through the media, it helps to shape the way people see and organize the world. Understanding the fuller meanings of the texts to which people pay attention helps to shape their worldview and the societies in which they live.

THE NEXT ROOM

by Mitchell Stephens

You are about to begin reading," wrote the novelist Italo Calvino.

Best to close the door; the TV is always on in the next room. Tell the others right away, "No, I don't want to watch TV!" Raise your voice—they won't hear you otherwise—"I'm reading! I don't want to be disturbed!" Maybe they haven't heard you, with all that racket; speak louder, yell: "I'm beginning to read ...!"

In this case, however, you are beginning to read a book that looks forward to the eclipse of reading by the offspring of TV.

It is only the opening to a longer program—the first ninety-six seconds of a one-hour 1995 ABC documentary about changes in American churches. In those ninety-six seconds fewer than two hundred words are spoken—some by the reporter, Peter Jennings, some by ministers and church members. A book or newspaper reader could probably digest twice as many words in that period of time.

Yet those ninety-six seconds, the work of a young producer named Roberta Goldberg, also feature fifty-one different images, most showing separate scenes: churchgoers praying, laughing, weeping and collapsing; a Christian stage show; a congregation joining in aerobics; ministers preaching; ministers using show-business techniques; ministers defending their use of show-business techniques. Intercut are pictures of religious icons, bending and blurring. Three candles are shown blowing out. Additional images are sometimes superimposed. Words from the Bible flash on the screen. Ethereal yet insistent music plays. Cameras dart here and there.

This piece uses techniques that have begun appearing with greater and greater frequency in some of the less prestigious corners of television and film—in promotional announcements, commercials, music videos, title sequences, sports highlights and trailers, and occasionally in news stories or on public TV. The piece has an almost ballet-like beauty, but it is not particularly profound. It is, after all, only the introduction to an otherwise traditional documentary; it lasts less than two minutes. (I will describe other, more ambitious examples later in the book.)

However, this segment of videotape, like its young cousins elsewhere on our screens, does manage to impart a remarkable amount of information and impressions in that short period of time—to the point where the more

READING NOTES

conventionally edited one-hour documentary that follows begins to seem superfluous. This brief ABC introduction, therefore, suggests that images—fast-cut moving images mixed with some words and music—have the potential to communicate at least as efficiently and effectively as printed words alone.

Although moving images are gaining responsibility for more and more of our communication, this is a suggestion most of us have great difficulty accepting.

Perhaps it was John F. Kennedy's handsome face or the opportunity most Americans had to watch his funeral. Maybe the turning point came with the burning huts of Vietnam, the flags and balloons of the Reagan presidency or Madonna's writhings on MTV. But at some point in the second half of the twentieth century—for perhaps the first time in human history—it began to seem as if images would gain the upper hand over words.

We know this. Evidence of the growing popularity of images has been difficult to ignore. It has been available in most of our bedrooms and living rooms, where the machine most responsible for the image's rise has long dominated the decor. Evidence has been available in the shift in home design from bookshelves to "entertainment centers," from libraries to "family rooms" or, more accurately, "TV rooms." Evidence has been available in our children's facility with remote controls and joysticks, and their lack of facility with language. Evidence has been available almost any evening in almost any town in the world, where a stroller will observe a blue light in most of the windows and a notable absence of porch sitters, gossip mongers and other strollers.

We are—old and young—hooked. While he was vice president of the United States, Dan Quayle embarked upon a minor crusade against television. It took him to an elementary school in Georgia. "Are you going to study hard?" the vice president asked a roomful of third-graders. "Yeah!" they shouted back. "And are you going to work hard and mind the teacher?" "Yeah!" And are you going to turn off the TV during school nights?" "No!" the students yelled. When children between the ages of four and size were asked whether they like television or their fathers better. 84 percent of those sampled chose TV.

Evidence of the image's growing dominance, particularly among the young, can be found too in my house, a word lover's house, where increasingly the TV is always on in the next room. (I am not immune to worries about this; nothing in the argument to come is meant to imply that my attempt to guide my children or myself through this transitional period has been easy.)

Television began its invasion about fifty years ago. The extent to which it has taken over—familiar as the statistics may be—remains dazzling. No medium or technology, before or after, "penetrated," as the researchers put it, our homes more quickly. It took seventy years before half of all American homes had a telephone. Apple sold its first all-in-one personal computer in 1977; IBM, which began selling computers to businesses in 1952, sold its first personal computer in 1981. It is true that processing chips are now imbedded in our cars and coffee makers; nevertheless, as this is written, personal computers themselves have still not found their way into half of America's homes, and a percentage of those that have made it there sit mostly unused. Yet it took only eight years, after the arrival of full-scale commercial television in 1947, before half of all American homes had a black-and-white television set. And disuse is not a fate likely to befall a TV.

A television set is now on in the average American home up to, depending on the time of year, eight hours a day—which means, subtracting time for work or school and sleep, basically all the time. We each sit in front of a TV an average of anywhere from two and a half to almost five hours a day, depending on which estimate or survey you believe. The average

READING NOTES

_____

_____

_____

_____

_____

fifth-grader *reports* (they likely are underestimating) spending almost seven times as much time each day watching television as reading. We are as attached, as addicted to television as we, as a society, have been to any other invention, communications medium, art form or drug.

Recently, it is true, television has begun to seem like yesterday's invention. Digital communications have mesmerized the technologically advanced and have won most of the press. Tens of millions of people have already begun using computers and the Internet to work, send written messages, shop, do research, and explore new corners of our culture—all with unprecedented speed and efficiency. This is certainly impressive. But television, which is less than a generation older than the computer, has already won over humankind.

Reliable global statistics are hard to come by, but the evidence indicates that almost three billion people are already watching television regularly for an average of more than two and a half hours a day, according to one international survey. That means most of the world's inhabitants are now devoting about halt their leisure time to an activity that did not exist two generations ago. Most of the rest are held back only by the lack of electricity or the money to buy a set.

Why? Television's unprecedented appeal rests in large part on the easily accessible, seemingly inexhaustible diversions it supplies. But it goes beyond that. We have not sufficiently recognized the power of moving images. There is a magic in their ability to appear on command in our homes, and there is a magic in them, a magic that may come to dwarf that of other forms of communication.

"The [World Wide] Web is going to be very important," computer pioneer Steve Jobs, cofounder of Apple Computer, was quoted as saying in 1996. But then he added, "It's certainly not going to be like the first time somebody saw a television. ... It's not going to be *that*

profound. It would be a mistake to underestimate the impact of our new digital communications systems, particularly their likely role in distributing moving images, but video remains the communications revolution of our time.

This does not mean we will continue to have what computer mavens dismiss as "dumb metal boxes" facing our couches—boxes to which we can do little more than change the channel and adjust the volume. Moving images undoubtedly will find new, more flexible, more clever means of presenting themselves. Silicon chips will be increasingly involved in their distribution. Perhaps we will soon locate our video at sites on the World Wide Web or some similarly interactive, global, cross-referenced, content-rich successor. Stations, networks, schedules and sets may all go the way of rabbit-ear antennas. However, if humankind's preferences over the past half century are any guide, whatever new screens and services do find their way into our homes in coming decades are going to be filled not so much with words or still graphics but with moving images.

The word *television* appears often in these pages. This is the form of moving images at which we have directed most of our attention and most of our criticism, the form that has conquered the world. However, this book views television as only one stage in a larger movement. Photography and film provided the initial thrust for the image's rise. And new kinds of moving images viewed in new ways are likely to lead to its triumph. A term is needed that encompasses the stages to come, that recognizes the increasing interchangeability of television and film, the coming "convergence," as the business pages put it, of television and the computer. The best alternative seems *video*— a compact word with a suitably broad meaning, derived from the Latin verb *videre* "to see."

When I talk of the video revolution, I mean video as content, not any particular size screen or variety of box.

READING NOTES

I mean that, by whatever improved means, we are going to continue staring at those magical moving images and obtaining more and more of our entertainment, information, art and ideas from them. "When I began here, I thought the writing was all that mattered," recalled the producer of that introduction to ABC's documentary on churches, Roberta Goldberg. "Now not only do I think the visuals matter, but I think they matter more than the writing." That too is what I mean.

What's missing from these pictures?

- Three people sit in a doctor's waiting room. One stares at the television that rests on an end table. The head of the second is wrapped in earphones. The third fiddles with a handheld video game.

- A couple of kids, waiting for bedtime, lie on the floor of a brightly painted room, squabbling over who gets to hold the remote control.

- Two hundred people sit in an airplane. Some have brought their own tapes, some doze; most stare up at small screens.

What is missing, of course, is the venerable activity you are engaged in right now. And such pictures are not difficult to supply. Reading is now missing from countless scenes it once dominated: at kitchen tables, on buses and trains, in beds at night, on couches, even in some classrooms.

When "the TV is always on in the next room," eventually large numbers of us stop yelling, put down what we were reading, and go into that room. The result—the opposite and (more or less) equal reaction to the arrival of the moving image—has been a significant lessening in the importance of the printed word.

The anecdotal evidence that print is in decline is copious and compelling. "When I go out socially in Washington," confided Daniel Boorstin, the historian and former librarian of Congress, "I'm careful not to embarrass my dinner companions by asking what they have read lately. Instead I say, 'I suppose you don't have much time to read books nowadays?'" Novelists perceive the same situation, with perhaps even more dismay: "There's been a drastic decline, even a disappearance of a serious readership," moaned Philip Roth.

This much-remarked-upon decline, nevertheless, is not easy to capture with statistics. Book seem to be doing reasonably well. According to the Book Industry Study Group, sales of adult trade books did drop in the mid 1990s, but this was after many years of steady increases. *Books in Print* now lists more than eighteen times as many titles as did its first edition, printed in 1948. And for a time the number of bookstores in the United States was growing at a rate second only to that of fast-food restaurants. Reports of the death of the book have been exaggerated.

Ah, but are those books actually being read? Not, in many cases, from cover to cover. The Gallup Poll found many more people in 1990 than in 1957 who said they are currently reading a book or novel, but many fewer than in 1975 who said they have completed a book in the past week. In a society where professional success now requires acquaintance with masses of esoteric information, books now are often purchased to be consulted, not read. Almost one quarter of the money spent on books in 1994 went for business, legal, medical, technical or religious books. Another large chunk was spent by or for the captive audiences in schools.

Fiction and general-interest nonfiction for adults represented only about $4.3 billion of the $18.8 billion book industry in 1994. Such trade books have also

READING NOTES

_____

_____

_____

_____

_____

been filling a function other than their ostensible one. Instead of being read, they have been replacing the bottle of scotch and the tie as gifts—with about the same chance of being opened as those ties had of being worn.

In 1985 Michael Kinsley, then with the *New Republic*, conducted an experiment. He hid little notes, offering a five-dollar reward to anyone who saw them, about three quarters of the way through seventy copies of certain select nonfiction books in Washington, D.C., bookstores. These were the books all of Washington seemed to be talking about. "Washington" was apparently basing its comments on the reviews and maybe a quick skim. No one called. "Fortunately for book-sellers," Kinsley wrote, "their prosperity depends on people buying books, not on people actually reading the bulky things."

Here is perhaps the most frightening of the statistics on books: According to the Gallup Poll, the number of Americans who admitted to having read *no* books of any kind during the past year—and this is not an easy thing to admit to a pollster—doubled from 1978 to 1990, from 8 to 16 percent. "I cannot live without books," Thomas Jefferson, certainly among the most dedicated readers of his era, once confessed to John Adams. More and more of us, apparently, can.

Magazines would appear better suited to life with television, if for no other reasons than that they require a smaller time commitment than books and that they themselves contain plenty of pictures. However, because magazines come in so many different varieties, gathering evidence to confirm or deny this surmise is not easy. The best indicator of whether we are spending more or less time with magazines may be time-use studies like those compiled by John Robinson at the University of Maryland. These show that the proportion of the population that reads a magazine on a typical day dropped from 38 percent in 1946 to 28 percent in 1985. Magazine publishers, however, can take some encouragement from the fact

that most of that drop occurred with the first onslaught of television in the 1950s.

The statistics on newspaper readership are much less ambiguous and much grimmer. According to those time-use studies published in *American Demographics*, the share of the adult population that "read a newspaper yesterday" declined from 85 percent in 1946 to 73 percent in 1965 to 55 percent in 1985. The numbers on per capita newspaper circulation and the percentage of American homes that receive a daily newspaper form similar graphs—graphs you could ski down.

"I'm not sure how much people read anymore," H. Ross Perot commented shortly before announcing his candidacy for the presidency in 1992. "What happens on TV is what really impacts on people."[18] During the 1996 presidential campaign, only 18 percent of a sample of voters in the United States said they received "most" of their information about the campaign from newspapers.

Those time-use studies actually discovered an increase of about thirteen minutes a week from 1965 to 1985 in the amount of time people say they spend reading books and magazines. But if you throw in newspapers, the total time people spent with reading as their primary activity has dropped more than 30 percent in those years—to less than three hours a week.

And this drop has occurred at the same time that the amount of formal education Americans obtain has been rising dramatically. The percentage of Americans over the age of twenty-four who have completed four years of high school has more than tripled since 1940, according to the Census Bureau's Current Population Survey. It increased from 69 percent to 82 percent just from 1980 to 1995. And since 1940 the percentage of Americans completing four years of college has increased by a factor of five. If education still stimulated the desire to read, all the statistics on reading would be expected to be shooting up. That they are not may say something about

READING NOTES

_____

_____

_____

_____

_____

the quality of our educational system and about the interests of the students it now attracts. It certainly says something about the word and its future.

Reading's troubles are not difficult to explain. A hundred years ago, on days when no circus was in town, people looking for entertainment had few alternatives: eating, drinking, strolling, procreating, singing, talking, reading. Those looking for information were restricted to the latter two. Many of our ancestors, to be sure, were unable to read, but many of those who could relied upon it, as Thomas Jefferson did, with a desperation that is difficult for us to imagine.

The printed word, in those days, had a unique power to transport. "There is no frigate like a book," wrote Emily Dickinson, "To take us lands away." Now, of course, that journey can be undertaken by a different route, one that allows us to *see* that which is beyond our direct experience. Another way of summarizing what has been happening to reading, and to our lives, is that the image is replacing the word as the predominant means of mental transport.

The image's ascent has certainly occupied its share of spoken and written words. Most of those words, however, are tinged with anxiety, annoyance, even anguish. We fret; we bemoan; we hope against hope; we indulge in righteous indignation. The revolution we are undergoing may be acknowledged, but only with chagrin. The photographer Richard Avedon recently dared state—on television—that "images are fast replacing words as our primary language." He did not display the requisite gloom. He was assaulted. "That, precisely, is the problem," thundered *New York Times* television critic John J. O'Connor, "as American culture drifts ever more distressingly into superficiality."

This is no easy subject. We are talking not only of the present, which is hard enough to see, but of the future. In which direction are we currently drifting? In which direction are we likely to drift? Formidable questions. Still, on issues of this importance, we should not have to settle for fretting, bemoaning, wishful thinking and indignation. The discussion does not have to be so windy and predictable.

I recently came upon a calender decorated with this quote from Patrick Henry: "I know of no way of judging the future but by the past." When pondering the image's rise, we have no difficulty working up nostalgia for the past, but we tend not to put much stock in the lessons of the past. Contemporary society—with its mastery of circuits and bits—chooses to think of its problems as unique. However, the video revolution is, by my reckoning, humankind's third major communications revolution, and the disruptions occasioned by the first two—writing and print—are surprisingly similar to those we are experiencing now. The stages in which the new technologies were adopted seem comparable, as does the profundity of the transformations they cause. Even the anxieties and anger sound familiar.

READING NOTES

_____

_____

_____

_____

_____

Chapter
(4)

Rules of the Game

"Give me the liberty to know, to utter, and to argue freely according to conscience above all liberties."

—JOHN MILTON

Communication is essential to social life. As social theorist Stuart Hall has noted, communication and language are essential components of the creation of meaning and meaningful interaction among people. It is through language and other symbol systems that people share the way they see the world and can determine if they understand the world in the same way that other individuals do. Communication can be thought of as the process in which people can share one another's perceptions of the world—even if they disagree about the meaning of what they see.

The word "language" itself can be used in a variety of ways. In the broadest sense, language can be defined as any formal system of symbols through which people can communicate meaning. In this way, visual images that communicate meaning can be thought of as languages. In this sense, there can be the language of movies and the language of fashion. Each involves a formal system though which meaning is shared among people and through which people can interact in a meaningful way.

Language can be used in many different ways, and communication can take place via many different media. Most fundamentally, language enables individuals to communicate with others, and the most common mechanism for people to communicate with one another is through speech. People talk to each other. When individuals communicate on a one-to-one basis through face-to-face communication, it is called interpersonal communication. When a single individual or communicator can send a message to many people at once, usually by using some kind of technology, it is called mass communication.

Because language and communication are so fundamental to the way people live with one another, structure their societies, and find meaning in the world, it should be no surprise that many rules have developed to control the way people communicate. Those rules have developed along two lines. First, governments regularly pass laws to control how people can express themselves and what people can say. In contemporary societies around the world, speech is always constrained to some degree by specific legal systems.

In addition to laws, however, speech is also constrained by ethical considerations. Since speech can do great harm, even if a person is allowed to say, print, or broadcast a particular kind of content, is it morally right to do so? Ethics deals with the moral question of right and wrong based on people's specific values. Communication often raises questions of right and wrong, so ethical considerations must be addressed.

The aims of this chapter are to

- sketch a short history of efforts to control speech,

- introduce students to basic issues in media law,

- address ethical issues raised by communication processes, and

- explore specific situations that have raised legal and ethical considerations involving communication.

Required Reading: "The Shadow Darkens," is an excerpt from *Technologies of Freedom* by Ithiel de Sola Pool, who argues that the specific regulatory constraints for different media technology are shaped by the dominant economic, social, and political environment in place when the technology initially emerges. Ithiel de Sola Pool was the founding chairman of the Political Science Department at the Massachusetts Institute of Technology (MIT) and the founder of the MIT Communications Forum. He believed that existing social and political thought underestimated the importance of communications and technological change. *Technologies of Freedom* (1983)

is considered a masterwork in defining the relationship of communications technology and human freedom.

WHY CONTROL SPEECH?

Communication serves many purposes and takes place in many different contexts. When one person talks to another person and intends only for that one individual to hear those words, it can be considered private speech. But when a person speaks to a large audience or transmits a message using technological means that enable the message to reach many more people, it can be considered public speech or public communication. The laws governing private communication and public communication are very different. In fact, many of the laws governing private communication are intended to keep the communication private and prevent third parties, often the government, from overhearing the communication.

The laws governing public communication are quite different. Public speech can be used in many different ways. Perhaps the most significant way public communication is used is to influence people, particularly in the way that societies are structured. Political speech, which includes everything from candidates delivering speech, to political commercials, to Web sites and Facebook pages, is one of the most powerful and significant forms of public communication. In addition to influencing people politically, public speech is a way for individual communicators to express their thoughts and visions of the world to other people. Communication, however, does not simply rely on words.

People can communicate visually by using images; through sound such as music; and through actions such as specific body movements, like dance. Communication that employs means other than words to create meaning is called expressive speech. As former U.S. Supreme Court Justice Robert Jackson said, symbols are "a shortcut from mind to mind." Expressive or symbolic speech involves conduct that communicates in a way that is analogous to speech—behavior intended to create meaning. For example, the prescribed method to discard a tattered U.S. flag is to burn it, which is not expressive speech. But if a person burns an U.S. flag to protest the U.S. government's involvement in a war, that action can be considered expressive speech (see Figure 4.1).

Finally, communication is essential to economic activity, production of goods, and the buying and selling of goods and services in the marketplace. Speech and expressive behavior related to economic activity is known as commercial speech. Political speech, expressive speech, and commercial speech are all regulated in different ways. Different kinds of laws control the different types of speech. Moreover, each type of speech invokes different ethical and other considerations.

With communication playing such a fundamental role in the ability of people to live together in society, the question arises: Why control speech anyway? Why shouldn't people just be allowed to say anything they want when they want to? The answer is that speech is inevitably and intricately intertwined with power. The ability to communicate with people involves the potential of persuading and motivating people to act. That is why the British philosopher John Stuart Mill argued that freedom of speech in an essential safeguard against tyranny.

Figure 4.1—*Expressive speech: The context of burning a U.S. flag determines whether the act symbolizes political protest.*

In fact, oppressive and totalitarian regimes around the world inevitably control speech to maintain their grip on power. For example, for 46 years, from 1948 until 1994, there was an apartheid government in South Africa in which a white minority ruled a black majority. During that time, one of the punishments meted out to political leaders opposing the regime was to limit them to talking to one person at a time. A similar punishment was handed out by the ruling junta in Myanmar, an Asian country once known as Burma, to its leading dissident, Aung San Suu Kyi, in 2009.

Governments can approach controlling speech in three ways. The most direct is to control content of speech, usually through censorship. Government officials review material before it is published or broadcast, and can forbid certain material from reaching the intended audience. Governments often use censorship during times of war and to limit the circulation of salacious material, such as pornography.

Speech also can be controlled by limiting access to the means communication. For example, in the United States, television and radio broadcasters must obtain licenses from the government. In return for those licenses, to some degree, the government can control the broadcaster. For example, during the George W. Bush administration, the Federal Communications Commission (FCC) decided that if certain proscribed words—so-called "foul language"—were uttered on broadcasts even in passing, the television networks, radio networks, or individual stations could be fined. This rule was upheld by the U.S. Supreme Court in 2009. Many, if not most, countries have television and radio networks controlled by the state.

The final way to control speech is to control who is allowed to speak. For example, for people to give medical or legal advice, they must be licensed, and those without a license can be punished. In the early 1980s, the United Nations Educational, Scientific, and Cultural Organization (UNESCO) proposed licensing journalists, as did Puerto Rico, which is a commonwealth of the United States.

Over time, governments have used all three approaches to controlling communication—controlling content, limiting access, and licensing speakers.

At the same time that governments around the world and throughout history have attempted to control communication, another set of rules governing speech has emerged as well. These rules revolve around the notion that individuals have the right to privacy. The right to privacy has three dimensions. The first dimension is that the government cannot "listen in" on private communications without cause. The second dimension is that the media cannot unreasonably intrude into people's lives. And the third dimension, though not typically associated with the right to privacy, is that communication between people in certain relationships is sacrosanct. For example, most conversations between a doctor and a patient or between a member of the clergy and a congregant can remain private under most circumstances. These kinds of conversations are known as privileged speech.

HISTORICAL DEVELOPMENT

Prior to the invention of the printing press, the control of speech was largely straightforward. If individuals uttered something that the government—or, in Europe, the Church—did not like, those individuals were duly punished. The most famous illustration of this approach to the control of speech came in 399 BC, when the philosopher Socrates was executed in Athens, Greece. Before he was put to death by being forced to drink hemlock, a poison, he is said to have uttered the words, "If you offered to let me off this time on condition I am not any longer to speak my mind ... I should say to you, 'Men of Athens, I shall obey the Gods rather than you.'"

But the absolute control of speech became more much more difficult after the invention of the printing press and movable type in 1450 made printed material much more available and

accessible to a wider audience. In England, where the traditions that ultimately became the cauldron from which American ideas about freedom of speech were developed, printing was introduced by William Caxton in 1476, well after it had appeared in Germany, France, and Italy. A second printer appeared in London in 1480. By the late 15th and early 16th centuries, books were selling briskly at county fairs and other venues. By the end of the 16th century, printed news books, mainly containing war news, began to appear. In 1590, 38 such news books were published. And in 1620, the first regularly printed news publication in English began to circulate. Once again, war, this time the Thirty Years' War, helped stimulate interest.

The English government's response to the spread of printing was swift. The underlying principle was that the ruler of England had the absolute right to control the publication of printed material. The Company of Stationers, which had been established as a guild in 1403 for book sellers, book binders, and illuminators, received a royal charter in 1557 and issued a monopoly over printing and book production, sharply limiting the number of printers allowed to operate. The Company of Stationers also was responsible for censoring materials unacceptable to the state and the church. By holding a monopoly on printing, the Company of Stationers ensured that once a member asserted ownership over a manuscript or copy, no other member would print it. Ownership was established by registering a copy with the Company of Stationers, establishing the concept of a copyright. Cases involving libelous or seditious speech were heard in a special court called the Court of the Star Chamber.

In 1641, the English Civil War erupted, pitting those who favored increasing the authority of Parliament against the Royalists. Called the War of Pamphlets, both sides printed pamphlets to attract supporters. In 1641, Parliament abolished the Court of the Star Chamber, which was replaced in 1643 by the Licensing Order. Under the Licensing Order, prepublication licensing of printed material and registration of printed material with the Company of Stationers was still required. Books offensive to the government could still be seized and destroyed. Offending authors could be arrested and imprisoned.

But in the short two years between the abolishment of the Court of the Star Chamber and the passage of the Licensing Order, the English experienced a short period free of censorship. In response to the passage of the Licensing Order, in 1644, the poet John Milton wrote a plea to Parliament, called *Areopagitica*, in which he mounted a spirited defense of freedom of speech. Milton, a supporter of Parliament in the English Civil War, argued that prepublication censorship was an excuse for the state to try to control thought. "[W]ho ever knew truth put to the worse in a free and open encounter?" he wrote. As long as the author and the publisher of a printed work were identified, punishment could be meted out after publication.

Milton was not alone in the campaign for freer speech. In the late 1600s, the philosopher John Locke was laying some of the philosophical foundations and intellectual arguments for democracy. In his essay *Concerning Human Understanding*, published in 1694, Locke opposed licensing the press and argued that governments and the governed had a social contract in which the government was supposed to serve the governed and not the other way around. Moreover, the people had inherent rights to life, liberty, and property. In 1695, the Licensing Order was allowed to expire.

The movement toward freer speech was the legacy that the U.S. colonies inherited as printing and newspapers began to appear in the colonies in the 1700s. But over time, the U.S. experience veered from the British conceptions of freedom of speech. The first sharp break came in 1735 with the trial of Peter Zenger, a New York City printer. Zenger had established a newspaper, the *New York Weekly Journal*, in 1733 that sharply criticized the governor of New York, William

Crosby. In 1734, Zenger was arrested on the charge of seditious libel, which meant that he had published charges that lessened respect for the government. After spending eight months in jail, Zenger finally came to trial. Although the law was clearly against Zenger, his lawyer Andrew Hamilton appealed directly to the jury, who acquitted Zenger. This case established that truth was an absolute defense against charges of libel and became a cornerstone of the people's right to criticize the government.

In 1765, the British government imposed a tax on printed material in the United States. The British had long imposed a tax on printed material in Britain, and the tax was seen as an effective way to raise revenues. Known as the Stamp Act because the law required publications to have a stamp that proved the tax had been paid, the law raised the ire of the American colonists, particularly printers, who felt that they were being taxed without having a say in the decision. Colonial leaders opposed to the tax called it "taxation without representation," and the phrase became one of the rallying cries that ultimately led to the American Revolution.

At odds with the British government and deeply influenced by the ideas of John Locke, when the United States' founders wrote the Constitution they included several sections governing speech and publication. The most famous is the First Amendment to the Constitution, which forbids Congress from making any laws abridging the freedom of speech or of the press. Part of what is called the Bill of Rights, the First Amendment represents perhaps the first time that the right of the people to speak was codified into law.

But the First Amendment is not the only section of the Constitution that addresses communication issues. Article 1 Section 5 requires that the proceedings of the U.S. Congress be published. While this requirement may seem unnecessary to include in the Constitution, suppression of reports about the activities of the British Parliament did not completely end until 1771. Article 1 Section 6 protects those in the House of Representatives and the Senate against punishment for speech while speaking on the floors of their respective houses, once again ensuring a right that was not always honored in Great Britain.

In addition, Article 1 Section 8 incorporates the protection of copyrights and trademarks into the Constitution, establishing the Post Office and post roads, which formed an important element in the communication network at the time. In the years following the ratification of the Constitution, the Federal government also subsidized the circulation of newspapers via the Post Office. In short, the Constitution protected political speech to a degree and helped facilitate its publication and circulation. It also recognized the commercial value of speech.

CREATING ROBUST DEBATE

Although a literal reading of the First Amendment would seem to indicate that Congress is forbidden to pass any laws curtailing the freedom of speech, in practice, that has not always been the case. In 1798, it appeared that the United States might go to war with France. As tensions increased, Congress passed four laws that were collective known as the Alien and Sedition Acts. The last of these laws, the Sedition Act, declared that any "false, scandalous, or malicious" printed material was a crime punishable by a fine or imprisonment. After the law was passed, at least 25 editors, primarily people supporting the opposition Democratic-Republican Party against the Federalists, who were then in power, were arrested and their newspapers shut down. Benjamin Franklin Bache, the grandson of Benjamin Franklin and editor of the *Philadelphia Democrat-Republican Aurora*, was among them. His arrest unleashed a firestorm of opposition to the laws, which were eventually allowed to lapse during the administration of President Thomas Jefferson.

Nonetheless, speech continued to be restricted in the United States during the 19th century. For

example, James Fenimore Cooper, a leading American novelist before the Civil War and author of *Last of the Mohicans,* initiated 18 libel suits between the years of 1839 and 1845, often in response to critical reviews of his work. Libel was still defined as any printed material that held a person up to scorn or ridicule or might provoke a person to a breach of peace. Eventually, the New York state legislature, echoing the Zenger case, passed a law establishing that truth was a defense against libel charges.

Indeed, although the U.S. Constitution forbids Congress from abridging the freedom of press and speech, in the 19th century, individual states did not feel so constrained. Prior to the American Civil War, Southern states tried to ban abolitionist newspapers. For example, in 1829 and 1830, the governors of Georgia and North Carolina respectively called on their legislatures to ban abolitionist newspapers and pamphlets. In 1830, Southern states began to censor the mail.

Moreover, throughout the 19th century, state judges invoked the doctrine of "bad tendency" to allow state laws restricting speech to be enforced. The doctrine of bad tendency holds that if a publication has the tendency to lead to an action that the state has a right to prohibit, the state can punish a person for publishing the material. The bad tendency concept led to the U.S. Supreme Court to uphold the conviction of Charles Schenck for distributing flyers opposing the military draft during World War I in violation of the Espionage Act of 1917. In that case, Justice Oliver Wendell Holmes wrote that since Schenck's speech constituted a "clear and present danger" of leading to a "substantive evil that Congress had the right to enjoin," he could be punished. Schenck was sentenced to ten years in jail.

A series of Supreme Court decisions beginning in the 1920s, however, began to enforce and enlarge the protections guaranteed in the First Amendment. In 1925, in *Gitlow v. New York*, the Supreme Court ruled that the First Amendment also restricted state governments from passing laws abridging the freedom of speech and the press. The Court based its decision on the Fourteenth Amendment, adopted after the Civil War, prohibiting any state from depriving "any person of life, liberty, or property, without due process of law." The rights of freedom of speech and freedom of the press were among those rights protected by the Fourteenth Amendment from impairment by the states.

Benjamin Gitlow, a Socialist, had been convicted of criminal anarchy for publishing a manifesto expressing his political ideology. Ironically, the Court upheld his conviction, despite its defense of the First Amendment, asserting that the state had the right to suppress speech calling for its illegal overthrow.

In 1931, in a significant case, *Near v. Minnesota*, the Court ruled that states could not restrain speech prior to its publication. Jay Near was the publisher of a newspaper, *The Saturday Press*, that routinely reported scandalous material. A complaint was filed against him under the Minnesota Public Nuisance Act, which allowed the court to issue a permanent ban on publishing similar newspapers by those who created "public nuisances" by publishing, selling, or distributing a "malicious, scandalous and defamatory newspaper." The Supreme Court overturned the Minnesota law, contending that "prior restraint" was unconstitutional.

Every "freeman," Chief Justice Charles Hughes wrote in the majority opinion, has the "right to lay what sentiments he pleases before the public." This right was tested in 1971, when *The New York Times* and the *Washington Post* obtained a history of the U.S. government's decision-making concerning the war in Vietnam. This entire history, which came to be known as the Pentagon Papers, was classified top secret and illegally copied by Daniel Ellsberg, a Department of Defense analyst who had compiled the history.

The Federal Government appealed to the U.S. District Court to block the publication of the Pentagon Papers. The case quickly made its way to the U.S. Supreme Court, which refused to block publication. The press, Justice Hugo Black

wrote in a concurring opinion in the case, *New York Times v. U.S.*, "was to serve the governed, not the governors. The government's power to censor the press was abolished so that the press would remain forever free to censure the Government." Consequently, any attempt at prior restraint was unconstitutional.

While the Court's decisions striking down attempts at prior restraint meant that people were free to publish what they wanted, at least when that speech regarded politics, it did not address when people could be punished for specific speech after publication. This issue was addressed in a major case in 1964 called *New York Times Co. v. Sullivan*. L. B. Sullivan was a safety commissioner in Montgomery, Alabama, responsible for supervising the police department. He claimed that a political advertisement placed by black citizens and clergymen in the *Times* that criticized the police for their conduct at Alabama State College was both false and damaged his reputation (see Figure 4.2).

Sullivan sued for libel, or the illegal act of making false statements that damage a person's reputation. An Alabama state court awarded Sullivan $500,000, but the U.S. Supreme Court overturned the decision, reasoning that the First Amendment was intended to protect robust debate and that within the context of robust debate, mistakes

Figure 4.2— *"Heed Their Rising Voices" was the headline of the political advertisement disputed in the famous First Amendment court case,* New York Times Co. v. Sullivan.

would be inevitable. To allow for the "breathing space" needed to guard against "self-censorship," even false speech about public officials that damaged their reputation was protected against punishment by the First Amendment.

A person could be sued for libel by a public official only, according to the *Sullivan* case, if it could be demonstrated the false speech was uttered with "actual malice." Actual malice was defined as knowing that the speech was false or the speaker demonstrated a reckless disregard for the truth or falsity of the speech. The *Sullivan* rule was later extended to cover public figures as well as public officials, and in *Gertz v. Welch* in 1974, the Supreme Court laid out who was subject to the standard laid out in Sullivan and who was not.

New York Times Co. v. Sullivan is considered the most important First Amendment decision of the 20th century. Several other public figures in the South had already filed suits against news media headquartered in the North. If Sullivan had prevailed, no doubt those suits would have had a chilling effect on coverage of the civil rights movement, and libel could have been used as a weapon to shut down press coverage to which public officials objected.

Of course, robust debate requires that the public have access to information to make informed decisions. A series of state and federal laws have been passed to ensure proactively that people can learn what their elected officials are doing.

The Freedom of Information Act (FOIA) was first passed in 1966 and subsequently amended several times, with the last set of amendments coming in 2002. The amendments passed in 1974, in the wake of the Watergate scandal and over the veto of President Gerald Ford, established the essence of the FOIA. In short, the law requires that the Federal government release records requested in writing by any citizen as long as the information does not fall into one of nine protected categories. Those categories include national defense information, commercial and trade secrets, information about government personnel, and other categories.

In 1976, the FOIA was amended as a part of the Government in the Sunshine Act.

The Sunshine Act requires that meetings of government agencies be open to public observation and that the public be alerted in advance about such meetings. As with the FOIA, there are ten exceptions to the law, whose purpose is to ensure that vital government business is not conducted in secret behind closed doors. All 50 states have also passed their own forms of the Sunshine and Freedom of Information Acts.

Taken together, the Sunshine and Freedom of Information laws mean that most government activities and records are available to the public. In most cases, information is reported to the public by journalists working for various news media. To ensure that journalists can report on issues of concern to the public without fear of punishment, reporters have pushed for the passage of shield laws, which would allow reporters to refuse to testify about the sources of their information, particularly confidential information.

Reporters argue that by forcing them to testify about sources who may have been involved in criminal wrongdoing or leaked confidential information even though they were not authorized to do so, sources would be less likely to talk to them and the public would not be informed. The idea behind shield laws is to establish that talking to reporters is a privileged category of speech, similar to talking to a doctor or a lawyer.

Currently, 36 states and the District of Columbia have passed some form of shield laws. But in the case *Branzberg v. Hayes,* which was decided in 1972, the U.S. Supreme Court decided that journalists did not have constitutional protection for refusing to reveal their sources. In the wake of the *Branzberg* decision, many journalists have been jailed for refusing to honor court subpoenas demanding to know the source of some information. For example, in 2005, Judith Miller, then a reporter for *The New York Times*, went to jail for 85 days for refusing to reveal which government official had improperly revealed the name of a covert CIA operative.

PROTECTION OF PRIVACY

The need to ensure robust debate concerning the great issues of the day and to protect the people who exercise their civic duty to participate in that debate is a significant element of the legal framework within which both mass and interpersonal communication take place. But if people entering the public sphere need legal protection, so do people who choose not to enter the public arena. Though it does not appear anywhere in the Constitution, over time, the notion that people have a right to privacy has developed.

The concept of a right to privacy was first crystallized in an article in the *Harvard Law Review* in 1890 written by Harvard University law professors Samuel Warren and Louis Brandeis, who later went on to become a Supreme Court justice. In it, Warren and Brandeis argued that people have the right to be left alone and protected from intrusion by the media. Consequently, the right to privacy was initially conceptualized as a right to be left alone by the media. This idea built on ideas contained in the Fourth and Fifth Amendments of the Constitution, which prohibit the government from searching people unless there is a compelling reason and from compelling people to testify against themselves.

In 1903, New York passed privacy legislation that prohibited the unauthorized use of an individual's name or picture for advertising or trade purposes, and two years later, Georgia became the first state to recognize a right to privacy. In a 1928 Supreme Court decision about a case that involved the surreptitious wiretapping of a telephone, Brandeis reasserted people's right to be left alone.

The right to privacy in terms of protection against the press has come to be seen as having at least four major components: People were protected against the public disclosure of private facts. People could not be presented in a false light. People's images could not be appropriated for commercial use. And people are protected against intrusion. Each of these concepts has been tested in the courts.

The right to privacy, however, has its limits, even for private citizens. In the case *Time, Inc. v. Hill* in 1967, the first privacy case to reach the Supreme Court, the Court ruled that for the Hill family to win its claim, the family had to prove that Time, Inc., the publisher of *Life* magazine, had acted with actual malice. In other words, the standard set in *Sullivan* had to be reached. The Hill family had been taken hostage and then later released. After their release, the family discouraged all further publicity about the case. Nevertheless a book was written about the ordeal and then turned into a play. As part of the publicity for the play, several re-enactments were photographed in the home in which the Hills had been taken hostage. The case involved the photo layout about the Hill family that appeared in *Life* magazine.

Furthermore, in the 1989 case *BJF v. Florida Star,* in which a rape victim claimed that a weekly newspaper in Florida published her name despite a Florida law forbidding the publication of rape victims' names in the mass media, the Supreme Court ruled that the law was unconstitutional. The First Amendment protects publication of legal information that is lawfully obtained, even if it discloses private facts, the Court stated.

The concept of privacy has taken on added meaning in the age of computers. Unauthorized distribution of private information over the Web and other electronic communications networks create new challenges for maintaining privacy rights (see Figure 4.3).

Figure 4.3—*Privacy rights are difficult to secure in our world of ubiquitous electronic communications.*

OBSCENE SPEECH

Although the First Amendment states that Congress should make no law abridging the freedom of speech and the press, in certain cases, the government can regulate the content of speech. The most obvious arena in which content is regulated is pornography. In 1873, at the urging of Andrew Comstock, the 29-year-old head of the New York Society for the Suppression of Vice, Congress made it a crime to send obscene materials, as well as materials relating to contraception and abortion, through the mail.

The law was popularly known as the "Comstock Law," and immediately after its passage, Comstock became a special agent of the Post Office, with the responsibility of enforcing the act. Over the next 42 years, Comstock successfully prosecuted thousands of people and confiscated tons of allegedly obscene material. By the turn of the century, 24 states had their own version of the Comstock Law. Not surprisingly, the law was challenged many times over the years.

The 1950s launched a period in which the U.S. Supreme Court struggled with obscenity and pornography. In the 1957 case, *Roth v. United States*, the Supreme Court for the first time defined obscenity, which it described in terms of the First Amendment as material whose "dominant theme taken as a whole appeals to the prurient interest" to the "average person, applying contemporary community standards."

In one of the most important challenges, in 1959, Grove Press published an unexpurgated version of D. H. Lawrence's book *Lady Chatterley's Lover*, which contained explicit descriptions of sex and used vulgar language. The U.S. Postmaster General banned it from the mails. However, the Supreme Court overturned the ban in 1959, ruling both that the book was not obscene and that the postmaster general was not qualified or authorized to determine if a book was obscene. Only material that was already judged to be obscene could be banned from the mail. The

Court's decision also lifted a government ban on two other controversial Grove Press books, *Tropic of Cancer* and *Fanny Hill*.

Finally, in the 1973 case of *Miller v. California*, the Court developed a three-part standard. Obscenity was defined as:

- work, when taken as a whole, that the average person, applying contemporary community standards, would find appeals to the prurient interest;

- work that depicts or describes, in a patently offensive way, sexual conduct or excretory function specifically defined by state law, and

- work that, taken as a whole, lacks serious literary, political, artistic, or scientific

REGULATING TELEVISION AND RADIO

When the First Amendment was instituted, print was the only mass medium, and even the circulations of the largest newspapers were limited to a few thousand copies. Although the invention of the telegraph and improvements in printing led to the development of newspapers whose circulation ran into the hundreds of thousands, print was still the dominant mass medium until the beginning of the 20th century. The emergence of broadcasting, first radio and then television, however, presented new challenges for the regulation of speech.

The first commercial radio broadcast took place in 1920 in Pittsburgh, Pennsylvania, when KDKA received a license to begin broadcasting. Consequently, for the first time since the days of the British control of the colonies, media outlets needed to be licensed by the government. The power to license broadcasters meant that the Federal government also had the power to deny licenses and thus could exercise considerable control over broadcasters despite the injunction in the First Amendment that Congress could not regulate speech.

The Federal government moved to regulate broadcasting for three reasons. First, wireless telegraph, as radio was first called, had military applications, and the military wanted to control it for its own use. During World War I, the U.S. Navy, in fact, took control of radio broadcasting. Second, during this period, the U.S. government was moving to regulate many aspects of the country's commercial and economic life, and control of a medium of communication seemed consistent with those efforts. The airways were seen as a public resource, and broadcasters had a public trust. It was the government's responsibility to make sure that broadcasters acted in the public interest.

Third, as the number of radio stations proliferated, they began to interfere with one another's broadcasts, creating chaos. The frequency spectrum within which radio operated was limited, and the Federal Government felt it had the responsibility to bring order to the growing radio market.

In 1927, Congress passed the Radio Act, which established the Federal Radio Commission (FRC). The FRC had the power to grant or deny licenses and to assign frequencies and power levels to different stations. In 1934, Congress enacted the Communications Act, creating the Federal Communications Commission (FCC) to regulate both radio and telephone service, and eventually television broadcasting as well. Like the FRC, the FCC had the power to grant and deny licenses, giving it enormous influence on broadcast operations.

Over the years, the FCC has developed many rules that critics believe infringe on their rights guaranteed under the First Amendment. For example, Section 315 of the Communications Act, which came to be called the Equal Time Rule, required that broadcasters provide an equal amount of airtime to major candidates running for political office and to treat each candidate equally in selling advertising time to them. The Fairness Doctrine required that if a radio or television station broadcast a controversial story, it must give time to all sides in the controversy. The

FCC also claimed the authority to regulate the content of television and radio. At times, it required stations to broadcast a set amount of educational programming. The agency limited the number of network shows that were broadcast between the hours of 7 p.m. and 11 p.m. The FCC further banned the use of "dirty words" on radio and television.

Most of the restrictions were challenged as unconstitutional in court. However, in almost all cases, the Supreme Court upheld the FCC's authority to regulate broadcasting. The Fairness Doctrine was allowed to lapse in the 1980s, but the Equal Time Rule is still enforced. Moreover the injunction against the use of specific language and images on television and radio continues to be enforced. In the 2009 case of *Fox Television Stations v. FCC*, the Court reasserted the Commission's power to fine stations that allowed expletives to be broadcast—even if those expletives were spontaneously uttered during a live broadcast (see Figure 4.4).

Interestingly, efforts to regulate the Internet have not been successful. In 1996, the Communications Decency Act (CDA) attempted to regulate indecent speech (which is banned from television and radio) as well as obscene speech, which is not protected by the First

Figure 4.4—*The Federal Communications Commission's original duty to regulate broadcasting frequencies was expanded to include regulation of broadcast program content as well.*

Amendment. However, the Supreme Court ruled in 1997 that the CDA was unconstitutional because the legislation had the potential to ban speech that was protected by the Constitution as well as speech that was not protected by the First Amendment. Communication via the Internet enjoys the same robust protection enjoyed by print, rather than being subjected to the regulations faced by broadcasting.

The FCC is not the only federal agency with the authority to regulate speech. Both the Food and Drug Administration (FDA) and the Federal Trade Commission (FTC) have the power to regulate advertising content. Indeed, the FDA was established in 1906 with the express charter to prohibit interstate commerce in misbranded food and drugs. The agency's authority was broadened over the years to include guarding against drug companies making false or misleading statements about the ingredients in drugs and therapeutic claims. The FTC was founded in 1915 with a charter to keep business competition fair and free. As a part of its responsibilities, the Commission is charged with preventing the dissemination of false and deceptive advertising of goods, drugs, curative devices, and cosmetics.

The threat of government regulations often leads specific industries to establish their own codes to govern speech. For example, the National Advertising Review Board was founded in 1971 to establish standards for truth and accuracy in national advertising. The board hears claims about companies that may have violated those standards, and the companies voluntarily comply with the board's findings. The Children's Advertising Review Unit was founded in 1974 to promote responsible advertising for children in conjunction with the National Advertising Review Council, which is made up of several of the leading advertising trade associations.

Perhaps the most prominent example of an industry's regulating itself to avoid regulation from the government is in the motion picture industry. In 1915, the Supreme Court ruled that movies were a business, not an art form (a ruling that was even-

tually overturned in 1952), and consequently not covered by the First Amendment. This allowed states and cities to censor movies, if they wished. From the 1930s to the 1960s, most major movie producers adhered to a production code developed by the Motion Picture Producers and Distributors Association, which later became the Motion Picture Association of America (MPAA).

In the 1960s, however, some movie directors began to chafe under the restrictions imposed by the code, which were seen as overly puritanical by many. In 1966, the British–American film *Blowup* was distributed without MPAA approval.

In response, pressure mounted to regulate the content of movies in the 1960s, and a U.S. Supreme Court decision upheld the right of state and local governments to prevent children from accessing books and movies that were constitutionally protected for adults. In 1968, the MPAA, in conjunction with the National Association of Theater Owners, introduced a voluntary ratings scheme ranging from G for films suitable for general audiences including children, to X. If a movie received an X rating, anybody under the age of 17 would be admitted to the movie theater. If a movie producer did not submit a film to the rating board, theater operators promised not to show it.

With revisions, the MPAA rating code successfully fended off the move for government regulations. Along the same lines, the video game and television industries also have instituted voluntary codes that do not necessarily regulate content but require labeling content geared to different audiences.

COMMERCIAL AND CORPORATE SPEECH

The reason that the FDA and FTC can regulate advertising is that advertising is considered commercial speech. Commercial speech is speech that is directed toward furthering economic activity. In the 1942 case *Valentine v. Christensen*, the Supreme Court asserted that commercial speech is not protected by the First Amendment. After all, business activity is regulated by the government. Commercial speech is just another aspect of business activity.

Over the next several decades, the Supreme Court backed away from that position. In *Bigelow v. Virginia*, decided in 1975, the Court recognized that advertising has an informational value, and therefore is worthy of at least First Amendment protection. In the case of *Central Hudson Gas and Electric Corp. v. Public Service Commission*, the Supreme Court established in 1980 a four-step analysis to determine if advertising could be regulated by the state. The four steps were:

- the speech had to truthful,

- the government interest in regulating the speech had to be substantial,

- the regulation of the advertising had to advance that interest, and

- the regulation could not be more extensive than necessary to advance the interest.

In a later case, the Supreme Court opined that the First Amendment protects most truthful, non-misleading advertising.

In all cases, however, the First Amendment does not protect misleading and untruthful advertising. In an interesting twist on the ban on misleading advertising, in 1998, Mark Kasky, a critic of Nike, the footwear company, accused Nike of running misleading advertising. Nike had launched a public relations and advertising campaign to defend itself against charges of engaging in exploitative labor practices in Europe. The case hinged on the issue of whether Nike's campaign constituted political or commercial speech.

In a four-to-three decision, the California Supreme Court ruled in favor of Kasky in the decision *Kasky v. Nike*. The U.S. Supreme Court first decided to hear the case and then changed its mind and did not hear the case. Kasky and Nike ultimately settled the suit, but the California Supreme Court's broad interpretation of commercial speech and the right to regulate it applies to companies operating in that state.

COPYRIGHT LAWS

In addition to the First Amendment, the right of authors to have exclusive rights to distribute their work, that is, to hold the copyright on a particular work, is also embedded in the Constitution. Copyright is intended to give people incentive to create material because they can be the primary beneficiaries of that material for a specific period of time.

Although the material that is copyrighted generally falls into the category of what is known as "intellectual property," copyright does not protect ideas from reuse by others; it protects the original expression of ideas in writing, images, sound, and so forth. For a work to be copyrighted, the expression must be original and fixed in a tangible medium, such as paper. If a person shares an idea for a film, for example, a producer could freely use that idea for the basis of a movie. However, if the person passed on a written synopsis for a film, it could be copyrighted and could not be used without the agreement of the author.

Over the years, copyright law has been modified in several ways. Under what is called the First Sale Doctrine, if a person purchases a copy or a facsimile of a copyrighted work, the purchaser has the right to resell it or rent it out. This doctrine enabled the development of the video-rental business, which relies on retailers buying DVDs and renting them to consumers without paying additional royalties to the copyright holders. This doctrine also protects college bookstores that buy back books and then resell them.

The unauthorized copying of copyrighted material, also known as piracy, emerged as a major issue with the growth of the Internet. With music and videos recorded in a digital format, it was easy for people to copy their CDs and make them available through file sharing programs. In the case of *A&M Records v. Napster* in 2001, the U.S. Court of Appeals for the Ninth Circuit ruled that peer-to-peer file sharing networks were guilty of copyright infringement by facilitating the unauthorized sharing of copyrighted material. After

Figure 4.5—*The Constitutional right to protect original creative works and other intellectual property from exploitation by others is vital in the information society.*

that decision, the Recording Industry Association of America began to vigorously prosecute people who pirated music via the Internet.

While copyright holders retain a large degree of control over their work for a long period of time, as long as 75 years, they do not retain total control. The Fair Use Doctrine stipulates that a limited amount of copyrighted material can be used for noncommercial purposes, such as being quoted in research papers or other books, as long as it does not interfere with the sale of the copyrighted material or otherwise exploit the creator of the material.

While the use of the copyright sign and registration of material with the U.S. Copyright Office is used as proof of ownership when copyright disputes arise, it is not required. All original expression is automatically protected (see Figure 4.5).

PROFESSIONAL ETHICS

Despite the seemingly absolute character of the First Amendment—"Congress shall make no law ... "—speech and communication is conducted in the United States within a complex legal framework, a framework as intricate or even more intricate than in countries in which speech is overtly controlled by the state. In addition to the legal environment, professionals working in communications industries such as journalism, advertising, public relations, and others take into account ethical considerations as they conduct their business.

Ethics is a set or theory of moral values. It is the discipline that addresses issues of right and wrong, good and bad. The word ethics comes from the Greek word *ethos*, which refers to the distinguishing character and guiding principles of a person, institution, or country. Ethical considerations often go beyond the law. Certain behavior might be legal, but still not ethical. That is, a person may be legally allowed to act in a certain way, but it would be seen as wrong to do so.

Ethics, or the notion of right and wrong, has many different sources. The most obvious foundation for right and wrong is religious. Indeed, the very basis of religion is the development of a moral code to which members are expected to adhere. Over the centuries, philosophers also have proposed systems of ethics. Though these systems are complicated and evolved, they are often succinctly summarized. The Greek philosopher Aristotle, for example, believed that ethical behavior was based on finding a midpoint, or the "golden mean," between extremes. In the 1550s, Italian political thinker Niccolo Machiavelli believed that people should pursue their enlightened self-interest. If everybody did what was in their own self-interest, the world would operate harmoniously. Some people have characterized Machiavelli's ideas as meaning that the ends can justify the means and that people can use any method to achieve their goal. "Enlightened self-interest" is the philosophical basis of the free-market system.

In the 1700s, Immanuel Kant contended that at the core of ethics was the search for rules that could be applied in every situation, without exception. His idea was called the categorical imperative, with the word categorical, in this case, meaning universal. In the 1800s, British thinker John Stuart Mill argued that people should behave in a way that produced the greatest good for the greatest number of people. This approach came to be called utilitarianism. In the 20th century, the American philosopher John Rawls built on the work of Kant to suggest that ethical behavior is only possible if everybody is treated equally, without regard for social or economic class. His approach involves using what is called the veil of ignorance. The veil of innocence proposes that a rule is just if everyone would agree to it given that they were made ignorant of their position in society, eliminating personal bias from social choices to guarantee the fairness of rules.

The general philosophical and religious systems of ethics broadly address the idea of what consists of a "good life" and how people should act to live a good life. What are people's obligations, duties, and responsibilities to themselves and others? These broad ideas, however, have to be translated into actions in very specific situations. Bringing ethical considerations to bear in a specific situation, such as a business setting, is called applied ethics.

In general, professionals in communications industries are said to have multiple sets of obligations or duties. They have an obligation to the company for which they work; their industry or profession; their customers, readers, or viewers; society at large; and their personal conscience. In some situations, those duties are in conflict, and the conflict must be resolved. To help guide people working in a specific industry, professional groups often develop codes of conduct and ethical standards. For example, the Society of Professional Journalists (SPJ) has developed an ethical code, which, among other things, asserts that professional journalists must seek truth and report it, minimize harm, act independently, and be accountable.

The Public Relations Society of America (PRSA) has developed a code of ethics for public relations practitioners. Its code includes the stipulations that public relations professionals should protect and advance the free flow of accurate information; promote healthy and fair competition; foster informed decision-making in a democratic society while providing the appropriate safeguards to protect confidential and private information; and avoid real, potential, or perceived conflicts of interest. Several trade groups have also proposed ethical guidelines for advertisers. For example, the American Advertising Federation asserts that advertising should be truth; advertising claims should be substantiated by evidence in hands of the advertiser; and advertisers should avoid making false or misleading claims about competitors.

Because the First Amendment prohibits the licensing of people involved in communications industries such as journalism and public relations, following these codes of ethics is often one of the primary ways professionals in those industries distinguish themselves from non-professionals. Nevertheless, ethical controversies routinely erupt in the media business.

For example, in the 1950s, when television was still a new medium, a contestant on the quiz show *The $64,000 Question* was coached by the producers, who wanted him to win because he attracted a large audience. The viewers believed that the contestant was answering the questions on his own. The coaching was considered unethical. When former football star O. J. Simpson was arrested on suspicion of murdering his wife in 1994, his image on the cover of *Time* magazine was darkened to make him seen more menacing. The manipulation of his photo was considered unethical.

In 2008, Pfizer ran an advertisement for its cholesterol drug, Lipitor, that featured a man rowing across a mountain lake. The voiceover said that it was Dr. Robert Jarvik, the inventor of artificial hearts. "When diet and exercise are not enough, adding Lipitor significantly lowers cholesterol," Dr. Jarvik said in the ad. However, Dr. Jarvik was not a cardiologist, and at the time the ad was created, he was not licensed to practice medicine. More problematic, the man actually rowing in the commercial was not Dr. Jarvik, but a stand-in. In fact, Dr. Jarvik never rowed. Pfizer reportedly spent millions of dollars airing the ad, which many found misleading and unethical.

The emergence of blogs as an important medium of communication has also led to ethical concerns. In 2006, it was revealed that a blog called Wal-Marting Across America, which was purportedly written by a couple traveling across country in a recreational vehicle, was actually created by a major public-relations company working on behalf of Wal-Mart.

The law was not violated in any of these episodes. Nonetheless, the deception involved in each case raised ethical red flags.

CONCLUSION

Communication plays a central role in the social, political, and economic life of the country. As a result, communication activities operate within a complex web of legal and ethical rules. In the United States, the First Amendment, which is both based on and serves as a break from British traditions, is the guidepost for most of the laws controlling communication. But even though the Constitution contains an absolute prohibition on Congress and the states passing laws abridging freedom of speech and the press, many laws and regulations have been put in place that do just that.

Broadcast media such as television and radio are regulated differently than print and the Internet. Political speech is regulated differently than commercial and corporate speech. The objective of many of the rules governing political speech, for example, is to create the conditions for robust debate. Many of the rules governing commercial speech are to ensure that the public is not deceived.

Perhaps as important as the legal restrictions are the ethical considerations that must be taken into account by people working in the communications industries. Since the First Amendment precludes the government's licensing of journalists or public relations practitioners, following ethical guidelines is one way that professionals in those industries distinguish themselves from non-professionals. Ethics is particularly important as blogging and other Web-based social media become more prominent.

The argument about how free speech should be and what constitutes ethical behavior is ongoing. Individuals must answer that question according to their own view of the world and of the question of right and wrong. Collectively, the answers to those questions decisively shape the character of a given society.

A SHADOW DARKENS

by Ithiel de Sola Pool

Civil liberty functions today in a changing technological context. For five hundred years a struggle was fought, and in a few countries won, for the right of people to speak and print freely, unlicensed, uncensored, and uncontrolled. But new technologies of electronic communication may now relegate old and freed media such as pamphlets, platforms, and periodicals to a corner of the public forum. Electronic modes of communication that enjoy lesser rights are moving to center stage. The new communication technologies have not inherited all the legal immunities that were won for the old. When wires, radio waves, satellites, and computers became major vehicles of discourse, regulation seemed to be a technical necessity. And so, as speech increasingly flows over those electronic media, the five-century growth of an unabridged right of citizens to speak without controls may be endangered.

Alarm over this trend is common, though understanding of it is rare. In 1980 the chairman of the American Federal Communications Commission (FCC) sent a shiver through print journalists when he raised the question of whether a newspaper delivered by teletext is an extension of print and thus as free as any other newspaper, or whether it is a broadcast and thus under the control of the government.[1] A reporter, discussing computerized information services, broached an issue with far-reaching implications for society when she asked, "Will traditional First Amendment freedom of the press apply to the signals sent out over telephone wires or television cables?"[2] William S. Paley, chairman of the Columbia Broadcasting System (CBS), warned the press: "Broadcasters and print people have been so busy improving and defining their own turf that it has escaped some of us how much we are being drawn together by the vast revolution in 'electronification' that is changing the face of the media today ... Convergence of delivery mechanisms for news and information raises anew some critical First Amendment questions ... Once the print media comes into the home through the television set, or an attachment, with an impact and basic content similar to that which the broadcasters now deliver, then the question of government regulation becomes paramount for print as well."[3] And Senator Bob Packwood proposed a new amendment to the Constitution extending First Amendment rights to the electronic media, on the assumption that they are not covered now.

READING NOTES

Although the first principle of communications law in the United States is the guarantee of freedom in the First Amendment, in fact this country has a trifurcated communications system. In three domains of communication—print, common carriage, and broadcasting—the law has evolved separately, and in each domain with but modest relation to the others.

In the domain of print and other means of communication that existed in the formative days of the nation, such as pulpits, periodicals, and public meetings, the First Amendment truly governs. In well over one hundred cases dealing with publishing, canvassing, public speeches, and associations, the Supreme Court has applied the First Amendment to the media that existed in the eighteenth century.

In the domain of common carriers, which includes the telephone, the telegraph, the postal system, and now some computer networks, a different set of policies has been applied, designed above all to ensure universal service and fair access by the public to the facilities of the carrier. That right of access is what defines a common carrier: it is obligated to serve all on equal terms without discrimination.

Finally, in the domain of broadcasting, Congress and the courts have established a highly regulated regime, very different from that of print. On the grounds of a supposed scarcity of usable frequencies in the radio spectrum, broadcasters are selected by the government for merit in its eyes, assigned a slice each of the spectrum of frequencies, and required to use that assignment fairly and for community welfare as defined by state authorities. The principles of common carriage and of the First Amendment have been applied to broadcasting in only atrophied form. For broadcasting, a politically managed system has been invented.

The electronic modes of twentieth century communication, whether they be carriers or broadcasters, have lost a large part of the eighteenth and nineteenth century constitutional protections of no prior restraint, no licenses, no special taxes, no regulations, and no laws. Every radio spectrum user, for example, must be licensed. This requirement started in 1912, almost a decade before the beginning of broadcasting, at a time when radio was used mainly for maritime communication. Because the United States Navy's communications were suffering interference, Congress, in an effort at remedy, imposed licensing on transmitters, thereby breaching a tradition that went back to John Milton against requiring licenses for communicating.

Regulation as a response to perceived technical problems has now reached the point where transmissions enclosed in wires or cables, and therefore causing no over-the-air interference, are also licensed and regulated. The FCC claims the right to control which broadcast stations a cablecaster may or must carry. Until the courts blew the whistle, the rules even barred a pay channel from performing movies that were more than three or less than ten years old. Telephone bills are taxed. A public network interconnecting computers must be licensed and, according to present interpretations of the 1934 Communications Act, may be denied a license if the government does not believe that it serves "the public convenience, interest, or necessity."

Both civil libertarians and free marketers are perturbed at the expanding scope of communications regulation. After computers became linked by communications networks, for example, the FCC spent several years figuring out how to avoid regulating the computer industry. The line of reasoning behind this laudable self-restraint, known as deregulation, has nothing to do, however, with freedom of speech. Deregulation, whatever its economic merits, is something much less than the First Amendment. The Constitution, in Article 1, Section 8, gives the federal government the right to regulate interstate commerce, but in the First Amendment, equally explicitly, it excludes one kind of commerce, namely communication, from government authority. Yet here is the FCC trying to figure out how it can avoid regulating the commerce of the computer industry (an authority Congress could have given, but never did) while continuing to regulate communications whenever it considers this necessary. The Constitution has been turned on its head.

The mystery is how the clear intent of the Constitution, so well and strictly enforced in the domain of print, has been so neglected in the electronic revolution. The answer lies partly in changes in the prevailing concerns and historical circumstances from the time of the founding fathers to the world of today; but it lies at least as much in the failure of Congress and the courts to understand the character of the new technologies. Judges and legislators have tried to fit technological innovations under conventional legal concepts. The errors of understanding by these scientific laymen, though honest, have been mammoth. They have sought to guide toward good purposes technologies they did not comprehend.

"It would seem," wrote Alexis de Tocqueville, "that if despotism were to be established among the democratic nations of our days ... it would be more extensive and more mild; it would degrade men without tormenting them." This is the kind of mild but degrading erosion of freedom that our system of communication faces today, not a rise of dictators or totalitarian movements. The threat in America, as Tocqueville perceived, is from well-intentioned policies, with results that are poorly foreseen. The danger is "tutelary power," which aims at the happiness of the people but also seeks to be the "arbiter of that happiness."[4]

Yet in a century and a half since Tocqueville wrote, the mild despotism that he saw in the wings of American politics has not become a reality. For all his understanding of the American political system, he missed one vital element of the picture. In the tension between tutelary and libertarian impulses that is built into American culture, a strong institutional dike has held back assaults on freedom. It is the first ten amendments to the Constitution. Extraordinary as this may seem, in Tocqueville's great two volumes there is nowhere a mention of the Bill of Rights!

The erosion of traditional freedoms that has occurred as government has striven to cope with problems of new communications media would not have surprised Tocqueville, for it is a story of how, in pursuit of the public good, a growing structure of controls has been imposed. But one part of the story would have surprised him, for it tells how a legal institution that he overlooked, namely the First Amendment, has up to now maintained the freedom and individualism that he saw as endangered.

A hundred and fifty years from now, today's fears about the future of free expression may prove as alarmist as Tocqueville's did. But there is reason to suspect that our situation is more ominous. What has changed in twentieth century communications is its technological base. Tocqueville wrote in a pluralistic society of small enterprises where the then new mass media consisted entirely of the printed press which the First Amendment protected. In the period since his day, new and mostly electronic media have proliferated in the form of great oligopolistic networks of common carriers and broadcasters. Regulation was natural response. Fortunately and strangely, as electronics advances further, another reversal is now taking place, toward growing decentralization and toward fragmentation of the audience of the newest media. The transitional era of giant media may nonetheless leave a permanent set of regulatory practices implanted on a system that is coming to have technical characteristics that would otherwise be conducive to freedom.

The causal relationships between technology and culture are a matter that social scientists have long debated. Some may question how far technological trends shape the political freedom or control under which communication takes place, believing, as does Daniel Bell, that each subsystem of society, such as techno-economics, polity, and culture, has its own heritage and axial principles and goes its own way.[5] Others contend, like Karl Marx or Ruth Benedict, that a deep commonality binds all aspects of a culture. Some argue that technology is neutral, used as the culture demands; others that the technology of the medium controls the message.

The interaction over the past two centuries between the changing technologies of communication and the practice of free speech, I would argue, fits a pattern that is sometimes described as "soft technological determinism." Freedom is fostered when the means of communication are dispersed, decentralized, and easily available, as are printing presses or microcomputers. Central control is more likely when the means of communication are concentrated, monopolized, and scarce, as are great networks. But the relationship between technology and institutions is not simple or unidirectional, nor are the effects immediate. Institutions that evolve in response to one technological environment persist and to some degree are later imposed on what may be a changed technology. The First Amendment came out of a pluralistic world of small communicators, but it shaped the present treatment of great national networks. Later on, systems of regulation that emerged for national common carriers

and for the use of "scarce" spectrum for broadcasting tended to be imposed on more recent generations of electronic technologies that no longer require them.

Simple versions of technological determinism fail to take account of the differences in the way things happen at different stages in the life cycle of a technology. When a new invention is made, such as the telephone or radio, its fundamental laws are usually not well understood. It is designed to suit institutions that already exist, but in its early stages if it is to be used at all, it must be used in whatever form it proved experimentally to work. Institutions for its use are thus designed around a technologically determined model. Later, when scientists have comprehended the fundamental theory, the early technological embodiment becomes simply a special case. Alternative devices can then be designed to meet human needs. Technology no longer need control. A 1920s motion picture had to be black and white, silent, pantomimic, and shown in a place of public assembly; there was no practical choice. A 1980s video can have whatever colors, sounds, and three-dimensional or synthetic effects are wanted, and can be seen in whatever location is desired. In the meantime, however, an industry has established studios, theaters, career lines, unions, funding, and advertising practices, all designed to use the technology that is in place. Change occurs, but the established institutions are a constraint on its direction and pace.

Today, in an era of advanced (and still advancing) electronic theory, it has become possible to build virtually any kind of communications device that one might wish, though at a price. The market, not technology, sets most limits. For example, technology no longer imposes licensing and government regulation. That pattern was established for electronic media a half-century ago, when there seemed to be no alternative,

READING NOTES

120

but the institutions of control then adopted persist. That is why today's alarms could turn out to be more portentous than Tocqueville's.

The key technological change, at the root of the social changes, is that communication, other than conversation face to face, is becoming overwhelmingly electronic. Not only is electronic communication growing faster than traditional media of publishing, but also the convergence of modes of delivery is bringing the press, journals, and books into the electronic world. One question raised by these changes is whether some social features are inherent in the electronic character of the emerging media. Is television the model of the future? Are electromagnetic pulses simply an alternative conduit to deliver whatever is wanted, or are there aspects of electronic technology that make it different from print—more centralized or more decentralized, more banal or more profound, more private or more government dependent?

The electronic transformation of the media occurs not in a vacuum but in a specific historical and legal context. Freedom for publishing has been one of America's proudest traditions. But just what is it that the courts have protected, and how does this differ from how the courts acted later when the media through which ideas flowed came to be the telegraph, telephone, television, or computers? What images did policy makers have of how each of these media works; how far were their images valid; and what happened to their images when the facts changed?

In each of the three parts of the American communications system—print, common carriers, and broadcasting—the law has rested on a perception of technology that is sometimes accurate, often inaccurate, and which changes slowly as technology changes fast. Each new advance in the technology of communications disturbs a status quo. It meets resistance from those whose dominance it threatens, but if use-ful, it begins to be adopted. Initially, because it is new and a full scientific mastery of the options is not yet at hand, the invention comes into use in a rather clumsy form. Technical laymen, such as judges, perceive the new technology in that early, clumsy form, which then becomes their image of its nature, possibilities, and use. This perception is an incubus on later understanding.

The courts and regulatory agencies in the American system (or other authorities elsewhere) enter as arbiters of the conflicts among entrepreneurs, interest groups, and political organizations battling for control of the new technology. The arbiters, applying familiar analogies from the past to their lay image of the new technology, create a partly old, partly new structure of rights and obligations. The telegraph was analogized to railroads, the telephone to the telegraph, and cable television to broadcasting. The legal system thus invented for each new technology may in some instances, like the First Amendment, be a *tour de force* of political creativity, but in other instances it may be less worthy. The system created can turn out to be inappropriate to more habile forms of the technology which gradually emerge as the technology progresses. This is when problems arise, as they are arising so acutely today.

Historically, the various media that are now converging have been differently organized and differently treated under the law. The outcome to be feared is that communications in the future may be unnecessarily regulated under the unfree tradition of law that has been applied so far to the electronic media. The clash between the print, common carrier, and broadcast models is likely to be a vehement communications policy issue in the next decades. Convergence of modes is upsetting the trifurcated system developed over the past two hundred years, and questions that had seemed to be settled centuries ago are being reopened, unfortunately sometimes not in a libertarian way.

READING NOTES

_____

_____

_____

_____

_____

The problem is worldwide. What is true for the United States is true, *mutatis mutandis*, for all free nations. All have the same three systems. All are in their way deferential to private publishing but allow government control or ownership of carriers and broadcasters. And all are moving into the era of electronic communication. So they face the same prospect of either freeing up their electronic media or else finding their major means of communication slipping back under political control.

The American case is unique only in the specific feature of the First Amendment and in the role of the courts in upholding it. The First Amendment, as interpreted by the courts, provides an anchor for freedom of the press and thus accentuates the difference between publishing and the electronic domain. Because of the unique power of the American courts, the issue in the United States unfolds largely in judicial decisions. But the same dilemmas and trends could be illustrated by citing declarations of policy and institutional structures in each advanced country.

If the boundaries between publishing, broadcasting, cable television, and the telephone network are indeed broken in the coming decades, then communications policies in all advanced countries must address the issue of which of the three models will dominate public policy regarding them. Public interest regulation could begin to extend over the print media as those media increasingly use regulated electronic channels. Conversely, concern for the traditional notion of a free press could lead to finding ways to free the electronic media from regulation. The policies adopted, even among free nations, will differ, though with much in common. The problems in all of them are very much the same.

The phrase "communications policy" rings oddly in a discussion of freedom from government. But freedom is also a policy. The question it poses is how to reduce the public control of communications in an electronic era. A policy of freedom aims at pluralism of expression rather than at dissemination of preferred ideas.

A communications policy, or indeed any policy, may be mapped on a few central topics:

> *Definition of the domain in which the policy operates*
>
> *Availability of resources*
>
> *Organization of access to resources*
>
> *Establishment and enforcement of norms and controls*
>
> *Problems at the system boundaries*

The *definition of the domain* of a communications policy requires consideration of the point at which human intercourse becomes something more than communication. In American law, at some point speech becomes action and thus no longer receives First Amendment protection. Similar issues arise as to whether under the law pornography is speech, and whether commercial speech is speech.

The *availability of resources* raises another set of questions. Tools, money, raw materials, and labor are all required in order to carry on communication. The press needs newsprint; broadcasters need spectrum. How much of these can be made available, and at what prices can they be had?

The *organization of access to these resources* can be by a market or by rationing by the state. There may be a diversity of sources of resources, or there may be a monopoly. How much freedom is allowed to those who control the resources to exercise choice about who gets what? Are resources taxed, are they subsidized, or neither? How is intellectual property defined, and how is it protected?

The *exercise of regulation and control* over communication is a central concern in any treatise on freedom. How much control are policy makers allowed to exercise? What are the limitations on them, such as the First Amendment? May they censor? May they license those who seek to communicate? What norms control the

READING NOTES

_____

_____

_____

_____

_____

things that communicators may say to each other? What is libel, what is slander, what violates privacy or security? Who is chosen to enforce these rules, and how?

The *problems encountered at the system boundaries* include the trans-border issues that arise when there is a conflict of laws about communications which cross frontiers. Censorship is often imposed for reasons of national security, cultural protection, and trade advantage. These issues, which have not been central in past First Amendment controversies, are likely to be of growing importance in the electronic era.

From the map of policy analysis can be extracted what social scientific? sometime call a mapping sentence, a brief but formal statement of the problem to be analyzed in this book. It seeks to understand the impact of resource availability, as affected both by technology and by the organization of access to the resources, upon freedom from regulation and control. The specific question to be answered is whether the electronic resources for communication can be as free of public regulation in the future as the platform and printing press have been in the past. Not a decade goes by in free countries, and not a day in the world, without grim oppressions that bring protesters once more to picket lines and demonstrations. Vigilance that must be so eternal becomes routine, and citizens grow callous.

The issue of the handling of the electronic media is the salient free speech problem for this decade, at least as important for this moment as were the last generation's issues for them, and as the next generation's will be for them too. But perhaps it is more than that. The move to electronic communication may be a turning point that history will remember. Just as in seventeenth and eighteenth century Great Britain and America a few tracts and acts set precedents for print by which we live today, so what we think and do today may frame the information system for a substantial period in the future.

In that future society the norms that govern information and communication will be even more crucial than in the past. Those who read, wrote, and published in the seventeenth and eighteenth centuries, and who shaped whatever heritage of art, literature, science, and history continues to matter today, were part of a small minority, well under one-tenth of the work force. Information activities now occupy the lives of much of the population. In advanced societies about half the work force are information processors.[6] It would be dire if the laws we make today governing the dominant mode of information handling in such an information society were subversive of its freedom. The onus is on us to determine whether free societies in the twenty-first century will conduct electronic communication under the conditions of freedom established for the domain of print through centuries of struggle, or whether that great achievement will become lost in a confusion about new technologies.

READING NOTES

_____

_____

_____

_____

_____

Section

2

THE IMPACT OF COMMUNICATION

Chapter 5

Communication and Community

"World community can only exist with world communication, which means something more than extensive software facilities scattered about the globe. It means common understanding, a common tradition, common ideas, and common ideals."

—Robert M. Hutchins

In his 1916 book *Democracy and Education*, noted American philosopher John Dewey observed that there are more than verbal ties among the words common, community, and communication. People live in community, he observed, by virtue of things they have in common, and communication is the process by which people come to possess things in common, particularly common understandings and visions of the world. Society, he argued, not only continues to exist by transmission, that is, by communication, but also can be understood to exist in communication. What that means is that people can recognize their common bonds, develop shared identities, and foster social relationships by communicating with each other.

This perspective is underscored by religious communities who excommunicate members who violate the precepts of that particular religious community. Violators are placed outside of communication and are no longer considered members of that community.

Different types of communication foster the development of different types of communities and complex social relationships. For example, oral communication and interpersonal interaction lead to the intense social interaction commonly associated with tribal culture. Writing sets the conditions for ongoing religious communities. It is not an accident that the oldest religious communities in the world have sacred books that serve to bind members to one another. The rise of print culture created by the printing press was deeply intertwined with the emergence of the concept of a nation-state, the development of political parties, and the launch of social movements. Television helped to generate fan communities, and, over time, the idea of the global village. The Internet provides the communication infrastructure for virtual communities—communities that exist only through their online linkages.

But different kinds of communication are only one factor that helps form community—the idea that people have things in common that join one to the other. Media types and content also function as glue to connect people. People who sing together, cheer together, or read the same books often feel important, if sometimes unspoken, social ties.

This chapter's aims include to

- explore the relationship of communication to building of community as well as social and national identity,

- examine how print media have been used to build political and social groups,

- look at the role of music in building specific communities,

- reflect on the rise of fan culture and what it means, and

- point out how the Internet is enabling new forms of community.

Required Reading: In the chapter, "'I Hear Singing in the Air': Singing as a Communication Strategy," Kerran L. Sanger argues that singing is a unique form of communication and that singing was an essential aspect of the persuasive strategy of the American civil rights movement in the 20th century.

COMMUNICATION AND COMMUNITY

Aristotle had the insight that communities are formed through communication. In his work *Politics*, he argued that every state is a community made up of households, which are also communities themselves. What he means by the word community is that the members hold something in common and, in certain perspectives, see themselves as one. It is speech and discussion of the just and the unjust, the useful and the harmful, that knit the households into a community. Therefore, Aristotle argued, a state should never be larger than a grouping in which all men can participate in its deliberations. The size and character of Aristotelian communities were dictated by the constraints imposed by face-to-face communication, which were significant.

As societies grew in size, Aristotle's vision could no longer serve to explain how communities come into existence or how communication creates and maintains communities. After all, even by the time of the Roman Empire, the sense of community—a shared identity, allegiance, and perhaps destiny—extended well beyond face-to-face communities. By the 12th century, popes could call on Christians to go on crusades to the Holy Land, and men responded to the call, at least in part because they identified with the Church.

Over time, several alternative theories suggesting both how communication forms communities and how communication makes communities possible were developed. In one line of thought with its roots in the idea of Jean Jacques Rousseau, people both are individuals with private lives and also have undifferentiated general identities as citizens or members of the public. Within a political context, the challenge is to keep private interests in check and allow people to act on their public impulses. To do so, states construct rituals, symbolic public displays and performances, and collective myths, which serve to reinforce the individual commitment to the public and minimize acting on private interests. In short, in this approach, communication creates community by suppressing individual concerns and privileging a public identity.

German philosopher Georg Hegel saw the role of communication in the creation of community differently. Rather than keeping a sense that each person was an individual with private interests in check, communication was the process through which each person could recognize and respect others. Through this mutual recognition and respect, communities could cohere. Through communication, individuals who are members of communities are created. Hegel's concept of the relationship of communication to community was more consistent with that of Aristotle, but it could be applied to communities of greaterscope. Indeed, American philosopher John Dewey, who was well-educated in the ideas of Hegel and Aristotle, argued that it was democracy, with its free press, free inquiry, free public education, freedom of association, and a regulated marketplace, that controlled the most dehumanizing aspects of industrialization and offered the ideal environment for personal development and the creation of community based on mutual recognition and respect among individuals.

But what exactly is a community? A community is not necessarily defined by geography. An American living in Europe, even an American born in Europe, is no less an American. Nor is a community necessarily defined by adherence to a strict set of ideas. Once again, in many communities, members disagree about a wide range of fundamental issues. While some communities, particularly religious communities, have limits to the extent that dissent is tolerated, many do not. Membership in a community frequently does not require performing a specific set of rituals.

As author Benedict Anderson has pointed out, people imagine themselves to be part of a community. They can imagine themselves part of a given community through the texts the community produces and to which its members pay attention in specific and learned ways. Consequently, newspapers and novels, music and art, even athletic events and spectacles, are vehicles through which people can imagine themselves as part of one community rather than another. In other words, New Yorkers attend to news about New York differently from people who see themselves as Philadelphians. As a result, communication processes are critical in the creation and maintenance of communities, both subgroups within the context of a larger community and the larger community itself.

How large a community can be created? With the development of international television networks and the Internet, people have begun to talk about the idea of a global village—the idea that people can imagine themselves as a part of a global community. Without global communication networks, being a part of a global community would be impossible. Prior to the widespread adoption of television in the 1950s, even national communication networks were slow and worked only intermittently. People's loyalties lay with smaller

Figure 5.1—*International television and the Internet facilitate communities around the world.*

groups, and participating in the communication networks of those groups helped them to construct their identities (see Figure 5.1).

THE AFRICAN AMERICAN PRESS AND THE CREATION OF COMMUNITY

In 1827, the African American community of New York was under attack. The *New York Enquirer*, established the year before by Mordecai M. Noah, a leader of a strident racist campaign stretching back to the early years of the decade, was attacking black men daily in its pages. The newspaper described African American men as lacking integrity and courage, calling them uncivil and indolent, and complained that Black Americans were adding to the city's number of paupers. As if that were not enough, the newspaper questioned the virtue and chastity of African American women and opposed the abolition of slavery. It even chastised people for freeing their slaves.

The attacks were not just venomous outbursts. In 1797, the New York state legislature had passed a law that banned slavery by 1827. The issue of slavery and what would happen when the last of the slaves were freed in New York was very much on the political agenda. Mordecai Noah had an answer. All African Americans, slave and free, should be deported to Africa.

The *Enquirer*'s attacks were not all that unusual or uncommon. After all, blacks were still enslaved in half the country, and in the other half, blacks were hardly seen as full participants in American society. But even if the *New York Enquirer*'s anti-black campaign was not very noteworthy, the response was. A group of free black men decided to establish their own weekly newspaper to respond. The reason they chose this course of action was simple. There was no other vehicle of communication open to them.

So on March 16, 1827, a representative group of African Americans launched *Freedom's Journal*. Its initial mandate was to confront the charges leveled against the black community by the white press. The newspaper's prospectus read in part: "Daily slandered, we think that there ought to be some channel of communion between us and the public, through which a single voice may be heard, in defense of the five hundred thousand free people of colour."

With that declaration, the founders of *Freedom's Journal* laid out what can be considered a rallying point for the community and ethnic press. The role of the black press and the media created by other ethnic groups is multifaceted. First, as the founders of *Freedom's Journal* noted, the press gives the community a voice in public affairs. It explains the specific community to the larger society and makes the views and concerns of the community known to those who are interested. Second, it provides a "communion," or a way for members of the community to share information and perspectives that are important to those in the community itself. In other words, the black press and other ethnic media explain the community to outsiders as well as to themselves.

Freedom's Journal was founded with the Reverend Samuel Cornish, a Presbyterian minister and well-known public speaker, as editor, and John B. Russwurm, one of the first African Americans to graduate from college in the United States when he graduated from Bowdoin College in 1826, as business manager. Cornish and Russwurm initially agreed on a platform that opposed slavery and colonization, but within a short period of time, their views began to diverge. After six months, Cornish resigned and Russwurm became the editor-in-chief as well as business manager. Russwurm's views continued to evolve, and he ultimately began to support colonization, which alienated many of the newspaper's original readers. In March 1829, *Freedom's Journal* was shuttered. In May of that year, Cornish resurrected the newspaper under the name *Rights of All*. But the new version of the paper lasted only until October of that year, when it too was closed.

Freedom's Journal's experience was repeated many times during the 19th century. Newspapers serving the African American community were launched, only to fail within several years. The black press faced many difficult challenges. The community that it served was not affluent, and literacy rates were low. Moreover, white advertisers were not interested in reaching the black community. Nonetheless, the black press demonstrated that it could have an impact both inside and outside the black community. For example, in 1847, Frederick Douglass, perhaps the first great national African American spokesperson for abolition, founded the *North Star*, a weekly newspaper based in Rochester, New York. The *North Star*'s platform was to "attack slavery in all its forms and aspects, advocate Universal Emancipation; exact the standard of public morality; promote the moral and intellectual improvement of the colored people; and to hasten the day of freedom to our three million enslaved fellow countryman." The *North Star* and its successors served as an important platform for Douglass as he became a celebrated spokesperson for the cause of abolition. He continued to publish his newspaper until 1860.

The years following the Civil War saw an upsurge in publishing in the black community. In 1887 alone, 68 newspapers were founded, and by 1890, around 575 publications produced and read by African Americans had been launched. Some were religious publications and others were political organs, but many were newspapers.

One of the most influential black journalists from this period was Ida B. Wells-Barnett. Born in Holly Springs, Mississippi, on July 16, 1862,

Wells-Barnett attended Rust College, a local school founded by the Freedmen's Bureau that provided instruction to people of all ages. In 1878, after an epidemic that claimed her parents and a younger brother, she left Rust and got a job as a teacher. Three years later, she relocated to Memphis, Tennessee, where she made headlines in both white and black newspapers in 1884, when she refused to relinquish her seat in the ladies' car and move to the "smoker" while riding on a train. Angry, she sued the railroad for assault and discrimination.

Wells-Barnett wrote about the court case in *The Living Way* and soon became a regular contributor—using the pen name "Iola"—to black newspapers and periodicals around the country. Wells purchased an interest in the Memphis *Free Speech and Headlight* in 1889 and assumed the editorial duties. The paper was co-owned by Reverend R. Nightingale, the pastor of Beale Street Baptist Church, who urged his large congregation to subscribe to the paper.

In May 1892, Wells wrote about the recent lynching of three men, including a good friend, who owned a Memphis grocery store. She also detailed her investigations of the latest hangings in Mississippi and Tennessee, concluding that mob violence was not really aimed at punishing African American men for raping white women but was a result of white fears of interracial relations and post-Reconstruction resentment of black progress. One week later, while Wells was in New York City visiting *New York Age* editor T. Thomas Fortune, who was considered the "dean" of black journalists in the period by virtue of his having worked for a time with Charles Dana of the *New York Sun*, she learned that a white mob had destroyed her office and run the business manager out of town.

Rather than returning to Memphis, she joined the *New York Age* and continued to write investigative articles about lynching. At the end of 1892, she wrote the first of three lengthy pamphlets documenting the number and causes of lynching, and outlining remedies: *Southern Horrors: Lynch Law in All Its Phases.* This was followed by *A Red Record* in 1895 and *Mob Rule in New Orleans* in 1900. Her efforts led to invitations to give dozens of public lectures on the subject, both in the United States and in the British Isles in 1893 and 1894, which were commented on in both the black and white press.

Despite the important role it played in the black community, the African American press continued to be characterized by small publications aimed at the elite black community and sympathetic whites. With a small audience, they usually operated on shaky financial ground. That changed when the *Chicago Defender* was launched in 1905. Its founder, Robert Abbott, emulated the approach of William Randolph Hearst, using sensational journalism to attract the masses. He began circulating his newspaper in the African American neighborhoods in Chicago, where 44,000 people lived crammed into a few blocks on the south side of the city. He also circulated the paper in the South, encouraging Southern blacks to move north. The *Defender* demonstrated that the black press could be a commercially viable, even lucrative, business venture. It breathed new life into the black press.

One of the most influential newspapers to follow along the trail blazed by the *Defender* was the *Pittsburgh Courier*. Founded in 1910 by Edwin Nathaniel Harleston, a security guard at an H. J. Heinz food packing plant, it gained prominence under the editorship of Robert Lee Vann. In the 1930s, Vann began to encourage blacks to shift their political allegiance away from the Republican Party to support Franklin Delano Roosevelt and the Democratic Party. But that support was not unequivocal. During World War II, the *Courier* won a national udience for its "Double V" campaign. Started in 1942, the Double V campaign called for a victory over the Nazis in Europe and a victory over racism at home. The campaign led to the *Courier* becoming the most widely circulated black newspaper of the period, with 270,000 readers, followed by the Baltimore *Afro-American* and then the *Defender*. At its height, there were as 14 editions of the

Courier circulated in states including Texas, Louisiana, Pennsylvania, Ohio, and New York.

The *Pittsburgh Courier* also campaigned tirelessly for the integration of major-league baseball. Its chief sportswriter, Wendell Smith, is credited with helping to pave the way for Jackie Robinson to become the first black major league ballplayer, playing for the Brooklyn Dodgers. Smith traveled and roomed with Robinson on several trips with the Dodgers.

After World War II, the black press became leading advocates for civil rights for blacks in the South and the rest of the country. Throughout the 1950s and 1960s, it offered the most sustained coverage of milestone events such as the efforts to desegregate public schools and universities in the South, the Freedom Riders in 1961, and the March on Washington for Jobs and Freedom in 1963 (see Figure 5.2).

As the economic strength of the black community grew during the 1950s and 1960s, it began to be served by other media as well. In 1942, John H. Johnson, then working as an assistant to the president at the Supreme Life Insurance Company, launched *Negro Digest*, a compendium of articles of interest to the black community modeled after *Reader's Digest*. The publication was a success, achieving a circulation of over 100,000 at its peak, but it did not have the same impact as his subsequent publication, *Ebony*, founded in 1945, which was modeled after *Life* magazine, one of the most successful magazines of its period. Initially focused on profiling economically successful African Americans, it soon branched out to report on the full range of issues of interest to the black community. In some ways, *Ebony* became a symbol of the growth of the black middle class.

The growth of cable television also provided new opportunities for the introduction of new media aimed at African American audiences. In the 1980s, Robert L. Johnson, a lobbyist for the cable television industry, launched Black Entertainment Television (BET) with the backing of John Malone, one of the most influential executives in the cable arena. The initial programming lineup consisted of music videos, original programming, and reruns of situation comedies of interest to the community. In the past 20 years, BET has created a number of new cable channels of interest to the black community.

The black media, obviously, did not create the black community. But the black press gave voice to the community and strove for its empowerment and advancement. It was a forum through which black leaders could debate the great issues and build support and solidarity that ultimately led to the inclusion of African Americans as full citizens in the United States. As the black community continually moved toward full empowerment, its success was reflected, in part, in the media geared for it.

THE IMMIGRANT PRESS

The black press is only one example of the media providing both a voice for a specific community and a way for the community to define itself. As wave after wave of immigrants arrived in the United States in the 19th and 20th centuries, newspapers, and sometimes radio stations, were established to serve those communities. As with the black press, the immigrant press played many different roles. It helped to acculturate newcomers into American society. It helped to

© JustASC, 2010. Shutterstock Inc.

Figure 5.2—*The black press laid the foundation for the American civil rights movement of the 1950s and 1960s.*

strengthen communal institutions serving those communities.—They served as mechanisms for keeping the culture and sometimes the language of the "old country" vibrant and immediate. And the immigrant press was a vehicle to defend the specific immigrant communities from the attacks of the dominant white American culture.

For example, one of the first publications in the United States published by and about Jews was *The Jew*, started in 1823 to fend off efforts by the American Society for Meliorating the Condition of the Jew (ASMCJ), an association of evangelical Christians dedicated to converting Jews to Christianity. In a stance that was remarkably similar to *Freedom's Journal*, which was started four years later, its editor, Solomon Jackson, wrote, "The right of defense, when attacked, is considered the first law of nature: it is not only inherent in man, but exists in equal strength in the insect and the reptile; hence the adage, 'tread on a worm and it will turn.' Israel has long been a 'worm and no man'; and has borne (to call it by no harsher name) the gainsaying of the Gentiles." *The Jew* was divided into three areas—theological defenses of Judaism, attacks on the ASMCJ, and an effort to combat innuendos and falsehoods spread about Jews and Judaism. It did not cover the news of the world or the news of the Jewish community.

The first successful traditional newspaper serving the Jewish community was the *Occident and American Jewish Advocate*, founded in 1843. Throughout the 19th century, the majority of Jewish publications were in English, even though by 1880, two-thirds of the Jews in the United States were from Germany. One of the primary objectives of the Jewish press at this time was to aid Jews in assimilating into the United States. With large-scale immigration from Russia and Eastern Europe in the first part of the 20th century, however, the character of the Jewish press changed. During this period, many publications printed in Yiddish, a combination of Hebrew and German spoken by these new Jewish immigrants, were launched. In 1916, there were five Yiddish newspapers in New York City alone.

The most prominent of the Yiddish newspapers was the *Daily Forward*, founded in 1897 and edited by Abraham Cahan. With a Socialist political orientation, during the 1920s and 1930s, the *Forward* had a circulation of around 270,000. It was a strong advocate of unions and workers' right, and played an important role in the formation of the International Ladies Garment Workers' Union (ILGWU). Its advice column, "A Bintel Brief," provided guidance to immigrants trying to get their grounding in the United States. The paper played an important role in supporting and promoting the arts in the Jewish community. Cahan himself was a novelist whose work was compared by the prominent critic W. D. Howell to that of Stephen Crane. Isaac Bashevis Singer, who eventually won a Nobel Prize for Literature, published much of his work first in the *Forward* (see Figure 5.3).

The experiences of other ethnic communities were similar. The Irish, the Italians, the Chinese, the Polish, and many other ethnic groups set up their own newspapers and other forms of communal communication. The Irish American press had two distinct orientations. Since the Irish dominated the Catholic Church in the United States in the 1800s, one group of Irish American publications was chiefly concerned with helping immigrants retain and strengthen their faith, particularly in the face of the strong anti-Catholic

© vhrinchenko, 2010. Shutterstock Inc.

Figure 5.3—*Immigrants to the United States used the free press to build communities.*

feeling common among Protestant Americans. The most prominent of the Catholic-oriented newspapers were the Boston *Pilot*, which was started in 1829 by the Catholic bishop of Boston and then sold in 1834 to two lay people.

Other Irish American newspapers had a more nationalist perspective. Between 1870 and 1913, Patrick Ford emerged as one of the most prominent and influential Irish journalists. As editor of the *Irish World*, which he founded in 1870, his newspaper became the voice of the Irish working class. Like other newspapers aimed toward immigrant communities, he advocated hard work and education as the keys to acceptance into American society. Moreover, he was a strong supporter of trade union activity, which was not uncommon among Irish American editors.

Ford even supported violent labor protests until the Haymarket Square massacre in 1886, in which a bomb was thrown during a rally in support of striking workers, killing eight police officers and some civilians. Worried that the violence would provoke a hostile reaction from the nativist community toward the Irish, who were deeply involved with union activity, Ford adopted a more conciliatory attitude toward the relationship between management and labor. Ford also offered political guidance to the Irish community, urging his readers to abandon their lock-step loyalty to the Democratic Party. Being identified with only one party, he argued, hurt their ability to compel politicians to address issues of interest to the Irish.

Virtually every immigrant community had its own newspapers, and many remain vibrant today. The *Italian Tribune* has been published since 1931 with a mission to provide a link for its readers to the Italian American community and their heritage, as well as to report on news of interest to Italian Americans. The first Chinese American newspaper, the *Golden Hills News*, was established in 1854 in San Francisco. But unlike with other immigrant communities, the number of Chinese speakers in the United States grew by 61 percent from 1990 to 2000, allowing the Chinese American press to grow and to improve quality. These publications are of great interest to the Chinese American community. Moreover, Chinese American newspapers have partnered with transnational publishing networks in China, Taiwan, and Hong Kong, which have given them exposure in the Asian markets. As a result, the United States has become the largest center for Chinese publishing outside of China, Taiwan, and Hong Kong.

The only non-English-speaking community that has grown more rapidly over the past twenty years than the Chinese has been the Hispanic community. The Hispanic community includes people from many different ethnic backgrounds; for example, immigrants from Cuba have had a very different experience both in their native country and in the United States than immigrants from Mexico. Nonetheless, the Spanish-language press in the United States can potentially cater to all Spanish-speaking immigrants. Indeed, the Hispanic community in the United States has grown to be such a significant factor that two television networks, *Telemundo* and *Univision*, have been created to serve it.

Clearly, newspapers and other forms of communication play critical parts in the life of immigrant communities, but the exact function changes from community to community. While most newspapers try to help immigrants adjust to life in the United States, some also try to maintain ties to the immigrants' country of origins. All try to preserve a sense of ethnic or religious identity. But in some cases, the immigrant community is still growing, so "preservation" is less important, while in other cases, after several generations have lived in the United States, people who have come from a specific country feel less attached to the country of their grandparents or great-grandparents. They feel primarily American and are less interested in the ethnic press.

COMMUNICATION AND CULTURAL CHANGE

Communication and the media are important mechanisms for maintaining a sense of community among immigrant groups. But communication is also the primary vehicle to effect social change within the larger community. Through speaking, publishing, demonstrating, and other ways of communicating, including such unremarkable ways as singing and dancing, people maintain the solidarity and recruit new supports for group's trying to restructure the interactions of specific communities. Three significant examples of the relationship of communication to changes in U.S. cultures can been seen in the acceptance of women, working people, and gays and lesbians as fully accepted citizens.

The Women's Movement

The Seneca Falls Convention of 1848 generally marks the start for the drive for women's rights in the United States. Women who had been active in the movement to abolish slavery were organized by Lucretia Mott to promote the idea that women also should have equal rights with men in the United States. At the convention, Elizabeth Cady Stanton presented the *Declaration of Sentiments*, which generally is considered the launching point for the women's suffrage movement. Modeled after the *Declaration of Independence*, Stanton's *Declaration* demanded, among other claims, a woman's right to full participation in the political system.

Between 1850 and 1900, at least 60 periodicals were started that supported a woman's right to vote. As a whole, these publications taught readers new ways to be—new ways to think, talk, dress, and name themselves. Without them, women would have remained isolated geographically, culturally, and socially. The new women's publications allowed women to form a national community of sorts to work for the changes they sought.

The first women's suffrage periodical, *The Lily*, was associated with the temperance movement. Its founder, Amelia Bloomer, proposed it when local temperance leaders restricted women to fund-raising and attending lectures by men. Bloomer's debut editorial read, "It is WOMAN that speaks through *The Lily*," promising that the monthly would be "a medium through which woman's thoughts and aspirations might

be developed." By January 1853, when its monthly circulation peaked at 4,0000, *The Lily's* motto advocated "Emancipation of Woman from Intemperance, Injustice, Prejudice, and Bigotry."

Perhaps the most famous women's suffrage periodical was the *Revolution*, though it only lasted from 1868 to 1870. Run by Elizabeth Cady Stanton and Susan B. Anthony, its motto was "Principle, not policy; Justice, not favors." A financier who loaned them money added a second motto: "Men, Their Rights and Nothing More; Women, Their Rights and Nothing Less." The *Revolution* represented and dramatized a "strong-minded" suffragist who was willful, determined, and contentious in style and tone. It won a reputation in the general press for being scrappy and feisty. After two years, Stanton and Anthony could no longer continue the newspaper and turned it over to a new publisher, who also could not keep it alive.

Anthony and Stanton were controversial even within the women's movement, and in 1869, a group of suffragists unhappy with their tactics formed the American Woman Suffrage Association. After Lucy Stone raised $10,000, the group launched the *Woman's Journal*, which was published from 1870 to 1931. The *Journal* merged in 1917 with the *Woman Voter*, which was the publication of New York City's Woman Suffrage Party, and the *National Suffrage News* to form the *Woman Citizen*.

The *Journal's* original motto was "Devoted to the Interests of Woman, to her education, industrial, legal, political equality and especially to her right of Suffrage." As opposed to other journals, it focused more specifically on suffrage, winning for women the right to vote. The *Journal* amassed strong support, and while it was not profitable, it survived through advertising revenue (but, unlike the *Revolution*, running only carefully chosen appropriate advertising), sales of stock, and fund-raising events.

Women won the right to vote when the 19th Amendment was ratified in 1920. But in practice, women's suffrage newspapers played a wider role than just agitating for a narrow political objective. They represented the interests of a universalized woman and were re-conceptualizing the role of women in society. In 1882, a writer for the *Woman's Journal* put it this way: The periodicals were "our own camping ground ... where we may indulge in private rehearsals and scan our own mistakes with a critical eye" (see Figure 5.4).

Books, magazines, and newspapers also played a pivotal role in what has been called the "second wave of feminism," which succeeded in reworking women's place in contemporary American society. A marker for the start of the second wave of feminism was the 1963 publication of the book *The Feminine Mystique* by Betty Friedan.

Based on interviews Friedan had conducted with her classmates from Smith College, Friedan argued that despite the cultural message of the times that women "never had it so good," many of these highly educated women were discontented, even though they could not determine exactly why. She criticized American women's magazines for propagating the idea that women could find happiness only through husbands, children, and homemaking.

The book hit a deep nerve as it challenged the "happy housewife" orientation of traditional women's magazines and their newspaper

counterparts—women's and society sections. In 1970, a group of feminists staged a sit-in at the *Ladies' Home Journal* offices in New York, demanding that the magazine deviate from its usual formula to carry articles on such subjects as abortion rights, balancing career and family, and prostitution.

In 1970, *Essence*, the first mass-circulation magazine for African American women, was created, and two years later, Gloria Steinem and others launched *Ms.*, a feminist publication intended for a national audience. By 1989, *Ms.* had a paid circulation of 543,000 per month and had turned the title "Ms." into an acceptable alternative to "Mrs." or "Miss". In the same way that "Mr." does not indicate marital status, neither does "Ms." Like *The Feminine Mystique*, *Ms.* played a central role in women's efforts to redefine themselves and their role in American society.

The Labor Movement and Communication

Women's long, hard road to equality was aided and abetted by the publications that women launched as well as their face-to-face meetings, conventions, and associations. During roughly the same period, working people also struggled to improve their position in society. As the United States industrialized during the 19th century, the owners of large factories often ruthlessly exploited workers. Working hours were long, conditions were poor, and protections for workers were few. Workers responded by organizing themselves into unions, which then often came under attack from management and others.

Like women and African Americans, workers launched newspapers and magazines both to organize themselves and to present their cases to the public at large. But labor also used other forms of communication to organize and build solidarity. One of the most effective was song.

When the folksinger Woodie Guthrie sang "You can't scare me, I'm sticking to the union"

© woodsy, 2010. Shutterstock Inc.

Figure 5.4—*Protest publications of the women's suffrage movement led to redefining the role of women in American society.*

in 1940, he gave voice to the millions of workers struggling to improve their lives through organizing. The Labor movement goes back to the 1800s, when there were few media outlets to voice their grievances. Newspapers were owned by anti-union publishers and unavailable to speak for the workers. Union organizers would hold group meetings in churches and homes. The songs help transform groups of strangers into a community of union brothers and sisters—regardless of whether they were in Pennsylvania, West Virginia, Utah, or Montana.

According to Joe Glazer, known as "Labor's Troubadour," who performed the songs of work and protest for 60 years, music played a significant role in the Labor movement. "It is not hard to understand the power of union music. Calls to stand up for one's rights and to fight for fair pay and working conditions can rouse any group that feels repressed in their jobs," he said, adding, "When you are in a struggle, it is very important to listen to music."

Many of the songs were based on old spirituals with Bible lyrics replaced by lyrics urging solidarity with the unions, Glazer noted. "'We are climbing Jacob's ladder' became 'We are building a strong union,' for example. 'Jesus is my captain, I shall not be moved' became 'The union is behind us, we shall not be moved.'"

The lyrics of Labor songs reflected the issues that union workers faced. Glazer wrote many of the songs that are still sung today, such as "Automation," which addressed worker fears of being supplanted by machines.

One of Glazer's best-known songs, "The Mill Was Made of Marble," was a commentary on the dreams of textile workers for a cleaner, safer mill. Glazer's song "Too Old to Work" came out of the early and ultimately successful efforts by unions to secure pension benefits. An excerpt of that song follows:

> You work in the factory all of your life. Try to provide for your kids and your wife. When you get too old to produce anymore, they hand you your hat and they show you the door. Too old to work, too old to work, when you're too old to work and you're too young to die. Who will take care of you, how'll you get by when you're too old to work and you're too young to die?

Music helped build unity among union members and gave them the sense they were fighting for the same goals. Music was important to build spirit and solidarity. Glazer explained that at union organizing meetings, the people would hear speeches on what they were fighting for. But hearing a song would get the crowd feeling they were connected.

There was one song that would always energize a crowd: "Solidarity Forever," written in 1915 by Ralph Chaplin, an organizer for the Industrial Workers of the World (IWW), a forerunner of the AFL-CIO. Chaplin wanted to write a song of revolution. He said it should show that workers would always unite to claim their rights. The song, written to the tune of "The Battle Hymn of the Republic," goes as follows:

> When the union's inspiration through the workers' blood shall run,
>
> There can be no power greater anywhere beneath the sun;
>
> Yet what force on earth is weaker than the feeble strength of one,
>
> But the union makes us strong.
>
> CHORUS:
>
> Solidarity forever,
>
> Solidarity forever,
>
> Solidarity forever,
>
> For the union makes us strong.
>
> Is there aught we hold in common with the greedy parasite,
>
> Who would lash us into serfdom and would crush us with his might?

Labor historian Lincoln Cushing describes Labor culture as the soul of working life. "It is the way we share the struggle and joy of earning our daily bread, and includes music, jokes, cartoons, posters, poetry, and murals. It can be noble or crude, insightful or clichéd. It can also be a very effective way to learn truths that may not be evident in surveys and questionnaires, and be the best medium for community building and shop floor organizing."

Joe Hill, an IWW organizer, was one of Labor's greatest songwriters. One of Joe Hill's best-known songs is a protest song based on the classic train song "Casey Jones." In Hill's version, Jones is not working for the railroad but "scabbing for the railroad." In Hill's version, Jones tries to break up a strike, but pays the price. His train crashes and Jones goes to heaven. But strike-breakers are not welcomed at the Pearly Gates, and Jones is sent to Hell by Angels' Union Local No. 23, as the song goes.

> *Casey Jones went to Hell a'flying;*
>
> *"Casey Jones," the Devil said, "Oh fine:*
>
> *Casey Jones, get busy shoveling sulphur;*
>
> *That's what you get for scabbing on the S.P. Line."*

Hill was later executed by a firing squad in Utah, although many believe the charges against him were false. His life was immortalized in the legendary Labor song, "I Dreamed I Saw Joe Hill Last Night." Written by Earl Robinson and Alfred Hayes, the song reaches out to thousands of Labor supporters who knew what Hill had gone through in trying to organize Utah copper miners. The song remains one of the most popular Labor songs today.

> *I dreamed I saw Joe Hill last night,*
>
> *alive as you and me.*
>
> *Says I "But Joe, you're ten years dead"*
>
> *"I never died" said he,*
>
> *"I never died" said he.*
>
> *"The Copper Bosses killed you Joe,*
>
> *They shot you Joe," says I.*
>
> *"Takes more than guns to kill a man"*

> *Says Joe "I didn't die"*
>
> *Says Joe "I didn't die"*
>
> *From San Diego up to Maine,*
>
> *In every mine and mill,*
>
> *Where working men defend their rights,*
>
> *It's there you'll find Joe Hill,*
>
> *It's there you'll find Joe Hill!*

The art and music of the Labor movement has manifested itself in many forms. In 1937, the International Ladies Garment Works Union in 1937 staged its own musical revue with sketches by various authors. The revue, *Needles and Pins*, had a cast recruited entirely from union members. The songs and sketches took on current events and union issues in a lighthearted manner. Most unions embraced music and had written their own songs. Probably the best-known is the song of the Ladies Garment Workers, "Look for the Union Label." The song was a reminder to shop for clothes made in the United States by union workers. Here is an excerpt from that song:

> *Look for the union label*
>
> *When you are buying a coat, dress, or blouse.*
>
> *Remember somewhere our union's sewing*
>
> *Our wages going to feed the kids and run the house,*
>
> *We work hard but who's complaining.*
>
> *Thanks to the I.L.G. we're paying our way.*
>
> *So, always look for the union label,*
>
> *It says we're able*
>
> *To make it in the U.S.A.*

Songs have an enduring quality that other media cannot match. John Steinbeck, the great author and labor supporter, explained why this is so: "The songs of the working people have always been their sharpest statement and the one statement which cannot be destroyed. You can burn books, buy newspapers, you can guard against handbills and pamphlets, but you cannot prevent singing."

That sentiment is seconded by Joe Hill: "A pamphlet, no matter how good, is never read more than once, but a song is learned by heart and repeated over and over; and I maintain that if a person can put a few cold, common sense facts into a song, and dress them up in a cloak of humor to take the dryness off of them, he will succeed in reaching a great number of workers."

The Gay and Lesbian Community

The communication processes through which culture changes can involve complex interplays among the activities of sub-communities, the news media, and the entertainment media. A striking example is the way that gay men and lesbians have been increasingly accepted into the mainstream American community. In the 1950s, novelist Alan Drury wrote the political thriller *Advise and Consent*, in which a central character, a U.S. senator, committed suicide because he was about to be exposed as having a same-sex escapade during World War II. The plotline was entirely plausible at the time. Although homosexuality has been an aspect of sexuality since Biblical times, in the United States in the middle of the 20th century, it could not even be mentioned. At the time, of course, married heterosexual couples were not allowed to be shown in the same bed on television either.

If homosexuality was seen as a deeply buried secret, it burst into public view on June 28, 1969, when the police in New York City raided the Stonewall Inn, a bar in which gay men liked to congregate. Although police raids on gay bars were commonplace—homosexuality was actually against the law at that time—in this case, the men fought back, and for the next several days, gay men and lesbians rioted, protesting against discrimination and police harassment. In what became known as the "Stonewall Riots," gays and lesbians took inspiration from the civil rights movement and the antiwar movement's defiance of authority to fight for fundamental rights. After the Stonewall Riots, the rights of gays and lesbians

to be left alone and not to be the subjected to discrimination was on the political agenda.

But as gays and lesbians pressed to be treated the same as every other U.S. citizen, publicly making that claim with the first Gay Pride Parade in New York in 1970, they were met with a fierce backlash, fueled in large part by religious conservatives. In 1977, when a law was passed in Florida's Miami-Dade County banning discrimination on the basis of sexual orientation, a campaign to repeal the ordinance was led by Anita Bryant, who was known at the time as the spokesperson for Florida orange juice.

For much of the next two decades, every step forward for equal rights for the gay and lesbian communities was met by fierce resistance. While gay community media such as *The Advocate* pressed the case for equality, the mainstream media were generally hostile to gays and lesbians. Established in 1967 initially as a newsletter for a gay-rights organization called Personal Rights in Defense and Education (PRIDE), T*he Advocate* is the most established newspaper serving the gay, lesbian, bisexual, and transgender (GBLT) community. It was started after a police raid on the Black Cat Tavern, a gay bar in Los Angeles.

But if the gay and lesbian communities found the mainstream basically inhospitable to their cause, the situation was different in the entertainment media. Johnny Carson, the very popular host of *The Tonight Show*, the dominant late-night television show in that period, began cracking jokes about Anita Bryant. Bryant was also mocked on the television show *The Golden Girls*, a situation comedy that featured four senior-citizen women. Celebrities such as Mary Tyler Moore and Barbra Streisand endorsed gay rights.

In the 1980s, AIDS became a national epidemic, and in 1985, beloved movie star Rock Hudson died of the disease. Hudson's friend, actress Elizabeth Taylor, considered one of the most beautiful women of the time, became a champion for AIDS victims.

During this period, gay characters began to show up in movies, on television, and on the stage.

In 1970, the movie *The Boys in the Band* was one of the first full-length feature films that focused on the lives of gay men. In it, a straight man inadvertently attends a party given by seven gay men. In 1975, the television show *Hot L Baltimore*, which showed the lives of people in the seedy Hotel Baltimore, featured a gay couple. They were the first gay couple on a network television series.

In the late 1980s, two men were shown slipping into bed at the end of an episode of the series *Thirtysomething*. By the 1990s, gay characters were routinely portrayed on television. The show *Will and Grace* featured a gay man and a woman who was his best friend. Ellen DeGeneres came out as a lesbian on her show, *Ellen*. By the 2000s, cable television had hit shows featuring primarily gay casts, such as *The L Word* and *Queer as Folk*.

Movies also were increasingly open to portraying gay men and women. In 1993, Tom Hanks, at that point one of the most popular and acclaimed actors in the United States, portrayed a gay lawyer with AIDS in the movie *Philadelphia*. In 2005, *Brokeback Mountain* was a story of two young cowboys who had an unanticipated gay encounter. The movie won three Academy Awards.

The political struggle for gay rights has not yet ended. But the gays' and lesbians' struggle for acceptance in the broader American culture has been assisted by their portrayal in the entertainment media, both on television and in the movies. When a beloved actor such as Rock Hudson is gay and an acclaimed actor such as Tom Hanks sympathetically portrays a gay character, being gay is no longer something that has to be hidden. It can be spoken and discussed openly and with pride. Ellen DeGeneres, whose first show was forced off the air after it was revealed that she was a lesbian 1990s, emerged as one of the most popular women on television for her daytime talk show by 2009. Research showed that she was almost as popular as the reigning queen of daytime television, Oprah Winfrey (see Figure 5.5).

NEW KINDS OF COMMUNITIES

The emergence of new media has enabled the creation of many different types of communities. One of the most interesting new social groupings is what are known as "fan communities" and "fan culture." Fan culture represents the evolution of what used to be called "fan clubs," but which have been enhanced because of the new methods of communication, particularly interactive communication, available. Put simply, fans make up a social network based on their interest in a particular "text." That text can be a sports team, a television show, a kind of music or a specific band, a video game, a book or books by a specific author, an entire genre such as science fiction literature, or many other kinds of texts that have some component of symbolic meanings. Fans develop a deep personal identification, both with the text itself and often with the other fans as well.

But being a fan can involve much more than simply appreciating, enjoying, or even knowing a lot about a particular text. With the growth first of television and then the Internet, fans have become able to interact with their texts more deeply and influence both the production and the meaning of specific texts. Perhaps the paradigmatic fan community is the community of "Trekkies," people who basically know everything

Figure 5.5—*The entertainment media helped to move forward the cause of gay and lesbian rights.*

there is to know about the television show *Star Trek* and the spinoffs and movies that followed. Trekkies hold conventions in which they dress in appropriate costumes and assume roles played in harmony with the fictional characters.

Within the scope of contemporary popular culture, Trekkies are often seen as social misfits who place far too much importance on a trivial and meaningless television show. Indeed, Trekkies were even mocked on the television show *Saturday Night Live* by guest host William Shatner, who played the lead role of Captain James Kirk on the original *Star Trek* series. "Get a life," he importuned the actors playing Trekkies.

However, digital media scholar Henry Jenkins and others provide an alternative perspective on fan culture. According to Jenkins, fan communities have specific characteristics. Fans engage with their selected texts deeply, giving them their undivided attention. Indeed, they engage with their texts in much the same way that a professor of literature might engage with Shakespeare, returning to specific texts over and over again, and translate this engagement into social interaction with other fans. Moreover, they develop both an emotional attachment and critical distance from the texts.

Moreover, fan communities develop as fans learn to "read" their texts in similar ways. In other words, they become acculturated into the fan community. Through communication, they build community and begin to see the world—at least the part of the world they share—through a similar interpretive lens. These intense interpretive practices lead to the construction of a "meta-text" that is usually richer than the original texts. Fans also will speak back to the creators of a specific text and obliterate the line between creator and consumer. Fan culture offers alternative social communities to its members.

The development of YouTube and other large-scale Web sites and blogs in which users create their own content has opened new vehicles for fan communities. Fans can now rework the texts to which they are devoted. As one reporter studying fans put it, no matter how obsessed somebody is with a piece of media, there is always somebody more obsessed, and that person is usually found on the Internet.

The idea that fans can rework content produced by others to reshape its meaning is called participatory culture. In fan communities, the fans no longer simply "consume"—that is read, watch, or listen to different products—they make those products their own and use them in their own ways, creating something new and vital. In the process, they build communities with other people doing the same thing. The Internet has provided a platform for all sorts of new fan communities. People can gather around new bands via their pages on Facebook or follow the blogs of their favorite writers, interacting directly with them through the comments section (see Figure 5.6).

Generally, fan communities, political movements, and of course geographic communities rely on some sort of face-to-face communication that either serves as the basis for, or is a result of, people interacting in other ways. The spread of the Internet has enabled a new kind of community, however, a community in which the participants only interact with one another online and never see or meet each other face-to-face. These kinds of social groups are known as virtual communities. The word virtual implies a particular quality for these communities. They operate as if they were real communities, but they are not. Some observers, however, argue that virtual communities are actually a new form of real communities.

Figure 5.6—*Participatory cultures on the Internet are redefining the idea of community.*

Virtual communities began to develop almost from the time that widespread computer networks began to develop. One of the first applications developed for computer networks was games—first simple shoot-'em-up games that could be played by multiple players in different locations, and then more complex role-playing games, where, once again, the players could be scattered across the country and even the world.

Even in these early days, in her books *The Second Self* and *Life on the Screen*, sociologist Sherry Turkle argued that the interactions people had with one another via computer networks were significant psychologically, and the identities players assumed in role-playing games represented important aspects of their personalities. In other words, people's interactions, personalities, and social interactions online were as "real" as their counterparts in the physical world.

As Internet technology improved and became more ubiquitous, the ways for people to meet and interact online grew. In the 1980s, people began to interact through what were called newsgroups, in which people with specific interests could post messages to a specific host computer, and that message would be redistributed to "subscribers" to that newsgroup. People with all sorts of interests ranging from sadomasochism to fine wines organized themselves around newsgroups. In the mid- to late 1980s, listservs, or automated e-mail lists, which once again allowed groups of people to communicate effortlessly with one another, became popular. That was followed by chat rooms, where people from different locations could interact with one another in real time. As with newsgroups, chat rooms covering a huge number of topics emerged.

Online communication among participants who had never met face-to-face became increasingly important in people's lives. In 1984, Stewart Brand, author of *The Whole Earth Catalogue* and a major figure in the counterculture of the 1960s and 1970s, established what he called *The Whole Earth 'Lectric Link*, known as The WELL. With a wide range of chat rooms and other communication mechanisms, The WELL became as significant a community to the participants as the towns in which they actually lived, if not more so. The WELL came to be seen as the seminal virtual community.

While the development of the World Wide Web in the 1990s continued to expand the number of participants in virtual communities, it was the creation of Facebook and Second Life that put a singular focus on the possibilities and possible impacts of virtual communities and social relationships conducted solely online. Created in 2005 by Mark Zuckerberg, then a student at Harvard University, and some of his friends, Facebook was first intended to be a computerized equivalent of the face book that colleges and universities printed to welcome their first-year students. Within a couple of years, Facebook mushroomed into a global social network and a primary method of communication for millions of high school and college students and then younger children and adults as well.

Two features of Facebook are particularly notable. First, people can create "fan pages" on very specific, even trivial, topics and attract interested people, basically in the blink of an eye. Second, people can "friend" one another, agreeing to link Facebook pages. The concept of "friending" has called into question the concept of what it means to be somebody's "friend." Many people on Facebook have significantly more than 500 "friends." Celebrities and politicians might have millions of "friends." Clearly, being a friend on Facebook does not necessarily have the same connotation as the traditional meaning of being a friend. Nonetheless, people who have "friended" one another on Facebook do have some sort of relationship and can be a part of some sort of community. The strength and social ties of an online community are not always clear.

Facebook pages usually have information and pictures about a person's life, which are accessible online. Even more anchored online are 3-D immersive social environments such as Second Life, a social world created by its members. People who join Second Life construct avatars to represent themselves in any way they would like. The avatars then interact with one another. On some level, any activity that can take place in the physical world can take place in Second Life, albeit virtually. The relationship of the avatar to the person who created and controls the avatar, as well as those of the social relationships built in Second Life to actual social relationships, is perplexing. In fact, in the early days of role-playing games—which can be considered the conceptual foundation for Second Life—Sherry Turkle once encountered an avatar that had been named "Sherry Turkle." Was the online Sherry Turkle as "real" as the sociologist Sherry Turkle? The answer depends, in part at least, on the context about which it is asked.

CONCLUSION

Communication is the essential human process for the development of community, or the idea that people both share something in common and are in some way linked to one another. Specific forms of communication enable different kinds of community. When people could communicate only orally, extended families, clans, and tribes were the primary form of communication. Written communication allowed for the development of religion and broadened people's sense of community.

As in most other areas of social life, the printing press and printing created a revolution in the idea of community. Over time, a sense of community developed to encompass nation-states. Regional languages gave way to single, dominant national languages, and large areas of land were ruled by a central government. In Western democracies, the rule of law rather than rule by a single individual became more commonplace.

Because different social groups could control the use of different media, subgroups use media to reinforce their sense of social identity. In particular, ethnic and racial minority groups use communication processes both to reinforce their sense of community and to present their perspectives to the larger community within which they live. Communication is critical to effect social and cultural change within broader communities.

The creation of the Internet has enabled the development of new kinds of communities. Fan communities, communities that gather around a specific social or cultural text, have the ability to use those texts in novel ways, creating new meanings for them and new kinds of communities around them. Further, the Internet has led to the creation of virtual communities, communities that function entirely and exclusively online.

"I HEAR SINGING IN THE AIR": SINGING AS COMMUNICATION STRATEGY

by Kerran L. Sanger

History has never known a protest movement so rich in song as the civil rights movement. Nor a movement in which songs are as important.[1]

During the years of the civil rights movement, activists sought strategies to communicate with one another as well as with people outside the movement's vanguard. Committed to nonviolence, the activists searched for potentially powerful forms of communication consistent with the ideals of the group. The people who made up the movement were, by and large, relatively powerless as individuals, but they chose to join together in acts designed to communicate their unified commitment to fight injustice. They eschewed sole reliance on traditional public address, opting often for actions that can be considered as purposeful, or rhetorical. These actions included sit-ins, mass demonstrations, Freedom Rides, and other forms of civil disobedience. And during all of these gatherings, whenever the activists met, they engaged in the behavior of singing, perhaps the most powerful rhetorical behavior of all in the civil rights movement.

This discussion of the act of singing presumes that the activists' choice to sing is interesting in its own right—in the United States, singing is not that common a communication option. The activists of the civil rights movement sang often, with clear purpose and great confidence. The freedom songs of the civil rights were sung during mass meetings, in jails, in churches, and in isolation, were sung by the elderly, by college students, by children, and by those of indeterminate age, were sung in fear, desperation, and jubilation. Activists saw these songs, such as "We Shall Overcome," "Keep Your Eyes on the Prize," and "Oh Freedom" as central to their success in opposing segregation and inequality. How do we know the activists felt this way? Listen. . .

Singing is the backbone and the balm of this movement.

[Singing] is like an angel watching over you.

READING NOTES

_____

_____

_____

_____

_____

This song represented the coming together ... You felt uplifted and involved in a great battle and a great struggle.

You sing the songs which symbolize transformation, which make that revolution of courage inside you.

The movement without songs would have been like birds without wings.

There was music in everything we did.

One cannot describe the vitality and emotion ... [singing] generates power that is indescribable.

When you got through singing ... you could walk over a bed of hot coals, and you wouldn't notice.

There is no armor more impenetrable than song.[2]

These claims are only a few that activists have made regarding the role of the freedom songs in their lives and their struggle. They have a great deal more to tell us about their singing—how it worked for them as a strategy and why it engendered such strong feelings among them. A thorough study of their testimony about singing indicates that the activists strongly believed the songs were an essential aspect of the total persuasive strategy of the civil rights movement. Before we turn to a close study of the song lyrics, it is important to understand what the behavior of singing meant for the activists.

That the activists felt song to provide them with a special power is evident in their testimony, where they asserted that song was central to the progress of the movement. Guy Carawan was Music Director at the Highlander Folk School and in that capacity he encouraged singing among civil rights activists. Carawan made bold claims regarding the power of the songs to accomplish great things in the movement:

> *Freedom songs today are sung in many kinds of situations: at mass meetings, prayer vigils, demonstrations, before Freedom Rides and Sit-Ins, in paddy wagons and jails, at conferences, work-shops and informal gatherings.*

> *They are sung to bolster spirits, to gain new courage and to increase the sense of unity. The singing sometimes disarms jail guards, policemen, bystanders and mob participants of their hostilities.[3]*

Bob Cohen, director of the Mississippi Caravan of Music, similarly addressed the far-reaching effects of the singing when he argued that "somehow you can go in the face of violence and death, cynicism and inaction of the FBI, the indifference of the Federal Government when you can sing with your band of brothers."[4] According to these activists, singing provided movement participants with significant power to face the internal enemies of fear and doubt as well as the external trials of the movement.

When the activists spoke of their singing and its effects, it was often in tones of awe, as if they could not quite believe what their singing could accomplish. In speaking of the unofficial anthem of the movement, "We Shall Overcome," Wyatt Tee Walker said simply that "it generates power that is indescribable."[5] Candie Carawan recounted her experience in jail and her realization there that songs could be more than a source of entertainment. She said, "Never had I heard such singing. Spirituals, pop tunes, hymns, and even slurpy old love songs all became so powerful."[6] Even onlookers to the movement, such as white journalist Pat Watters, were affected by the mood of the mass meetings—"mystical, inspired and excited, ecstatic"—and the music there that "cannot be described—or recaptured."[7] These people, and seemingly all others who experienced the singing of the civil rights movement, cast song as a motive force in that struggle, a force giving the participants the strength to move forward and to involve others.

The songs figured so greatly in the minds of some activists that they expressed doubt that the movement could progress or succeed without singing. Bernice Reagon, for instance, claimed that "by the end of the Freedom Rides, the songs of the Sit-ins, bus and jail

READING NOTES

_____

_____

_____

_____

_____

experiences were considered essential for organizing. No mass meeting could be successfully carried off without songs."[8] Both Cordell Reagon and Student Nonviolent Coordinating Committee (SNCC) field secretary Charles Jones remarked on the centrality of the songs to the campaign in Albany, Georgia. According to Reagon,

> *without the songs, the Albany movement could not have been. They sang these songs on the [picket] line and off the line, day in and day out, and went to bed humming "We Shall Overcome."*

Jones's words echoed Reagon's when he said simply "there could have been no Albany Movement without music."[9] In singing, activists felt they had found an activity that united them, shielded them from harm, and gave them the very power and strength to move forward.

It might be argued, of course, that the activists had no evidence of any link between singing and the powers they attributed to it. The important consideration is not whether singing actually allowed activists to accomplish all the things they claimed for it but, rather, that they *believed* it did. If activists believed singing provided them with the strength to face difficult situations, then when they sang, they were likely to find that, in fact, they did feel stronger. The claims they made about the communicative power of song fostered an attitude toward singing among participants in the movement, and gave this form of communication enormous power in their lives—the power that comes with expectations.

Scholars suggest that singing differs from other forms of communication, in that it more fully involves those who take part. Rhetorical critics argue that musical sound engages human feeling in significant ways because its kinesthetic appeal promotes a physiological and psychological response.[10] In many forms of demonstration, civil rights activists were involved both by their physical presence and by the act of protest—whether it was marching, sitting-in, or swaying with the music of a song. In addition, when the activists sang, their involvement grew to include not only their presence and physical movement, all rhetorical insofar as they constituted purposeful action, but the voicing of their commitment as well.

Singing was most often engaged in during other types of demonstration, which added another layer of communication to the mass marches. The communication of the movement was usually much more than a single voice speaking in a quiet room to silent listeners. Instead, it was a rich mixture of singing, listening, marching, swaying, and other symbolic acts. The involvement was much greater and, potentially, much more influential when communication had several layers of expression.

Singing was, perhaps, most important to activists when other symbolic acts were denied them. According to the activists, some of the most fervent and inspired singing in the movement took place in the cells of Parchman Penitentiary and the Hinds County Jail in Mississippi where the Freedom Riders were imprisoned. In jail, many other forms of direct action were denied the activists but, in singing, they were able to find a positive rhetorical place between passivity and acts of violence. Euvester Simpson referred to time she spent in jail as a result of trying to register to vote, and remarked that the "only way we could get through that ordeal was to sing any song that came to mind."[11] By singing, the activists continued to communicate their refusal to be rendered impotent or to be drawn to the level of their adversaries. Their jailers recognized the power that their prisoners held when they sang and often threatened the activists. Zinn reported that:

> *Charles Sherrod had been taken with a group of demonstrators to "Terrible" Terrell County, escorted there by Sheriff Zeke Mathews, who announced: "There'll be no damn singin' and no damn prayin' in my jail."[12]*

READING NOTES

_____

_____

_____

_____

_____

For civil rights activists, the choice of music as a mode of communication was a choice consistent with their desire to act and their belief that song was essentially symbolic act. It complemented the other acts of the civil rights movement and sometimes stood alone, or combined with prayer, as the only positive communication outlet available to the protestors.

The activists' belief in the power of song and its "correctness" for meeting their needs meant that activists often chose singing even when other options, like speaking, were available. In their comments, activists equated song with speech or, often, asserted that song did for them what speech could not. Bob Cohen's description of Fannie Lou Hamer indicated that, for this particular black leader, song was used in essentially the same way that speeches were:

> When Mrs. Hamer finishes singing a few freedom songs one is aware that he has truly heard a fine political speech, stripped of the usual rhetoric and filled with the anger and determination of the civil rights movement. And on the other hand in her speeches there is the constant thunder and drive of music.[13]

Cohen's comments equated political speaking and singing but he also subtly argued for the superiority of singing when he claimed that song retained its power without the bombast and meaningless words so often associated with political speaking.

Speech was insufficient not only for black leaders like Hamer but for the average person as well, according to the activists. Bernice Reagon claimed that, in Albany, Georgia "masses of people had much to say about their condition and found the language with which to speak in the songs."[14] Whether the implication here was that these people were inarticulate in their speaking or that they were not listened to when they spoke is less important than the assertion that they found an outlet to overcome such difficulties.

Activists also described themselves as turning to song when they were so overwhelmed by one emotion or another that speaking seemed not to fulfill their desire to communicate. One described a preacher as follows:

> The sermon began as a talk and ended as a song. The preacher jumped up and down and had tears running down his face. He finally was overcome by the sheer power of his words and started singing
>
> "This Little Light of Mine" in the middle of a sentence.[15]

Josh Dunson, in his book *Freedom in the Air*, also commented on the tendency for song to take over when speech fell short, saying, "often, emotion is too strong to come out in words, so a new song is born."[16] The activists promoted their songs as providing a special outlet for their excitement and fears, an outlet unavailable elsewhere.

As an outlet for strong emotion, song became, according to the activists, more forceful and vital than speech. Although logic dictates that southern police would have as much power to silence singing activists as chanting or speaking activists, movement participants felt the singing was less likely to be quelled. Bernice Reagon argued that "with a song, there was nothing they could do to block what we were saying," while Willie Peacock also commented that, when activists sang, "there is nothing the police can do to stop you. They can put you in jail, but you can sing in jail."[17] Reagon seems to have summed up the attitude of the activists when she said, simply, that, for blacks in the civil rights movement, "the songs were more powerful than spoken conversation."[18]

The commentary of the songleaders indicates that they emphatically did not conceive of the singing that accompanied nearly every aspect of the movement as

READING NOTES

_____

_____

_____

_____

_____

148

merely expressive or as entertainment. Although these are often accepted as the functions of song, the singers in the civil rights movement held the strong belief that song communicated and, in fact, did so in ways that surpassed speech.

It is worthwhile to know that the activists held strong faith in their singing but questions remain regarding the source of the power of song. What about singing made that particular behavior stand out as powerful in the activists' minds? It is clear that the special appeal of singing came, in part, from the long tradition of protest singing in African-American culture.

THE AFRICAN AMERICAN SONG TRADITION

The songs sung during the civil rights movement were drawn, primarily, from black tradition. Some had their roots in the songs of slavery and in the years immediately following the Civil War. Others appeared later in African American tradition, as gospel songs. Still others came to the tradition from black laborers who took part in the labor movements of the 1930s and 1940s, where protest singing was considered an important aspect of the struggle. The existence of such a long-standing tradition created a special context for singing in the civil rights movement.

The tradition of singing among Africans and African Americans is a long and tenacious one. When the first Africans were brought to America in large numbers as slaves, they brought with them a musical tradition that has remained important in black life, and that differs from many Western conceptions of music.[19] Black music scholars argue that in many African cultures, music has traditionally been a pervasive element in daily life. John Lovell wrote of the African tradition of the "integrating of every action and thought into song, and of song into every thought and action,"[20] and

Gerhard Putschogl concurred, saying that, "it cannot be stressed enough that black music and 'black life' cannot be separated. Both influence and depend on each other."[21] Scholars also note the extent to which all people, not just designated "entertainers," made singing one of their primary forms of communication in African cultures. As Lovell put it, the "African rarely plays *for* someone as Westerners do; he usually plays *with* someone. An inactive audience to a musical performance simply does not exist."[22]

ENDNOTES

1. Karen Lebacqz, *Professional Ethics* (Nashville: Abingdon, 1985), 77–91.

2. From "Which Side Are You On?"

3. From "Keep Your Eyes on the Prize" and "Michael Row the Boat Ashore."

4. From "Come By Here" and "Keep Your Eyes on the Prize."

5. From "Do What the Spirit Say Do," "I Love Everybody," and "Hallelujah, I'm A-Traveling."

6. From "We Shall Overcome." "I Love Everybody." "Come By Here," and "I Love Everybody."

7. First two examples from "Come By Here." Third example from "Michael Row the Boat Ashore."

8. From "Over My Head I See Freedom in the Air" and "This Little Light of Mine."

9. From "Which Side Are You On?"

10. From "Hallelujah. I'm A-Traveling," "I'm On My Way to Freedom Land," and "Jacob's Ladder."

11. W. Edson Richmond, "The American Lyric Tradition," in *Our Living Traditions: An Introduction to American Folklore*, ed. Tristram P. Coffin (New York: Basic, 1968), 95.

12. Roger Abrahams and George Foss, *Anglo-American Folksong Style* (Englewood Cliffs: Prentice-Hall, 1968), 87.

13. Abrahams and Foss, *Anglo-American Folksong*, 37.

14. Abrahams and Foss, *Anglo-American Folksong*, 49, 57.

READING NOTES

_____

_____

_____

_____

_____

15. Carroll Arnold, *Criticism of Oral Rhetoric* (Columbus, OII: Merrill, 1974), 144.

16. David King Dunaway, *How Can I Keep From Singing?: Pete Seeger* (New York: Da Capo, 1981), 236.

17. From "Ain't Gonna Let Nobody Turn Me 'Round" and "Hallelujah, I'm A-Traveling."

18. From "Michael Row the Boat Ashore."

19. Roderick P. Hart, *Modern Rhetorical Criticism* (Glenview, IL: Scott, Foresman, 1990), 351.

20. Guy Carawan and Candie Carawan, *We Shall Overcome!: Songs of the Southern Freedom Movement* (New York: Oak, 1963), 8; Carawan and Carawan, *We Shall Overcome*, 8; Esau Jenkins in Guy Carawan and Candie Carawan, *Freedom Is a Constant Struggle: Songs of the Freedom Movement* (New York: Oak, 1968), 135; Julius Lester in Bernice Johnson Reagon, "Songs of the Civil Rights Movement 1955-1965: A Study in Culture History" (Ph.D. diss., Howard University, Washington, D.C., 1975), 161; Reagon, "Songs of the Civil Rights Movement," 132; Bernice Johnson Reagon, booklet accompanying three phonodises, *Voices of the Civil Rights Movement: Black American Freedom Songs 1960-1966* (Washington: Smithsonian Institution, Program in Black American Culture, 1980), 6.

21. Willie Peacock in Pete Seeger and Bob Reiser, *Everybody Says Freedom* (New York: W.W. Norton, 1989), 180; Jane Stembridge in Seeger and Reiser, *Everybody Says*, 36.

22. Hollis Watkins in Seeger and Reiser, *Everybody Says*, 179-180.

READING NOTES

_____

_____

_____

_____

_____

Chapter
(6)

Communication and Politics

"Were it left to me to decide whether we should have a government without newspapers, or newspapers without a government, I should not hesitate a moment to prefer the latter."

— THOMAS JEFFERSON

On February 27, 1860, in the middle of a cold and snowy winter, Abraham Lincoln, then a relatively obscure politician from Illinois, gave a speech before 1,500 people at Cooper Union in New York City. He was not yet a candidate, much less the front-runner, seeking the Republican nomination for the presidency. Established just a year earlier, Cooper Union was a radical new experiment in higher education in the United States, founded on its benefactor Peter Cooper's belief that education should be free. Lincoln had been invited to address the audience by the Young Men's Republican Union, which included Horace Greeley and William Cullen Bryant, two major newspapers editors at the time, on its board of directors. Both Greeley and Bryant opposed the efforts of William Seward, the governor of New York, to secure the Republican nomination for the presidency. At that point, Seward was seen as the favored candidate.

Constructed in some ways like a lawyer's brief and absent flowery language, Lincoln spoke for more than an hour. In the speech, Lincoln defended the right of the Federal government to control slavery in the federal territories, attacked the Southern states for threatening to secede from the Union if a Republican were elected president, and ended with a call to action for Republicans, closing the speech with the lines "Let us have faith that right makes might, and in that faith, let us, to the end, dare to do our duty as we understand it."

The audience's response was electrifying. One attendee reported that although he was not very impressed by Lincoln when he rose to speak, by the end, "I was on my feet like the rest, yelling like a wild Indian, cheering this wonderful man." The entire speech was printed in several New York newspapers—*The New York Times* ran it on its front page—and circulated throughout the country as campaign literature. The speech, historians agree, set Lincoln on the road that resulted in his winning the Republican presidential nomination that summer and the Presidential election itself that fall.

On July 27, 2004, an obscure state senator from Illinois who was running for the U.S. Senate was selected to give the keynote address to the Democratic National Convention that would nominate Senator John Kerry, a Democrat from Massachusetts, as a candidate for the presidency of the United States. On that night, Barack Obama delivered a variation of what had been his standard stump speech.

In a memorable passage, Obama said, "... there's not a liberal America and a conservative America; there's the United States of America. There's not a black America and white America and Latino America and Asian America; there's the United States of America. The pundits like to slice and dice our country into red states and blue states: red states for Republicans, blue States for Democrats. But I've got news for them, too. We worship an awesome God in the blue states, and we don't like federal agents poking around our libraries in the red states. We coach Little League in the blue states and, yes, we've got some gay friends in the red states. There are patriots who opposed the war in Iraq, and there are patriots who supported the war in Iraq. We are one people, all of us pledging allegiance to the stars and stripes, all of us defending the United States of America."

Broadcast live by television to millions of people, the impact was electrifying. It was immediately clear than a new political star had emerged onto the stage of national politics. That year, Obama won his Senate race with 70 percent of the vote. In 2008, he was elected president of the United States, the first African American to hold that office.

Open and free communication is essential to democracy. One of the primary reasons that the First Amendment was added to the U.S. Constitution was to protect and safeguard robust political speech. In some ways, political

communication has remained consistent over time. Both Lincoln and Obama delivered powerful addresses in person to specific audiences that catapulted their careers to the highest level. On the other hand, political communication has radically changed. A transcript and news of Lincoln's speech traveled relatively slowly through the country, printed and reprinted in newspapers in cities large and small. Obama's speech was seen as it was delivered by millions of people and then was the subject of nearly endless commentary, also on television, during the course of the next several days. The changes in the methods of communication, as well as the consistency, are significant.

This chapter's aims to

- examine the close links between media systems and the political process,

- chronicle several key episodes in which the media had a major political impact,

- identify the mass media as the mechanism through which people have a voice in public affairs, and

- understand the media strategies people use to influence the public agenda.

Required Reading: Since the 1990s, blogs and online media have played an increasingly significant role in political communication. Talking Points Memo (www.talkingpointsmemo.com) is a leading liberal blog while Red States (www.redstate.com) claims to be the conservative blog most widely read on Capitol Hill. Along the same lines, The Huffington Post (www.huffingtonpost.com) covers politics from a liberal perspective while Politico.com (www.politico.com) has a slightly right-of-center tilt, according to some observers. For more than half a century, the mainstream media claimed to be politically neutral. But with the development of the blogosphere and the increase in ratings in the conservatively oriented Fox News and the more liberal MSNBC cable networks, political neutral media appear to be losing their audience.

REVOLUTIONARY COMMUNICATION

On March 23, 1775, Patrick Henry, a radical advocate for American independence, gave a speech to the Virginia House of Burgesses, the lower house of the colony's legislative assembly. Meeting at St. John's Church in Richmond, the delegates were debating how to respond to the approaching British Army. Henry introduced resolutions calling for the colony to arm a militia for its defense. According to Henry's biographer William Wirt, Henry closed his speech with rousing words that have lived on in American history.

"I know not what course others may take," Henry is reported to have said. "But as for me, give me liberty, or give me death!" The chamber erupted after his speech and narrowly passed the resolution. Virginia thus joined Massachusetts in defiance of the British.

Henry's stirring speech was not delivered to a general audience, nor was it meant to arouse public sentiment. The speech was given as a part of a debate in the state legislature and meant to influence the debate being conducted by elected delegates. In fact, during the founding of the United States, most significant political communication was conducted among the propertied elite and not aimed at the people. Writing letters was a common way for elites to communicate with each other, as was closed meetings. Indeed, the Continental Congresses, the Constitutional Convention that drafted the U.S. Constitution, and even (until 1794) the U.S. Senate met behind closed doors.

Political discourse was not completely confined to the elite in the colonies, however. After the imposition of the Stamp Act in 1765, which required colonists to pay a tax on all legal documents, licenses, playing cards and newspapers, vocal opposition to British rule began to rise. Though the amount raised by the tax, proceeds from which were intended to pay for the defense of the colonial frontier, was not great, the idea that the British Parliament could impose a tax on the colonies without the approval of the colonial legislatures touched off a storm of protests and helped fuel the drive for independence.

In response to the Stamp Act and other taxes imposed by the British government in London that seemed onerous or unjust, the colonists developed several methods of communication to express their opinions and rally popular opinion. They formed committees of correspondence, widening the community of readers who would receive regular updates about events in different towns. They convened congresses and conventions to debate and air their grievances. While newspapers were small, local, and generally issued weekly or less frequently, they freely published material that first appeared elsewhere, often anonymously, making it hard to punish an author of offensive materials. Newspapers played a role in the development of a relatively informal, multilayered national news exchange.

Another important form of political communication of the period was the pamphlet. Once again, often written anonymously, popular pamphlets circulated widely. *Common Sense* by Thomas Paine was the most prominent of the pamphlets published in the Revolutionary War period. Described as the most influential tract of the American Revolution, *Common Sense* was published anonymously in January 1776. Placing blame for the "suffering" in the colonies directly on King George III, Paine called for an immediate declaration of independence. Written in plain language, the 48-page pamphlet was clearly aimed at the general, literate public and not just the elite. It clearly resonated with public sentiment. *Common Sense* sold more than 100,000 copies in the first three months after its publication and 500,000 copies in the first year.

The founders of the United States clearly envisioned a political system in which popular sentiment was tempered by more dispassionate and reasoned discourse. The House of Representatives was supposed to represent popular opinion. The Senate was intended to be a more deliberative body. Congress was supposed to provide a check on the president, and the president checked the Congress. After 1801, the Supreme Court assumed the role of guardian of the Constitution.

Within this scheme, the press is supposed to supply the information needed by an informed electorate as well as be agents of robust debate. To ensure these goals were achieved, postal rates for newspapers were subsidized, making it very inexpensive for them to circulate widely, and the First Amendment was passed, ensuring robust debate without fear of retribution, at least not on the federal level (see Figure 6.1).

However, almost as soon as the U.S. Constitution was passed in 1787, the leaders of the revolution fractured into competing factions over the issue of the role of the Federal government in national life and its relationship to state governments. One camp, led by Alexander Hamilton, argued for a strong central government. The Federalists, as this group came to be called, had promulgated their vision of the role of the national government in a series of essays that had appeared in the *New York Independent Journal* from October 1787 to April 1788, while the Constitution was in the process of ratification by the states. In total, 85 essays were written by Hamilton, James Madison,

Figure 6.1—*Speech and press freedoms guaranteed by the First Amendment to the U.S. Constitution allow for robust public debate about government and politics.*

and John Jay under the pen name "Publius," suggesting that a strong central government as envisioned in the proposed constitution would help protect the rights of the people from the whims of an unpredictable majority and would allow the United States to better compete on the world stage.

After the ratification of the Constitution, however, the actual role of the Federal government was subject to heated dispute. With the French Revolution and its revolutionary ideals setting the context, Thomas Jefferson and James Madison argued that centralized power was dangerous and anti-republican and that each state should have a larger say in its own affairs. To the dismay of George Washington, two political parties—the Federalists, led by Hamilton and John Adams, and the Democrat-Republicans, led by Jefferson and Madison—emerged and were quickly attacking each other.

In this period, newspapers emerged that became one of the chief weapons of attack for both political parties. In 1789, John Fenno set up the *Gazette of the United States*, in part to promote the ideas of the Federalist Party. In response, Benjamin Franklin Bache established the *Aurora* in Philadelphia in 1790. The exchanges in the newspapers were harsh and vituperative, hardly the sort of reasoned debate envisioned as the touchstone of democracy. Leaders of both parties were charged with all sorts of chicanery ranging from graft to sexual improprieties. Because the United States was the first democratic country in the modern world, the idea of a loyal opposition had not yet been invented. Attacks in newspapers were seen as treason.

In 1798, during the administration of John Adams, Congress passed the Sedition Act, which made it a crime to write maliciously about the Federal government and bring it into contempt. Following the passage of the act, several Republican editors were jailed. The law was allowed to lapse when Thomas Jefferson assumed office.

THE EMERGENCE OF POPULAR DEMOCRACY

For the next generation, relatively small and expensive newspapers were among the chief vehicles for political communications. These newspapers were often subsidized by the holders of political office and received printing contracts from the party with which they were aligned. But by the 1830s, several factors began to reshape political communication. First, the property qualifications for the right to vote were dropped, expanding the electorate to all white men. Second, the United States was beginning to industrialize, migration to large urban centers was accelerating, and literacy rates were climbing.

In response to these factors and improvements in printing technology, in the mid-1830s, entrepreneurial journalists such as James Gordon Bennett and Benjamin Day in New York, and others in Boston, Philadelphia, Baltimore, and elsewhere, cut the price of their daily newspapers to a penny from the six cents it had been before. The impact was immediate and twofold. Average circulations climbed by a factor of ten, to 30,000 copies per day or more. Newspapers were no longer dependent on political or commercial patrons and the printing contracts they could provide to survive. They became commercially independent, which meant they could be more independent politically as well.

The same changes that led to the "penny press" also influenced the practice of politics and political communication in other ways. In 1817, Martin Van Buren, a leading politician in New York, established the first statewide political machine. Deftly using political patronage to place allies into key government positions, he and a group of men associated with him were able to control much of New York politics for a generation. Using the same tactics, Van Buren established the first national political party, the Democratic Party, arguing that a national party was needed to mediate between the conflicting interests of the North and South. Having a permanent party, however, meant that political organizing became an ongoing activity.

Tammany Hall in New York was a leading example of the rise of the permanent party. Founded in the late 1700s as a social hall, by the 1830s, it had become the headquarters for the Democratic Party in New York City. The politicians associated with Tammany Hall actively helped new immigrant groups such as the Irish find jobs, particularly in newly formed police and fire departments, and acculturate to the United States. In return, those immigrants became the party's "foot soldiers" to get out the votes in elections.

The ongoing state and local parties also communicated with each other on a national level. In 1831, the Anti-Masonic Party, which had been formed to oppose Freemasonry, a secret fraternity that had its roots in Scotland in the 16th century, met in Baltimore to nominate its candidate for the presidency of the United States, selecting William Wirt. It was the first national nominating convention and represented a break from the past, in which parties' Congressional delegations selected the candidates. Under the convention system, locally elected delegates chose the candidates. The larger political parties saw the value of the convention as an organizing tool; in December 1831, the National Republican Party nominated Henry Clay of Kentucky as its candidate for the presidency, and in May of 1832, more than 300 delegates of the Democratic Party met once again in Baltimore to nominate Martin Van Buren as a candidate for the vice presidency. It was a foregone conclusion that Andrew Jackson, the incumbent president, would be re-nominated for that post.

By 1840, a relatively modern notion of a political campaign had developed. While candidates still did not hit the campaign trail to solicit votes—that would not happen until the campaign of William Jennings Bryan in 1896—other aspects of campaigning were evident. William Henry Harrison's successful run for the presidency in

1840 was marked by huge processions in his name, campaign songs, buttons, and campaign newspapers printed specifically to support him. Harrison even delivered some speeches to select audiences. Although Harrison was from a well-established Virginia family, a campaign image as a frontiersman was crafted for him. With the country mired in a deep economic depression, Harrison won a convincing victory over the incumbent, Martin Van Buren.

By the middle of the 19th century, the basic contours of political communication in the United States were set. Major newspapers were commercially independent, but allied with one party or another. The parties themselves were responsible for campaigning and using the communications tools available to them to create a story and image for the candidate. Abraham Lincoln, for example, was a highly paid railroad lawyer. But during the campaign of 1860, he became known to the public as the "rail-splitter" (see Figure 6.2).

The nickname originated in the Illinois State Republican Convention in May 1860, when Richard J. Oglesby, later governor of Illinois, and John Hanks, who had lived with the Lincolns, marched into the convention hall with two fence rails and a sign that read, "Abraham Lincoln, The Rail Candidate for President in 1860." The idea was to capitalize on Lincoln's humble origins to attract votes. It worked—the image was spread by Republican-oriented newspapers in many parts of the country.

MEDIA EXPANSION

Throughout the 19th century, several technological developments led to the expansion of newspapers. In 1844, Samuel F. B. Morse publically demonstrated the power of the telegraph, transmitting news of the Whig presidential nominating convention in Baltimore in 1844 to Washington, D.C. While everybody knew that Henry Clay would be nominated for the presidency, the vice presidential candidate, Theodore Frelinghuysen, was largely unknown. The news by telegraph was confirmed by the news that arrived by railroad one hour later. The development of the telegraph had a profound impact on newspapers. Suddenly, for news, time and space collapsed.

Though newspapers had competed since the 1830s to be first with the story, that competition became much more heated in the telegraph era. Moreover, news from Europe and other distant lands could arrive much sooner. News reports from the Crimean War in 1854 arrived in London as quickly as reports to the government and led to widespread criticism of the way the war was conducted. Making use of telegraph technology was expensive, giving an advantage to larger, better-financed newspapers (see Figure 6.3).

Following the Civil War, improvements in printing technology and typesetting made it possible to produce newspapers more quickly, and in the 1880s, similarly to the 1830s, newspaper circulations again jumped tenfold. The largest

© Gary Blakeley (Lincoln/flag), Kenneth V. Pilon (newspaper articles), James Steidl (press), 2010. Shutterstock Inc.

Figure 6.2—*By the mid-1800s, newspapers were aligned with political parties and influenced elections.*

© Anyka, 2010. Shutterstock Inc.

Figure 6.3—*Newspapers in the 1800s used the telegraph to get the story first.*

newspapers, such as the *New York World*, had daily circulations of 500,000 or more. At that point, newspapers played a central role in the political process. In 1872, Horace Greeley, the longtime editor of the *New York Tribune*, was nominated as a candidate for presidency by the Liberal Republican and Democratic Parties. In 1892, his successor at the newspaper, Whitelaw Reid, was nominated by the Republicans for the vice presidency. Clearly, newspapers were deeply integrated in the political process.

As newspapers grew in size and scope, editors argued that they had the responsibility to lead public opinion and should not be bound by the ideas of the political party with whom they were identified. In 1884, disgusted by the nomination of James G. Blaine, whom they saw as corrupt, as the Republican candidate for the presidency, a group of activists and newspapers usually aligned with the Republicans instead supported the Democratic nominee, Grover Cleveland.

These editors were derisively labeled "Mugwumps" by Charles Dana, editor of the *New York Sun*. "Mugwump" came from an Indian word for "kingpin," but others said they deserved the label because they had their "mugs" in one party and their "wumps" in the other party. Though scorned at the time, the Mugwumps were later embraced as a model of political independence for newspapers.

THE RISE OF ROADCASTING

Newspapers and political party organizations and campaigns remained the dominant form of political communication through the beginning of the 20th century. In several elections, particularly the election of 1912, William Randolph Hearst extended his newspaper chain to new cities to take advantage of the interest in newspapers generated by the heat of campaigns. In 1920, however, a new medium emerged—radio. As with the telegraph, one of the first pieces of information broadcast by a commercial radio station had to do with politics, in this case the presidential election results, when station KDKA in

Pittsburgh broadcast the winner of the contest between Warren G. Harding and James Cox. Before they held elective office, both Harding and Cox were newspaper publishers from Ohio.

Within ten years, radios were found in more than 45 percent of all U.S. households, and ten years after that, in 1940, more than 80 percent of all U.S households had radios. The potential impact of radio on politics was immediately apparent. For the first time, thousands and then millions of people could actually hear a candidate's voice. Radio significantly shrank the perceived distance between the candidates and the voters. With that in mind, Congress quickly moved to regulate radio, establishing the Federal Radio Commission (FRC) in 1926, which ultimately became the Federal Communications Commission (FCC) in 1934, both to license radio stations and to ensure that radio stations operated in the public interest. In this case, the public interest required that one political party would not have more access to radio than the other, and the Radio Act of 1927 mandated that stations give equal opportunities to political candidates.

The Federal government was determined to keep a tight leash on radio. Moreover, newspapers viewed radio as a serious potential rival. In the early 1930s, the Associated Press began to refuse to supply news reports to radio stations, and charged newspapers that owned radio stations extra. Other wire services simply refused to do business with radio stations too. In 1933, representatives from radio, newspapers, and wire services struck a deal that effectively kept radio out of the newsgathering business.

If the potential of radio as a medium of political communication was not fully realized, the same could not be said of television, which was first demonstrated in the 1930s but truly started to emerge from the laboratory after World War II. In 1948, the Democratic National Convention was broadcast by a small network of television stations up and down the East Coast.

In 1952, the impact of television in politics began to be felt. That year, a little-known U.S. senator from Tennessee, Estes Kefauver, headed a special committee charged with investigating organized crime. The committee's hearings were televised, catapulting Kefauver to national prominence. He used that prominence to run for the presidency that year and in 1956 was selected as the running mate for Adlai Stevenson, the losing Democratic candidate for president. Also in 1952, Dwight D. Eisenhower, the former Supreme Commander of the Allied troops in Europe during World War II, aired commercials on television to support his ultimate candidacy for the presidency.

Over the next several decades, television became the dominant medium for political campaigns, while newspapers remained the primary source for in-depth political news between elections. Like radio, television was mandated by the FCC to provide equal time for candidates, a regulation known as the Equal Time Rule. Moreover, if somebody was attacked on a television or radio broadcast, that person would have the right to reply according to a regulation known as the Fairness Doctrine.

The Fairness Doctrine did not apply to newspapers. However, in the 1950s and 1960s, as many newspapers failed, the survivors began to cover the news more objectively, and their news pages would not favor one party over the other. Support for specific political or policy positions, or particular candidates, was reserved for the editorial page.

The shift to television as the vehicle for political campaigning had a profound influence on the practice of politics. On the one hand, the way a candidate looked and performed on television, and the effectiveness of the television commercials their campaigns crafted, became increasingly important. On the other hand, political parties and their organizations became less important. Candidates, who had to raise enormous amounts of money to fund television commercials, became increasingly independent of the parties with which they were affiliated. Finally, the shift to television put pressure on the parties to change the way they nominated candidates for the presidency. Since the 1830s, candidates had been selected

in conventions primarily by the leadership of the party. In 1972, the Democratic Party passed a series of rules that required that delegates to the national nominating convention be largely, though not entirely, selected by primary campaigns. With a long primary season, the effective use of media to campaign became even more important.

In the 1980s and 1990s, with the emergence of Cable News Network and other cable news stations, the amount of time on television that could be devoted to politics increased significantly. Shows such as *Crossfire* on CNN would feature prominent political personalities being peppered with questions by a liberal pundit and a conservative pundit.

C-SPAN, the Cable-Satellite Public Affairs Network, which is funded by the cable networks, began televising the deliberations of both houses of the U.S. Congress, including speeches members would give to virtually empty chambers directed to the listening audience. Over time, commentators such as Bill O'Reilly on Fox News and Rush Limbaugh on radio were able to attract large and significant audiences.

Finally, as the Internet and the World Wide Web became commonplace, bloggers began to assert themselves politically. The Huffington Post and the Daily Kos, as well as Matt Drudge, could have an impact on the political agenda of the day. In a way, political communication has come full circle, with the lonely pamphleteer ala Thomas Paine able to profoundly influence political events. But now, the pamphleteer writes a blog.

KEY EVENTS IN POLITICAL COMMUNICATION

In some ways, the evolution of political communication—and of communication systems in general, as well as evolution in general—can best be described as a process of punctuated equilibrium. That means that systems stay constant for long periods of time and then are subjected to great upheavals. Once those upheavals have run their course, a new equilibrium is established. The way political communication has changed over time as the makeup of communications systems has changed can perhaps best be understood by exploring what have become paradigmatic events in politics and understanding the place of the communication processes in those events.

For example, the anniversary of July 4, 1776 is celebrated as Independence Day in the United States even though the American Revolution had started a year earlier, for on that day, Congress adopted the Declaration of Independence after declaring independence from Great Britain two days earlier. The Declaration was printed as a broadside, a single, large sheet of paper printed on one side. Broadsides were often used to publish public notices, advertisements, and the words to popular ballads and songs (see Figure 6.4).

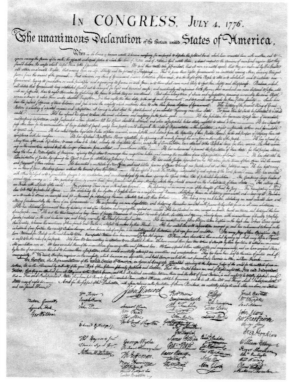

Figure 6.4—*The culmination of American revolutionary political discourse, the Declaration of Independence, was printed as a broadside and distributed throughout the rebel colonies.*

On July 5, John Hancock, the president of the Continental Congress, sent copies of the broadside to the legislatures in Delaware and New Jersey, the two colonies closest to Pennsylvania. On July 6, the *Pennsylvania Evening Post* printed the Declaration in a newspaper for the first time. And on July 8, the Declaration was read aloud in public for the first time; George Washington had it read to the army in New York on July 9. Congress voted to apply its seal to the Declaration on July 19, and the signers actually signed the document starting on August 2. From there, it wended its way through the states, now declared independent. The initial audiences for the Declaration of Independence were the people of Philadelphia and then the legislatures of the states, as political activity was still largely confined to a small elite class.

The overall framework for political communication was not much different in 1863, when Abraham Lincoln delivered what may be the most famous speech in U.S. history—the Gettysburg Address. A short speech of around 260 words (different versions of the address have slightly different word counts), Lincoln himself did not think that his speech would be long remembered. After all, he had been invited late to the ceremony at the Gettysburg's Soldiers' National cemetery, and he was paired with one of the great orators of the time, Edward Everett. And, in fact, the initial reaction to the speech was mixed. Some people felt that by speaking for less than three minutes, Lincoln had insulted those killed in the battle.

The following day, *The New York Times* carried a chronological account of the event and the remarks of each speaker, except for the keynote speech by Everett, which apparently was too long to reprint. It did note where the audience applauded for Lincoln and that the president received sustained applause at the end of the speech. But there is no indication that this would emerge as one of the most stirring speeches in U.S. history.

On the other hand, Edward Everett grasped the impact of Lincoln's words immediately, writing to the president afterward, "I should be glad, if I could flatter myself that I came as near to the central idea of the occasion, in two hours, as you did in two minutes." The Gettysburg Address made its way slowly through the United States. In 1864, George Bancroft, the preeminent historian of the time, a former Secretary of the Navy and the founder of the U.S. Naval Academy, requested a copy of the address for an anthology he was putting together called *Autograph Leaves of Our Country's Authors.* However, because the copy Lincoln sent him was written on both sides of the paper, it could not be used in the anthology.

In fact, five different versions of the address exist. Three were written for charitable reasons, including the Bliss version, which, because it is signed and dated by Lincoln, has become the standard version. Alexander Bliss was George Bancroft's son in law and the publisher of *Autograph Leaves of Our Country's Authors.* The address's place in American culture was ultimately fixed when it became a tradition for American schoolchildren to memorize it to commemorate Lincoln's birthday each February 12. As with the Declaration of Independence, the Gettysburg Address moved slowly through the country as it was reprinted in different formats, and ultimately was widely recited.

By the end of the 1800s, the impact of newspapers was much more immediate. Perhaps the most telling example of the power of the press to influence political events is the Spanish–American War of 1898. The Democratic Party and the newspapers associated with it, particularly the mass-circulation newspapers the *New York Journal,* owned by William Randolph Hearst, and the *New York World,* owned by Joseph Pulitzer, had long clamored for the United States to end Spain's colonial domination of Cuba.

When the *U.S.S. Maine* was sunk in the Cuban port of Havana, the clamoring for war intensified. In a story that is almost certainly not true but is deeply embedded in the lore of journalism, when a reporter and photographer Hearst had sent to report on the U.S. military action against Cuba reported back that nothing much was

happening, Hearst supposedly cabled, "You supply the pictures, I will supply the war."

Ultimately, President William McKinley, a Republican, did decide to move against Spain. And while pressure from Democratic newspapers probably was not the decisive factor, that did not stop Hearst from crowing on the front page of the *Journal* when hostilities broke out, "How do you like our war now?"

The Declaration of Independence, the Gettysburg Address, and the events leading to the start of the Spanish–American War represent political communication in an era of print culture. Broadcasting changed political communication in radical and profound ways. In some ways, broadcasting allowed the electorate to hear and see candidates and politicians in a much more intimate fashion. In other ways, broadcasting sapped the vitality and authenticity of political debate.

THE IMPACT OF BROADCASTING

With the development and spread of radio, campaigning and political communication gained a dimension that it had never before had. Candidates had started actively campaigning for political office only at the end of the 19th century. On the presidential level, active campaigning was pioneered by William Jennings Bryan, who was the Democratic candidate in 1896, 1900, and 1908. In his first run for the presidency, Bryan faced an uphill fight. The Democrats, who held the White House, were widely blamed for an economic recession that gripped the country. Moreover, large factions in the party disagreed with Bryan on critical economic questions. The usual campaign support provided by Democratic-oriented newspapers was split.

Bryan decided that he needed to bring his message directly to the people. Riding a train, he addressed audiences in small towns from the train's back platform. The technique became known as a "whistle-stop" campaign, and it marked the first time that relatively large numbers of people could actually hear a candidate speak.

Radio changed all that. Suddenly, huge numbers of people across the country could actually listen to the president. The ability to communicate directly through radio gave the president added power and authority, as demonstrated by the effectiveness of President Franklin Delano Roosevelt's fireside addresses during the Great Depression. In total, Roosevelt delivered around 30 talks to the American people through radio. Although he regularly communicated through newspapers as well—Roosevelt convened 337 press conferences in his first term in office and 374 in his second—it was through the fireside chats that he developed an almost personal bond with millions of Americans from all social classes. Moreover, it was through the fireside chats—so named because the quintessential image was of family members sitting close to their fireplace huddled around the radio listening to the president—that Roosevelt worked to restore confidence in the United States and in the future (see Figure 6.5).

Radio became an element of the mix of political communication still dominated by print media such as newspapers and magazines. However, as television spread like wildfire during the 1950s, it became clear that it would become the dominant medium for political communication. Like radio,

Figure 6.5—*Radio made politics up close and personal for millions of listeners.*

television seemed to allow voters to get a more intimate and personal view of the candidate. They could try to determine who the person behind the candidacy was, rather than simply what the person's positions were. The importance of this new kind of assessment was tested in the 1960 presidential campaign between Richard M. Nixon and John F. Kennedy.

Nixon, the sitting vice president and formerly a senator, was an experienced, veteran politician. He was widely viewed as crafty and tough. Kennedy had only been in the Senate for seven years when he ran for office. Many viewed him as a lightweight politician with few achievements to his credit.

Nixon and Kennedy agreed to hold three televised debates to allow the American people to judge them side-by-side. In one of the debates, Nixon looked as if he badly needed a shave. He looked pale and overtired. Kennedy, on the other hand, projected a fresh and vital image. According to the commonly held wisdom, post-debate polling showed that people who listened to the radio thought that Nixon had won the debate, but those who watched it on television felt that Kennedy had won. When Kennedy won the election by the slimmest of margins, pundits credited his performance on television for his victory.

Over the decades that followed, televised debates became centerpieces of political campaigns at both the state and national levels. But televised debates have to be structured to suit television and the viewing habits of those who watch. So unlike the great debates of the pre-television era, candidates are sharply restricted in the amount of time they can use for any one answer. Moreover, candidates do not address each other, but are asked questions by mutually acceptable moderators. As a result, televised debates are less like real debates and more like side-by-side interviews in which the candidates provide scripted answers to obvious questions.

As television became the most powerful channel of communication and the most powerful platform for advertising in the country, candidates also began to air commercials exhorting voters to vote for them or, as often, against their opponents. Raising doubts about the opponent as opposed to saying something positive about the candidate airing the ad is called "negative advertising." Throughout the 1950s, much political advertising consisted of repetitive jingles with catchy words such as "You like Ike; I like Ike; everybody likes Ike," which ran in both 1952 and 1956 on behalf of Dwight D. Eisenhower. In 1964, however, the campaign of Lyndon Johnson showed how powerful a well-crafted negative ad could be.

That year, an ad entitled "Daisy" showed a young girl picking the petals off a daisy and miscounting her way to ten. She was the epitome of young innocence. When she reached ten, an authoritative male voice in the background started to count down from ten. When the voice reached one, the camera zoomed into the eye of the child, where an image of an exploding atomic bomb was shown. Those were the stakes, Lyndon Johnson's voice then said: People must love one another or die. The implicit argument of the ad was that Johnson's Republican opponent, Senator Barry Goldwater of Arizona, would lead the country into a nuclear war. The Goldwater campaign cried foul, but the point was made. Though the ad ran on television only once, it became a part of advertising history.

Television had a major impact not only on political campaigning, but also on the way that the news could influence political events. In the 1950s and early 1960s, as the civil rights movement spread across the South, televised reports of the police in Southern towns attacking peaceful protesters galvanized support for the movement in the North. In the late 1960s, reports from Vietnam helped to turn public sentiment against the war. For the first time, people could view, in their living rooms on a nightly basis, actual footage of an ongoing war.

As it became clearer and clearer that the war was not going well for the Americans, support for the war dried up. In 1968, the anchor of the *CBS Evening Report*, Walter Cronkite, who was

Figure 6.6—*The Vietnam War stirred fierce public debate about the U.S. government's war policy and about television coverage of the war.*

considered the most trusted man in America, opined that the United States was trapped in a stalemate in Vietnam. Lyndon Johnson was watching and commented to his aide that if Walter Cronkite had turned against the war, Middle America had turned against the war as well. Johnson decided not to run for reelection (see Figure 6.6).

ONLINE NEWS MEDIA

Television remains the dominant medium for politics. Television is coupled with urban newspapers such as *The New York Times* and the *Washington Post*, and is called the "mainstream" media and at other times the "megaphone" media because it still commands the most attention nationally. Indeed, for a political issue truly to gain a national audience, it has to make its way into a televised broadcast, usually by one or more of the major networks—CBS, NBC, or ABC. Significant news that appears first on CNN, MSNBC, or Fox News Channel almost inevitably appears on the networks as well.

Moreover, with professional prowess and technological infrastructure that includes access tosatellite broadcasting to bring viewers to news scenes, television news provides information that sometimes is better than the U.S. government's information. When the Berlin Wall fell in 1989, the U.S. Secretary of Defense at the time admitted that he only knew what he saw on CNN. And after Hurricane Katrina struck in 2005, the Secretary of Homeland Security claimed that he had no reports of refugees huddled in the Superdome sports stadium in New Orleans, while CNN and other networks were broadcasting pictures of them. In fact, the contradictions in what the government was saying and what the networks were broadcasting throughout the aftermath in Katrina led to a crisis of confidence in the administration of then-President George W. Bush.

Though television still commands the most attention for political events, with the spread of the Internet, more people can get their voices heard than through television alone. The sources of news have widened. The ability of the Internet to be the medium through which critical information can be released first was demonstrated in 1998, when Matt Drudge, who ran a Web site popular with journalists that was filled with political gossip and other interesting tidbits of information he found by surfing the Internet, was tipped off that *Newsweek* magazine was holding a story that President Bill Clinton had had an affair with an intern and had lied about it to a grand jury. By publishing the tip on his Web site, Drudge touched off a firestorm of activity that ultimately led to President Clinton's impeachment.

In the years that followed that event, an easy way to publish information on the Internet called blogging emerged, and tens of thousands of people began to blog. Web sites that aggregated bloggers such as The Huffington Post and the Daily Kos became part of the daily reading habits for journalists, politicians, and a significant general audience. Working through the mainstream media, bloggers have been able to influence the national political agenda.

For example, in the 2004 presidential campaign, Dan Rather, then the anchor of the *CBS Evening News* and one of the most prominent journalists on television, reported that *CBS News* had uncovered documents that purported to show that President Bush had neglected to fulfill his commitments in the National Guard during the war in Vietnam. The story was a bombshell, in particular because President Bush was running against a decorated war hero whose record had come under scurrilous attack during the campaign.

Immediately after Rather aired his report, a group of bloggers began to denounce it as false. In the end, Rather had to withdraw the report and resign his position. The power of what has come to be called the "blogosphere" had been established.

CITIZEN MEDIA

Political communication, however, is not confined to just politicians and campaigns. Ordinary citizens have long worked to place issues on the political agenda and to agitate for change. Historically, these citizen groups have used the communication tools available to them to push for their causes. They would band together into associations such as the National Association for the Advancement of Colored People (NAACP), which was founded in 1909, and became the leading organization promoting civil rights, integration, and social equality. The Sierra Club was established in 1892, making it the oldest and one of the most powerful organizations promoting the protection of the environment.

In their early days, organizations such as these typically held meetings and rallies and published pamphlets and newspapers promoting their causes. If an issue was particularly acute, they held demonstrations to make their voices clearly heard by their elected officials. Such was the case during the civil rights movement, when the 1963 March on Washington for Jobs and Freedom captivated the nation. The words from Martin Luther King, Jr.'s "I Have a Dream" speech calling for racial equality and harmony are still widely quoted and have become a regular part of Martin Luther King Day celebrations.

Toward the end of the 1960s and early 1970s, people opposed to the war in Vietnam regularly took to the streets in massive numbers. In both the civil rights movement and the antiwar movement demonstrations, speeches were only one form of communication used. A whole genre of protest songs developed as well and, for a time, protest music was a popular category.

The Internet has greatly enhanced people's ability to interact with each other politically as well as for politicians and officeholders to interact with the public. During President Clinton's impeachment process in the late 1990s, an organization called MoveOn.org lobbied hard for the president to be censured for his actions and the impeachment proceedings to be dismissed. The group's main point was that it was time to "move on." Working only through the Internet, it attracted the support of hundreds of thousands of people. After the impeachment proceedings concluded with President Clinton's being acquitted, MoveOn.org formed a political action committee to continue to influence the political agenda.

The Internet and other new communication technologies also have had an impact on the way candidates campaign and the way officeholders communicate with the public. During the presidential election of 2008, Barack Obama attracted millions of people who "friended" Obama on Facebook. As part of his embrace of new communication technologies, Obama announced his selection of a running mate for vice president via a text message to his supporters. During the war between Israel and the Palestinians in the Gaza Strip in the winter of 2008 to 2009, the Israeli Embassy in New York conducted a question-and-answer session with the public worldwide using Twitter (see Figure 6.7).

Figure 6.7—*Political candidates reach out to the public via new communication technologies.*

CONCLUSION

One of the cardinal principles of democracy is that the best decisions are made following robust debated in which a multitude of voices are heard. In the contemporary world, robust debate depends on effective communication systems that are open for people to use. The communication processes associated with political communication have developed significantly over time as new media have emerged.

During the founding of the American republic, political communication consisted primarily of correspondence among the elite; speeches in legislatures, conventions, and congresses; and the reprinting of those letters and speeches in small newspapers. Starting in the 1830s and for nearly 100 years after that, mass circulation newspapers assumed a more powerful voice in political affairs, both in the way news was gathered and in their editorial voices. Speeches to large crowds also became much more important, as did campaigning. Starting in the 1920s, politicians used radio to connect in a personal way with millions of listeners. In the 1950s and 1960s, television became the most important communication platform for politics. And starting in the 1990s, the Internet has played a role in political discourse.

However, even as new media for political communication emerged, the old forms of political communication remain powerful. An effective speech can have a powerful impact on events. Speeches by prominent politicians may be shown live on television, such as a president's State of the Union address, and snippets can be seen over and over again on YouTube and other Web sites. President Barack Obama updated Franklin Roosevelt's idea of the radio "fireside chat" by having weekly White House audio-video addresses posted on YouTube. But despite the developments in communication technology, oral communication—the speech—is still significant.

However, the emergence of new communications platforms has an impact on the nature and content of political communication. In what may be the most famous debates in U.S. political history,

Abraham Lincoln squared off against Stephen Douglas in a race for the U.S. Senate seat from Illinois in 1858. Ironically, senators were not elected by the people in those days but selected by state legislatures. Nonetheless, Lincoln and Douglas debated for hours. In fact, the format called for the first speaker to speak for one hour and the second speaker to respond for 90 minutes. The first speaker then had 30 minutes for a rebuttal. In some cases, the debates were attended by more than 10,000 people.

Televised debates have become a regular part of many political campaigns. But the candidates cannot speak for an hour or a half-hour. Because of the demands and expectations that come with television, if a candidate has five minutes to make a point, that is considered a long time. But five minutes is a long time compared to the way people interact with each other over Twitter. The key to politics in a democracy, however, is interaction, and communication is the foundation of that interaction.

Chapter 7

Communication and the Marketplace

"In our factory, we make lipstick. In our advertising, we sell hope."

—CHARLES REVSON

In the 19th century, the Rothschild family had the richest private family fortune in Europe, with a net worth in current terms of hundreds of billions or perhaps even a trillion dollars. The founder of this international financial dynasty was Mayer Rothschild, who was born in Frankfurt, Germany, in 1744, the son of a moneychanger. He founded a bank and installed each of his sons in a major European city to conduct business.

An essential part of Rothschild's success was the private communication network the family developed to exchange information about the various markets they served. During the Napoleonic wars in the early 1800s, the Rothschilds played an instrumental role in financing the British war effort. According to a popular myth, the Rothschilds' private communication network allowed them to learn that the Duke of Wellington had defeated Napoleon a day before the British government itself learned of the victory. With this advance knowledge, legend has it, Rothschild was able to make a significant profit buying and selling British government securities. In truth, Rothschild learned of Wellington's victory when the information became public knowledge.

While subsequent research has shown the legend of Rothschild's advance knowledge of Wellington's victory to be not only false, but also propagated by anti-Semites determined to damage the Rothschilds' reputation, it is true that commerce and the efficient functioning of the marketplace, particularly in modern economies, depend on the free and timely flow of truthful, accurate information accessible to all members of the public. For example, in the United States, the Securities and Exchange Commission, which regulates the stock markets, requires public companies to make public a great deal of financial information so investors can have an accurate picture of a company's operation. Indeed, in the 1975 case *Bigelow v. Virginia*, the U.S. Supreme Court ruled that the First Amendment protected truthful commercial speech—that is, speech aimed at fostering economic activity—because that kind of speech was of interest to diverse audiences. The contemporary marketplace could not function without the unimpeded flow of accurate information.

This chapter explores the relationship of communication processes, systems, and industries to the marketplace. It will

- develop a framework for understanding media in the modern economy.

- link the development of communications systems with the development of the modern economy,

- trace the role of advertising and public relations in the marketplace, and

- examine the role of communication in globalization.

Required Reading: In *Translating Advertising: Painting the Tip of an Iceberg*, Marieke de Mooij demonstrates that the ways consumers behave and communicate are heavily dependent on their cultural values, presenting a challenge to global companies. Effective advertising must use a culturally appropriate style; simply translating advertising copy into different languages is insufficient.

THE EXCHANGE ECONOMY

The way an economy produces goods and services needed to sustain life or to pursue what members of a given society feel is a "good life" plays a central—some argue dominant—role in the social structure and culture of that society. Karl Marx argued that the economic structure, which he called the "relations of production," was the primary determinant of the essential nature of a society. The culture associated with feudal society in the Middle Ages in Europe, which was based on a hierarchical set of relationships and obligations flowing down from a monarch to lesser nobility to serfs and peasants at the bottom of the hierarchy, was driven by its primarily agrarian economy. People were tied to their land. Entry into skilled crafts was sharply limited.

There was no general public education. And religion—Roman Catholicism in most of Europe—played a central role in people's lives. Wealth was measured largely by how much natural resources—particularly land and gold—a person controlled. According to Marx, the political, cultural, and social structure of feudalism was necessary to support its economic structure.

Starting in the late 1400s, however, feudal economies began to break down. With improvements in transportation systems and the development of postal systems that ensured regular communication among major cities, trade within local economies and among the economies of different cities and countries began to assume a great role. The growth of trade increased the potential markets for manufactured goods. Soon, a goldsmith, for example, could conceivably sell products throughout Europe and not just in a specific town or region.

The growth of demand for manufactured goods led Adam Smith to observe in his book, *The Wealth of Nations*, published in 1776, that true wealth was not obtained in the control of natural resources, but through the application of human labor to the world. Human labor increased value. In one of his most famous examples, Smith studied a pin factory that was able to produce pins forty times faster than any other pin factory in the area and therefore sell them for a much lower price. The secret, Smith observed, was in the efficient use of labor. Instead of each worker performing each step needed to produce a single pin, the more efficient factory had divided the production process into a series of steps. Each worker only performed one task, becoming expert in that task. Smith called that process the division of labor.

As the production of goods became more efficient, the essential character of the economy in Europe began to shift. As opposed to feudal economies, in which serfs were obligated to relinquish large portions of their crops to the lords of the manors on which they lived, exchange emerged as a central feature of economic activity. Manufacturers would produce a single item to sell and then purchase the other items needed to live a good life. Money became the central medium of exchange.

The term "commodity" came to be used for any good that was exchanged for money. While producers, including farmers, miners, and manufacturers, exchanged goods for money, most people did not have goods to exchange. Instead, they exchanged their labor for money—that is, for wages, or a salary. Because labor is exchanged for money, it also can be thought of as a commodity. And because value is produced by the application of labor, the difference between the cost of manufacturing a product, including the cost of labor, and the price at which it can be sold is called the surplus value, or profit. Fundamentally, modern economies are organized around the exchange of goods and services for a profit.

MEDIA PRODUCTS AS COMMODITIES

The mass media play a complex role in an exchange economy. On the one hand, the information and entertainment products associated with the media are commodities for exchange. For example, people buy tickets to watch a movie, or buy books. The value added by labor to a movie is obvious. Without the work of the director, actors, and literally hundreds of other workers, the movie and the entertainment it provides would not exist at all. In the same way, an author writes a book that is then edited, printed, bound, distributed, marketed and sold, and eventually purchased by the consumer. A bound and printed book that a person can purchase in a bookstore is usually worth more than a raw manuscript. Even an e-book that has been edited and published by a reputable publisher is usually worth more than a book-length manuscript posted to the Internet. Interestingly, while a printed book often costs more than an e-book, the profit or surplus value of the e-book is greater because the costs of production are less. The difference in profit suggests that the value added to a book by printing it may be diminishing.

But actual media content such as books or movies is only one kind of product, or commodity, produced by the media. The mass media also produce audiences—and get audiences' attention, which they sell to advertisers. Because a commodity is something that is exchanged for money, when a company buys a commercial on a television program, it is buying the time and attention of the audience watching that television show. The same holds true for advertisements in newspapers, magazines, and radio. While televisions and radio shows transmit information and entertainment, the actual commodity exchanged for money is the audience. The more people watch a television show, the more expensive it is to buy time for a commercial.

So there are two kinds of commodities associated with the media. Media content itself can be a commodity, and the audience gathered by the media can be a commodity. The key to understanding what is being exchanged is identifying where money changes hands. For example, consumers purchase books and DVDs, they pay for music they download from iTunes, and they purchase tickets to movies, the theater, concerts, and other live performances. On other hand, people do not pay to watch broadcast television or radio, they do not pay for newspapers that are circulated for free, nor do they pay to read billboards. In those cases, the audience is the commodity. To a large degree, outside of e-commerce sites, the commodity produced on the Internet is attention. For example, it costs a user nothing to search the Internet using Google. However, providing the ability to deliver an advertising message related to the information a user is searching for is, in aggregate worth a great deal, as Google's remarkable growth has demonstrated.

Many media kinds of media can be thought of as hybrids in which both content and audience attention are being purchased. For example, people subscribe to newspapers and magazines for the informative and entertaining content they provide. In addition, when advertisers buy space in newspapers and magazines, they are buying the readers' attention. Cable television also can be thought of as a hybrid. While some premium channels such as HBO are sold purely as content, most cable channels such as the Food Network and The History Channel generate both subscription revenue from cable providers and advertising revenue.

COMMUNICATION AND THE EXCHANGE ECONOMY

The production and consumption of media content is only one aspect of the relationship of the media to the exchange economy. In fact, the emergence and development of the exchange economy and capitalism are intricately intertwined with the development of media systems, particularly printing. Similarly, the acceleration and globalization of capitalism is intertwined with the growth of broadcasting and then the Internet.

Writing—the symbolic representation of language—began to develop between 3300 and 3400 BC or perhaps even before that. Scholars believe that the first book of the Old Testament of the Bible, perhaps the best known and most widely circulated of the ancient manuscripts, was probably recorded around 1400 to 1500 BC. For the next 3,000 years or so, ancient manuscripts such as the Bible had to be painstakingly reproduced by hand. It could take a monk as many as 20 years to copy a single significant tract. Even shorter manuscripts could take months to copy. As a result, few books were in circulation. Literacy, reading, and the knowledge that comes with those skills were confined to a narrow educated elite primarily found within the church.

In the 1400s, an improved road system in Europe, and postal systems that were created to take advantage of improved transportation, allowed for increased trade among people living in what eventually grew into the major cities of Europe. Better roads meant that letters could be delivered more reliably and on a regular schedule. As a result, correspondents in different cities began to send letters to their counterparts elsewhere to report on market conditions and prices as well as other notable events. Because the information

could be valuable, some recipients of these "newsletters" would have them re-copied and distributed to a wider audience, sometimes selling the copies for a modest price.

Gutenberg's invention of movable type in the mid-1400s made an impact on the burgeoning European market economy in several ways. First, the cost to reproduce a manuscript began to fall. Instead of taking years to make a single copy, Gutenberg produced between 180 and 200 copies of a Bible with 42 lines per page in about two years. Although it is hard to imagine, that represented a dramatic improvement in the ability to produce books, and consequently, a broader market for books began to develop (see Figure 7.1).

At that point, what is called "the virtuous cycle" of capitalism was launched. As more books were produced and more types of books became more available, the desire to become literate spread. As more people learned to read, the demand for books increased. As the market for books broadened, more people were attracted to enter the field to produce books, and printing processes were improved, making it less expensive to produce books, stoking additional demand, as more people felt the need to be able to read. As the book publishing industry grew, people began to fill additional tasks required to make and sell books, serving as editors, bookbinders, publishers, and booksellers. Finally, because printing was

Figure 7.1—*Gutenberg's invention of mass printing technology stimulated rapid expansion of the market economy in 15th century europe.*

© Kenneth V. Pilon (chronicle), T-Design (statue), 2010. Shutterstock Inc.

a new industry, it was not controlled by a guild structure. Consequently, more people could launch their own presses, supplying more books and increasing demand.

Interestingly, printing technology was applied not only to books. Entrepreneurs began to create patterns on cloth, enabling middle-class and even agricultural workers to wear clothes that were not either brown or dyed some other color. Cloth could be printed with floral patterns or simply a design of bright colors. The ability to print on cloth put the idea of fashion within the reach of the growing manufacturing class, which ultimately would evolve into the European *bourgeoisie*, or middle class.

The idea of fashion is inextricably linked to the distribution of information. Fashion represents what is new, different, and appealing to those with the social power to make choices. To be fashionable requires a person to know what is "in style" in different places. As a result, people in different towns and cities wanted to be aware of what people were wearing elsewhere as cloth with different patterns became more widely available. Fashion, by definition, also relies on new products being regularly introduced to the marketplace and is coupled with a sense of change. In many cases, what is fashionable is what is new. What is old and traditional is de facto "unfashionable." The idea that people should buy what is the latest and greatest is essential to the exchange economy, as it stimulates the production of new commodities—that is, new products for exchange.

The desire to learn about what people were buying elsewhere led to a demand for more and better information. Starting in the 1500s, people began to print newsletters instead of copying them by hand. Merchants and bankers established fixed networks of agents who reported information, and that information would be compiled, printed, circulated throughout the network, and sold to others.

Throughout the 1600s, printed material became more widespread. In addition to newsletters, a market for pamphlets developed. Moreover, merchants

began to print posters, circulars, and handbills to promote their goods. By the middle of the 1600s in England, weekly newspapers began to appear, along with small advertisements for goods for sale, including toothpaste. And by the early 1800s, the market for printed material was robust enough support the publication of daily newspapers as well as to support the emergence of a new printed product called the novel. The new form was pioneered by Daniel Defoe with his novel *Moll Flanders* and by Samuel Richardson, who published *Pamela, or Virtue Rewarded* in 1740. *Pamela* is considered by many to be the first true novel in English.

THE INDUSTRIAL REVOLUTION

While the conceptual underpinnings for the exchange economy were in place by the mid-1700s, with the print media at the forefront of that revolution, the wholesale move to capitalism as the dominant economic structure began in earnest in the early 1800s. The rotative steam engine, which could produce rotary motion using steam power, was patented in England in 1781 (a steam pumping device had been invented in 1698). Developed by James Watt, it represented a marked improvement in efficiency. Nevertheless, commercial acceptance of Watt's steam engine was slow. In 1800, there were only 321 steam engines in operation, primarily in new industries such as the cotton trade, and in mining and canals, which could not function without steam power.

As steam-engine technology improved over time, however, it began to be deployed more widely. Because steam power was used in cotton factories, cotton factories were much more efficient than the factories used for the production of wool, and cotton began to displace wool as the textile of choice for clothing. In 1807, Robert Fulton demonstrated how effectively steam power could be applied to boats, when his ship, the *Clermont*, traveled the 150 miles from New York City to Albany in 32 hours. In 1812, Frederik Koenig developed a steam-driven printing process that could print 400 sheets of paper per hour. And in

1832, Richard Hoe invented the cylinder press, which increased production by a factor of ten with its ability to print 4,000 pages per hour.

The mechanization of production driven by steam power had many deep and wide-ranging repercussions. First, and perhaps most important, goods could be mass-produced. The ability to mass-produce goods applied to printed material as well as other commodities. In the mid-1830s, the circulations of the largest daily newspapers in the United States jumped from 5,000 to as much as 50,000. The jump was fueled by both the ability to produce many more newspapers quickly and the ability of publishers to cut the price of newspapers from six cents to one cent. Mass newspapers launched in the 1830s became known as the "penny press." The improved technology and the drop in price once again led to the virtuous cycle of capitalism. A drop in price sparked an increase in demand, which led to more competition and more products available, which led to increased demand.

The same process was under way in book publishing. In 1852, the novel *Uncle Tom's Cabin*, by Harriet Beecher Stowe, sold 300,000 copies in the first year and became one of the most politically influential novels ever written. Some historians believe that Stowe's novel helped inflame popular support for the abolition of slavery. The mass production and widespread distribution of *Uncle Tom's Cabin* was made possible by steam-driven printing presses as well as other technological innovations.

The mechanization of production meant that many goods were standardized. For example, consumer items such as clothing no longer had to be made entirely by hand. Cloth could be mass-produced and then cut into standard sizes to be assembled. Because output increased dramatically, manufacturers had to expand their market reach. And with the invention of steam-powered railroads in the 1830, large quantities of goods could be more widely distributed and were more widely available.

New forms of retailing emerged to capitalize on the opportunities presented by mass production. Starting in the 1840s and continuing through the 1880s, department stores with such well-known names as Macy's, Alexander's, Lord and Taylor, and John Wannamaker's were established in major cities in the United States. The department store is predicated on providing a wide range of goods to customers. Moreover, department stores competed not on the availability of specific goods, which had generally been the case prior to their development, but on price. Department stores offered fixed prices with which they tried to attract customers.

Department stores and the ability to distribute goods widely completely revolutionized retailing and the selling of consumer products. Department stores, which attempted to draw customers from wider areas than smaller shops with which they competed, had to continually promote both their goods in multiple product categories and their prices. Manufacturers who could distribute their products nationally had to devise strategies to ensure that consumers everywhere would be aware of and even familiar with their products. National brands began to emerge, and not infrequently, the awareness of a brand was the key differentiator in consumers' minds among products.

MEDIA AND RETAILING

The increased production of goods and the retailing revolution was accompanied by a dramatic shift in advertising, particularly in newspapers and magazines. While advertising had long been a component of newspapers, the rise of department stores meant that urban newspapers became the most efficient way to reach potential consumers in a consistent way. Indeed, newspapers became as important as word of mouth in directing consumers' purchases.

In generally the same period, as in the 1830s, improvements in printing technology, paper-making, and typesetting made it less expensive to produce newspapers. In the 1880s, once again, newspaper publishing companies cut the price of a single copy of a newspaper to one cent. And once again, circulations increased by a factor of ten to as many as 500,000 or more copies sold on a good news day.

With the cut in price, the revenue mix for newspapers changed, with advertising accounting for two-thirds of a newspaper's revenue and circulation accounting for around one-third. The change in the newspaper business model put new pressure on publishers to attract large audiences. The higher the number of readers, the more a newspaper could charge for advertising, the reasoning went. Classified advertising—a few lines of type offering an item for sale or a home for rent—also became more significant as people proved to be very willing to spend a small amount of money to reach a large audience.

The increased reliance on advertising as a revenue source created tension between the editorial side of the newspaper, which saw the newspaper's responsibility to serve the public interest and lead public opinion, and the business side of the operation, which did not want potential advertisers to be offended. Some scholars have argued that in this period, newspapers began to move away from the political orientations with which they had been generally identified.

As newspapers grew in size to accommodate the growth in advertising, they also began to include more kinds of information. Reporting on sporting events grew, as did reporting on issues of concern for women. And with the increased revenue, newspaper publishers such as E. W. Scripps and William Randolph Hearst began to establish chains of newspapers, with different newspapers in major cities across the country. For example, in 1873, E.W. Scripps and his half-sister Ellen began to work with his brother James, who had founded the *Detroit News*. Scripps went on to set up the *Cleveland Press* and eventually owned newspapers in 25 cities. In 1887, William Randolph Hearst's father gave young William control of the *San Francisco Examiner*, which his father had purchased in 1880. In 1896, Hearst bought the *New York Morning Journal*, and, by the mid-1920s, he had a chain of 28 newspapers, including papers in Los Angeles, Boston, Chicago, and Washington, D.C.

Newspapers were not the only medium to benefit from the growth of advertising. The national distribution of consumer goods led to new opportunities for magazines. Traditionally, many magazines had a tentative relationship with advertising. Some felt that advertising hurt their images and did not appeal to the elite readers they wanted to attract. And because the most visible magazines circulated nationally, local and regional companies were not that interested in advertising in them.

But the same factors that revolutionized advertising in newspapers had an impact in magazine publishing as well. Improved printing and production techniques, and an improved transportation infrastructure, made it possible to cut the cover prices of magazines and build much larger audiences. Manufacturers whose products were distributed nationally and who wished to establish a brand identity saw magazines as a viable advertising platform. In 1883, Cyrus Curtis established the *Ladies' Home Journal* with the avowed purpose of serving as a vehicle of national advertising. In one of the first national advertising campaigns, in 1887 an issue of *Ladies Home Journal* carried an advertisement about Ivory Soap, and by 1891, it had a circulation of over 600,000 readers.

Newspapers and magazine were only one part of the advertising media mix for brands such as Quaker Oats, which was headquartered in Cedar Rapids, Iowa, and manufactured the first mass-marketed breakfast cereal, and the company that invented the first condensed soup, Campbell's, located in Camden, New Jersey. In additional to newspapers and magazines, these companies, which sold their products nationally, were promoted on billboards, streetcars, handbills, and elsewhere. Moreover, the companies developed innovative packaging to reassure consumers that they would always receive the same high-quality product. They would also sponsor events, give away free samples, and sponsor booths in country fairs. Brand recognition became a competitive advantage.

ADVERTISING AND PUBLIC RELATIONS AGENCIES

Before the end of the 1880s, commercial communication had become quite complex. Manufacturers and merchants who wanted to advertise had to manage a range of media including newspapers and magazines, and needed to develop a mix of approaches to communicate their messages. As a result, there was a need to professionalize advertising and to make it more efficient. Even simply placing an advertisement in different newspapers could be complex. Large cities could have more than a half dozen newspapers. Moreover, advertisers could craft more complex messages using color printing and graphics (see Figure 7.2).

The first step in the process of professionalization came years before in 1849 when Volney B. Palmer established what is often remembered as the first advertising agency. The agency did not fit the mold of advertising agencies today. Palmer started his career selling advertising space for specific newspapers. He was what is called an "ad space sales person." Palmer then had a new idea.

Figure 7.2—*Advertisers' need to promote their brands stimulated improvements in print graphics for newspapers and magazines.*

He bought up large blocks of space from different newspapers and began to solicit advertisements from companies with which to fill that space. He would also suggest to companies where they should place their ads for them to have the most effect, offered to create advertisements for them at no charge, and verified ad placements. Because he was a large buyer of space, he demanded a fee, and later a commission, from the newspapers for each ad he sold and placed with their newspapers.

P. T. Barnum demonstrated the potential power of advertising when he brought Jenny Lind, dubbed the "Swedish Nightingale," to the United States in 1850. Before her arrival, Lind was unknown to American audiences. But through his effective use of advertising, handbills, and broadsides, Barnum drummed up so much interest in the singer that 30,000 fans met her when she arrived at the docks in New York.

N. W. Ayer and Son was the first advertising agency that worked primarily for manufacturers and retailers instead of the newspapers and magazines that published their ads. Founded in 1869 in Philadelphia by Francis Wayland Ayer and named for his father, the company helped create, write, produce, and place ads in different newspapers and magazines for its clients. It also guaranteed the lowest possible rates for the placement of advertising and eventually began to collect a 15 percent commission on the advertising placed. In 1880s, the company began compiling a directory of newspapers and magazines in the United States so advertisers could effectively compare rates. And in 1892, N. W. Ayer began to team writers with artists in creative teams to produce advertisements, a structure that remains in place today.

Many of the elements still associated with advertising were created in this period. The first ad for Smith Brother's cough drops was placed in a Poughkeepsie, New York, newspaper. An illustration of the two brothers appeared in the ad with the names "Trade" and "Mark." In 1856, the first full-page advertisement ran in a newspaper, promoting a new literary newspaper. In 1870, the Reverend Henry Ward

Beecher, the brother of Catherine Beecher and Harriet Beecher Stowe, and remembered as perhaps the most famous man in the United States at the time, endorsed Waltham watches in an advertisement running in *Harper's Weekly*. In 1912, N. W. Ayer coined the slogan "When it rains it pours" for Morton Salt, whose commercial image today is still a little girl with an umbrella; and in 1921, Ayer penned the line "I would walk a mile for a Camel" for Camel cigarettes.

As the commercial environment became more complex and competitive by the turn of the century, it became increasingly clear that advertising would only serve as one method, albeit a dominant one, through which companies could communicate with their customers and the public at large. As the Progressive movement gained political strength in this era, companies realized that promoting their products was not enough; they also had to project good images for their companies. Having the public feel positively about a company, or at least not feel hostile to it, would provide commercial benefits.

In 1904, Ivy Ledbetter Lee and George Parker, two former newspaper reporters, formed an agency to guide public opinion, using the slogan "Accuracy, Authenticity, and Interest." While it was the third public relations agency to be founded, in 1906, Lee issued a declaration of principle in which he argued that public relations practitioners have an obligation to the public as well as to the company for which they work. When the Pennsylvania Railroad had an accident that same year, Lee issued a press release describing the details of the event. In 1914, Lee was retained by John D. Rockefeller, then one of the richest men in the world, to represent his family and his company, Standard Oil. When a strike at a Rockefeller-owned mine in Ludlow, Colorado, resulted in the killing of some of the strikers, Lee insisted that Rockefeller personally visit the site. When Rockefeller was pilloried in the press as a robber baron, Lee had him release a list of the charitable contributions that he had made.

In 1923, Edward Bernays, the nephew of Sigmund Freud, wrote *Crystallizing Public Opinion* and began to promote the term public relations counsel. Bernays was responsible for several memorable public relations campaigns. In 1927, he developed the idea for a Golden Jubilee to celebrate the 50th anniversary of Thomas Edison's "invention" of the light bulb. Edison, however, had not invented the light bulb (though he was the one to make it commercially viable). Nonetheless, Bernays succeeded in getting Edison's face on a postage stamp. And in 1929, Bernays, who was working on behalf of the American Tobacco Company, organized what has become known as the Torches of Freedom campaign, in which women marched down Fifth Avenue in New York in the annual Easter parade smoking Lucky Strike cigarettes. Smoking became a symbol of women's drive for equality.

Advertising and public relations played a significant role in the major changes the economy underwent in the period between 1850 and 1920. In fact, the companies that ultimately grew to be the largest in the country, including Procter & Gamble, Coca-Cola, Nabisco, and others, achieved their prominence in part because of their effective use of advertising.

RADIO AND TELEVISION

The 1870s through the 1920s were a period of remarkable economic growth in the United States. The country began the installation of its electrical grid for power generation. Thomas Edison created a commercially viable electrical light bulb. In 1830, there were 23 miles of railroad tracks in the United States. By 1870, there were 52,000 miles of track. Between 1880 and 1890 alone, another 70,000 miles of track were laid. The Ford Motor Company was set up in 1903 and would pioneer the mass manufacturing of automobiles.

Print advertising played an important role in the creation of the consumer culture that enabled other technological developments. But the introduction of commercial radio in the 1920s and television in the 1950s increased the importance of advertising exponentially. Commercial radio can be seen as the first consumer electronics product to experience explosive growth. From 1922 to 1930, the number of radio receivers in households grew from 60,000 to 13 million. At that point, half of all urban households had radios.

The growth of commercial advertising on radio was slow. In 1925, less than five percent of radio stations were owned by private corporations, and nobody was quite sure how radio stations would be able to make money. In the early 1920s, the U.S. Department of Commerce passed regulations forbidding direct marketing via the radio, limiting radio's range as an advertising medium. In the middle of that decade, however, department stores, which were selling radio receivers, began to lend their weight to the commercialization of the industry. In fact, many department stores applied for and received their own licenses to broadcast, and their stations would attract hundreds of customers to tour their studios and purchase radios as well as other goods.

In the 1930s, regulations passed by the Federal government favored the creation of national radio networks. Moreover, independent radio stations did not have the talent or expertise to create radio programming. As a result, advertising agencies such as J. Walter Thompson created radio departments to script and produce radio shows and commercials for its clients.

In that decade, advertiser-supported radio came to dominate the field. And when television came of age in the 1950s, the same economic model as the one used in radio prevailed. In fact, the national radio networks NBC and CBS dominated the development of television, and, once again, advertising agencies developed both television shows and commercials for their clients. Often, the sponsor's name would be in the name of the show, such as the *Camel News Caravan*, the *Texaco Star Theater*, or the *Hallmark Hall of Fame*.

As television production became more complicated and expensive, a single advertiser rarely could sponsor a television show on its own.

Specialized companies and the networks themselves became responsible for developing the programming, while advertising agencies created ads that appeared in them. Within a short period of time, television became the most important advertising medium in the country, and expenditures in advertising jumped significantly.

In 1920, the year commercial radio was introduced, total advertising expenditures in the United States totaled $2.4 billion, with advertising in newspapers, magazines, and radio accounting for $830 million. In 1947, when television first started making inroads, total advertising expenditures were $5.7 billion, with newspapers, magazines, radio, and television accounting for $3.6 billion of the total. In 1970, total advertising expenditures were $19.5 billion, with television, radio, newspapers, and magazines representing $12.7 billion. And in the year 2006, advertising expenditures in the United States were approximately $282 billion, with television, radio, newspapers, and magazines accounting for $150 billion.

The proliferation of advertising and commercial speech in general has had a significant cultural impact. Social critics argue that advertising has undermined important social values, claiming that advertising fosters stereotypes, unwarranted consumption of unnecessary products, and a distorted view of the world. As media systems and brands became global, critics asserted that advertising propagated American values and the expensive at the expense of values embodied in other cultures. Also, pressure from advertisers could slant the news and information available to citizens (see Figure 7.3).

While a spirited debate about the impact of advertising is warranted, there can be no doubt that advertising and public relations are integral elements of the modern economy. Developing a great new product is not enough to succeed in the marketplace. Companies and organizations of all kinds must effectively communicate their messages as well.

Figure 7.3—Integral to the modern economy, advertising and public relations bring us both desired information about commerce and undesired consequences.

THE RISE OF THE ENTERTAINMENT INDUSTRY

The wholesale integration of advertising and public relations into the general economy is only one aspect of the role of communications and mass media in the marketplace. Over the same time period, entertainment, driven initially by movies and recorded music, emerged as one of the most significant industries in the country. Although Thomas Edison filed his first patent for recording sound in Great Britain in 1877, it was first conceived as a tool for dictating business letters. Not until the early part of the 20th century did playing music become the phonograph's primary application and did phonographs and records become widely available for home use.

The social impact of the ability to record music was dramatic, if uneven. On the one hand, after music became a staple of radio programming, new forms of music became accessible to wide audiences. For example, jazz became popular in the 1920s to a large extent because the record industry made it available. In the 1930s, a whole series of stars such as Bing Crosby, Ella Fitzgerald, and the Andrews Sisters became very popular. On the other hand, technical limitations through the 1940s limited the impact of recorded music. Until 1948, records only contained three to four minutes of music per side, and sound quality was relatively

poor. Nevertheless, the music industry in the 1920s and 1930s began to revolutionize popular culture.

Motion pictures represented an even bigger revolution. Similar to the phonograph, motion pictures were first developed in 1870s and 1880s, with several people working on the problem of capturing motion on film. As with the phonograph, Thomas Edison is remembered as having the most influential role in their creation. Motion pictures were first demonstrated to the public in the U.S. in 1893 at the Brooklyn Institute of Arts and Sciences, when a 30-second scene of a blacksmith was shown using kinetoscope technology. The kinetoscope used an individual viewer rather than a projector.

The kinetoscope was soon replaced by film technology, and in France, two brothers, Auguste-Marie and Louis-Jean Lumiere, created a portable movie camera that could also be used as projector. While roll film had been created by George Eastman in1884 and improved by Hannibal Goodwin in 1889, the Lumiere brothers established standards for film speeds and format that would be widely adopted. In 1895, the first private screening of a movie took place. The image of an oncoming train reportedly caused a stampede by the movie's audience.

As with the phonograph, the full potential for film developed over time. At first, because of technical limitations, films were restricted to short scenes basically showing everyday life and mundane events. In 1902, however, another Frenchman, Georges Melies, demonstrated the potential of film to tell a story using film when he made *A Trip to the Moon*. His ideas about film narrative were extended by Edwin Porter, who made *The Great Train Robbery* in 1903. A 16-minute production with 14 scenes, the film was a tale about a group of outlaws who rob a train, killing everybody who gets in their way and then being killed by the posse who pursued them. The film established editing as a central device to creating film narratives. In 1915, D. W. Griffith produced and directed *Birth of a Nation*, the first full-length feature film to use many of the techniques still used in filmmaking.

Along with improvements in film technology, the market for movies began to grow rapidly in the first decade of the 20th century. In 1905, the first movie theater in the United States opened in Pittsburgh. Called a nickelodeon, a combination of the price of entry and the Greek word for "theater," 450 people watched *The Great Train Robbery* the first day, and more than 1,500 lined up to enter the second day. Movies had become a popular craze, and by 1908, there were more than 8,000 nickelodeons.

But making motion pictures was becoming more sophisticated and more expensive. Following his success with *The Birth of a Nation*, D.W. Griffith made a film called *Intolerance*, which cost more than $500,000 to produce. To execute the project, which turned out to be a commercial failure, Griffith had to attract outside investors. To succeed, films also needed to be distributed to the ever-expanding network of theaters. By the mid-1920s, a handful of movie production companies had expanded to include the financing of films, distribution of films, and ownership of a chain of theaters. The five largest, known as the "Big Five" or "majors," were Twentieth Century Fox, RKO, Paramount Pictures, Warner Brothers, and Metro-Goldwyn-Mayer. Three smaller companies—Universal, Columbia, and United Artists—did not own their own theaters and were known as the "Little Three."

Those companies came to be called "movie studios," and because the majors were generally vertically integrated, managing the process from production to theatrical release, they tightly controlled the entire industry, establishing its economic structure. At the same time, as movies became an increasingly important element in popular culture, the movie industry began to produce a new class of celebrity.

Many historians consider Mary Pickford to be the first true movie star. Born in 1892, at age 17 she got a job working for D. W. Griffith and burst into public consciousness in 1915, when she appeared in 11 films. She was stunningly beautiful and virtually invented the role of movie star. Others soon followed her, including Pickford's husband

Charlie Chaplin, Douglas Fairbanks, and Rudolph Valentino. In fact, Pickford established United Artists with Chaplin and Fairbanks. From that point, movie actors and actresses assumed perhaps the most visible roles in popular culture. In the early 21st century, top actors could receive as much as $20 million to star in a film. Over the decades, there has been an ongoing tension between the studios and the stars.

Even though movie studios were forced to divest themselves of their theaters in a major government antitrust case in 1948, they still played a critical role in the financing and distribution of movies. After a significant dip in business in the 1950s because of competition from television, the film industry began to steady itself in the 1960s and then resumed its growth. Not adjusted for inflation, in 1975, Steven Spielberg's movie *Jaws* became the first film to top $100 million in total box-office receipts. In 2002, the movie *Spider-Man* passed the $100 million mark in a single weekend. And in less than four months following its release in December 2009, *Avatar* by James Cameron earned $2.7 billion worldwide. Adjusted for inflation, about 40 films have made more than $500 million at the box office.

THE RISE OF MEDIA CONGLOMERATES

Through much of the 1940s, the 1950s, and much of the 1960s, media companies generally operated within their own domains. In part, that was because of government regulations that prevented a company associated with one medium from moving into new areas. For example, as radio and then television broadcasting became more important media, newspapers tried to move in aggressively. But their efforts were limited by federal regulations. Along the same lines, federal regulations limited movie studios' involvement with television production.

In one of the first successful efforts at diversification, in 1955, the Walt Disney Company opened Disneyland, a theme park in Anaheim, California, based on its movie characters. The company also successfully launched a television production operation that included a Sunday-night anthology show called *The Wonderful World of Color* in 1954. When the show aired a miniseries about the frontiersman Davy Crockett in 1955, it spawned a Davy Crockett merchandising craze, with tens of thousands of young boys buying Davy Crockett headgear. The show's theme song, "The Ballad of Davy Crockett," was the hit record of the year. In 1955, Disney launched *The Mickey Mouse Club*, which became the longest-running variety show on television. Contemporary singers such as Britney Spears, Christina Aguilera, and Justin Timberlake starred on *The Mickey Mouse Club* early in their careers.

While Disney pioneered diversification, Warner Brothers, under the leadership of Steve Ross, launched the process that has led to the rise of the media conglomerate, companies that own and operate media companies in many different fields. Like Disney, Warner Brothers launched a small television production unit in the 1950s, producing *Hawaiian Eye* and *Surfside Six*. Nevertheless, the company was never fully committed to television production.

In the late 1950s, Warner Brothers launched Warner Brothers Records, primarily to promote its own stars, whether they could sing or not. In 1963, the company bought Frank Sinatra's record company, Reprise, and promptly began to lose millions of dollars. In 1966, Jack Warner sold the company to Canadian investors, who sold it two years later to a conglomerate called Kinney National Company, run by Steve Ross. Kinney owned a wide range of companies, including a talent agency, parking lots, and funeral parlors. Ross became head of the studio. Jettisoning the other businesses Kinney owned, he renamed the company Warner Communications. The studio worked with the biggest movie stars of the time, including Paul Newman and Clint Eastwood. It also had a series of successful movies based on comic-book characters such as *Superman* and *Batman*, who appeared in D. C. Comics, which Warner also owned.

In the 1970s and 1980s, Ross began to acquire media-related companies such as the video game maker Atari and the Six Flags theme parks. In the 1980s, under the administration of President Ronald Reagan, the Federal government began to loosen its controls concerning how large media companies could grow. And in his last big deal before he died, in 1989, Ross merged Warner Communications with Time, Inc., the publisher of *Time* magazine, *People* magazine, and *Sports Illustrated*, as well as many other magazines. In addition, the combined company also owned several cable systems, record companies, a book-publishing company, and several cable channels, including HBO, Nickelodeon, and MTV, in whose establishment Ross was instrumental.

Ross died in 1992, but Time Warner, as the company was then called, continued on its acquisition spree. In 1996, it purchased Turner Broadcasting, founded by cable visionary Ted Turner and the operator of CNN, Turner Classic Movies, Cartoon Network, and other cable networks, as well as several foreign language cable networks abroad. Both Time Warner and Turner had video operations too. Then, in 2000, in a $164 billion deal, Time Warner was acquired by America Online, the largest provider of online services at the time. That deal did not work out, as the collapse of the technology bubble in 2000 and the growth of the World Wide Web sapped AOL's business. In 2009, Time Warner spun off AOL into a separate company.

Steve Ross pioneered the idea of a media conglomerate, but others traveled down the same road. Starting with newspapers in Australia, Rupert Murdoch built his company, News Corp., into an international conglomerate with newspapers, cable broadcasting and production, television networks and production, satellite broadcasting, and other media properties operating in virtually every part of the globe. Sumner Redstone turned Viacom into a similar type of operation. In the 1990s, both Disney and Viacom tripled in size.

These conglomerates enjoyed huge competitive advantages in the media world, not only because of their sheer size and economic clout, but also because of opportunities for cross-promotion among the media companies within the conglomerate, and also because they facilitated the combination of media products in new and exciting ways (see Figure 7.4).

By the end of the 1990s, critics warned that a small number of transnational, U.S.-based companies were dominating the global commercial media market, controlling much of the world's film production, television production, cable-channel ownership, cable- and satellite-system ownership, book publishing, magazine publishing, and music production. These critics argued that media concentration stifled alternative voices in the marketplace and was a threat to democracy. In 2010, Disney, Time Warner, News Corp., and Comcast, which purchased NBC/Universal and Viacom, dominated the media industries. Together, they have a market capitalization of more than $200 billion.

The Internet, however, is having a dramatic impact on media economics. The rise of the World Wide Web and the economic recession that started in 2008 seriously damaged print pub-

Figure 7.4—*Media conglomerates can deliver a total, integrated news/entertainment experience within a single corporate enterprise.*

lications, and many newspapers and magazines went out of business. And the same time, new devices and online-based channels of communication such as the iPod, Facebook, MySpace, YouTube, and Google have grown in importance.

The iPod has revolutionized music by allowing people to download single songs instead of buying albums. New musical groups can now find fans through their MySpace or Facebook pages rather than having to rely on getting a recording contract from a record label. While neither YouTube nor Google produce content, they make content produced by others easier to locate. Google has emerged as the largest advertising-supported platform in the world, with a market capitalization of $180 billion in the spring of 2010, or nearly as big as the five largest media conglomerates combined. As an advertising platform, Google appears to advertisers as being more efficient—messages are delivered as consumers are looking for related information—and other advertising-supported and hybrid media have scrambled to find ways to compete.

THE GLOBALIZATION OF THE MEDIA

Globalization represents the idea that the entire world can be considered a single place and even a single community. It presupposes that people everywhere share at least some common values and respond similarly to at least some common events or situations. The idea of a global market is two-fold. First, the idea is that a single product can meet a need, or that people will be responsive to it, virtually anywhere in the world. For example, Coca-Cola is sold in nearly every country in the world. Second, globalization refers to the idea that economic activity in one country can have a profound effect on other countries. For example, in 2010, as a global fiscal crisis entered its second year, there were reports that Greece might default on its national debt. The extent of the problem was hidden by U.S.-based international bankers such as Goldman Sachs. If Greece, which is a relatively small country, failed to pay back its loans, the impact would be felt throughout Europe and the world.

Globalization, of course, depends on a global communications infrastructure. The technology to communicate globally has been in place for a considerable period of time. Satellite communication and broadcasting was launched in the early 1960s. The power of satellite broadcasting was demonstrated when CNN broadcast the fall of the Berlin Wall, a symbol of division in Europe, live. It also broadcast live the start of the first Gulf War in 1991.

With the proliferation of the Internet, global communications have become less expensive and more efficient. Web sites are generally accessible anywhere in the world. By using Skype, people can talk to each other via voice or video chat at very low, if any, cost. It has become commonplace for television and radio outlets to broadcast program segments transmitted over Skype.

Nonetheless, many questions about globalization remain unanswered. Some observers feel that globalization represents primarily the export of American values at the expense of local and traditional values. Others argue that while products might be global—people everywhere may drink Coca-Cola—markets are local; that is, Coca-Cola has to be sold differently in different areas. Markets are driven by culture, custom, and language. But translating an ad into a different language is not enough to make it resonate with a local community. Most global companies, however, are more product-oriented than market-oriented.

Media companies play three roles in globalization. They provide the communications infrastructure by which all major companies can communicate their commercial messages to their potential customers. They also create content that is available around the world. With Google and other services, the media, particularly the Internet, serve as an international advertising platform. And while there has been a strong backlash against globalization, it seems that, with the growth in the sophistication of communications technology, Marshall McLuhan's vision of a "Global Village" might someday be realized.

Because U.S.-based media conglomerates produce an overwhelming amount of content, critics worry that the global village will be dominated by the United States. But the flow of content is not unidirectional. *American Idol*, the most popular television show in the first decade of the 21st century, originated in the United Kingdom under the name *Pop Idol*. In fact, the entire genre of reality television has its roots in Europe. Interesting, McLuhan first coined the term "Global Village" around the same time that the Beatles and other British groups such as the Rolling Stones dominated popular music internationally.

CONCLUSION

The free flow of commercial communication plays a vital role in an exchange economy. Through advertising and public relations, the producers of goods and services can communicate their messages to their potential customers as well as to a wide range of other stakeholders and interested parties. The critical need for commercial communication is one of the reasons that advertising revenues have skyrocketed in the past two decades.

In addition, the media represent a giant industry itself. While five large companies dominate the production and distribution of media content, and employ hundreds of thousands of people or more, millions more people are creating news publications, books, magazines, films, audio and music, and Web sites that they hope will find an audience that they can inform or entertain.

The media industries are on the cutting edge of the largest economic and social trends in the world. They are at the forefront of globalization, and the impact of media content is fiercely debated. Indeed, while many see the age of the "Global Village" as a positive dream rapidly coming closer to reality, others see the media industries as threats to democracy.

TRANSLATING ADVERTISING
Painting the Tip of an Iceberg

by Marieke de Mooij

Abstract. Translating advertising copy is like painting the tip of an iceberg. What you see are the words, but there is a lot behind the words that must be understood to transfer advertising from one culture to another. This paper demonstrates that consumer behaviour and the way consumers communicate are heavily dependent on their cultural values. For advertising, one important distinction is between low- and high-context communication, which can help us understand that people categorize the world in different ways. Another important influence of culture is on consumers' needs, motives and emotions. Variations in interpersonal communication styles are reflected in advertising styles. Thus, effective advertising uses a culturally appropriate advertising style. For example, in Europe and Asia these styles are very different from US advertising style, of which rhetoric is an integral part. Another idea which is expanded in the present paper is that the persuasive communication function of advertising is biased toward rational claims. This is the sort of style that can be translated, but translating does not necessarily render such advertising appropriate for other cultures.

With increased global trade and the emergence of the global company the idea was born that it would be cost-effective to develop all advertising in the home country of the company for use in other countries, either in the English language or translated into many different languages. But it is not only languages that vary across the globe; consumers' needs, and the way advertising appeals to these needs, also do. Recent decades saw a heated debate on how to cope with these differences. In 1983, Harvard professor Ted Levitt published an article entitled 'The Globalization of Markets' in which he argued that consumer wants and needs had homogenized. The assumed causes of homogenization were convergence of national wealth, technology and emerging global media. However, no empirical evidence has yet been presented to support the argument that homogenization of tastes, needs and motives of consumers across the world has occurred. On the contrary, there is recent evidence of

READING NOTES

_____

_____

_____

_____

_____

increased heterogenization of consumer behaviour with increased wealth (De Mooij 2003). Although several advertising managers at the time doubted the homogenization thesis and thus the effectiveness of global advertising, the global media committee of the International Advertising Association called global advertising a breakthrough marketing tool. According to its members "no longer will there be a different advertising campaign for each country and each language of the world" (Keegan *et al.* 1992:20).

At the turn of the century practice had shown that standardized global advertising is not equally effective in all markets. Much of it is wasted in markets where consumer values are different from the values promoted in the advertising message. As a result, the Coca-Cola Company, which had been the prototypical global advertiser, decided in 2000 to get closer to local markets. Coca-Cola's CEO Douglas Daft was quoted as saying: "We kept standardizing our practices, while local sensitivity had become absolutely essential to success" (Daft 2000). Such sensitivity is essential when adapting or translating ads developed in one culture for use in others (Anholt 2000:5):

> *Translating advertising copy is like painting the tip of an iceberg and hoping the whole thing will turn red. What makes copy work is not the words themselves, but subtle combinations of those words, and most of all the echoes and repercussions of those words within the mind of the reader. These are precisely the subtleties which translation fails to convey. Advertising is not made of words, but made of culture.*

ADVERTISING ACROSS CULTURES

According to McCracken (1988:77),

> *advertising works as a potential method of meaning transfer by bringing the consumer good and a representation of the culturally constituted world together within the frame of a particular advertisement. The creative director of an agency seeks to conjoin these two elements in such a way that the viewer/reader glimpses an essential similarity between them. When this symbolic equivalence is successfully established, the viewer or reader attributes certain properties known to exist in the culturally-constituted world to the consumer good.*

Advertising has developed its own particular systems of meaning. These are by no means universal across borders but are often culturally defined and frequently vary from country to country. This suggests a difference in the way advertising is composed and read: that is, a difference in advertising codes. It also suggests that where a different language is spoken, there is likely to be a different set of symbolic references, including myths, history, humour and the arts. Any advertisement that does not tap into such references is likely to be a blander proposition than one that does (Becatelli and Swindells 1998). In different cultures people have different *schemata*, i.e. structures of knowledge a person possesses about objects, events, people or phenomena. For acquired information to be placed in memory, it must be encoded according to existing schemata. These schemata are often linked to both a typical language concept and a specific product category (Müller 1998). If the advertising message does not fit the consumers' schema, they will ignore the message, and the ad is consequently wasted.

As well as being viewed as transfer of meaning, in American advertising theory advertisements are also viewed as persuasive communication, of which rhetoric is an integral part. The persuasive communication function of advertising is biased toward rational claims and a direct address of the public. All elements of advertising, words and pictures, tend to be evaluated on the basis of their persuasive role in the sales process. This is the typical approach of the culture of origin of advertising theory, the United States. Although in other cultures sales will also be the ultimate goal of advertising, the role of advertising in the sales process is often different. In Asian countries, for example, the role of advertising is to build a relationship between the company and consumers. An indirect approach serves that purpose better than a direct approach that turns consumers off, instead of persuading them.

As in any communication process, both the advertising message and the schemata of the consumer are influenced by their culture, and it is difficult to transfer advertising to other cultures without understanding how culture operates.

CULTURE

Culture is the glue that binds groups together. Without cultural patterns, organized systems of significant symbols, people would have difficulty living together. The anthropologist Clifford Geertz (1973:44) views culture as a set of control mechanisms—plans, recipes, rules, instructions (what computer engineers call 'programs')—for governing behaviour. People are dependent upon the control mechanisms of culture for ordering their behaviour.

Consumers are products of their culture and culture cannot be separated from the individual: it is not a system of abstract values that exists independently of individuals. Neither can culture be separated from historical context. Culture includes shared beliefs, attitudes, norms, roles and values found among speakers of a particular language who live during the same historical period in a specific geographic region. Language, time and place all help define culture (Triandis 1995).

Cultures can be described according to specific *characteristics* or categorized into *value categories* or *dimensions*

of national culture. Dimensions are generally developed from large numbers of variables by statistical data reduction methods (e.g. factor analysis) and provide scales on which countries are scored. Dimensions that order cultures meaningfully must be empirically verifiable and more or less independent. Two categorizations are most relevant for cross-cultural communications, the distinction between high and low context communication and Hofstede's (2001) dimensions of national culture.

Context and communication

The anthropologist Edward Hall (1976, 1984) distinguished patterns of culture according to context, space, time and information flow. In particular, the concept of context is useful for understanding differences in communication across cultures because it explains the degree of directness of communication. In a *high-context communication* message most of the information is either part of the context or internalized in the person; very little is made explicit as part of the message. Information in a *low-context communication* message is carried in the explicit code of the message. To the observer, an unknown high-context culture can be completely mystifying because symbols, not known to the observer, play such an important role. Thus, high context culture communication is also defined as inaccessible. Low-context communication cultures are characterized by explicit verbal messages. Effective verbal communication is expected to be direct and unambiguous. Low-context communication cultures demonstrate positive attitudes towards words, argumentation and rhetoric, whereas high-context communication cultures can be characterized by symbolism or indirect verbal expression (De Mooij 1998).

Hofstede's dimensions of national culture

Hofstede (1991) developed a model of five dimensions of national culture that helps to explain basic

_____

_____

_____

_____

_____

value differences. This model distinguishes cultures according to five dimensions: Power Distance, Individualism/Collectivism, Masculinity/Femininity, Uncertainty Avoidance, and Long-Term Orientation. The dimensions are measured on a scale from 0 to 100. The model is based on quantitative research and gives scores for 75 countries and regions. In the second edition of his book *Culture's Consequences*, Hofstede (2001) describes over 200 external comparative studies and replications that have supported his indexes. The dimensions can be used to explain differences in people's needs and motives, communication styles, language structure, metaphors and concepts used in advertising and in literature across different countries. For those readers who are unfamiliar with the model, a brief description of the five dimensions follows, including examples from literature.

Power distance is the extent to which less powerful members of a society accept that power is distributed unequally. In large power-distance cultures (e.g. France, Belgium, Portugal, Italy, Spain, Russia and the whole of Asia and South America), everyone has their rightful place in society and there is respect for elders and people in authority. There are dependence relationships between young and old, parents and children, and teachers and students. Demonstration of social position is important, so ownership of status objects to demonstrate one's position in society is more important in cultures of large power distance than in cultures of small power distance (e.g. Great Britain, Germany, the Netherlands and Scandinavia). A good example from literature is the Italian Pinocchio, by Carlo Collodi, who is an obedient and dependent child compared with the nephews of Disney's Donald Duck, who are much more independent and less obedient.

In *individualistic* cultures, people look after themselves and their immediate family only and want to differentiate themselves from others. There is a need for privacy. In *collectivistic* cultures people belong to in-groups who look after them in exchange for loyalty. People prefer to conform to the norms adopted by others instead of differentiating themselves from others. In individualistic cultures the person is viewed as an independent, autonomous entity with a distinctive set of attributes, (traits, abilities, motives and values). In collectivistic cultures individuals are fundamentally dependent on each other. The self cannot be separated from others and the surrounding social context. Self-reflection is more common among individualists than collectivists because for the latter their relationships to others are more important than self-knowledge. Hofstede suggested a correlation between collectivism and high-context in cultures. In collectivistic cultures, information flows more easily among members of groups and there is less need for explicit communication than in individualistic cultures. North Americans and Northern Europeans are individualists: in the south of Europe people are moderately collectivist Asians, Latin Americans and Africans are collectivists.

The fear of loss of privacy is reflected in George Orwell's *1984*. The essence of much drama in western (individualist) literature is an internal struggle within the hero ("to be or not to be"). Chinese essayist Bin Xin has noted that real tragedy has never existed in Chinese literature because the Chinese had hardly any internal struggles with their own mind (Li 2001).

In *masculine* cultures the dominant values are achievement and success. The dominant values in *feminine* cultures are caring for others and quality of life. In masculine cultures status products and brands are important for demonstrating success. Men and women have distinct roles. Feminine cultures have a people orientation, small is beautiful and status is not so important.

READING NOTES

_____

_____

_____

_____

_____

The roles of men and women overlap. Examples of masculine cultures include the US, Great Britain, Germany, Italy, Mexico and Japan. Examples of feminine cultures include the Netherlands, Scandinavian countries, Portugal, Spain, Chile and Thailand. Femininity is reflected in the classic *Don Quixote*, in which women are relatively equal to men. A classic example of masculinity is the Italian *Casanova*.

Uncertainty avoidance is the extent to which people feel threatened by uncertainty and ambiguity and try to avoid them. In cultures of strong uncertainty avoidance, there is a need for rules, rituals and formality to structure life. Competence is a strong value resulting in belief in experts, as opposed to weak uncertainty avoidance cultures characterized by belief in generalists. In weak uncertainty avoidance cultures people tend to be more innovative and less bureaucratic. Southern and Eastern European countries as well as Japan score high on uncertainty avoidance, while England, Scandinavia and Singapore score low. Strong uncertainty avoidance is reflected in the novel *Das Schloss* (The Castle) by Franz Kafka, in the way the main character K. is affected by bureaucracy. *Alice in Wonderland*, where the most unreal things happen, is a typical work to originate in a culture of weak uncertainty avoidance, namely England. It is also no surprise that the same culture produced the Harry Potter books.

The fifth dimension, *long term orientation* versus *short term orientation*, distinguishes between long-term thinking and short-term thinking. Other elements include pragmatism, perseverance and thrift. This dimension distinguishes mainly between Western short-term oriented and East Asian long-term oriented cultures. In Europe, the differences are small but in some cases significant. The Netherlands and Norway score relatively high, and Spain scores lowest.

Hofstede's model is particularly useful for understanding consumer behaviour because his country scores can be used for statistical analysis of consumption data, opinions and attitude measures in consumer surveys. Thus, cross cultural differences of the various aspects that drive consumer behaviour and that are used in advertising—needs, motives and emotions—can be explained by these cultural dimensions. Language is a means to express these aspects, but language as such is also defined by culture.

LANGUAGE

The ideal global advertisement is the same everywhere, and in the English language. Behind this ideal is the assumption that worldwide most people know enough English to be able to understand the message. English language understanding, however is overestimated. A second best approach is to translate advertising that is centrally developed, usually in the English language. Advertising, however, is more than words.

English language understanding

Some companies subtitle English language television commercials, others translate most of the text except for some fragments and pay offs (short statements on what the company or brand stands for) that serve as cues to convey an international image. Yet, the spread of English as a second language tends to be overestimated. Whereas in 2001, 79% of the Danes and 75% of the Dutch said they spoke English well enough to take part in a conversation, only 18% of the Spanish, 22% of the Portuguese, 32% of the French, and 44% of the Germans said they did. Speaking a foreign language correlates with low uncertainty avoidance. Both for the general public and young people, 58% of

187

variance is explained by low uncertainty avoidance.[1] In high uncertainty avoidance cultures, even when people do speak a little of a foreign language, they are reluctant to try because they are afraid to make mistakes.

Furthermore, the consumer often does not have a sufficient command of English to understand a native English or American speaker, which can cause misunderstanding in international advertising. To give just one example, a UK commercial for Bacardi Breezer in spring 2002 was also aired in the Netherlands. It included a reference to a tomcat. The word for tomcat (*kater*) in the Netherlands also means 'hangover' (probably not intended to be communicated as an effect of the alcoholic beverage advertised). In addition, the tomcat in the advert is asked whether he has been chasing birds (—chasing women in English), a wordplay that is beyond the understanding of most people in the Netherlands.

A study by Gerritsen and Binsen (2001) among young people in the Netherlands showed that Dutch young people (14–17 years old) do not know the meaning of many English language words that are regularly used in the Dutch language. Examples include words like *blazer, entertainment, image, research, sophisticated,* and *strapless.* The word *blazer* was thought to mean 'remote control' or 'laser pistol', *entertainment* to mean 'working with a computer', *image* to mean 'energy, brains, health, appearance', *research* to mean 'rubbish', *sophisticated* to mean 'ugly, hysterical, aggressive', and *strapless* was thought to mean 'whorish'. A former pay off by the electronics company Philips. "Philips invents for you", was understood as meaning "Philips invites you". The watch brand Swatch used the term *boreproof*, which was understood to mean 'drill-proof'. In another study (Gerritsen *et al.* 1999), respondents were confident that they can understand English, but over half could not write down what was said in the ads and only one third understood the meaning of English fragments in TV commercials. Fa's "The spirit of freshness" was understood as meaning 'the spirit of fitness'. The L'Oreal Studioline copy "style and love for my hair, invisi'gel FX" was decoded as 'style grow of my hair' and 'invisual terrifies'. Seiko's "lifetime precision without a battery" was understood to mean that it 'goes slow'. Thus, English language elements in advertising make advertisements less easily understood than those worded purely in Dutch.

Finally, a survey among 11000 14–49 year old Germans in September 2003 showed that German consumers also understand little of the English language used in advertising. Only 59% of respondents could properly translate McDonald's slogan "Every time a good time". The pay off "Multi Utilities" by the energy company RWE was understood as a reference to the multicultural society. And Esso's pay off "We are drivers too" was translated as 'We are two motorists' (Verbeek 2003)!

Language and culture

Concepts and ideas in advertising are embedded in the culture in which they originate. Words and sentences elaborated for one culture are not necessarily meaningful for another culture. Western advertising, for example, tends to use efficient value-expressive language to help recognition and memory. Yet some terms that efficiently refer to specific behaviour in one language do not exist in other languages. For example, in English it is possible to combine a number of diverse types of behaviour under the adjectives *artistic* or *liberal.* These devices do not exist in some other languages, for example in Chinese. The separate behaviours referred to *do* exist in China, but there is apparently no encompassing term for them (Semin and Zwier 1997). An item that cannot easily be replaced with a linguistically or conceptually equivalent one in translation most likely expresses culturally significant values that cannot directly be translated into copy for an ad in another culture. One language represents only one cultural framework. Speakers of

READING NOTES

different languages not only say things differently, they also experience things differently; and the fact that there are rarely direct translations (especially for abstract words) is a reflection of this (Garcia 1998). The ultimate consequence of all this is that the more meaningful advertising is in its source culture, the less translatable it becomes.

Language also reflects the way people communicate with each other. At different language acquisition stages, children do not learn language per se; rather they learn the various patterns and styles of language interaction that enable them to function as competent communicators in different situations. They develop a culture-specific communication style that is, for example, direct and explicit in individualistic cultures or indirect and implicit in collectivistic cultures. Examples of expressions linked with the direct style include categorical words like *absolutely, certainly* and *positively*. By contrast, cultural assumptions of interdependence and harmony require that collectivists limit themselves to implicit and even ambiguous use of words, using modals like *maybe, perhaps*, or *probably* (Gudykunst and Ting-Toomey 1988). English is the only language in the world that spells / with a capital letter. This phenomenon may reflect the fact that the roots of individualism lie in England (Macfarlane 1978). There is no Chinese or Japanese equivalent for the English *I*. In Japanese, different words are used to refer to the self, depending on the social situation, the speaker's gender, age and the other social attributes relative to the listener. The terms reflect status differences, and the speaker usually attempts to elevate the status of the other while reducing his or her own status by choosing the correct wording. Similarly, there are different terms for *you*, depending on the social context (Triandis 1995).

Language reflects values, and the expression of values therefore varies according to the language used. Several studies have shown that forcing bilinguals to complete a test in their second language can often mean that they will express the values stereotypically associated with that language (Giles and Franklyn-Stokes 1989). In a projective test in both languages, the narratives of French American bilinguals were more romantic and emotional in French than in English (*ibid*). The reverse can happen with respondents who strongly identify with their cultural group. When students in Hong Kong were asked to complete a values test in either English or Cantonese, they expressed more traditional Chinese values in English than in Chinese (Giles and Franklyn-Stokes 1989). Translations can therefore introduce bias in value research. The fact that bilinguals express different values when using different languages is likely to influence the translations of questions, among other things. The existing system of using translation and back translation may not be able to correct for value expression variations. Some questions are simply untranslatable, as is arguably the case with the following two statements that appeared in the original VALS[2] questionnaire in the United States; these could not be translated into British English and were borrowed in their original forms: "I am a born-again Christian" and "I like to think I am a bit of a swinger" (Williams 1991).

Language structure

Kashima and Kashima (1998), who studied the relationship between pronoun drop and culture, demonstrated how the structure of language reflects cultural outlook. In some languages—including English—the use of subject pronouns is obligatory: *I* or *you* must be mentioned. By contrast, other languages do not require explicit encoding of subject pronouns, and these words can be dropped by the speaker if he or she deems it appropriate to do so. In some Indo-European languages such as Spanish, personal pronouns are not obligatory, partly because the referents can be recovered from verb inflections. This phenomenon is called *pronoun drop*. Explicit use of *I* signals emphasis. Its absence reduces the prominence of the speaker's person. Dropping the subject pronoun (*I*, *we* or *you*) was found to correlate significantly with low individualism. Thus, languages which license pronoun drop are associated with lower levels of individualism than those that require the use of personal pronouns such as *I* or *you*.

The view that language reflects culture contradicts the Sapir-Whorf hypothesis, which states that the structure of language influences culture via perception and categorization. This would imply that people's worldview and social behaviour depend on the structure and characteristics of the language they speak (Usunier 1996). Related to this is the assumption that certain thought processes are more likely to occur in one language than in another because of the structure of the language. One example is the idea that more concrete styles of thought are found in collectivistic cultures, whereas in individualistic cultures thought is more abstract because it is not necessarily linked to the social environment (Semin and Zwier 1997). This view was used to explain why, for example, the Chinese place relatively greater emphasis on concrete attributes when evaluating products than on abstract affective (emotional) aspects (Malhotra and McCort 2001).

Translating pay offs and brand names

Advertising is a means of developing strong brands. When companies decide to go international, one of the first things they have to consider is how to internationalize their brand name and pay offs. The latter are often kept in English, a practice that results from the western need for consistency. In collectivistic cultures, people are more inclined to adapt their communication to the situation. Examples include "Wanadoo, positive generation" and "Ford Mondeo, designed for living". Earlier in this article examples were given of how such English language statements are often misinterpreted. A literal translation is often not a good solution, precisely because of the interdependence of language and culture.

Grammar and writing systems have consequences for perception and memory. For example, Chinese native speakers rely more on visual representations, whereas English speakers rely primarily on phonological representations (verbal sounds). In English, the sound system is used to encode the brand name and facilitate memory recall. Explicit repetition of words enables consumers to recall the brand name. Examples include "If anyone can, Canon can" and "O_2, (pronounced as O two) see what you can do", both used as pay offs in ads in the United Kingdom, as well as in other countries (such as France) where people pronounce the brand name differently and as a result it doesn't rhyme with the rest of the expression. When Western companies translate pay offs, their own focus on sound and pronunciation makes them adapt their brand names to other cultures more vocally than visually. Thus, Motorola is pronounced as *me de lou la* in Cantonese, which means 'nothing to take'. Peugeot's *416* is pronounced the same as *si yi lu*, which means 'die all along the road' in some Southern Chinese dialects (Li 2001).

Chinese consumers are more likely to recall information when the visual rather than phonological memory trace is accessed. Schmitt *et al.* (1994) found that Chinese native speakers were more likely to recall brands when they could write them down than when they generated a spoken response. The authors suggest that marketers, instead of translating Western brand names into Chinese via sound, should enhance the natural tendency of Chinese consumers to rely on visual representations. Visually distinct brand name transcription or calligraphy and logo designs that enforce the written word should prove more effective in China, whereas for English native speakers the sound qualities of brand names should be exploited by the use of jingles and onomatopoeic names (resembling the sound made by the object).

Transferring brand names to other countries can be hazardous. The most frequently mentioned example is

190

that of the Ford Nova, which in Spanish means 'doesn't go'. Naming practices are different among nations and languages, and this includes brand naming practice. For example, Chinese has more homonyms than many Western languages. To translate a Western brand name one has to choose suitable characters among those homonyms. Thus Coca-Cola uses *kekou kele*, which means 'tasty and happy'. Culturally, the Chinese prefer names that express goodwill, while Western names are usually viewed simply as codes to label brands. Chinese brand names tend to have meaning, for example a name like *Liu shen wan* means 'it includes six herbs'. Many brand names encode meanings such as 'lucky', 'gold' or 'good'.

Li (2001) sums up three ways to translate brand names. The first is pronunciation-oriented, without the intention to encode specific meaning. For example, *Nokia* becomes *Nuojiya*, which carries no meaning. The second involves creating a meaningful name like *Coca-Cola*. A good example is *Ericsson: Ai* (meaning 'love', 'like to') *li* ('to set', 'establish') *xin* ('trust'). A further example is *Hewlett Packard: Ilui* ('benefit') *pu* ('popular'). The third strategy is to replace the brand name with another one that possesses the desired attributes. For example, the Finnish machinery brand name *Kone* was changed into *Tong Li* ('general power').

Language and categorization

How people categorize products and brands should be properly reflected in advertising to make the message understood. The structures of different languages affect categorization and judgement (Zhang and Schmitt 1998). Unlike Indo-European languages, Asian languages like Chinese, Japanese and Korean are *classifier* languages. A classifier is a measure that is used in conjunction with numerals (one, two, three, etc.) or determiners (a, the, that, this) and that refers to common physical features of objects, such as shape, size, thickness, length, as well as other perceptual or conceptual properties associated with objects, including 'bendability' and 'graspability'. Classifiers categorize a given object into a larger set of objects and describe classes of objects. As such they are different from adjectives that describe specific instances within a class. Adjectives answer the question "What kind of object is it?" whereas classifiers answer the question "What kind of object is this a member of?" Classifiers are used in Chinese, Japanese, Korean and Thai languages as well as Navajo and Yucatan-Mayan languages. Some languages, such as Japanese, have classifiers that are generally of broader scope than classifiers of other languages (e.g. Chinese). Compared to English native speakers, Chinese speakers perceive objects that share a classifier as more similar than objects that do not share a classifier (Schmitt and Zhang 1998).

In advertising in classifier languages, objects are more positively evaluated when they are combined with a visual cue related to the classifier. An example is the difference in judgement of pictures of 'graspable' objects (brush, cane, umbrella, broom) using the classifier *ba* in Chinese. A picture showing only the object is judged less positively than one showing the object with a hand (Zhang and Schmitt 1998). The classifier system thus has to be exploited carefully since it can have positive and negative effects. For example, a classifier for pipe-like thick objects will lead to positive expectations for lipstick, but a classifier for long, thin objects can lead to negative expectations, implying that the lipstick in question will provide less quantity and will not last long (Schmitt and Zhang 1998).

NEEDS, MOTIVES AND EMOTIONS

Advertising influences consumers partly by giving information but mostly by appealing to needs, motives and emotions. Consumption can be driven by functional or social needs. Clothes satisfy a functional need; fashion satisfies a social need. A house serves a functional need; a home serves a social need. A car may satisfy a functional need but the type of car one chooses can satisfy a social need. Understanding variations in people's needs and motives is important for developing effective advertising.

People's behaviour is not determined only by their needs and motivations, but also by their surroundings, and the context in which they make decisions. People in different cultures can do the same thing for different reasons or motives, and people in different countries may do different things for the same reasons. Many global standard products or product features which are assumed to be culture-free are bought for different reasons across different cultures. A good example is individualized ring tones that were offered by Nokia to Chinese consumers. These are interesting for people of individualistic cultures who want to demonstrate their uniqueness, but not so interesting for the collectivistic Chinese who prefer to be in harmony with the other members of the group (Li 2001).

Differences in sensitivity to certain product attributes and variation in motives for buying can be explained by the underlying cultural values that vary by product category. For example, for mineral water a generic motive is purity; for soft drinks and alcoholic beverages it is status. For cars, motives vary between safety, status, design and being environmentally friendly, all based on different cultural values. Motives for buying can be recognized in the appeals used in advertising. When culturally relevant motives are used in an ad, translating the ad as it stands will not be sufficient, and the appeal itself may have to be adapted.

This also applies to emotions in advertising. The concept of global advertising was based on the assumed universality of basic emotions such as happiness, anger and fear. Much research on emotions has been designed to test the hypothesis of universality. Basic emotions were supposed to be part of the human potential and, therefore, universal. One argument in favour of universal basic emotions is that most languages possess limited sets of central *emotion-labelling* words which refer to a small number of commonly experienced emotions. Examples of such words in English include *anger, fear, sadness,* and *joy.* Specific English words underpin psychologists' theories of emotion, but we must remember that words for emotions vary from one culture to another. English words often assumed to denote natural basic categories of emotion have no equivalents in some other languages, and other languages provide commonly used emotion words with no direct equivalent in English. Even where there appears to be an equivalent, seemingly equivalent words may cover different concepts. Anger, for example, appears to be natural in western cultures, but even across western cultures the content varies. The American experience of anger is specific to American culture, stressing the expression of one's rights, goals and needs. Anger occurs when these are blocked, and the person has a sense of "I was treated unfairly". By contrast, in collectivistic cultures anger might constitute a different experience because it produces separation and disconnection where connection and interdependence are so important (Markus *et al.* 1996).

Another argument relating to universality is based on research on *recognition of facial expressions.* People from different cultures can recognize facial expressions in similar ways. The question is whether it is justified to take facial expression as an index of the presence of emotions, because it is possible that in some societies emotions occur without facial expressions whereas in others facial expressions occur without emotions (Russell 1995). Seeing a facial expression allows an observer to draw a conclusion about a situation, but one specific facial expression is not necessarily connected to one specific emotion. For example, a smile is generally viewed as an expression of happiness. However, seeing a friend can make a person smile, but this does not imply that the person is happy. He or she can in fact be sad or lonely. Facial

READING NOTES

_____

_____

_____

_____

_____

expressions, then, are only a crude measurement of emotions, and labelling a facial expression is not the same as conceptualizing emotion. Yet, many people in Western cultures implicitly believe that certain categories of emotion are 'natural' and that specific facial actions inherently express these emotions.

In judging other people's behaviour and emotional expression context plays an important role. In particular, in collectivistic cultures people may judge emotional expression differently according to the context or event surrounding the emotional expression. This also applies to emotions in advertising, where the meaning of communication depends on the context. The problem is that operationalizing context is a difficult task, as context does not have a specific, fixed meaning. This aspect of context doesn't facilitate the measurement of teffects of emotional appeals across cultures. A frequently applied approach to measuring the effects of emotional appeals in advertising involves using alternative (mock) advertisements with different textual appeals, keeping the pictures constant—not realizing that a picture can have different meanings across cultures. Since a picture serves as context for the words, respondents are likely to interpret the meaning of the words in line with their different interpretations of the context (De Mooij 2003). So the same picture may lead to different interpretations of the text.

COMMUNICATION STYLES

Not only do appeals and motives in advertising vary, there are also different communication styles that are reflected in advertising styles. The strongest distinction is between direct and indirect communication. For example, in collectivistic cultures where indirect communication prevails, more metaphors are used than in individualistic cultures. Metaphors of one culture are not necessarily understood in other cultures. A global ad by the Korean LG showing an old man with a baby on a

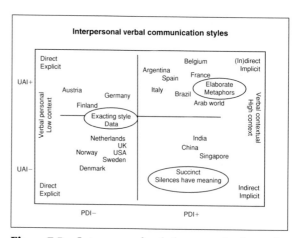

Figure 7.5—*Interpersonal verbal communication styles.*

mountain top will be understood in Asia as a reflection of continuity and long-term orientation, but in the US and in Europe the ad is unlikely to be understood in the same way. Similarly, a squirrel in a forest in an ad by Nokia aimed at the Finns symbolized good reception and free movement in a deep and distant forest. The Chinese understood it as depicting an animal that lives far away from people and completely missed the symbolic role of the squirrel.

The prevailing advertising styles of cultures follow interpersonal communication styles. Gudykunst and Ting-Toomey (1988) offer the best description of how dimensions of culture explain variations in verbal communication styles. They distinguish between verbal personal and verbal contexual style according to the importance of context. Another distinction is between elaborate, exacting and succinct verbal style. Figure 7.5 clusters countries according to two of Hofstede's cultural dimensions that explain interpersonal communication styles: power distance and uncertainty avoidance.

Verbal personal style covers individual-centred language that characterizes the cultures in the quadrants on the left. *Verbal contextual style* covers role-centred language found in the cultures in the quadrants on the right. Verbal personal style enhances the 'I' identity, is person-oriented (e.g. in English), whereas verbal contextual style emphasizes context-related role identity (e.g. Japanese, Chinese). The two styles focus on personhood vs. situation or status. Verbal personal style is linked with low power distance (equal status) and individualism (low-context), whereas verbal contextual style is linked with high power distance (hierarchical human relationships) and collectivism (high context). Verbal contextual style includes different ways of addressing different people, according to their status (as in Japanese).

Elaborate verbal style refers to the use of rich, expressive language, *Exacting* or *precise style* is a style where no more and no less information than required is given. *Succinct* or *understated style* includes the use of understatements, pauses and silences. Stretches of silence carry meaning. High-context cultures of moderate to strong uncertainty avoidance orientation tend to use the elaborate style. Arab cultures draw on this elaborate style of verbal communication, using metaphors, long arrays of adjectives, flowery expressions and proverbs. Low-context cultures of weak uncertainty avoidance (e.g. USA, UK) tend to use an exacting style. The succinct style is found in high-context cultures of strong uncertainty avoidance (e.g. Japan).

In advertising in individualistic cultures, the direct communication style uses the personal pronouns "you" or "we", whereas in collectivistic cultures the indirect style is preferred, drawing on indirect devices such as symbolism and metaphors. There are, however, variations in indirectness among collectivistic cultures. The Singaporean Chinese, for example, are more direct than the Taiwanese (Bresnahan 1999). This is confirmed in a study by Cutler *et al.* (1997), who examined advertisements from eight different countries (US, UK, France, India, Japan, Turkey, Taiwan/Hong Kong, and Korea) and measured the use of a direct, personalized headline in which the public are addressed by "you" or "your".

Mapping advertising styles

Applying the concept of interpersonal communication styles to advertising, the position of various countries can be mapped out as in Figure 7.6. Advertising styles in the lower and upper left hand quadrant are associated with individualistic cultures of small power distance. Advertising style is *direct explicit*, and *personal*. The uniqueness of the person or the brand, and the importance of identity and personality are reflected in this style. These advertising styles are typical of the US and the countries of northwest Europe, which show a preference for direct and explicit forms of communication such as the personalized 'lecture' style in advertising. This is the type of advertising in which an identified presenter endorses the product. Ads are carefully directed to focus on the personality of the endorser.

In cultures of strong uncertainty avoidance, positioned in the upper left hand quadrant, advertising is more *serious* and *structured*. The execution of the visuals will be detailed, often including demonstration of how the product works. This is the style of Germanic cultures, where visuals are more exact and more information and data are provided than in weak uncertainty avoidance cultures. In the weak uncertainty avoidance cultures of the lower left hand quadrant, where ambiguity is tolerated, more humour is used in advertising. In the masculine cultures (US, UK), known personalities or celebrities are used to present the product, whereas in the feminine cultures (Scandinavia, The Netherlands) the personality of the presenter is downplayed.

The two quadrants on the right include direct-implicit and indirect-implicit styles. The upper right hand

READING NOTES

_____

_____

_____

_____

_____

194

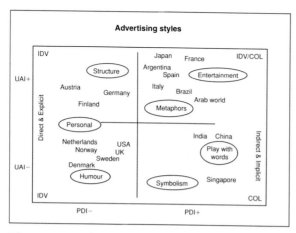

Figure 7.6—*Advertising styles.*

quadrant covers several styles because it includes cultures that combine high power distance and high uncertainty avoidance with individualism (e.g. France and Belgium), as well as cultures that combine these two dimensions with collectivism (e.g. Spain, Brazil). France and Belgium show a mix of direct and indirect implicit communication styles that express both uniqueness and inaccessibility. *Inaccessibility* is recognized in the frequent references in advertising to other forms of communications such as films, art or even advertising by others. In the other countries communication is *indirect and implicit*, is less likely to offend and thus upholds public face. Meaning is in the context. Communication is subdued and works on likeability, not on persuasion. If celebrities are involved, they are not likely to address the audience directly; they play a more symbolic role, and are simply associated with the product rather than endorse in a direct way. *Visual metaphors* and *symbols* are used to create context and to position the product or brand in its 'proper place', as one would expect in large power distance cultures.

The advertising style of collectivistic cultures of medium to large power distance and weak to moderate uncertainty avoidance in the lower right hand quadrant must reinforce group norms and help maintain face. *Visuals*, (visual) *wordplay*, and *symbolism* are important in advertising in these cultures, but the audience can be directly addressed. Advertising in Hong Kong, Singapore and India tends to follow this style. These cultures prefer relatively direct modes of communication, which can be explained by low uncertainty avoidance. Chinese consumers like visual as well as straightforward and vivid ads with images (Shuqian 1992). For India, the direct communication style is confirmed by Roland (1988:284), who states that "Indian modes of communication operate more overtly on more levels simultaneously than do the Japanese".

CONCLUSION

Advertising consists of concepts, ideas, copy and visuals. A concept or idea that is relevant for one culture isn't necessarily relevant for others. In some cultures an idea is mainly expressed by visuals, in others by words. Historically, much attention has been paid to advertising copy because of the Anglo-European heritage of advertising practice and theory. This has made people believe that most advertising can be translated. Current knowledge of the influence of culture on people's perception, memory and communication styles is likely to change that belief. If advertising is translated at all, the translator should closely co-operate with the copywriter/art director team and not only translate but also advise about culture-specific aspects of both languages.

MARIEKE DE MOOIJ
Westerenban 44, 4328 IIE Burgh Haamstede. The Netherlands.
mdemooij@zeelandnet.nl

READING NOTES

_____

_____

_____

_____

_____

ENDNOTES

1. Based on data from Eurobarometer Surveys: *Eurobarometer Standard #55* and *The Young Europeans* (2001), Brussels: European Commission Directorate. http://europa.eu.int/comm/public opinion/standard_en.htm.

2. VALS stands for 'Values and Life-styles', a segmentation system developed by SRI International in Menlo Park, California.

REFERENCES

Anholt, Simon (2000) *Another One Bites the Grass. Making Sense of International Advertising*, New York: John Wiley & Sons.

Becatelli, Ian and Alan Swindells (1998) 'Developing Better Pan-European Campaigns', *Admap* (March): 12–14.

Bresnahan, Mary Jiang, Rie Ohashi, Wen Ying Liu, Reiko Nebashi and Chao-Chih Liao (1999) 'A Comparison of Response Styles in Singapore and Taiwan', *Journal of Cross-Cultural Psychology* 30: 342–58.

Cutler, Bob D., S. Altan Erdem and Rajshekhar G. Javalgi (1997) 'Advertiser's Relative Reliance on Collectivism-Individualism Appeals: A Cross-Cultural Study', *Journal of International Consumer Marketing* 9: 43–55.

Daft, Douglas (2000) 'Back to Classic Coke', *Personal View*, *Financial Times*, March 27, http://news.ft.com.

De Mooij, Marieke (1998) *Global Marketing and Advertising. Understanding Cultural Paradoxes*, Thousand Oaks, CA: Sage Publications.

—— (2003) *Consumer Behavior and Culture Consequences for Global Marketing and Advertising*, Thousand Oaks, CA: Sage Publications Inc.

Eurobarometer 55 and The Young Europeans (2001) Brussels: European Commission Directorate.

García, Sara (1998) 'When is a Cat not a Cat?', *Admap* (October): 40–42.

Geertz, Clifford (1973) *The Interpretation of Cultures*, New York: Basic Books.

Gerritsen, Marinel, Inge Gijsbers, Hubert Korzilius and Frank Van Meurs (1999) 'Engels in Nederlandse TV reclame' [English in Dutch TV advertising], *Onze Taal* 1: 17–19.

Gerritsen, Marinel and Frank Jansen (2001) *Teloorgang of Survival?* [Loss or survival?], *Onze Taal* 2/3: 40–42.

Giles, Howard and Arlene Franklyn-Stokes (1989) 'Communicator Characteristics', in Kete Asante Molefi and William B. Gudykunst (eds) *Handbook of International and Intercultural Communication*, Newbury Park, CA: Sage Publications.

Gudykunst, William B. and Stella Ting-Toomey (1988) *Culture and Interpersonal Communication*, Thousand Oaks, CA: Sage Publications.

Hall, Edward (1976) *Beyond Culture*, New York: Doubleday.

—— (1984) *The Dance of Life*, New York: Doubleday.

Hofstede, Geert (1991) *Cultures and Organizations. Software of the Mind*, London: McGrawHill.

—— (2001) *Culture's Consequences*, Thousand Oaks, CA: Sage Publications, second edition.

Kashima, Emiko S. and Yoshihisa Kashima (1998) 'Culture and Language. The Case of Cultural Dimensions and Personal Pronoun Use', *Journal of Cross-Cultural Psychology* 29: 461–86.

Keegan, Warren, Sandra Moriarty and Tom Duncan (1992) *Marketing*, Englewood Cliffs, NJ: Prentice Hall.

Levitt, Theodore (1983) 'The Globalization of Markets'. *Harvard Business Review* (May-June): 2–11.

Li, Zhenyi (2001) *Cultural Impact on International Branding. A Case of Marketing Finnish Mobile Phones in China*, Doctoral Dissertation, University of Jyväskylä, Finland.

Macfarlane, Alan (1978) *The Origins of English Individualism*, Oxford, UK: Blackwell.

Malhotra, Naresh K. and Daniel J. McCort (2001) 'A Cross-Cultural Comparison of Behavioral Intention Models', *International Marketing Review* 18: 235–69.

Markus, Hazel, Shinobu Kitayama and Gary R. VandenBos (1996) 'The Mutual Interactions of Culture and Emotion', *Psychology Update Psychiatric Services* 47: 225–26.

McCracken, Grant (1988) *Culture and Consumption: New Approaches to the Symbolic Character of Consumer Goods and Activities*, Bloomington: Indiana University Press.

Müller, Wendeling (1998) 'Verlust von Werbewirkung durch Standardisierung' [Loss of Advertising Effectiveness through Standardization], *Absatzwirtschaft* 9: 80–88.

READING NOTES

_____

_____

_____

_____

Roland, Alan (1988) *In Search of Self in India and Japan*, Princeton University Press.

Russell, James A. (1995) 'Facial Expressions of Emotion: What Lies Beyond Minimal Universality?', *Psychological Bulletin* 118: 379–91.

Schmitt, Bernd H., Yigang Pan and Nader T. Tavassoli (1994) 'Language and Consumer Memory: The Impact of Linguistic Differences Between Chinese and English', *Journal of Consumer Research* 21: 419–31.

Schmitt, Bernd H. and Shi Zhang (1998) 'Language Structure and Categorization: A Study of Classifiers in Consumer Cognition, Judgment, and Choice', *Journal of Consumer Research* 25: 108–22.

Semin, Gün R. and Sandra Zwier (1997) 'Social Cognition', in John W. Berry, Marshall H. Segall and Cigdem Kagitcibasi (eds) *Handbook of Cross-Cultural Psychology*, Volume 3. Boston: Allyn and Bacon.

Shuqian, Tan (1992) 'China Reform and Consumers' Changes', Unpublished paper presented at the *IAA Word Congress*, Barcelona.

Triandis, Harry C. (1995) *Individualism & Collectivism*, Boulder: Westview Press.

Usunier, Jean-Claude (1996) *International Marketing, A Cultural Approach*, Harlow, UK: Pearson Education.

Verbeek, Hans (2003) 'Duitsers begrijpen Engelse Slogans niet' [Germans do not understand English slogans], *Adformatie* 39(25): 16.

Williams, Jim (1991) 'Constant Questions or Constant Meanings? Assessing Intercultural Motivations in Alcoholic Drinks', *Marketing and Research Today* (August): 169–77.

Zhang, Shi and Bernd Schmitt (1998) 'Language-Dependent Classification: The Mental Representation of Classifiers in Cognition, Memory and Evaluations', *Journal of Experimental Psychology: Applied* 4: 375–85.

READING NOTES

_____

_____

_____

_____

_____

Chapter 8

Celebrity Culture

"Celebrities, like other commodities, have a built-in obsolescence. They take the national stage, do their act and leave."

—NEAL GABLER

In 1968, pop artist Andy Warhol proclaimed, "In the future, everybody will be famous for fifteen minutes." In 1988, the editors of *People* magazine wrote that the future was now. By 1998, Warhol's future was even more "now," and by 2010, anybody with a video on YouTube could be catapulted into international fame within a matter of days.

Warhol was reflecting on the proliferation of the mass media and the access it provides to an ever-greater array of people. Once communication networks were the exclusive domain of the literate elite, which represented a miniscule percentage of the population, largely the clergy and the nobility. With each successive new communication technology, an increasing number of people could communicate with wider audiences. Newspapers, the movies, television, and now the Internet opened communication networks to new groups of producers and consumers. With social media such as Facebook and YouTube, any clever teenager—or even younger children— can communicate with potentially hundreds of millions of people (see Figure 8.1).

Open access to communication networks has changed the nature of fame and celebrities, and their relationships to their audiences. In the past, the media spotlight seemed to focus on people because of some sort of accomplishment. In the 1870s, Henry Ward Beecher, a Congregationalist minister, might have been the most famous man in the United States—or at least that is what his biographer claimed. But Beecher won his fame through his fierce support for civil rights and women's rights, and through his impassioned sermons in defense of evolution and immigration. His church, the Plymouth Church in Brooklyn, was one of the first megachurches in the United States, drawing 2,500 people a week. It had purchased rifles—they became known as Beecher's Bibles—for those opposing slavery in Kansas and Nebraska in the 1850s. It was attended at one time or another by Abraham Lincoln, Walt Whitman, and Mark Twain.

Figure 8.1—*The growth of celebrity culture is inextricably linked to the rise of the modern mass media.*

In 1870s, however, Beecher's fame metamorphosed into notoriety. In that year, Beecher was tried on charges that he had committed adultery with his friend's wife, Elizabeth Tilton. As the story goes, Tilton confessed to her husband that she had had an amorous relationship with Beecher. Tilton later told Elizabeth Cady Stanton, a leader of the women's rights movements who, in turn, told Victoria Woodhull, another feminist and publisher of a widely read newspaper, *Woodhull and Claflin's Weekly*. In the pages of the newspaper, Woodhull had preached the virtues of free love, a stance that Beecher had denounced from the pulpit. So when Woodhull heard of Beecher's affair with Tilton, she published an article declaring that Beecher was secretly practicing the free love principles he had earlier excoriated.

The charges created a national sensation. Woodhull was arrested for publishing obscene material. Beecher was investigated by his church and exonerated. Tilton's husband, Theodore Tilton, however was excommunicated by the church. He sued Beecher for "criminal conversation" with his wife; a trial began in 1875 and lasted six months, but the jury could not agree on a verdict.

Two years later, when she repeated her claim that she had had an affair with Beecher, Elizabeth Tilton was also excommunicated while a second investigation by the church once again exonerated Beecher, who remained a popular national figure until his death in 1887. The story of Henry Ward Beecher is a useful marker of the subtle shift that was underway in American culture. In the end Beecher was a celebrity, a curious mixture of fame seasoned with notoriety.

Henry Ward Beecher's celebrity was driven in part by the dominant mass medium of his time—newspapers. For example, in 1875, *The New York Times* published complete transcripts of the daily trial proceedings as well as a pamphlet giving a complete review of the evidence in the case. For all of his achievements, without the obsessive newspaper coverage of his trial for adultery, it is unlikely that Beecher would have been considered the most famous man of his time.

In the current media environment, celebrity usually relies much less on accomplishments and more on notoriety. Consider the case of Paris Hilton, a young socialite and the granddaughter of billionaire Conrad Hilton, the founder of the Hilton Hotel chain. After an undistinguished career as a model, Hilton became a well-known fixture in the New York club scene, being dubbed by the New York tabloid newspapers as the "It Girl," a reference to the Hollywood silent era film star Clara Bow.

In 2003, Hilton signed a deal to do a reality television show called *The Simple Life* with her friend Nicole Richie, the daughter of singer Lionel Richie. The premise of the show was simple. What would happen if two New York debutantes had to live in the rural South and live like regular people do—working at low-paid jobs and shopping at places such as Wal-Mart? The idea came from a 1960s sitcom called *Green Acres*.

Before the first episode was aired, however, a sex tape "starring" Hilton surfaced on the Internet. From that moment on, Hilton was a celebrity. *The Simple Life* ran for several years, and Hilton was a regular at "red carpet" celebrity events. Hilton followed up *The Simple Life* with another reality show in which people compete to be Hilton's new "best friend forever," or BFF.

In fact, her celebrity was so great that her friend Kim Kardashian also able was launch a reality show, *Keeping Up with the Kardashians*, which basically followed the lives of Kardashian, her sisters, and to a lesser extent, her parents. While her stepfather, Bruce Jenner, is a former Olympic athlete, and various celebrities and major-league athletes come in and out of their lives, the Kardashians are known not for what they have done, but mainly for clawing their way into the media spotlight.

Indeed, a growing number of celebrities such as Kim Kardashian are completely "manufactured" by the media. After Kate Gosselin gave birth to sextuplets—an experience that was aired on the Learning Channel on cable television—her life was turned into a reality television show called *Jon and Kate Plus Eight* (she had already had two children before the sextuplets). Jon and Kate had no other notable accomplishment other than having eight children. But as their marriage started falling apart, the media relentlessly covered the messy breakup.

The couple saw their marital discourse unfold on hundreds of Web sites, entertainment news shows, and magazine covers. The media were quick to portray Jon as a heartless monster who abandoned his children to pursue a hedonistic lifestyle. The media assiduously informed millions of people of every development in their saga through the Internet, cable television, and magazines. The reason? Their story apparently was very entertaining.

The media, entertainment, and celebrity are inextricably linked in very complicated ways. The media direct the audience's attention to specific people and not to others. Celebrities, the focus of media attention, play significant roles in every aspect of social life from the marketplace to politics, and, of course, culture.

This chapter will

- outline the development of the idea of celebrity,

- examine the relationship of the media to the creation of celebrity,

- provide snapshots of celebrities from different periods, and

- explore the power that celebrities have in public life.

Required Reading: In the article "The Imaginary Social World and the Use of Media Figures in Advertising," Neil Alperstein explores the role celebrities play in advertising and in people's imagination. Celebrity spokespeople in advertising create illusions of intimacy and enable viewers to cultivate imaginary social relationship with media figures.

THE DEFINITION OF CELEBRITY

There have always been heroes—Odysseus of Homer's *The Iliad* and *The Odyssey*, Jason in search of the Golden Fleece, and so on. And there has always been fame. The cultural historian and film critic Leo Braudy has argued that Alexander the Great is perhaps Western civilization's first famous person. While it is true that Alexander III of Macedonia established the greatest empire of its time through conquest, manipulation, and strategic communication, he also created the image of Alexander "the Great," the sobriquet by which he is known to modern generations. Julius Caesar also relied not solely on his military conquests and rule of Rome to spread his name and his impact throughout the Roman Empire. He also actively created an image for himself.

The human impulse toward fame—the desire, even the hunger, to stand out from the crowd, to be known by people whom the person does not know—seems deeply rooted in the human psyche. But for much of history, the mechanisms to achieve fame were limited. People were rooted in a rigid social structure from which they could not extricate themselves. Even in the few instances in which people could overcome the accidents of their births, usually in a time of war—such as William Wallace in Scotland and Joan of Arc in France—there were few vehicles to truly spread the word about an individual's exploits.

Fame was largely restricted to those who were born to power, and even then, the scope of one's fame was confined to the elite classes of society. While the literate class could write treatises and poetry, the circulation of those works was narrow. Portraiture and painting could capture a person's image, but at least until the Renaissance, painting in Europe was largely devoted to religious motifs. Kings and other rulers could imprint their visages on coins, but those coins contained almost no informational value about the person.

As in so many other aspects of social life, the invention of the printing press changed the process for becoming famous. From the beginning, printing expanded the reach and audience for communication. Fame and celebrity rely on the ability to attract and maintain an audience. Without an audience, there is no fame, nor is there celebrity. New communications media enable new vehicles for building audiences for famous celebrities.

The impact printing had on the ability to command an audience can be seen in the literary marketplace in the 18th century. Prior to the 18th century, writers had to either be independently wealthy or find a patron to support and publish their work. As books became less expensive to produce in the 1700s, it became possible for writers to support themselves through the sale of their books. By the 1770s, English writer Samuel Johnson, who compiled the first *Dictionary of the English Language*, proclaimed to his biographer James Boswell that the age of aristocratic patronage for literary production was at an end because of book sales.

However, the shift to the marketplace to support production of books raised several issues for writers. Under the patronage system, a writer had only to appeal to one person, the patron. In the new environment, writers had to satisfy a much wider reading public, whose tastes were more difficult to determine in advance. Readers faced challenges as well. No longer could a reader anticipate the worth of a particular work based on knowledge of the patron. Books were privately circulated less often, with private circulation lists representing only a small fraction of the reading public. With the shift in the economic foundation of book publishing, there was no clear measure of literary quality.

The response to these challenges was the rise of literary magazines, whose pages were filled with book reviews written by critics assessing the merit of a given work. In London of the mid-1740s, for example, excluding newspapers, there were 30 periodicals that published book reviews. Twenty years later, that number had risen to 75. At least two magazines devoted themselves exclusively to reviewing new publications.

Made possible by lower-cost printing technologies, the reach of those periodicals was impressive in their day. In 1742, *Joseph Andrews*, written by Henry Fielding, one of the first English-language novels, sold 6,500 copies. The most popular magazine at the time, *Gentleman's Magazine*, circulated 3,500 copies monthly.

The growth of periodicals to review books enlarged the reading public. Moreover, it enabled writers such as Henry Fielding, Daniel Defoe, and Jonathan Swift to attract relatively large audiences. Moreover, those audiences remained in place to receive the author's subsequent works. Writers could build their reputations. With the help of the periodicals reviewing their books, they could become famous and celebrated. In fact, the term *celebrity*, which was once used to designate somebody who had performed certain rites and rituals, first took on its modern meaning at this time.

But what is the difference between *fame* and *celebrity*? Fame is driven by the unique characteristics and achievements of an individual that have been brought to the attention of a broad public. Fame is defined both by the achievement of the person and the community within which he or she is known. People can be famous within their professional community, for example, or within their city or other small community of people.

Celebrity involves the creation of a public image that commands widespread attention yet is not the same as a person's private life. Somebody is famous when many people know of the person's accomplishments. A person is a celebrity when many people think that they actually know the person, although their knowledge is limited to the way the individual appears to the public. Celebrities hold a place in the popular imagination. People believe they have relationships with celebrities—although those relationships are only imaginary. Indeed, the cultivation of these imaginary social relationships is an integral part of the production of celebrity.

Fame can be gained in many ways, including through word-of-mouth communication. The production of celebrity—the creation of a public persona—relies on the existence and exploitation of the channels of mass communication. While at one point celebrity was often linked in some way to fame, in the contemporary, highly mediated environment of the 21st century, an increasing number of people can create public personas completely unfettered to any actual accomplishments. Many people believe that they have relationships with Paris Hilton and actually care about who will be her next BFF, simply because she has a "reality" television show that they find amusing to watch.

CELEBRITY IN EIGHTEENTH-CENTURY AMERICA

All countries need heroes—people who take on mythic characteristics and serve as emblems for the national character. According to Amy Henderson, cultural historian at the Smithsonian National Portrait Gallery, the effort by the media to create heroes is part of a much larger enterprise to derive a mythic national character by focusing on military heroes, romantic fictional protagonists, and eminent statesmen who embodied the ideals of virtue and self-reliance. Heroes of the Revolutionary War era in America were meant to give the nation a sense of historical legitimacy.

Above all other figures of the Revolutionary generation, George Washington stood as the great embodiment of national virtue, the symbol of the fledgling nation's essential worthiness. But who was George Washington? Prior to his role in the American Revolution, Washington had a relatively undistinguished career. A surveyor and a planter, he won his first military commission at age 20 through family connections. His early military career in the British Army was marked largely by defeats. He was unable to win a commission in the regular British Army, as opposed to the militia. His wealth was acquired largely through his marriage.

Although not generally remembered today, the U.S. army under Washington's command struggled mightily, staggering from defeat to defeat in the early years of the revolution. During his tenure as president, he had to put down a rebellion led by distillers in Pennsylvania, and he was regularly denounced by his political opponents as a monarchist intent on become the king of America.

After his death, however, Washington and his image were transformed. The process began with a eulogy delivered by Henry Lee, which was widely circulated in pamphlet form. Washington, said Lee, "was first in war, first in peace, and first in the hearts of his countrymen." Then, in the words that are critical to understanding the transformation of Washington from being merely famous to being a celebrity, Lee continued, "he was second to none in the humble and endearing scenes of private life. Pious, just, humane, temperate and sincere—uniform, dignified and commanding—his example was as edifying to all around him as were the effects of that example lasting."

In the years to come—through written and oral accounts of Washington's younger years; through paintings, statues, and engravings; with music, ceremonies, and holidays in his honor; through schoolbooks and even bank notes—Americans came to "know" Washington. The "real" Washington, the private Washington, was no longer what mattered. All that mattered was the public image of Washington constructed through the media (see Figure 8.2).

Washington, of course, was not the only celebrity constructed by the media in 18th century America. Frontiersman Daniel Boone was a hugely popular figure who explored and opened up large parts of the United States that lay west of the Appalachian

Figure 8.2—*The celebrity-making media transformed George Washington from a famous general and political leader into the mythic founder of the nation.*

Mountains. Boone led a colorful life, blazing trails, fighting Indians, and embodying the American impulse to move west in many ways. But he became an iconic figure and the United States' first folk hero with the publication of John Filson's "The Adventures of Colonel Daniel Boon," part of his book *The Discovery, Settlement and Present State of Kentucke*. Though Filson had interviewed Boone, he embellished his account considerably, adding long philosophical dialogues and other literary flourishes. The book was translated into French and German, making Boone an international figure. One of his adventures served as the basis for James Fenimore Cooper's novel *The Last of the Mohicans*.

In 1833, Timothy Flint also interviewed Boone and published his *Biographical Memoir of Daniel Boone, the First Settler of Kentucky*. Flint's book greatly exaggerated Boone's feats. It had him fighting a bear barehanded, swinging on vines through trees to escape Indians, and other fanciful adventures. Though Boone's own family thought the accounts ridiculous, the book caught the popular imagination. The stories were recycled though countless cheap novels and young adult literature, and later through comic strips, radio programs, and films. Eventually, the Walt Disney Company produced a television series called *Daniel Boone* that ran for six years starting in 1964. The theme song of the show claimed that Daniel Boone was a "big man" in a "coonskin cap," even though he was neither big nor did he wear a coonskin cap.

Writer Washington Irving wrote that Americans "want something to rally round; some brilliant light to allure them from afar. They want something to attract and concentrate their affections." The celebrity of George Washington and Daniel Boone showed that Irving was right.

THE INVENTION OF MASS CELEBRITY

The first half of the 1800s was a period of great innovation in communication technologies. The invention of the steam-powered press and improved papermaking techniques led to the emergence of the penny press, which had circulations ten times greater than earlier newspapers. In 1840, the introduction of the telegraph severed the link between information and transportation. Information could be sent from Maine to Texas in just a matter of minutes or hours (depending on how it was routed) rather than a matter of weeks or months. Once the transatlantic cable was completed in 1866, information could flow freely between the United States and Europe.

In 1839, after a decade or more of work, Frenchman Louis Daguerre unveiled a viable approach to photography. Suddenly, realistic images of people's faces could become familiar to people whom they had never met. By the middle of the century, calling cards with people's photographs were commonplace. Abraham Lincoln opined that he was elected, in part, because of the calling card create for him by photographer Matthew Brady.

With photography, people could experience images of a thing without experiencing the thing itself. In 1859, Oliver Wendell Holmes suggested that photography would enable people to capture the surface of everything but the substance of nothing. Photography would make it easier to disseminate people's faces than their ideas.

These new communications technologies led to two significant developments. First, as newspapers and magazines grew in size and shrank in costs, competition grew. The publication that could provide the most enticing package of information would attract the most readers and prosper financially. Public discourse would no longer be confined to politics, business, and crime. All aspects of social life potentially became raw material for newspapers (although society news had started to make its way into newspapers as early as the 1830s.) Second, the gap between a person's public image and the person's private life grew. The media could present people's public lives—their public faces, so to speak—but even if the media reported details of people's private lives—and they did—the audience, which was growing larger and larger, still did not really know the public figures. They only knew what the media told them.

Consequently, public figures and celebrities played two roles in the growth of the media. First, different publications competed to report information about personalities who commanded the public attention. Once a figure had gained public prominence, the media wanted even more information about that person to ensure that readers would still pay attention to that publication. Celebrities in the 19th century print media played the same role that movie stars played through most of the 20th century. They attracted an audience to the media.

But the nascent mass media of newspapers and magazines were not the only players who wanted to attract audiences. A mass consumer market was beginning to emerge, and marketers of all kinds were learning how to use the media to draw attention for whatever it was they were promoting. Perhaps the first master of the art of using the media to create celebrities was P.T. Barnum, who is best known today for saying that there is "a sucker born every minute," although that line was actually said by somebody else in response to one of Barnum's stunts.

Born in Connecticut, Barnum moved to New York City in 1834 and embarked on a career in entertainment, first by creating a variety troupe and then purchasing a museum to display "human curiosities," such as General Tom Thumb, a joke-telling "little person," whom Barnum billed as the smallest person to walk alone. Thumb started to perform when he was four years old, although Barnum claimed he was 11. Tom Thumb eventually performed for Queen Victoria of England, an event that represented quite a publicity coup. While Barnum had just exaggerated Tom Thumb, many of the other curiosities Barnum showed to the public were outright frauds. Nonetheless, through the effective use of publicity, by the mid-1840s, Barnum's Museum was attracting 400,000 visitors a year.

One of the greatest testaments to Barnum's ability to create stars was the triumphant American tour of Jenny Lind. Born in Sweden around 1820, by age 17, she was a prominent singer in the Royal Swedish Opera, and by 20, a member of the Royal

Swedish Academy of Music. During the 1840s, she toured through Europe and in 1847 performed for Queen Victoria. In 1849, while performing in London, Barnum became aware of the large crowds Lind was drawing. He decided to bring her to the United States for a tour. The problem was that as popular as Lind was in Europe, she was little known to Americans.

But through Barnum's deft use of publicity, including hiring his own critics to review her performances in England before she set sail for America, he was able to generate a crowd of more than 40,000 people to greet her when she arrived in New York in 1850. A few days after she landed, a friend took the first photograph of Lind at the studios of Matthew Brady. In all, Lind gave 93 concerts and earned $250,000, a princely handsome sum in those days. Barnum himself earned at least $500,000.

P. T. Barnum represented something new in U.S. culture. Not only could he generate a pandemonium of attention for individuals, Barnum also made promotion itself a form of entertainment. His autobiography, *The Life of P.T. Barnum*, was first published in 1854, when he was 44, and went through numerous printings. Barnum dubbed himself the "King of Humbug" and saw nothing wrong with vigorous promotion, as long as the audience members were amused and felt they received value for their money.

Well-established as an impresario, Barnum embarked in the late 1840s on an effort to make attending the theater a respectable middle-class activity. Prior to that, going to the theater was seen as morally questionable. To change that image, he built the largest theater in New York City and called it the Moral Lecture Room. The first play he staged there, *The Drunkard*, was basically a lecture on temperance. He followed that show with an array of melodramas, farces, and other theatrical performance.

He staged watered-down versions of Shakespeare plays and a sanitized version of Harriet Beecher Stowe's antislavery novel *Uncle Tom's Cabin*, making it acceptable to family audiences. To attract those audiences, he offered matinee showings, so families could attend the theater during the day.

During this period, entertainers began to emerge as subjects for national adoration and fascination. In one newspaper article from the late 1880s, a journalist remarked on the rising popularity of stage actors, "It is remarkable how much attention the stage and things pertaining to it are receiving nowadays from the magazines."

Magazines started writing about the Barrymore family—a multigenerational theatrical family whose matriarch, Louisa Lane Drew, owned the Arch Street Theater in Philadelphia—and other leading lights of the theatre. During this period, the nation seemed to be able to "get to know" dozens of theatrical performers through articles about them printed in illustrated magazines.

THE TRIUMPH OF ENTERTAINMENT

As the United States urbanized in the 19th century, cities could support larger theaters. With the growth of railroads, traveling shows could more easily barnstorm across the country to smaller towns and hamlets. Always the innovator, P. T. Barnum was the first to move a circus around the nation via rail. Ever the self-promoter, he dubbed the circus "The Greatest Show on Earth." It featured a jumbo elephant.

The efforts of Barnum and other entertainment promoters were aided and abetted by newspapers and magazines looking to fill their pages with appealing material. As newspapers in the 1880s printed more pages daily, they broadened their coverage of events to include entertainment, human-interest stories, society gossip, and photographs. But when photographers invaded the wedding of Harvard University law professor Samuel Warren's daughter and plastered the pictures all over the Boston newspapers, Warren was incensed by the invasion. He and his colleague Louis Brandeis, who later became a justice of the U.S. Supreme Court, published an article in the *Harvard Law Review* in

1890 arguing that Americans had a right to privacy, which meant a right not to be bothered by the press.

Trying to preserve a sense of privacy within the expanding media environment was a losing battle. While newspapers and magazines had strong grips on the public's attention span, emergence of radio, the recording industry, and motion pictures in the 1920s and 1930s revolutionized the role of entertainment in American social life. Radio, phonographs, and movies were qualitatively different media from print. With radio, listeners actually heard a singer's voice. So, while thousands might have attended the concerts of Jenny Lind and heard her sing once, millions of people actually heard the voices of Al Jolson and Bing Crosby through their recordings. Crosby became an instant national sensation after he signed a contract for a 15-minute broadcast with CBS Radio in 1931.

Referred to as "crooning," Crosby's soft voice and engaging style was perfect for radio broadcasting. In sharp contrast to the big Irish and Italian tenors whose voices filled large auditoriums, a crooner's softer delivery was just right for the limited technology of the day. Microphones for radio and music recording could not have loud volume. Crooning emphasized subtle vocal nuances and phrasing that had not been heard before. The audience loved this different way of singing, which did not damage the equipment. Bing Crosby and the male singers who followed, perhaps most notably Frank Sinatra, became heartthrobs for women across the country.

Radio and the recording industry broadened the kinds of music available to the public. In the 1920s, a genre of music with its roots in the African-American and Creole cultures of Louisiana made its way to New York City and was embraced by the cultural avant-garde. The music was called "jazz." Despite harsh criticism from the musical establishment of the time, jazz emerged as a quintessentially American form of music because it could be marketed via records beyond its geographical roots.

Indeed, music was changed fundamentally by the spread of radio and records. Light and melodic songs were always a part of popular culture, propagated primarily through sheet music that people could play. Starting in the mid-1880s, many U.S. sheet-music publishers set up shop in the same district in New York City, which came to be called Tin Pan Alley. But by the 1930s, radio and phonographs supplanted sheet music as the mechanism to distribute new music. As radio became established as a major media in the late 1930s, the press quickly started giving radio personalities star treatment. Singers, comedians, and bandleaders became household names. People faithfully listened to shows featuring bandleaders, such as Tommy Dorsey and Benny Goodman, and comedians, such as Jack Benny and Fred Allen.

Companies emerged to market aggressively the records of the most popular singers of the day. Not surprisingly, the most promising market for this new technology and new music was the youth audience. Starting in the 1920s, if not before, young people in their teens and early twenties began to emerge as a dynamic, important market to be cultivated. The 1920s marked an important era in the establishment of what is known today as youth culture.

Music was not the only area of entertainment that was revolutionized by radio. Radio also broadened the reach of sports. While sports coverage in newspapers had expanded in the 1880s, the radio broadcast of baseball games, horse racing, and boxing in the 1920s increased their audiences exponentially. The first baseball game was broadcast on August 5, 1921, by KDKA in Pittsburgh, Pennsylvania, as the Pittsburgh Pirates defeated the Philadelphia Phillies 8 to 5. The World Series between the New York Yankees and the New York Giants was broadcast by KDKA and WJZ of Newark, New Jersey, and called by the famed sportswriter Grantland Rice.

Rice was not at the ballpark, however. Instead, he received a telegram after each play, from which he would reconstruct the action. The pace of baseball allowed it to overcome the limitations of the technology at the time. Baseball players, who until that time were seen as somewhat disreputable, soon became national icons. In the late 1920s, when a reporter pointed out to home-run slugger Babe Ruth that he was making more money than President Herbert Hoover, Ruth opined he was worth it because he had had a better year than Hoover.

Baseball was not the only sport to claim a bigger footprint in American life through radio broadcasting. Broadcasts of horse racing and boxing also attracted huge numbers of listeners. In the 1930s, the races of thoroughbred horses such as War Admiral and Seabiscuit were avidly followed from coast to coast. When the two horses had a match race in 1938, the entire nation stopped to listen to the radio broadcast of the event. Even schools stopped classes so students could hear the event (see Figure 8.3). In boxing, two fights between American heavyweight champion Joe Louis and German champ Max Schmeling in 1936 and 1938 were broadcast to worldwide radio audiences and were trumpeted as a struggle between Western democracies and Fascism.

If radio had the power to increase the popularity of sports, it also had the power to destroy sports. Before the advent of radio, wrestling was among the three most popular sports in the United States. During the early part of the century, wrestlers toured the nation and attracted huge crowds. Wrestling events were staged in the largest theatres and opera houses. Wrestling was slowly transforming from a legitimate martial-arts sport into its current format as carefully staged entertainment.

The wrestlers would sometimes have legitimate matches, known as "shoots," while other times, the competition was fixed, with the outcome pre-determined. But wrestling was a visual event that did not translate when radio started broadcasting matches. As radio became more popular, wrestling declined, essentially going out of business. The sport would reemerge in the 1950s, however, thanks to the growth of another medium: television.

Wrestling and television were perfect for each other. Few families had television sets in the 1950s, and several families would commonly gather together at someone's home to watch tiny black and white screens. Television networks loved the fact that wrestling matches cost little to produce, and wrestling promoters were eager to stage matches most days of the week. Even news stories exposing wrestling as "fixed" did little to stop the popularity of wrestling.

Indeed, the relationship between the popularity of sports and the media to broadcast them is critical. While college football was popularly covered in newspapers since the 1880s, professional football did not realized its full potential to gather fans until the National Football League signed a

© Margo Harrison (horse), Cheryl Ann Quigley (horse race), 2010. Shutterstock Inc.

Figure 8.3—*Champion thoroughbred racehorse Seabiscuit inspired millions of Depression-era radio listeners, proving that animals also could become media celebrities.*

league-wide contract to televise games and innovations such as the instant replay became commonplace. The popularity of basketball also was aided greatly when games were more regularly broadcast on television.

THE INVENTION OF MOVIE STARS

Both radio and the music industry manufactured national celebrities and conveyed feelings of intimacy with the audience that helped to develop the idea of a youth culture. However, their impact on popular culture was not as great as that of the movies. People were drawn by movie stars in the era of the silent films, but even more so after the release of the movie *The Jazz Singer* in 1927, the first full-length motion picture with synchronized dialogue, in which viewers could not only hear a performer's voice but also see the performer's face. Movie stars became national icons, treated almost as if they were royalty.

Mary Pickford was perhaps the first great female movie star in the United States. Born in 1892, Pickford was part of a theatrical family, touring the country and acting in mediocre plays produced by undistinguished companies. In 1907, she landed a supporting role in a play on Broadway and then was signed by movie director D. W. Griffith to work for his company, Biograph, which produced silent films.

Pickford moved with the Biograph production team to Los Angeles in 1910 and over the next six years worked prodigiously with the early pioneers of the movie industry, including Griffith, Adolf Zukor, who founded Paramount Pictures, Carl Laemmle, whose company served as the foundation for Universal Pictures, and others. She recruited her friend Lillian Gish to work in the industry as well.

As was typical in those years, Pickford played both small and large parts. And while in the early years the names of the actors and actresses were not even listed in a film's credits, the audiences noticed Pickford. In 1916, she signed a contract with Zukor that gave her control over the production of her films and a salary of $10,000 a week. In contrast, at that time, the vice president of the United States earned $12,000 a year.

Two years later, however, she left Paramount and formed her own company called United Artists with other film stars, including Charlie Chaplin, Douglas Fairbanks and D. W. Griffith. In total, Pickford starred in 52 feature films, and throughout much of the 1910s and 1920s, she was considered the most famous woman in the world. Her 1920 film *Pollyanna* grossed more than $1 million at the box office.

Pickford's career as an actress came to an end when she underestimated how popular sound would be in the movies. She had likened sound in movies to putting lipstick on the Venus de Milo. She also made the mistake of appearing in a 1929 film without her trademark curls. Instead, her hair was cut in a fashionable bob. Her fans were shocked.

Mary Pickford's success and celebrity illustrate the changes that movies brought to entertainment. She had been, at best, a third-rate theatrical actress, but the movies made her a star of the first magnitude, earning more money in a year than most theatrical actors could dream of earning in a lifetime. Her production was prodigious, but the primary goal of each movie was to attract as large an audience as possible. Because the movies are a democratic form of entertainment, Pickford was idolized by the masses.

THE GOSSIP INDUSTRY

With the growth of movies, people in the audience wanted to know more about the personal lives of the stars they saw on the silver screen. As the perceived distance between entertainers and their audiences narrowed with the addition of sound, the thirst for personal information about the stars grew.

In addition to coverage in New York tabloid magazines, other magazines were created that developed themselves to cover celebrities. *Photoplay* emerged as the most popular and most powerful magazine covering the film industry and its stars. During the 1920s and 1930s, its circulation reached more than 200,000 readers. *Photoplay's* editors created a format that would set a precedent for almost all celebrity magazines that followed.

Credited with inventing celebrity media, the publication essentially launched the practice of intensive press coverage of the most popular film stars, a practice that was extended and enhanced during the 1980s and 1990s with the launch of *People* magazine, *US Weekly*, and others. The goal of the celebrity magazines is to show the "human" side of the stars. As one regular feature in *US* puts it, the idea is to show that stars are people "just like us."

As part of its influence, *Photoplay* published articles by the most famous gossip columnists of the day, including the "queen" of gossip, Louella Parsons. No one before had enjoyed the power of Parsons' influence in Hollywood. A writer for William Randolph Hearst in the 1920s, Parsons started out, like most female writers at that time, writing "light reading" articles. She remained a minor player in the Hearst media empire, until Hearst discovered that people actually wanted to read about motion-picture stars.

Parsons arrived in Hollywood at the same time that films became a major U.S. industry and film stars had large followings. She established herself as the social and moral arbiter of Hollywood. Her judgments were considered the final word in most cases, and her disfavor was feared more than that of movie critics. Her column was followed religiously by millions of readers as well as movie-industry insiders, giving her a unique type and degree of power.

Parsons' influence reached its height when the studio system controlled Hollywood and a mere handful of moguls wielded the power of professional life and death over the stars. The studios needed someone who would portray their stars in a positive light, so they catered to everything that Parsons and her competitor, Hedda Hopper, demanded.

The press and studios became fused into one giant star-making machine that portrayed film stars as the quintessence of glamour. The studios relied heavily on the press to maintain its control of both the industry and the nation's imagination, creating a symbiotic relationship with a few, well-placed columnists to make sure the public heard only what the movie executives wanted them to hear. Publicity agents were eager to get their clients on the covers of coveted magazines and also fed information to the columnists.

Gossip was not restricted to print publications. Walter Winchell, credited by some with inventing the modern gossip column, started his career in 1920 when he wrote for the *Vaudeville News*. He moved to the *New York Evening Graphic* in 1924 and began writing about the personal relationships of celebrities—who was seeing whom, who was getting married, who was getting divorced, and so on.

Winchell made his radio debut in 1930 with a 15-minute show on Saks on Broadway on the CBS radio network. Known for his machine-gun-like, staccato delivery through the 1950s, virtually everyone in America knew his name. Fed by press agents, tipsters, legmen, and ghostwriters, he possessed an extraordinary ability to make a Broadway show a hit, create overnight celebrities, or enhance or destroy a political career. FBI Director J. Edgar Hoover supplied scoops and favors in return for Winchell's support. Upon Winchell's death in 1972, a front-page obituary in *The New York Times* eulogized him as "the country's best-known, widely read journalist as well as its most influential."

The celebrity economic system that Parsons and Winchell helped established remains firmly in place today, supplemented or even led by television shows, Web sites, and Web 2.0 technologies such as Twitter. The lineup consists of television shows such as *Entertainment Tonight, Access Hollywood,* and *Inside Edition,* and Web sites such as TMZ.com and PerezHilton.com. The concept of celebrity media is unchanged from the era of

Parsons and Winchell. Audiences want to know the inside scoop about a celebrity, particularly when the celebrity might be misbehaving.

Periodically, contemporary celebrities such as Lindsay Lohan, Britney Spears, and Angelina Jolie experience round-the-clock coverage of their every move. Every day, crews of young reporters armed with cameras and microphones search the streets of Los Angeles for some film star dressed in shabby clothes, inebriated, or walking into a restaurant—or, better yet, into a hotel with somebody who isn't their spouse. Their efforts are supplemented by thousands of fans who are only too willing to snap pictures on their cell phones of celebrities misbehaving and to upload them to a gossip Web site (see Figure 8.4).

MASS-MEDIATED CELEBRITY

While most celebrities have their roots in the entertainment industry, media mechanisms are in place to turn virtually anyone into a celebrity. Some pundits argue that the age of mass-media celebrity began when a shy pilot from Minnesota astonished millions in 1927 by flying his airplane, the *Spirit of St. Louis*, solo across the Atlantic Ocean. From that moment, the media had an insatiable appetite for any news it could learn about him.

Figure 8.4—*In the 21st century participatory media culture, any fan with a cell phone or digital camera can become a paparazzi.*

Charles Lindbergh was only 25 years old when he accomplished his feat. The flight of the *Spirit of St. Louis* gripped the public, and the media went to extraordinary lengths to celebrate the young man. *Time* magazine event invented a new honor, "Man of the Year," to commemorate Lindbergh's feat and to promote the publication. The media could not get enough of Lindbergh, who married Anne Morrow, the daughter of a U.S. diplomat. It was a storybook romance. She even learned to fly.

The media were equally relentless when the Lindberghs had to endure the tragedy of having their first son kidnapped and killed. As the events of the kidnapping unfolded, the press treated the Lindberghs as commodities to be exploited, with no respect for their privacy and no regard for the terrible grief that they were experiencing. The Lindberghs were horrified to find out that, after the baby's remains were found, reporters snuck into the morgue and photographed the body. The subsequent murder trial itself stirred up such a media frenzy that Lindbergh worried about the safety of his second son, Jon.

Often, the only way Lindbergh could escape the press was to climb into a plane and fly away. Despite flirtations with Fascism and anti-Semitism, he remained a popular figure throughout his life. Even into his 70s, a rare public appearance by Lindbergh would have people running to see him, with people clamoring to shake his hand.

Lindbergh was the prototype of what is now called an "instant celebrity." In the blink of an eye, an ordinary person is elevated into sudden prominence. With the spread of television and then the Internet, the chance of any individual to become an instant celebrity grew.

In the 1950s, long before reality television converted ordinary citizens into instant celebrities, the television viewing audience was mesmerized by a new form of programming—the "big-money" quiz show. In the quiz shows, ordinary people would compete for prizes by answers questions or facing other challenges. From its premiere on CBS in June 1955, *The $64,000 Question* was an immediate sensation, racking up some of the highest ratings in television history up to that time. Its success spawned a spin-off, *The $64,000 Challenge*, and a litter of like-minded shows: *The Big Surprise, Dotto, Tic Tac Dough*, and *Twenty-One*.

While the success of these shows was anticipated, what was not expected was how winning contestants became instant celebrities, who were hounded by the media as if they were rock-and-roll or movie stars. Part of the public adoration stemmed from the great drama that surrounded the quiz shows, in which average citizens performed under great pressure, trying to succeed while sweating profusely under the hot studio lights. Through that adoration, the public transformed college professors into national figures.

But the televisions quiz shows of the 1950s were not exactly what they presented themselves as. The most notorious episode, which has come to be called the "quiz show scandal," involved NBC's *Twenty-One*, a quiz show based on the game of blackjack, and Charles Van Doren, an English professor at Columbia University. Van Doren was the most popular contestant of the quiz show era. He was an authentic celebrity phenomenon featured on the cover of *Time* magazine—one of the great celebrity achievements of the era. Commentators praised his all-American good looks. Van Doren even obtained a permanent spot on NBC's morning show *Today*, in which he discussed non-Euclidean geometry and recited 17th century poetry.

Van Doren was a natural showman on *Twenty-One*. He engaged the audience by seeming to struggle to answer questions. He would mutter to himself, taking out a handkerchief to wipe his sweating brow. Then, suddenly, he would proclaim, "Oh, I know!" There was one problem with his elaborate performance: He knew the answers in advance. The quiz shows were fixed. Van Doren was not the only one who was part of the charade. The losing contestants also participated. However, one of them became disgruntled and spilled the beans.

Herbert Stempel, Van Doren's former nemesis on *Twenty-One*, exposed the quiz show fraud, saying how he agreed to lose graciously. A New York grand jury was convened to investigate Stempel's allegations. The bad publicity destroyed the quiz shows ratings. The quiz show producers, Van Doren, and the other big-money winners steadfastly maintained their innocence. But additional disgruntled former contestants came forward to expose the fraud.

Everyone got into the act of condemning the crooked quiz shows. Congressional hearings investigated the quiz show scandals, fueling continued media coverage. According to the trade magazine *Variety*, the firestorm resulting from the quiz show scandals "injured broadcasting more than anything ever before in the public eye."

Television did more than just elevate ordinary people to celebrity status. It put actors, actresses, talk show hosts, newscasters, and game show hosts into people's living rooms day after day. When housewives reported that the tremendously popular daytime television personality Arthur Godfrey seemed to them like a close personal friend or member of the family, such pseudo-relationships became known to social scientists as parasocial interaction. Celebrities and entertainers became household figures and imaginary friends and confidantes.

For example, in 1972, Walter Cronkite, the anchor of the CBS News, was voted the most trusted man in America in a national opinion poll. In the 1970s, Robert Young, who played the fictional doctor Marcus Welby on a popular television series, was considered to be a medical expert by some. In middle of the show's run, Young starred in a series of television commercials in which he said, "I am not a doctor, but I play one on TV." His role as a doctor on television presumably helped his credibility with the viewers. In the 1990s, when Jennifer Aniston, one of the stars of the hit television show *Friends*, decided to change her hairstyle, tens of thousands of women followed suit.

Not only did television bring celebrities into people's homes every night, but also it brought viewers into celebrities' homes. In the early 1950s, fabled CBS newscaster Edward R. Murrow hosted a show called *Person to Person*, in which Murrow chatted informally with famous people such as former president Harry S. Truman, movie star Marilyn Monroe, and author John Steinbeck, in the intimacy of their own homes. The concept was picked up in the 1980s, with *Lifestyles of the Rich and Famous*, when Robin Leach would interview and tour the homes of extremely wealthy people, opening to cameras the extravagant living places of entertainers, major league athletes, and titans of business. The same idea was put to use in the MTV hit *Cribs*, which first aired in 2000 and also featured tours of the over-the-top mansions of entertainers and other celebrities, such as Mariah Carey, whose New York City penthouse was the subject of the most-watched episode in the first five years the show was on the air.

Television made celebrity more pervasive and more constant in everyday life. As cable television became widespread and the number of channels people could access jumped from three to seven to more than a 100 or even 200, the need to fill airtime grew intense. One solution was reality, or unscripted, television, in which regular people were brought together to compete in some away—a race, a contest, for a date, an apprenticeship with business executive Donald Trump, and many other premises. In true Warholian fashion, scores of people every television season receive their "15 minutes" of stardom on television.

While television considerably broadened access to the channels of mass communication, the Internet made it possible for virtually anyone to win worldwide acclaim in a matter of moments. In 2009, on the British reality talent show *Britain's Got Talent*, the audience and the judges were ready to laugh at a matronly, poorly dressed middle-aged woman who stepped to the microphone. One of the regular elements of the tryout portion of show is to present contestants who cannot carry a tune but are totally oblivious to their lack of talent. This contestant seemed to be in that category.

But when she began to sing, listeners heard an astonishingly beautiful voice. One judge's jaw literally dropped. Another judge sat back in his chair, as if pushed back by the power of the voice. Within days, a video on YouTube of Susan Boyle's performance "went viral" and was seen by tens of millions of people around the world.

YouTube, Facebook, and other social media offer new possibilities for creating celebrity. But fame via the Internet seems to be even more short-lived than Andy Warhol anticipated. Fifteen minutes of attention on the Internet is quite a long time.

CONCLUSION

The growth of new channels of communication has changed the nature and scope of entertainment and celebrity, even changing the nature of who commands attention in society and why. Sociologist Leo Lowenthal surveyed the biographical articles that appeared in the *Saturday Evening Post* and *Colliers*, two national general interest magazines, between 1901 and 1941, and reported his findings in his book, *Radio Research, 1942–1943*. In the years 1901 through 1914, 74 percent of the magazines' subjects came from traditional fields such as politics, business, and the professions. But after 1922, more than half came from the world of entertainment: sports figures such as Joe Louis and Babe Ruth, and movie stars such as Mary Pickford and Charlie Chaplin. The shift toward sports and entertainment celebrities is evidence of radio's impact on making celebrities.

Some critics contend that the role entertainment plays in society has exacted a considerable cost. In the words of media scholar Neil Postman, "we are amusing ourselves to death." The sheer glut of entertainment has made it difficult to pay attention to and to think about the more important and more authentic aspects of being human. In fact, other media critics contend that the amount of time that people, particularly young people, spend watching television, playing video games, and surfing the Internet has led to a situation in which the parasocial interactions with celebrities and other

Figure 8.5—*Children blur together real and imaginary worlds presented in the media.*

people encountered through the media seem as real as face-to-face relationships with other, real people in their lives. The separation between what is real and authentic, and what is mediated and artificial, has dissolved (see Figure 8.5).

From the middle of the 1800s, when P. T. Barnum began to invent the techniques used to attract audiences by entertaining them, to the creation of YouTube, except for sports and some select popular singers, mediated performance has become more important than live performance. In the middle of the 19th century in Paris, the annual art exhibit would draw tens of thousands of people. Impressionists painters like Edouard Manet could scandalize an entire nation with a new and provocative painting. Today, many people could not name prominent painters, much less be familiar with their works. In the late 1800s, visual artists on stage were cultural superstars. In today's world, not a single actor commands national attention through only work in the theater. But movie actors since the 1920s and television actors since the 1950s have commanded huge audiences, regardless of their actual acting ability.

The family situation comedy was one of the earliest successful genres on television. Viewers were introduced to television housewives such as June Cleaver from the show *Leave It to Beaver* and Harriet Nelson from *Ozzie and Harriet*. Now, reality television viewers get to meet the "real housewives" of Orange County, California, New York, New Jersey, and Atlanta. The explosion of media has created numerous celebrities whose claim to fame is the everyday nature of their lives.

Chefs, truck drivers, lumberjacks, real-estate agents, fashion consultants, and others have become overnight celebrities. An MTV series *Jersey Shore*, about young residents from New Jersey, made household names of people such as "The Situation" and "Sooki." These "celebrities" were formerly indistinguishable young people whom most could not pick out of a crowd. Yet thousands of fans await their latest post on Twitter.

The media spend considerable time and effort trying to portray celebrities as "regular" people with mundane, everyday lives. Television coverage of the Olympics, for example, routinely features extended profiles of the athletes intended to show them "up close and personal." By knowing the personal details of celebrities, people feel as though they have a relationship with them. Viewers truly care who becomes the next American Idol, as millions of people vote for their favorite each week.

At the same time, millions of people imagine that they might become the next American Idol some day. With the development of new communications technologies and the entertainment industries they enable, celebrities are transformed from being oddities to residing at the core of the mediated environment in which people live.

THE IMAGINARY SOCIAL WORLD AND USE OF MEDIA FIGURES IN ADVERTISING

by Neil Alperstein

In order to be a member in good standing of U.S. society, one should possess information about people one has never actually met, including knowledge of media figures. Caughey (1984) described the importance of such knowledge:

> In Europe during World War II, strangers dressed in American uniforms and speaking fluent English might be Americans lost from their own units or German spies. Standard interrogation questions designed to test American affiliations included inquiries about persons the individual could not be expected actually to know—for example, 'Who plays first base for the Philadelphia Phillies?' Answering such questions successfully was literally of life or death significance. (31)

The knowledge of media figures—individuals with whom we are familiar, but have not actually met—is an important part of everyday social interaction and distinguishes outsiders from insiders in U.S. society (Allen, 1982). In addition to knowing about media figures, people feel strongly about them. "People characterize unmet media figures as if they were intimately involved with them, and in a sense they are—they engage in pseudo-social interactions with them" (Caughey, 1984: 33).

This chapter describes the nature of imaginary social relationships with media figures appearing in advertising. It is concerned with the degree of connectedness to media figures that may range from mere awareness to deep and abiding loyalty. The ways in which individuals utilize those connections to media figures, not necessarily as a basis upon which to make decisions about products, but rather to mediate their imaginary relationships, is discussed.

MEDIA FIGURE FUNCTIONS

Klapp (1964) claimed media figures perform three major functions for their audiences. "First, they function as an emotional outlet providing a portal for both positive and negative feelings to be vented. Second, they function as role models that an individual may incorporate into his or her own make-up. Third, media figures may

READING NOTES

influence individuals to behave in certain ways; live in a particular lifestyle, for example" (34). The model through which media figures emerge, which klapp referred to as a dialectic, does not identify why someone becomes a media figure; some people become media figures even though they would rather not. The celebrity-making process takes place in the form of a public drama that is in constant flux as new faces regularly appear on the scene. Advertising is an ideal, if not likely, place for this drama to occur.

Fowles (1996) described four ways in which individuals regard media figures in advertising. First, media figures "encapsulate and personify the normalizing services of popular culture" (117). By normalize he meant both to satisfy emotional needs and to confirm social norms. Second, individuals overlay the repeated exposure of the media figure with certain personality traits. In this sense, individuals reintegrate the media figure into their own lives through the idealization of certain qualities they appreciate. Third, individuals can utilize the media figure as a talking point in social discourse. And, fourth, Fowles suggested that media figures are a means by which individuals celebrate the world of popular culture, a world that is elevated from the mundane qualities of ordinary life.

Although interaction with media figures may take place in various media contexts, the ever-changing nature of advertising, and the dramatic conventions on which it is based (Esslin, 1987), make advertising an ideal place for this interaction to occur. Consider, for example, the consumer who is a long-standing fan of Jerry Seinfeld, whose imaginary social relationship grew through his long-running sitcom and who obtains an American Express card because Jerry Seinfeld is a guy you can "trust" and a "good guy." The importance of this pseudosocial interaction and evidence regarding the functions of celebrities from cultural (Caughey, 1984; Schickel, 1985; Schudson, 1984; Zeitlin, 1979), and marketing perspectives (Joseph, 1982; Rubin, Mayer, & Friedman, 1982) is well documented.

MEDIA FIGURES AND EMULATION

The use of testimonials by advertisers dates back to their unsavory connection to patent medicines in the 19th century. In the 1880s, the British company, Pears' Soap, used the concept of association—connecting cleanliness and godliness to their product—by obtaining an endorsement from U.S. preacher Henry Ward Beecher. Pears' later created an emotional connection to the product by having the actress Lillie Langtry endorse Pears' (Twitchell, 2000). However, it was not until the 1920s that advertisers featured famous people as product endorsers. Actresses Joan Crawford, Clara Bow, and Janet Gaynor were among the first celebrities to promote products (Fox, 1984). At that time, the rationale given by advertising agencies for using celebrities was "the spirit of emulation" (90).

The rise of performers as cultural figureheads is largely a 20th-century phenomenon that parallels the rise of popular culture and advertising (Fowles, 1996). The star system from which the early endorsers emerged was closely tied to the growing popularity of film and the birth of modern consumer culture: rising incomes, discretionary spending, increased leisure time, a rapid increase in new technologies, growth of urban areas, and women entering the workplace (Gamson, 1994). Early celebrity endorsers served merely to introduce products and recommend them to consumers. Mullan (1997) described how a review of popular magazines of the 1920s indicates a shift away from heroes to a new category of celebrities. This amplifies Daniel Boorstin's (1962/1992) widely accepted definition of celebrity—persons known for their well-known-ness.

Jamieson and Campbell (2001) suggested the following about the way media figures in advertising build associations that make their behavior worth emulating:

> *When celebrities appear in commercials, they are often there to testify to the worth of*

READING NOTES

_____

_____

_____

_____

_____

a product. Sometimes they function as pseudo-authorities. What qualifies Ed McMahon as an expert on mayonnaise, motorcycles, or sunglasses? At best, celebrities speaking outside their field of achievement give testimony about their ordinary experience, experiences no more authoritative than yours and mine, about how coffee tastes or how well a detergent works. Often, the celebrity not only tells us why he or she uses the product but also hints that if we want to be like him or her, we ought to use this product. (237)

Fowles (1996) reported that entertainers receive about 60% of their income from advertising. In addition to appearing in advertisements, media figures make personal appearances, promote their own product lines, and hawk merchandise from movies in which they have appeared, among other promotional activities.

THE ILLUSION OF INTIMACY

In contemporary U.S. society, emulation provides only a partial explanation for the use of media figures in advertising. At times, advertisements, along with other media content, create the illusion of interpersonal contact when media figures speak directly out of the television and address audiences personally. Horton and Wohl (1956) defined this as a form of social interaction—"intimacy at a distance." Levy (1979) suggested that such interactions may be demonstrated by the audience's reaction to meanings attributed to a media figure. From a cultural perspective, this artificial involvement is an elementary form of social activity that Snow (1988) concludes has gained a "taken-for-granted status" (204).

Advertisements at times create the illusion of participating when spokespersons speak directly to the audience as if to address them personally. Caughey (1984)

described this illusion as an important part of everyday American life in which "media consumption directly parallels actual social interaction" (37). Schickel (1985) referred to the "illusion of intimacy between the television viewer and the celebrity spokesperson" to explain how celebrities become viewers' friends (4).[1] As culture is the result of people acting through social forms, an imaginary social relationship may connect audiences to a celebrity who appears in an advertisement, a concept advanced by Caughey (1984).

P. Berger and Luckmann (1966) described this participation in "multiple realities" as a play form that helps us to make sense of reality. Gamson (1994) said:

a good chunk of the audience reads the celebrity text in its own language, recognizing and often playing with the blurriness of its vocabulary. They leave open the question of authenticity and along with it the question of merit. For them, celebrity is not a prestige system, nor a postmodern hall of mirrors, but much as it is in the celebrity-watching tourist circuit, a game. (173)

The role that advertising plays in this process is to interrupt and then extend the game as members of an audience move from one reality, news or entertainment programming, to "supermarkets, bathrooms and bars" (Caughey, 1984: 34). This is not, however, a passive experience, but one that resembles interactions in actual social relationships. As the individual takes on the role of objectified others he or she assigns a complimentary role to the media figure that might include father figure, good citizen, or lover, among others. Although advertising may temporarily take the viewer, reader, or listener out of his or her ordinary experience, the advertisements are locked into the values, motives, and roles embedded in contemporary U.S. middle-class society. In this sense, audience members get to interact with individuals that they may hold in very high esteem in the context of their everyday lives.

READING NOTES

Although Schudson (1984) supported the notion of divine power for media figures. Caughey categorized their influence more in the realm of middle-class values. It is, to some degree, a question of idolatry versus identification. As individuals operate within these multiple realities they may for a time become the media figure; that is they may closely identify with the celebrity. The following example is of a young athlete who, for a time, is transformed into a movie character.

> There's a movie called Rudy about a small guy whose life goal is to be on the Notre Dame football team. Because he's small there isn't much chance of him making the team. But the guy, Rudy, perseveres and eventually gets on the team and plays. At the end of the movie where Rudy's involved in the last play of the game, you hear the fans yelling "Rudy, Rudy, Rudy." The movie is based on the real-life experiences of this guy. And, I had the same experience. When I was in high school, I was considered too small to make the football team, but I wanted to play and persevered the same way Rudy did. I totally identified with the character and when I played my friends would shout "Rudy, Rudy, Rudy." I became Rudy.

This example demonstrates how the connection to the media figure transcends media consumption. This is not uncommon as Caughey (1984) said, "Even when the TV is turned off, the book closed, or the newspaper thrown away, people continue to engage in artificial relationships with the figures they have 'met' in the media" (39).

MEDIA FIGURES AS CULTURAL REFERENTS

Schudson (1984) described how the audience viewing a media figure in an advertisement draws on other frames in which the celebrity has appeared in order to give meaning to this experience. In other words, viewers generally do not initially learn about celebrities through appearances in advertising but in some other media context or form that is part of their larger system of referents. Reeves (1987) confirmed that meanings ascribed to a media figure may come in part from knowledge gained from some other appearance. Schudson (1984) claimed that the media figure's appearance in an advertisement, which itself contributes to intertextual complexity, is "highly abstracted and self-contained" (211). Personalities have to "appear, suggesting a pulling back into well-established characters" (213). Advertising "simplifies and typifies. It does not claim to picture reality as it is but reality as it should be—life and lives worth emulating" (215). Emulation is not simply, as Veblen (1973) described it, conspicuous consumption or the subordinate trying to emulate the superordinate. The notion of emulation has grown more complicated by the diversity of American culture and the complexity of the individual's experience with commercial media. Rather than imitating the powerful, Douglas and Isherwood (1996) saw cultural consumption as a means of expression. Goods and services carry with them symbolic expression whose importance may be expressed through association with media figures. In this sense, the media figure provides a symbolic and communicative connection to the goods and services being advertised. In other words, media figures may confer value on an object within the information system of advertising.

This abstraction may be the inducement—wonder that leads to consent—for the viewer to enter into a pseudosocial interaction with a media figure appearing in an advertisement. This is a significant cultural function even if media figures only temporarily take audiences beyond their actual everyday experiences. In this sense, audiences get to interact with individuals they may hold in very high esteem even in the context of their everyday lives, which Altheide and Snow (1979) suggested may be boring when compared to the highly entertaining situations depicted within the dramatic conventions of mass media and in advertising. Boredom may provide a partial explanation why media figures appearing in advertising, as well as those appearing in entertainment and news programming, take viewers beyond actual experience. Additionally, it may be that a media figure's repeated appearances have a cumulative effect as a pseudosocial relationship develops between the media figure and the viewer or reader. The accumulation of pseudosocial experience leads to an intertextual layering through which the relationship may take on greater meaning and dimension Caughey (1984) posited that the social world of Americans includes more media figures than actual persons.

EXPERIENCING MEDIA FIGURES

Generally, individuals describe media consumption in terms of being transported to another, sometimes disorienting, world in which they may become "involved" in the interactions of those who appear in programming and advertising. Horton and Wohl (1956) described this as creating a bond of intimacy. This experience is closely tied to the notion of suspension of disbelief in which individuals are out of touch with the actual world and in touch with their imaginary social world. Horton and Wohl reported that the fan develops loyalty to the media figure over time, as the fan sees the media figure as reliable and predictable. Reduction theory (C. Berger, 1985) similarly suggests that over time relationships develop through a process of increased certainty (C. Berger & Calabrese, 1975). Providing certainty in a relatively unstable world may be one of the more important roles media figures play in the culture. Appearance of media figures in advertising is a form of expression that as Douglas and Isherwood (1996) said, "make visible and stable the categories of the culture" (38).

Although some individuals rely on the certainty and predictability of media figures in their imaginary relationships, others indicate a more complex dimension, one that combines intimacy with a measure of skepticism. There is a natural tension within the imaginary social relationship, a dimension of which expands on Sunnafrank's (1986) conclusion that found closeness could be increased or decreased depending on the information learned. Gamson (1994) developed a typology of "celebrity-watching audiences" which he used to explain why some individuals become more involved with media figures than others. He referred to the "traditional believer" as one type of individual that "deflects reasoned evaluations ... in favor of fantasy or personal-identification relationships" (192).

EXPLORING IMAGINARY SOCIAL RELATIONSHIPS

It may be accurate to depict, as Schudson (1984) did, a character that on the screen or page is flattened by the one-dimensional media world that turns that character into an abstraction. This abstraction, according to Schudson, limits the audience in the ways in which it connects to the media figure. Media figures may be seen as attractive, interesting, or charismatic individuals. "Credibility of the media figure may encourage individuals to believe in the quality of a product, or believe in their own inadequacy and thus develop a need for a product, or they may be reminded of their own inadequacies that may be helped by a product" (Schudson, 1984: 224). Schudson maintained that the object of a celebrity endorsement is not intended to lead to a direct influence on the purchase of a product, but rather to connect the product to the "superhuman world of the gods" (228). However, informants indicate through their descriptions of imaginary social relationships with media figures, they inflate those images—adding dimension to the interaction—as evidenced in the descriptions of their attraction to media figures.[2] Informants generally learn about or enter into these relationships through the media figure's repeated appearances in news, entertainment programming, or sports events. Repeated exposure, however, does not equate with a deep and abiding relationship as informants indicate media figures may operate on several levels ranging from early impressions—both positive and negative—to physical or social attraction that holds some potential for modeling or imitative behavior. For individuals involved in these varying degrees of relationship, media figure appearances in advertising serve a variety of functions. One basic function of their repeated appearances and subsequent exposure to the audience is the maintenance of the relationship with the media figure. Individuals also may have used the media figure's appearance in the advertisement to further explore their attraction, to question some aspect of the media figure's character or role, or to reinforce or diminish feelings toward the media figure. Therefore, the media figure's appearance in the advertisement may serve as a mediating role: to keep the relationship current and to enliven, reinforce, or alter existing attitudes toward the media figure. In this sense, the relationship with the media figure can be meaningful, but individuals can also remake or unmake meaning, variations that need to be accounted for in any meaning-making system.

Over the past decade product endorsements by media figures have become routine. McAllister (1996) pointed to the following examples from the sitcom Seinfeld:

> When Seinfeld was the hip show, advertisers rushed to use these characterizations to make the show a referent system: Julia Louis-Dreyfus redoes her Elaine characterization on commercials for Nice 'n Easy hair treatments; Jerry Seinfeld makes observations worthy of his stand-up routine on American Express commercials; Jason Alexander is a George—like character on Rold Gold Pretzel commercials, and George's parents pitch the wonders of AT&T; Michael Richards maintains his Kramer persona in Pepsi commercials. (114)

Informants know of a large number of media figures appearing in advertisements, and express familiarity with fictional characters appearing in advertisements. These fictional characters included Madge the manicurist, the Maytag repairman, Sarah Tucker, and Morris the cat, to name a few. Informats are able to cite a range of media figures they may have been introduced to through appearances in the media, for whom they have over time developed great admiration, and who appear in advertising: Gillian Anderson, Joe Namath, Fran Drescher, Bill Cosby, Joan Lunden, and Joan Rivers to name a few. The following exemplifies an informant's attraction toward Gillian Anderson:

> Gillian Anderson did this ad for Saturn cars. She plays a savvy professional who is in the market to buy a reliable new car. In the commercial every car dealer she goes to treats her like an idiot, then she goes to the Saturn dealer and is treated like an equal. By the end of the commercial she not only buys a Saturn but is now selling them, playfully showing guys the vanity mirror. I saw this ad as I was about to graduate from college, and of course I recognized Gillian Anderson from the X-Files. I got the idea to apply to Saturn for a job not only because I loved the product and knew a lot about it, but because Gillian Anderson did too. I respect Gillian Anderson. She is close to my age and we both have a conservative image, but possess a definite wild side. I can't say how seeing her in the commercial affected my purchase of the car, but it certainly affirmed in my mind that I was making the right decision.

READING NOTES

_____

_____

_____

_____

_____

A homemaker recalls her reaction toward seeing the former Good Morning America co-host, Joan Lunden in a commercial:

> I regard Joan Lunden as a trusted friend. I choose to watch her primarily because I like her style. When she happens to be sick or on vacation I miss her. I've suffered through her pregnancies, and when I had children of my own, I bought Beechnut baby food based on her recommendation. I don't think she's some kind of goddess whose words I have to obey, but I do think she's an intelligent, responsible person, and I respect her opinion. When she starred in Mother's Day on cable I watched and I suppose I'll watch her on the show Everyday, as well. I especially enjoyed the clip at the beginning of the program showing her going through her daily routine: waking up, getting to work, exercising, grocery shopping, etc. I suppose she does affect my behavior because she gives me confidence. She seems normal, and she has also attained goals that I value: She's a bright, attractive woman with a happy family and successful career. So if she can do it, I can too. I will stop to watch Joan Lunden in a commercial because it's like having a friend in for coffee. I trust her and enjoy seeing her and her baby. Because I like the product, I feel vindicated whenever a Beechnut commercial comes on. When the Alar scare cropped up, Beechnut reassured consumers they didn't use that pesticide—of course not—Joan wouldn't speak for a company that did.

The informant describes the relationship as safe and predictable—one that had grown over a number of years. That safety and predictability extends from the media figure's appearances in entertainment and news programming into her advertising appearances and denotes an intertextual complexity connected through the various frames in which the media figure is experienced. A college student's description of an imaginary social relationship with Bill Cosby,[3] who many Americans have grown to admire over a long period of time, also exemplifies this predictability:

> Bill Cosby is a fine example of the well-rounded celebrity. He possesses many attributes he has applied to his career. The way in which he presents himself is unique because of the way he shares himself and his personality in everything he does. I admire Bill Cosby because of his individuality. He is the ideal model for Black youth to model themselves after. I try very hard to make my own character like him. I feel that Cosby and I share that characteristic of trying to be different. Bill's personality is an important factor when it comes to his well-rounded character. There is a time and place for everything and Bill Cosby observes this. He shares humor and sincerity whenever the time or whatever the occasion. He seems to know when and when not to. He exhibits self-control. I try to exhibit this attribute and I hope to be as successful as Bill Cosby. Also, his accomplishments in the media field have been a tremendous reflection on the Black community because he's a positive character. I hope to be able to accomplish as much in my life as he has in his. What a fulfilled life of goal conquering!

Informants express an awareness of particular aspects of Bill Cosby's life, chief among them, that he holds a doctorate in education. This, they say, translates into his unique ability to deal with children in advertisements. They not only admire the media figure, they used his appearance in advertising to reinforce some generally held belief and to find significant meaning in the experience. Informants refer to Bill Cosby, and to other media figures, as people to whom they feel close. Using first names—referring to Bill Cosby as

READING NOTES

_____

_____

_____

_____

_____

Bill, for example—implies a familiarity that parallels other imaginary experiences with media figures, primary of which are fantasies and dreams.

ENHANCING, DIMINISHING, AND MAINTAINING IMAGINARY RELATIONSHIPS

Fowles (1996) suggested that when media figures appear in advertisements they carry "certain valuable contextual inferences."

> *The performers have found their fame within the domain of popular culture, and when they reappear in the domain of advertising, they to one degree or another bring with themselves an aura of entertainment and diversion. When Candice Bergen testifies to the advantages of Sprint telephone service, the much enjoyed "Murphy Brown" is testifying also, when the retired Larry Bird appears in a Nike commerical, the active Larry Bird, memorable leader of the Celtics, is there too. (128–129)*

The bond of intimacy that may develop through repeated media appearances would be expected to continue into the media figure's appearance in an advertisement. The appearance, however, may also serve as a meta-communicative signal (Glenn & Knapp, 1987) that may disrupt the individual's suspension of disbelief and increase uncertainty about the media figure. Self-professed fans of particular media figures appearing in advertising express an expectation that the media figure will look or act a certain way, or might appear in expected contexts. There is an expectation regarding the synergy between a spokesperson, the product, the message, the context of the advertisement, and the medium of communication. Informants point to the synergy between Frank Perdue of the Purdue Chicken Company, because he looks like a chicken." Joan Rivers is admired because

she is straightforward," "outspoken," "blunt," or a "smart-ass." The physical resemblance of Frank Perdue to a chicken connects him to the product he promotes. Joan Rivers, as a straightforward and outspoken individual, was certainly consistent with promoting a phone service attempting to break through the advertising clutter and distinguish itself among the competition and certainly these attributes contribute to her success selling products via the Home Shopping Network. Candice Bergen played the same sarcastic role of Murphy Brown when she was spokesperson for Sprint. And, Sprint's current spokesperson, Sela Ward, displays the same independent mindedness in their advertisements, as does her character on the television series Once and Again.

Inconsistency among these variables of celebrity character, product, message, and medium serves as a signal that something is not quite right. Fowles (1996) said "Endorsements succeed only when consumers feel that meanings can shift along unimpeded paths from performer to product—either because of an inherent affinity between the two or because of the ingenuity of the agency's creative team, or both" (131). Strong identification with the celebrity is not enough for consumers to positively evaluate a product or its usefulness to them. As one informant reported:

> *My relationship with Joe Namath goes back to his legendary status with my favorite football team, the New York Jets. During his career he was able to go beyond the status of star regional athlete to enter the realm of the national folk hero. He did this by combining traditional football talent with a unique personality and sense of style that seemed to reflect the new nonconformist mood of the country.*

This individual suggests that Namath "cashed in" by selling everything from men's cologne to pantyhose. Of his appearance in a Nike shoe advertisement he says:

READING NOTES

_____

_____

_____

_____

_____

I don't know if I feel betrayed in any way, but part of the shine has certainly come off of one of my heroes whose actions and statements are now compromised by the lure of financial gain. By opening himself up to the highest bidder I feel that Joe Namath is no longer "free" to express the individualism that first attracted me to him.

Some advertisers apparently understand this interaction and in some instances use antagonism to gain viewers' attention. Informants point to the following examples: John McEnroe, the "bad boy of tennis," and Larry Hagman, who played J. R. Ewing on Dallas. In instances where these two media figures have appeared in advertisements, the advertiser uses the inverse of the stereotypical fan relationship to gain attention. One informant describes Fran Dresher, who appeared in the television program The Nanny, as "someone possessing all of the traits I try to avoid in a friend."

She is everything that I am not. She annoys me. Her voice sends a jolt through my spine that has me quickly reaching for the omnipotent remote control. She reminds me of my nosy neighbor and one of my college roommates. When I see her in a commercial, I am briefly transported to the days in college when I lived in a house with five other women—a bitter-sweet remembrance. This experience is both pleasurable and an irritation.

The Jenny Craig Company selected Monica Lewinsky, fresh from the Clinton scandal, as their spokesperson hoping to take advantage of her notoriety. "Some Jenny Craig franchises refused to pay for the ads. 'As a person who has been successful on our program, she'd done great,' said a franchise owner. But as a person to look up to there are certainly some issues there. ... I wouldn't be pleased if my daughter came home and said I want to be just like Monica Lewinsky" (cited in Jamieson & Campbell, 2001: 238). Inversion has the potential to attract attention, but the advertisement also can repel those for whom the inversion is transparent.

If predictability were simple to construct and maintain, advertisers would certainly take advantage of such ritualized encounters (Sunnafrank, 1986). However, because imaginary social relationships are dynamic, the nature of such encounters—the advertisement as the point of interaction—may be beyond the advertiser's control. In the following instance, a young man reported losing, then regaining, respect for Bill Cosby when he chose not to appear in an advertisement.

I think the way Bill Cosby was doing Coke commercials was misleading. I think I read in a magazine that he really didn't like the new Coke or drink the new Coke. Now that I don't see him doing any more commercials for Coke, I can respect him more and I would be more likely to buy a product he endorsed, if I was interested in the product.

A re-evaluation that the media figure has not sold out reinforces that he or she has integrity and allows the relationship to remain in its predictable mold.

Sometimes informants report extreme emotional reactions such as being "horrified" or watching "in disbelief" when they have seen a media figure appear in an advertisement; something is askew regarding their personal expectations for a media figure. This negative appraisal may, for a time, causes audiences to pay closer attention to the advertisement, or at least part of the message as they question something about the media figure, like the appropriateness of the appearance in an advertisement. Over a short period of time not believing that Bill Cosby likes Coke, for example, may create tension in the relationship. This tension may build over repeated exposure to the advertisement as evidenced by several informants' highly emotional reactions to these instances.

If the relationship is important, individuals may attempt to reconcile the conflicts that emerge between

READING NOTES

223

all of these elements. This is evidenced in the earlier description of the reaction to Bill Cosby choosing not to appear in Coke commercials. The tension between what is expected of the media figure and the media figure's "unexpected" behavior is important to advertisers attempting to get the audience's attention and may be emotionally unsettling for audiences involved in long-term imaginary relationships. For example, one Gen-Xer recalls the positive impact Orson Welles had on his life prior to his appearance on a wine advertisement:

> *Orson Welles demonstrated his independence from mainstream ideas and showed a willingness to suffer the consequences of pursuing his own course, traits that I have tried to develop within myself through the inspiration of figures like Welles. His emphasis on quality at the expense of acclaim led him to be a rather obscure figure for much of his professional career... . It has led me to develop some-what of a maverick attitude toward society, resulting in my taking unpopular stands on issues, both social and professional ones. While this has sometimes gotten me into trouble, I hope it has also earned me the same kind of grudging respect frequently accorded Welles.*

The informant, having recalled seeing Welles in a wine advertisement, describes this re-evaluation of the actor as "seriously disillusioning." He says he felt cheated: "It was not a happy experience." Even though some individuals show great admiration for a media figure, they remain suspicious of advertising's motives. C. Berger and Calabrese (1975) maintained that attraction should increase through repeated exposure. When audiences, however, are very familiar with a media figure, through repeated appearances in news, sports, or entertainment programming, they may react quite negatiely to that media figure's appearance in an advertisement. A young woman's reaction to Linda Ellerbee's appearance in a Maxwell House coffee advertisement serves as a case in point:

> *I believe part of my attraction to news is that as a major link between me and the world. It has been a vehicle that has released powerful personal emotions. It has brought stories of events that have genuinely shocked me, saddened me, stopped me in my tracks. The fact that Linda Ellerbee did a Maxwell House coffee commercial offends my sensibilities. How dare someone use the mantle of journalistic respectability to promote a single product. Somehow the fact that she was involved in news programming makes her more respectable and objective in your eyes, which makes her promotion of a product seem narrow, limited, money-grubbing, and objectionable. Since I've never had any cause to take Willard Scott [the weather reporter] seriously, I just see him as another media figure turning a quick buck.*

One homemaker reported that she cannot accept the inconsistency between the "bad guy" role an actor portrays on a soap opera and his "good guy" role in a television commercial:

> *I remember that guy who plays Tad Martin, a playboy on All My Children, doing a commercial for Woolite. I couldn't believe it. I said, what's a dog like him doing in a commercial for a product that is supposed to be gentle and soft? It made me hate him more.*

Informants' descriptions of this inconsistency suggest a range of potential reactions. The immediate result of this inconsistency is the expression of disbelief in the advertisement's message and questioning of their feelings about the media figure. The individuals might also have questioned how this new role would impact the media figure's career, and therefore the relationship.

READING NOTES

_____

_____

_____

_____

_____

Till and Shimp (1998) used an associative memory framework to study transfer of feelings from media figure to audience. Although the advertiser expects there to be a transfer of positive feelings toward the product endorser to the brand, they found a correlation between negative feelings toward the product endorser and lower evaluations of the brand. Even if predictability and certainty resulted from past experience with the media figure, informants maintain that this had little to do with the media figure's authority to make product claims or to proclaim product virtues. As one woman succinctly put it, "who can be an authority on Coke? If you drink it, you're an authority." The individual added:

> That Pizza Hut commerical where those celebrities just sit up there and eat pizza. I don't care who it is ... the noises they are making ... I'm ready to go eat. ... It's only because I've been to Pizza Hut that things are already established for me that make it easy to make the decision.

Audiences may initially be drawn to an advertisement for its entertainment value, or because of values with which they identify. The message, however, may be rejected in some fashion as the initial attraction is counterbalanced by the media figure's perceived expertise or authority. Questioning the media figure's authority to make product claims is an important aspect of the imaginary social interaction. An elementary school teacher states in reaction to a media figure's appearance in an office copier commercial: "What does he [the celebrity] know about copiers?" A homemaker says: "And what about that yogurt commercial with all those celebrities speaking French. ... What's that say's name? ... who you know has never eaten yogurt in his life!" Individuals who could not provide a rationale for the media figure's authority may have used existing beliefs about the media figure to question the product and some aspects of the relationship. This kind of skepticism appears to help individuals to distance

themselves from the perceived power of advertising (and media figures who appear in advertisements) to persuade. This questioning is an important matter for audiences and may play a larger cultural role. As such the media figure's appearance may serve as a warning, signaling audiences to be vary of what is to follow. Individuals express a desire to separate the celebrity from the sales pitch. Other qualities or attributes—social or physical—of the media figure appear to be significant to audiences in physical and maintaining their attention. In cases where the media figure appears to have authority the individual does not perceive the media figure to possess, the individual may reject at least part of the message. This situation holds the potential for re-evaluation of the relationship.

AUDIENCE AWARENESS OF THE CELEBRITY SYSTEM

Individuals display an astute awareness of the "system" in which media figures operate, and they use advertising appearances in a dialectical manner in order to adjust their knowledge and beliefs about media figures. Appearances in advertising, therefore, become part of the explanation process in which audiences understand what is going on in a media figure's life. Informants report varying, often contradictory, reasons why media figures appear in advertisements. These reasons are similar to those reported in the literature—money, exposure, and versatility.

Individuals say a media figure's appearance in an advertisement at the same time that an actor is performing in a current entertainment program serves as a signal, perhaps indicating that she or he was about to leave the series. A college student provided the following example:

> Like Nina who left All My Children and started doing Neet commercials. Maybe nothing is going on with their character at the

225

time, so they do commercials if they are getting ready to leave the show—appearing in advertisements—their managers can show that the actor can be versatile. Maybe he's a playboy on the soap but he can act sentimental in some other role. Maybe appearing in the commercial will lead to another role.

A homemaker explains her understanding of the reasons why some actors appear in advertisements and others do not:

The majority of older actors don't do commercials, except for comediennes. For many actors who have been at it so long, it's not dignified enough to do commercials. Others will do commercials for charities, like Bob Hope. He did do commercials for Gulf, Exxon ... or is it Texaco? Maybe he was just been doing them for years and thinks that's just part of his role. I would say that older actors don't do them and younger actors do, because the younger ones are at the bottom of the ladder and have to gain respect.

Whether accurate or not, this general perception suggests audiences may use the appearance to further understand the media system in which advertising operates. A college student says, "If you are already established and you appear in an advertisement, it may mean that everything is not right in your career. Advertising is a place on the entertainment ladder to work your way up from." McAllister (1996) echoed this when he said, "Advertisers love to use motion picture celebrities as referent systems. Movie stars know, however, that appearing in commercials dilutes their star quality. When you see a movie star shilling for a product, the glamour and allure of the star decreases" (57). Other informants say advertising is the place celebrities begin the long road down. And yet others conclude that advertising is just a stopping off place— a place to wait for good roles. Therefore, there is little

inherent significance regarding Jane (Josie Bissett) from television's Melrose Place appearing in advertisements for an underarm deodorant or make-up. What is of significance is what audiences do with the appearance as a part of their imaginary social interaction. The appearance may become fodder for gossip— grist for the mill, but it also might play a more significant role in helping individuals to make sense of their world. As further evidence, a homemaker speaks following description:

The system is not set up for the celebrity to step forward and say, "I want to do this because I believe in the product." It's oriented toward the business side where they will say, "Let's get so-and-so to do this commercial because it will work."

Perspectives may vary somewhat as to why a media figure appears in an advertisement, but rationalizing the appearance is an important interaction in the imaginary social relationship. Individuals also use such appearances to make value judgments about the capitalist system. As one middle-aged man put it, "I don't see how it (appearing in advertisements) could be deceitful. It's acting. It's a job." The informant adds, "Actors appearing in commercials may be seen by producers and obtain other acting jobs, making the process totally acceptable." Some informants also acknowledge that some celebrities will not do commercials because "it's beneath them ... they don't believe in the product or they don't need the money. Some do have morals and standards and won't budge. ... Money doesn't affect them."

Individuals use media figures to make moral judgments about society. The general notions that "it's okay to make lots of money doing small tasks" (advertisements), that a certain level of "deceit is acceptable," and that "we (individuals) are responsible for being able to discern the truth from lies" were reinforced through appearances of media figures in advertisements. "If the

READING NOTES

_____

_____

_____

_____

_____

celebrity had no connection to the product and doesn't use it—that's not deceitful," one informant says. "She's just trying to make money." Media figures appearances in advertising, therefore, are far from taken as "art for art's sake." The meaning ascribed to these appearances suggests the audience is wary. This is further evidence that the aesthetic level is only one level on which audiences approach the appearance of media figures in advertising.

CONCLUSION

If advertising is relatively timeless and placeless, as Schudson (1984) suggested, audiences may ground their experience of the advertisement in an imaginary social relationship. Such pseudo relationships serve as compensation for experience that the audience otherwise cannot have, Part of the meaning comes through the predictability of a media figure's repeated appearances in advertisements. The path toward the social construction of reality, at least as far as media figures appearing in advertising, is not a straightforward or simple one. Some individuals demonstrate a strong attraction to and unyielding faith in certain media figures. Other individuals, who displayed a long term attraction, sometimes express an uncertainty about the media figure's appearance in advertisements. This skepticism does not necessarily affect feelings for a media figure, as the individual may seek a rationale as to why the media figure appeared in an advertisement. Product purveyors have grown somewhat skeptical of the use of media figures as endorsers. Public embarrassment, exemplified in the case of O. J. Simpson (indicted and later acquitted on charges of murder), resulted in a libility for the brand. This has resulted in the trend toward using deceased celebrities who are scandal proof (Goldman, 1994).

Paralleling relationships in real life, audiences can balance positive feelings for media figures with negative or neutral attitudes towards their appearances in advertisements. Furthermore, the advertiser's attempt to associate a media figure with a product may serve as a meta-communicative signal that, while gaining audience attention may also hold the potential to increase uncertainty. The connections between product and media figure, therefore, are part of the complex dimension of experience. The aesthetic connection is just one factor audiences use to evaluate the media figure's performance or appearance in an advertisement, and in the broader sense to make judgments about advertising and the capitalist system.

Schudson (1984) concluded, "consumers in front of a television screen are relatively unwary" (227). This is what allows, he suggests, the advertisement to be successful. However, even if the media figure's appearance in the advertisement is flattened, viewers make up the difference—fill in the gap—through their pseudosocial interactions. Repeated appearances across programming create an intertextual web that can be likened to the complex system of actual social relationships. The advertisement itself is a means by which audiences can "reach out and touch someone" to form relationships, alter existing relationships, and, perhaps end relationships. Advertising, which is hardly neutral territory, is a point at which many media experiences converge. The confluence of information, gossip, and past media experiences sometimes come together at this juncture to provide meaning to the viewer involved in an imaginary social relationship. Gamson (1994) supported this conclusion when he said:

> *Playing with culture offers participants the chance to work through in a free realm everyday life experiences that typically appear in arenas of consequence. Celebrities are*

READING NOTES

particularly suited to these games precisely because they are encoded in a semifictional language: audiences can easily play evaluation and judgment games "as if" with real people but without an ultimate authority [gossip], or they can play at the borders between real and not real [detectives]. (185)

In a sense, audiences' actual social situations are interconnected to multiple realities; advertising is just one of them. Enculturation into this imaginary social interaction begins at an early age (James & McCain, 1982; Reid & Frazer, 1980). Appearances by media figures in advertising are just one form in our mass mediated culture where audiences participate in the give and take with a multitude of media figures.

Attracted to some of these media figures, audiences incorporate them into their imaginary social worlds.

ENDNOTES

1. An informant wondered why his daughter always played close to the glow of the television screen. He reported that she only paid attention to what was going on when the commercials came on. After observing her, the informant became aware that she was paying attention because unlike dramatic programming, the people in the commercials were talking directly to her.

2. See the Appendix for an explanation of the ethnographic method utilized to collect and interpret the imaginary social relationships described in this chapter.

3. Bill Cosby was a spokesperson for Jello for 27 years.

READING NOTES

_____

_____

_____

_____

_____

Section

3

© Monkey Business Images, 2010. Shutterstock Inc.

PRODUCING AND CONSUMING MEDIA

Chapter 9

Communication as Storytelling

"Storytelling reveals meaning without committing the error of defining it."

—HANNAH ARENDT

Stories are both the form and content of the media, and provide cultural links to the most ancient human traditions. The narrative form of plot, characters, tension, development, and resolution entertains and informs audiences, anchors the media in literary and artistic traditions, spawns celebrities, drives advertising sales, recounts history, and encompasses the American ethos. Media stories grab our attention, stimulate our thoughts and feelings, and occasionally impel us to action. Telling stories is what the mass media do.

This chapter's aims include to

- establish the centrality of narrative and storytelling in social life,

- investigate the different ways stories are created, disseminated, and preserved in communities,

- identify differences among the media in enabling and constraining storytelling, and

- give examples of media storytellers at work.

Required Reading: Technically and aesthetically, D.W. Griffith's landmark 1915 feature film *The Birth of a Nation* set the standard for audiovisual storytelling, but morally and socially it presented the worst message that Hollywood had to offer: racist stereotyping of blacks, valorization of the Ku Klux Klan, legitimization of segregationist Jim Crow laws in the South, and systematic discrimination against African Americans throughout the nation. In "The Good Lynching and *Birth of the Nation*," Michele Faith Wallace probes these contradictions of this cinematic milestone in the history of mass-media storytelling, which exemplify the ethical challenges raised by the media's extraordinary power over the audience still with us today.

THE DIALOGIC DOMAIN

Humans are not the sole storytelling animal species; a counterpoint is the "waggle" foraging dance of honeybees, and another the mating song of blue whales. However, human storytelling surpasses the instinctual behavior of other animals and expresses the innate human need for the companionship, a condition known to philosophers as intersubjectivity. If a person lived in complete isolation without meeting another human being, that person nonetheless would imagine other people with a similar perspective on the world. The dialogue of intrapersonal communication, or talking to one's self, is natural behavior. This basic need to communicate is illustrated with humor and pathos by *Cast Away* (2000), a DreamWorks/Twentieth Century Fox motion picture directed by Robert Zemeckis. Driven by his need for companionship, a marooned man, played by Tom Hanks, recognizes a kindred spirit in a volleyball named "Wilson."

The dialogic domain—the mode of connecting with others—is omnipresent and shapes human symbolic thinking regardless of communication means. The act of speaking implicitly means to have the Other present. Media stories put one in the present moment in communion with storytellers of the past, traversing time and space. The modern mass media have led scholars to rediscover old oral traditions—a new orality, that is, oral community, rooted in the most ancient cultures.

One of the jobs of storytellers, from Homer to reality television, has been to preserve social values for the younger generation. As cultural anthropologist Jean Gebser observed, storytellers speak from a collective consciousness in identification with the tribe, a total subjectivity characterized by the cycles and rhythms of nature. The story is told and retold against the backdrop of an unchanging universe. The story is preserved in the telling and augmented by each voice. Homer's great stories *The Iliad* and *The Odyssey*, were recited orally by generations of storytellers before being written, as were the Judeo-Christian Bible, Islamic Koran, and Jewish Talmud. Each retelling of these ancient stories added to the collective consciousness of the community associated with them.

American cultural historian Walter Ong has observed that the act of affixing oral stories in writing disrupts the oral life world. Writing separates the speaker from the story by stripping away the sounds of the words and by supplanting the listener's spatially ambivalent aural experience with the writer's outward-directed point of view. Beginning with Gutenberg's printing press in 1450, the mass production of the printed word made possible such notions as objectivity, fact, truth, point of view, history, and education, but it also deprived the tribal collective memory of the sounds and rhythms of the storyteller.

The ancient Greek and Roman myths are well known to generations of American schoolchildren who have read the classics primer *Mythology: Timeless Tales of Gods and Heroes* by German-American classicist Edith Hamilton. Myths, said Hamilton, are universal and timeless human stories. German anthropologist Adolph Bastian proposed the idea that the Greek and Roman myths had behind them universal "elementary ideas" common to all cultures. French anthropologist Claude Lévi-Strauss called these common cultural ideas mythemes. Based on his ethnographic field studies of primitive cultures around the world, Lévi-Strauss concluded that universal laws governed all myths and all human thought. Based on Lévi-Strauss's work and Swiss psychiatrist Carl Jung's concept of archetypes, American mythologist Joseph Campbell studied comparative mythologies and concluded that all of the world's religions reflected the same transcendent truths, or spiritual meaning of life. Shortly before he died, Campbell completed a series of interviews with Bill Moyers for American public television entitled *The Power of Myth*, which raised awareness of the role of myth in the mass media.

Journalist and scholar Jack Lule wrote in his book *Daily News, Eternal Stories: The Mythological Role of Journalism* that journalism's role in society is to tell stories that maintain essential myths. He identifies seven master myths in the news, which are extensions of Jung's mythological archetypes: the

Victim, the Scapegoat, the Good Mother, the Hero, the Trickster, the Other World, and the Flood. An example of the Hero myth is the news media's idolizing of St. Louis Cardinals baseball star Mark McGuire during his chase of the single-season home run record in 1998. McGuire the Hero became the Trickster when accusations that he used performance-enhancing steroids surfaced in the media seven years later. The hero's fall from grace kept McGuire from being voted into the Baseball Hall of Fame when he became eligible in 2007.

Mythopoeia is English philologist J. R. R. Tolkien's term for fiction styled like myth, as exemplified by his epic three-volume novel *The Lord of the Rings*. Tolkien's created his vast and deep fantasy world to replace the Celtic myths that were lost when the Normans conquered the British Isles a thousand years earlier. Tolkien's friend C. S. Lewis wrote a similar mythic novel, *The Chronicles of Narnia*, in seven volumes. Both stories became popular motion pictures.

George Lucas, the writer and producer of the *Star Wars* films, credited Joseph Campbell's popular book *The Hero with a Thousand Faces* (1949) as a strong influence on his story ideas. In turn, Campbell credited Lucas's films with popularizing the study of monomyths, fundamental stories shared by all the world's great religions. In the *Star Wars* story, the hero (Luke Skywalker) embarks on a quest (defeat the Empire) with the aid of a mentor (Obi-Wan Kenobi), consults an Oracle (Yoda), overcomes temptation (the Dark Side of the Force), reaches an apotheosis (becomes a Jedi knight), faces his father (Darth Vader), and fulfills a prophecy (overthrows the Emperor). These story elements seem familiar because they tap into the collective consciousness.

TRUTH, FICTION, AND LYING

Storytelling has many jobs in society. The traditional job of nonfiction genres, such as journalism and documentary, is to tell what is true by verification of facts and clarification of the speaker's credibility. However, facts do not necessarily add up to the truth. A set of accurate, verifiable facts might give a false or misleading story. When it comes to capital-T "Truth," a culture generally turns to its poets and novelists, whose stories communicate an eternal veracity through fictional means.

In recent years, the fiction—nonfiction line has been blurred. "Based on actual events" is a favored marketing strategy for fiction stories, whereas nonfiction news and documentary sometimes use fictional storytelling devices, such as made-up characters and reenactments with actors. Even books that have been marketed as memoirs such as *A Million Little Pieces* by James Frey, which became a huge best seller after it was promoted on The Oprah Winfrey Show, was revealed to contain a great deal of fiction in it.

Journalists and documentarians serve as society's gatekeepers to decide which events are reported to the public. Gatekeeping is necessary because the media never have enough space or time to convey all available news. As gatekeepers, reporters and editors traditionally rate news as important or "hard" if it has timeliness, proximity to the audience, prominence, conflict, novelty, or audience impact (see Figure 9.1). The hard news stories chosen for publication or airing influence the public's perception of importance, the public agenda. Except for those rare occasions when reporters are eyewitnesses to events, verification of stories and sources for hard news is essential to win the public's trust.

"Soft news" or "feature news" is human-interest or celebrity stories that can keep until tomorrow. They tend to be long, in-depth stories that take more time to write and produce than hard news, such as profiles of people or organizations, personal memoirs, or diaries, typically published in popular magazines, newspaper Sunday supplements, and reality television. The audience generally prefers soft news because it is more entertaining than hard news. Fighting to recoup audience share, the traditional hard-news media have "softened" their delivery and content.

Among mainstream news media, television was first to soften its hard news product, particularly since the late 1980s when cable made inroads into

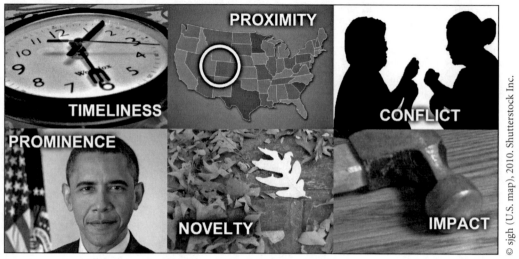

Figure 9.1—*Traditional "hard news" values.*

its dominant audience share. Storytelling techniques borrowed from the tabloid newspapers began to appear in newscasts, such as flashy graphics, sensational headlines, dramatic first-person narratives, and increased celebrity and entertainment news. Within a decade, such techniques were deemed acceptable for hard news on television. At the same time, newsgathering operations and overseas news bureaus were slashed because their high costs were not warranted in the softer news environment. The one hard news value that the audience still seemed to value was timeliness, so stations and networks emphasized live coverage, even when the story itself did not seem to warrant the extra expense of transmitting live pictures.

Print news got softer, too, but for different reasons from television. Partly because of television's influence, readers began to favor more visual, easier to digest news. The Gannett newspaper chain led the way in 1982 with the launch of its national daily newspaper *USA Today,* which targeted business readers on-the-go with crisp writing, color printing, plenty of photos, infographics, color-cued indexing, and high quality sports and entertainment news. Other newspapers, clinging to traditional ideas of hard news, were slow to follow suit, and Gannett lost money for many

years, but eventually nearly all newspapers, local and national, followed *USA Today's* lead.

Documentary storytelling is different from news. Documentaries tend to be longer, more in-depth, and more retrospective, whereas news focuses on what is happening now and works against deadline. As an eyewitness to events, a documentarian's job is to convey a sense of reality to the audience. The cutting-edge medium for documentaries is the World Wide Web, which surpasses the linear media of film and television in its interactivity and complex linking possibilities. An example of a Web documentary produced by Fusionspark Media (see Figure 9.2) about the New Jersey pinelands, an endangered natural resource that supported the advocacy work of the Pinelands Preservation Alliance. Some documentarians embrace a neutral point of view regarding their subjects, while others openly advocate for particular causes. In recent years, documentary films such as *Super Size Me* (2004), *An Inconvenient Truth* (2004), and *Fahrenheit 9/11* (2006) have garnered large audiences, thereby shaping public opinion and influencing government policy.

Newspapering originally was an apprenticeship trade learned on the job. After World War II, the

Figure 9.2—*A new, nonlinear storytelling genre, the Web documentary, provides interactivity and complex linking possibilities for projects such as the Pinelands Preservation Alliance.*

Figure 9.3—*State of the blogosphere in 2008.*

launch of U.S. university journalism programs began to professionalize the field. The 1947 Commission on Freedom of the Press, a panel of scholars and journalists chaired by University of Chicago President Robert Hutchins, examined the state of the mass media, found it wanting, and reaffirmed the media's social responsibility in a democratic society. For the next half-century, professional journalists claimed truth telling in public affairs as their exclusive social function, a claim backed by their gatekeeping role.

Starting in the 1990s, "citizen journalism" on the Web shattered journalism's monopoly, democratized truth telling, and blurred the distinction between news and opinion. Weblogs or "blogs" posting personal opinion columns such as The Huffington Post, Gizmodo, and Mashable! proliferated in this century (see Figure 9.3). In addition to posting opinion, some bloggers do original reporting and research. Bloggers see themselves as compensating for shortcomings of the professional news media, but without the journalist's obligation to verify content and sources. This

democratizing of news and opinion has changed the truth-telling equation. Truth no longer equals what journalists say it is—if it ever did. Without professional journalists as intermediaries between the audience and its information sources, citizens must rely on their own sense of credibility to decide what is true.

Newsrooms of the various communications media require different skills. Print, broadcast, the Internet, and wireless technologies such as cellular phones and iPods all require specialized technical skills and address audiences uniquely. In the 1990s, major news organizations experimented with merging newsrooms of the various media to reach new audiences, to share information resources, to economize, and to make news more entertaining. This convergence of newsrooms put pressure on the journalists to become fluent storytellers in multiple media channels.

Some much-heralded experiments at converging newsrooms of different media into unified operations were only partially successful. An example is the Tribune Company's Chicago-based news organizations, the *Chicago Tribune,* WGN Radio and TV, and Tribune Interactive Web properties. The Tribune experiment ran out of time, because overinvestment in newspapers and broadcast properties forced the company into bankruptcy in December 2008.

Despite the promise of convergence, most U.S. professional newsrooms still are not converged. With increasing costs of operation and declining readership, many U.S. newspapers shed most of their newsroom employees and struggled to develop new income streams from the Internet to replace subscription and newsstand losses. Newspapers' woes were primarily a matter of financial expectations. Profit margins dropped from double-digit percentages in the 1990s to half that a decade later—still substantial, but disappointing to investors. Those newspapers that did not adjust went out of business. A national debate raged about whether newspapers would survive without charging customers for access to their content on the Web.

Convergence with the Web helped television news. Network and local television had been losing audience share to cable since the mid-1980s, forcing news programs to become more entertaining to win back viewers. They added more anchor chat, eye-popping graphics, and recreation of events containing fictional elements—strategies that softened journalistic standards and reduced the news "hole" (time for actual news content). Webcasting companion news stories enabled broadcasters to provide more content, and audience interaction with their Web sites enriched market data for advertisers. With newspapers in peril, magazine costs increasing, and television rapidly adapting to the Web, the only reasonable conclusion is that Internet-based news will dominate in the future.

FAMOUS MEDIA DECEPTIONS

The history of the mass media is colored by notorious cases of false storytelling. In most cases, unvigilant coworkers aided the liars. These hoaxes damaged the credibility of the mass media and caused the media professionals to reexamine their practices. Here is a brief survey of some of the most infamous media hoaxes, perpetuated in many different media

The "Great Moon" hoax (1835) was a series of six stories published by the *New York Sun* (motto: "It Shines For All") about the discovery of civilized life on the moon, falsely attributed to the preeminent astronomer of the time, Sir John Hershel. Eventually debunked, this hoax showed that these "penny press"-era readers of the first true mass-circulation newspapers trusted the printed word, however farfetched. The ethics lesson from this hoax is that newspapers (and other news media later) have a social responsibility to verify what they report as news.

The quiz show scandals (1958 to 1959) were recounted in the 1994 Hollywood Pictures production *Quiz Show*, directed by Robert Redford. In the first decade of U.S. television broadcasting quiz shows garnered huge audiences and equally huge ad revenues. However, the bubble burst in 1958, when a disgruntled ex-contestant on NBC's *Twenty-One* announced to the public that the game was rigged. Congress passed a law criminalizing the fixing of any form of media contest. Quiz shows all but disappeared from prime-time television, but returned more popular than ever in 1999 with *Who Wants To Be a Millionaire?*

The Howard Hughes autobiography hoax (1972) was recounted in the 2007 Miramax film *The Hoax*, directed by Lasse Hällstrom. Clifford Irving was a promising novelist waiting for his big break. He decided to take a shortcut to success and faked an autobiography of Howard Hughes, a reclusive billionaire who had disappeared from public view for years. Irving was betting that Hughes would not sacrifice his anonymity to debunk the hoax, but he lost the bet. After Irving signed a publishing contract with McGraw-Hill and accepted a $765,000 advance to great public fanfare, Hughes telephoned McGraw-Hill and denied everything.

Irving and his accomplice Richard Suskind were prosecuted, returned the money, and spent time in prison. Following his release, Irving continued to write books and had several best sellers. Ironically, when the film based on his memoir was released in 2007, Irving complained that it was not accurate.

The Janet Cooke scandal (1980) was a great embarrassment for the *Washington Post*, famous for uncovering the Watergate scandal that forced President Richard Nixon's resignation in 1974. Janet Cooke was a young African American star in the *Post* newsroom. "Jimmy's World," her series of investigative stories about an eight-year-old heroin addict in Washington, D.C., won a Pulitzer Prize, the most prestigious award for professional journalists. Later, when city officials were unable to find the hapless child, Cooke admitted that, while her basic reporting was accurate, she had invented the character of Jimmy to make the stories more dramatic. Cooke returned the prize and resigned. Thereafter, the *Washington Post* tightened its verification rules for investigative reports based on anonymous sources.

The Hitler diaries hoax (1983) was about financial greed. West German journalist Gerd Heidemann and conman Konrad Kujau were convicted of forgery and embezzlement for accepting ten million German marks from the newsmagazine *Stern* for their faked diaries of the former Nazi dictator Adolph Hitler. As in the Hughes autobiography hoax, the media buyers, including the U.S. newsmagazine *Newsweek*, were reluctant to admit they had been taken in by a hoax. However, when forensic evidence conclusively proved the fabrications, all the editors involved resigned their positions. Heidemann and Kujau each served 42 months in prison.

The Stephen Glass (1998), Jayson Blair (2003), and Jack Kelley (2004) scandals signaled a disturbing resurgence of professional liars in three highly respected news publications. Glass was caught by his own editors at the *New Republic* after fabricating parts of 27 major investigative feature stories, and possibly more. As in previous scandals, Glass's colleagues were reluctant to disbelieve their young star. After his firing, Glass pursued a law career, an ironic choice given his transgression. His scandal was recounted in the 2003 Lions Gate film *Shattered Glass,* directed by Billy Ray.

Jayson Blair resigned from *The New York Times* in 2003 after his editors discovered that he had plagiarized and faked parts of 36 national news stories. A lengthy report of the *Times'* investigative commission was printed on the newspaper's front page and concluded that this "low point in the 152-year history of the newspaper" was caused by breakdowns in newsroom procedures.

Figure 9.4—*The audience relies on insiders to maintain the integrity of the media and to expose hoaxes when they are perpetrated.*

Foreign correspondent Jack Kelley resigned from *USA Today* in 2003 without admitting guilt after an internal investigation showed that he had been faking datelines, inventing sources, and embellishing story details for three years. Kelley had been with the paper since 1982 and was nominated five times for the Pulitzer Prize. *USA Today's* investigators concluded that Kelley's star status in the newsroom discouraged others from taking complaints about Kelley's work seriously. Kelley dismissed the charges as professional jealousy.

These infamous media hoaxes and scandals reveal a pattern. In most cases, safeguards to ensure truth telling were set aside or short-circuited because the person involved became a celebrity, a rising star. Stars make the best liars because they command the biggest audiences (see Figure 9.4).

MEDIA STORYTELLING TECHNIQUES

Since before recorded history, humans have listened to stories to make sense out of life. Storytelling is what ties together discrete events and gives meaning to a sequence of sheer happenings. A story is both what is told and why it is told. The result is that a listener understands what happened. Listeners want to understand, want to get meaning from their lives, so they listen for stories in the media. The media world provides many more stories of greater variety than are available in direct social relations. Four types of media stories are described in this section: oral histories, screenwriting, genres, and transmedia stories.

Oral Histories

Personal stories based on the spoken word are sometimes called oral histories, a structured form of storytelling used in truth-telling genres such as news, documentary, and fiction based on fact. For example, the U.S. Holocaust Museum's oral history collection has oral histories of more than 9,000 survivors of the Nazi Holocaust. These oral histories, including audio and video, enable the public to hear the personal stories of victims, witnesses, and perpetrators of Nazi crimes against humanity. Each person's oral history is one tile in a mosaic of the total Holocaust experience.

This sample oral history from the Museum's collection describes a woman's deportation from the Jewish Ghetto in Lodz, Poland, to a concentration camp:

> When we walked through the ghetto to work after the entire ghetto was empty, it was a very weird feeling. Empty streets, open windows, flowing curtains blowing with the wind. No people. Once we thought that we saw a glimmer of somebody in the window, or a candle or something and, of course, we averted our eyes not to give away to the German escorts that somebody was there. In November of 1944 came our time, we had to be taken out. The entire population of our hospital was walked to the place where the cattle cars were, and we were loaded. It was a horrible thing because people had to stand. There was no place to sit or squat. If somebody was sick or even dying, he died on his feet standing up. It was just unbearable. Water was the worst ... the lack of water, the thirst was the worst.

The oral historian's procedure should transparently convey the speaker's story. Some speakers need an interviewer's guidance to be clear and complete. The normal sequence starts with a pre-interview, which guides archival research and development of questions for the main oral history interview. The interviewer looks for a quiet, non-distracting, comfortable interview location that will evoke the speaker's voice to the past. The interviewer strives to travel with the speaker into the past while maintaining a critical perspective. The interview concludes by tracking the speaker's life since the events described. Details such as the spelling of names and places, release forms, and archiving the interview recording are attended to afterward.

Oral histories are a rich source of personal storytelling that is distinctly different from novel writing or screenwriting, because they do not require an expert storyteller, only the vivid memories of the speaker.

Screenwriting

Screenplays are different from books or short stories because they describe only what is heard or seen by a mass media audience, refrain from elaborate descriptions or internal dialogue, and use present tense verbs. Here is an example of an original story episode from *Moby Dick* by Herman Melville:

> "Thou damned whale! Thus, I give up the spear!"
>
> The harpoon was darted; the stricken whale flew forward; with igniting velocity the line ran through the groove;—ran foul. Ahab stooped to clear it; he did clear it; but the flying turn caught him round the neck, and voicelessly as Turkish mutes bowstring their victim, he was shot out of the boat, ere the crew knew he was gone. Next instant, the heavy eye-splice in the rope's final end flew out of the stark-empty tub, knocked down an oarsman, and smiting the sea, disappeared in its depths.

This is the same episode written as a screenplay:

> Ahab cusses the whale, flings his harpoon, and is pulled under by the lurching behemoth.

Courtesy of the U.S. Holocaust Memorial Museum, Washington, D.C.

The basic screenplay has three acts. The first act, called the exposition, sets the story universe, opens with a propitious or auspicious occasion, and gives a defining action for the protagonist. An example of exposition in *The Godfather* (1972; screenplay by novelist Mario Puzo and director Francis Ford Coppola, assisted by Robert Towne) is the family wedding spectacle, which introduces the Corleone crime family's cast of characters and establishes Michael as the returning war-hero son who tells his girlfriend, "That's my family, Kay. It's not me."

The first act ends with an irrevocable act, or point of no return: Michael's assassination of the mobster and crooked police captain. The second act is when the protagonist, pushed beyond the point of no return, tries something new and fails, the low moment in the story (Michael's Sicilian bride being killed by the car bomb meant for him, the event that seals his fate to become the Godfather). The third act starts with the protagonist's taking charge to alter the course of events (Michael returns to become the family's Don, or leader of the crime family), followed by the story climax (Michael settles all scores with the family's enemies). The story concludes with affirmation that the protagonist is forever changed (Michael Corleone is now the Don of the family and lies to his wife to protect her).

Genres

Genres, or story types, are comprehensive structures that provide whole frameworks of understanding to the mass media audience. They help audiences better understand media content with which they are interacting. Contrary to the presumption that genres limit creativity, they can be powerful weapons in the hands of a media producer.

A popular television storytelling genre is the situation comedy, or "sitcom." Television writer and producer Norman Lear created a remarkable string of hit sitcoms from 1972 to 1977. Lear's first hit, *All in the Family,* for CBS-TV, topped primetime ratings five years running and broke new ground both thematically and technically for the situation comedy television genre. It was the first American sitcom to explore contentious social issues such as racism, breast cancer, menopause, women's liberation, homosexuality, and impotence. It also popularized the economical production technique of videotaping before a live studio audience.

Lear's concept for *All in the Family* was based on the British series *Till Death Us Do Part,* but with a strong male lead character (Archie Bunker), ostensibly patterned after Lear's own father, instead of the dominant female character in the British series. Lear's next hit, *Sanford and Son* (NBC), also was based on a British show, *Steptoe and Son.* He followed with two successful "spin-off" shows based on *All in the Family* supporting characters, *Maude* (CBS) and *The Jeffersons* (CBS), as well as *Good Times* (CBS) and *One Day at a Time* (CBS).

Lear's string of hits established him as the leading producer of U.S. prime time television entertainment in the early 1970s. He began to experiment with edgier show concepts with strong female characters, including *Hot L Baltimore* (ABC), *Mary Hartman, Mary Hartman,* and *All That Glitters.* Created by Ann Marcus, Daniel Gregory Browne, and Jerry Adelman, the soap opera parody *Mary Hartman, Mary Hartman,* starring Louise Lasser and Mary Kay Place, ran five nights a week for 325 episodes during 1976 and 1977. The show was directed by Joan Darling, who was one of few female directors in Hollywood.

The premise of the first episode was Mary Hartman's numbed reaction to wailing sirens responding to the mass murder of a neighboring family, including their goats and chickens. The show's deadpan, tongue-in-cheek satire and controversial topics scared off the networks, so Lear sold the show individually to 40 independent stations, which aired it late at night. Though not commercial hits, Lear's experimental sitcoms were critical successes, raised the social consciousness, and help to liberalize broadcasting standards for story content.

Genres for television commercials, popular songs, books, magazines, sales brochures, Web sites, and video games all can be used like shorthand to efficiently manage audiences' expectations, or they can be used to surprise the audience with intentional formula violations. An example of the creative violation of genre expectations was director Alfred Hitchcock's 1960 movie *Psycho*.

When actress Janet Leigh succumbed to sudden brutality halfway through *Psycho,* audiences were disbelieving that the marquee female lead would meet her demise so early in the story. Paramount Studios used this plot twist as a promotional gimmick in ads featuring Hitchcock's beseeching the audience to keep the film's secret. *Psycho* became a smash hit and was lauded by critics.

Transmedia Stories

Transmedia stories are a phenomenon that was started by the Web-based marketing of *The Blair Witch Project* (1999), a small-budget independent film directed by Daniel Myrick and Eduardo Sánchez that became a big hit because of its Web site. The Web site was crafted to appear as a serious documentary about a witch case in Burkittsville, Maryland. The filmmakers said the goal of their Web site was to create a fake legend to stimulate curiosity about the upcoming film release. Following the lead of *Blair Witch Project,* which grossed nearly $250 million worldwide, film directors Larry and Andy Wachowski broadened the transmedia strategy for their film trilogy—*The Matrix* (1999), *The Matrix Reloaded* (2003), and *The Matrix Revolutions* (2003)—to cultivate loyal fans for their mythical science-fiction saga. Combined box office revenues from the three films were more than $1.6 billion worldwide. The Wachowski brothers ascribe much of their success to their transmedia storytelling approach.

Popular culture scholar Henry Jenkins cites the Wachowskis' *Matrix* franchise of three Warner Brothers film releases, DVDs, Web sites, video games, comics, and animated spin-off films as a ground breaking effort in "synergistic storytelling." The Wachowskis planted bits of their saga across various media, forcing fans on a transmedia hunt to piece their story together. Casual viewers were frustrated that the three theatrical films did not add up, but transmedia fans looked eagerly to the auxiliary media for background, additional characters, and story clues missing from the films.

The fans posted blogs to share their story clues and to posit their own interpretations of *The Matrix.* The Wachowskis encouraged other artists to develop new plotlines and characters for the *Matrix* saga in comics, two video games, a massive multiplayer game set in "the Matrix," and a program of nine animated films produced by the Wachowskis and directed by leading Asian animators, called *The Animatrix* (2003). The *Matrix* transmedia phenomenon is an example of "collective intelligence," according to Jenkins.

A strong motive for media convergence and transmedia storytelling is cross-media marketing, and the *Matrix* franchise is no exception. However, the Wachowskis also attempted to reinvent media storytelling by inviting the collaborating marketers to be co-creators of the Matrix saga. This collaborative authorship allows licensing companies in the various auxiliary media to capitalize on the strengths of their respective media with new characters and stories, instead of the unoriginal replications of film content normally licensed in cross-promotion deals. For example, one of the *Matrix* animated shorts introduced a new character, the Kid, whose adventures ran parallel to that of the main hero, Neo. Another example of collaborative authorship was the 2005 game *The Matrix Online*, in which Morpheus, Neo's mentor, is killed off while trying to recover Neo's body, that had been carried away by the machines at the end of *Revolutions.*

The Wachowskis cited Tolkien's *The Lord of the Rings* as a major influence. Similar to Middle Earth, the *Matrix*'s universe is rich with complex possibilities. In addition to collaboration by franchise marketers, fans all over the world maintain a virtual knowledge community of blogs with new *Matrix* interpretations, original side plots and spin-offs, franchise news, and speculations about the future. The *Matrix* phenomenon is seen as part of a larger trend of serialization in media storytelling—continuing stories across many episodes to satisfy a loyal audience. Other good examples of successful serialization in books and movies are the *Harry Potter* series by J.K. Rowling, the Fox Network's action/drama show *24*, and the reality show *American Idol*, also on Fox.

MEDIA STORYTELLERS

The mass media are mythmaking engines. With the passage of time, stories take on a life of their own with each telling. The amplification effect of the mass media spreads the stories rapidly through the audience, accelerating a story's growth toward mythic universality. The following famous cases of media storytellers illustrate stories that outgrew their tellers and took on lives of their own: The Filmmaker as Ethnographer, The Sports Writer as Mythmaker, and The Media Mogul as Legend.

The Filmmaker as Ethnographer

Nanook of the North (1922) is revered as the first feature-length documentary film and an important ethnographic study of the Inuit people of North America, but filmmaker Robert Flaherty had different intentions. He wanted to make an entertaining fiction film about the Inuit— "A story of life and love in the actual Arctic." Flaherty spent several years in the Arctic researching his topic. From his experiences, he knit together a fictional, romanticized story of a typical Eskimo family from a past that no longer existed. His story took liberties with reality. For example, he repressed Inuit polygamy and their ongoing assimilation of the white man's ways (see Figure 9.5).

The protagonist Nanook was portrayed by Flaherty's Inuit friend Allakariallak. Flaherty staged many scenes for the camera, including a cutaway set of an igloo interior, Nanook emerging from the igloo on cue the next morning, and faked a struggle to pull a seal through a hole in the ice. To increase the drama, Flaherty forced Allakariallak to use spears in the dramatic walrus scene, a dangerously ineffective weapon that the Inuit had long since replaced with firearms.

Despite Flaherty's desire to portray the struggles of the Inuit people with respect, *Nanook of the North* takes a condescending point of view toward the Inuit. For example, an opening title perpetuates the stereotype of the primitive

Figure 9.5—Promotional poster for the 1922 documentary film Nanook of the North *by Robert J. Flaherty, Pathé Pictures.*

savage, unfettered by the cares of civilization: "Nanook, the Happy-Go-Lucky Eskimo." On the contrary, Allakariallak and his family often were on the brink of starvation, and Allakariallak himself died of hunger not long after filming was completed. Another condescending portrayal is when Nanook encounters a fur trader's gramophone and tries to bite into the disk.

The audience interpreted *Nanook* as a documentary because of its astonishing technical achievement in difficult conditions and because it was the first film to show real Eskimos. Because they assumed that Flaherty intended to produce a documentary, scholars criticized the filmmaker for distorting the reality of his subjects' lives. Nevertheless, *Nanook of the North* stands as a great, if misunderstood, example of ethnographic storytelling.

The Sports Writer as Mythmaker

Grantland Rice was a sports writer in the 1920s, an era when the rising U.S. middle class embraced sports figures such as Babe Ruth in baseball, Knute Rockne in football, Bobby Jones in golf, and Jack Dempsey in boxing as its new heroes. Rice's specialty was literary metaphors, which he showered on the players he most admired, such as in his famous description of a Notre Dame—Army football game, published on October 18, 1924, in the *New York Herald Tribune*:

> Outlined against a blue, gray October sky, the Four Horsemen rode again. In dramatic lore, they were known as Famine, Pestilence, Destruction, and Death. These are only aliases. Their real names are Stuhldreher, Miller, Crowley, and Layden. They formed the crest of the South Bend cyclone before which another fighting Army team was swept over the precipice of the Polo Grounds this afternoon.

Rice's literary allusion to the Bible was courtesy of the Rudolph Valentino film *The Four Horsemen of the Apocalypse* released three years before. Rice's flowery, heroic writing style elevated sports to a mythic level. Notre Dame's Stuhldreher, Miller, Crowley, and Layden were known as the "Four Horsemen" for the rest of their lives. They honored Rice, the "Dean of American Sports Writers," at his funeral in 1954.

The Media Mogul as Legend

Actor-director Orson Welles was the boy wonder of Hollywood at 25 years old when he co-wrote, directed, and starred in his first motion picture, *Citizen Kane* (1941), later regarded for its innovative techniques as one of cinema's great masterpieces. However, *Citizen Kane* was nearly destroyed before it was released. The film's dark story about a newspaper magnate's rise to power and failed private life was patterned after William Randolph Hearst, head of Hearst Corporation, the first and largest U.S. media chain of its time, with 28 newspapers claiming one-fifth of newspaper readers nationwide, a cartoon syndicate, book publishing, magazines, radio stations, a movie studio, and real estate, lumber, and mining interests.

When the Hearst Corporation's gossip columnist Hedda Hopper found out about *Citizen Kane*, she told her boss, who became furious and tried to have the film destroyed. Hearst offered $800,000 to Welles's studio, RKO Pictures, to destroy all prints and negatives of the film. When RKO refused, Hearst tried to stop the film at the box office. He ordered his newspapers not to accept advertising and to pan the film. He used his connections in the movie business to get some major theater chains to refuse to carry the film.

Hearst launched a smear campaign against Welles that was as skilled and ruthless as the film that enraged him. Hearst had his publicity people spread rumors that Welles was a Communist and unpatriotic. Welles was an easy target because of his open contempt for Hollywood. The tactics not only hurt the film's profits and chances for critical acclaim. *Citizen Kane* made money at the box office, but fell short of RKO's expectations. Nominated for eight Academy Awards in 1942, *Citizen Kane* won only for Best Original Screenplay by Herman J. Mankiewicz and Welles. The director and film were booed at the awards ceremony. Dismayed by the industry's reception, RKO quietly retired the film to its vault. It was decades before scholars would resurrect the film's reputation worldwide.

The young, overconfident Welles relished controversy and had expected trouble from Hearst over the film, but he underestimated the media baron's power and vindictiveness, which was equal to the fictional Kane's. The conflict with Hearst over *Citizen Kane* ruined Welles's reputation with the movie studios, and he was never again given total control over his film projects, which he had enjoyed with *Citizen Kane.* For his part, Hearst's sabotage campaign against the film got some revenge in the short term, but forever associated Hearst with the Kane legend in the public's memory, as evidenced by a biography by W. A. Swanberg, *Citizen Hearst,* published in 1961.

CONCLUSION

This chapter establishes the centrality of narrative and storytelling in social life. The modern media are a technological equivalent to the ancient tribal circle and have resurrected the oral tradition, extending universal monomyths into fiction and nonfiction genres. *Star Wars, The Lord of the Rings,* and other blockbuster movies have story elements that can be traced back to ancient myths. Even journalism can be seen as a society's process of maintaining shared myths.

The traditional boundary between fiction and nonfiction is becoming blurred in the media. The drive to attract audiences in an increasingly competitive media market has led television news and newspapers to increase the entertainment value of their products, sometimes at the cost of hard news coverage and in-depth reporting. The occasional media hoax complicates the credibility of all media professionals. With the rapid rise of Web blogs in the media mix, opinion is becoming as important, or perhaps more important, than facts and accuracy. Consumers are increasingly on their own to decide what is important and who is right.

Media storytellers have available a wide variety techniques to captivate their audiences, including oral histories, screenwriting, genres, and transmedia stories, each with their own strengths and applications. Past stories set up a framework of expectations for plot and character that media writer may use to guide or surprise their audiences.

Storytelling is an essential media skill. Media convergence has increased demand for storytellers who can shape their stories for multiple audiences across several media, including print, audio-video, and Web. Major commercial successes such as *The Blair Witch Project* and *The Matrix* franchise point the way to further experimentation with transmedia storytelling. The possibilities are limitless.

THE GOOD LYNCHING AND THE BIRTH OF A NATION: DISCOURSES AND AESTHETICS OF JIM CROW

by Michele Faith Wallace

Abstract: The Birth of a Nation (1915) *is a landmark in the development of the feature film and in the history of American racial discourse in the Jim Crow period. This article proposes that the corrective for our current perspective on* The Birth of a Nation *is that we more thoroughly study how the techniques of feature film inscribe and underwrite dominant racial ideologies.*

The integration of former slaves and their offspring into mainstream society was an ill-fated and irresolvable problem for the United States during the same period as the U.S. film industry was being established—that is, in the first two decades of the twentieth century. Yet material related to the plight of African Americans was rarely present in cinematic narrative. When it was present, it was frequently in the context of a performance by whites in blackface or by blacks in situations that were denigrating. Compounding the problem, scholars have tended to ignore issues of race in silent films.

Recent research on silent film has tended to focus on the technological and formal aspects of the medium and not, for the most part, on its narrative content. Scholars have seemed to suggest that the silent film narrative is predictable, formulaic, and therefore of little intellectual interest.[1] A breakthrough in this thinking occurred at the 2002 meeting of the Society for Cinema and Media Studies in Minneapolis, where Alison McMahan presented three previously unseen Alice Guy Blaché films. Among the three films was a fascinating twelve-minute 35mm silent entitled *A Fool and His Money* (1912), also known as *Darktown Aristocrats*. The film features an entirely black cast with James Russell, the so-called Cakewalk King, in the lead role of Sam. The question McMahan posed was whether *A Fool and His Money* was made with a black audience in mind, given that the film is gently humorous and not at all offensive.[2]

The company of *A Fool and His Money* performs a set comedic piece, probably borrowed more or less intact from a stage production. Especially impressive is the work of James Russell, who manipulates the camera's focus like a seasoned film actor. Russell plays Sam, who is frustrated in his pursuit of Lindy, the well-off daughter of a retired

READING NOTES

era yet widely viewed as antiblack propaganda. This film's continued notoriety challenges all our most beloved notions of the intrinsically moral character of aesthetic masterpieces.

It would be one thing if *The Birth of a Nation* were merely the best of a thousand or even a hundred similarly racist or similarly virulent films and therefore represented a larger trend in silent film production. But as far as we know, it is the only historical epic focused on the fear of so-called Negro domination in the Reconstruction era.

From its first appearance, *Birth* inspired controversy and violent feelings in both its adherents and its detractors, and it continues to do so.[4] As such, *Birth* is a fascinating polemic, the analysis of which I like to think will expose the soft underbelly of an unfathomable conundrum that remains at the heart of the future of cinema studies: why does academic discussion of this film remain so endlessly important and yet so hopelessly inadequate to the task of ameliorating the textual racism this discussion seeks to diagnose?

The Genesis of *The Birth of a Nation*

The difficulty of explaining the origins of *Birth* stems from the many strands of its genesis and history. We know that D. W. Griffith based the film on *The Clansmen* and *The Leopard's Spots*, two rabidly racist novels by Thomas Dixon. Dixon, a preacher turned novelist. epitomized the most virulently racist and sadistic thinking of the early years of the twentieth century. Griffith, in contrast, seems to have been a rather conventional Southern Democrat. Dixon was bent on and obsessed with white genealogical purity; Griffith, although a white supremacist, was more concerned with establishing himself as an innovative artist in a revolutionary new medium.

At the behest of numerous censorship boards, as well as the NAACP, several of the most objectionably racist

"public porter." When he accidentally locates some money, Sam spends it foolishly getting dressed up to impress Lindy. In the end, Sam is tricked out of his money in a crooked poker game when a card is passed under the table to his opponent.

Whether the film is concerned with race, or even a race film, is unclear, although it seems unlikely that film audiences were as racially segregated in 1912, particularly in New York and other metropolitan areas, as is sometimes suggested. But even if race was only a minor concern in this and other silent films, that does not mean it was of no concern at all.

Even today, U.S. cinema only rarely addresses race as a subject matter. When it seems to do so, as in *Imitation of Life* (John Stahl, 1934, and Douglas Sirk, 1959), *To Kill a Mockingbird* (Robert Mulligan, 1962), and *Mississippi Burning* (Alan Parker, 1988), the historical bottom line is invariably softened and aestheticized beyond recognition. An exception to this trend is found in a few of the works that have survived from the silent period. In these few films, colorblindness is temporarily reversed.[3]

The most significant case in point is D. W. Griffith's *The Birth of a Nation* (1915), a masterpiece of the silent and controversial scenes in the film were cut from the final version. Among these scenes—for reasons we shall never know—were some that featured Mme. Sul-te-Wan, a mixed-blood black and Native American actress. She still appears in a number of crowd scenes and is instantly recognizable by her long straight hair and dark, angular features.

Born Nelly Conley, Sul-te-Wan spent her childhood in Louisville, Kentucky, where her mother worked as a maid for two actresses who encouraged Sul-te-Wan to be a performer. When Sul-te-Wan was later abandoned by her husband and left stranded in Los Angeles with no work and three children, she pursued Griffith, who was also from Louisville, and persuaded him to give her work. He was so impressed with her abilities that he gave her a small role in *Birth*. Deliah Beasley, a contemporary commentator, described Sul-te-Wan's role as evidence of "the advancement of the Negro from antebellum days to the present period . ... [Madame] appeared as a rich colored lady, finely gowned and owner of a Negro colony of educated colored citizens, who not only owned their own land, but she drove her own coach and four-in-hand."[5]

How such a scene fit in with the *Birth* we watch today is not difficult to imagine if we remember that Griffith's intention was partly to show the undeserved and unearned prosperity of blacks during Reconstruction. That Beasley mistake the "lost" scenes for a critique of black behavior at the turn of the century rather than during Reconstruction, which is the film's actual subject, suggests the temporal confusion the film invites. This is to not to say that there were no wealthy blacks at the turn of the century, for there were definitely pockets of black affluence in the South, and not all black communities experienced economic and social decline at the same pace.

Though Sul-te-Wan gets no credit for her role in *Birth*, she went on to have an active career in Hollywood for sixty more years and may indeed have been the first black woman to be a contract player in the industry. Like the black actor Noble Johnson, who was one of the founders of the black-owned Lincoln Motion Picture Company, Sul-te-Wan played a variety of roles: Indian princesses, monsters, witches, half-breeds, and gypsies. Nonetheless, not many cinema histories list Sul-te-Wan among their entries. Could it be that most critiques of racism, which aim for an impossible ideal of colorblindness continue to render the social and cultural histories of bodies of color (e.g., black women) invisible?[6]

Beasley's comments about *Birth* hint at the reason the film continues to arouse strong emotions despite its eighty-eight-year history: a problem has never been resolved in popular culture discourse—that is, to use historian Grace Hale's phrasing, how to correct "the legitimating narratives of origin for the culture of segregation." Hale explains:

> *The effort required to make a fiction into a truth would shape the development of twentieth-century southern culture, projecting a screen of common racial identity and white supremacy over the myriad varieties of class, gender, and locality. And the first boundary to become permeable in the reinscription of race, uncoupled from slavery, as the single most important social category of southern life was the orderly division of time into past, present, and future.*[7]

As historian Jim Cullen points out the Civil War (and the histories that followed) is known to most Americans through popular culture, not through professional or "responsible" historical literature.[8] One reason for this lack of knowledge of the war, and of race relations from then until the 1960s, may be because all Americans do not share a common history. An obfuscating cloud has blocked the development of anything like a national consensus about the

READING NOTES

247

history of race relations, even for those of us whose ancestors have been here for centuries.

Black People as Invisible

In his novel *Invisible Man*, Ralph Ellison suggests that black people became invisible after the Civil War. They became invisible (at least as cognitive beings) in the relatively new technologies of media, photography, and film through which knowledge was increasingly disseminated. However, being invisible did not mean that blacks were nonexistent in these media; rather, their status paralleled and reflected their marginal status in the broader society.

As Orlando Patterson has pointed out, in every culture it takes generations after emancipation or manumission for the effects of slavery to fade.[9] The corollary to this is a period of "symbolic death," sometimes marked by stereotypes, representational stagnation, chaos, or structured absence. The realities of the lives of blacks were kept in the shadows, where they continued to be viewed by most of the American public as largely irrelevant to the course of American events and sensibilities.

Birth is rarely shown publicly because it presents an emotionally charged historical argument in an aesthetically dynamic package. Griffith accomplishes this in part by using black-and-white nitrate film, perhaps the most lovely medium ever invented, and by emphasizing classical whiteness as a racial ideal. (Two recent authors, Richard Dyer and Kirk Savage, have written compellingly on how whiteness as a nineteenth-century racial ideal was borrowed in part from Greek statuary and in part from the palette of Renaissance and Baroque painters.[10])

In addition to using nitrate film, two technical innovations contribute to *Birth*'s profound impact. The first is, of course, Griffith's manipulation of film grammar through editing and montage. The second is his deployment of the well-worn and well-known generic capacities of melodrama.

In *Birth*, as in *Intolerance* (1916), *Broken Blossoms* (1919), and *Way Down East* (1922), Griffith defined the basic components of the melodramatic modern movie: a light realistic touch combined with unfathomable pathos.[11] No genre is better able to translate myriad complicated and ultimately irresolvable problems into the chaotic swirl typical of personal relations.

Whatever one may think of how Griffith deployed melodrama and appealed to the baser instincts of popular culture, *The Birth of a Nation* has always been, and always will be, an important American film because of its aesthetic legacy. The film is also crucial to comprehending this country's "other" history—the failure of Reconstruction, which is rarely taught or even recounted.

The Myth of the Black Brute

In *Birth*, Gus (Walter Long), sometimes known as the "black brute," is considered guilty of killing Flora (Mae Marsh), the youngest of the Cameron siblings, when he accidentally chases her off the edge of a cliff. She jumps off the cliff because the alternative, to be in Gus's embrace, is unthinkable.

While grieving her loss, her older brother Ben (Henry Walthall) is inspired by some children playing hide-and-seek to invent what becomes the costume of the Ku Klux Klan. Ben thus becomes the leader of a pack of Klansmen who apprehend Gus and, in an elaborately hand-tinted night scene, lynch him.

The notorious Gus has been at the crux of an argument about the image of blacks in film since the initial release of *Birth*. Gus, we are told, was the first black to show aggression toward whites in cinema, behavior considered so provocative that it was not

Griffith exploited the formal and narrative structures of melodrama in Birth of a Nation, as evidenced in this family scene.

shown again until the Blaxploitation films of the 1960s and '70s.

In the 1914 version of *Uncle Tom's Cabin* (Edwin S. Porter), a black male slave picks up a pistol and shoots Simon Legree dead, grasping the fired gun to his chest in a subsequent close-up. The biggest difference between this nameless slave and Gus is that the *Uncle Tom's Cabin* slave is played by a phenotypically black male, whereas Gus is so transparently a Caucasian done up in blackface as to appear clownish to anybody not in the grip of the "Confederate myth."[12]

The Confederate Myth

The Birth of a Nation can roughly be divided into three parts: (1) before the war, (2) during the war, and (3) after the war. The first part presents a nostalgic picture of antebellum life, both in the South among the Camerons and in the North among the Stonemans, yet neither setting is perfectly idyllic.[13]

Flora (Mac Marsh), a flower of southern womanhood, throws herself off a cliff rather than succumb to Gus's sexual advances.

The scenes involving the Stonemans are split between the senator's daughter's apartment in Boston and the home of his mulatto mistress, Lydia. Lydia (Mary Alden), to whom we are introduced in one of the earliest scenes in the film, has delusions of grandeur and annoys Stoneman's political visitors by attempting to trick them into treating her like a lady, which she is not.

Lydia's race and questionable moral character are visually marked in three ways. First, although played by a white actress, she wears dark makeup. Second, she is clothed like a gypsy or other colorful ethnic with a

_____

_____

_____

_____

_____

Mary Alden, a white actress in dark makeup, as the Stonemans' mulatto housekeeper in The Birth of a Nation.

"The Little Colonel" (Henry P. Walthall) recovers from his war wounds with the help of his mother (Josephine Crowell) and Elsie (Lillian Gish), the woman he adores.

head wrap and a peasant dress. Third, her gestures are exaggeratedly exotic and elaborate. At one point, she falls to her knees, tearing her clothes from her shoulders in an obvious translation of the overacting of stage conventions when they are transferred to the screen. Few film scholars have commented on Lydia's behavior or on her role in subsequent action.[14]

Silas Lynch, the male mulatto, played by a white man (George Siegmann) in brown face, plays a much larger role in the narrative. He has a wanton appetite for power and revenge and is invited to participate in the Reconstruction government in South Carolina. Lydia seems sinister, but only in a vague way. Lynch's role as a villain is much more palpable.

Senator Stoneman (modeled after Thaddeus Stevens), is also portrayed as a less than positive character. But in Griffith and Dixon's estimation, his major problem is that he is surrounded by people of mixed blood who are intrinsically untrustworthy.

This point might be missed even after several viewings since cause and effect are not precisely delineated and

because of Griffith's characteristic manipulation of film grammar, particularly in the chase scenes. Nonetheless, the reign of terror of the elite mulatto children of the former plantation class is the basis of an important subplot. It is not at all clear how the Camerons figure in this subplot since their house appears to be on a small in-town street, not on a plantation, and, of course, the elder Cameron is not a plantation owner but a doctor. When one reads Thomas Dixon's *The Clansman* and *The Leopard's Spots*, the potential dangers that could occur with the emergence of mulattoes and mongrel races is spelled out much more clearly.

Early in the film, when the Stoneman boys go to visit the Cameron boys in Piedmont, South Carolina, all seems to be bliss. Mammy and a trusted elderly male slave, both white actors in blackface, are shown to be close members of the household. The rest of the slaves primarily played by phenotypically black actors, appear to be working happily in the fields and, as the intertitles note, they benefit from "the two-hour interval given for dinner, out of

READING NOTES

_____

_____

_____

_____

_____

their working day from six till six." Yet there are subtle hints of difficulties a close shot of a skirmish between a black puppy and a white kitten at Dr. Cameron's feet is accompanied by an intertitle that reads "Hostilities," and when Ben Cameron sees the locket photo of Elsie Stoneman, he immediately falls in love with her, refuses to return it to her brother Phil, and puts it in his breast pocket, where it will remain throughout the Civil War.

Slaves and masters are shown as happy with one another. One sign of their contentment, which appears in subsequent plantation films, is the presence of barefoot and raggedly dressed black children, who run and play behind carriages carrying white folks. Yet despite this peaceful facade, there is a "gathering storm," or, as Griffith expresses in the intertitles, "The power of the sovereign states, established when Lord Cornwallis surrendered to the individual colonies in 1781, is threatened by the new administration." If the North wins the election, the South will be forced to go to war.

Whiteness as Right and Beautiful

From the outset, the viewer is positioned to notice the poetic, gleaming beauty of the young, delicately boned white Camerons and Stonemans and how cruel it will be for them to be divided by the war. In this and subsequent films, Griffith is decidedly antiwar, albeit in favor of white male honor, bravery, and chivalry. In a series of elaborate battle scenes, in which the two younger Cameron and Stoneman boys die melodramatically in one another's arms. Ben Cameron, the Little Colonel, is dramatically rescued by Union soldier Phil (Elmer Clifton), the older Stoneman boy. Ben survives to be nursed by none other than Elsie (Lillian Gish), whose picture he still carries in his pocket. Ben wakes to find her, a vision of ethereal loveliness, the light filtering through her golden hair, singing to him at his bedside.

Mrs. Cameron pleads with President Lincoln (Joseph Henabery) to commute her son's death sentence.

Of the scenes that take place at the end of the war, perhaps the most significant is the one in which Mrs. Cameron (Josephine Crowell) goes with Elsie to plead for the life of her son Ben, who has been sentenced to death. Abraham Lincoln (Joseph Henabery), whom Griffith calls "the great heart," quite naturally grants Ben a reprieve. Lincoln's administrative generosity is juxtaposed, scene by scene, with the rampant vigilante justice of the hog-wild Union troops in Piedmont, who ransack the Cameron home and almost (but not quite) have their way with the Cameron women.

Among these squads of marauders are soldiers played by black actors, led by either a white or a white person in blackface. The contrasting look of the blackface actors and those with black skin lends an even greater sense of chaos to the actions of the Union regiments. A wounded Ben Cameron returns home just in time to prevent further disaster.

In another major scene linking the first part of the film to the second part, Elsie and Senator Stoneman look on in horror as Lincoln is assassinated. As Dr. Cameron puts it, "Our best friend is gone. What is to become of us now?" Radical Reconstruction, or what Thomas Dixon and many other southerners called "Negro rule," followed hard on the heels of Lincoln's assassination. Griffith presents a series of scenes to illustrate how badly blacks behaved after passage of the Thirteenth Amendment, when they were freed and given the vote, and after passage of the Fourteenth and Fifteenth Amendments, when they were given free access to public facilities. These scenes include large numbers of phenotypically black actors, along with some in blackface, aggressively groveling and grimacing. The freed slaves throw down their sacks in the cotton fields to dance and frolic all day. Black members of the state legislature are shown seated with their bare feet on their desks, openly drinking whiskey. Blacks are shown selling their votes outright or simply unable to comprehend what voting means. Black demonstrators are shown with picket signs demanding mixed marriages.

Elsie and Senator Stoneman look on in horror as Lincoln is assassinated in Ford's Theater in a recreation of the event in **The Birth of a Nation.**

Lynching in American Photography

Lynching was one of the major topics in U.S. news reports at the time of the release of *Birth*, in 1915. Such episodes were extensively reported on in local newspapers. Particularly around 1915, huge, festive crowds, including women and young children, often turned out ot witness these hangings, in which victims were sometimes tortured, slowly burned alive, or castrated, their body parts distributed among the crowds as keepsakes. A great deal is known about these events from journalists such as Ida B. Wells. who did what they could to arouse antilynching sentiments among responsible Americans.[15]

Recently, lynching has been dramatically represented in the book *Without Sanctuary*,[16] which includes postcard-size photographs of lynch victims, most of them shown dead. One is struck by the youth and beauty of the average victim (one almost never sees such men in silent film) and, in contrast, the oddly sinister faces of the white men, boys, girls, and women posing proudly with the corpses. (In comparison, the lynching in *Birth* is comparatively pristine and carefully choreographed.) Produced as mementos of the events and widely distributed via mail as picture postcards, these images show huge crowds of people milling around in broad daylight. At the center of the photographs, we see the mutilated bodies of the victims—blacks, usually men—either hanging from a rope or badly burned on a pyre of smoking wood. Sometimes the photos which were collected by the antiquarian dealer James Allen, are marked by the names of the photographers who took them. Sometimes they include messages to friends and relatives, such as "He killed Earl's grandma. She was Florence's mother. Give this to Bird from Aunt Myrtle." or "Warning: The answer of the Anglo-Saxon race to black brutes who would attack the womanhood of the South." These images have since circulated as curiosities and collectibles in the South and North. Virtually none of the perpetrators of these vigilante crimes, some of which were based on

READING NOTES

trumped-up charges of rape and murder, some on no charges at all, have ever been prosecuted.[17]

We who are black have all seen images of lynchings in daylight, with large, festive crowds taking part in the torture of the victim. Griffith, and perhaps even Dixon, might have seen such public lynchings as wanton, savage events, unlike the "good" lynching meted out to Gus in *Birth*. A private affair, Gus's execution occurs at night in an orderly and ritualized manner and is performed by white men dressed in full Klan regalia.

For the audiences of 1915, who were mostly too young to have experienced the events of the Civil War but were nonetheless familiar with the carnage and devastation, the film's romanticization of the Klan must have obfuscated not only the historically remote events of Reconstruction in the South but also the Gilded Age of progressivism and westward expansion under Presidents William McKinley, Theodore Roosevelt, and Woodrow Wilson.[18]

The History of Reconstruction

For lack of a convincing and viable alternative popular discourse, the dominant account of Reconstruction tells us that the post—Civil War period was one in which the freed slaves, having been forcibly kept illiterate and uncivilized by their masters, showed themselves to be unprepared for the awesome responsibilities and mundane difficulties of freedom. Meanwhile, unscrupulous blacks (or educated mulattoes, some of whom happened to look white) and white "carpetbaggers" from both the North and South took advantage of federal funds and protection to grab all they could steal.

The first really significant historical correction to this picture was W. E. B. DuBois's account in 1935.[19] DuBois's conclusion was that by allowing Reconstruction to end prematurely, the federal government essentially made peace with the South; the North traded economic contingency for "states' rights," leaving former slaves poor, defenseless, and illiterate. Yet, unlike *The*

Birth of a Nation, Uncle Tom's Cabin, or *Gone with the Wind* (1939), DuBois's book was never a bestseller, even among black readers.

According to historian James Loewen, violence by whites against blacks, not the ignorance of the former slaves, was the chief problem of the postwar decade:

> *Textbooks written between about 1890 and the 1960s … painted an unappealing portrait of oppressive Republican rule in the postwar period, a picture that we might call the Confederate myth of Reconstruction. For years black families kept the truth about Reconstruction alive. The aging slaves whose stories were recorded by WPA [Works Progress Administration] writers in the 1930s remained proud of blacks' roles during Reconstruction. Some still remembered the names of African Americans elected to office sixty years earlier. "I know folks think the books tell the truth," said an 88-year-old former slave, "but they shore don't." As those who knew Reconstruction from personal experience died off, however, even in the black community the textbook view took over.[20]*

It was no accident that Griffith, who originally came from Kentucky, a border state, chose to set his drama in South Carolina, the most pro-slavery state from the earliest days of the Union, the first state to secede from the Union, and the only state where blacks outnumbered whites. More blacks were elected to the state legislature of South Carolina under Reconstruction than in any other state in the country.

As late as the 1960s, the American historical establishment was still in a quandary over the reasons Reconstruction was such a failure. It fell to black historian John Hope Franklin to make the most significant correction in the record. As Franklin explains it, blacks made substantial and noteworthy contributions during Reconstruction despite the obstacles put in their way by whites who would not abandon the goals of the Confederacy.[21]

The 1970s was the first period when American historians began to substantially revise what Loewen calls the "Confederate myth" in regard not only to Reconstruction but to the effects of slavery in general. Historians such as John Blassingame, Eugene Genovese. David Brion Davis, and Herbert Gutman finally began to base their accounts of the antebellum period on narratives written or dictated by slaves and on the hundreds of interviews with former slaves collected by the WPA in the 1930s.[22] It became intellectually fashionable to write about what Genovese dubbed "the world the slaves made." It would be another decade before the privileging of the perspectives of male slaves over females would be laid to rest by Angela Davis, Deborah Grey White, Brenda Stevenson, and Patricia Morton. It has now become almost conventional in scholarly discussion of slavery to emphasize slaves' accounts of their own lives.[23]

Until the 1970s, however, American social scientists (some of whom were black, such as E. Franklin Frazier) often assumed that blacks had, more or less, been reduced to the psychological equivalent of a comedic caricature as imagined by Stanley Elkin in *Slavery*. Elkin suggests that the "Sambo" stereotype was an empirical reality. Blacks, he claims, were so degraded by the experience of slavery that all vestiges of character, culture, family values, ethics, and morality were uprooted. Elkin compares the Sambo figure to the so-called degraded personalities of some of the victims of the concentration camps in Germany during World War II.[24]

The question is, What does it take to turn a human being into a thing? Is this even possible? I do not believe so. Paul Lawrence Dunbar, a turn-of-the-century black writer whose parents were slaves, has written a number of extraordinary short stories (which are rarely read these days and are out of print) in which a plantation is depicted as haunted by the spirits of slaves hidden in trees, birds, or animals. How slaves survived, and how well, particularly in the U.S., where the population was able to regenerate itself without depending on continuously importing new slaves from Africa, is an open question, especially given the current high rates of prison incarceration among black youths (although the Rockefeller drug laws explain some of those statistics).

Elkin's unpopular argument merits further investigation into posttraumatic stress disorder in survivors, particularly survivors of multigenerational trauma. Literary scholars, beginning with the collection *The Slave's Narrative*, and continuing with a range of other texts, some of which seek to reconstruct the emotional life of slaves, have thus far done the best work in the area.[25] But even more crucial than our perception of the role of slavery, the Civil War, and Reconstruction to our understanding of the cultural politics that produced *The Birth of a Nation* is our knowledge of the years between 1890 and 1920.

Blackface as an Assimilation Ritual

In 1890, *Uncle Tom's Cabin* was still the text on race relations most familiar to the widest American audience. The initial publication of Harriet Beecher Stowe's book in 1852 closely followed the consolidation of a popular cultural phenomenon called blackface minstrelsy, in which white performers blackened their faces with burnt cork and put on fright wigs. What admixture of observation and imagination was the basis for such performances, no one has ever determined conclusively.[26]

Eric Lott suggests that blackface was, in particular, a favorite immigrant pastime and assimilation-initiation ritual. Before the Civil War, blackface minstrelsy troupes were mostly white. After the war, black performers, many of whom had acquired their skills during the antebellum period, took over, transforming and expanding blackface minstrelsy conventions in an

READING NOTES

open-ended process that then drifted into burlesque, vaudeville, and musical theater.

One of the main texts these minstrelsy companies performed in a variety of adaptations, was *Uncle Tom's Cabin*. Since Harriet Beecher Stowe, a religious abolitionist, wanted nothing to do with the stage, she declined to participate in the writing of a dramatic adaptation. Because copyright laws were not nearly as stringent as they are today, Stowe's unwillingness to get involved with dramatic productions of *Uncle Tom's Cabin* seems to have opened the door to a virtually endless series of spinoffs, a few of which completely undid Stowe's abolitionist intentions. According to Lott, the narrative of *Uncle Tom's Cabin* became a veritable battleground for interpretations of the pros and cons of southern slavery.[27]

After emancipation, black performers began to appear in white blackface minstrelsy troupes and also to form their own troupes, which traveled throughout the North and the South, as well as to the Caribbean, Latin America, Europe, Australia, and even South Africa. On tour, in tent shows and circuses, and on the nation's stages, blackface minstrelsy was the dominant means by which many black musicians, actors, comedians, and dancers first learned and had a chance to practice their craft. To compete with white minstrels, these performers advertised themselves as "the real thing." Scholars continue to insist that they were unduly pressured to render themselves as childlike, comedic, and even absurd.[28]

Post-Reconstruction Era

When Reconstruction ended, former Confederates managed to reassume local power in the South. Between 1890 and 1907, every southern and border state "legally" disenfranchised the vast majority of its African American citizens. Lynchings rose to an all-time high. In 1896, the Supreme Court upheld

A scene from the 1926 adaptation of Uncle Tom's Cabin (Harry A. Pollard).

segregation in *Plessy v. Ferguson*, the infamous "separate but equal" decision.[29]

After slavery, those blacks who were educated tended to advance first. They became the doctors, lawyers, teachers, skilled professionals, and craftspeople in the newly freed communities. Much more often than we care to admit, these blacks, including some of the most militant and politically radical, were partly white and therefore light-skinned, some so light and so mixed that they could pass for white. That some of these blacks were virtually indistinguishable from whites was an important element in Dixon and Griffith's nightmare of race mixing and of mulattoes, taking over the United States.

At least ten film adaptations were made of *Uncle Tom's Cabin*, all during the silent period before 1927. In the seventh of these, released a year before *The Birth of a Nation*, Uncle Tom was finally played by a black person, the famous minstrelsy actor and songwriter Sam Lucas. Now seventy years old, he had been the first black to play Uncle Tom on stage.

Uncle Tom's Cabin shares with *The Birth of a Nation* a preoccupation with the plight of mulattoes. There is one prominent male mulatto, George (Irving Cummings), and two prominent female mulattoes, Eliza, who runs across the ice to freedom, clutching her son to her breast, and Cassy, the mistress and housekeeper of Simon Legree, the drunken slaveholder who whips Uncle Tom to death.

In the 1914 film version of *Uncle Tom's Cabin*, all the mulattoes are played by either white actors or actors of color who appear to be white. But unlike Griffith's Lydia and Silas Lynch, Eliza, George, and Cassy never grimace or laugh hysterically; nor are their faces darkened or distorted to diminish their appearance as white. Also unlike *Birth*, in the 1914 version of *Uncle Tom's Cabin*, most of the other parts for blacks are played by phenotypically black people with admirable dignity. The only role rendered in blackface—and it is not surprising given the film's conjuncture of issues of gender, race, and sexuality—is the little slave girl, Topsy. As in Stowe's novel, Topsy is utterly comedic. Dressed in a burlap bag, her hair standing on end, and continually in motion, she is rendered largely as she was in the first *Uncle Tom's Cabin*, released in 1903.

Griffith, Dixon, Stowe, and indeed the rank and file of white abolitionists were not substantially in disagreement about the cultural and social inferiority of the full-blooded or nearly full-blooded African black. The difference among them was one of perspective. Stowe and the abolitionists argued that blacks were essentially harmless children who needed the benevolent guidance of whites, whereas demagogues, such as Thomas Dixon, felt blacks presented specific dangers as workers and voters. The concern was that mixed-race blacks, such as Griffith's Silas and Lydia (the ancestors of Eliza and George), who combined the immorality of the black race with the ingenuity of whiteness, could tip the balance in a negative direction if they were not exterminated. Whether or not Griffith believed in a "final solution" is

not clear, although *Birth* did encourage the rebirth of an incendiary twentieth-century Ku Klux Klan.

Stowe's view was that blacks who looked white and who were literate and educated and thus behaved like whites should be treated as white, because they were, after all, white. For Dixon and Griffith, such a prospect was terrifying, perhaps because, unlike Stowe, they were working-class white men and afraid they would have to give up ground to the descendants of former slaves. Dixon and Griffith were also afraid that racial impurity would lead to cultural degeneration and, ultimately, white invisibility.

Dixon and Griffith dearly wanted to believe that there was an intrinsic order to the natural universe, as Charles Darwin had described it, but events must have seemed to be overtaking the scientists' abilities to update their theories.[30] Both Dixon and Griffith must have had George, Eliza, and Cassy in mind when they created Lydia and Silas. The iconography of Cassy is so similar to that of Lydia that they might be related. Leslie Fiedler reports that in a performance of *Uncle Tom's Cabin* in 1903 Thomas Dixon was incensed by what he saw as the historical distortions of life under slavery.[31] At that time, Dixon publicly vowed to ameliorate this false impression by writing a trilogy on the Civil War.

Jim Crow and White Supremacy

The ideological and cultural battle over how to enforce white supremacy preceded the theatrical tours of Thomas Dixon's adaptations of *The Leopard's Skin* (1902) and *The Clansman* (1905). The skirmishes continued well after the release of *Birth*, as sporadic lynchings and race riots occurred following the return of black soldiers who had fought abroad in World War I.

Dixon's narratives had many sources; there was no lack of material illustrating the spread of white supremacy, lynching, and white vigilantism around

READING NOTES

_____

_____

_____

_____

_____

The white mob prepares to lynch Gas for his sexual pursuit and "murder" of Flora.

the turn of the century. Histoman Glenda Elizabeth Gilmore points to certain correspondences between events in Wilmington, North Carolina, in 1898 and the plot of Thomas Dixon's novels and, by extension, of *The Birth of a Nation.*[32]

In 1898. Wilmington became the ideal place to test the feasibility of the white supremacist campaign to block blacks from voting in the South. Wihnington was a port city with a large black middle class and many black public officials. After the Republicans and Populists won control of the state legislature in 1894, blacks, as well as white Republicans and Populists, won local posts previously held by Democrats. In the 1897 election, Republicans won the majority on the board of aldermen and got to choose the mayor as well. The Dixie Democrats challenged the Republicans in the state supreme court, which had ruled in favor of the Republicans, so the white supremacists were spoiling for revenge.

Then, in August 1898, in the only black daily in the state, the *Daily Record*, editor Alexander Manly responded to an excerpt from a speech by racist agitator Rebecca Latimer Felton that had been printed in the white-controlled *Wilmington Messenger*. Felton had accused white men in the rural South of being soft on black men who raped white women. In her view, lynching black men was the only remedy.

In response, Manly argued that white women lied about being raped at least half the time and that white men also raped black women. Why was it worse for a black man to rape a white woman than for a white man to rape a black woman? "The morals of the poor white people are on a par with their colored neighbors of like conditions," Manly wrote. White newspapers proceeded to reprint Manly's statements each day until the election, often as the lead-in to reports about local "outrages," such as incidents of black women refusing to move aside for white women on the sidewalks or other indignities perpetrated by no longer humble blacks.

As Gilmore recounts the story in *Cender and Jim Crow*, Alfred Moore Waddell, a Confederate colonel and formerly a moderate Reconstruction politician, had become the leader of the Wilmington White Government League, a "cross-class alliance of white men" who were extensively armed. Warning against an alleged plot by blacks to take over the city, Waddell insisted "we are going to protect our firesides and our loved ones or die in the attempt." He and his men promised to drive Manly and all the black politicians from Wilmington. "Go to the polls tomorrow," Waddell beseeched his audiences, "and if you find the Negro out voting, tell him to leave the polls, and if he refuses, kill him."[33] Meanwhile, white businessmen had already black-mailed Governor Russell, a Republican, into removing the names of Republican were running seared and Democrats were sweeping into office.

After the election, a white mob burned Manly's press, hunted down prominent blacks, and either shot them or ran them out of town. The Wilmington Light

READING NOTES

Infantry soon swelled the ranks of the mob. By the end of the day, ten blacks were dead and Waddell had seized the mayor's office. As presented in *The Birth of a Nation*, the point had been to scare blacks into never trying to vote again.

Meanwhile, blacks were fleeing Wilmington In New Bern, whites climbed up a water tower, where they could shoot blacks as they were trying to get on trains. Poor blacks, including four hundred women and children, fled to the woods, where they remained for several days. Black congressman George White begged for federal intervention but to no avail. As part of the national Afro-American Council, Ida B. Wells-Barnett met with President McKinley to beg him to speak out, again to no avail. "Today we are mourners in a strange land with no protection near," an anonymous black women wrote the president. "I cannot sign my name and live."[34]

Without support forthcoming from McKinley, the white Republicans panicked and called for a "lily-white" party.[35] Within a month, 1,400 blacks had left Wilmington, and six months later, they were still leaving by the scores. Once they left, whites immediately confiscated the blacks' property for unpaid taxes.

Conclusion

The Birth of a Nation has stood not only as a dominant fictional account of Reconstruction but as an apologia for the nearly one hundred year-reign of Jim Crow segregation and white supremacist politics that followed in the South and effectively dominated social policies in the West and North. *Birth* remains distinct from most other cultural ephemera about racism in that it has somehow continued to occupy our interest, whereas other cultural artifacts—the postcards, the plays, and so forth—have not. *Birth* continues to be a source of fascination precisely because of its formal brilliance. Why the myths it recounts survive in public discourse is less clear. Those people who might benefit most from a

rigorous study of *The Birth of a Nation* invariably choose to avoid its examination. I can no longer imagine life without my knowledge of Jim Crow culture, history, and politics in the South or without being able to draw upon archival references and an intellectual genealogy largely prompted by my first bewildered viewing of *The Birth of a Nation* fifteen years ago. Indeed, analysis of *Birth* in the context of Griffith's exemplary career as a filmmaker—and in the context of the history and historiography of American silent cinema—must surely be one of the ideal places to begin the long-overdue analysis of race in U.S. cinema studies.

ENDNOTES

1. Silent film scholars often seem preoccupied with cataloging and describing technological and aesthetic innovations. Among these are the genesis of the seamless "chronological" narrative, the formation of the studio and the star system, and the emergence of the dominant genres. Content analysis is sometimes dismissed as unimaginative and crude work. There are, of course, some notable exceptions, particularly with regard to working-class and other polemical themes, such as Kevin Brownlow's *Behind the Mask of Innocence: Films of Social Conscience in the Silent Era* (Berkeley: University of California Press, 1990): Kay Sloan's *The Loud Silents: Origins of the Social Problem Film* (Urbana: University of Illinois Press, 1988); Steven J. Ross's *Working-Class Hollywood: Silent Film and the Shaping of Class in America* (Princeton: University of Princeton Press, 1998); Martin S. Pernick's *The Black Stork: Eugenics and the Death of "Defective" Babies in American Medicine and Motion Pictures since* 1915 (New York: Oxford University Press, 1996); and Gregory Waller's *Main Street Amusements: Movies and Commercial Entertainment in a Southern City, 1896–1930* (Washington, D.C.: Smithsonian Institution Press, 1995).

2. Alison McMahan, *Alice Guy Blaché: Lost Visionary of the Cinema* (New York: Continuum Books, 2002), 149–53.

3. First, one should take into account depictions of peoples of color who were not African American. See in particular Charles Musser's detailed compendium on the earliest Edison films in *Edison Motion Pictures 1890–1900: An Annotated Filmography* (Washington, D.C.: Smithsonian Institution Press, 1997). Also, since this article was written, several books have been published on blacks in silent films. These include Bruce Chadwick, *The*

READING NOTES

Reel Civil War: Mythmaking in American Film (New York: Vintage, 2002); Barbara Tepa Lupack, *Literary Adaptations in Black American Cinema: From Micheaux to Morrison* (Rochester, N.Y.: University of Rochester Press, 2002); Anna Everett, *Returning the Gaze: A Genealogy of Black Film Criticism, 1909–1949* (Durham, N.C.: Duke University Press, 2001); Charlene B. Regester, *Black Entertainers in African American Newspaper Articles*, vol. 1 (Jefferson, N.C.: McFarland; 2002); Pearl Bowser, Jane Gaines, and Charles Musser, eds. *The World of Oscar Micheaux's Silents* (Bloomington: Indiana University Press, 2001). Pearl Bowser and Louis Spence, *Writing Himself into History: Oscar Micheaux, His Silent Films, and His Audiences* (New Brunswick, N.J.: Rutgers University Press, 2000), Jane Gaines, *Fire and Desire: Mixed-Race Movies in the Silent Era* (Chicago: University of Chicago Press, 2001); Linda Williams, *Playing the Race Card: Melodrama of Black and White, from Uncle Tom to O.J. Simpson* (Princeton: Princeton University Press, 2001); and Gerald R. Butters, Jr., *Black Manhood on the Silent Screen* (Lawrence: University Press of Kansas, 2002).

4. See, for example, Lary May, *Screening out the Past: The Birth of Mass Culture and the Motion Picture Industry* (Chicago: University of Chicago Press, 1983); Robert Lang, ed., *The Birth of a Nation* (New Brunswick, N.J.: Rutgers University Press, 1994); Robert Sklar, *Movie-Made America: A Cultural History of American Movies*, rev. and updated (New York: Vintage, 1994); David Platt, ed., *Celluloid Power: Social Film Criticism, from "The Birth of a Nation" to "Judgment at Nuremberg"* (Metuchen, N.J.: Scarecrow Press, 1992); Richard Schickel, *D. W. Griffith: An American Life* (New York: Limelight Editions, 1994); Daniel Bernardi, ed., *The Birth of Whiteness: Race and the Emergence of U.S. Cinema* (New Brunswick, N.J.: Rutgers University Press, 1996); and Thomas Cripps, *Slow Fade to Black* (New York: Oxford University Press, 1974).

5. Darlene Clark Hine, Elsa Barkley Brown, and Rosalyn Terborg-Penn, eds., *Encyclopedia of Black Women: An Historical Encyclopedia* (Brooklyn, N.Y.: Carlson Publishing, 1993), 1129–32.

6. In *Slow Fade to Black*, Thomas Cripps mentions Mme. Sul-te-Wan several times in the context of discussing the small colony of black performers in Hollywood at the time *The Birth of a Nation* was being filmed.

7. Grace Elizabeth Hale, *Making Whiteness: The Culture of Segregation in the South, 1890–1940* (New York: Pantheon, 1998), 48.

8. Jim Cullen, *The Civil War in Popular Culture* (Washington, D.C.: Smithsonian Institution Press, 1995), 18.

9. Orlando Patterson, *Slavery and Social Death: A Comparative Study* (New York: Oxford University Press, 1982), 13, 244–61.

10. Richard Dyer, *White* (New York: Routledge, 1997), 1–40, and Kirk Savage, *Standing Soldiers, Kneeling Slaves: Race, War, and Monument in Nineteenth-Century America* (Princeton: Princeton University Press, 1997). 8–9. To get some idea of the variation among human beings in nature as opposed to the rather rigid formulas for their appearance we have been shown in classic Hollywood cinema since Griffith's day all one need do is think about the fact that all dogs, despite their endless variety of shapes, sizes, colors, and fur, belong to a single species. The apparent differences in behavior and function among dogs have been deliberately bred, whereas this is not the case in humans. Yet we remain (I suspect) equally diverse and all the more unpredictable as a species.

11. A. Nicholas Vardae, "Realism and Romance: D. W. Griffith," in Marcia Landy, ed., *Imitations of Life: A Reader on Film and TV Melodrama* (Detroit: Wayne State University Press, 1991), 353–61.

12. Michele Wallace, "Oscar Micheaux's *Within Our Gates: The Possibilities for Alternative Visions*," in Pearl Bowser, Jane Gaines, and Charlie Musser, eds., *Oscar Micheaux and His Circle: African-American Filmmaking and Race Cinema of the Silent Era* (Bloomington: Indiana University Press, 2001), 53–66; and "*Uncle Tom's Cabin*: Before and after the Jim Crow Era," *Drama Review* 44, no. 1 (spring 2000): 137–56.

13. John Cuniberti, *"The Birth of a Nation": A Formal Shot-by-Shot Analysis together with Microfiche*, Cinema Editions on Microfiche, 1979.

14. I owe my knowledge of this material to a lecture given by Sandy Lewis-Flitterman in the Columbia Film Seminar at the Museum of Modern Art, spring 1994.

15. Jacqueline Jones Royster, ed., *Southern Horrors and Other Writings: The Anti-Lynching Campaign of Ida B. Wells, 1892–1900* (Boston: Bedford Books, 1996). Ida B. Wells was a journalist who proselytized against lynching via a series of self-published pamphlets resulting often from her firsthand investigations of lynching scenes and the communities in which they occurred. This book contains the full text of Wells's three most prominent pamphlets: "Southern Horrors: Lynch Law in All Its Phases," "A Red Record," and "Mob Rule in New Orleans." One of the most interesting things about her accounts for readers today is that, in an attempt to disarm critics, she drew heavily on published accounts called from local and national newspapers.

Historian Linda O. McMurray has written as excellent biography of Wells. See McMurray, *To Keep the Waters Troubled:*

READING NOTES

The Life of Ida B. Wells (New York: Oxford University Press, 1998). Also see Anne P. Rice, ed., *Witnessing Lynching: American Writers Respond* (New Brunswiel N.J.: Rutgers University Press, forthcoming). This volume contains antilyching writings by American authors, including Wells, published from 1889 through 1935.

16. James Allen et al., *Without Sanctuary: Lynching Photography in America* (Santa Fe, N.M.: Twin Palm Publishers, 2000). See also Wallace, "Passing, Lynching, and Jim Crow: A Genealogy of Race and Gender in U.S. Visual Culture, 1895–1929," Ph.D. dissertation, New York University, 1999, for a discussion of visual issues of lynching, and Rice, "Introduction: The Contest over Memory," in Rice, *Witnessing Lynching.*

17. Allen's collection appeared first in a finely made, limited-edition book that sold for $60; only four thousand copies were printed. The collection will be permanently housed at the Robert Woodruff Library at Emory University in Atlanta, where it will be made available to researchers.

18. Nell I. Painter, *Standing at Armageddon: The United States, 1877–1919* (New York: Norton, 1987).

19. W. E. B. DuBois, *Black Reconstruction: An Essay toward a History of the Part Which Black Folk Played in the Attempt to Reconstruct Democracy in America, 1860–1880* (New York: Russell Co., 1935): *The Souls of Black Folk: Essays and Sketches* (1903, reprint; New York; Vintage, 1990); and *The Suppression of the African Slave Trade to the United States of America, 1638–1870* (1896, reprint; Baton Rouge: Louisiana State University Press, 1969).

20. James Loewen, *Lies My Teacher Told Me: Everything Your American History Textbook Got Wrong* (New York: New Press, 1994).

21. John Hope Franklin, *Reconstruction after the Civil War* (Chicago: University of Chicago Press, 1961), and Franklin, *From Slavery to Freedom: A History of Negro Americans*, 3rd ed. (New York: Knopf, 1967).

22. Eugene Genovese, *Roll, Jordan, Roll. The World the Slaves Made* (New York: Pantheon, 1974); Herbert Gutman, *The Black Family in Slavery and Freedom, 1750–1925* (New York: Pantheon, 1976); John Blassingame, *The Slave Community: Plantation Life in the Antebellum South* (New York: Oxford University Press, 1979); and George Rawick, *From Sundown to Sunup: The Making of the Black Community* (Westport, Conn.: Greenwood Press, 1972) served as the introduction to the twenty-volume set of WPA slave narratives.

23. A few recent examples include the PBS documentary series *Africans in America*, Toni Morrison's novel *Beloved*, and its recent film adaptation directed by Jonathan Demme.

24. Stanley Elkin, *Slavery: A Problem in American Institutional and Intellectual Life*, 3rd ed., (Chicago: University of Chicago Press, 1976) 98–115, 305–06.

25. See John W. Blassingame, Charles T. Davis, and Henry Louis Gates, Jr., eds. *The Slave's Narrative* (New York: Oxford University Press. 1985). Particularly instructive has been Jean Fagin Yellin's annotated version of Harriet Ann Jacob. *Incidents in the Life of a Slave Girl* (Cambridge: Harvard University Press, 1987).

26. Erie Lott, *Love and Theft: Blackface Minstrelsy and the American Working Class* (New York: Oxford University Press, 1993); Robert C. Toll, *Blacking Up: The Minstrel Show in Nineteenth-Century America* (New York: Oxford University Press, 1974); and Annemarie Bean, James V. Hatch, and Brooks McNamara, eds., *Inside the Minstrel Mask: Readings in Nineteenth-Century Blackface Minstrelsy* (Hanover N.H.: Weslcyan University Press, 1996).

27. Lott, *Love and Theft*, 211–13.

28. See Michele Faith Wallace, "Bamboozled: The Archive," in *Dark Designs and Visual Culture* (Durham, N.C.: Duke University Press, forthcoming). Also see Mel Watkins, *On the Real Side: Laughing, Lying, and Signifying—The Underground Tradition of African-American Humor That Transformed American Culture, from Slavery to Richard Pryor* (New York: Simon & Schuster, 1994).

29. Wallace, "Passing, Lynching, and Jim Crow."

30. See Edward J. Larson, *Sex, Race, and Science: Eugenics in the Deep South* (Baltimore: Johns Hopkins University Press, 1995).

31. Leslie Fiedler, *The Inadvertent Epic: From "Uncle Tom's Cabin" to "Roots"* (New York: Simon & Schuster, 1980).

32. Glenda Elizabeth Gilmore, *Gender and Jim Crow: Women and the Politics of White Supremacy in North Carolina, 1896–1920* (Chapel Hill: University of North Carolina Press, 1996), 134–38.

33. Ibid., 105–08. Similar racially antagonistic outbursts took place all over the South, as well as in communities in the West and in mid-Atlantic states from 1880 through the 1920s, as part of the process of general disfranchisement and eastration of the political aspirations of the black population. See Michael Perlman, *Struggle for Mastery: Disfranchisement in the South, 1888–1909* (Chapel Hill: University of North Carolina Press, 2001) for a relevant historical bibliography.

34. Gilmore, *Gender and Jim Crow*, 113.

35. Ibid., 113–14.

READING NOTES

_____

_____

_____

_____

Chapter 10

Evolution of Media Systems

"A new medium of verbal communication not only does not wipe out the old, but actually reinforces the older medium or media. However, in doing so it transforms the old, so that the old is no longer what it used to be." — Walter Ong

This chapter is about technology. It also is about the business of selling innovation. And it is about change. Walter Ong, a Jesuit priest and communication scholar at St. Louis University, devoted his professional life to the study of technology, innovation, and change. His quotation above presents one of his most important ideas about the evolution of media systems, that the invention of new systems changes our understanding of the old systems.

Knowing how technologies evolved in the past provides insights into the patterns of change and future developments. Key inventions, events, and forces both stimulated and inhibited change. The Industrial Revolution of the 1800s, together with key scientific discoveries in physics and chemistry, spurred transportation and telecommunications innovations in that century. The two world wars in the 20th century escalated innovation in broadcasting and telecommunications and spurred the U.S. lead in global media. The pace of change has increased, so that the present era is marked by continuous innovation, the only constant being change itself.

This chapter will:

- survey forces that shaped the development of communications technologies in the United States,

- spotlight some significant communications inventions and inventors,

- apply the theories of diffusion of innovations to communications technologies, and

- consider the major shifts in human thought and communication brought about by technological innovation.

Rather than giving separate histories of the technologies, the following discussion examines the communications media as a whole with an emphasis on the theme of change. It contextualizes history to the current media world and serves as a basis to speculate about the future of mass communications. To help the reader sort out the sequence of events, a brief chronology of communications technology is provided at the end of the chapter. The bunching of digital technology innovations in the late 20th century vividly shows the escalating pace of change in the electronic media.

Required Reading: Following Walter Ong's idea that new communication technologies serve to redefine old ones, Henry Jenkins' chapter, "Democratizing Television? The Politics of Participation," from his book *Convergence Culture* discusses the recent trend of consumer-modified media. Some audience members do not just sit back and passively taking in their media products; they slice and dice them, create personalized versions, discuss them in fan groups, and pressure the producers for new releases that reflect their interests. Some producers have learned how to use such consumer participation to their advantage. Jenkins calls this new trend "participatory media," and it is revolutionizing the media business.

No single factor can explain the evolution of communications technologies. A complex interplay of concurrent technological, economic, and sociological forces have promoted innovation at some times and blocked it at other times. The fundamental factor driving communications technology innovations has been the human urge to communicate, but other factors must be present for innovation to occur, including motivation of personal self-interest, ingenuity, enabling resources, access to markets, and removal of inhibitions.

Technological inventions helped the U.S. mass media to grow into an economic and cultural force to dominate the worldwide flow of information and entertainment in the 20th century. The developing U.S. media enjoyed several advantages compared to their competitors in Western Europe and Asia—a free enterprise system, plentiful raw materials, economic stimulation from parallel growth in transportation and markets, relative isolation from international political upheavals, a superior educational system, immigration of some of the world's top scientific research minds seeking the freedom and the capital that the United States offered, and constitutional protection for free expression.

At times, lack of government involvement worked to the disadvantage of U.S. communications technology companies competing with government-run foreign competitors. Occasionally, the United States lost its technological lead to other countries organized more efficiently to take advantage of media inventions. For example, Japan claimed leadership of the consumer-electronics industry in the 1970s; the Minitel videotex service run by the French and British postal systems in the 1980s outstripped anything available at the time in the United States, and the adoption of mobile telephone technologies in Western Europe and Asia in the 1990s was faster than the U.S. Nevertheless, U.S. communications technology companies, and particularly providers of content for transmission via the media, generally have emerged as competitive leaders in the world markets.

PRIVATE GAIN VERSUS PUBLIC GOOD

Both *Time* magazine and A&E cable network recognized German goldsmith Johannes Gutenberg as the most influential person of the second millennium for his invention of the movable type printing press. All that he wanted from his invention was a return on his investment. After his business venture to manufacture Bibles failed to make a profit, Gutenberg lost some of this printing equipment in a lawsuit brought by his business partner, who was opening his own print shop with Gutenberg's presses and apprentice. Imitators of the Gutenberg flatbed printing press propagated rapidly throughout Germany, then into Italy, France, and the rest of Europe.

By the end of the 15th century, hundreds of books had been mass-produced, one page at a time, on hand-powered wooden presses (see Figure 10.1). Printing press design improved only modestly for nearly four hundred years, until steam power was added during the Industrial Revolution in the 19th century.

The evolution of the printing press set a pattern for communications technology discoveries to come. Taking advantage of propitious circumstances, innovators risked precious resources in hopes of a big personal return. If an innovator's timing is right and if he or she has the resources needed to get the invention to a receptive market, the inventor presumably reaps the rewards. If not, a better-positioned competitor will come along and enjoy the benefits.

Gutenberg's invention reduced the cost of print media by substantially increasing the efficiency of reproducing texts while maintaining quality as compared to hand-lettering. Despite his efficiency breakthrough, Gutenberg's Bibles still required hundreds of hours of highly skilled labor to produce and thus were priced beyond the means of most people.

Figure 10.1—*Gutenberg-style flatbed printing press.*

Though print publications were not yet affordable for the masses, the Gutenberg press greatly broadened the market for books and other kinds of printing. In 1484, governments began to print proclamations and in the early 1500s, news books chronicling events in Europe began to circulate. The first daily newspaper in England began publication in 1702. With the greater availability of printed material, literacy rates began to climb, creating a virtuous cycle in which more printed material made literacy more desirable and increased the number of literate people, in turn increasing the demand for more printed products.

In the 1830s, steam engines sped up the printing process sufficiently to reduce the purchase price of a daily newspaper to a penny—affordable for most average citizens. A series of inventors since then have increased the efficiency of presses by replacing Gutenberg's flat press with a rotating drum, adding images and color, and moving printing technology to consumers' computer desktops. Papermaking techniques were also improved, and in the late 1880s, typesetting was further mechanized. Each invention was motivated by self-interest to gain a market advantage in the printing business by increasing the efficiency and improving the quality of communication.

But communications technologies are evolutionary. With virtual publishing for the screen, and the fast and easy digital distribution of text and pictures on the Web, mobile devices, and e-book readers, print is threatened with obsolescence, or, at a minimum, playing a far reduced role in the circulation of words and images. The first mass print medium to face the pinch of competition from the Web was newspapers in the late 1990s. Several factors have led to the problems newspapers face. They have lost lucrative classified advertising to online e-commerce Web sites, such as eBay, and CraigsList.org and job search sites like Monster.com. Classified advertising was an important revenue stream for newspapers. The indexing, searchability, and hyperlinking of digital text outweigh print-on-paper's physical advantages and nostalgic appeal. In the future, online delivery of information through devices such as Amazon's Kindle and the iPad from Apple Corporation could revolutionize the concept of a book and threaten libraries as seats of knowledge. In the digital age, information is valued less for its permanence and credibility, and more for its convenience and utility. Information-sharing and collaborative Web sites such as Wikipedia represent the post-print mentality.

A few communications technology innovations seem to have been motivated by a desire to serve the common good rather than self-interest. An important early example was in 1839, when the French government purchased the patent for Louis Daguerre's silver-on-copper plate photographic process called daguerreotype and turned it over to the public domain. The invention became the basis for modern photography. Another example of selfless innovation occurred in 1971. University of Illinois student Michael Hart started Project Gutenberg, a nonprofit group dedicated to digitizing and archiving e-books from public domain texts. Volunteers keyboarded texts manually until 1989, when document scanners and character recognition software sped up the digitizing process. The Project now claims more than 30,000 items—three times Hart's goal—and offers Web downloads to portable media devices.

Project Gutenberg has spurred several imitators. The largest is Google Books, which includes more than ten million public domain books and counting. Some people who are nostalgic about physical books view digitization of books as a threat to the survival of the medium. The role of printing in the production of a book might be reduced, but online indexing and retrieval of digitized books—though perhaps far removed from Gutenberg's original flatbed printing-press technology—could reaffirm the book's historical role as the repository and disseminator of human knowledge. In perhaps the most spectacular act for the public good in the history of communications technology, in 1990 the inventor of the World Wide Web for global information sharing over the Internet decided not to seek personal profit from his creation and gave it to the world. British computer scientist Tim Berners-Lee launched the Web from his office computer at CERN, the European Organization for Nuclear Research in Geneva, Switzerland, and has worked tirelessly ever since to keep the Web open, nonproprietary, and free. For both his genius and his generosity, Berners-Lee has been showered with numerous international honors and millions of dollars worth of technology prizes. Perhaps the highest praise was offered by *Time* magazine, which called his achievement "almost Gutenbergian."

MOTIVATIONS FOR INNOVATION

Communications technology inventors typically respond to their own inventions with an impulse contrary to the spirit of innovation: They try to restrain free diffusion of their inventions to keep profits for themselves. The most common strategy is patent protection. Thomas Edison patented his Kinetoscope peephole movie viewer in 1889 and aggressively pursued patent infringement lawsuits to preserve his U.S. monopoly in movie technology. He later sought to repress importation of European experiments with screen projection of movies, which he perceived as a threat to his Kinetoscope parlors.

Edison formed the Motion Picture Patents Company with the inventor of motion-picture film, George Eastman, in 1908. Known as the Edison Trust, the company sought to control the motion-picture market under the guise of maintaining quality standards. To evade the Trust's investigators operating out of Edison's home base of New Jersey, competitors moved their moviemaking operations to California, which offered year-round sunny weather for filming. Thus, Edison's effort to restrict free enterprise had the reverse effect of stimulating technology diffusion in the growth of the Hollywood movie industry. In 1915, a federal district court broke up Edison's Trust for illegal restraint of trade, making Hollywood's victory complete.

Hollywood movie studios pursued their own unfair trade practices to discourage independent operators by vertically integrating all phases of production, distribution, and exhibition. Independent producers had limited access to movie theaters. In 1948, the U.S. Supreme Court ruled that the movie studios had to sell off their theater chains.

The linear model of innovation looks like this: invention → innovation → diffusion. In this paradigm, Edison and Eastman's motion-picture technology is known as a manufacturer innovation, in which an agent innovates in order to sell the innovation. Despite the Edison Trust's best efforts to inhibit competition, movie technology diffused in parts of the world beyond their control and fostered a worldwide entertainment industry.

Other examples of communications technology innovations are known as end-user innovations, in which an agent develops a new technology for personal or in-house use. Berners-Lee's World Wide Web represents an end-user innovation, which tends to diffuse into society more rapidly than manufacturer innovations because of the inventor's cooperation or outright encouragement. End-user innovations also foster more collaboration among users to refine and extend the technology.

A famous incubator of innovation in communications technology, particularly computer technology, is the Palo Alto Research Center in California (PARC). Founded by the Xerox Corporation, PARC scientists invented several key computer technologies, including laser printing (1969), the graphical user interface, or GUI (1973), and Ethernet local area networking technology (1976). As an end-user innovation, Ethernet was first developed primarily to link desktop computers at PARC to a new high-cost laser printer. Xerox allowed other companies to commercialize the technology.

In fact, PARC often did not recognize the commercial value of its inventions. Perhaps the most striking example is its invention of the graphical user interface. Pronounced "gooey," the GUI was an important innovation because it made computers much more user-friendly. Tens of

thousand computers were in use around the world the 1970s, but Xerox was unsuccessful in marketing PARC's new interface to others. Apple Computer co-founder Steve Jobs heard about PARC's GUI project and negotiated visits to their labs in exchange for Apple corporate stock options. Jobs was so impressed with what he saw that he immediately formed a design team to create a GUI computer for consumers, and Apple's Macintosh computer, the first commercially successful personal computer to use a GUI was released in 1984.

Apple licensed parts of its GUI for Microsoft Corporation's Windows operating system. When Windows was upgraded to resemble the Macintosh more closely, Apple seemed to forget that it had benefited from PARC's user-innovator mindset and switched to a manufacturer-innovator attitude. Apple sued Microsoft for copyright infringement, arguing that Windows had stolen the "look and feel" of the Mac GUI. A federal court rejected Apple's suit in 1994 because of the original Apple-Microsoft licensing agreement. Xerox's suit against Apple for the same infringement was rejected because a three-year statute of limitations on its invention had expired.

MOTIVATIONS FOR RESTRAINING INNOVATION

Communications technology innovators with significant market share are tempted to employ unfair business practices to repress competing products, thereby arresting technological advances. Such was the case in the 1940s, when David Sarnoff, chief executive officer of the Radio Corporation of America (RCA), conspired to repress FM (frequency modulation) radio, invented by Edwin Armstrong in 1936. Because FM had superior sound quality, it was a threat to RCA's dominant position in the AM (amplitude modulation) radio market.

Sarnoff convinced the Federal Communications Commission (FCC) to reallocate the FM portion of the broadcast spectrum for use by television broadcasters, which made all of Armstrong's FM receivers obsolete. Sarnoff convinced American Telephone and Telegraph (AT&T) to support his proposed spectrum change, because blocking FM relay technology would force radio stations to continue to rent AT&T's telephone lines. RCA further frustrated Armstrong by filing its own patent for FM radio.

After years of struggle, Armstrong despaired over his failure to achieve popular acceptance of his invention and committed suicide in 1954. Armstrong's heirs renewed the patent fight against RCA and eventually prevailed. Stereo sound was added in 1961. FM radio overtook AM in popularity by the 1980s.

The U.S. music-recording industry sought to restrain innovation in the 1990s when peer-to-peer digital file sharing (P2P) over the Internet threatened profits from music CD sales. The U.S. Digital Millennium Copyright Act (1998) made it illegal to record copyrighted music through file sharing. As a consequence, the first P2P site, Napster, was shut down in 2001, driving the public to other P2P sites that sprang up rapidly.

Manufacturers since have encoded their music recordings with digital rights-management copy-protection software. They also have threatened individual large-volume P2P users with legal action, targeting college students as the biggest abusers. A widespread backlash to these aggressive tactics has created a major public relations problem for the music industry. In response, some artists choose to distribute their music free over the Internet to curry the public's favor.

The music industry responded belatedly to file-sharing technology by offering its own Internet music-distribution services, such as Apple's iTunes, launched in 2001. Download music sales grew rapidly, boosted by new, personal media players such as the iPod, packaged with iTunes. However, new revenue for the music companies from music downloads has not offset revenue losses from the precipitous drop in CD sales since 1995, forcing major record store chains such as Tower Records into bankruptcy.

Because inexpensive digital technology enables music artists to produce and distribute their own recordings over the Internet, they no longer seek traditional recording contracts from the record labels. The new business model is the "360 deal," incorporating all of the artist's income streams, including sales of recorded music and live performances, and providing to the artist direct advances, marketing, promotion, and touring expenses.

To survive the transition from CD to file-sharing, the global media conglomerates that control four-fifths of music sales—EMI, Sony BMG, Universal Music Group, and Warner Music Group—are exploring ways to develop Internet-based distribution of their music that provides increased convenience and flexibility not available by existing means, legal or otherwise. Youth, the key demographic group for music, has demonstrated that they are not satisfied with a passive listening experience. They seek to make their favorite music truly their own by compiling personal play lists, composing custom mixes, and posting their own music videos on media servers such as YouTube.com. Such audience behaviors have evolved beyond consumption to participation.

The evolution of recorded music provides a specific snapshot of the general evolution of media systems. Mentioned in the Bible, making music is a fundamental human activity and people have been playing musical instruments together for as long as there have been instruments. In the late 1880s, Edison invented a way to record sound, and though he did not intend for it to record music, ultimately music proved to be the first great application for what became known as the phonograph or record player.

From the 1920s on, phonograph technology consistently improved in terms of sound reproduction and other factors. Moreover, the cost for record players dropped, the manufacturing process for records improved, and playtimes extended to more than an hour. The changes were incremental, however, as records were easily scratched, which hurt the sound quality.

In the early 1980s, recorded music went digital with the introduction of the compact disc. The sound reproduction on CDs was far superior to records, the discs themselves were more robust, and tracks could be random-accessed. Perhaps most significantly, the digital reproduction process of CDs produced a listening experience that was nearly identical the original performance.

Compact discs were the primary medium for recorded music until the Internet became pervasive. At that point, many people opted to download the songs they wanted from the Internet, rather than buying compact discs that would have songs that they did not like along with the songs that they wanted. Moreover, portable music devices like the iPod and other MP3 players could store much more music and were much more compact and more convenient than portable CD players. Now there are online music services such as Rhapsody and Pandora, which, for a flat monthly fee, give access to nearly every music recording ever made, effectively eliminating the need to have a physical music collection.

At each phase of the evolution of music recording technology, different companies held dominant positions. In the early days of the phonograph, the Victor Talking Machine Company pretty much controlled the market. With the invention of the compact disc, companies such as Phillips and Sony played significant roles in the music industry. The commercial market for digitally downloading music was virtually invented by Apple. Now, the business is spread across a number of Internet companies.

Interestingly, some people still collect and play records. The market for CDs is still functioning, although it is smaller than before. But the market for digitally downloading music is still expanding. Technological innovation in communications often does not completely eliminate earlier technologies, but can radically alter their role in the marketplace.

There is an ironic twist to the evolution of recorded music technology. Although sound quality improved dramatically with the move to compact discs, when the Internet emerged as an important distribution mechanism for music, many people began to listen to music on the computers and then on their cell phones. Very often, the listening experience is far inferior on a computer or cell phone than it is on a dedicated listening device such as a CD player.

Virtually all communication technologies have gone through an evolutionary process similar to that of recorded music. When television was first introduced to the public it consisted of live broadcasting only. Television sets were large but the screens were small and the picture was a grainy black and white.

Some of the key technological developments that have contributed to the current television-watching experience include the invention of videotape, which made it cost-effective to pre-record shows; color, which dramatically improved the viewing experience; satellite broadcasting, which meant that shows could be easily broadcast across large distances and news events around the world could be broadcast in real time; cable, which increased the number of channels available in the home exponentially; and high definition receiving technology, which improved the picture quality. Interestingly, with the introduction of high definition and improved monitor technology, television sets have gotten much larger and thinner than before, with 40 and 50 inch screens commonplace in many homes. On the other hand, people are willing to watch their favorite show on the screens of the cell phones as well.

A THEORY OF COMMUNICATIONS TECHNOLOGY DIFFUSION

To have a significant impact on society, enough consumers must adopt communications technologies to form a viable marketplace. Indeed, Robert Metcalfe, the inventor of the Ethernet computer networking protocol that allowed personal computers to be efficiently hooked together, proposed what came to be called Metcalfe's law. He suggested that the value of a telecommunications network is proportional to the square of the number of connected users of the system. In other words, the value of a communications network increases much more rapidly than the simple increase in the number of users. The growth of new networks such as Facebook and Linked In for business users generally supports Metcalfe's insight.

The adoption rate for new technology is influenced by a variety of technical, strategic, and environmental factors. By taking these factors into account, diffusion theory can predict how rapidly a technology innovation will be adopted. Inventors who seek to sell their inventions are aware of the importance of bringing early adopters on board to help sell their products. In some cases, innovators try to achieve a "de facto" standard by being first to market. Otherwise, they might be forced to outlast competitors in a costly format war. In other cases, competitors cooperate with each other, sometimes with government intervention, to establish a technical standard for mutual benefit of all.

Communication theorist Everett Rogers wrote about how and why innovation, which he defined as "an idea, practice, or object that is perceived as new by an individual or other unit of adoption," spread through cultures in his important 1962 book *Diffusion of Innovations*. He synthesized diffusion studies from anthropology, sociology, agriculture, education, and medicine to propose an overarching theory of five stages of adoption of innovation. Though meant as a general theory, it can be applied to all communication technologies (see Figure 10.2):

1. Innovators are the first persons to adopt a new communications technology; they tend to be young risk-takers, have advanced education, wealth, and high social class.

2. Early adopters are next group to embrace innovation. They are similar to innovators in youth and social status and function as opinion leaders because they have more influential standing in society and better connections with the media than the innovators group.

3. Early majority adopters tend to be somewhat older and have above-average social position and some contact with early adopters.

4. Late majority adopters tend to be older and have lower social status, approach innovations with great skepticism, and adopt them only after the majority does.

5. Laggards are the last to adopt an innovation. They generally resist change, are advanced in age, are focused on traditional ways, and have the lowest social status, smallest incomes, and fewest interpersonal relationships.

Modeling the diffusion of a communications technology innovation is complicated by the fact that most technologies do not wait for market saturation before additional improvements become available, so that a revised version of an innovation might already be introduced by the time that the majority of adopters is interested in the original release. Because the credibility

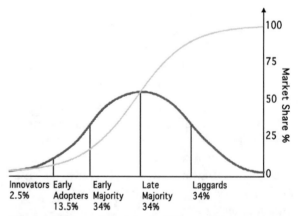

Figure 10.2—*A model of diffusion of innovations showing successive groups of consumers (dark-gray curve) adopting new technology and market share (light-gray curve) approaching saturation.*

of early-adopter opinion leaders already is established, upgrades might be embraced by end users more rapidly than the original release, particularly if the response of early adopters is negative, as was the case in 2007 with introduction of the Vista version of Microsoft's Windows operating system, for example.

Microsoft argued that criticisms of Vista were ungrounded, but nevertheless, its corporate customers were slow to convert to the new system version. Ironically, Vista's problems helped initial sales of the next version of the Windows operating system, Windows 7, in 2009. Some innovators capitalize on the predictability of escalating adoption cycles by holding back some extra features from a product's initial release, which probably are not needed to convince early adopters, so that the features can be added later in the adoption cycle as an extra enticement to resistant late adopters.

The mass media, especially the World Wide Web, can influence the diffusion process by disseminating information to innovators and early adopters, and by providing forums for opinion leaders to influence the majority. Indeed, in Rogers' formulation, the diffusion of innovation is primarily a communications process. Early adopters in the use of new communications on the Web such as blogs and social networks were able to enhance their roles as opinion-makers as their views on other innovations could be accessed more quickly and by wider audiences and consequently had a major impact on people's decision to use whatever was new.

A classic example of diffusion of communications technology innovations is the adoption of home videocassette recorders, or VCRs, in the United States. Diffusion of home VCRs went through the five stages of Rogers' theory, leaving a format war unresolved until the late adopters had their say. U.S. companies initially led in design and manufacture of videotape technologies for professional broadcasters, but Japanese electronics companies caught up by the 1970s and geared up for the lucrative U.S. home market.

Sony Corporation introduced its Betamax home video recorder to the U.S. consumer market in 1975, followed six months later by the video home system (VHS) recorder manufactured by Matsushita, at the time, the parent company of the well-known consumer electronic brand JVC and Panasonic. The marketplace battle that retarded technological development and corporate profits earlier in the century, between Thomas Edison's cylinder-based phonograph and Victor Corporation's disc-based Victrola, was a warning for the Japanese manufacturers to cooperate on the development of home VCRs, but Sony jumped to market with its technically superior product. "Innovators" bought the Betamax immediately and gave Sony 100 percent of the market, and Betamax continued to dominate with early-adopter purchases even after JVC launched its VHS recorder.

However, when Matsushita agreed to manufacture a VHS unit that would record four hours, the length of a typical U.S. football game and more than long enough for Hollywood movies, and when the purchase price was set below Betamax, sales among majority adopters began to shift in favor of VHS.

Sony was unwilling to sacrifice recording quality for length, but it turned out that U.S. consumers valued extended recording time over quality. VHS had a 75 percent market share by 1981. Sony began to market its own VHS recorders in 1988, sounding the death knell of Betamax.

There have been dozens of format wars in communications technology, and more can be expected in the future. Recent format wars include cellular technology, where TDMA, CDMA, and GSM formats meant cell phones could only work on specific systems in different geographical area (as late as 2010, cell phones used on the Verizon system still don't routinely work in Europe), streaming media formats for the Internet (QuickTime, Windows Media, RealMedia, and many others causing hardware and software incompatibilities), and high-definition optical video discs (Blu-ray beat HD-DVD in 2008).

PATHS OF LEAST RESISTANCE

The history of U.S. long-distance telecommunications is one of a few dominant corporations taking paths of least resistance to achieve de facto standards through monopolistic practices. Unlike Europe, where telegraph and telephone services were part of government-run postal systems, American wired communication remained private enterprise, and both experienced initial vigorous, open competition that fostered technological innovations.

Large capitalization and shrewd—some might say predatory—business practices eventually gave Western Union and American Bell Telephone Company monopoly control of the long-distance telegraph and telephone networks, respectively.

After others had demonstrated the practicality of the electrical telegraph, Samuel Morse and Alfred Vail's version of the telegraph received U.S. government backing in 1837 because its single wires were cheaper to install than the two-wire systems. Congress appropriated funds for an experimental line from Washington, D.C. to Baltimore, Maryland. Seven years were required for procurement of rights-of-way and construction of the 40-mile line. In 1844, Morse's demonstration message, quoting the Bible, was "What hath God wrought?" (see Figure 10.3).

Following existing transportation lines for commerce—roads, railroads, and sea lanes—the Morse telegraph spread rapidly in the East, then in California. Industrialist Jeptha Wade bought up several early competing telegraph companies and founded the Western Union Telegraph Company.

Figure 10.3—*Samuel Morse's demonstration message to Alfred Vail on May 24, 1844, over their first telegraph line was written in the Morse Code signaling alphabet invented by Vail.*

Western Union completed construction of the first transcontinental telegraph line in 1861, preceding the transcontinental railroad by eight years and hastening the railroad's construction. Because of its early dominance of long-distance telephone lines, Western Union enjoyed near-monopoly control of the U.S. long-distance telegram business.

Efforts to discover how to send multiple telegraph messages simultaneously led to invention of the acoustical telephone. Alexander Graham Bell was awarded the U.S. patent in 1876. The following year, Thomas Edison came up with a much-improved design. The Bell-Edison concern bought Western Union in 1879 to take advantage of the latter's network of wires and became AT&T. Large capitalization and shrewd business practices eventually gave AT&T monopoly control of the long-distance telegraph and telephone networks. The Kingsbury Commitment of 1913, a letter written by a vice president of AT&T to the attorney general of the United States to resolve several antitrust issues, formalized AT&T's monopoly of U.S. long-distance telephony as a government-regulated utility. The company was allowed to retain its subsidiary regional telephone companies, but was required to spin off Western Union.

Once AT&T assumed monopoly control of the telephone system, the pace of innovation began to slow. Even in the 1950s and 1960s, it was very costly to make long distance calls. Telephones were hardwired into walls, and there had been very little improvement in basic features such as dialing mechanisms and handset style.

That situation began to change in the late 1960s and 1970s. An FCC decision in 1968 gave entrepreneur Tom Carter the right to connect devices directly to the AT&T network. This ruling allowed for the use of telephone answering machines, fax machines, and other new telephony equipment. Carter had won an earlier ruling allowing for devices to be attached to handsets, a ruling that enabled the development of acoustical modems.

A more fundamental challenge to AT&T's monopoly positions began in 1963, when another innovator, John Groeken, the owner of Microwave Communications, Inc. (MCI) petitioned the FCC to allow him to build a private microwave communication network between St. Louis and Chicago. AT&T and some of its subsidiaries opposed the position, launching a long and protracted corporate battle. In 1968, in a four-to-three decision, the FCC approved MCI's petition. AT&T immediately saw MCI as a threat to its monopoly position. On the other hand, William McGowan, who had joined MCI as chairman and chief executive officer in 1968, saw an opportunity to build a nationwide communication system to compete with AT&T. After a protracted legal battle, MCI cracked AT&T's monopoly in the 1980s and emerged as a competitive alternative for long distance services.

In 1984, the Federal government forced AT&T to split off its regional telephone companies, or "Baby Bells," to stimulate competition and technological innovation in the stagnant telephone market. The results were striking. As telephone rates plunged, new services such as call waiting, caller ID, voicemail, and others were added rapidly. The telephone industry in the late 1980s served as a case study for the benefits of deregulation and competition.

At that time, however, telephone companies found themselves competing with cable television companies as well. With the growth of the Internet in the mid-1990s, the overall telecommunications regulatory structure was called into question. Both the telephone companies and the cable companies, for example, wanted to be able to provide high-speed Internet services to the home.

The U.S. government's response was the U.S. Telecommunications Act of 1996, which deregulated the telephone, cable television, and wireless telephone businesses, allowed companies to compete for local as well as long-distance telephone service and to offer telephone–wireless–cable–Internet service bundles. Because bigger have certain built-in advantages in the telecommunications industry, the unintended result of removing ownership restrictions has been to foster the consolidation of the industry into the hands of a few major companies such as Verizon, AT&T, and Comcast.

THE IMPACT OF TECHNOLOGY ON HUMAN CONSCIOUSNESS

The writings of Jean Gebser (*The Ever-Present Origin*, 1949, 1985), Marshall McLuhan (*Gutenberg Galaxy: The Making of Typographic Man*, 1962), and Walter Ong (*Orality & Literacy: The Technologizing of the Word*, 1982) give substantial evidence for the lasting impact of communications technologies on society and consciousness. Starting with writing and continuing to the present, the periodic introduction of new communications media have brought momentous changes to society.

Archeological evidence collected from around the globe reveals a magic-mythic consciousness in the oral traditions of prehistorical, pre-literate humans. Ancient cultures were in tune to the natural rhythms of their aural environments. The magic-mythic consciousness was grounded in the cycles of day–night, life–death, and the seasons of the year. Individuals strove to identify with and to become immersed in the clan and the clan with nature. Ancient people passed down their cultural values orally through myths spoken around the fire circle. These stories became the great myths of the world—timeless and eternal. Some oral cultures around the world have survived with these sound-centered stories intact.

The development of written languages in ancient cultures began to privilege seeing over hearing. In 15th century Europe, sight-oriented technologies such as optics, ballistics, and the printing press gradually caused seeing to overcome the old ways and their ancient attunement to the earth and nature. A cultural emphasis on vision is known as ocularcentrism. Technology-enhanced vision showed not only what can be seen in the present moment, but also what is just out of reach, beyond the horizons of experience. This new ability to envision possible futures led to learning, research, education, and social mobility. With a fixed viewpoint, it was possible to project one's perspective into space, and therefore also into time, a development called perspectival thinking. In Europe, perspectival thinking first arose in the early Renaissance Italian city-states with the new science of gunpowder weapons known as ballistics, and later in paintings and drawings by artists such as Leonardo DaVinci (see Figure 10.4).

The mass distribution of books and the spread of literacy in 15th century Europe had repercussions that went far beyond the dissemination of the Christian Bible. Printed texts introduced new ways of thinking about the world to the masses, who could read and come to their own conclusions about the world without relying on priests. The popular demand for schooling exploded. Educational institutions sprang up throughout Europe, and rationalism, empiricism, and systematic scientific research flourished. Print also allows the work of scientists, philosophers, authors, poets, painters, and composers to be recognized and perpetuated on a mass scale.

In the vision-centered culture wrought by print, individual citizens became alienated from the collective. Five centuries later, vision continues to be emphasized in the mass media's surveillance role of watching the culture and the audience's voyeur role of peeping on private moments exposed by the media.

Courtesy of Library of Congress

Figure 10.4—*Perspectival thinking is seen in a preparatory drawing by Leonardo DaVinci for his painting, The Adoration of the Magi (circa 1481, Uffizi Gallery, Florence, Italy).*

Some scholars have criticized the modern communications technologies for causing fragmentation and alienation of human experience. However, Gebser, McLuhan, and Ong all were more optimistic about the effects of communications technology and believed that humanity eventually will morph into an integral, collective consciousness—a "global village."

CONCLUSION

Each evolution of communication systems brings changes in social life and human consciousness. Printing played an integral role in the emergence of science, the Protestant Reformation, the English Civil War, and the development of the nation-state. The impact of technological innovations in printing in the 19th century—including steam-powered presses, rotary feed, improved papers, photography, mechanical typesetting, and color printing—helped to create urban and national markets, to reorder American politics, and to foster universal education.

The evolutionary cycle in communications technology is relatively consistent across media systems. New technology is introduced, disrupting the old ways, and follows a predictable pattern of diffusion through society. The technology is used first by innovators and then early adopters and slowly spreads to other groups. As the technology diffuses, innovators add features and functionality that improve the base technology. This process kicks off what is called the virtuous circle, in which improved technology attracts an increased number of users and the greater number of users create incentives to improve the technology.

The rate of technological change is accelerating rapidly. To date, three great communications platforms have been created. The first was print; the second, broadcasting; and the third is computer-based communication. It took more than 400 years for essential innovations in print—such as improved high-speed presses, improved paper-making, mechanical typesetting, color printing and others—to develop. In broadcasting, it took around 40 years for the technological pieces to be put into place. Within 20 years, the Internet moved from being basically a hard-to-use computer network serving the military, scientific, and academic communities to a worldwide communication system with hundreds of millions of users. Moreover, new applications are now being developed at a frantic pace. The past ten years has seen the emergence of blogging, social networks, Twitter, podcasting, YouTube video services, iTunes, Wikipedia, RSS feeds, and more.

The major changes in communications systems have produced major changes in social life and human consciousness. The early generations of Facebook users frequently have more than 500 "friends" on the network, which calls into question the traditional concept of friend. Politicians pay attention to bloggers in the same way they used to pay attention to major newspapers. Amazon.com is a major retailer even though it does not have a single store. As long as the world evolves, so will communications systems and technologies, and the possibilities provided by them.

BRIEF CHRONOLOGY OF MEDIA TECHNOLOGY FIRSTS

1440—German metal smith Johannes Gutenberg invents the movable-type printing press.

1690—Benjamin Harris's *Publick Occurrences both Foreign and Domestick* in Boston is the first newspaper in the British colonies in North America.

1741—In Philadelphia, the first U.S. magazines are Andrew Bradford's *American Magazine* and Benjamin Franklin's *General Magazine*.

1791—The *First Amendment to the U.S. Constitution*, the original and longest-lasting codification of legal rights to freedom of expression, is ratified by the thirteen United States.

1796—Bavarian author Alois Senefelder invents lithographic printing of images on flat stones, which replaces woodblock printing as the preferred method to reproduce artwork.

1825—Frenchman Joseph Nicéphor Niépce invents chemical photography.

1833—The steam-powered printing press is invented, based on Gutenberg's flatbed design.

1835—Englishman George Baxter receives a patent for the first commercially successful color printing system.

1837—Americans Samuel Morse and Alfred Vail invent the electromagnetic telegraph over single copper wire and the Morse Code signaling alphabet.

1839—The French government buys Louis Daguerre's patent for his silver-on-copper photography called the daguerreotype and release it to the public domain.

1843—Richard Hoe of New York City invents the rotary printing press, many times faster than the flatbed press.

1848—The Associated Press of New York establishes the first wire service in which subscribers share local news items.

1860—The Pony Express fast mail service operates for only eighteen months by horseback riders from St. Joseph, Missouri, to Sacramento, California, before it is made obsolete by the first U.S. transcontinental telegraph line in 1861.

1861—Scottish physicist James Clerk Maxwell invents color still photography.

1866—The first transatlantic telegraph cable is laid.

1867—Edward Calahan of the American Telegraph Company invents the first telegraph printing device.

1875—English writer Robert Barclay invents offset printing to transfer lithographic images from flat stones to rotary press.

1876—Alexander Graham Bell invents the first practical telephone.

1877—Thomas Edison invents the cylinder-based phonograph and makes the first recording of the human voice.

1878—English photographer Eadweard Muybridge captures motion of a cantering horse in a series of still photographs.

1884—George Eastman of Rochester, New York, invents photographic film, replacing glass and metal plates as the holder for camera images.

1886—German inventor Ottmar Mergenthaler invents the linotype machine for automatically setting type for printing.

1888—Emile Berliner of Alexander Graham Bell's telephone laboratories invents the gramophone, a precursor to the 1906 Victrola disc-based record player that eventually overtakes Edison's phonograph in popularity.

1889—Thomas Edison's laboratory invents the Kinetoscope motion-picture peephole viewer.

1894—Frenchman Léon Bouly invents the cinématographe, the first motion-picture camera, developing machine, and projector all in one device.

1896—Italian Guglielmo Marconi invents wireless radio.

1901—George Eastman's Kodak Brownie became the first mass-market still camera.

1903—The first marketable color photographic system, Autochrome, is patented by Auguste-Marie and Louis-Jean Lumiere and is marketed four years later.

1906—Canadian inventor Reginald Fessenden makes the first radio voice transmission.

1906—In Illinois, Lee De Forest invents the first electronic communication device, the Audion vacuum tube.

1915—The first modern feature film, *The Birth of a Nation* directed by D.W. Griffith, establishes both the art of cinematic editing and Hollywood's stereotyping of African Americans.

1920—KDKA in Pittsburgh, Pennsylvania, is the first licensed commercial radio station, although a few noncommercial stations had been operating years earlier.

1925—Julius Lillenfeld invents the transistor, a semiconductor that can replace vacuum tubes.

1926—RCA launches the National Broadcasting Company (NBC), the first U.S. broadcast network.

1927—NBC is split into the "red" and "blue" radio networks, and a third network is launched, William Paley's Columbia Broadcasting System (CBS).

1927—*The Jazz Singer* starring Al Jolson is the first sound motion picture.

1927—Philo Farnsworth and Vladimir Zworkin independently invent electronic television.

1934—The U.S. Communications Act establishes the FCC to regulate broadcasting.

1936—Columbia University scientist Edwin Armstrong invents FM radio.

1939—RCA demonstrates television broadcasting at the New York World's Fair.

1939—In New York City, Pocket Books introduces mass-market paperback books.

1941—U.S. standards for broadcast television (SDTV) are established.

1946—John Mauchly and J. Presper Eckert at the University of Pennsylvania invent the first general-purpose electronic computer, the ENIAC, for the U.S. military.

1948—The U.S. government forces film studios to sell their theaters.

1949—American physicists William Shockley, John Bardeen, and William Brattain develop the modern solid-state transistor, which becomes the basis of the computing and telecommunications industries.

1956—Ampex Corporation introduces the first videotape recorder for broadcasters.

1958—The first stereo long-playing (LP) records are sold.

1958—Jack Kilby of Texas Instruments demonstrates the first working integrated circuit, enabling modern electronic media.

1960—Haloid/Xerox introduces the first commercial photocopy machine, based on a 1942 invention by Chester Carlson.

1965—IntelSat I is the first geosynchronous Earth orbital satellite for television, telephone, and telefascimile transmissions.

1967—The U.S. government establishes the Corporation for Public Broadcasting, which later launches public television and National Public Radio.

1969—The charge-coupled device (CCD) for digital photography is invented by Willard Boyle and George E. Smith at AT&T Bell Labs.

1969—Xerox researcher Gary Starkweather invents the laser printer.

1969—The U.S. Department of Defense launches ARPANET, the first national computer network.

1970—The Digital Equipment Corporation invents the dot matrix printer.

1970—Corning Glass researchers invented fiber optic cable capable of carrying 65,000 times more information than copper cable (see Figure 10.5).

1971—Intel Corporation engineers invent the first microprocessor or computer-in-a-chip (see Figure 10.6).

1971—University of Illinois student Michael Hart starts the nonprofit Project Gutenberg for creating electronic books, or e-books, from public-domain texts.

1972—The world's first commercial, ready-to-use personal computer, the Micral N, is invented in France.

1973—The Xerox Palo Alto Research Center develops the computer graphical user interface that will inspire the Apple Macintosh operating system and later Microsoft Windows.

1973—Motorola invents and demonstrates the world's first handheld mobile telephone.

1975—Time, Inc., launches HBO, the first cable television service over satellite.

1975—Sony's Betamax is the first videotape recorder for consumers.

1976—JVC introduces its VHS home videotape recorder, which edges Betamax out of the consumer market by 1988.

1979—CompuServe is the first consumer online service provider.

1980—Turner Broadcasting in Atlanta launches CNN, the first cable news service.

1982—The Gannett Corporation launches *USA Today*, the first U.S. national newspaper.

1982—Compact discs (CDs) are the first digital audio format for the home market.

1984—Apple Computer introduces its Macintosh personal computer for desktop publishing.

Figure 10.5—*Fiber optic cables laid in the oceans carry Internet messages around the globe.*

Figure 10.6—*Invented in 1971, the microprocessor or computer-in-a-chip enabled miniaturized, portable computing devices such as personal media players and cellular phones.*

1985—Stewart Brand and Larry Brilliant start the first online social network, Whole Earth 'Lectronic Link (WELL).

1993—Briton Tim Berners-Lee gives his World Wide Web to the public domain.

1993—The first text messaging over cellular services is offered to European consumers.

1994—Jeff Bezos founds the hugely successful online merchandiser Amazon.com.

1995—The U.S. government relinquishes control over the Internet.

1996—The Telecommunications Act deregulates U.S. communications media.

1997—The MP3 digital audio file compression format spurs music distribution over the Internet and on personal media players.

1997—Toshiba introduces the DVD optical data storage disc in the United States based on an industry consortium technical standard.

1998—Stanford Ph.D. students Larry Page and Sergey Brin launch the Google Internet search service.

1999—Digital video recorders (DVRs) are introduced to consumers.

1999—College student Shawn Fanning launches his free Napster program for sharing music on the Internet, to be shut down as illegal two years later.

1999—*Star Wars: The Phantom Menace* is the first movie digitally distributed to theaters.

2001—Jimmy Wales launches the Wikipedia open encyclopedia on the Internet.

2001—Apple Computer launches iTunes and the iPod, which will become the best-selling digital media player.

2002—Competing satellite radio services XM and Sirius begin.

2003—eUniverse launches the MySpace social networking Web site.

2003—Verizon Wireless and AT&T Mobility are first to offer wideband third-generation (3G) digital mobile telephone services in the United States.

2004—Harvard student Mark Zuckerberg launches his social networking Web site Facebook.

2004—Media programs distributed over the Web (podcasts) become popular.

2005—Three computer engineers launch the YouTube online video sharing service, which is purchased a year later by Google.

2006—The free social networking and microblogging service Twitter is launched.

2008—With support from the major film studios, Blu-ray becomes the worldwide technical standard for high-definition video on optical storage disc.

2009—By FCC order, the Advanced Television Standard or HDTV replaces SDTV.

2009—The first broadband fourth-generation (4G) mobile telephone services are offered in Sweden and Norway.

CONCLUSION

DEMOCRATIZING TELEVISION? THE POLITICS OF PARTICIPATION

by Henry Jenkins

In August 2005, former Democratic vice president Albert Gore helped to launch a new cable news network, Current. The network's stated goal was to encourage the active participation of young people as citizen journalists; viewers were intended not simply to consume Current's programming but also to participate in its production, selection, and distribution. As Gore explained at a press conference in late 2004, "We are about empowering this generation of young people in the 18-to-34 population to engage in a dialogue of democracy and to tell their stories of what's going on in their lives, in the dominant medium of our time. The Internet opened a floodgate for young people, whose passions are finally being heard, but TV hasn't followed suit. ... Our aim is to give young people a voice, to democratize television."[1] The network estimates that as much as 25 percent of the content they air will come from their viewers. Amateur media producers will upload digital videos to a Web site; visitors to the site will be able to evaluate each submission, and those which receive the strongest support from viewers will make it onto the airwaves.

The idea of reader-moderated news content is not new. Slashdot was one of the first sites to experiment with user-moderation, gathering a wealth of information with a five-person paid staff, mostly part time, by empowering readers not only to submit their own stories but to work collectively to determine the relative value of each submission. Slashdot's focus is explicitly on technology and culture, and so it became a focal point for information about Internet privacy issues, the debates over mandatory filters in public libraries, the open-source movement, and so forth. Slashdot attracts an estimated 1.1 million unique users per month, and some 250,000 per day, constituting a user base as large as that of many of the nation's leading online general interest and technology-centered news sites.[2] Yet, this would be the first time that something like the Slashdot model was being applied to television.

Even before the network reached the air, Current's promise to "democratize television" became a focal point for debates about the politics of participation. Cara Mertes, the executive producer for the PBS documentary program *POV*, itself an icon of the struggle to get alternative perspectives on television, asked, "What are you

READING NOTES

_____

_____

_____

_____

_____

talking about when you say 'democratizing the media'? Is it using media to further democratic ends, to create an environment conducive to the democratic process through unity, empathy and civil discourse? Or does it mean handing over the means of production, which is the logic of public access?"[3] Was Current going to be democratic in its content (focusing on the kinds of information that a democratic society needs to function), its effects (mobilizing young people to participate more fully in the democratic process), its values (fostering rational discourse and a stronger sense of social contract), or its process (expanding access to the means of media production and distribution)?

Others pushed further, arguing that market pressures, the demand to satisfy advertisers and placate stockholders, would ensure that no commercial network could possibly be as democratic on any of these levels as the Gore operation was promising. Any truly democratic form of broadcasting would necessarily arise outside corporate media and would likely see corporate America as its primary target for reform. Even if the network remained true to its goals, they argued, those most drawn to the alternative media perspective would be skeptical of any media channel shaped by traditional corporate gatekeepers. A growing number of Web services—such as participatoryculture.org and ourmedia.org—were making it easier for amateur media makers to gain visibility via the Web without having to turn over exclusive rights to their material to a network funded by some of the wealthiest men and women in the country. In a society where blogs—both text based and video enhanced—were thriving, why would anyone need to put their content on television?

Others expressed disappointment in the network's volunteeristic approach. Original plans to pay a large number of independent filmmakers to become roaming correspondents had given way to a plan to allow amateurs to submit material for consideration and then get paid upon acceptance. The first plan,

critics argued, would have sustained an infrastructure to support alternative media production; the other would lead to little more than a glorified public access station.

The network defended itself as a work in progress—one that was doing what it could to democratize a medium while working under market conditions. A spokesman for the network observed, "For some people, the perfect is always the enemy of the good."[4] Current might not change everything about television, they pleaded, but it could make a difference. Gore held firm in his belief that enabling audience-generated content had the potential to diversify civic discourse: "I personally believe that when this medium is connected to the grassroots storytellers that are out there, it will have an impact on the kinds of things that are discussed and the way they are discussed."[5]

At about the same time, the British Broadcasting Company was embracing an even more radical vision of how consumers might relate to its content. The first signs of this new policy had come through a speech made by Ashley Highfield, director of BBC New Media & Technology, in October 2003, explaining how the widespread adoption of broadband and digital technologies will impact the ways his network serves its public:

Future TV may be unrecognizable from today, defined not just by linear TV channels, packaged and scheduled by television executives, but instead will resemble more of a kaleidoscope, thousands of streams of content, some indistinguishable as actual channels. These streams will mix together broadcasters' content and programs, and our viewers' contributions. At the simplest level—audiences will want to organize and reorganize content the way they want it. They'll add comments to our programs, vote on them, and generally mess about with them. But at another level,

READING NOTES

audiences will want to create these streams of video themselves from scratch, with or without our help. At this end of the spectrum, the traditional "monologue broadcaster" to "grateful viewer" relationship will break down.[6]

By 2005, the BBC was digitizing large segments of its archive and making the streaming content available via the Web.[7] The BBC was also encouraging grassroots experimentation with ways to annotate and index these materials. Current's path led from the Web—where many could share what they created—into broadcast media, where many could consume what a few had created. The BBC efforts were moving in the other direction, opening up television content to the more participatory impulses shaping digital culture.

Both were in a sense promoting what this book has been calling convergence culture. Convergence does not depend on any specific delivery mechanism. Rather, convergence represents a paradigm shift—a move from medium-specific content toward content that flows across multiple media channels, toward the increased interdependence of communications systems, toward multiple ways of accessing media content, and toward ever more complex relations between top-down corporate media and bottom-up participatory culture. Despite the rhetoric about "democratizing television," this shift is being driven by economic calculations and not by some broad mission to empower the public. Media industries are embracing convergence for a number of reasons: because convergence-based strategies exploit the advantages of media conglomeration; because convergence creates multiple ways of selling content to consumers; because convergence cements consumer loyalty at a time when the fragmentation of the marketplace and the rise of file sharing threaten old ways of doing business. In some cases, convergence is being pushed by

corporations as a way of shaping consumer behavior. In other cases, convergence is being pushed by consumers who are demanding that media companies be more responsive to their tastes and interests. Yet, whatever its motivations, convergence is changing the ways in which media industries operate and the ways average people think about their relation to media. We are in a critical moment of transition during which the old rules are open to change and companies may be forced to renegotiate their relationship to consumers. The question is whether the public is ready to push for greater participation or willing to settle for the same old relations to mass media.

Writing in 1991, W. Russell Neuman sought to examine the ways that consumer "habit" or what he called "the psychology of the mass audience, the semi-attentive, entertainment-oriented mind-set of day-to-day media behavior" would slow down the interactive potentials of emerging digital technologies.[8] In his model, the technology was ready at hand but the culture was not ready to embrace it: "The new developments in horizontal, user-controlled media that allow the user to amend, reformat, store, copy, forward to others, and comment on the flow of ideas do not rule out mass communications. Quite the contrary, they complement the traditional mass media."[9] The public will not rethink their relationship to media content overnight, and the media industries will not relinquish their stranglehold on culture without a fight.

Today, we are more apt to hear the opposite claim—that early adopters are racing ahead of technological developments. No sooner is a new technology—say, Google Maps—released to the public than diverse grassroots communities begin to tinker with it, expanding its functionality, hacking its code, and pushing it into a more participatory direction. Indeed, many industry leaders argue that the main reason that television cannot continue to operate in the same old ways is that the broadcasters are losing younger

READING NOTES

_____

_____

_____

_____

_____

viewers, who expect greater influence over the media they consume. Speaking at MIT in April 2004, Betsy Frank, executive vice president for research and planning at MTV Networks, described these consumers as "media-actives" whom she characterized as "the group of people born since the mid-70s who've never known a world without cable television, the vcr, or the internet, who have never had to settle for forced choice or least objectionable program, who grew up with a 'what I want when I want it' view attitude towards media, and as a result, take a much more active role in their media choices."[10] Nothing that "their fingerprints are on the remote," she said that the media industry was scrambling to make sense of and respond to sharp declines in television viewership among the highly valued 18–27 male demographic as they defected from television toward more interactive and participatory media channels.

This book has sought to document a moment of transition during which at least some segments of the public have learned what it means to live within a convergence culture. Betsy Frank and other industry thinkers still tend to emphasize changes that are occurring within individuals, whereas this book's argument is that the greatest changes are occurring within consumption communities. The biggest change may be the shift from individualized and personalized media consumption toward consumption as a networked practice.

Personalized media was one of the ideals of the digital revolution in the early 1990s: digital media was going to "liberate" us from the "tyranny" of mass media, allowing us to consume only content we found personally meaningful. Conservative ideologue turned digital theorist George Gilder argues that the intrinsic properties of the computer pushed toward ever more decentralization and personalization. Compared to the one-size-fits-all diet of the broadcast networks, the coming media age would be a "feast of niches and specialties."[11] An era of customized and interactive content, he argues, would appeal to our highest ambitions and not our lowest, as we enter "a new age of individualism."[12] Consider Gilder's ideal of "first choice media" as yet another model for how we might democratize television.

By contrast, this book has argued that convergence encourages participation and collective intelligence, a view nicely summed up by the *New York Times's* Marshall Sella: "With the aid of the Internet, the loftiest dream for television is being realized: an odd brand of interactivity. Television began as a one-way street winding from producers to consumers, but that street is now becoming two-way. A man with one machine (a TV) is doomed to isolation, but a man with two machines (TV and a computer) can belong to a community."[13] Each of the case studies shows what happens when people who have access to multiple machines consume—and produce—media together, when they pool their insights and information, mobilize to promote common interests, and function as grassroots intermediaries ensuring that important messages and interesting content circulate more broadly. Rather than talking about personal media, perhaps we should be talking about communal media—media that become part of our lives as members of communities, whether experienced face-to-face at the most local level or over the Net.

Throughout the book, I have shown that convergence culture is enabling new forms of participation and collaboration. For Lévy, the power to participate within knowledge communities exists alongside the power that the nation-state exerts over its citizens and that corporations within commodity capitalism exert over its workers and consumers. For Lévy, at his most utopain, this emerging power to participate serves as a strong corrective to those traditional sources of power, though they will also seek ways to turn it toward their own ends. We are just learning how to exercise that power—individually and collectively— and we are still fighting to define the terms under

READING NOTES

_____

_____

_____

_____

_____

which we will be allowed to participate. Many fear this power; others embrace it. There are no guarantees that we will use our new power any more responsibly than nation-states or corporations have exercised theirs. We are trying to hammer out the ethical codes and social contracts that will determine how we will relate to one another just as we are trying to determine how this power will insert itself into the entertainment system or into the political process. Part of what we must do is figure out how—and why—groups with different backgrounds, agendas, perspectives, and knowledge can listen to one another and work together toward the common good. We have a lot to learn.

Right now, we are learning how to apply these new participatory skills through our relation to commercial entertainment—or, more precisely, right now some groups of early adopters are testing the waters and mapping out directions where many more of us are apt to follow. These skills are being applied to popular culture first for two reasons: on the one hand, because the stakes are so low; and on the other, because playing with popular culture is a lot more fun than playing with more serious matters. Yet, as we saw in looking at Campaign 2004, what we learn through spoiling *Survivor* or remaking *Star Wars* may quickly get applied to political activism or education or the workplace.

In the late 1980s and early 1990s, cultural scholars, myself included, depicted media fandom as an important test site for ideas about active consumption and grassroots creativity. We were drawn toward the idea of "fan culture" as operating in the shadows of, in response to, as well as an alternative to commercial culture. Fan culture was defined through the appropriation and transformation of materials borrowed from mass culture; it was the application of folk culture practices to mass culture content.[14] Across the past decade, the Web has brought these consumers from the margins of the media industry into the spotlight; research into fandom has been embraced by

important thinkers in the legal and business communities. What might once have been seen as "rogue readers" are now Kevin Roberts's "inspirational consumers." Participation is understood as part of the normal ways that media operate, while the current debates center around the terms of our participation. Just as studying fan culture helped us to understand the innovations that occur on the fringes of the media industry, we may also want to look at the structures of fan communities as showing us new ways of thinking about citizenship and collaboration. The political effects of these fan communities come not simply through the production and circulation of new ideas (the critical reading of favorite texts) but also through access to new social structures (collective intelligence) and new models of cultural production (participatory culture).

Have I gone too far? Am I granting too much power here to these consumption communities? Perhaps. But keep in mind that I am not really trying to predict the future. I want to avoid the kind of grand claims about the withering away of mass media institutions that make the rhetoric of the digital revolution seem silly a decade later. Rather, I am trying to point toward the democratic potentials found in some contemporary cultural trends. There is nothing inevitable about the outcome. Everything is up for grabs. Pierre Lévy described his ideal of collective intelligence as a "realizable utopia," and so it is. I think of myself as a critical utopian. As a utopian, I want to identify possibilities within our culture that might lead toward a better, more just society. My experiences as a fan have changed how I think about media politics, helping me to look for and promote unrealized potentials rather than reject out of hand anything that doesn't rise to my standards. Fandom, after all, is born of a balance between fascination and frustration: if media content didn't fascinate us, there would be no desire to engage with it; but if it didn't frustrate us on some level, there would be no drive to rewrite or remake it. Today,

READING NOTES

I hear a great deal of frustration about the state of our media culture, yet surprisingly few people talk about how we might rewrite it.

But pointing to those opportunities for change is not enough in and of itself. One must also identify the various barriers that block the realization of those possibilities and look for ways to route around them. Having a sense of what a more ideal society looks like gives one a yardstick for determining what we must do to achieve our goals. Here, this book has offered specific case studies of groups who are already achieving some of the promises of collective intelligence or of a more participatory culture. I do not mean for us to read these groups as typical of the average consumer (if such a thing exists in an era of niche media and fragmented culture). Rather, we should read these case studies as demonstrations of what it is possible to do in the context of convergence culture.

This approach differs dramatically from what I call critical pessimism. Critical pessimists, such as media critics Mark Crispin Miller, Noam Chomsky, and Robert McChesney, focus primarily on the obstacles to achieving a more democratic society. In the process, they often exaggerate the power of big media in order to frighten readers into taking action. I don't disagree with their concern about media concentration, but the way they frame the debate is self-defeating insofar as it disempowers consumers even as it seeks to mobilize them. Far too much media reform rhetoric rests on melodramatic discourse about victimization and vulnerability, seduction and manipulation, "propaganda machines" and "weapons of mass deception." Again and again, this version of the media reform movement has ignored the complexity of the public's relationship to popular culture and sided with those opposed to a more diverse and participatory culture. The politics of critical utopianism is founded on a notion of empowerment; the politics of critical pessimism on a politics of victimization. One focuses on what we are doing with media, and the other on what media is doing to us. As with previous revolutions, the media reform movement is gaining momentum at a time when people are starting to feel more empowered, not when they are at their weakest.

Media concentration is a very real problem that potentially stifles many of the developments I have been describing across this book. Concentration is bad because it stifles competition and places media industries above the demands of their consumers. Concentration is bad because it lowers diversity—important in terms of popular culture, essential in terms of news. Concentration is bad because it lowers the incentives for companies to negotiate with their consumers and raises the barriers to their participation. Big concentrated media can ignore their audience (at least up to a point); smaller niche media must accommodate us.

That said, the fight over media concentration is only one struggle that should concern media reformers. The potentials of a more participatory media culture are also worth fighting for. Right now, convergence culture is throwing media into flux, expanding the opportunities for grassroots groups to speak back to the mass media. Put all of our efforts into battling the conglomerates and this window of opportunity will have passed. That is why it is so important to fight against the corporate copyright regime, to argue against censorship and moral panic that would pathologize these emerging forms of participation, to publicize the best practices of these online communities, to expand access and participation to groups that are otherwise being left behind, and to promote forms of media literacy education that help all children to develop the skills needed to become full participants in their culture.

If early readers are any indication, the most controversial claim in this book may be my operating assumption that increasing participation in popular culture is a good thing. Too many critical pessimists are still

READING NOTES

_____

_____

_____

_____

_____

locked into the old politics of culture jamming. Resistance becomes an end in and of itself rather than a tool to ensure cultural diversity and corporate responsibility. The debate keeps getting framed as if the only true alternative were to opt out of media altogether and live in the woods, eating acorns and lizards and reading only books published on recycled paper by small alternative presses. But what would it mean to tap media power for our own purposes? Is ideological and aesthetic purity really more valuable than transforming our culture?

A politics of participation starts from the assumption that we may have greater collective bargaining power if we form consumption communities. Consider the example of the Sequential Tarts. Started in 1997, www.sequentialtart.com serves as an advocacy group for female consumers frustrated by their historical neglect or patronizing treatment by the comics industry. Marcia Allas, the current editor of Sequential Tart, explained: "In the early days we wanted to change the apparent perception of the female reader of comics. ... We wanted to show what we already knew—that the female audience for comics, while probably smaller than the male audience, is both diverse and has a collectively large disposable income."[15] In her study of Sequential Tart, scholar and sometime contributor Kimberly M. De Vries argues that the group self-consciously rejects the negative stereotypes about female comics readers constructed by men in and around the comics industry but also the well-meaning but equally constraining stereotypes constructed by the first generation of feminist critics of comics.[16] The Sequential Tarts defend the pleasures women take in comics even as they critique negative representations of women. The Web zine combines interviews with comics creators, retailers, and industry leaders, reviews of current publications, and critical essays about gender and comics. It showcases industry practices that attract or repel women, spotlights the work of smaller presses that often fell through the cracks,

and promotes books that reflect their readers' tastes and interests. The Sequential Tarts are increasingly courted by publishers or individual artists who feel they have content that female readers might embrace and have helped to make the main stream publishers more attentive to this often underserved market.

The Sequential Tarts represent a new kind of consumer advocacy group—one that seeks to diversify content and make mass media more responsive to its consumers. This is not to say that commercial media will ever truly operate according to democratic principles. Media companies don't need to share our ideals in order to change their practice. What will motivate the media companies is their own economic interests. What will motivate consumer-based politics will be our shared cultural and political interests. But we can't change much of anything it we are not on speaking terms with people inside the media industry. A politics of confrontation must give way to one focused on tactieal collaboration. The old model, which many wisely dismissed, was that consumers vote with their pocketbooks. The new model is that we are collectively changing the nature of the marketplace, and in so doing we are pressuring companies to change the products they are creating and the ways they relate to their consumers.

We still do not have any models for what a mature, fully realized knowledge culture would look like. But popular culture may provide as with prototypes. A case in point is Warren Ellis's comic-book series, *Global Frequency*. Set in the near future, *Global Frequency* depicts a multiracial, multinational organization of ordinary people who contribute their services on an ad hoc basis. As Ellis explains, "You could be sitting there watching the news and suddenly hear an unusual cell phone lone, and within moments you might see your neighbor leaving the house in a hurry, wearing a jacket or a shirt with the distinctive Global Frequency symbol ... or, hell, your girlfriend might

READING NOTES

_____

_____

_____

_____

_____

answer the phone ... and promise to explain later. ... Anyone could be on the Global Frequency, and you'd never know until they got the call."[17] Ellis rejects the mighty demigods and elite groups of the superhero tradition and inelead depicts the twenty-first-century equivalent of a volunteer fire department. Ellis conceived of the story in the wake of September 11 as in alternative to calls for increased state power and paternalistic constraints on communications: *Global Frequency* doesn't imagine the government saving its citizens from whatever Big Bad is out there. Rather, as Ellis explains, "*Global Frequency* is about us saving ourselves." Each pasue focuses on a different set of characters in a different location, examining what it means for *Global Frequency* members personally and professionally to contribute their labor to a cause larger than themselves. The only recurring characters are those at the communications but who contact the volunteers. Once *Frequency* participants are called into action, most of the key decisions get made on site as the volunteers are allowed to act on their localized knowledge. Most of the challenges come, appropriately enough, from the debris left behind by the collapse of the military-industrial complex and the end of the cold war—"The had mad things in the dark that the public never found out about." In other words, the citizen soldiers use distributed knowledge to overcome the dangers of government secrecy.

Ellis's Global Frequency Network closely mirrors what journalist and digital activist Howard Rheingold has to say about smart mobs: "Smart mobs consist of people who are able to act in concert even if they don't know each other. The people who make up smart mobs cooperate in ways never before possible because they carry devices that possess both communication and computing capabilities. ... Groups of people using these tools will gain new forms of social power."[18] In Manila and in Madrid, activists, using cell phones, were able to rally massive numbers of supporters in opposition to governments who might otherwise have controlled discourse on the mass media; these efforts resulted in transformations of power. In Boston, we are seeing home schoolers use these same technologies to organize field trips on the fly that deliver dozens of kids and their parents to a museum or historic site in a matter of a few hours.

Other writers, such as science fiction writer Cory Doctorow, describe such groups as "adhocracies." The polar opposite of a bureaucracy, an adhocracy is an organization characterized by a lack of hierarchy. In it, each person contributes to confronting a particular problem as needed based on his or her knowledge and abilities, and leadership roles shift as tasks change. An adhocracy, thus, is a knowledge culture that turns information into action. Doctorow's science fiction novel *Down and Out in the Magic Kingdom* depicts a future when the fans run Disney World, public support becomes the most important kind of currency, and debates about popular culture become the focus of politics.[19]

Ellis's vision of the Global Frequency Network and Doctorow's vision of a grassroots Disney World are far out there—well beyond anything we've seen in the real world yet. But fans put some of what they learned from *Global Frequency* into action: tapping a range of communications channels to push the networks and production company to try to get a television series on the air.[20] Consider this to be another example of what it would mean to "democratize television." Mark Burnett, *Survivor's* executive producer, had taken an option on adopting the comic books for television; Warner Bros. had already announced plans to air *Global Frequency* as a midseason replacement, which then got postponed and later canceled. A copy of the series pilot was leaked on the Internet, circulating as an illegal download on BitTorrent, where it became the focus of a grassroots effort to get the series back into production. John Rogers, the show's head writer and producer, said that the massive response to the

READING NOTES

_____

_____

_____

_____

_____

never-aired series was giving the producers leverage to push for the pilot's distribution on DVD and potentially to sell the series to another network. Studio and network executives predictably cited concerns about what the consumers were doing "Whether the pilot was picked up or not, it is still the property of Warner Bros. Entertainment and we take the protection of all of our intellectual property seriously. ... While Warner Bros. Entertainment values feedback from consumers, copyright infringement is not a productive way to try to influence a corporate decision." Rogers wrote about his encounters with the *Global Frequency* fans in his blog: "It changes the way I'll do my next project. ... I would put my pilot out on the internet in a heartbeat. Want five more? Come buy the boxed set." Rogers's comments invite us to imagine a time when small niches of consumers who are willing to commit their money to a cause might ensure the production of a minority-interest program. From a producer's perspective, such a scheme would be attractive since television series are made at a loss for the first several seasons until the production company accumulates enough episodes to sell a syndication package. DVD lowers that risk by allowing producers to sell the series one season at a time and even to package and sell unaired episodes. Selling directly to the consumer would allow producers to recoup their costs even earlier in the production cycle.

People in the entertainment industry are talking a lot these days about what *Wired* reporter Chris Anderson calls "The Long Tail."[21] Anderson argues that as distribution costs lower, as companies can keep more and more backlist titles in circulation, and as niche communities can use he Web to mobilize around titles that satisfy their particular interests, then the greatest profit will be made by those companies that generate the most diverse content and keep it available at the most reasonable prices. If Anderson is right, then niche-content stands a much better chance of turning a profit than ever before. The Long Tail model assumes an increasingly savvy media consumer, one who will actively seek out content of interest and who will take pride in being able to recommend that content to friends.

Imagine a subscription-based model in which viewers commit to pay a monthly fee to watch a season of episodes delivered into their homes via broadband. A pilot could be produced to test the waters, and if the response looked positive, subscriptions could be sold for a show that had gotten enough subscribers to defer the company's initial production costs. Early subscribers would get a package price, others would pay more on a pay-per-view basis, which would cover the next phase of production. Others could buy access to individual episodes. Distribution could be on a DVD mailed directly to your home or via streaming media (perhaps you could simply download it onto your iPod).

It was the announcement that ABC-Disney was going to be offering recent episodes of cult television series (such as *Lost* and *Desperate Housewives*) for purchase and download via the Apple Music Store that really took these discussions to the next level. Other networks quickly followed with their own download packages. Within the first twenty days, there were more than a million television episodes downloaded. The video iPod seems emblematic of the new convergence culture—not because everyone believes the small screen of the iPod is the ideal vehicle for watching broadcast content but because the ability to download reruns on demand represents a major shift in the relationship between consumers and media content.

Writing in *Slate*, media analyst Ivan Askwith described some of the implications of television downloads:

> *As iTunes and its inevitable competitors offer more broadcast-television content, producers ... won't have to compromise their programs to meet broadcast requirments.*

READING NOTES

Episode lengths can vary as needed, content can be darker, more topical, and more explicit. ... Audiences already expect director's cuts and deleted scenes on DVDs. It's not hard to imagine that the networks might one day air a "broadcast cut" of an episode, then encourage viewers to download the longer, racier director's cut the next afternoon. ... While DVDs now give viewers the chance to catch up between seasons, on-demand television will allow anyone to catch up at any time, quickly and legally. Producers will no longer have to choose between alienating new viewers with a complex storyline or alienating the established audience by rehashing details from previous episodes. ... Direct downloads will give fans of endangered shows the chance to vote with their wallets while a show is still on the air. And when a program does go off the air, direct payments from fans might provide enough revenue to keep it in production as an online-only venture.[22]

Almost immediately, fans of canceled series, such as *The West Wing* and *Arrested Development*, have begun to embrace such a model as a way to sustain the shows' production, pledging money to support shows they want to watch.[23] Cult-television producers have begun to talk openly about bypassing the networks and selling their series directly to their most loyal consumers. One can imagine independent media producers using downloads as a way of distributing content that would never make it onto commercial television. And, of course, once you distribute via the Web, television instantly becomes global, paving the way for international producers to sell their content directly to American consumers. Google and Yahoo! began cutting deals with media producers in the hope that they might be able to profit from this new economy in television downloads. All of this came too late for

Global Frequency, and so far the producers of *The West Wing* and *Arrested Development* have not trusted their fates to such a subscription-based model. Yet, many feel that sooner or later some producer will test the waters, much as ABC-Disney did with its video iPod announcement. And once again, there are likely to be many others waiting in the wings to pounce on the proposition once they can measure public response to the deal. What was once a fan-boy fantasy now seems closer and closer to reality.

While producers, analysts, and fans have used the fate of *Global Frequency* to explore how we might rethink the distribution of television content, the series premise also offers us some tools for thinking about the new kinds of knowledge communities that this book has discussed. If one wants to see a real-world example of something like the Global Frequency Network, take a look at the Wikipedia—a grassroots, multinational effort to build a free encyclopedia on the Internet written collaboratively from an army of volunteers, working in roughly two hundred different languages. So far, adhocracy principles have been embraced by the open-source movement, where software engineers worldwide collaborate on projects for the common good. The Wikipedia project represents the application of these open-source principles to the production and management of knowledge. The Wikipedia contains more than 1.6 million articles and receives around 60 million hits per day.[24]

Perhaps the most interesting and controversial aspect of the Wikipedia project has been the ways it shifts what counts as knowledge (from the kinds of topics sanctioned by traditional encyclopedias to a much broader range of topics relevant to specialized interest groups and subcultures) and the ways it shifts what counts as expertise (from recognized academic authorities to something close to Lévy's concept of collective intelligence). Some worry that the encyclopedia will contain much inaccurate information, but the

READING NOTES

_____

_____

_____

_____

_____

Wikipedia community, at its best, functions as a self-correcting adhocracy. Any knowledge that gets posted can and most likely will be revised and corrected by other readers.

For this process to work, all involved must try for inclusiveness and respect diversity. The Wikipedia project has found it necessary to develop both a politics and an ethics—a set of community norms—about knowledge sharing:

> Probably, as we grow, nearly every view on every subject will (eventually) be found among our authors and readership. ... But since Wikipedia is a community-built, international resource, we surely cannot expect our collaborators to agree in all cases, or even in many cases, on what constitutes human knowledge in a strict sense. ... We must make an effort to present these conflicting theories fairly, without advocating any one of them. ... When it is clear to readers that we do not expect them to adopt any particular opinion, this is conducive to our readers' feeling free to make up their own minds for themselves, and thus to encourage in them intellectual independence. So totalitarian governments and dogmatic institutions everywhere have reason to be opposed to Wikipedia. ... We, the creators of Wikipedia trust readers' competence to form their own opinions themselves. Texts that present the merits of multiple viewpoints fairly, without demanding that the reader accept any one of them, are liberating.[25]

You probably won't believe in the Wikipedia unless you try it, but the process works. The process works because more and more people are taking seriously their obligations as participants to the community as a whole: not everyone does so yet; we can see various flame wars as people with very different politics and

ethics interact within the same knowledge communities. Such disputes often foreground those conflicting assumptions, forcing people to reflect more deeply on their choices. What was once taken for granted must now be articulated. What emerges might be called a moral economy of information: that is, a sense of mutual obligations and shared expectations about what constitutes good citizenship within a knowledge community.

We might think of fan fiction communities as the literary equivalent of the Wikipedia: around any given media property, writers are constructing a range of different interpretations that get expressed through stories. Sharing of these stories opens up new possibilities in the text. Here, individual contributions do not have to be neutral; participants simply have to agree to disagree, and, indeed, many fans come to value the sheer diversity of versions of the same characters and situations. On the other hand, mass media has tended to use its tight control over intellectual property to rein in competing interpretations, resulting in a world where there is one official version. Such tight controls increase the coherence of the franchise and protect the producers' economic interests, yet the culture is impoverished through such regulation. Fanliction repairs the damage caused by an increasingly privatized culture. Consider, for example, this statement made by a fan:

> What I love about fandom is the freedom we have allowed ourselves to create and recreate our characters over and over again. Fanfic rarely sits still. It's like a living, evolving thing, taking on its own life, one story building on another, each writer's reality bouncing off another's and maybe even melding together to form a whole new creation. ... I find that fandom can be extremely creative because we have the ability to keep changing our characters and giving them a

READING NOTES

_____

_____

_____

_____

_____

new life over and over. We can kill and resurrect them as often as we like. We can change their personalities and how they react to situations. We can take a character and make him charming and sweet or cold-blooded and cruel. We can give them an infinite, always-changing life rather than the single life of their original creation.[26]

Fans reject the idea of a definitive version produced, authorized, and regulated by some media conglomerate. Instead, fans envision a world where all of us can participate in the creation and circulation of central cultural myths. Here, the right to participate in the culture is assumed to be "the freedom we have allowed ourselves," not a privilege granted by a benevolent company, not something they are prepared to barter away for better sound files or free Web hosting. Fans also reject the studio's assumption that intellectual property is a "limited good," to be lightly controlled lest it dilute its value. Instead, they embrace an understanding of intellectual property as "shareware," something that accrues value as it moves across different contexts, gets retold in various ways, attracts multiple audiences, and opens itself up to a proliferation of alternative meanings.

Nobody is anticipating a point where all bureaucracies will become adhocracies. Concentrated power is apt to remain concentrated. But we will see adhocracy principles applied to more and more different kinds of projects. Such experiments thrive within convergence culture, which creates a context where viewers—individually and collectively—can reshape and recontextualize massmedia content. Most of this activity will occur around the edges of commercial culture through grassroots or niche media industries such as comics or games. On that scale, small groups like the Sequential Tarts can make a material difference. On that scale, entrepreneurs have an incentive to give their consumers greater opportunities to shape the content and participate in its distribution. As we move closer to the older and more mass market media industries, corporate resistance to grassroots participation increases: the stakes are too high to experiment, and the economic impact of any given consumption community lessens. Yet, within these media companies, there are still potential allies who for their own reasons may want to appeal to audience support to strengthen their hands in their negotiations around the boardroom table. A media industry struggling to hold on to its core audience in the face of competition from other media may be forced to take greater risks to accommodate consumer interests.

As we have seen across the book, convergence culture is highly generative: some ideas spread top down, starting with commercial media and being adopted and appropriated by a range of different publics as they spread outward across the culture. Others emerge bottom up from various sites of participatory culture and getting pulled into the mainstream if the media industries see some way of profiting from it. The power of the grassroots media is that it diversifies; the power of broadcast media is that it amplifies. That's why we should be concerned with the flow between the two: expanding the potentials for participation represents the greatest opportunity for cultural diversity. Throw away the powers of broadcasting and one has only cultural fragmentation. The power of participation comes not from destroying commercial culture but from writing over it, modding it, amending it, expanding it, adding greater diversity of perspective, and then recirculating it, feeding it back into the mainstream of media.

Read in those terms, participation becomes an important political right. In the American context, one could argue that First Amendment protections of the right to speech, press, belief, and assembly represent a more abstract right to participate in a democratic culture. After all, the First Amendment emerged in the context

READING NOTES

---

of a thriving folk culture, where it was assumed that songs and stories would get retold many different times for many different purposes. The country's founding documents were written by men who appropriated the names of classical orators or mythic heroes. Over time, freedom of the press increasingly came to rest with those who could afford to buy printing presses. The emergence of new media technologies supports a democratic urge to allow more people to create and circulate media. Sometimes the media are designed to respond to mass media content—positively or negatively—and sometimes grassroots creativity goes places no one in the media industry could have imagined. The challenge is to rethink our understanding of the First Amendment to recognize this expanded opportunity to participate. We should thus regard those things that block participation—whether commercial or governmental—as important obstacles to route around if we are going to "democratize television" or any other aspect of our culture. We have identified some of those obstacles in the book, most centrally the challenges, surrounding corporate control over intellectual property and the need for a clearer definition of the kinds of fair-use rights held by amateur artists, writers, journalists, and critics, who want to share work inspired or incited by existing media content.

Another core obstacle might be described as the participation gap. So far, much of the discussion of the digital divide has emphasized problems of access, seeing the issue primarily in technical terms—but a medium is more than a technology. As activists have sought a variety of means to broaden access to digital media, they have created a hodgepodge of different opportunities for participation. Some have extended access to these resources through the home, and others have limited, filtered, regulated access through schools and public libraries. Now, we need to confront the cultural factors that diminish the likelihood that different groups will participate. Race, class, language differences amplify these inequalities in opportunities for participation. One reason we see early adopters is not only that some groups feel more confidence in engaging with new technologies but also that some groups seem more comfortable going public with their views about culture.

Historically, public education in the United States was a product of the need to distribute the skills and knowledge necessary to train informed citizens. The participation gap becomes much more important as we think about what it would mean to foster the skills and knowledge needed by monitorial citizens: here, the challenge is not simply being able to read and write, but being able to participate in the deliberations over what issues matter, what knowledge counts, and what ways of knowing command authority and respect. The ideal of the in-formed citizen is breaking down because there is simply too much for any individual to know. The ideal of monitorial citizenship depends on developing new skills in collaboration and a new ethic of knowledge sharing that will allow us to deliberate together.[27]

Right now, people are learning how to participate in such knowledge cultures outside of any formal educational setting. Much of this learning takes place in the affinity spaces that are emerging around popular culture. The emergence of these knowledge cultures partially reflects the demands these texts place on consumers (the complexity of transmedia entertainment, for example), but they also reflect the de-mands consumers place on media (the hunger for complexity, the need for community, the desire to rewrite core stories). Many schools remain openly hostile to these kinds of experiences, continuing to promote autonomous problem solvers and self-contained learners. Here, unauthorized collaboration is cheating. As I finish writing this book, my own focus is increasingly being

READING NOTES

_____

_____

_____

_____

drawn toward the importance of media literacy education. Many media literacy activists still act as if the role of mass media had remained unchanged by the introduction of new media technologies. Media are read primarily as threats rather than as resources. More focus is placed on the dangers of manipulation rather than the possibilities of participation, on restricting access—turning off the television, saying no to Nintendo—rather than in expanding skills at deploying media for one's own ends, rewriting the core stories our culture has given us. One of the ways we can shape the future of media culture is by resisting such disempowering approaches to media literacy education. We need to rethink the goals of media education so that young people can come to think of themselves as cultural producers and participants and not simply as consumers, critical or otherwise. To achieve this goal, we also need media education for adults. Parents, for example, receive plenty of advice on whether they should allow their kids to have a television set in their room or how many hours a week they should allow their kids to consume media. Yet, they receive almost no advice on how they can help their kids build a meaningful relationship with media.

Welcome to convergence culture, where old and new media collide, where grassroots and corporate media intersect, where the power of the media producer and the power of the media consumer interact in unpredictable ways. Convergence culture is the future, but it is taking shape now. Consumers will be more powerful within convergence culture—but only if they recognize and use that power as both consumers and citizens, as full participants in our culture.

READING NOTES

_____

_____

_____

_____

_____

Chapter 11

Aesthetics and Production

"People still underestimate the value of content. ... Content is king."

—Michael Eisner, former CEO, Walt Disney Company

Despite momentous changes in technology, corporate structures and ownership, channels of distribution, and job roles, the core activity of the media business is producing news, entertainment, and educational content for its audiences. Content is the meaningful symbolic representations that inform, amuse, and interest viewers, listeners, readers, and users. Contrary to the presumption that audiences are passive, people must interact with media content on some level.

When analyzing media, observers often term call that interaction "consuming" media. In other words, media content has three distinct phases for analysis—the production of content, the distribution of content, and the consumption of content. Each phase, however, as an impact on the others. Recorded music can be played over the radio, on a CD player, on an iPod or MP3 player, on a computer, and in other ways—but regardless of the channel of communication or distribution, the music itself is why people use those devices in the daily lives. The means can vary, but the end result is the same—interaction with media content. And the public apparently has an insatiable appetite for content.

This chapter offers an overview of media aesthetics and production. In general, aesthetics is the branch of philosophy that addresses the nature and expression of beauty and art. What makes a painting great? What is the definition of beauty? Traditional aesthetics explores those sorts of questions. In the sense that it is used in media production, aesthetics refers to the creative choices in constructing media messages that achieve the audience effects desired by the producer. In other words, aesthetics are those choices that define a media product as effective or ineffective at a specific point of time and within a specific context.

Production is the creative process for making media products according to one's aesthetic choices. Aesthetics is the parameters and production the process by which media content is created.

Aesthetics and production considerations have an impact on message creation in every media channel—movies, television, radio, recordings, newspapers, magazines, books, advertising, public relations, the Web, video games, social media, and virtual-reality worlds. As surely as a painter wields brush on canvas to make a scene come to life, a media producer paints with sights, sounds, motions, and words to stimulate the audience's imagination.

Media production is a complex and collaborative process that requires many forms of creativity to achieve the producer's goal of having an intended effect on an audience. Although the author of a book or the director of a movie might seem to be the sole creative spirit, in fact, the production of all media products requires teams of people exercising many forms of creativity.

The aims of this chapter are to

- define media production as purposeful communication to audiences.

- explain how humans experience mediated communication.

- describe production skills and phases of the production process common to all media, and

- introduce an aesthetic system for the mass media.

Required Reading: In "The Culture and Business of Cross-media Production," computer- and video-games expert Espen Aarseth argues that the worldwide entertainment industry has changed the creative process. Media content such as games, films, novels, animated movies, T-shirts, action figures, perfumes, and amusement park rides now are driven not by the creator's individual choices but by the content's potential for maximizing profits across media platforms. Aarseth goes on to present a model of cross-media content transfer in which some content transfers easier than others. Media franchises such as *The Matrix, Pirates of the Caribbean, The Lord of the Rings, Harry Potter*, and *Death Jr.* are described.

MAKING MEDIA

Making media products is a popular and often deeply rewarding activity because it satisfies the creative impulse—the impulse to bring something new into the world, something that makes a difference to other people. Almost all successful media producers share a curiosity about the media world and are always on the hunt for the next new concept or approach.

Of course, few ideas in media culture are totally new. As explained by creativity scholar Robert Weisberg, imagining an old idea in a new context can be creative. Some people argue that there are seven archetypal story plots: the quest story, the coming-of-age story, the voyage-and-return story, comedy and tragedy in the classical sense of the terms, overcoming the monster, and the rags-to-riches story. But just because those archetypes exist, it does not mean that a book and movie such as *The Lord of the Rings*, which combines several of the archetypes, is not original, extremely creative and deeply moving. There are also recognizable archetypal characters, such as the willing or unwilling hero, the anti-hero, the fallen mentor, and so on.

Along the same lines, Aristotle described the six elements of drama—character, action (or plot), ideas, language, music, and spectacle. The key to creating great drama is understanding how those elements can work together and combining them in new and creative ways.

Content works on another levels as well. Media content is symbolic communication, consisting of representations and recombinations of the world, not the world itself. Meaning is created through the media producer's combinations of representations, transmitted by the channel of communication, and understood by the receiver. Meanings for cultural symbols are not fixed in time, but are constantly morphing. Even remakes of existing content, such as popular movies and television shows, can be creative and original in how they reshape old ideas to appeal to new audiences. Often, as a story is recast from one medium to another—for example, the folk tale of *Beauty and the Beast* was made into a book, a theatrical film, an animated movie, and a stage musical—each iteration of the story will be creative and meaningful in its own way.

THE MEDIATED EXPERIENCE

The media producer's job is to craft messages that catch the audience's attention, impart information, sway emotions, and impel action. These goals require that the producer understand how audiences experience the media messages. Artists, philosophers, and psychologists since the 1800s have discovered four principles of human experience that apply to media audiences: "aboutness," context, selective sensing, and gestalt. These concepts can serve as a useful framework for the analysis of media productions.

"Aboutness" is the outward-directed quality of human sensation, thought, and feelings. The core is the focus of attention; the field is everything outside the core; and the horizon limits the field. All possible objects of human experience, including the media, have the same core–field-horizon structure. Having a core of experience means that people cannot focus attention on everything at once. There always is a field or background for what being looked at, listened to, or thought about. The field is known as the lived world, a sort of stage for the drama of life, from which we draw all of our stories, emotions, hopes, and cares. In a way, the experiential field helps the core by constituting what the core is not, like a target to a bull's-eye (see Figure 11.1).

The artists' term for the core–field relationship is figure–ground. Sometimes, a shift of focus can bring about an inversion of figure–ground, in which the former ground transforms into figure. Psychologists call these figure–ground inversions multistable phenomena, as exemplified by the well-known illustration of a white water goblet set against two black faces looking at each other; one can see either the goblet or the faces, but not both simultaneously. Media producers can capitalize on figure–ground reversals in their logo designs, story plots, or multilayered images to elicit messages of greater richness and complexity (see Figure 11.2).

Horizons limit sensation, beyond which humans cannot see, hear, touch, and so forth. In a landscape picture, a horizon of houses, trees, mountains, or perhaps the curvature of the Earth, limits far seeing. Memories also have horizons, both spatial and temporal, which imagination can stretch to a degree but never totally surpass. According to philosophers such as Michel Foucault, Roland Barthes, and Jacques Derrida, language is the horizon of thought itself. Foucault famously said "Language is oppression." In other words, indescribable experiences do not matter.

Foucault's statement means that media production should begin with clear statements of the communication goals and target audience, and keep the goals and audience at the core of the entire production process. If producers cannot tell themselves and their clients what they are aiming at, they are likely to miss their targets.

The field powerfully influences the audience's core experience of a media message. The field

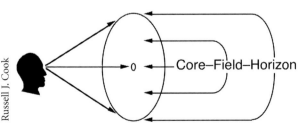

Figure 11.1—*The structure of mediated experience.*

Figure 11.2—*A multistable visual phenomenon.*

contextualizes the core with field elements, such as connotations for language, gestures, and images; logistics such as ambient lighting or interfering noise; and interpretive frames that might resonate with the media message, such as a "mad cow" disease news story followed by a fast-food commercial. Schramm's *Shared Experience Model of Communication* accounts for these contextual factors with overlapping spheres of experience for the sender and receiver, indicating that successful communication is dependent on the commonality of language, culture, media habits, personal values, and so forth (see Figure 11.3).

Horizons of media messages also are contextual. Having a horizon is a reminder of the world beyond, which is chock full of personal and cultural references. For visual media, the presentation format (page, screen, package, publication, etc.) contextualizes a rectangular-shaped media experience with an awareness of a coextensive aesthetic space beyond the frame. Sound media also have horizons, which are the unheard sounds beyond the range of hearing.

Recapping, mediated experience is structured with both an "aboutness" (core) and a context (field/horizon). The third important principle of human experience that applies to the media is selective sensing, which is the intentional shifting of attention from core to core in the experiential field. Thanks to proto-humans' survival conditioning to find food and to avoid becoming food for other species, humans have inherited an ability to focus on specific sights and sounds, and to tune out other stimuli. In the mass media's jungle of sensations, selective sensing is a survival skill, too.

Audience members are able to push various media messages to the background while focusing on particular items of interest—for example, the name of a celebrity, a song beat, line of dialogue, or a vibrant color. This rapid time-sharing of attention to simultaneous communication channels explains why a college student can appear to watch television, surf the Web, listen to an iPod, and text on a cellular phone, all at the same time.

Gestalt is a psychological word for the innate human desire to find the unifying elements of a complex phenomena—to "connect the dots" of the parts into a satisfactory whole whose meaning is greater than the sum of the parts. Gestalts are the meaning frames for media messages. They incorporate background, "big-picture" questions of significance, direction, and purpose. Without gestalts for a mass-media program, audience members become disoriented and suffer information overload. Gestalts also are the organizing principle of memory. Single sensations trigger bundles of memories stored in the human brain, such as the pleasing aroma of mother's apple pie bringing a flood of childhood recollections.

Gestalts in the mass media take on numerous forms. Taken together, color schemes, vector lines, selective typography, and pictorial balance create a visual gestalt known as composition in graphic designs. Melody and harmony are give meaning to sound. Strongly motivated behaviors and stereotypes make story characters comprehensible.

The aesthetics principles of aboutness, context, selective sensing, and gestalt all are consequences of the core–field–horizon structure of mediated experience. This structure is a useful framework for aesthetic analysis of the media, or making a the judgment that certain media content "works."

MEDIA PRODUCTION SKILLS TOOLKIT

Just as a carpenter or plumber carries a kit of essential tools designed to perform crucial functions on the job, diversified media producers pack

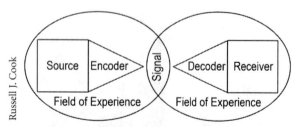

Figure 11.3—*Wilbur Schramm's* Shared Experience Model of Communication (1954).

a personal "toolkit" of three essential production skills: writing, concepting, and computing.

The ability to write well is an essential skill for all creative media. Even graphic designers need to be good writers to rationalize their designs and to pitch to their clients. The three most important issues of effective production writing are targeting the audience, accommodating technical requirements, and conciseness. First, targeting a specific audience helps a scriptwriter or copy-editor to choose words that speak the audience's language. The more narrowly the audience is defined, the sharper and more effective the language then can be used to address that audience. Second, the production writer should know the medium's technical parameters to take advantage of its possibilities while working within its limits. Third, concise writing improves clarity of meaning and purpose, which helps the production team and the audience to get the message.

"Concepting" can be described as thinking in pictures, or the ability to imagine the finished content from script directions. One way to learn concepting is to obtain the screenplays and scripts for feature films and compare the plans to how the final films turned out. Two forms of visual concepting—comping for print layouts and storyboarding for film, video, and interactive media—are generally essential to the production process. "Comps" are thumbnail drawings of graphic designs. Storyboards are rough, cartoon-like visualizations of the action in commercials, television shows, and the movies. Both forms of concepting visual designs help to work out aesthetic problems and pitch ideas to the client. Some DVD releases of feature films come with storyboard extra features, such as *Men in Black* (1997) and *Gladiator* (2000). Because of media convergence, computing plays a central role in production. Computers can be used for everything from researching audiences, writing headlines and copy, shooting and touching up photographs, choosing typography, designing logos, laying out publications and promotions, recording sounds and music, editing movies and radio shows, burning DVDs and Blu-ray discs, and building Web sites. Computer technology

helps producers to work anywhere and for a smaller investment than ever before. Media producers can take portable hardware such as laptop computers, miniaturized cameras, and digital sound recorders almost anywhere, and send back project drafts to clients over the Internet.

Humans live in the real, analog world of paper, voices, walking the dog, and making grilled cheese sandwiches, whereas computers operate in the virtual, digital world of zeros and ones. Almost all mass media are delivered digitally, so some information and signals from the human analog world must undergo *analog-to-digital conversion* to be usable by the media producer. Analog-to-digital conversion hardware that plug into computers include scanners for documents and photographic prints, audio interfaces for capturing microphone feeds, and analog video converter boxes.

The major movie studios have converted almost entirely from analog to digital production and distribution to save money, increase convenience, and improve quality. More and more Hollywood and independent features are being shot digitally, and all features are edited digitally after analog-to-digital conversion. For nostalgic types who prefer the "film look" to digital for still or motion applications, computer software and photographic techniques have been developed to simulate the film look digitally for both still and motion applications. The reverse conversion from digital to analog is a technological challenge for print graphic designers, especially in screen presentation of colors for print production of newspapers, magazines, book, brochures, poster, and the like. Most computer displays use the red–green–blue color model and are notoriously inconsistent in presentation of design colors, whereas processing uses the yan–magenta–yellow–black color model.

THE PRODUCTION PROCESS

Whether the media content is a sales brochure, news report, magazine article, radio play, or video game, the production process roughly follows the same general pattern of ideation, proposing, planning and gathering resources, producing/financing, directing or creating, editing, testing, marketing, and distributing. The actual techniques used in each step might vary depending on the project. However, the sequence of steps is generally consistent.

Sometimes the steps are grouped into three broad stages—pre-production, production, and post-production. Each stage is important in creating and delivering the content to its intended audience and having at least the potential of having the audience understand the content in the intended way. A breakdown at any stage will negatively impact the production, and in each stage, creativity can play an important role.

Pre-Production

The first step is generating an idea; all production starts with an initial concept. But the ways ideas are generated can differ for each medium. For example, a single author usually comes up with the idea for a book. Television, however, usually employs groups of people who generate ideas for specific episodes in a weekly series, for example. Ideation is a term often used in the advertising community to describe coming up with a concept for an ad.

Once a media producer has an idea, that idea has to be proposed to other people. Media content frequently is produced within large and complex networks. Ideas for movies have to be "green lighted" by the studios. While a novelist can write a novel independently, it will not be published without proposing it to a publisher.

The next step is planning and gathering resources. This step might involve outlining a story in more detail or writing a script. It could include storyboarding a commercial. It could mean doing additional research. It also could mean assembling a production crew as well as talent. All these activities take money, usually other people's money, or financing. Of course, because the costs of actually writing a book could be low, the would-be author can self-finance that kind of project. Musicians can distribute music over the

Internet, using low-end computers to mix the music. This also can be self-financed. Movie director Robert Townsend self-financed his first film, *Hollywood Shuffle*, using credit cards. On the other hand, James Cameron's blockbuster movie *Avatar* cost $500 million to make.

Technological breakthroughs, particularly the emergence of computer-based communications networks, have had a radical impact on media production. In computer-based networks, particularly the World Wide Web and cellular telephone works, all content—words, audio, video, and graphics—are in a digital format. All can be created using computer-controlled technology and all can be played back on computer-controlled devices. This collapsing of all media types into a digital format is called *technological convergence.*

Technological convergence allows producers to create a single media product and release it in multiple forms for multiple markets, greatly expanding the potential audience. The emergence of converged media has made pre-production planning more critical because communicators might have to provide their content in several different formats.

Film and television are multi-format environments in which the original version is shot in the highest resolution necessary, usually for theater screens, and then translated into lower resolutions for video and online release. Still photography for print media and advertising is planned into the same converged-media production process. The photographer might also need to be able to shoot motion video for companion video games, extra features, and cable promotions in addition to stills.

Production

Once the production planning has been completed and necessary resources have been gathered—in other words, once pre-production is done—the project goes into production. Time needed for production can vary greatly. A song can take as little as a few minutes to produce; a news broadcast will be created in a day; a 30-minute primetime television episode usually needs a week; a movie might take several weeks or even months just to shoot; and a book can take years to write. Production in each medium is unique.

Production job titles vary according to the medium and the size of the production team. In the movies, the person in charge of pre-production is the producer, and the director takes change during the production stage. Some directors who want more control of their projects also serve as producer. The title executive producer usually is give to people who provided the financing. Other motion media such as video games tend to have similar roles.

The job titles for print production are very different. The person in change of pre-production of a graphic production might have the title of creative director, while the supervisor of production—person who actually executes the design—might be called the graphic artist or design director. Regardless, the stages of production will be the same.

Post-Production

The last step of the process is post-production. This consists of editing, refining, and evaluating the product. A book might have to be revised. Once compiled, scenes in a movie might need to be reshot or the musical soundtrack added later. Testing the product with audience—sometimes through formal research and sometimes by sending it to reviewers—and then marketing and distributing the content also are part of post-production. Feedback from the audience might lead to further changes. Post-production is a continuous process of refinement to obtain the best possible product. The work enters as raw materials and exits as a highly refined whole. Sometimes the end product comes out very similar to the original concept, but most for most productions, the contributions of many different people in collaboration result in a something new and different.

Interestingly, there is a reverse relationship of the stages: post-production strategies will have an impact on the production itself, and production needs will determine pre-production planning. To put the puzzle together in post-production editing, one must gather the right puzzle pieces during the production phase, which in turn should guide pre-production planning. In a strange way, then, one should start with the desired end product and work backward to figure out how to begin.

Consider movies, for example. The production of a movie and perhaps even its meaning is changed if it is to be released in a high-definition IMAX theater, a regular movie theater, television, Blu-ray disc, or video streaming on the Web. Means of distribution also is important in the music industry. Promoting and selling music via the Internet has allowed many new bands to find audiences interested in their music.

AESTHETIC ANALYSIS OF MEDIA

Aesthetics generally refers to analyzing, appreciating, and judging the worth of art. Is the art good, or bad? Applying aesthetic analysis to the media is somewhat different. The valid aesthetic question for the media is about effectiveness as communication, not about good or bad: "Do the aesthetic qualities of this media artifact communicate the producer's intended message to the target audience?"

The rules of aesthetics for art or the media are not fixed in time. For example, when the French Impressionists began displaying their work in the 1860s, one critic opined, "Without line, there is no form, and without form, how can reality be represented?" Based on the critic's understanding of the purpose of art—to represent reality—he judged that Impressionism was not art. However, the Impressionists were cutting-edge for the 1860s. The Impressionists did not paint reality; they painted light as it was reflected by objects to the observer's eye. The wrong-headed critic failed to judge Impressionist art on its own terms. The Impressionists are now seen as the starting point of modern Western art.

Similarly, in the media, hip-hop music was denigrated when the first rap recording, Sugar Hill Gang's "Rapper's Delight," was released in 1979. Hip hop's new sound, its de-emphasis of lyricism, and its controversial lyrics expressing the frustrations of urban life caused some critics to dismiss it as not music—a shortsighted judgment, given hip hop's international acceptance within a decade. Like hip hop music and Impressionist art, all popular media should be judged on their own terms.

Aesthetic analysis in audiovisual communication can be broken down into six analytical fields or stages. These six fields are like layers of a cake that blend together while baking to produce the whole dessert. Like bakers, media producers need to know the recipe for producing a good cake. This section gives the list of aesthetic ingredients and cooking instructions for mediated communication according to two leading authorities on applied media aesthetics, Rudolph Arnheim, author of *Art and Visual Perception: A Psychology of the Creative Eye* (1954), and Herbert Zettl, author of *Sight Sound Motion: Applied Media Aesthetics* (2008). The six analytic fields are not components of the messages themselves; rather, they are ways of examining the audience's mediated experience.

Aesthetic Field Zero: Sound

The title "field zero" for sound refers to sound's lack of dimensionality and its primordial aspect as the origin of the sensory world. Sound seems to be all around the listener; aesthetically, it invades the core of experience from the field and merges the two. Sound is primordial; human beings hear first and then see, so sound sets the mood and tone for the visual experience. This principle is obvious to anyone who has tried different soundtracks for a video and found the music transforming (see Figure 11.4).

Media professionals use sound effects to make screen experiences seem real. In the heyday of radio plays, families used to sit together at home in rapt attention while "watching" the radio console.

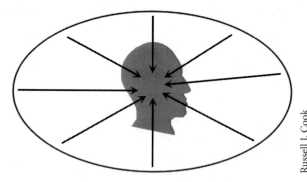

Russell J. Cook

Figure 11.4—*Aesthetic field zero: Sound seems to be all around the listener.*

Television news and sports punctuate their motion graphics and picture transitions with "swooshes" and "zaps." Motion-picture music scores cue the audience's emotional responses, while sound effects make the experiences immediate. Even photographs and text descriptions can make the audience "hear" environmental sounds. In short, sound gives the sense of here and now.

Compared to the visual field, sound has relatively few parameters for analysis: frequency (pitch), duration, rhythm, timbre (instrumentation), texture, attack and decay (pre- and post-echo), major and minor key, melody and harmony. Hearing seems less accessible to analysis because of a cultural bias in favor of seeing, which arose during the Italian Renaissance. Human perspectival thinking, literacy, and empirical rational science all stress vision as the preferred epistemological sense. In the common vernacular, "I see" is equated to knowing or understanding. In everyday experience, hearing actually is as powerful as seeing for knowing and feeling about the world. A close inspection of movies and TV shows will reveal this fact. However, hearing is "overlooked" because we have fewer words for it.

Aesthetic Field One: Light, Shadow, and Color

The fact that light is needed for sight is elementary. However, light energy itself is invisible except as it illuminates objects. Shadows are needed to make light visible. Therefore, shadow and light are equal partners in the first aesthetic field. Light is a form of electromagnetic radiation detectable by the human eye and represented as a narrow band of the electromagnetic spectrum. Other forms of electromagnetic radiation include infrared (heat), ultraviolet, radio waves, microwaves, gamma rays, and x-rays, all traveling at the same speed but at different frequencies and wavelengths (see Figure 11.5).

Digital still and video cameras can shoot in most natural light, regardless of how dim. Various filters and gels can be added for special effects and to balance color. The most important job of the photographer is arranging lighting, which is thought of as painting with light. Light sources vary in color hue or "temperature". Candles are reddish, television lights orangish, the sun and sky blueish. For accurate color reproduction, cameras for still or motion photography must be balanced to the color of the light source (see Figure 11.6).

Shadows give shape to things. Attached shadows cast by an object onto itself show the object's texture. By their angles, cast shadows indicate the direction of light and, if cast by the sun, the time of day and season of the year. Shadows also can indicate spatial depth. In graphics, the drop-shadow effect helps text to stand out from its background. Without shadows, an image lacks definition and depth, so shadows are a photographer's friend.

The 17th century Dutch painter Rembrandt Van Rijn perfected the expressive use of deep shadows

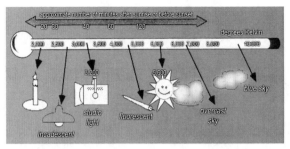

Figure 11.6—*The color temperature scale.*

from chiaroscuro lighting, which was imitated by the German Expressionist film director Fritz Lang in *M* (1931) and later by Hollywood *film noir* cinematographer Gregg Toland in *Citizen Kane* (1941). A notable modern example of chiaroscuro is Frank Miller's graphic novel *Sin City* (1991–1992) and film version (2005).

White light can be refracted or split by a prism into all the colors of the spectrum. Conversely, all the colors of the spectrum together will produce white light. This mixing of colors of light is called additive. The mixing of colored pigments for printing on paper is called *subtractive*, because light reflecting from the page is blocked by the ink from reflecting back to the eye.

Screen technologies that project light, such as motion pictures, video, and the Web, work with additive color mixing. The additive primary colors are red, green, and blue (RGB). The subtractive primary colors for print media such as graphic design, newspapers, magazines, and books are cyan, magenta, and yellow (CMY). Black (K) is added for text to save money on color inks. When overprinted, CMYK can produce all of the colors of the spectrum, including red, green, and blue. Media producers often must work in both color-mixing systems. Color-management hardware and software can help to manage the color conversion from display to printer (see Figure 11.7).

Two contextual factors for color perception more powerful than physiology are composition and culture. Perception of color brightness, hue, and saturation are affected strongly by surrounding colors. For example, the same blue rectangle will

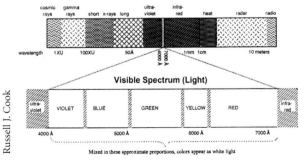

Figure 11.5—*The electromagnetic spectrum.*

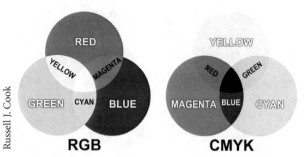

Figure 11.7—*RGB and CMYK color-mixing systems.*

look brighter when surrounded by black than when surrounded by white. Color perception also is conditioned by culture. In the West, black shows solemnity and respect at funerals, whereas East Asians wear white at funerals, and African cultures wear white and red.

An example of effective color use is the 1995 Columbia Pictures production of *Dolores Claiborne*, directed by Taylor Hackford. The movie is based on a novel by Stephen King about a mother and daughter struggling with repressed memories of their abusive husband/father. Hackford and his director of photography, Gabriel Beristain, showed the present awash in blue-gray colors of overcast skies, symbolizing spiritual repression. In contrast, the past was rendered as warm, sunlit flashbacks that did not yet know the father's evil. The color symbolism climaxes with an eclipse of the sun as the father falls to his death.

Aesthetic Field Two: Shape and Area

Graphic designers compose their pictures in the two-dimensional picture plane defined by geometry's horizontal (X) and vertical (Y) axes. The principles of pictorial design apply to all visual media, from printed matter to Panavision film. In addition to arranging shapes and areas, the graphic designer also manipulates typography, photography, and ergonomics to craft media messages. The discussion of depth in the pictorial plane is reserved for the next section concerning the third aesthetic field, represented by geometry's third axis (Z) (see Figure 11.8).

A picture frame, whether a computer screen or a newspaper's page trim, is the outer horizon of the visual field. Most pictures are rectangular for convenience of technology, not because rectangles are aesthetically superior to other shapes. The standard frame for screen media in the United States changed in 2009 from the old television standard proportion or aspect of 4:3 (width to height) to the new high-definition television aspect of 16:9. The wider format is much closer to the ideal compositional shape (rarely achieved) of the fuzzy oval conforming to human binocular vision. Theatrical motion pictures are 1.85:1 or wider to allow viewers to lose themselves in the screen experience and to forget about their worldly cares (see Figure 11.9).

Sometimes, the screen world seems to extend beyond the mediated frame edge, like a window onto a wider world. This effect of the frame edge is barely noticed, except for instances when people would like to peek around the edge, and would be shocked if a the world did not in fact continue.

Figure 11.8—*X–Y–Z axes of geometric space.*

Figure 11.9—*Screen aspect ratios.*

The term for "seeing with" the obscured part of a contiguous image is psychological closure. The mind completes or "closes" the mediated world by seeing it as extending beyond the medium's window. Premature closure occurs when graphic elements, such as the top of a person's head, align with the frame edge, which has the effect of reminding the viewer of the aesthetic outer horizon.

Two-dimensional design issues can be subsumed into an overarching metaphor of forces in the physical world: gravity of graphic mass, vectors, and frame edge magnetism. The "weight" of a compositional shape is determined by its graphic mass—a combination of its size, density, and complexity. A large shape is heavier than a small one; a dense shape heavier than one less dense, and a simple shape heavier than a complex one. The heavier an object, the stronger its aesthetic gravitational pull on other objects and on the aesthetic magnetism of the frame edge. Because terrestrial beings are accustomed to the downward pull of gravity, heavy graphic masses high in the frame strain to stay afloat (see Figure 11.10).

Straining against Earth's gravity, human bodily comportment strongly influences the perception of forces in graphic designs employed in different mass media. Horizontal shapes appear at rest, vertical shapes appear to "stand up," and diagonal shapes appear ready to spring into action.

As shown in Figure 11.10, vectors are arrows of force that direct the viewer's attention within a pictorial composition. Any linear elements, such as slats of a picket fence, columns on a building, or road signs, could function as compositional vectors leading the viewer's attention to the center of importance. Single lines of text in a graphic design usually function as graphic vectors, whereas blocks of text usually function as textured graphic masses.

Generally, but not always, vectors that lead the viewer's attention away from the center of importance are considered to be poor compositional design because they confuse the viewer. (Occasionally, the communication goal *is* to confuse the viewer, in which case diverging vectors would be good composition.) Because humans make visual contact by looking at each other in the eye, the pictured eye glance of a person or animal, known as an index vector, is perhaps the most powerful of all compositional devices.

Pictures that are a mirror image along a vertical central axis are called horizontally symmetrical and evoke the body symmetries of animals and humans. In everyday life, horizontally symmetrical scenes are rare and create psychological tension, as if the graphic weight of the scene is teetering from side to side. For that reason, most graphic designs in the mass media, such as Web pages, advertising layouts, or book jackets, are asymmetrical. The ancient Greeks formulated the most revered formula for asymmetrical pictorial designs found in nature, known as the *golden section*. The golden section defines four ideal locations for center of interest in a pictorial frame. The locations are off-center, but not extremely so. Some commercial still photographers are known to rely on the golden section to create interesting compositions (see Figure 11.11).

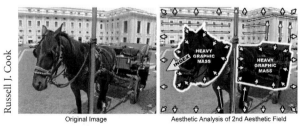

Figure 11.10—*Graphic mass, vectors, and frame magnetism.*

Figure 11.11—*The golden section. Place center of attention at 3/5ths–2/5ths for harmonious balance.*

Russell J. Cook

Chapter 11 | Aesthetics and Production 301

In fact, all subject locations in the frame—symmetrical or not—have the potential to communicate effectively to the viewer if the overall pictorial design accounts properly for gravitational forces, vectors, and closure of the two-dimensional aesthetic field.

Aesthetic Field Three: Volume and Depth

In general, the deeper a mediated communication message, the more engaging the aesthetic experience for the audience. Volumes and spatial depth can appear in still pictures as well as in motion media. Rarely is a picture seen as totally flat, and being able to see *into* a picture gives a more engaging aesthetic experience Several aesthetic depth cues to enhance the sense of depth are considered briefly in this section.

Relative size is the most fundamental depth cue, learned by human adolescents at an early age. Size can be deceiving, however, so a reference object for relative size is helpful, such as a person standing in front of an architectural monument to clarify its scale for the viewer. The stained-glass artists and tapestry weavers of medieval Europe did not comprehend relative size as a depth cue, so they failed to show background objects as smaller than foreground objects. However, they were able to indicate distances by use of two other depth cues, height in plane and overlapping shapes, in which objects farther away tend to appear higher in the two-dimensional pictorial frame and to be hidden by foreground objects.

Aerial perspective is a separation of foreground and background objects by atmospheric effects. Air refracts light, causing color desaturation and softening of focus. Greater scene depth enhances the effect, as does air pollution or moisture. A famous example of aerial perspective is Leonardo da Vinci's painting of the *Mona Lisa* (1503–1506), in which hazy Italian hills and rivers seem to recede to great distances behind the central figure (see Figure 11.12).

A lens-generated version of aerial perspective *is rack focus*, in which a shadow depth of field blurs

Courtesy of Library of Congress

Figure 11.12—*Aerial perspective in* Mona Lisa *by Leonardo da Vinci.*

the background behind a sharply focused foreground object.

Linear perspective cues depth by converging lines that seem to recede to a distant destination called a vanishing point. Linear perspective was invented by Italian Renaissance military engineers who developed the science of ballistics to plot the path of projectiles shot from cannons.

In fact, artist Leonardo da Vinci's day job was as a ballistics engineer for the Duke of Milan. (da Vinci wrote the first scientific treatise on aerial and linear perspective.) At first, artists struggling to perceive space traced reflected images on mirrors or set up wooden helper contraptions with movable arms to make the receding lines explicit.

As linear perspective became more common in painting, the general populace learned to see in spatial depth and also to think in temporal depth.

By privileging the viewpoint of an individual person in both space and time, linear perspective contributed a conceptual landscape for new ideas of human freedom, education, and mass media, which emerged during the late Renaissance (see Figure 11.13).

Photographers use different focal-length lenses to achieve depth effects. A wide-angle lens, which has a short focal-length, shows the widest possible view with exaggerated depth and everything in focus, whereas the *telephoto* lens brings close objects near, collapses depths, and makes selective focus possible. Cinematographer Gregg Toland used wide-angle lenses and deep focus in Orson Welles's RKO film production *Citizen Kane* (1941). In contrast, cinematographer Dante Spinotti for Michael Mann's Universal Pictures production *Public Enemies* (2009) achieved a claustrophobic effect with telephoto shots and selective focus.

Aesthetic Field Four: Time and Motion

The most fundamental property of time is its elasticity. Time stretches or condenses, depending on the experiencer's attention to the moment. A boring lecture might seem to stretch on endlessly, whereas a gripping, fast-paced movie might seem to go by in a snap. Sound and picture rhythms make one more conscious of time's passage. Generally speaking, the more involved an audience is in a media message and less involved in the seconds ticking away, the more quickly time will seem to pass.

Down through history, time has been represented in Western culture by a vector for the horizontal orientation of human action on the Earth's surface. The time line's now-point is constantly giving way to the next now-point on the time line. The future is the direction of the time traveler's frontal space. The past is the origin of the time vector behind the traveler. In a nostalgic moment, one might "turn around" one's consciousness to reflect on the past.

A vertical vector representing the experiencer's mental engagement also extends from the now-point. If the now-point vector is tall and is pointing straight up, it represents intense involvement in the present moment. A now-point vector leaning toward the future represents relative boredom. A now-point vector that is lying down on the time line represents a totally bored experiencer who is "watching the clock" (see Figure 11.14).

The time line metaphor is used by video-editing computer software, in which the editor drops rectangular blocks representing individual "shots" onto the time line. The shot widths indicate their duration in minutes and seconds. A shot captured by a video camcorder typically has one video track for the picture and two audio tracks for stereophonic sound. However, additional tracks for video and audio might be added as horizontal layers to the time line to accommodate more complex audiovisual constructions.

Figure 11.13—*Linear perspective intensifies the perception of three-dimensional depth in two-dimensional media.*

Figure 11.14—*Aesthetic time line.*

Transitions between shots might be instantaneous or might extend over time as wipes or dissolves. Special effects such as fast or slow motion might be achieved simply by squeezing or stretch the shot blocks (see Figure 11.15).

Given that real life does not have "edits" (even for sleep), it is a marvel of mediated communication that the audience has learned to make sense out of an edited television show, movie, or video game. Standard editorial practice calls for a distinct change of camera angle at the point of an edit from shot to shot, which modern viewers are able to understand as changes of viewpoint, an understanding analogous to physical movement of their bodies to the new viewing location in mediated space. The more edits in a media program, the more psychic energy is expended by viewers to shift their viewpoint mentally, and the more they become engaged aesthetically in the media event. All of this occurs without the viewer's direct consciousness.

Media scholars such as Jean Baudrillard and Marshall McLuhan have suggested that modern technology has morphed human perception of time. Electricity brought light into the terrifying night. Heating and air-conditioning of homes, workplaces, and automobiles overcame seasonal variance. Birth control and importation of off-season food overcame biological constraints. High-speed travel and virtual reality traversed previously impassable distances. Around-the-clock shopping and mass-media access catered to personal schedules and individual whim. All of this convenience came at the cost of cutting off

the human experience from the rhythms of nature. The mass media continue to fragment and to dislocate temporal experience.

Aesthetic Field Five: Synaesthesis (Field Integration)

Synaesthesis is a philosophy term meaning the merging of the senses in everyday life. Only in reflection and analysis do the aesthetic fields appear separately. In life, they produce an integrated whole experience. Integration begins at a very young age in humans. At a young age, infants in their cribs learn to correlate objects they can touch with similar-appearing objects just out of reach. Thus, vision becomes an extension of touch. Another sensory integration, that of smell and taste, is well known to anyone who has salivated over aromas from the kitchen. Hearing and vision are integrated by normal life experience and reinforced in mediated communication by the pairing of pictures and sounds.

Rhythmically, synchronized pictures, and sounds can be integrated so completely that one can "hear" colors or "see" sounds. For example, a blaring brass trumpet might evoke visions of strongly saturated colors, or a picture of raindrops in a pond might sound like a harp being plucked. Media producers often use these natural picture-sound equivalencies to create a more compelling aesthetic experience. At other times, they choose to have pictures and sounds work against each other in what are called *contrapuntal* structures, which will create a disorienting or disconnect mood.

Complex editing effects for marrying picture and sound are called *montage*. Soviet Russian film directors of the 1920s, such as Sergei Eisenstein (1898–1948), Dziga Vertov (1896–1954), and Lev Kuleshov (1899–1970), contributed the first serious montage theories. Their ideas are still in use today by movie directors such as Andy and Larry Wachowski (*The Matrix*, Warner Brothers, 1999) and Joel and Ethan Coen (*No Country for Old Men*, Miramax, 2007).

Synaesthesis applies to the media in another way. Audiences take in mediated communication as an

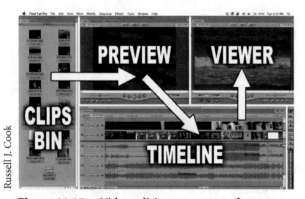

Russell J. Cook

Figure 11.15—*Video-editing computer software.*

integrated experience—sensory, emotional, and intellectual—a total aesthetic package. Analyzing the experience using the tools of the six aesthetic fields introduces an entirely different mode that brings the aesthetic experience to an abrupt halt. After analyzing the constituent parts of the experience to understand how they work, a producer cannot accurately decide the aesthetic merit of the experience without reassembling the parts into a synaesthetic whole, just as one cannot savor a dish of fine cuisine by reading its recipe. As the old proverb says, "the proof of the pudding is in the tasting."

PRODUCTION CAREERS

Before entering the competitive media production business, do a personal career inventory. You will need good personal communication skills (writing, researching, and speaking), an ability to think audiovisually, experience in media design, diversified computer hardware and software skills, broad liberal arts knowledge, and understanding of how design can address the goals of clients and employers. Most importantly, to get a job in production, you will need a production portfolio that demonstrates skill, versatility, and creativity in the professional area into which you hope to enter. Every media designer should have his or her own portfolio website, with custom Web domain name.

In addition to computer expertise, creativity, and a portfolio Web site, media production job appli-

cants need to understand how production supports the overall goals of a media organization. Media employers find such "bottom line"-oriented prospects rare but desirable, so a course in economics and/or marketing can give a competitive edge. Strategic thinking about producing to target audiences, achieve communication goals, and adding to your media organization's bottom line leads to media products that *work* and will get *you* work.

CONCLUSION

The production of content is at the core of every communications industry, from in-your-face infomercials to the most sublime love songs. Without a continuous supply of fresh, attractive, professionally-crafted entertainment and information, the mass media soon would lose their audiences. Content is a producer's symbolic expression intended to affect an anonymous mass audience in specific ways. To get messages across as intended, it is important for producers to understand how people experience mediated content.

The creation of mass-distributed content proceeds step by step. Those steps are basically the same regardless of what is produced. Although the scope is dramatically different, the steps to produce and to distribute a simple sales flyer are not unlike the steps involved in producing and distributing a complex feature film. Both can be highly collaborative processes requiring careful attention to each step in the process from concept to execution to dissemination.

Applied media aesthetics provides a set of concepts to judge the media's communication effectiveness. A producer's choices of sights, sounds, and motions must communicate effectively to the target audience in order for the media production to succeed. Because the audiovisual experience of the world through movies, television, computer games, the Web, and even e-books is so different from normal life, media producers should learn how their aesthetic choices impact the mediated experiences of their audiences. Every choice can make a difference.

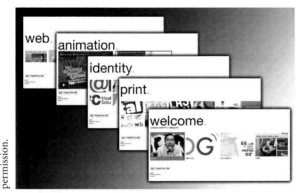

Figure 11.16—*A sample media production portfolio Web site.*

THE CULTURE AND BUSINESS OF CROSS-MEDIA PRODUCTIONS

by Espen Aarseth

INTRODUCTION

Today, the culture industries are not driven by storytelling, art, or visionary individuals. The Walt Disney era's focus on end-user experience is replaced by the entertainment industry's need to minimize risk in the face of rising cost of production and advertising, which means that no stand-alone product, whether film, game, or even comic book is worth risking the investment. The risk has to be spread across media, and beyond, to secure the bottom line.

In this paper some of the relations between media content and cross media production is explored, with the focus on movies and games, and implications for cultural theory are critically discussed. The main observation is that the medium no longer is the message (if it ever was), instead, in the words of cross-media producers David Alpert and Rick Jacobs "Movies are now no longer free-standing IP [intellectual property]; they are one piece in a marketing assault". Or, as Jay Lemke (2004) puts it: "maximizing profits compels a strategy of crossing over across as many of these media as possible."

Today, risk-adverse producers and investors seek to capitalize on the marketing by co-launching concepts through multiple media: The game, the film, the novel, the animated movie, the T-shirt, the action figure, the perfume, the amusement park ride etc. Typical examples are the *Lord of the Rings* and the *Harry Potter* cross-productions. Films like *The Matrix* are followed by a game and the animation film *Animatrix*; this has caught on to the extent that the *Chronicles of Riddick* game/film is accompanied by an animated DVD named on the package, ridiculously[1], "Ani Riddick".

Another example of this is the concept/license "Death Jr." Not a film, not a game, not a comic book, not an action figure, but all of the above, and more.[2] As a Sony PlayStation Portable (PSP) launch title. Death Jr. is a prime example of how concept licenses, rather than content, move between media platforms. This paper will examine what implications this has for the types of message that can be reproduced.

Using Cawelti's theory (1976) of popular genres, the paper will present a model of cross-media content transfer, showing what must be left behind in content/concept migrations across media, and the role and importance of games as a nexus in this exchange. Will games replace movies as the economical terminal platform (book->comic->film->game) or has game technology and the Hollywood-comparable cost of game production already redefined the cycle? Story, game or sculpture? We need to develop a critical language to address and analyze cross-media assets and their cultural cycles.

The analysis presented here is focused on comparative studies of content. To gain a full perspective on the "poetics" of cross-media productions, however, this ought to be accompanied by a study of the cross-media industry: the economics of cross-media financing, licensing, marketing and distribution.

TRANSFERRING "CONTENT" — MIGRATION, FRANCHISE, BRANDING

"Content" is a tricky word. When used it usually signals the importance of something other than that it refers to, usually the container. Those who actually focus on the "content"—say, a professor of literature or visual art, would never use the word to describe their object; the "content of Shakespeare" or "the content of Botticelli". It is used when something other than the "content" is the main focus, such as the medium and its material, technological, social or political conditions. In this paper, however, the focus is on the content-side of content, and not on the container-aspect. However, the key question is whether content can be transferred between media, so here, too, the term is mostly used negatively.

What is a crossmedia production? There are two forms, synchronous and asynchronous, which we might also see as the "strong" and "weak" versions:

Crossmedia productions that produce the media versions in parallel, and productions that take place sequentially, as a migration between media, and where the first instance usually is seen as the original content. At some point the latter becomes merely an *adaptation*, where a work is translated from one medium to another, without any plan for such transfer at the time of first creation. The distinction between adaptation and crossmedia production can be difficult to maintain, however, as many works may have been made with crossmedia migration in mind. Typically, low-cost media such as books afford a later transfer to high-cost media (movies) that often depends upon, and is initiated by, the success of the initial product, while high-cost media products afford simultaneous transfers to low-cost media (e.g. novelizations and comic book versions). It should be pointed out that crossmedia productions do not have to be entertainment, but could be documentary, journalistic or didactic instead, but the present perspective will be limited to entertainment crossmedia productions and properties that involve a game in their chain of output.

Historically, it is possible to trace crossmedia productions back to antiquity, where a play or poem in manuscript form, both intended to be performed and read, in principle could be seen as an early example. Similarly, 18th century sheet music allowing upper-class families to recreate contemporary chamber music compositions in their homes might be seen as an early parallel to the music recording industry or the home VCR revolution of the early 80es.[3] This is not the place to give an account of the history of crossmedia production, but it should be noted that the principle is old and covers many genres and types of content.

Before the advent of commercial games some three decades ago, movies were the normal terminal in the chain of crossmedia migration. An intellectual property might start as a play, a novel or a comic book, or even as a song or a painting, and would migrate up the cost chain and end up as a Hollywood movie.

An obvious example is Tracy Chevallier's novel *Girl with a Pearl Earring* (1999), based on Vermeer's 1665 painting, and turned into a movie directed by Peter Webber in 2003, with Scarlett Johansson in the title role. Here we note how Vermeer's visual style bypasses a link in the chain and informs the movie directly.

Today, however, game productions are starting to rival movie productions in terms of cost, and therefore also the position on top of the cost chain. Movies and computer games are now the most interesting cross-media pair, because in addition to being rather different in terms of cognitive and social affordances, their modes of production are more alike than most other output types. According to David Alpert and Rick Jacobs (2004), the average cost of a Hollywood film in 2003 was $63.8 million. In addition, another $39 million was used to market each movie, making the total $103M. Game productions are still less costly on average, but may start to reach comparable figures in the near future, as the "third generation consoles" (the PlayStation 3, the Xbox360 and the Nintendo Revolution) dramatically increase the need for animation labor because of the more demanding graphics resolutions and formats such as High Definition TV.

As Alpert and Jacobs (2004) point out, movies are increasingly remade, not originals:

—Novels (Harry Potter)

—Comics (Spider Man)

—Games (Tomb Raider, Doom)

—TV Shows (Starsky and Hutch)

—Remakes (Italian Job)

—Ride (Pirates of the Caribbean)

The reason for this, they claim, is that *pre-awareness* reduces risk, by making the marketing of the movie less costly and more effective. And as we see in the games industry, the same trend exists there; most bestselling titles are sequels or movie franchises, often both. Given this financial logic, where cost-recovery is the core value of the operation, certain observations can be framed about the types of transformations afforded by the crossmedia industry:

1. A single-medium launch is a lost opportunity, a flawed business plan

2. The health and timeliness of the overall production and launch is more important than the integrity of an individual piece

3. The individual pieces should add to the total franchise/brand awareness

4. Ease of transfer (crossability) becomes a critical aspect of the operation

Therefore, the somewhat romantic notion of "crossmedia content" should be replaced with the more accurate term "crossmedia branding," which may include transfer of the content to a greater or lesser degree.

How is content transferred? Does it even have to be? The logic of advertising suggests that the logo is all you need to brand successfully (e.g. "Batman candy"). However, audience acceptance is also critical to the health of the brand, and the fulfillment of audience expectations clearly depends on medium conventions and affordances. In other words, producers cannot stray too far from audience expectations if they wish to keep the brand healthy. This was clearly seen in Tim Burton's risky lead casting of the comic actor Michael Keaton in the first *Batman* movie, which was met with significant pre-launch skepticism, especially among fans of the comic book. In that case the product was strong enough to succeed, but a less successful example may be found in the game *Enter the Matrix* (2003) whose greatest disappointment may have been the simple fact that the audience's expectations of a *Matrix* game franchise far exceeded the actual game's ability to outshine its competition, especially since *Max*

READING NOTES

_____

_____

_____

_____

_____

Payne, two years earlier, had implemented the "bullet time" effect of the first movie. Although *Enter The Matrix* made a profit, it was also the most highly shop-returned game ever, and it did not get great reviews, which made the license owner, Warner Bros., unhappy enough to suggest that licensed games that did not receive good review ratings would be penalized by higher royalty fees, to prevent brand damage.

WHAT TRANSFERS?

To fully investigate the aesthetic mechanisms of content transfer, many examples are needed. In this paper, relatively few are used, so the conclusions reached must remain tentative and in need of further verification. Clearly, a content migration from one medium to another depends on a number of factors, making each case special. However, some general observations can be made, even at the outset: Adaptations are not always successful. Financial success can sometimes be due to substantial marketing and pre-awareness, rather than high quality, but at the cost of possible brand damage. And since production companies have a fairly realistic sense of what will work, they select projects with the best chances for success. In the film-to-game business, it is easy to spot the pattern: Only certain types of film become games. Keywords here are action, science fiction, horror, war; in other words, spatial spectacle. Interestingly, games don't seem to afford the transfer of many genres that we recognize from book-to-film: romance, psycho-drama, period/historical, biography. Successful book-to-film transfers such as *Remains of the Day* or comic-book to film transfers such as *Ghostworld* will never make the leap to game, and for good reason: the narrative affinities and affordances shared by books and films are not shared by games. In other words, we are not witnessing crossmedia storytelling, but rather crossmedia spectacle-making.

One interesting example is Walt Disney's last amusement park ride from Disneyland, *Pirates of the Caribbean* (1973). This is a boat ride through a spectacular series of tableaus, showing (among other things) grinning skeletons, mounds of gold and treasure, imprisoned pirates, a sea to land cannon battle, the sacking of a town, and pirates celebrating and singing the famous "Yo ho, yo ho! A pirate's life for me!" In time for its 30-year anniversary, Disney released a film (subtitled *The Curse of the Black Pearl*) *and* a game bearing the same title, but without a sub-title. Comparing these three works, however reveals that there is almost nothing in common between any of them, except the title and the brand logo. The characters of the film, staring Johnny Depp, Keira Knightley, and Orlando Bloom, do not figure in either the game or the ride. A few individual tableaus from the ride, such as the cannon battle and the jailed pirates trying to lure the keys from a dog, can be seen briefly in the film, but most of the tableaus are not transferred. The film tells a story of love, inheritance, and release from immortality, themes not found in the ride or the game. In fact, the only element from the film found in the game is the voice of Keira Knightley, used as voiceover. This is understandable given the fact that the game was commissioned by Disney very late in the production process, and was conceived independently as the follow-up to a strategy/RPG (role playing game) hybrid called *Sea Dogs*, and was originally destined to become *Sea Dogs II*. More striking, then, is the lack of overlap between the ride and the film. Even rides with "narrative" content, such as the *Peter Pan* or the *Winnie-the-Pooh* rides in Disneyland, or *The Mummy* or *Jurassic Park* rides at Universal Studios in Hollywood, do not recapture tellable story moments that would be associated with the books or the films of the same name. The rides depend on pre-awareness of the narrative, but offers nothing narrative in return. Amusement park rides, obviously, are not narratives, but obey other laws of presentation. To get a deeper perspective of this, let us turn to popular fiction theorist John Cawelti, who makes a distinction between two levels of popular fiction, 1) the level of

READING NOTES

310

cultural convention, where we find the stereotypes, characters, the clichés and the environment (e.g. Europe in the Middle Ages, the Wild West), and 2) the level of the underlying structure, which is a series of events (boy meets girls, boy loses girl etc). Only the latter is where the story is actually told, but the amusement park rides and the games contain the first level without really affording the latter.

This can be seen even more clearly when we look at the transfers that actually work across the story-game frontier. Book-film-game transfers do exist, and perhaps the best examples here are the *Lord of the Rings* and *Harry Potter* franchises. If we study these carefully, we see that all elements that transfer between book and film may not travel all the way to the game. The actual events of the books are usually transferred reasonably faithfully to the films, except where length dictates that elements may be removed to shorten the viewing time. In the games however, the storylines from the books/films are not recapitulated faithfully, if at all.

Again, Cawelti's model applies, with the layer of cultural conventions being transferred, but the underlying narrative structure not at all, or bent almost out of recognition. Playing Gandalf in the Electronic Arts 2003 *Return of the King* game involves zapping orcs endlessly and performing ninja-like moves with sword and staff, but with none of the inventiveness and dignity that the narrative Gandalf would have displayed. Are we playing Gandalf, or merely a Gandalf-like puppet? On the other hand, one would also have hoped that the rich, beautiful world of Middle-earth would have been more freely explorable in the game, but instead we are served a very linear action corridor, a unicursal labyrinth that offers as much individual choice as a train ride.

Harry Potter games such as the *Chamber of Secrets* (2002) are more openly explorable, since one can wander around Hogwarth and explore in a multicursal

fashion, but here also the transfer of narrative events from the book are nowhere as faithful as in the movie. Furthermore, the main game event elements, such as collecting jelly beans and fighting various monsters, are not derived from the narrative works, and correspond to nothing in them. Again, Cawelti can be used to describe a transfer that, like chemical warfare, kills the people (or turns them into brainless zombies) but leaves the buildings untouched.

A possible alternative to the sequential media migration can be found in the crossmedia franchise *Death, jr*. *Death, jr*. is not a movie, comic book, game, T-shirt, action figure, belt-buckle, or piece of jewelry, but rather, all of the above. *Death, jr*. started life as a game engine demo, and was soon licenced for several simultaneous media productions. Even before any audience had gotten to know this new phenomenon, it made money on cross-licencing rights. The idea behind Death, jr. is very simple: he is just a normal kid going to school, but with a very special father, the grim reaper. Death, jr. is the logical offspring of crossmedia productions and one which offers a flexibility of freedom that already established franchises cannot match, but in terms of pre-awareness, it is still quite a risk. Death, jr. offers an alternative model to the other examples here, which should throw new light on the evolution of the culture industry into the age of crossmedia. Unfortunately, the PSP game, launched in August 2005, was not a success, so the future for the Death Jr franchise looks a bit grim at the time of writing.

LOST IN TRANSLATION

According to David Alpert and Rick Jacobs, there are three things to look for in the evaluation of a possible film-to-game transfer: 1) Iconic characters with high recognition value; 2) an interesting universe, and 3) a "high concept" that would translate into a gameplay mechanic. If you have all three, you may be able to

Element	Ride to movie	Book to movie	Movie to game	Game to movie
Storyline	No	Ok	Not really	No
Events	Hardly	Ok	Hardly	Ok
Universe	Ok	Ok	Ok	Ok
Character	No	Ok	Partly	Expanded

make an interesting game, but it is still difficult. What is lacking from this formula, of course, is story. Partly because you don't really need it, if you have these key ingredients, and partly because, as the *LOTR* and *Harry Potter* examples show, you can't really use it anyway. You can transfer characters (up to a point) and universes (unproblematically), and any kind of action gimmick such as bullet time; but for games to work, gameplay, not story, is key. A predefined story will mess up the game if followed too slavishly. Therefore the method is to extract the spectacular, the spatial and the idiosyncratic, and develop events and waypoints that will nod to the story of the original work, while keeping a firm eye on the bottom line of gameplay quality.

CROSSMEDIA TRANSFER TABLE

Previous commentators on crossmedia (e.g. Jenkins 2003, Klastrup and Tosca 2004) have pointed out that "world" is a key transferable element, especially when it comes to game transfers. Here I have preferred to use the more open word "universe", as it allows for the possibility of only a rudimentary compatibility between the content of two productions. However, even here, the term is a metaphor at best. There is no "world" or "universe" as such being transferred between media platforms, only partial and more or less faithfully represented elements. The orcs and

elves of Blizzard's *Warcraft* universe is clearly not identical to the orcs and elves of Tolkien's Middle-earth, so Cawelti's idea of a "cultural convention" seems more appropriate when describing the kinship between the various Tolkien-derived (and semi-derived) universes, or even between the universes by a single creator, such as Richard Garriott's various *Ultima* games.

CONCLUSION

This preliminary study shows that crossmedia transfer happens relatively smoothly between forms that are alike, such as books and films, and less so between forms that have strong structural differences, such as amusement park rides, games and narratives. There may be examples that contradict this or tell a different story, but the economically grounded practice of the entertainment industry gives a good indication of what is and is not viable. Cawelti's model provides a very relevant indicator of what can and cannot be translated easily, and is a good way to get past the confusing notion of storytelling, and instead focus on, and attempting to understand, universe-building, character-construction, and the translation of concepts into media-specific mechanisms. This way, we can also begin to see what traditional authors have been doing when they construct the universes they use to grow their narratives.

READING NOTES

_____

_____

_____

_____

_____

Crossmedia productions come in many shapes, and depend on a large number of arts: storytelling, game design, and concept development among them. But a good sense for business may be the most important one. To understand this market-driven logic, the research strategy seems simple enough: Follow the money!

ENDNOTES

1. The animated short film directed by Peter Chung was called "Dark Fury" (2004) and "ani Riddick" completely misses the elegant wordplay of the "animatrix" title, but the logic of pre-awareness dictated an Animatrix-like name, to signal a similar relationship between this product and the main films.

2. http://www.deathjr.com/

3. About the latter, see Wasser 2001.

REFERENCES

Alpert, David and Rick Jacobs, 2004. "Videogames & Licensing in the Hollywood Film Market" Presentation at the Korea Games Conference, Seoul, October 16th.

Cawelti, John (1976). *Adventure, Mystery, and Romance. Formula Stories as Art and Popular Culture.* The University of Chicago Press.

Jenkins, Henry (2003). "Transmedia Storytelling" in *Technology Review.* Boston: MIT Press. January 15. http://www.technologyreview.com/articles/03/01/wo_jenkins011503.asp?p=1

Klastrup, Lisbeth and Susana Tosca (2004), "Transmedial worlds—rethinking cyberworld design" in Proceedings, International Conference on Cyberworlds 2004. IEEEE Compuater Society, Los Alamitos, California. http://www.itu.dk/people/klastrup/klastruptosca_transworlds.pdf

Lemke, Jay (2004). "Critical Analysis across Media: Games, Franchises, and the New Cultural Order" presented at the First International Conference on Critical Discourse Analysis, Valencia 2004 http://www-personal.umich.edu/~jaylemke/papers/Franchises/Valencia-CDA-Franchises.htm

Wasser, Frederick (2001). *Veni, Vidi, Video: The Hollywood Empire and the VCR.*

Austin: University of Texas Press.

READING NOTES

Section

4

© Florian ISPAS, 2010. Used under License from Shutterstock, Inc.

MEDIA INDUSTRIES AND CAREERS

Chapter 12

Media Industries

"It is difficult, indeed dangerous, to underestimate the huge changes this (digital) revolution will bring or the power of developing technologies to build and destroy—not just companies, but whole countries."

—RUPERT MURDOCH, CHAIRMAN AND CHIEF EXECUTIVE OFFICER, NEWS CORP.

Rupert Murdoch's News Corporation is one of the largest companies in the world. It owns major newspaper, magazine, broadcasting, cable, publishing, and Internet properties on five continents. He and his company are leaders in trying to navigate media industries through the shift to digital information and networks.

Throughout most of their histories in the pre-digital, analog world, the communications industries developed more or less independently, with their own business structures, distribution systems, and production cultures. The individual media industries grew according to the social and regulatory environments that existed when the medium came into its own. For example, newspapers started during the revolutionary era, when New World colonists were fighting England's interference in their lives and businesses. That spirit of independence was codified in the First Amendment to the United States Constitution (1791), which secured the role of the free press as an independent government watchdog. Consequently, newspapers and magazines developed in the United States with little government control, as opposed to other places in the world where censorship and government ownership are the norm. The United States shines as a country where freedom of the press is a living concept.

In contrast to the print media, the U.S. broadcast media evolved with an expectation of government regulation and control of content. Broadcasting spent its infancy during the 1930s and 1940s, a time when the federal government had a growing presence in everyday matters. The Federal Communications Commission (FCC) was established in 1934 to regulate broadcast radio and television. The FCC imposes fines for what it deems unsuitable programming on the grounds that the broadcasting frequencies belong to all citizens, and therefore broadcasters must operate "in the public interest." When cable television matured much later, during the 1980s, deregulation was in favor, so cable enjoyed much greater freedom from government regulation of content as compared to radio and television.

Since the early 1990s, however, the boundaries separating the traditional mass-media industries have all but disappeared. People listen to music and read newspapers on cellular telephones, watch television on iPods, play video games on high-definition television, listen to radio on computers, and read books on handheld devices such as the Amazon Kindle and the Apple iPad—often using several of these devices simultaneously. The days of distributing media content exclusively over one communications channel are long gone.

This chapter provides a tour of the various communications industries within the context of media convergence and differing social and regulatory environments. The chapter embraces the following two learning aims regarding U.S. media industries, which are to

- sketch key moments and actors in the histories of different media industries, and

- explain how and why the media industries converged.

Required Reading: In the companion reading for this chapter, media scholar Mark Deuze describes how convergence of the traditional media industries and new audience-participatory cultures are changing the media landscape. Media businesses have moved away from the old industrial model of manufacturing and distributing media content and toward a model of creative networking. Audiences have a bigger, more active, and more influential role than ever before in deciding what media content is produced, how it is delivered, and how it can be customized for the audience's own purposes.

NEWSPAPERS

Newspapers were the dominant mass medium throughout most of U.S. history. From its peak in the 1940s, the newspaper industry began to experience an attrition in the number of newspapers published and the percentage of the population that read them, increasing operating costs, and competition for advertising revenues from television. Many newspapers, particularly afternoon editions, went out of business, merged with competitors, or were bought up by out-of-town chains. Currently most U.S. cities and towns have only one daily newspaper left.

The earliest newspapers in the British North American colonies offered mostly international news from England and suffered censorship from the governmental authorities. Most of them did not last long. The first multi-page newspaper in America was published in 1690 by Benjamin Harris, who had previously edited a newspaper in London. Called *Publick Occurrences Both Forreign and Domestick*, it was shut down after one day because Harris had not obtained a license from the government to print it. In 1721, James Franklin, Benjamin Franklin's brother, started The *New England Courant*, first printed in 1721 by James Franklin. It was one of the first independent newspapers in the American colonies. Franklin soon was involved in a number of controversies including criticizing the government for promoting inoculating people against small pox, while failing to protect Boston citizens from pirates. It was shut down in 1727. Nevertheless, newspapers soon appeared in most of the colonies, and larger cities enjoyed reading several different papers. These early newspapers were usually no more than four pages long. They were filled primarily with short news items.

One paper, John Peter Zenger's *New York Weekly Journal*, which began and printing in 1733, would help to build a foundation for freedom of the press. Zenger, a young German-born printer, began criticizing the colony's governor, who, in turn, had Zenger arrested for seditious libel. At the printer's trial in August 1775, the judge instructed the jury that under the law's definition of seditious libel, criticism of the government was libelous, even if it was true. The jury ignored the judge's instructions and found Zenger innocent.

Newspapers gained readers when Americans started debating separation from England—an issue that the colonists saw as essential to their lives. When the Revolutionary War broke out, dozens of papers were being published. By the time the war ended in 1783, an estimated 43 newspapers were operating. The founders of the United States felt that a free and unencumbered press was considered critical to self-government. Consequently, the First Amendment to the U.S. Constitution guaranteed freedom of speech and the press and the right of the people to assemble peacefully.

By the end of the century, fueled by further technological advances, newspapers enjoyed explosive growth in the number of papers and readers. The first cylinder press, invented in Germany by Frederick Koenig, was first used in the United States in 1825. By 1835, steam engines were used to drive presses, making it possible to push circulations even higher. What was impressive was that newspapers provided inexpensive information to their readers. Advances in mechanical papermaking technology dramatically increased the availability of newsprint at low costs. Papers would cost as little as one cent. "Penny press" newspapers meant that average working people could buy a paper, greatly expanding potential reading audiences. The *New York Herald* in 1835 was selling 20,000 copies a day. The 1850 census catalogued 2,526 different newspapers.

Publishers reached out to all Americans, regardless of class, reflecting a more egalitarian philosophy. The *Baltimore Sun's* motto was "It Shines for All."

As readership and income rose, newspapers started building their staffs, hiring correspondents. Newspapers started covering trials, especially if the case involved sordid events, such as a murder. Coverage of war also increased with correspondents reporting on the Mexican and Civil Wars.

Newspaper reporting took a major step forward with the invention of the telegraph. Samuel Morse's device enabled newspapers to report on out-of-town news developments within days or even hours, instead of weeks. With the successful completion of a transatlantic cable in 1866, American newspapers could print news from Europe with similar promptness.

Moreover, as mass circulation transformed newspapers into valuable businesses with large staffs, they started to be seen less as vehicles for one person's opinions and more as providers of information. The rise of the wire services, which distributed stories to many different papers, helped reduce the emphasis on personal opinion in news stories. Newspapers began to see themselves as vehicles for objective journalism.

Despite outrageous reporting on many occasions, newspaper reporters and editors started thinking of themselves as part of a profession with its own standards. The first school of journalism was founded at the University of Missouri in 1904. The American Society of Newspaper Editors drafted the "Canons of Journalism" in 1923, which included this dictum: "News reports should be free from opinion or bias of any kind."

Besides the telegraph, one other technological advance first used in 1886 would greatly affect the newspaper industry: the introduction of the Linotype machine, which would improve dramatically the ability of newspapers to quickly create entire pages of type. Linotype machines were designed to speed up several of the processes in printing. Before this, workers known as typesetters, or "compositors," would have to spend many hours assembling words by picking up one piece of type at a time, and then return the type—one piece at a time—to the cases when printing was finished.

The Linotype eliminated the necessity for individual pieces of type by creating an entire line of type that could be quickly stacked with other lines to create a news article. The machine's operator would use a keyboard to call into position individual characters, punctuation marks, and the spaces between words. The Linotype enabled newspapers to print several editions during the day.

Newspapers commonly had an early edition, sometimes called a "bulldog" edition, and then later editions as the day proceeded. Each edition would use a color—usually red, blue, or green—to denote how late into the evening they were printed. Each edition could be changed within hours when there were breaking stories or if front-page stories needed to be updated to reflect new developments. Newspapers could bring much more immediacy to their stories.

Another hallmark of the new U.S. newspaper industry has been the growth of newspaper chains, which gave publishers such as William Randolph Hearst tremendous influence over political and social issues.

Hearst started his chain in San Francisco and then acquired another paper in New York. Eventually, his chain would expand to 30 papers nationwide, giving him enormous influence over public opinion. Hearst is perhaps best known for pushing American public opinion in favor of a war with Spain in 1898, using so-called "yellow" journalism—sensationalized stories with exaggerated and dubious facts—to convince the American public of the need to invade Spanish possessions around the world, such as the Philippines and Cuba.

Those early newspaper chains were big for their times, but they pale in comparison to some of today's newspaper conglomerates. Gannett, which is best known for publishing USA Today, has 84 daily newspapers and nearly 850 magazines and nondaily publications, and operates 23 television stations in the United States. However, in the first half of the 20th century, the news-paper chains could hold sway over the public through their ability to publish newspapers with the same viewpoint in key U.S. markets.

Even when there were large numbers of daily newspapers circulating in major cities, many groups felt these papers were not representing their points of view and interests. One solution, especially for immigrant groups who were still more comfortable in another language, was to publish newspapers of their own. One of the first foreign-language newspapers in America was a German newspaper that Ben Franklin helped start in Germantown, near Philadelphia. Early Spanish-language newspapers appeared in New Orleans in 1808 and Texas in 1813.

The first Native American newspaper, the *Cherokee Phoenix*, was printed in Georgia in 1828. The *Jewish Daily Forward*, printed in Yiddish, first appeared in New York in 1897 but was printing local editions in eleven other cities by 1923. With the waves of immigration to U.S. cities in the first decades of the 20th century came an increased market for foreign-language papers. African Americans also have sought alternatives to mainstream newspapers, beginning with *Freedom's Journal* and the *North Star*. Ida B. Wells-Barnett fought for the rights of blacks and women in the paper *Free Speech* in Memphis and then in the *New York Age* and the *Chicago Conservator*. The *Chicago Defender*, a major black newspaper, began publishing in 1905, the *Amsterdam News* in New York in 1909, and the *Pittsburgh Courier* in 1910.

These papers provided news stories and features that were simply not available in the mainstream papers. When Jackie Robinson became the first black baseball player in the Major Leagues, the *Courier* expanded its sports to make sure readers in Pittsburgh and outside the city could read about the baseball star's performances.

Among the early women's-rights newspapers were the *Lily*, which was published by Amelia Bloomer from 1849 to 1859, and Elizabeth Cady Stanton's the *Revolution*, from 1868 to 1871, for which Susan B. Anthony served as business manager.

The anti–Vietnam War protests and the cultural upheavals of the 1960s also produced a number of colorful and experimental alternative newspapers, including the *Berkeley Barb*, the *San Francisco Oracle*, the *Seed* in Chicago, the *East Village Other* in New York, and the *Los Angeles Free Press*. The "granddaddy" of alternative papers is New York's *Village Voice*, which was launched in 1955. The *Voice* provided a platform for many great journalists, giving them leeway to write in a vibrant, exciting style that came to be known as New Journalism.

By the second half of the 20th century, newspapers started seeing a decline in readership. Facing competition from television and other sources, many papers were forced to close. The United States had 267 fewer newspapers in 1990 than it had in 1940. By 1992, only 37 cities in the United States had separately-owned, competing daily newspapers. A UNESCO survey in the 1980s found that the United States had slipped to 19th among countries the world in per-capita newspaper circulation, down from its number one ranking in the 19th century.

In recent years, publishers have tried different approaches to make newspapers more viable. One of the more notable efforts was the Gannett Corporation's launching in 1982 of *USA Today*. Gannett's concept was to produce a more user-friendly newspaper than the competition. *USA Today* emphasizes shorter, punchier stories. Rarely, if ever, does a news story jump to another page. The paper also makes extensive use of graphics. Critics referred to *USA Today* as "McPaper," in a reference to McDonald's hamburger fare. However, the newspaper has influenced some competitors to follow its approach, and *USA Today* remains a major player in the newspaper business.

The economic recession in 2008 hit many newspapers hard. Traditional sources of advertising dried up quickly and several newspapers shuttered their doors. Others had to reduce the size of their newspapers in every dimension—thinner paper, narrower pages, less space for news, and a smaller staff covering a shrinking geographic area and range of topics. For example, during 2009, the *Baltimore Sun* cut the size of its food section to two pages. The section's editors were forced to forego publishing recipes for the first time in the paper's 173-year history. The section editor received an outpouring of angry complaints from long-time readers.

Other papers are trying to resolve their space problems by having certain topics covered by a Web site, rather than in print. The *Washington Post* is experimenting with this approach for two very different topics. To provide adequate coverage of swimming as a sport, the newspaper has created a Web site, Reachforthewall.com, that is devoted to competitive swimming news. In a similar vein, the *Post* is expanding its coverage of health issues through an interactive Web site, Washingtonpost.com/wellness.

Web-based publications eliminate much of the traditional production and distribution staff. A Web-only paper cuts out a number of individuals, sharply reducing costs. Some of the more successful Web-based magazines, such as Salon.com and TheDailyBeast.com, maintain small full-time staffs and rely for much of their content on independent bloggers—the Web's equivalent of free-lance reporters.

Looking toward the future, many people are espousing alternative business models for the newspaper industry. One suggestion is to allow newspapers to convert from for-profit corporations into non-profit organizations, similar to radio stations affiliated to National Public Radio. Non-profit status would mean the newspapers would be exempt from some federal and state taxes, which would boost their revenues.

The non-profit approach has sparked a debate over whether the government would be subsidizing newspapers. However, the government has been indirectly subsidizing print media for decades by authorizing reduced postal rates for sending the publications through the U.S. Postal Service.

TELEVISION

Throughout the late 1800s, as telegraphy became commonplace and the telephone began to make its way into the marketplace, inventors began to think about sending moving images over electrical wires as well. In 1884, a German engineering student named Paul Nipkow developed and patented a mechanical device that could transmit images. In the early 1900s, Philo Farnsworth and the Russian émigré Vladimir Zworkin, working independently, began exploring how to transmit images electronically using vacuum tubes. And in 1927, the Bell Telephone Company and the U.S. Department of Commerce conducted the first long distance use of television that took place between Washington, D.C., and New York City. That same year, Farnsworth filed patent papers for a complete television system and the following year, the Federal Radio Commission issued its first television broadcasting license to Charles Jenkins, who discontinued developing a mechanical television system and adopted the electronic system devised by Farnsworth and Zworkin. Jenkins broadcast the first television commercial in 1930 on station W3XK in Wheaton, Maryland.

Television remained an experimental technology through much of the 1930s. But David Sarnoff, president of the Radio Corporation of America, parent of the largest radio network in the country, realized the potential of television as an entertainment medium and poured millions of dollars into its technical refinement, despite much diminished economic activity during the Great Depression. RCA premiered its electronic television at the 1939 New York World's Fair, and its subsidiary, NBC, began regularly scheduled telecasting. NBC's chief competitor, CBS, followed soon after with its own television broadcasting.

© DeshaCAM, 2010. Shutterstock Inc.

In those days, the manufacturers of television sets in the United States—RCA, General Electric, DuMont, Philco, and a handful of others—produced the programming, literally inventing the medium. Initially, television entertainment was a hybrid of recycled radio dramas and stage productions. However, as young authors started writing new plays specifically for television, some great productions emerged. New shows such as *The Actors' Studio* originated from primitive but innovative two-camera television studios located primarily in New York City. These shows would showcase many young actors destined to become movie stars, such as James Dean, Paul Newman, Burgess Meredith, and Marlon Brando. Some of the outstanding writers who wrote for television included Rod Serling, Paddy Chayevsky, Gore Vidal, and Reginald Rose. These writers and others would go on to enjoy great success as novelists and screenwriters.

Perhaps the quintessential Golden Era television drama is Paddy Chayevsky's *Marty* on The Philco Television Playhouse on NBC, which starred Rod Steiger and Nancy Marchland, later known as Olivia, the mother of Tony Soprano on the groundbreaking HBO series *The Sopranos*. Steiger later would win an Oscar for his portrayal of a Southern police chief in the powerful feature film *In the Heat of the Night*.

Marty is a love story about two ordinary characters, Marty and Clare, and their mundane lives. The title character is a butcher who lives with his mother. In a famous scene, Marty and his buddy plan their evening. The dialogue consists of the two saying to each other, "What do you want to do?" "I dunno. What do you want to do?" This strong, stark, realistic type of drama anticipated series such as *The Wire* shown on cable decades later. Shortly after its phenomenal television success, *Marty* became a successful feature film in 1955, which won Chayevsky his first Academy Award for best screenplay.

The Golden Era also included some memorable comedy shows, such as Sid Cesar's *Show of Shows*, which became the role model for later sketch comedy shows such as *Saturday Night Live*. Some early hits, such as *I Love Lucy*, are still being watched today through reruns. Jackie Gleason popularized comedies based on the daily struggles of working-class people with *The Honeymooners*. Stand-up comic Milton Berle became television's first superstar by hosting the comedy-variety show *Texaco Star Theater*. Berle was so popular that he became known as "Mr. Television." Historians credit Berle's popularity for a huge spike in the sale of television sets.

By the mid-1950s, television audiences started to grow tremendously. At the time, viewers could choose from shows on four national networks—NBC, CBS, ABC, and DuMont (which would later become the basis for the Fox network). In addition to a hugely successful entertainment medium, television began to have a major impact on politics.

In 1952 vice presidential candidate Richard Nixon became the first politician to use the relatively new medium to address the American public directly, saving his public career in the process. He took to the air to defend himself from accusations that he had misused campaign funds. He looked the camera square in the eye and claimed that his life was an open book for the public to inspect. His wife Pat even wore a plain, respectable, Republican cloth coat, he said. Facetiously, he admitted that he had received one gift that he refused to return: a cocker black-and-white spaniel puppy that his daughter named "Checkers." The message was clear: he was one of the people.

Television's audience reach saved Nixon's political career. There was no way he could have gotten the same access simultaneously to millions of American homes through the print media. The event, which became known the "Checkers Speech," established a precedent for future contrite politicians, entertainers, and athletics to deliver the own *mea culpa* on the small screen.

Television was not so kind to Nixon in 1960, when he was perceived to have lost the first televised presidential campaign debates to John Kennedy. However, having learned his lessons well, he would go on to use television advertising effectively in winning the U.S. presidency in 1968.

Coverage of public affairs and government gave television its credibility as a source for news. When television started covering live events, it captivated American viewers during historic moments. One such moment, the Army–McCarthy hearings, would prove emphatically that live television was a powerful tool for informing the public.

Three months after the irresponsible red-baiting of Senator Joseph McCarthy of Wisconsin was exposed and excoriated by Edward R. Murrow on the CBS television news program *See It Now*, the senator continued to make unsubstantiated attacks on his political enemies. McCarthy went so far as to accuse the U.S. Army of Communist infiltration, when it refused to give special treatment to one of his legislative aides, who had been drafted. However, public opinion was beginning to swing against McCarthy, and the military refused to be intimidated and hired a prominent Boston attorney, Joseph N. Welch.

The Army–McCarthy Senate hearings were broadcast "gavel to gavel" on the ABC and DuMont networks from April 22 to June 17, 1954. The nationally televised congressional inquiry became a landmark in the emerging nexus of television and American politics. The 36 days of hearings created unprecedented drama on television as Welch challenged McCarthy's repeated charges that the Army was harboring Communists. The climax of the hearing came on June 9, when McCarthy insinuated that a young associate of Welch was a Communist sympathizer. It was the last straw for Welch, who responded to the senator's slurs with this famous reply:

"Until this moment, Senator, I think I never gauged your cruelty or recklessness … . Have you no sense of decency, sir, at long last? Have you left no sense of decency?" The unscripted confrontation showed that television could be a major force in national politics and could serve the public interest. The importance of the broadcasts was not lost on the press. *The New York Times* television critic Jack Gould wrote: "Last week may be remembered as the week that broadcasting recaptured its soul."

The networks and other programmers imported popular entertainment genres from radio, such as Westerns, soap operas, situation comedies, and dramas featuring doctors, lawyers, cops, and detectives. Based on a popular CBS radio serial, the hugely popular television Western, *Gunsmoke,* starring B-movie actor James Arness, spurred many imitators. Arness' Marshall Matt Dillon kept the peace in Dodge City for at total of 635 weekly episodes over two decades beginning in 1955—the longest running, live action primetime drama on American television.

Gunsmoke's production process was typical of many network shows of the period. Arness' own company, Filmaster Productions, filmed the show on movie studio lots and sold it to the network. Filmaster produced other hit Westerns for CBS, including *Have Gun Will Travel* and *Death Valley Days.* Shows such as *Gunsmoke* signaled Hollywood's strategy to cope with competition from the networks: if you can't beat 'em, produce their programs. This cross-media cooperation between movies and television initiated a trend toward media convergence that eventually resulted in the vertically-integrated media conglomerates that rule the 21st century media world.

With technological improvements such as videotape recording and electronic editing, television matured into the dominant entertainment medium, sometimes capturing huge audiences. In 1967 the final episode of the ABC dramatic series *The Fugitive*—in which Dr. Richard Kimble, played by David Janssen, finally caught up with his wife's killer after a five-year chase—captured 46 percent of households and a 72 percent share, a record that stood until the "Who Done It" episode of *Dallas* grabbed a 53 rating and 76 share in 1980, which in turn was eclipsed by *M*A*S*H* ("Goodbye and Farewell," 60 share and 77 share) in 1983.

The premise of *The Fugitive* was very similar to a notorious real-life case of Dr. Sam Sheppard, an Ohio doctor who was convicted of murdering his wife. In 1966 the U.S. Supreme Court ruled that Sheppard had not received a fair trial, setting an important precedent in media law and leading to the doctor's release from prison and eventual acquittal. Television's fugitive still had another year to run before he would be cleared.

The Fugitive's producer, the highly successful Quinn Martin, had a record string of 21 straight years of primetime shows.

The CBS primetime line-up became dominated by situation comedies on a rural theme appealing to older audiences, such as *The Beverly Hillbillies, Mayberry R.F.D, Petticoat Junction,* and *Green Acres.* Responding to advertisers who were looking for younger, more affluent urban viewers, the network axed all of these highly-rated shows in 1971 in what industry analysts nicknamed the "Rural Purge." They were replaced with a new, hipper line-up in established programming genres, including *All in the Family, Barnaby Jones, The Bob Newhart Show, Cannon, Kojak, The Mary Tyler Moore Show,* and *M*A*S*H.* The new shows, plus top-rated news programs *CBS Evening News with Walter Cronkite* and *60 Minutes,* made CBS the ratings king throughout the 1970s.

In the mid-1980s, broadcast television experienced is own competition crisis. Ratings for over-the-air programming dropped as viewers switched to the new cable services, such as WTBS, HBO, and CNN. The networks slashed their budgets and looked for lower-cost programming. News magazine shows and reality-based shows such as *Entertainment Tonight, Dateline NBC, Who Wants to Be a Millionaire?,* and *American Idol* eventually emerged as their solution.

The cable networks began to offer their own productions, trumpeting high quality and daring subject matter, such as HBO's *The Sopranos.* The resulting competition for viewers between broadcast and cable spawned a string of slickly-produced dramas, such as *X-Files* on the Fox Network and *ER* and *West Wing* on NBC. Situation comedies such as *Taxi, Cheers, Frasier, Seinfeld, Friends,* and *Sex and the City* garnered large audiences and launched the movie careers of their stars. The distinction between the networks and the cable services blurred in the 1990s as they joined forces within media conglomerates, and as more households got cable.

Another genre of television programming capitalized on the open-ended nature of live television. From the first U.S. sports telecast in 1939, a college football game on NBC, televised sports experienced a steady rise of popularity and advertising revenues, pushed technological advances such as instant replay and infographics, established professional football and basketball as American institutions, and made athletes into highly paid entertainers.

American football's frenetic pace and visual spectacle turned out to be a perfect fit for television, whereas the radio-era American pastime of baseball seemed boring to many when they watched it on the small screen. When the American and National Football Leagues merged to leverage their incomes from broadcast rights in the 1960s, the new Super Bowl championship game became an annual global media spectacle that generated record global audiences and advertising revenues. Football went primetime when ABC's programming genius Roone Arledge, creator of the award-winning *ABC Wide World of Sports,* launched *Monday Night Football* in 1970.

Cable news came into its own during the 1990 Persian Gulf War, when CNN reporters Bernard Shaw, John Holliman, and Peter Arnett broadcasted live from the ninth floor of a downtown Baghdad hotel, as U.S. bombs rained down on the city. Cable news became the American public's preferred source for news, as it was when the World Trade Center and the Pentagon were devastated on 9/11, when U.S. forces invaded Iraq in 2003, when Hurricane Katrina devastated New Orleans in 2005, and when Michael Jackson died in 2009.

MOVIES

Playing tough-guy detective Sam Spade, Humphrey Bogart uttered the classic line: [This is] "the stuff that dreams are made of." He was referring to a solid gold statue in the shape of a falcon. However, the line also seems to sum up the meaning of motion pictures. People see their dreams and nightmares in the movies; often, they also see their own lives and the lives of their ancestors.

Movie technology has evolved from short silent films to three-hour epics that create the illusion of reality through stereoscopic, three-dimensional effects. Throughout this evolution, the medium has fulfilled a variety of needs and gratifications for the audience. Movies reflect society's issues, addressing them in a way that has sparked social change. Films have served as propaganda and as an education tool. They also have entertained, which is probably their primary role. During the Great Depression, people went to movie theaters in droves to watch light comedies and musicals as a way to forget their own problems. A theater filled with people laughing at movies such as the Marx Brothers' *Duck Soup* or Preston Sturges' *Sullivan's Travels* could be golden.

Movie production had it roots on the east coast. By 1908 most of the key patents were owned by the Motion Picture Patents Company, also known as the Edison Trust. The Trust made it difficult for independent producers to compete. To escape the trust, several producers moved to a small town outside of Los Angeles called Hollywood. The perpetually sunny skies there provided ideal conditions for filming. The rest is history. Hollywood become America's film capital, while movie actors such as Mary Pickford, Charlie Chaplin, and Douglas Fairbanks became better known and more beloved than political leaders.

Far away, in Moscow and Berlin, Russian and German filmmakers were experimenting with

© BLANKartist, 2010. Shutterstock Inc.

serious themes and innovative techniques. The Russians were using motion pictures as a form of propaganda, such as Sergei Eisenstein's *Battleship Potemkin*, which recreated a workers' uprising in pre-Revolutionary Russia. Eisenstein's theories of montage influenced later filmmakers such as Brian De Palma *(The Untouchables)* and Michael Mann *(Heat)*. German audiences were captivated by expressive use of light and shadow in films such as *The Cabinet of Dr. Caligari* and *Metropolis*, the first horror film and the first science-fiction film, respectively.

American filmmakers perfected visual storytelling during the pre-sound era with classics such as D.W. Griffith's *Birth of a Nation*, Lon Chaney's *Phantom of the Opera*, and Buster Keaton's *The General*. Perhaps the greatest director and movie star of the era, Charlie Chaplin, eschewed dialogue for his first sound film, *Modern Times*, because he felt that the sound of speech would detract from his Tramp character's universal appeal.

Sound on film catapulted the Hollywood movie studios to new heights of profitability and power. MGM's Louis B. Mayer and the other studio CEOs ran their corporations as virtual fiefdoms, controlling every aspect of talent acquisition and development, production, and distribution. It became known as the era of the producer. Stars such as Bette Davis and Clark Gable worked under ironclad contracts and could be suspended for not accepting assigned parts.

Just when the studios began to face competition from the new force in entertainment media—television—the Supreme Court in 1948 ruled that the studios' control of the great majority of U.S. movie theaters violated Federal antitrust laws and ordered them to divest. The ruling reduced the big eight's grip on the industry and created opportunities for independent producers, including production companies of many movie stars. The independents flourished beginning in the 1960s, sparked a wave of innovation, and started the era of the director.

In post-World War I, several state and local governments moved to censor and control the content of movies, worried that motion pictures would corrupt moral values. A 1915 Supreme Court ruling, *Mutual Film Corporation v. Industrial Commission of Ohio*, stated that movies were not an art form and not protected by the First Amendment. In response, an industry group later known as the Motion Picture Association of America adopted its Production Code, which told studios what they could do and say on screen, down to the smallest details. Nicknamed the "Hays Code" for its creator, the Republican National Committee chairman William Hayes, the code became the bane of sex, violence, foul language, and controversial subjects in the movies, such as Jane swimming nude in 1934's *Tarzan and His Mate* or Rhett Butler's exclamation, "Frankly, my dear, I don't give a damn," in 1935's *Gone with the Wind*—the latter being permitted only after a long battle.

By the 1950s, several developments led to dissolution of the Production Code. The studios' grip on the movie business had weakened, as more directors insisted on making their films without interference, foreign films with forbidden subjects and nudity began to be imported, and the Supreme Court overturned its *Mutual* decision. With the restrictions of the Production code removed, the Hollywood studios began to offer edgier content that audiences could not see on television.

Still fearing government censorship, the Motion Picture Association of America replaced the Production Code with a voluntary ratings system, which would advise theaters and parents on the suitability of films for younger audiences. The MPAA movie ratings have been criticized for inconsistency and general ineffectiveness, but they persist.

In the 1970s, a series of "blockbuster" movies—*The Godfather* (1972), *The Exorcist* (1973), *Jaws* (1975), and *Star Wars* (1977)—so-named because lines of movie-goers lined up around the block, raised the specter of the Hollywood megahit and established two young former classmates at the University of California School of Cinematic Arts, George Lucas and Steven Spielberg, as the crown princes of Hollywood. The two would collaborate on several projects in years to come, including the *Indiana Jones* and *Jurassic Park* films and Industrial Light and Magic, Lucas' cutting-edge special effects laboratory.

Two applications of digital technology to moviemaking revolutionized the industry starting in the 1990s. Computer generated imagery, or CGI, produce realistic-looking, three-dimensional special effects that were much cheaper to produce that physical effects and launched a string of fantasy films and animations of astounding technical quality. *Jurassic Park* (1993) and *Forest Gump* (1994) convincingly combined CGI with live action with a process known as motion capture. Toy Story (1995) from the Pixar animation studio, later purchased by Disney, was the first feature entirely generated by computers. Each of *Toy Story's* frames, representing a tiny fraction of a second, were 1536 pixels wide by 922 pixels high and required about three hours of supercomputer processing to render after design was completed. Director James Cameron employed extensive CGI in his 1997 megahit, *Titanic,* and then pushed the technological envelope to stereoscopic 3D in *Avatar* (2009). Home 3D digital televisions and disk formats started to be offered to consumers at this time.

The other digital revolution in the movie business was less noticeable to audiences than CGI but probably far more significant: films began to be distributed as digital files and video-projected in theaters, which promised to save the movie industry billions of dollars of film print and shipping costs, improve projection quality, and increase exhibition scheduling options. Customized versions of movies for different markets might also be a possibility.

DOCUMENTARY FILMS

With smaller budgets and audiences, documentary filmmakers' claim to fame lies in the social significance of their films rather than their commercial impact. Some critics argue that the small audiences prevent documentaries from making a difference, and that the emotional impact of fiction films is potentially greater. However, a few documentaries have made unique contributions to the history of the cinema.

Early documentary features—such as American explorer Robert Flaherty's *Nanook of the North* (1922) and Leni Riefenstahl's films for Adolph Hitler, *Triumph of the Will* (1935) and *Olympia* (1938)—showed how cinema could be harnessed to tell compelling stories about real subjects. The Franklin Roosevelt administration hired documentary filmmakers and photographers to drum up public support for its New Deal programs and for the U.S. war effort during World War II, with films such as *The River, The Plow That Broke the Plains,* and *Why We Fight,* a series of propaganda films by Hollywood director Frank Capra.

Following the war, CBS journalist Edward R. Murrow and his producer, Fred Friendly, launched television's first news magazine series, *See It Now,* which brought numerous documentaries to the small screen, including programs exonerating Lieutenant Milo Ridulovich of false charges and exposing Senator Joseph McCarthy's demagoguery. Murrow's last major piece for CBS was the 1961 landmark one-hour documentary film *Harvest of Shame,* which used extensive on-location footage to expose harsh working conditions faced by migratory farm workers.

In later years, with investigative shows such as *60 Minutes,* CBS would claim proudly that it was the "network of Murrow," but the historical record reveals that the journalist had been disillusioned by the network's dwindling support. Later, CBS News gave free reign to its correspondent Charles Kuralt in his *On the Road* series of mini-documentaries on the lives of everyday Americans, but Kuralt assiduously avoided any controversies that would bring the heavy hand of the head office.

In the 1980s, when the FCC suspended its Fairness Doctrine, stations no longer were requi-red to air programs on controversies in their communities, so documentaries all but disappeared from U.S. airwaves, except for those funded by the National Endowment for the Humanities (NEH) and National Endowment for the Arts (NEA) for broadcast on the Public Broadcasting Service. An important early PBS documentary project, the 1970 *cinema vérité* documentary called *An American Family,* about the daily life of a California family, was a precursor to reality television such as *The Real World.* Other significant documentaries shown on PBS included the 11-part series *Vietnam: A Television History* (1983) and the 14-hour *Eyes on the Prize* (1986, 1989).

Documentary films would achieve unprecedented popularity when filmmaker Ken Burns presented his 11-hour documentary series *The Civil War,* first run on public television in 1990. The filmmaker combined interviews, readings from diaries, reconstructions of historic clashes, and famous people to portray voices of the Civil War characters. His pan-and-scan animation of photographs was so effective that it became known as the "Ken Burns effect." The series achieved the highest ratings ever for PBS, averaging more than 14 million viewers each evening.

The commercial success of Michael Moore's documentaries has ushered in an era of opportunity for documentaries to obtain theatrical release. The first film of the ex-auto worker from Michigan was *Roger and Me* (1989), about the mismanagement of General Motors, followed by the Academy Award-winning *Bowling for Columbine* (2002) about a mass murder at a high school, and *Fahrenheit 9/11* (2004) about the terrorist attacks of September 11 and their aftermath, the highest-grossing U.S. documentary of all time, earning more than $200 million worldwide. Moore's successes led the way for *Super Size Me* (2004) about eating junk food, *March of the Penguins* (2005), and *An Inconvenient Truth* (2006) about global warming, which won an Academy Award and directly contributed to its presenter, Al Gore, receiving the Nobel Peace Prize.

RADIO

As noted by the Pew Center's Project for Excellence in Journalism, "radio is well on its way to becoming something altogether new—a medium called audio." Radio is well suited for transformation. Voice and music fit well with new mobile technology platforms.

Westinghouse launched the first radio station, a 100-watt transmitter in Pittsburgh, in 1920. It was given the call sign KDKA by the Commerce Department. The station is still on the air today. One of its first broadcasts announced election results—showing listeners that radio could provide important news more rapidly than news-papers. In the 1930s, it was decided to give call signs starting with "W" to stations east of the Mississippi River and "K" for west of the Mississippi.

Almost immediately radio stations began to cooperate with each other to share programming by forming networks. The first radio network combined six stations in the Midwest in 1925. The government then took the unusual step of allocating frequencies to high-power "clear" channels whose signals could reach many states and even further in the evening.

The National Broadcasting Company (NBC) was formed in 1926, owned jointly by RCA, General Electric, and Westinghouse. NBC grew so quickly that it had to form two separate networks—a "blue" and a "red" network. The blue network would later become the basis for the American Broadcasting Corporation (ABC).

The Columbia Broadcasting System (CBS) was the second national radio network, boasting 47 affiliates in 1927, which received programming in exchange for ad time sold to national advertisers. NBC countered with coast-to-coast programming that same year.

© Gts, 2010. Shutterstock Inc.

Because there were no precedents for broadcasting, people working in the new medium of radio had to invent ways of doing things. Radio stations began diversify their schedules with different kinds of programs offered at set times of the day—music, sports, news, drama, and comedy. Radio would become the launching pad for many of America's greatest talents, including the Marx Brothers, Frank Sinatra, Orson Welles, Neil Simon, and many more.

The power of radio to influence public opinion was demonstrated by two public figures in the 1930s. In an early form of conservative talk radio, Father Charles Coughlin, a Roman Catholic priest from suburban Detroit, started broadcasting vitriolic attacks on President Franklin D. Roosevelt on radio station WJR in Detroit. He had been a Roosevelt supporter, but grew impatient went the president's New Deal policies did not relieve workers' plights fast enough. Because WJR had a "clear channel" transmitter, its reach increased after dark to a much as a third of the national radio audience. Coughlin had a huge following, with up to 80,000 letters per week from listeners.

On the air, Coughlin was an outspoken isolationist. He began attacking Jews, atheists, and Communists in speeches that sounded similar to those of Nazi propaganda minister Joseph Goebbels in Germany. He even accused Jews of a conspiracy to cause the Great Depression. The Church tried to distance itself from its renegade priest but, for its part, did nothing to silence him. When World War II started in Europe, the government threatened to revoke WJR's license, and Coughlin lost his mouthpiece.

The other man who demonstrated the power of radio was Franklin Roosevelt. His "fireside chats" over the radio helped millions of American listeners to cope, first with the economic depression, and then with the world war.

Radio captivated listeners with its immediacy. Some of the most important moments in history were announced to Americans first by radio, such as the *Hindenburg* disaster in 1937, when a hydrogen-filled German airship exploded into flames while trying to land in New Jersey, as radio announcer Herbert Morrison exclaimed in a voice wrenched with emotion, "[I]t's a terrific crash, ladies and gentlemen. It's smoke, and it's in flames now; and the frame is crashing to the ground, not quite to the mooring mast. Oh, the humanity!"

The compelling nature of radio's immediacy was demonstrated definitively on Halloween night, October 30, 1938, in a notorious episode in which thousands of radio listeners were duped into believing that hostile Martians were invading the Earth, and as a consequence fled their homes in panic. Orson Welles, the young, brash director of the Mercury Theater on the Air, produced and starred in a radio adaptation of H.G. Wells' novel, *War of the Worlds,* in the form of a mock-news report. To demonstrate to his cast the mood he wanted for the production, Welles played a voice recording of Herbert Morrison's report of the Hindenburg disaster, and he staged his story in New Jersey, not far from where the airship exploded. Upon hearing of the panic that his radio drama caused, Welles confessed embarrassment, but secretly he was delighted at the power he had wielded over his audience.

In the aftermath of the *War of the Worlds* panic, public opinion expert Hadley Cantril led a team of researchers, including one of the show's scriptwriters, to examine the psychological effects of the episode. They concluded that, contrary to the "Hypodermic Needle" theory of mass communication that was popular at the time, the effect of the radio program was not all-powerful, but rather, depended on the propensities of individual listeners, and whether they happened to be tuned in during program breaks.

Americans relied on radio to keep up with global developments during World War II. CBS Radio correspondent Edward R. Murrow became a national celebrity when he provided regular reports of the bombing of London, often with the sound of explosions in the background. The audience was electrified as it never had been before. Because the idea of broadcasting the news on location was so new, Murrow assembled a crack team of former newspaper reporters who knew how to get the story, and who become legends in broadcast journalism: William L. Shirer, Eric Sevareid, Charles Collingwood, and Howard K. Smith became known as "Murrow's Boys."

The U.S. public also first heard about the attack on Pearl Harbor by radio, with legendary CBS radio journalist John Charles Daly announcing the news to a shocked public. They listened with rapt attention again the next day to a live radio broadcast of President Franklin Roosevelt's address to congress, as he condemned the surprise Japanese attack as a "date that will live in infamy."

The FM radio transmitter was invented in 1933, offering clearer sound with less static and interference than AM. (AM stands for "amplitude modulation" and FM for "frequency modulation.") However, efforts to promote this superior form of radio were blocked by the corporate establishment, such as RCA's Sarnoff, who wanted to protect his company's huge investments in AM equipment and stations. Audiences for FM were so small, licenses for FM stations could be purchased for as little as five dollars. FM remained a secondary player in communications despite such advances as FM stereo, which began in 1961. Radios started to have an FM band included with the AM band in the late 1950s and 1960s. FM radio also benefitted when automakers started including AM/FM radios as standard equipment in their cars. By the 1970s, the FM audience size surpassed that of AM, with more than 2,000 FM stations broadcasting in the United States. AM in recent years has become primarily a place for talk radio.

While traditional radio broadcasts have lost their audiences, radio remains a vibrant medium thanks to individuals and corporations that have combined radio with the power of the computer. Internet radio has empowered smaller stations. Sitting down in front of a computer, someone can listen to radio broadcasts from any part of the world, from Lubbock, Texas, to London, England.

One-man radio stations also are possible with the Internet. Web sites such as Pandora, SHOUTcast, MTV, LIVE365, and Rhapsody give listeners a seemingly endless choice of stations and formats. However, new music performance royalties imposed by the Digital Millennium Copyright Act of 1998 threatened to strap small operators with overly burdensome fees. A decade of policy debates ensued, during which listenership and revenues for Internet radio grew dramatically. In 2009 the Federal government announced that the royalties for digital play would be based on revenues collected. Many nonprofit college and university radios stations streaming their content on the Web breathed a collective sigh of relief.

Talk radio has been around since the medium's inception. In a move to prevent demagogues such as Father Coughlin from controlling the airwaves, the FCC instituted the Fairness Doctrine in 1949, which required licensed radio and television stations to devote airtime to programs that discussed "controversial matters of public interest" and to present contrasting views on those matters. The FCC did not specify what stations had to do to comply with the doctrine. Contrary to the doctrine's intended purpose, its requirement to offer opposing viewpoints created a large financial burden on the stations that had a chilling effect, and stations tended to avoid controversy.

The politically conservative administration of President Ronald Reagan pushed for deregulation of private industry, and in 1987 the FCC announced it would no longer enforce the Fairness Doctrine. Democratic congressional attempts to pass a Fairness Doctrine law were vetoed by Reagan's successor, George H.W. Bush. As a consequence, talk-radio commentators were free to express their biases, so long as they observed the other broadcasting regulations still in force.

Reflecting the trend in most media, talk radio is ideologically splintered, with talk-show hosts reflecting the spectrum of political viewpoints. The number of radio stations that carry at least some talk shows, which include everything from political talk to sports to advice shows, grew by a third in 2008, to 2,056 from 1,370 the year before, according to *Inside Radio* magazine.

MAGAZINES

American magazines give readers seemingly endless choices in topic, format, and viewpoint. Gradually, the magazine industry abandoned the traditional general-news format that it started with and moved toward specialized, "niche" publications. In the process, the industry created a medium that is ideal for advertisers to target consumers with very specific tastes.

Because of the magazine industry's overall direction toward narrowcasting, the current environment is becoming difficult for the national news weeklies that for so long have dominated the industry. *Time, Newsweek,* and *U.S. News & World Report* are being forced to reinvent themselves. Their process of transformation mirrors a

© Denis Vrublevski, 2010. Shutterstock Inc.

similar experience of a half century ago, when the general-readership picture magazines *Life, Look,* and *The Saturday Evening Post* could not compete as low-cover-price weeklies with television for advertising revenues and folded.

The continued strong health of specialized publications is evident to anyone who visits a local Borders or Barnes & Noble. What is impressive is the degree to which specialization has evolved. There are not only magazines for musicians, but also highly specialized magazines that focus on only acoustic guitars or only electric ones, classical guitarists, emerging musicians, bass players, drummers, synthesizers, or traditional keyboards.

In a similar vein, new magazine titles take popular subjects, such as cars, lifestyle, gardening, cooking, fashion, or sports, and emphasize a specific slice of the subject. Someone can find not only a magazine devote solely to trucks, but also a magazine exclusively about off-road 4 × 4 trucks.

The Pew Center's Project for Excellence in Journalism (PEJ) has reported that the audience for magazines, while varying markedly by category, has been enduring a slow, steady erosion of circulations since the 1990s. Twenty-three percent of adult Americans in 2008 said they read a magazine of some kind the day before—a drop of nearly a third from 33 percent in 1994, the first year the survey was conducted. However, a small group of niche publications that target narrow segments of the population managed to add readers.

In a similar vein, advertising revenues for magazines also have declined. The PEJ reported that the biggest declines came in reduced ad buying by automakers, pharmaceutical companies, and financial services providers. With general-news magazines faltering and niche publication prospering, it is not surprising that specialized news magazines are growing both in popularity and in share of advertising business.

The history of the modern magazine goes back to the 1700s. According to legend, Englishman Daniel Defoe, the author of *Robinson Crusoe,* published the first magazine, *The Review,* in London. Defoe reported on domestic politics, including the goings-on in Parliament. He got into serious trouble when he criticized the Church of England's policies. The first magazine to be published in America and to last more than a year was *The American Magazine and Historical Chronicle*, which was published in Boston between 1743 and 1746. From the beginning, magazine readers liked pictures. In the 1800s, illustrated magazines such as *Harper's Monthly* sent sketch artists to cover community events, just as news photographers are now. For the printing presses, their drawings were engraved by hand or etched with acid on copper and wood, using a number of sophisticated new techniques to simulate gray tones with only black ink. The etching process was tedious, but produced elaborately textured images, more beautiful than you would expect from the few that are reproduced today.

By the mid-1850s, magazines became well established in America. Around 600 weekly publications were available. Many of the magazines offered serialization of popular books and poems of the day, such as Harriet Beecher Stowe's *Uncle Tom's Cabin* and Edgar Allan Poe's *The Raven*. Similarly to newspapers, improvements in printing technology allowed magazines to be sold at low cost, boosting readership. Historians also note that, in the late 1800s in the United States, a higher number of Americans were benefiting from compulsory education, which meant an increasing number of people could read. Individual magazine issues typically were passed along to additional readers.

Until the 1880s, magazines were expensive, partly because printing technology limited even the most popular to a run of 100,000 copies; it simply took too long to push any more paper through a press. Then, technological developments in typography, printing, and distribution caused the cover price of magazines to drop dramatically. For example, *The Saturday Evening Post* sold for only five cents a copy. Magazines also became more popular among all economic classes when technology made it easier to add illustrations and photography. The combination of pictures, evolving styles of journalism, and the new technology

of offset printing and color process made high-power advertising layouts possible, giving new impetus to that fledgling industry.

Suddenly, magazines were very attractive to advertisers. Before the turn of the 20th century, even the most popular magazines carried only a small amount of what we call "classified advertising," and almost no large display ads. Mass-market magazines all came to depend on advertising to survive. Advertising exploded, which made it possible to sell magazines below production cost. In turn, the prices of magazines could be lowered, increasing circulation further. Advertisers discovered that with full pages and the new language of design, there was room for pictures, slogans, headlines, and the psychic symbols of "soft-selling." Graphic design came to mean sophisticated visual means of developing impact.

With the start of the 20th century, a new form of journalism emerged that reported on the harsh working and living conditions that many Americans faced, especially those who had recently emigrated from Europe. The journalists that reported on injustice in magazines were known as "muckrakers" and established the journalistic tradition of reporting on corporate and political corruption. Among the more famous muckrakers was Upton Sinclair, who reported on the unsanitary conditions in meatpacking houses. Sinclair's articles spurred the Federal government to enact the Pure Food and Drug Act, as well as the Meat Inspection Act.

Other outstanding muckrakers included Ida M. Tarbell, who wrote about John D. Rockefeller's corrupt business practices and how the Standard Oil Company illegally controlled the oil industry. Her articles in *McClure's* would lead to enactment of antitrust legislation and the breakup of Standard Oil, probably the most powerful company in America at the time. Magazines wrote exposés on a wide array of issues, including worker safety, the rise in child prostitution, and corruption in unions.

About the same time, another type of magazine was starting to emerge in America that offered outstanding journalism and high-quality photography. One of the most successful examples of this type of magazine was the *National Geographic*, which was launched in 1888 nine months after the National Geographic Society was founded. With bright, glossy photos and stories about exotic, faraway places, *National Geographic* opened doors to new cultures. It also was one of the first sponsored publications. The magazine is "free" as part of an Society membership. The Society uses proceeds from the magazine to pursue cultural and wildlife research, and to produce their famous documentary films.

Other sponsored publications rank among the most popular publications in America. AARP offers its members *AARP the Magazine*, which typically ranks among the top five U.S. periodicals with the highest circulations.

In today's market for specialized publications, it seems that many of the more successful fall into a handful of categories. For more serious readers, magazines such as *Harper's* and *Atlantic Monthly* provide extended articles that deeply analyze entire issues. These magazines, which date back to the 1850s, typically go into depth on cultural and political issues. At the same time, their influence among selected audiences can be significant. The *New Republic*, *Mother Jones*, and *Progressive* have liberal traditions. Others, such as the *National Review* and *Weekly Standard*, appeal to conservatives.

A long-standing part of the magazine industry is trade publications, whose audiences are professionals working in specialized areas. By not writing for a general audience, these publications can provide more in-depth and sophisticated coverage of pending issues within a particular profession or industry. An issue that would not rate coverage in a newspaper could receive extensive coverage in a trade magazine. One of the largest of these publications is *Accounting Today*, read only by certified public accountants, enjoys consistently high readership and is filled with plenty of ads.

Trade magazine journalists work under tremendous pressure. Reporters and editors must find news and information that their audience needs; otherwise, subscribers will go elsewhere. Also known as *business publications*, these magazines are relied upon by a wide variety of professionals to stay current with developments in their fields. Trade publications often will preview products and services, provide statistics, report leadership changes in the business, and alert readers to significant changes in regulation.

There are a few specialized magazines that are hard to classify, but nevertheless enjoy great popularity. Leading this group is the U.S. edition of a British publication, *The Economist*. First published in 1843, *The Economist* covers both U.S. and international news. Like many British publications, *The Economist* practices advocacy journalism, rather than objective reporting, giving a slant to its news coverage. The *Week*, another British-owned publication, uses a different approach to the news magazine by employing a staff of 20 editors who combine the prior week's news developments into a weekly summary.

Many of the more successful specialized publications are aimed at female audiences. In the magazine industry, insiders refer to the "Seven Sisters": *Better Homes & Gardens*, *Family Circle*, *Good Housekeeping*, *Ladies' Home Journal*, *McCall's*, *Redbook*, and *Women's Day*. The popularity of the publications peaked in 1979, when they had a combined circulation of 45 million readers. Faced with steady circulation slippage, the Seven Sisters are in a period of self-examination. Among some of the anticipated adjustments is a change in the magazines' voice, from promoting safe, middle-of-the-road values, such as motherhood, to a more assertive style reflecting women's engagements in the workplace.

The magazine industry also offers publications primarily aimed at men. Among these magazines are two classics: *Esquire* and *Playboy*. *Esquire* was the first major "glossy" men's magazine. Founded in 1933, *Esquire* featured pinups and impressive literary features. In the last half of the 20th century, *Esquire* became the launching pad for New Journalism, a vibrant form of narrative nonfiction that added excitement to magazine writing.

Several outstanding former newspaper writers embraced the new writing technique, including Tom Wolfe, Gay Talese, and Richard Ben Cramer. *Esquire* became their launching pad.

In 1953, Hugh Hefner, who was originally on the staff of *Esquire,* founded *Playboy.* The first edition contained nude photos of Marilyn Monroe—before she became a famous movie actress. Hefner did not put a date on the magazine because he did not know if there would ever be a second edition. However, it sold out as soon as it hit the newsstands. The magazine developed a history of publishing short stories by such notable writers as Arthur C. Clarke. More than a collection of nude photos and superior writing, *Playboy* played a significant role in changing American attitudes toward sex and contributed to the U.S. cultural revolution of the 1960s.

Rolling Stone is another magazine that has had an impact on American culture. *Rolling Stone* was started as a counterculture magazine in San Francisco during the 1964 "summer of love" by 21-year-old Jann Wenner, who thought that starting a music magazine would help him to meet John Lennon. *Rolling Stone* celebrated sex, drugs, and rock and roll, but it also raised important political and cultural issues of the day from the youth culture's perspective. *Rolling Stone* attracted a different breed of writers, who saw journalism as an extension of rock music's rebellious spirit. "*Rolling Stone* is not just about music, but also about the things and attitudes that the music embraces," wrote Wenner in the first issue.

As *Washington Post* media critic Peter Carlson put it: "In its glory, *Rolling Stone* was the conscience, if not the voice, of its generation. The stories it broke or covered in ways the establishment press wouldn't included such disturbing ones as the fiasco at the Rolling Stones' mammoth [December 1969] Altamont outdoor concert, which included the murder of a spectator by a Hell's Angel."

For outstanding journalism, *The New Yorker* holds a significant position. The magazine remains a vehicle for thoughtful, insightful writing. Some of the best writing of all types—political, humor, sports, fashion, biography, humor—can be found within the magazine's pages. *The New Yorker* also has been the home for some of the greatest journalists of the past 85 years.

When the magazine was founded in 1925, it became an immediate hit among a growing number of educated middle-class and upper-middle-class Americans, in and around New York City. Its editor, Harold Ross, guaranteed that his new publication would serve sophisticated readers. *The New Yorker* "is not edited for the old lady in Dubuque," he said.

While humor writing initially was *The New Yorker's* strong suit, the magazine soon established itself as a preeminent forum for serious journalism and fiction. In subsequent decades, the magazine published short stories by many of the most respected writers of the 20th and 21st centuries, many destined for greatness, such as James Thurber, E.B. White, John Updike, John Cheever, H.L. Mencken, Vladimir Nabokov, Mary McCarthy, and J.D. Salinger.

THE INTERNET

As the United States moved into the 21st century, the Internet became more intertwined in people's daily existence. It is hard to imagine life without the World Wide Web. The Internet's roots are in national security. As a part of its Cold War competition with what was then called the Soviet Union, the U.S. government decided that it

needed a computer network that could continue to operate even if part of the network was destroyed in an attack. This goal set in motion a series of developments that would ultimately led to the Web and all that it entails, from e-mail to YouTube. The network that became known as the Internet was a collaboration of government, academia, and the private sector.

For example, the government made a key contribution to development of the Internet through forward-thinking bureaus such as the Defense Advanced Research Projects Agency (DARPA). In the late 1960s and early 1970s, DARPA funded many innovations that ultimately became part of the Internet, including protocols that allowed computers made by one manufacturer to send and receive information from computers built by another manufacture. In the early 1970s, Ray Tomlinson of Bolt, Beranek and Newman, now BBN Technologies, a research and development company that works closely with the U.S. government, created the first e-mail program.

One of the key technological breakthroughs that enable the growth of the Internet was the standardization of the way information would be sent through the network. In 1983, Vinton Cerf of Stanford University and Bob Kahn from DARPA developed the computer protocol that allows computers to interconnect—TCP/IP (transmission control protocol/Internet protocol)—which is the digital glue that holds the Internet together.

TCP/IP allowed a broad array of computers to "talk" to each other. But at the time, computers were still hard to use and information was hard to find. What people needed was a flexible way to locate, display, and share information.

In the late 1980s and early 1990s, Tim Berners-Lee, a researcher at CERN, a European nuclear physics lab, developed protocols that answered this need. He called his technology the World Wide Web, and he created a new type of computer application for the Web that he called a browser. In the next few years, several different universities and other non-profit organizations developed browsers with graphical user interfaces. Because Berners-Lee

worked hard to keep his invention free and open to the public, use of the Web exploded.

While the great milestones of most other communications media were marked by content that has an impact on the audience, it is new applications have truly marked the Internet's growth and use. The email and the World Wide Web were the first great applications. Then in 1996, Larry Page and Sergey Brin, graduate students at Stanford University, began collaborating on a search engine that would allow people to find information more efficiently on the World Wide Web. Their goal certainly was not modest: they merely wanted to organize all the information on the Web and then perhaps in the world. They eventually named their search engine Google, derived from the word googol, a mathematical term for a one followed by 100 zeros. By 1998, Google was recognized for its ability to return extremely relevant results. Google would go on to not only be the most widely used search engine, but also to revolutionize advertising on the Web by pioneering what is called pay-per-click advertising. With pay-per-click, advertisers pay Google only after end-users clicks on their ads.

In the late 1990s, an easy, low-cost way to post diary-like information on the Web was developed—first called Weblogs and then blogs. Within five years, millions of people were blogging and following other people's blogs.

In 2001, Jimmy Wales and Larry Sanger used the concept and technology of a "wiki," essentially an online document that anybody can modify, to launch Wikipedia, an online encyclopedia. The idea was that the entries in Wikipedia would be developed and policed for accuracy by anybody with an interest in a specific subject. The concept worked. As of mid-2010, Wikipedia consisted of 15 million articles in 200 languages contributed and edited by more than one million people.

Other dynamic applications of Web technology were developed such as YouTube, in which people can easily post and find videos. And in 2003, Facebook, was founded by a Harvard student, Mark Zuckerberg. A social networking site that essentially let's people create personal Web pages, link them, and communicate easily with whoever is linked to the page, started out as a hobby that Zuckerberg originally called "Hot or Not." The concept was an instant success, and soon thousands of Harvard students were signing up. Within months, Facebook was extended to Stanford and Yale. Three fellow Harvard students, Eduardo Saverin, Dustin Moskovitz, and Chris Hughes, helped Zuckerberg to expand the enterprise nationally. The four dropped out of Harvard to run the company. Facebook eventually became a fixture at most universities in the United States and Canada. More than 500 million people around the world now have joined Facebook and use it regularly as a primary source of information, generating annual revenues from Internet advertising in excess of $800 million.

Creative thinkers are developing novel communications mechanisms that people had no idea they needed until they became available. For example, work began in 2006 on Twitter, which dubs itself a micro-messaging service. The idea was to use short messaging code, not unlike text messages on cell phones, to allow people in your social group to know where you are or what you are feeling at all time. While many people scratched their heads and wondered why anybody would want to constantly update their lives online, the concept was a hit with celebrities and politicians and the millions of people who follow them. In fact, it is currently a primary mechanism for celebrities to react to news about them or to make public announcements.

The possibilities for the Internet seem without limit. Entire libraries can be accessed from the Internet. Federal and state legislation and court decisions are easily obtained from the Internet. Not so long ago, a few publishing companies controlled access to court rulings, requiring people to pay for copies of a court decision—including those of the U.S. Supreme Court. Now they're available for free on the Web.

The Library of Congress has been working at creating the World Digital Library, a project that is receiving large financial support from Google. The Library of Congress says the concept behind the digital library is to give everyone access to "rare and unique cultural materials." Another ongoing Library of Congress project is the American Memory Project, an effort that has been digitizing American documents, images, sound recordings, and more. The collection contains more than 10 million items that can be searched or browsed as a whole. The two Library of Congress projects are but two of many examples of intellectual cross-fertilization inspired by the Internet.

Finally, established companies and organizations of all sizes have Web sites and are getting involved with social media such as Facebook and Twitter. With all these applications, and with more undoubtedly being hatched, the Internet has become a central, indispensible, multifaceted communications platform that supports multibillion dollar industries.

BOOKS

Writing is one of the most basic of human communication processes and humans have been writing in one sense or another almost from the beginning of human history. Twenty-two thousand cuneiform tablets chronicling the history of the kings of Assyria dating from the seventh century BC were found on the site of the ancient city of Nineveh. Papyrus was used for writing in ancient Egypt and some scrolls, such as the history of the rule of Ramses III, stretched more than 100 feet.

Between the second and fourth centuries, the scroll was replaced by the codex. Individual pages were attached to each other at the back. This led to easier access to information. Other innovations at the time were the separating of words and the use of capitalization and punctuation, making easier to read books silently. Later, the idea of a table of contents was developed.

But while the back form of the book was in place nearly 1500 years ago, the emergence of the modern book is intrinsically tied to the development of the printing press and moveable type in the 15th century. As it became easier to print and manufacture books, the motivation for people to

Shutterstock# 24495127

read grew and an industry to satisfy that need grew as well.

One of the first book publishers in America to use modern manufacturing techniques was Harper Brothers, first founded as J. & J. Harper in 1817. In 1837, the company published Edgar Allen Poe's *Pym on Nantucket* and in 1840 published Richard Henry Dana's *Two Years Before the Mast*. Harper's was also the American book publisher for English authors Emily and Charlotte Bronte and William Thackeray, bringing such classics as *Wuthering Heights*, *Jane Eyre*, and *Vanity Fair* to American readers.

Another early American publishing house was Charles Scribner's Sons. Founded in 1846 by Charles Scribner and Isaac Baker under the name "Baker and Scribner." Scribner was a graduate of Princeton University and the publishing house was one of the first in America that did not grow out of a printing operation or as an offshoot of a retail book operation. The aim was to publish American authors and the first book it produced was *The Puritans and Their Principles* by Edwin

Hall. The first bestseller was *Napoleon and His Marshals* by the Reverend J.T. Headley. Scribners would go on to serve as the publisher for leading American writers such as F. Scott Fitzgerald, Ernest Hemingway, Edith Wharton, Thomas Wolfe, Kurt Vonnegut, and Stephen King.

Both Harper Brothers, now part of Harper and Row, and Scribners are still in business. But as a sign of just some of the changes in the book publishing industry, both are owned by major media conglomerates.

There can be little doubt about the significant social, political, and culture roles books play in modern and contemporary society. For example, Harriet Beecher Stowe wrote the antislavery novel *Uncle Tom's Cabin* in 1852, depicting the harsh realities of slavery and inflaming antislavery sentiments. One of the best selling novels of the 19th century, Stowe's book helped intensify the abolitionist cause. *The Education of Henry Adams*, written in 1918 by the great-grandson of President John Adams, provided one of the first records of the social, technological, political, and intellectual changes that occurred over Adams's lifetime. *The Education* also examined the intellectual and political life of the late 19th century.

The Man Nobody Knows was a different, more controversial type of book, but it grabbed the attention of the reading public. Written by an advertising executive, Bruce Fairchild Barton, the book contended that Jesus Christ was the founder of modern business. Written in 1925, the book fueled the attitude among many Americans that great wealth was a sign of God's blessing. Barton wrote about how Jesus created an organization that conquered the world, assisted by a board of directors (the Apostles) whom Jesus handpicked. The book tried to change the image of Jesus from a kind and gentle person to a tough, hard-nosed businessman. Though Barton's message was not for everyone, *The Man Nobody Knows* was one of the best selling nonfiction books of the 20th century.

Born in China of missionary parents, John Hersey received an Ivy-League education and went on to study at Cambridge. Then he landed a summer job as the private secretary and driver for the famed "muckraking" writer novelist Sinclair Lewis. His boss' high-level connections led to a job for Hersey at *Time* magazine, where he was hired after he wrote an essay on the magazine's dismal quality. Hersey served as a correspondent for *Time* and *Life* during World War II. At the end of the war, Hersey came upon an account written by a Jesuit missionary who had survived the U.S. atomic bombing of the Japanese city of Hiroshima at the end of World War II. He found the priest, who introduced Hersey to other survivors. The resulting book was a milestone in nonfiction literature.

Hersey examined the horror of nuclear war in human terms in his book *Hiroshima,* considered the precursor to the "new journalism" or "literary journalism" genre that emerged in the 1960s. Hersey reported on the lives of six survivors of the bombing. He told how the people got through their day. Hersey introduced his book to the reading public as a series of articles in *The New Yorker* in 1946. Many Americans were moved by Hersey's lean prose style, which was calculated to fit his topic, and the book sparked debate over future nuclear warfare at a time when the United States was escalating its nuclear arsenal. The Book-of-the-Month Club, the largest book buyer in America at the time, gave a free copy of *Hiroshima* to all of its members. Noted historian David McCullough said of the Pulitzer Prize-winning Hersey, "He has given us the century in a great shelf of brilliant work, and we are all his beneficiaries."

Over the decades, other great books have influenced society by shedding light on an issue and, in some cases, inspiring Americans to take action:

- In *The Organization Man,* published in 1956, *Fortune* magazine writer William H. Whyte caused Americans to stop and think about their regimented lives, or, as author Michael Lewis put it, "the deplorable, metronomic life of the American businessman." Whyte saw individual citizens being buried alive by the prevailing bureaucracy. His critique planted the seeds for the

lifestyle changes of the 1960s and 1970s, including telecommuting, casual Fridays, and a more relaxed work environment.

- Theodore H. White's *The Making of the President* (1960) was a breakthrough in political writing. White was the first reporter to devote himself entirely to covering the presidential primaries up close. When John F. Kennedy won a crucial West Virginia primary, he watched the results on a hotel television with White sitting next to him—a scene that is difficult to imagine taking place today. *The Making of the President* gave fascinating inside glimpses into the world of politics and launched a new category of books that analyze presidential elections.

- Consumerism experienced a rebirth, thanks partially to Ralph Nader's *Unsafe at Any Speed.* The 1965 book is best known for causing the demise of the Chevrolet Corvair, which was General Motors' model to compete with another popular small car, the Volkswagen Beetle. Nader claimed the car was poorly designed and that its components made the car more likely to cause crashes. The book made a national hero of Nader, who was harassed by detectives hired by GM. One year after the book's release, the president of GM publicly apologized to Nader at a congressional hearing. The book and incident would lead to the Clean Air Act and tougher car safety rules, such as mandatory seat belts and air bags.

The best selling book of all time is the Holy Bible, with estimated copies sold in excess of 2.5 billion worldwide, followed by *Quotations from Chairman Mao (The Little Red Book)* and the Koran at 800 million each. Other all-time best sellers have been *A Tale of Two Cities* by Charles Dickens (200 million), *Scouting for Boys* by Robert Baden-Powell (150 million), *Lord of the Rings* by J.R.R. Tolkien (150 million), *The Da Vinci Code* by Dan Brown (80 million), and *The Catcher in the Rye* by J.D. Salinger (65 million).

J.K. Rowling's seven *Harry Potter* books have sold more than 400 million copies worldwide.

Despite the *Harry Potter* phenomenon that resuscitated the children's literature market, the book industry's biggest challenge has been the loss of younger readers. A survey of 17,000 persons by the Census Bureau in 2002 showed a distinct decline among younger people in reading literature. Some observers feel the growth of video games and particularly online media are the cause in the decline of reading, though, as could be expected, others disagree.

PUBLIC RELATIONS

Public relations involves shaping and maintaining the image of a company, organization, or individual in the public's eyes. By the middle of the 20th century, maintaining good public relations was widely recognized as a critical function for almost any organization—business, nonprofit, or governmental. Corporate executives, entertainers, sports figures, directors of charities, religious leaders, and U.S. presidents alike all have recognized the value of public relations for achieving their goals.

Public relations is very much a part of daily life in modern societies. At the heart of public relations is interpersonal communication—striving to communicate effectively with others. The P.R. professional simply practices that ethos for the benefit of his or her client organization. The goals of public relations vary according to the client—from raising awareness of an emerging issue, to motivating the public to take action, to informing the public about an emergency situation. Some of the longest-lasting campaigns have had the single goal of keeping an organization in the public eye.

Nascent forms of public relations have been practiced since the birth of the American nation. American colonists calling themselves the "Sons of Liberty"—including Paul Revere, Patrick Henry, John Hancock, John Adams, Samuel Adams, and Benjamin Edes—used public relations tactics to sway people to the cause of independence. They actively resisted British rule with a campaign of newspaper editorials, broadsheets, pamphlets, letter writing, and public demonstrations. Several of the Sons were printers, including Edes, publisher of the *Boston Gazette*. Freedom of the press became a central issue in the patriots' resistance campaign, when the British imposed the Stamp Act of 1765, which levied taxes on all printing paper.

The Sons staged public stunts, such as erecting "liberty poles" in city streets, burning custom officers in effigy, and dumping a shipload of tea into Boston harbor to protest the Tea Act of 1773. After Congress approved the final wording of the Declaration of Independence in Philadelphia on July 4, 1776, the handwritten draft was taken to the print shop of John Dunlap and printed as a broadsheet. Copies were circulated throughout the colonies and reprinted in newspapers.

Advances in print technology in the 1800s not only made books, newspapers, and magazines affordable to the masses, but also they helped to create the first American folk heroes—such as frontiersmen Davy Crockett, Buffalo Bill Cody, and General George Armstrong Custer. Their feats of daring were trumpeted by best-selling biographies, dime novels, and "penny dreadful" pulp magazines. Custer's fame also was spread by an advertising campaign of Anheuser-Bush, in which the beer company ordered reprints of a dramatic painting that depicted "Custer's Last Stand" and had them hung in many U.S. saloons.

The media personas of Crockett, Cody, and Custer had only a vague resemblance to the men's' actual lives, despite their active seeking of publicity. Crockett served as legislator, Cody was a travelling show impresario, and Custer craved appointment to higher rank. How these men were portrayed in the media over the years depended on the public's prevailing mood—sometimes "natural men," sometimes "founding fathers," and sometimes "Indian fighters."

As the field modernized in the beginning of the 20th century, publicists coming from the ranks of journalism, such as Ivy Lee and Edward Bernays, sought ways to clean up the field's reputation. Ivy Ledbetter Lee, with partner George Parker, opened a public relations counseling office in 1905, and took on high profile clients, such as industrialist John D. Rockefeller, the Pennsylvania Railroad, and the American Red Cross. He believed that public relations had a public responsibility in addition to its duty to serve the client. To Lee, a former newspaperman, the public was best served by keeping the press informed. His Declaration of Principles of 1906 stressed openness and accuracy: "This is not a secret press bureau. All our work is done in the open. We aim to supply news. This is not an advertising agency. If you think any of our matter ought properly to go to your business office, do not use it. Our matter is accurate. Further details on any subject treated will be supplied promptly, and any editor will be assisted most carefully in verifying directly any statement of fact."

Lee's Declaration is regarded by some observers as the beginning of modern public relations. Historian Eric F. Goldman wrote that Lee's Declaration marked the emergence of the second stage of public relations, in which the public was no longer to be ignored, in the traditional manner of business, nor fooled, in the continuing manner of the press agent. The public was to be informed.

Describing himself as a "physician to corporate bodies," Lee saw himself as protecting his clients from their own worst impulses toward secrecy and manipulation, shunning deceptive practices such as ghostwriting press releases, disguising ads as news stories, and repressing factual information that might be damaging to the client. His principles helped to make U.S. corporations more public-spirited and humanitarian.

When the United States entered World War I in 1917, there was strong opposition from isolationists who viewed the conflict as a European war. To boost support for the war effort, the U.S. government created the Committee on Public Information (CPI), which was known as the "Creel Committee" in honor of its foreman, George Creel, a legend in the annals of public relations. Creel already had a reputation within the emerging profession because of his work raising funds for the American Red Cross.

At the same time, many of President Woodrow Wilson's military leaders wanted to impose strict censorship to give the government control of the press. Creel argued against this policy and convinced the president to develop a coherent pro-war policy instead. Creel contended that the government needed an aggressive public relations policy to counter Germany's propaganda.

Creel felt that public relations was an essential component of a war campaign. As he wrote in his memoir, "It was the fight for the minds of men, for the 'conquest of their convictions,' and the battle-line ran through every home in every country. It was in this recognition of public opinion as a major force that the Great War differed most essentially from all previous conflicts." Creel's committee, in effect, had to sell the war to the American public, an effort that set a precedent for other conflicts to follow.

The CPI launched a series of public-service announcements that included the famous phrase, "Make the world safe for democracy." Creel innovated several P.R. techniques, such as training a corps of public speakers, called "Four-Minute Men," who would go into movie theatres, churches, and county fairs. They would urge support for the war while asking people to buy war bonds or donate blood. According to the committee's records, 75,000 Four-Minute men and women made a total of 7,555,190 speeches in 1917 and 1918.

The CPI further established a Division of Pictorial Publicity that produced posters urging people to buy bonds or enlist in the army. Germany was depicted as a bloodthirsty savage, "the Hun." A team of graphic artists turned out 1,438 different designs for posters, window cards, newspaper advertisements, cartoons, seals, and buttons. Of all of the posters, the best known is of Uncle Sam saying "I Want You," drawn by illustrator James Montgomery Flagg.

The efforts of Lee, Bernays, Creel, and others brought public acceptance to public relations; however, the image of P.R. men as "spin doctors" with malevolent influence on the audience lingered. What was needed was recognition of public relations' role in organizational leadership, which was achieved when Arthur W. Page was appointed vice president of public relations for AT&T in 1927.

Page was well prepared for his new position. After graduation from Harvard in 1905, he wrote for the magazine *World's Work* published by his father's company, Doubleday, Page and Co. When his father was appointed U.S. ambassador to England in 1905, the young Page was promoted to editor of the magazine and eventually vice president of Doubleday. Page's former Harvard classmate, Walter Gifford, was president of AT&T and offered Page a job as vice president of public relations for the telecommunications giant. Page accepted the position on the condition that he would have a say in policy development.

AT&T had a government-sanctioned monopoly of the U.S. telephone industry and needed to cultivate the public's trust. Appointing a P.R. man of integrity to high executive office helped that effort. Page created a public relations staff and standard procedures for how AT&T would react to public opinion and communicate persuasively to the public. "Public relations is everybody's job," he said. Page's public relations corporate infrastructure was credited as the key factor that enabled AT&T to emerge unscathed from close scrutiny of the monopoly's practices by the new Federal Communications Commission in 1935.

The fourth stage of development of public relations as a true profession was marked by the establishment of the Public Relations Society of America, chartered in New York City in 1947. The PRSA sought to maintain standards of conduct for P.R. professionals, to promote continuing education for its members, to provide a forum for exchange of information and ideas, and to encourage growth of the profession through its adjunct organization for college and university students, the Public Relations Student Society of America. The PRSA publishes two periodicals for its 21,000 members, the monthly tabloid *Public Relations Tactics* and the quarterly magazine *Public Relations Strategist*. The PRSA's *Code of Ethics* calls for its members to

- protect and advance the free flow of accurate and truthful information,

- foster informed decision making through open communication,

- protect confidential and private information,

- promote healthy and fair competition among professionals,

- avoid conflicts of interest, and

- work to strengthen the public's trust in the profession.

With the PRSA showing the way, public relations developed into a global industry employing hundreds of thousands of people worldwide and offices around the world. In fact, any form of organizational communication is now nearly synonymous with the field. Strategies and tactics of public relations expanded rapidly to address new media technologies. A former television producer for the U.S. Army and national manager of CBS Television News, Chester Berger started the nation's first communications management consulting firm in 1955 and led the industry in using television to achieve public relations goals.

Following the civil rights movement of the 1960s, the stage was set for the field of public relations to diversify. Moss Kendrix was born in Atlanta, Georgia, in 1917. He attended the city's Morehouse College and became editor of the student newspaper, *The Maroon Tiger*. Upon graduation in 1939, he was accepted into Howard University's law school, but chose instead to start his career in journalism. He was drafted into the Army in 1941 and served for the War Finance Office, traveling many times across the country with African American celebrities such as Duke Ellington and Billy Eckstine to promote war bonds. He often spoke on CBS radio. After directing the Republic of Liberia's Centennial Celebration in 1944, Kendrix launched his own public relations firm. He went on to a distinguished career in corporate P.R. with a specialty in targeting African-American consumers. Kendrix's client list included the Coca-Cola Company, Carnation, the National Dental Association, and Ford Motor Company. His firm's letterhead proudly announced the mantra, "What the Public Thinks Counts!"

An innovative, holistic approach to marketing communications emerged in the mid-1990s: integrated marketing communication or IMC. This new approach combined P.R. with other tools in the corporate "marketing mix," including advertising, sales promotion, and personal selling activities. Most of the largest P.R. firms such as Ketchum and Fleishman-Hillard either combined with leading advertising agencies or formed their own. IMC strategies called for tight integration of all aspects of a marketer's operations and fits with the general trend away from "broadcasting" and toward "narrowcasting." The target of promotional activity now was the individual customer.

ADVERTISING

Advertising in America goes back to colonial days when the primary form of advertisement was the posting of messages that offered services or goods. Some historians credit Benjamin Franklin with introducing illustrated ads to the colonies. He would use woodcuts of sailing ships to make ads in his *Philadelphia Gazette* and *Poor Richard's Almanac* more eye-catching.

The sales pitch in Franklin's ads for his stove would not be out of place in today's ads: "Fireplaces with small openings cause drafts or cold air to rush in at every crevice, and 'tis very uncomfortable as well as dangerous to sit against any such crevice. ... Women, particularly, from this cause (as they sit much in the house) get colds in the head, rheums, and defluxions which fall into their jaws and gums, and have destroyed early, many a fine set of teeth in these northern colonies. Great and bright fires do also very much contribute to damaging the eyes, dry and shrivel the skin, bring on early the appearance of old age."

As newspapers flourished in America, advertising became a key revenue source. For example, James Gordon Bennett, publisher of the *New York Herald* from 1835 to 1867, discovered that he could reduce the price of his newspapers, which led to a wider circulation and then he could charge higher prices for advertisements. Bennett printed ads on the same page as the news stories, making sure that readers saw the ads as they went through a daily paper.

By the mid to late 19th century, emerging advertising agencies, such as J. Walter Thompson, started collecting circulation figures of newspapers and magazines, and based their commissions on readership. Initially, the agencies would place ads in newspapers for their clients, and then began preparing the advertising copy themselves. As the 20th century began, a handful of advertising agencies began offering what is today known as mass-communicated advertising.

As railroads crisscrossed America, national markets began to emerge. Companies found that customers remembered their products more easily when ads included a slogan or catchy phrase. Ivory Soap told everyone that its product was "99 and 44/100 percent pure." Slogans helped modernize advertising, which had primarily consisted of lengthy texts. Advertisements had emphasized the importance of their products in long pieces of copy. A short, memorable catchphrase was found to be just as effective as its lengthier counterpart.

One of the earliest agencies, N.W. Ayer in Philadelphia, created slogans that are still part of the American vernacular, such as " "I'd walk a mile for a Camel," for R.J. Reynolds in 1921; "A diamond is forever," for DeBeers in 1948; "Reach out and touch someone," for AT&T in 1979; and "Be all you can be," for the U.S. Army in 1981. In addition to slogans, companies found they could boost market by building a brand identity for a product. Many brand names that are still around were launched as the 19th century ended, including Campbell's Soup, Quaker Oats, and Lipton Tea. As Duke University Professor William O'Barr explained, "As brands emerged in the late 1800s in America, advertising played a significant role in imbuing commodities with specific meanings. Ivory soap was no longer called 'white soap,' but had its own name. It had a distinctive appearance, logo, and package design that hasn't changed much over the years. Other soaps and cleaning products were also some of the earliest successful brands. Pears' soap, a competitor to Ivory, was promoted with romantic images of perfect people in a dreamy world."

Advertising also was a major factor in bolstering the growth of radio. Radio added a new dimension to advertising with the introduction of jingles and the spoken word. Ads agencies reinvented themselves by incorporating broadcast production departments, often writing both commercials and the programming for their clients. Early radio stars frequently delivered the commercial messages during their shows.

From its modest beginnings to the present, advertising has been able to change the daily habits of Americans. For example, before World War II, orange juice was not a popular breakfast drink. During the war, frozen orange juice from concentrate was invented, but it lacked the "fresh" taste of freshly squeezed orange juice. A relentless ad campaign by Florida orange growers convinced Americans that frozen orange juice was "part of a balanced breakfast," changing people's eating habits.

The Federal government in the early 1960s wanted Americans to drink more coffee. The United States was trying to support several Latin American governments through a coffee price-support program that depended on greater U.S. coffee consumption. An advertising campaign was launched that created a new concept, "the coffee break," which helped convinced the public that they needed to stop during their workday and drink coffee.

Other famous advertisement campaigns changed the public's perception toward a variety of products. For decades, women were portrayed in a poor light if they dyed their hair blond. "Peroxide blonde" or "bleach-bottle blonde" were derogatory phrases thrown at women who wanted to lighten their hair color. Clairol launched an aggressive advertising campaign to change that negative view. Two of its more famous slogans was "Blondes have more fun" and "Only her hairdresser knows for sure." Later, Clairol promoted the idea of going blond to a younger audience by calling its hair-lightener product "Summer Blonde." The products made the idea of dyeing one's hair seem more natural.

Sometimes, ads were used to change the image the public had for a product. When Philip Morris initially introduced Marlboro cigarettes to the public in 1924, they were marketed as a product for women. However, after World War II, Marlboros' image was reinvented by using ads featuring rugged cowboys, with the musical score from the film *The Magnificent Seven* in the background. The "Marlboro Man" helped to make the cigarette brand the most popular in the world. The ad campaign was followed up with a year-long promotion called the "Marlboro Adventure Team," with point-of-sale materials and merchandizing of a catalogue of Marlboro gear, including clothing, cowboy and auto racing paraphernalia, belt buckles, and lighters, all emblazoned with the Marlboro logo.

Governments in the 20th century also found that advertising could change the public's opinion of what was acceptable in society. Prior to World War II, the great majority of U.S. women had never worked outside their homes. When war broke out, thousands of manufacturing plants suddenly were converted from peacetime goods to war production to meet the government's call for weapons and munitions. Because men were being drafted into the armed services, it soon became evident that the country would need women to work in the factories. The government launched an ad campaign featuring "Rosie the Riveter," first introduced in a popular song that became a national hit. The lyrics went: "All the day long / Whether rain or shine / She's part of the assembly line / She's making history / Working for victory / Rosie the Riveter."

Ironically, the same advertising strategy was used after the war to encourage women to give up their jobs and stay home. The government saw millions of soldiers returning from the war and felt women would take away jobs from the veterans. Women who continued to work for a wage were ostracized for leaving their children alone at home.

In the last half of the 20th century, advertising also became a way to support public policies, nonprofit groups, and other popular campaigns. Many of the ads were created for the Ad Council, a nonprofit organization that was started in 1942. Using advertisements to support worthy causes, rather than sell products, the Ad Council is famous for such advertising icons as Smokey the Bear and his famous warning, "Only You Can Prevent Forest Fires." At the time, accidental fires accounted for nine out of ten forest fires and destroyed millions of acres every year. The council originally used Walt Disney's Bambi, but later brought in Smokey the Bear, after a bear that lived in the National Zoo in Washington, D.C. Since its inception, Smokey's forest-fire prevention campaign has helped to the number of acres lost annually from 22 million to 4 million.

Over the decades, ads have reflected the times in which they were created. During the 1950s,

people worried about standing out. Ads tried to convince people that buying a certain product would make them feel that they belonged to the larger social group. For example, one campaign said, "Everyone is buying a Chevrolet; shouldn't you?" Ads also played on fears that the listener would make some grievous social error. Housewives worried that their husbands would be shamed in public because their shirt collars were discolored. "Ring around the collar" was a heavily repeated ad slogan.

In the 1960s and 1970s, when America experience immense social change, advertising appeals flaunted rebelliousness and encouraged people to think for themselves. A memorable example was the "Think Small" ad campaign for Volkswagen "Beetle," which urged people to reject materialism by buying their automobiles. The print ads featured a black-and-white photograph of the car in a large empty space, with the two-word slogan and no other embellishment—a daring concept of William Bernbach of Doyle Dane Bernbach (DDB) that was carried over to Volkswagen's television commercials.

This trend toward nonconformity probably reached its zenith when Apple Computer showed its legendary "1984" television commercial during the third quarter of Super Bowl XVIII between the Washington Redskins and Oakland Raiders. The ad was conceived by the Chiat/Day agency in New York City (now part of TWBA), produced by Fairbanks Films, and directed by Ridley Scott, who would go on to a distinguished career directing feature films. The commercial showed a bleak, futuristic scene in which seemly thousands of people with shaved heads in gray clothes were forced to watch a Big Brother figure (an allusion to Apple's chief competitor, IBM) on an enormous television screen—a scene inspired by George Orwell's novel *Nineteen Eighty-Four*.

In the commercial, while the dejected people watch the giant screen, a lone woman with long blond hair, dressed in a tank top, breaks into the room and is chased by storm troopers. She runs to the front of the screen and hurls a huge hammer, shattering the television. As the screen explodes, the audience reacts with stunned silence and is bathed in a blinding white light. The voiceover announces, "On January 24th, Apple Computer will introduce the Macintosh. And you'll see why 1984 won't be like '1984.' " Although the ad was aired only one time and never showed the product, *Advertising Age* named it the greatest commercial of all time in 1995.

CONCLUSION

Although each communications industry has a separate and unique development path, with the growth of the Internet and computer-based communication, the boundaries between the industries are blurring in a process called media convergence. The convergence has had a huge impact on how media industries do business. It has transformed job roles and what it means to work in the media, including increased expectations of new workers.

The primary tool in the age of media convergence is the computer—for the desktop, then the laptop, followed by smart phones such as the Blackberry and the iPhone and tablet computers such as the iPad. Computer technology is used to create content, transmit content, and receive contents.

Because the Internet is international, it challenges the regulatory environment in countries around the world. In 2010, for example, Google pulled out of the Chinese market because the Chinese government had insisted on both censoring search results and using Google records to try to track down dissidents.

But media convergence and changes in the rules governing communication also has led to media consolidation, with five major media companies dominating the world market. Consolidation does not always live up to expectations, however. AOL Time Warner was formed in 2000 when the largest media content provider—Time Warner—

purchased the largest Internet service provider—America Online—for $164 billion, with AOL's Steve Case as chairman. The merger created the largest global media conglomerate to that point. The company's executives and industry analysts alike predicted that AOL's commanding market presence in the Internet services industry, combined with Time Warner's massive and vertically-integrated supply of media content, would be a match made in media heaven.

The executives and analysts did not foresee that AOL would loose its competitive advantage in the Internet services market to broadband providers Comcast and Verizon, nor did they recognize that the two corporate cultures were incompatible. Within three years, "AOL" was dropped from the company's name and Case was out. In 2009 Time Warner spun off AOL as an independent company, which has been trying to reconfigure itself in the communications marketplace ever since. The significance of the episode has not been lost on other companies, who now scrutinize merger opportunities with a more critical eye.

Some media critics who are wary of threats to our democracy, such as Noam Chomsky and Robert W. McChesney, argue that the concentration of media ownership has been a bad thing, because there are fewer independent voices in the public affairs mix and because media content has be homogenized into the least common denominator. It could be that the groundswell of opinion liberated by Internet blogging, which puts a powerful communications tool in the hands of average citizens, will serve to counteract homogenization of big media, and indeed, might have arisen in response to it.

Each of the media industries has a rich past and unclear future. However, because of the process of convergence, they will experience the future together. As new generations of young professionals vie to make their own marks in the ever-changing media world, knowing the paths that the industries have traveled will help guide them in the future.

MEDIA INDUSTRIES, WORK AND LIFE

by Mark Deuze

Abstract. Convergence culture, as a concept, articulates a shift in the way global media industries operate, and how people as audiences interact with them. It recognizes contemporary media culture as a primarily participatory culture. In turn, this assumption renders notions of production and consumption of (mass, mediated) culture not just theoretically problematic—as has been established earlier in disciplines as varied as communication studies, cultural geography and media anthropology—but also less than useful on a practical level when making sense of the role media play in people's everyday lives. This paper explores the practical applications of convergence culture from the perspectives of media workers, suggesting not so much the use of 'new' categories, but rather an alignment of production, mediation and consumption as constituent practices in all experience of (in) media life.

MEDIA INDUSTRIES, WORK AND LIFE

The media industries, in the broadest sense, can be seen as the key drivers and accelerators of a global culturalization of economies. Media are our window to the world, yet also function as its mirror; media reflect and direct at the same time. Theorizing the way the media industries operate is understanding the elements of the human condition in the information age—living in a world that can be considered a *mediapolis*: a mediated public space where media underpin and overarch the experiences of everyday life (Silverstone, 2007). As such, the convergence of production and consumption of media across companies, channels, genres and technologies is an expression of the convergence of all aspects of everyday life: work and play, the local and the global, self and social identity (especially in the use of social networking sites and participation in virtual worlds). The media as cultural industries act as trend amplifiers by flexibly adapting to a globalizing marketplace for products and a global production network for creative labour (Power and Scott, 2004). This perspective builds on a suggestion in my work that media should not be seen as some-how located outside of lived experience—for example as the artefacts we use to connect to each other via the Internet, or as messages that are transmitted or decoded that

READING NOTES

may or may not have effects on people, but rather should be seen as intrinsically part of it. Our life should perhaps be seen as lived *in*, rather than *with*, media—a *media life*.

In a way, this point of view differs not much from earlier suggestions, such as Marshall McLuhan's view on media as extensions of man, the forms and structures of which affect how we perceive and understand the world around us, Byron Reeves and Clifford Nass's notion of media as equating real life in terms of how people interact with media as social actors, and Michael Callon and Bruno Latour's insistence on the agency of nonhumans (including computer software, hardware and technical standards) when studying any kind of social relations. Similarly, authors as varied as Neil Postman, Terje Rasmussen, Stig Hjarvard, and Paul Levinson have developed more or less comprehensive perspectives on media and social theory (Hesmondhalgh and Toynbee, 2008), media ecology (Strate, 2006) and mediatizaton (Lundby, 2009) that supersede the existence of media in a material sense—aiming to explore how changes and developments in society interact with, and are 'softly' determined by, trends in media (production, use and content). My suggestion is, however, that until recently most of these perspectives were mainly theoretical exercises, with exceptions not necessarily induced from observed and lived experience. In today's media culture, where people increasingly move through the world assembling (more or less deliberately) a deeply individualized media system—in other words: living in their own *personal information space*—such a viewpoint can form the basis of (empirical) investigation and understanding of everyday life.

A *media life* perspective unsettles the key organizing categories of the study of communication and the role of media in people's lives: production, content and consumption. Certainly, the problematic nature of such categories has been argued in the past. One could think of Stuart Hall's notion of media as encoded and decoded with (invariably contested) meanings to challenge a dominant paradigm where mediated messages were generally seen as transmitted; James Carey's equally formidable challenge to the transmission model of communication by emphasizing the ritualistic nature of the way people use media and technology to make sense of their world; and the field of media anthropology stressing the linked and circular nature of the production and consumption of culture. Scholars in media studies, informatics and economic geography similarly have critically articulated the categories of media production and consumption with the parameters of the capitalist (and distinctly cosmopolitan) project, rather than with the material practice or lived experience of how people actually use and make media. Several other terms have been suggested to overcome the perceived production–consumption dichotomy, such as Jesús Martín-Barbero's notion of media as a process where each and every person produces meaning, and Nick Couldry's more recent suggestion of media as practice, explicitly focusing on decentring media research and engaging more deliberately with questions of how knowledge and actions are produced by people through their direct or indirect engagement with media. A media life perspective would assume that people generally do not make sense of their meaning-making processes and usage practices with media in terms of production and consumption. It furthermore aims to discuss media practices less in terms of specific technological affordances, instead opting to see how media in fact are used and appropriated in the organization of everyday life.

Beyond theoretical and operational consequences, a third consideration of a media life based ontology of contemporary reality can be made regarding the widely suggested convergence of culture and economy in modern life, emblematic of a more networked

READING NOTES

---

individualist culture (as Manuel Castells argues), expressive of an increasingly post-materialist society (following the work of Ronald Inglehart and, more recently, Roland Benedikter). This in turn connects to a broad and influential strand of thinking—both in academia and professional fields—regarding the increasing significance of culture in the economy (cf. Jean Baudrillard's suggestion of the sign-value of a commodity predominating its use-value), as well as in politics (articulating a Giddensian primacy of life politics and self-interested engagement over party politics and elections). Néstor García Canclini (2001) among others, observes along these lines a global reconstruction of world culture and local creativity under the paradigms of technology and the market, and advocates vigilance in this process. More concretely, such viewpoints can be linked to Maurizio Lazzerato's critique of the rise of *immaterial labour* as the new form of work organization in contemporary global capitalist society. Immaterial labour refers to the changes taking place in workers' labour processes in the manufacturing, knowledge and creative industries (including, for example, journalism and advertising), where the time-tested craftsmanship involved in direct labour tends to shift to the currently more privileged yet self-deleterious skills of the information age, involving cybernetics computers and mediated communication. Immaterial labour also refers to a parallel process of commoditization of activities that can be roughly labelled as traditionally being part of the realm of social skills: assigning status and building reputations (within specific communities of interest); and maintaining and structuring social relations (in teams and networks)—including identity play and performance. Nick Couldry, Göran Bolin, and others have extended these notions to articulate a perspective on immaterial media landscapes—where what is produced by people can be seen as existing increasingly in the realm of views, attitudes, symbols and ideas, yet has direct consequences for social and political realities.

This in turn has contributed to an equally recent *spatial turn* in media studies, emphasizing (the co-creation of) media and space/place relationships (Adams, 2009).

There runs a parallel argument alongside these and other more or less recent observations about the apparent immaterial, post-materialist and dematerialized, *weightless* nature of contemporary society (as in a reduction in the quantity of materials required to serve economic functions, including factories, machines and labour), attributing primacy to the largely informational and symbolic nature of life's processes, which in turn to some extent explains the significance of media as benchmarks for finding and circulating meaning. Indeed, contemporary social theory is suffused with claims-making about our increasingly liquid, ephemeral, self-reflexive, mobile, and otherwise less than stable, permanent, or tangible modern times (see in particular Bauman, 2000, 2007; Urry, 2007). The dissolution of communications' key sense-making categories—production and consumption—seem to fit nicely within this broader debate, and thus fit within processes of theoretical abstraction about the boundary-erasing nature of contemporary life as well as practical observation of the concurrent exposure to media people enjoy today. The media life perspective engages on both these levels.

In this essay, the study of media industries is considered in a context of what appear to be increasingly complex and boundary-breaking relationships between media companies, media technologies, media producers and consumers—what Henry Jenkins (2006) describes as a convergence culture. This particular approach is presented here as flowing from a more abstract appreciation of the role of media in everyday life, as people's lives are seen as lived in media—an ontological turn that presumes to build on and perhaps extend many existing theoretical, operational and organizational debates about the structure and conditions of

READING NOTES

_____

_____

_____

_____

_____

contemporary existence as described, however briefly and insufficiently, above.

In the current convergence culture—within which all media industries operate—the key question for theorizing media industries must be how we can adequately explain the process, content and consequences of consumption and production when people's contemporary media practices seem to include both at the same time. Further, the blurring of real or perceived boundaries between makers and users in an increasingly participatory media culture challenges consensual notions of what it means to work in the media industries (Deuze, 2007). This convergence can be seen as driven by an industry desperate for strong customer relationships, technologies that are increasingly cheap and easy to use, and a media culture that privileges an active audience (Turow, 2005). After considering more or less traditional theories of media industry studies—looking at the political economy of the industry and considering the different roles of audiences—I develop convergence culture as a third perspective. Although this perspective allows for a more mixed, hybrid and complex understanding of the roles, functions and work of media industries in society, it is not without problems—particularly regarding the co-optation of all creativity by corporations, and the colonization of consumer/producer agency by markets (Deuze, 2009). After these critical considerations, the essay concludes with discussing possible consequences for further research.

MEDIA INDUSTRIES AND SOCIETY

Beyond the crucial role media industries play in everyday life and the significance of their products and production networks in the global marketplace, another reason for carefully examining the media business and its workers is its influence on the cultural economy of contemporary cities. Cultural and creative industries tend to cluster close to certain urban regions—such as

Los Angeles, New York, Vancouver, Brisbane, Milan, Wellington, Munich and Manchester—and thus catalyse a flurry of economic, cultural and social activities in those regions. This, in turn, has led many local and regional governments to invest in public relations campaigns, profiling themselves as creative or media cities. Creative industries are attracted to, and attract, investors and generate business for restaurants, clubs, theatres, galleries, and other ingredients of cultural and economic life. Media thus are not only central to an understanding of everyday life in terms of the aesthetic quality and the utility they bring to information, entertainment and communication, they are also key to analysing the converging economic and cultural environment of the world's post-industrial urban spaces. Much of the work in the media industries is interconnected on a global scale through international co-production, outsourcing, offshoring and subcontracting practices. Combined with their role as accelerators of urban regeneration, these interconnected creative clusters contribute to a shift in power away from states and national territories to a transnationally converging cultural economy and economy of culture (Du Gay and Pryke, 2002).

Whereas the media industries generally operate on the premise of aggregating audiences for advertisers (while assuming to provide people with something in return for their work as audiences, such as services like news, information, entertainment), today the audience is not just a mass market to transmit messages to—it is also an increasingly segmented and fragmented public to collaborate with in the co-creation of content and experiences. Among creatives and brand managers in many if not most ad agencies the contemporary focus is on interactive advertising, which can be defined as the paid and unpaid presentation and promotion of sponsored products, services and ideas involving mutual action between consumers and producers (Leckenby and Li, 2000). Marketing communicators brainstorm about the potential of 'social', 'upstream' or even 'spherical' marketing (Svensson, 2005), which

350

refers to the strategic process of identifying and fulfilling consumer needs early in product development, up to and including customers and users at various stages in the total production and product innovation cycle. In journalism, editors of news publications actively consider adding what is called 'citizen journalism' to their websites, allowing members of the audience to respond, comment and submit their own news. In particular, convergence culture has been part of the organization of work in the computer and video game industries. Game publishers often consider their consumers as co-developers, where product innovation and development largely depends on online consumer communities. In the music and recording industry, both mainstream bands like Radiohead and Nine Inch Nails as well as so-called 'indie' acts on a local level, sidestep traditional cultural intermediaries such as record labels to directly interact, and collaborate with fans online (for example in terms of album cover design, concert set lists, mixing and remixing processes, and even album pricing). Media industries increasingly make use of this generally 'productive' consumer behaviour, which means that the role of creative labour and the management of cultural production taking place within such organizations is becoming increasingly complex as well. The ongoing merger of production and consumption across the various media, cultural and creative industries signals the emergence of a global convergence culture, based on an increasingly participatory and interactive engagement between different media forms and industries, between people and their media, as well as between professional and amateur media makers.

In short, when conceptualizing media industries, one is struck by the simultaneous occurrence of many instances of what we could call convergence:

- Convergence of *place*, as in the sites of media production

- Convergence of *identity*, as in notions of professional identity versus the cult of the amateur

- Convergence of *experience*, as in the way people interact with, give meaning to, and even actively make their media as a window to the world.

MEDIA INDUSTRIES AND WORK

The ecosystem of media organizations consists of a combination of (large and small) public service and for-profit companies dealing with the industrial and creative production and circulation of culture. In terms of media work, this culture refers not only to the production of spoken and written words, audio, still or moving images, buy (and increasingly) also to providing platforms for people to produce and exchange their own content. In contemporary definitions of what the work within these industries involves, four elements tend to get mixed up, which to some extent makes an adequate assessment of media industries rather difficult: content, connectivity, creativity and commerce—which all translate into the production of culture. Media industries produce content, yes, but also invest in platforms for connectivity—where fans and audiences provide free labour (Terranova, 2000). Media work is culture creation, and it tends to take place within a distinctly commercial context.

As argued before, in the current digital and networked global media ecosystem the roles played by advertisers, media producers and content consumers are converging. Through the widespread use of these networks the boundaries blur not only between geographical regions (households, cities), and between types of regions (local, global) and domains (private, public), but also between the dimensions that constitute regions themselves—such as material, symbolic and imaginary spaces (Falkheimer and Jansson, 2006). The production system of the media industry is a case in point, as it has become networked on a 'translocal' scale, integrating different locales of cultural production into a global production system, integrating and localizing cultural values and regional symbols across dispersed markets. Many industries—such as computer and video game development, motion pictures and television—offshore, subcontract and outsource various elements in the production process to save costs and redistribute risks. Examples are, securing international co-financing deals for television projects, filming and post-producing a movie at several locations (often in different countries), moving an editorial division or marketing department of a news organization to another part of the world (a practice called 'remote control journalism'),[1] mixing music recorded in Los Angeles in a studio outside London, localizing game titles set in one regional, cultural or national context in another part of the world, adding local soundtracks and hit songs to generic advertising campaigns generated for global brands, separating out the marketing and distribution of titles, and so on. It is important to note that within these networked forms of production people generally do not move across borders—ideas, skills and values do. In this sense, the globalization of production networks in the media industries can be considered a supercharged example of the broader trends in the mutual construction of social and spatial relationships in and through media.

In terms of media work, then, convergence relates to:

- The *inclusion* of various stakeholders—professional producers, audiences, sources, sponsors—in the (co-)creation of media content and experiences

- The *integration* of various media industries in a global production network

- The *immaterialization* or media production practices—as skills, values and ideas rather than people or machines move across such networks

- The *coordination* between distinctly different goals—creativity, commerce, content and connectivity—in the media production process.

CONVERGENCE CULTURE

In today's digital culture, media work can be seen as a stomping ground for the forces of increasingly differentiated production and innovation processes, and the complex interaction and integration between work, life and play, all of which get expressed in, and are facilitated by, the rapid development of new information and communication technologies. This convergence is not just a technological process. Media convergence must also be seen as having a cultural logic of its own, blurring the lines between economics (work) and culture (meaning); between production and consumption; between the competition and cooperation ('coopetition') implied in creativity, commerce, content and connectivity; between making media and using media; and between active or passive spectatorship of mediated culture.

When combined with ongoing efforts throughout the media industries to develop multimedia formats (either through mergers and integrating different company units, or by the increasingly popular networking of the production process across numerous subcontracted business partners), producer-consumer convergence poses significant challenges to theorizing media industries. Traditional frames of reference interpret these trends from distinctly different perspectives, looking at either the industry (political economy) or the audience (reception analysis). As mentioned earlier, the literature for some time now has clearly signalled the reductionist and ineffective nature of such approaches (see also Jenkins and Deuze, 2008).

One way that the increasing use of user-generated content in professional media production can be seen is as an example of the global media industries' attempts to secure, harness, and thus win back control over the circulation and consumption of culture. It can thus be viewed as evidence of the increasing rationalization and (thus) homogenization of all forms of public communication (including news and entertainment) in the hands of fewer and fewer multinational companies. However, such a traditional political economy of industry belies three contemporary developments in the structure and organization of media industries: vertical disintegration (partly because of failed synergies); media deconcentration; and outsourcing.

Although most of the major media corporations and production businesses consolidated their holdings into large corporate conglomerations in the 1990s, at the same time a parallel development of media deconcentration and corporate dysfunctionalism has been recorded. Research in various media industries consistently suggests that infighting and turf wars, slow centralized decision-making processes, mismanagement, difficulties in building or sustaining a knowledge-sharing work culture, as well as a general lack of cooperation among different media properties within the same corporation or holding firm, are among the key reasons why mergers or efforts towards achieving synergies in the cultural industries generally fail or do not deliver the expected results. Partly in a response to these failures, but also in an attempt to develop flexible strategies to cope with increasingly unpredictable and complex markets, a trend toward flexibilization of production and labour is accelerating throughout the media industries, which in turn signals less power over the creative process flowing from large media conglomerates, and increases co-creative relationships

between media professionals inside and outside of firms, as well as between consumers and producers of media. Whether in the movies, advertising, in journalism or video game development, most of the work in these industries is done by independent contractors, loosely affiliated teams, temporarily hired work groups, or otherwise contingently-employed labour, often spread across translocally-situated contexts (Hesmondhalgh, 2006). The roles of all those companies, networks and individuals in the creative process of the media industries converge (and diverge) in countless unpredictable, confusing and complex ways. My reading of the industry perspective on convergence culture does not assume that large corporations control all aspects of the production of news or entertainment. However, neither has the global market completely opened up to hundreds of thousands of small or independent companies. This complex and symbiotic two-tier production system runs throughout the cultural and creative industries, where corporations can have independent companies under long-term contracts, and where the same multinational companies can completely outsource production or acquire a show or movie after production elsewhere, and where ownership of different media properties has a tendency to change quickly.

Not only does this perspective on convergence culture from the view of the industry offer us a more complex, hybrid and colourful palette for looking at the production of culture, it also opens the door to include the audience, the consumer and the user into our framework for understanding the collisions and collusions of 'old' and 'new' in the contemporary media ecology.

The extent to which this convergence culture plays a significant role in the entire media ecology, including and interpellating the audience as a productive force in the creation and circulation of culture, can be illustrated by countless studies (for example in Europe conducted by the OECD, and in the US by the Pew Research Center's Internet & American Life Project)

READING NOTES

suggesting that, today, the majority of people *make* media when they *use* media (including but not limited to maintaining a blog; creating or working on a personal webpage; sharing original content such as artwork, photos, stories, or videos online; and remixing content found online). Media co-creation furthermore takes place in perhaps more modest terms, ranging from the customization of media devices (ringtones, wallpapers, screensavers, channel programming) to the often passionate production of fan movies, citizen journalism sites, online video mashups, and computer game modifications (or 'mods'). It must be clear that contemporary citizen-consumers demand the right to participate—or at the very least are constructed in such a way across all media industries.

With the gradual development of industrial standards and financially successful practices for media companies embracing audiences as co-creators of content, a glimpse is offered on the possible outcomes of the suggested convergence between sender and receiver from the perspective of the industry. Considering the corporate enclosure of the information commons, one has to note the triangular tactics of increasingly enforced restrictive regulation of copyright as a form of property, disintermediating practices of soliticiting users' free labour in the creative process, and opaque uses of social media to establish new ways of 'taming' or controlling the otherwise unpredictable behaviour of consumers. This is not to say that Internet users step blindly into such traps, nor that, when they do, companies are necessarily successful in harnessing their creativity. Indeed, the strategic or tactical opposition among certain individuals or groups of users to some extent feeds into the deliberate construction of consumers as 'unpredictable masses' by the contemporary mainstream in marketing and corporate communication. A traditional audience perspective would focus on the behaviour of audiences as either successful consumers, or as active in a strict sense of meaning-making. In a context of convergence culture, one could add a more explicit reference to emerging read/write multimedia literacies (Hartley, 2007) with a necessity to articulate legal rights and protections for the producing consumer—what Aoki (1993) has described as audience 'recoding' rights. Such approaches seem to be more responsive to the emerging complex relationships between media industries, their producers and the consumers.[2]

DISCUSSION

This essay has suggested how convergence culture takes place on both sides of the media spectrum: production and consumption. Within this spectrum, the distinctions between the traditional role-players in the creative process are dissolving. The key to understanding the currently emerging relationships between media consumers and producers, or between media owners and media workers (whether paid or voluntarist), is their complexity. These relationships are constantly reconfigured in a convergence culture, and at times are both reciprocal and antagonistic. Such liquid relationships are seldom stable, generally temporary and, at the very least, unpredictable. Lev Manovich (2005) calls this a 'culture of remix and remixability', where user-generated content exists both within and outside commercial contexts, and supports as well as subverts corporate control. While this may be true, it is safe to say that professionals—and the companies that employ them—are better protected and more powerful in negotiating terms of service than the average consumer is. The work that citizen-consumers do as part of what Von Hippel calls 'user-innovation communities' (2005: 103ff.), operating in a system of what Benkler describes as 'commons-based peer production' (2006: 60), is at least in part dependent on, contingent with and benefiting to, the market-driven efforts of the multinational media enterprise.

READING NOTES

_____

_____

_____

_____

_____

Faced with intense competition, an increasingly critical and unpredictable user, and heightened commercial pressures from a global market, media companies dismantle their production operations into a flexible global network of temporary affiliations in order to focus more on controlling distribution and access in a context of increasingly precarious labour conditions for media workers. At the same time, the audience seems to be quite content with, on the one hand spending more time with media than ever before, while, on the other hand, at the same time repurposing, remixing and creating their own media in the process. Media technologies contribute to converging the industrial and creative processes associated with both these trends, and suggest in their generally networked, remixable, customizable and portable form the need for a perspective on media production and consumption that is both aware of the interchangeable nature of these categories, and manages to articulate these artefacts and activities with broader arrangements in contemporary society. Jenkins's notion of a convergence culture can thus be seen as a fascinating case study to articulate broader concerns about the categories, perspectives and paradigms in the field of media and communication studies. With the media life framework as briefly explored at the outset of this piece, I hope to have offered a possible entry for this discussion. It is certainly one that I intend to explore further.

ENDNOTES

1. See http://deuze.blogspot.com/2006/11/remote-control-journalism.html

2. The culturally convergent practices of media industries, remixing professional content and user-generated content in the creative process, led *The Economist* (of 20 April 2006) to ask the fundamental question: what is a media company? Traditionally, media companies would be seen as audience aggregators: engaging in the production of content aimed as mass

audiences. Considering the social, technological and economic trends outlined above, such a definition has become problematic. Instead of audiences', media businesses today talk about 'networks', emphasizing media work as a practice that would (or should) generate endless opportunities for people to form communities of interest around content. This creates interesting dysfunctional family effects within large media corporations, where some parts of the firm are actively restructuring to meet the demands of what *The Economist* describes as a race to become 'the most liquid media marketplace, while other sectors of the company are still very much in the process of developing intricate Digital Rights Management (DRM) software intended to prevent all this arguably profitable audience activity from actually taking off (Benkler, 2006).

REFERENCES

Adams, Paul C. (2009) *Geographies of Media and Communication.* Somerset: Wiley-Blackwell.

Aoki, Keith (1993) Adrift in the Intertext: Authorship and Audience "Recording" Rights', *Chicago-Kent Law Review* 68.

Balnaves, Mark, Mayrhofer, Debra and Shoesmith Brian (2004) 'Media Professions and the New Humanism', *Continuum: Journal of Media & Cultural Studies* 18(2): 191–203.

Bauman, Zygmunt (2000) *Liquid Modernity.* Cambridge: Polity Press.

Bauman, Zygmunt (2007) *Liquid Life.* Cambridge: Polity Press.

Benkler, Yochai (2006) *The Wealth of Networks.* New Haven, CT: Yale University Press.

Canclini, Néstor Garcìa (2001) *Consumers and Citizens: Globalization and Multicultural Conflicts.* Minneapolis: University of Minnesota Press.

Deuze, Mark (2007) *Media Work.* Cambridge: Polity Press.

Deuze, Mark (2009) 'Convergence Culture and Media Work', in A. Perren and J. Holt (eds) *Media Industries: History, Method, and Theory.* Malden: Blackwell.

Du Gay, Paul and Pryke, Michael (eds) (2002) *Cultural Economy: Cultural Analysis and Commercial Life.* London: Sage.

Falkheimer, Jesper and André Jansson (eds) (2006) *Geographies of Communication: The Spatial Turn in Media Studies.* Göteborg: Nordicom.

READING NOTES

_____

_____

_____

_____

Hartley, John (2007) '"There are Other Ways of Being in the Truth": The Uses of Multimedia Literacy', *International Journal of Cultural Studies* 10(1): 135–44.

Hesmondhalgh, David (ed.)(2006) *Media Production*. Maidenhead and Milton Keynes: The Open University Press.

Hesmondhalgh, David and Toynbee, Jason (eds) (2008) *The Media and Social Theory*. London: Routledge.

Jenkins, Henry (2006) *Convergence Culture: Where Old and New Media Collide*. New York: New York University Press.

Jenkins, Henry and Deuze, Mark (2008) 'Convergence Culture', *Convergence* 14(1): 5–12.

Keen, Andrew (2008) *The Cult of the Amateur*. New York: Broadway Business.

Leckenby, John and Li, Hairong (2000) 'Why We Need the *Journal of Interactive Advertising*', *Journal of Interactive Advertising* 1(1). www.jiad.org/vol1/no1/editors/index.htm.

Lundby, Knut (ed.) (2009) *Mediatization: Concept, Changes, Consequences*. New York: Peter Lang.

Manovich, Lev (2005) *Remixability*. October–November 2005. www.manovich.net/DOCS/Remix_modular.doc

Power, Dominic and Scott, Allen (eds) (2004) *Cultural Industries and the Production of Culture*. London: Routledge.

Silverstone, Roger (2007) *Media and Morality: On the Rise of the Mediapolis*. Cambridge: Polity Press.

Strate, Lance (2006) *Echoes and Reflections: On Media Ecology as a Field of Study*. Cresskill, NJ: Hampton Press.

Svensson, Göran (2005) 'The Spherical Marketing Concept: A Revitalization of the Marketing Concept', *European Journal of Marketing* 39(1/2): 5–15.

Terranova, Tiziana (2000) 'Free Labour: Producing Culture for the Digital Economy', *Social Text* 18(2): 33–57.

Turow, Joseph (2005) 'Audience Construction and Culture Production: Marketing Surveillance in the Digital Age', *The Annals of the American Academy of Political and Social Sciences* 597: 103–21.

Urry, John (2007) *Mobilities*. Cambridge: Polity Press.

Von Hippel, Eric (2005) *Democratizing Innovations*. Boston: MIT Press.

READING NOTES

Chapter 13

Media Careers

"It's a wonderful life. You get paid to do what other folks do for pleasure: read, write, travel, meet all kinds of people, and learn a lot about things that interest you. It's true that newspaper work can be hard, sometimes tedious. But there's this payoff: It's work that matters."

—JENNIE BUCKNER, EDITOR OF THE *CHARLOTTE OBSERVER*

Communications is a huge, youth-oriented arena that invites the curious, creative, and industrious to find a place. Media careers are competitive and demand dedication and perseverance, but the reward is a chance to touch millions of lives. Communications jobs aligned with the older technologies are constantly being updated and redefined by the new media. Current examples are the transitions from traditional newspapers to online media and from broadcasting to "narrowcasting." Because younger audiences tend to anticipate mainstream media-consumption patterns, employers will pay a premium to hire college graduates who have new media skills and knowledge.

As the various media industries integrate in a process known as convergence, most communications jobs these days involve both print and electronic media. These can be exciting jobs in which you are working on a magazine article or documentary one day and then on a Web site the next. An advertising or public relations campaign probably will involve several media simultaneously. Journalists must know how to cast their news stories for print, broadcast, and online audiences.

A career in communications will take you to amazing places and introduce you to fascinating people. You can prepare for the challenges and opportunities of media work by developing a diverse skill set. Your goal is to make choices that bring out your best.

The learning aims of this chapter include to

- examine the current conditions of major media industries,

- suggest some career opportunities within those industries,

- describe the range of skills media professionals need, and
- recommend job-hunting strategies.

Required Reading: This chapter is accompanied by Mark Bowden's profile for *Atlantic Monthly* of television writer/producer David Simon. Bowden describes Simon as "the angriest man in television" because of Simon's passionate advocacy of social justice. Simon is a former newspaper police-beat reporter turned screenwriter who forged his close personal encounters of life on the streets into scripts for the NBC-TV drama series *Homicide* and Home Box Office's *The Corner*. His next project was the urban drama series *The Wire*, hailed by critics as one of broadcasting's finest accomplishments. *The Wire*'s gritty, fictional depiction of inner-city Baltimore features Simon's various alter egos battling institutional indifference in government, education, and the press to dramatize the plight of America's working poor. In 2010, Simon created another critically acclaimed dramatic series, *Treme,* about life in New Orleans shortly after Hurricane Katrina.

THE INTERNET

Publishing for the Internet, sometimes called "new media," has exploded on the World Wide Web since the late 1990s. Nearly every business, nonprofit organization, interest group, and government organization in the United States has a presence on the Web, so the demand for Internet publishing professionals is tremendous.

While being young might be a disadvantage in other fields, it is the norm in Internet publishing. Many of the most prominent Web professionals are in their twenties or thirties. Some college students, and even high school students, run their own successful Web-design businesses. For example, a high school student worked after school in a Boston flower shop. The shop owners decided they needed an e-commerce Web site, but could not afford to pay to develop one. They offered the young man a percentage of their business if he

would create a site for them. He agreed, and the site eventually grew into the hugely successful Gifts.com, which he continued to manage for the owners while he attended college. After college, he sold his part of the business back to the owners for $250,000, which he used to pay off his college debt.

E-commerce, or online sales, is growing rapidly in the United States and the world. Companies harness the Internet to increase profits and reduce operating costs in a variety of ways. Like the Boston flower shop, existing retailers can expand their reach without building more stores. Companies such as Amazon.com run hugely successful retail operations without any storefronts at all.

As a result, online advertising offers many career opportunities. The Web has been the fastest-growing advertising medium in recent years. Advertisers like the low cost compared to other media and the Web's ability to target likely customers by tracking users who click on their ads. Employment opportunities abound for designers and producers with computer and Internet skills not only online, but also in print, including for books, magazines, newspapers, press kits, posters, brochures, calendars, flyers, and packaging. Desktop publishers typically design page layouts and logotypes, create graphic illustrations, convert photographs into digital images, and manipulate the text and images to display information in an attractive and readable format. Desktop publishing enables even the smallest businesses and organizations to do their own printing in-house, but they do not necessarily have design expertise, which means there is an even greater need than before for graphic designers who know how to use these tools.

Blogging is also an emerging opportunity on the Web. Anyone with a networked computer can launch a blog at no cost on a site such as blogger.com or wordpress.com. Once your blog has started, it is up to you to attract an audience. Some blogs and fan Web sites build communities, such as www.WouldYouBelieve.com

for fans of the original television series *Get Smart*. Many bloggers do not make money from their work initially, but, with the Web's global reach, they have the potential of earning significant income from their writing via online advertising.

Another appealing aspect to writing for the Internet is that innovation is welcomed. Enterprising writers can develop so-called "hyper-local" blogs and Web sites that present information in an interesting way. For example, a Chicago journalist's blog, on www.EveryBlock.com, melds public police data with Google maps to show neighborhood crime patterns in 15 U.S. cities. Another example of an ingenious blog is www.BaristaNet.com, where a pair of former newspapermen, calling themselves "baristas," serve up a mix of community-contributed news and their own sense of humor to suburban New Jerseyites.

Anthony Moor, lead local editor at Yahoo!, sees a bright future in online-media jobs. He says that as media companies lay off traditional workers, they hire more online writers and designers. He noticed "a healthy supply of digital jobs still up for grabs" at media companies such as The New York Times Company, the Tribune Company including the *Los Angeles Times*, and MTV cable networks. Moor recommends that students start their own blogs to learn how the blogosphere intersects with the news industry.

Aspiring designers should acquire Web design and authoring skills, such as coding Web sites in HTML (hypertext markup language), using Web authoring tools such as Adobe Dreamweaver, designing vector-based illustrations with tools such as Adobe Illustrator, editing digital photographs with Adobe Photoshop, producing podcasts, or creating a Flash presentation. Knowing how to optimize Web sites for Web search engines such as Google and Yahoo!, and how to use Web content management systems such as Joomla.com, also will pay dividends. The bottom line is that diversified communications skill sets will open doors for you in the online-media world.

MAGAZINE PUBLISHING

The incredible diversity of magazines today makes magazine publishing an appealing place for young communications professionals to find careers in writing, editing, designing, or advertising. There is a magazine for almost every consumer special interest (such as *Car and Driver* or *Popular Photography*), how-to and motivational magazines (*O, The Oprah Magazine,* or *Martha Stewart Living*), trade and professional magazines (*Billboard* or *Variety*), public relations magazines (American Airlines' *American Way*), research journals (the *New England Journal of Medicine* or *Communication Research*), city magazines (*New York*), women's magazines (*Cosmopolitan*), fashion magazines for men and women (*GQ* and *Vogue*), general interest magazines (*Vanity Fair and The New Yorker*), comic books, or Webzines (niche publications with small audiences), and so on.

Many of the most prominent magazines are owned by media conglomerates, such as Time Warner or Hearst Corporation. Thousands of titles such as *Good Housekeeping* and *Glamour* have international editions. New York City has a large concentration of magazine publishers, so that is a great place to hunt for a magazine job.

The U.S. magazine industry estimates that the average person reads 12 magazines per month, with many of those copies being shared with friends (pass-along circulation). Not only can magazines address specific audience segments, but also they can turn out custom versions of the same issue for different parts of the country or different types of readers. For example, a business magazine such as *The Economist* could print the headline "Top Investment Opportunities" on its cover for its upscale home subscribers, while offering "Getting into the Stock Market" on its newsstand edition. Audience segmentation enables the magazine industry to serve nearly every specific audience.

Two nonprofit groups track magazine circulation figures: the Audit Bureau of Circulations for North America and BPA International for other countries. The AARP, an association for retired persons, published the two public relations magazines with the largest U.S. circulations, with more than 36 million readers combined. They are free with AARP membership. The third-largest magazine circulation belongs to another free public relations publication, the *Costco Connection,* with more than eight million readers, followed by two traditional titles, *Better Homes and Gardens* and *Reader's Digest,* with more than seven million readers each. Almost all magazines get about three-fourths of their revenue from advertising, except for *Consumer Reports,* which is published by the nonprofit Consumers Union and is entirely subscription-supported in its print and online editions.

Most magazine companies are organized into editorial, advertising, and circulation departments, with a deputy editor or manager in charge of each department and the editor-in-chief or executive editor in charge of all. Some also have an online department. Monthly magazines, such as *Atlantic Monthly, Playboy,* or *Highlights for Children,* generally have few full-time writers on staff and instead hire self-employed, freelance writers to produce individual pieces for the magazine.

Editors typically assign stories to writers, but their freelancers also can pitch their own ideas for stories. Many freelancers write simultaneously for several different magazines and build up a special expertise in certain topics, such as education, national defense, the environment, medicine, economics, or law. Freelancers also contribute photography and illustrations, editorial cartoons, and crossword puzzles, as well as reviews of the arts, movies, restaurants, and music recordings.

An example of a successful freelance magazine writer is Mark Bowden, a former reporter for the *Philadelphia Inquirer,* who writes investigative journalism for *Vanity Fair,* the *Atlantic Monthly, Men's Journal, Sports Illustrated,* and *Rolling Stone.* Bowden was assigned by the *Inquirer* to cover the U.S. military intervention in Somalia in 1993. He gathered his articles into a 1999 book, *Black Hawk Down,* which became a best seller and was adapted into a Columbia Pictures motion picture directed by Ridley Scott and

released in 2001. This chapter's required reading is Bowden's *Atlantic Monthly* article about his friend and fellow journalist David Simon.

Magazines stress visual style and impact, so there are many great career opportunities for graphic artists and Web designers in the magazine industry. Most layout and design is done in-house, with the occasional special issue assigned to a freelancer. A magazine's art director generally supervises its layout and graphic look. In magazines such as *Vogue,* the art director is often as important a decision maker as the editor-in-chief of the magazine.

The business operations in a magazine are headed by the publisher. The key departments are advertising sales and circulation. Magazines are going online to sell subscriptions, provide supplementary content, offer gateways to marketing partners, tie in blogs and social media that cultivate interactions from readers, and sell archived articles. The publisher is responsible for making sure a magazine succeeds economically.

ADVERTISING

A key part of marketing is advertising—the presentation or promotion of ideas, goods, or services by a business or nonprofit organization. Advertising is ubiquitous in our society and employs millions of workers worldwide. Regardless of fluctuations in overall economic activity, the proportion of U.S. income spent on advertising has remained consistent over the decades at about 2.5 percent of the nation's gross domestic product, which is a measure of the total economic productivity. From a peak of $264.5 billion in 2007, U.S. advertising spending fell to $222.5 billion in 2009 during the global economic recession, followed by a gradual recovery. Since its inception in the late 1990s, Internet advertising has grown rapidly, while newspaper and magazine advertising has declined.

Amid a prevailing economic downturn, the National Football League's Super Bowl XLIV in 2010 between the Indianapolis Colts and the

New Orleans Saints nevertheless set an all-time record for advertising revenues from a single event. The game's 106.5 million viewers comprised the largest U.S. television audience in history, topping the final episode of the television show *M*A*S*H* in 1983. CBS Network aired almost 48 minutes of advertising messages during the game, with dot-com companies the largest category of advertiser and Anheuser-Busch the top single advertiser.

CBS charged $2.8 million for airing a single 30-second spot, not including production costs. Consumers contributed to the creativity with four Super Bowl ads for Doritos brand snacks. In addition to commercials, numerous brands got exposure through in-stadium, scoreboard, and program placement; souvenir and novelty sales; and magazine, newspaper, and online promotions. For example, Reebok enjoyed 580 on-screen occurrences of its brand during the game for a total duration of more than 23 minutes, according to Nielsen Audience Research.

Most media, including television, general interest magazines, newspapers, and billboards, traditionally have charged for advertising according to the number of audience members exposed to an ad at "cost per thousand" exposures, or CPM (the "M" is from the French word *mille*). Media convergence is causing that approach of "broadcasting" an advertising message to be reconsidered.

The problem with broadcasting an advertising message to a general audience is circulation waste. Early retailer and pioneering advertiser John Wanamaker memorably said, "Half the money I spend on advertising is wasted; the trouble is I don't know which half." Advertising clients now want to reach likely purchasers in specific audience segments with media such as direct mail, cable, special interest magazines, radio, newspaper supplements, and the Internet. The new revenue models for target marketing figure advertising costs based not on exposures, but instead on customer responses such as inquiries or purchases.

More than 13,000 advertising agencies are based in the United States, ranging from small, specialized firms to huge global concerns. Manhattan's Madison Avenue has been synonymous with the industry, but recently, agencies have moved elsewhere to find lower rents. Some of the more successful agencies are located in relatively small cities, such as the Martin Agency in Richmond, Virginia. Among the five largest U.S. advertising firms in terms of billings, or fees charged, the Martin Agency is best known for its memorable campaigns for GEICO Insurance, including the GEICO cavemen and Martin the Gecko.

Twenty-seven ad agencies reside in Minnesota, including offices of BBDO Worldwide, Campbell Mithun, and Carmichael Lynch, and have banded together to co-sponsor a Web site, MinneAdpolis.com, proclaiming Minneapolis the "City of Advertising." The Web site greets readers: "The black shirt and skinny jeans are a dead giveaway. You, my friend, are in advertising. And you've come to the right place: Minneapolis is a mecca for your type."

Most full-service ad agencies have departments for accounts, research, creative, and media. An account manager represents various clients at the agency and must thoroughly understand their businesses and markets, and come up with fresh promotional strategies. The account managers turn to the research department to gather data about targeted consumers. Researchers gather valuable measurements of demographics (audience characteristics), psychographics (attitudes, beliefs, and motivations), and positioning (the specific customer type for the client). Research helps the agency to convince its clients that the ads they produce will work. Once the creative department has executed the ads, the media department purchases time and space in the mass media.

While these job roles in ad agencies vary in their specific duties, all require general business acumen, strong speaking and writing skills, creativity, demonstrated leadership experience, computer spreadsheet skills, organizational experience, enthusiasm, and a hunger to succeed. Many agencies offer internships so they can preview up-and-coming talent. Candidates should prepare a physical and Web portfolio of their advertising projects, copywriting, layouts, market research, and campaigns. Perhaps most important, to communicate great enthusiasm and preparedness, candidates should research the agency's principal personnel, main clients, promotional specialties, and track record in the business.

Advertisers are always looking for creative, non-traditional ways to promote their products, from specialty ads on pens and T-shirts to blimps to product placement in movies to celebrity branding to sponsorships of sports stadiums. In 1982, sales of Hershey's peanut butter candy Reese's Pieces took off with placement in the blockbuster film *E.T.: The Extra-Terrestrial*, after Hershey's competitor, the Mars Candy Company, turned down director Steven Spielberg's offer to feature its market-leading M&Ms in the film.

In fall 2006, CBS Television advertised its new fall lineup of shows by imprinting slogans on 35 million eggs sold in grocery stores. Television reality shows *The Biggest Loser*, *American Idol*, and *Extreme Makeover: Home Edition* regularly have many product placements.

New media are transforming advertising into more interactive, personal experiences, perfect for targeting younger audiences. In a cutting-edge strategy known as *viral marketing*, promotions are spread person-to-person via existing interpersonal and online social networks. Successful viral-marketing campaigns promoted the cable show *Mystery Science Theater 3000*, the independent feature film *The Blair Witch Project*, and chicken sandwiches through Burger King's "Subservient Chicken" campaign. Web 2.0 sites such as Twitter, Facebook, MySpace, and YouTube are prime vehicles for viral marketing.

BOOK PUBLISHING

Despite tremendous changes in the book-publishing business, the book medium is alive and well. Bowker, the publisher of the *Books in Print* database, estimates there were more than 275,000 new U.S. titles and editions published in 2008. On-demand book printing increased a staggering 132 percent to more than 285,000 books printed. The largest on-demand book printer is Lightning Source, with a digital library of more than 600,000 books.

The U.S. book industry is dominated by five global media conglomerates beholden to investors: Bertelsmann AG, Pearson, News Corporation, Time Warner, and Holtzbrinck. In addition, there are thousands of smaller publishing houses with more esoteric concerns, such as promoting appreciation of poetry, preserving the family publishing business, or serving a niche or focused audience.

E-books are on the verge of transforming the industry by reducing costs of production and distribution and increasing reader convenience, but at present, most readers still prefer their books on paper. Amazon's Kindle e-book reader has become a popular consumer electronics device, and in 2010, Apple released the iPad tablet computer that also could serve as an e-book reader. The bookseller Barnes & Noble and the consumer electronics giant Sony also have released e-book readers.

Publishers have four general book categories: educational, reference, and professional are the first three, with trade books making up the rest. Many smaller publishers specialize in certain categories and subjects. For example, Sage Publications in Newbury Park, California, specializes in college textbooks and reference books, as well as print and online academic journals. Books come in several forms besides cloth cover and paperback, including audio books on CD and online, e-books for portable electronic reading devices and online, mobile books for cell phones and MP3 players. Accessible publishing serves impaired readers with technologies such as Braille, audio books, specialized fonts, and digital talking books. This flood of new formats has triggered a debate over whether online reading is qualitatively different from print.

Publishing houses employ full-time editors to acquire books by negotiating with authors, develop manuscript projects, obtain copyright permissions, copyedit and fact-check, design and lay out the books, and promote them. Many book publishers employ freelancers for editing, proofing, layout, design, and other production aspects. Three-quarters of book editors are women.

Book editors need a good eye for storytelling, a good ear for language, an attention to detail, and an ability to work well with creative individuals. They should be avid readers themselves. They are always learning something new from the books they edit. Most book editors are working on multiple titles at the same time, each of which generally takes from nine to 12 months of copyediting, designing, and proofing before publication. The average book sells a few thousand copies, but every editor is on the lookout for the next million-selling blockbuster.

The other major role for book publishers is promoting their products. As book editor Jeanette Perez of HarperCollins said, "Working closely with the authors is, for me, the best part of the job. But once the editing process is finished, my role changes from editor to salesperson and marketer." Publishers try to promote their books through a combination of Web sites, jacket blurbs, magazine and newspaper reviews, excerpts in periodicals, author book tours, and best seller lists. After the promotional campaign, when most of a book's sales occur, a book will go to the publisher's *backlist.*

The changing nature of the modern book editor's role has created entrepreneurial opportunities for writing coaches, literary scouts, and agents. The role of the literary agent has grown enormously in the book industry. The large publishers receive so many book proposals that it is almost impossible to get a book considered without an agent. Waiting for their first book contract can be frustrating for authors, but Perez at HarperCollins encourages them to keep trying: "I think it's really helpful when writers join workshops or take a writing class. That way they can get the early criticism they need as well as make contacts in the writing world." Cultural, literary, and civic groups such as the Literary Group International

(literarygroup.com) or the CityLit Project in Baltimore, Maryland (citylitproject.com), are great for author networking.

Although online booksellers such Amazon.com and BarnesandNoble.com are challenging for dominance, the big chain bookstores, such as Barnes & Noble, Books-A-Million, and Borders Books and Music, still sell more than half of all books in the United States. Independent bookstores, such as the Strand Book Store in New York City, Politics and Prose in Washington, D.C., and Tattered Cover in Denver, Colorado, also can play a vital role in helping a book gain a national audience as they cater to influential tastemakers.

Print-on-demand (POD) books are ideally suited to online booksellers because there are no inventory costs, and they can be shipped nearly as quickly as preprinted books. Lightning Source offers the Espresso Book Machine, a compact, desktop book-printing kiosk that can print books on demand while the customer waits. Traditional bookstores, such as Borders or Barnes & Noble, carry POD books, although they do not like them because of smaller profits on special orders. POD enables micropublishing at Loyola University Maryland, where Apprentice House, the only U.S. book publisher run by college students, issues several titles each year in conjunction with the university's book publishing course sequence housed in its department of communication.

PUBLIC RELATIONS

More than a half-million Americans work in public relations. Some work in the 6,000-plus public relations agencies across the United States. The three agencies with the most employees are Weber Shandwick (New York City), Fleishman-Hillard (St. Louis), and Ketchum (New York City), with offices in other U.S. cities and around the world as well. Eighty percent of all large companies and nonprofit organizations have their own public relations departments.

Public relations practitioners who work for individual companies as opposed to a public relations agency can be known as press secretaries, information officers, public affairs specialists, or communication specialists. They keep the public informed about the activities of their agencies. One of the most visible public relations practitioners is the White House press secretary, who holds a daily briefing for reporters and is available to respond to press inquiries involving the presidency.

Public relations professionals serve as advocates for manufacturers, retailers, charities, other non-profits, business and professional associations, universities, colleges, private high schools, churches and synagogues, hospitals, political parties and candidates, government lobbying groups, think tanks, community activists, and even media companies—in short, just about any type of organization with a story to tell. Public relations professionals operate at all levels of communication to establish positive relationships with the public—from interpersonal to mass communication. E-mail, the Web, and online social media have revolutionized public relations work by allowing public relations practitioners to reach out to the public directly and to rely less on other media. However, most public relations work still is done the old-fashioned way.

The main functions of public relations are news management, community relations and relationship building, crisis management, and lobbying. Each of these functions entails research, counseling, and communication activities. The internal and external groups of interest are typically called publics.

News management includes the publicity activities most people associate with public relations: writing news releases, preparing press kits, producing VNRs (video news releases), contacting news organizations (media relations), staging publicity stunts, leaking information and launching "trial balloons" to try out ideas on the public, granting exclusives to specific media, holding news conferences, and negotiating corporate sponsorships for public institutions such as sports teams or the arts. Compared to paid advertising, print and video news releases have the

advantage of acquiring the credibility of the news organizations that publish or broadcast them, but the disadvantage of loss of control over the message. A news release should be composed to look and sound like news and be delivered when and how the media want and need it. Releases that are ready-to-use are more likely to get into the news and to be used as-is without editing. Publicity agents need to know the news business inside out, including writing in appropriate journalistic style, cultivating newsroom contacts, and knowing daily publication and broadcast deadlines.

Press kits include a news release, brochures, maps, photographs, leadership profiles, and other information about the sponsor. VNRs include recorded interview samples, which broadcasters call "sound bites" or "actualities," with full identification; illustrative video, or "B-roll;" a sample broadcast news script; and a finished, ready-to-use video news package at various lengths, such as two minutes, one minute, and 30 seconds. VNRs formerly were shipped on broadcast-quality videotapes, but now DVDs are cheaper and easier for PR people to produce and news departments to use. Contact television stations in advance to get their video technical requirements.

The community-relations function of public relations includes cultivating partnerships with community and government groups, fundraising, publishing newsletters and magazines, scheduling speaking engagements and preparing speeches for organization officials, sponsoring public initiatives and giving awards consistent with the client's or employer's message and values, donating to charities, and responding to the public's queries or complaints. Public relations staff usually also are responsible for maintaining good internal relations between management and employees by publishing newsletters and staging information sessions and social events.

Crisis management is a specialized function of public relations that is rarely needed but requires constant readiness, for only well-prepared organizations are likely to survive a serious emergency with their public images intact. Lobbying is public relations aimed at legislators. Lobbyists represent companies or entire industries and insure that their client's views are taken into account when legislation that will have an impact on them is being crafted. Though lobbyists have their own image problem as people criticize them for representing private interests and the expense of the public interest, they serve an essential role in a democracy, and their right to represent their clients is protected by the First Amendment. Because lawmakers' support can be so important to their clients, Washington lobbyists are among the best-paid public relations professionals.

Most entry-level public relations specialists hold an undergraduate degree in journalism or communication. Work experience in electronic or print journalism is desirable, as is knowledge of the employer's specific operation—information technology, health care, science, engineering, sales, or finance, for example. College students should seek networking and development opportunities with the local chapter of the Public Relations Student Society of America, affiliated with the PRSA, or the International Association of Business Communicators (IABC).

A unique aspect of public relations work as compared to other media careers is its quasi-professional status through accreditation established in 1965 by the PRSA. Professionals with "APR" (Accredited in Public Relations) after their names have worked in the field for at least five years, have been recommended by an accredited PRSA member, and have passed an extensive written and oral examination. The IABC has its own certification program, called Accredited Business Communicator (ABC). While many people without APR or ABC certifications do good public relations work, having such professional stamps of approval tells the world that you hold high ethical and professional standards, which might make a difference in mid-career advancement opportunities.

Public relations specialists must show creativity, initiative, and good judgment, and have the ability to write and to speak clearly and convincingly. Decision-making, problem-solving, and research skills also are important. People who choose public relations as a career should be outgoing and self-confident, understand human psychology, and be enthusiastic about what they do. They should be competitive, yet able to function as part of a team, and be open to new ideas.

RADIO

The Federal Telecommunications Act of 1996 relaxed station ownership restrictions, and the ownership changes that followed led to elimination of many local radio announcer jobs. Old dreams of becoming a radio disc jockey are now tempered by the reality that most chain-operated radio stations no longer employ local on-air talent. Instead, listeners hear voices they do not realize are coming from corporate broadcast centers in other cities.

For example, Clear Channel Communications, Inc. owns six of the eight stations licensed to broadcast in the Wheeling, West Virginia, market. All six are run out of one facility by a computer technician operating the stations' automated systems and one announcer, who insert the station identification, local ads, and news breaks into the corporate feed. Computerized *voice-tracking* makes out-of-town "cyber-jocks" sound as if they originate in Wheeling, without ever having actually visited there. Listeners hear a big-city sound with nationally known radio personalities, such as Tom Joyner and Don Imus. These turnkey networks allow Clear Channel to lay off most of the local staff, thereby reducing costs and maximizing dividends for its stockholders.

Radio properties are attractive to big media because radio programming formats can target specific consumer markets ("narrowcasting"). The radio audience-measurement company Arbitron tracks 54 different radio formats. The Country format is programmed at about 13 percent of stations nationwide, followed by News Talk (11 percent), Adult Contemporary (7 percent), Pop Contemporary Hits Radio (6 percent), Classic Rock (5 percent), and Urban Adult Contemporary (4 percent). Radio station groups can diversify their audiences by combining formats. Of the dozens of radio groups in the United States, Clear Channel is largest, with about 900 out of a total of 10,000 commercial radio stations. Clear Channel's stations are connected to its Web radio network called iHeartRadio, a name chosen to respond to Clear Channel's anti-local reputation. About a third of its stations simulcast on HD digital radio, primarily for the benefit of car listeners.

A growth area in the radio business is nationally-syndicated (or "networked") entertainment programming. The largest program provider, Premiere Radio Network, a Clear Channel subsidiary, syndicates 70 programs weekly to more than 7,800 radio affiliates reaching more than 180 million listeners. Premiere's feature personalities include Rush Limbaugh, Glenn Beck, and Dan Patrick. Many radio personalities have crossover cable television shows.

Radio is ubiquitous at home, in cars, at work, and for people engaging in leisure activities. According to a 2009 report from Nielsen, about 80 percent of Americans listen to broadcast radio, with another 15 percent tuning in to satellite radio. Of an average of about 109 minutes per day listening to broadcast radio, a whopping 94 minutes is in automobiles during morning and afternoon drive-time. Web radio is small but growing at nine percent of the (mostly younger) audience, and is responsible for a slow but steady decline in broadcast radio listenership.

There are thousands of radio stations that stream their programming on the Web, and thousands more Web-only stations, such as Yahoo! Music, AOL Music, Rhapsody, MTV, SHOUTcast, and Pandora. Pandora.com is described as an automated music listening service with a library of 700,000 tracks. Pandora has a two subscription plans: free with ads, or fee-based without ads. *The New York Times* reported in March 2010 that Pandora had 48 million users who listened an average of nearly 12 hours per month.

After Sirius and XM satellite radio services merged in 2008, Sirius XM claimed more than 18 million subscribers. Satellite radio is especially popular with people who drive a lot, such as long-haul truck drivers. Customers pay either monthly or a one-time fee for the lifetime of the receiver and for that fee can listen to hundreds of channels. Moreover, they do not have to find a new channel carrying the same content as they travel from city to city. Some XM channels programmed by Clear Channel have commercials, while Sirius is commercial-free.

National Public Radio (NPR) is a programming service for local noncommercial stations owned by states and municipalities, universities, public libraries, school boards, and other nonprofit community groups. NPR and the public radio stations formerly got most of their funding from the federal government, but now they rely primarily on listener and corporate donations, and selling their programs. Stations pay NPR $6,000 in annual dues plus fees for individual programs, the most popular being two daily news programs, *All Things Considered* and *Morning Edition*. According to the Radio Research Consortium, public radio accounts for about five percent of U.S. radio listeners. In other countries, public radio stations are run by the government and dominate their radio systems.

Radio station program directors decide what type of music will be played and supervise on-air personnel. Producers coordinate the activities of on-air personalities, production staff, and news editors. With unscripted talk shows, producers must be ready to deal with unforeseen developments at a moment's notice. Producers also program the station's Web site and streaming audio.

The Federal Communications Commission (FCC) requires over-the-air broadcast radio stations to have an engineer in charge of the station's terrestrial transmitter and tower. Most stations forge collaborations with local newspapers and/or television stations for news coverage of local events and the city council.

The aspect of radio-station operations that has grown during ownership concentration is advertising and promotions. Sales personnel handle local accounts, call on retailers, offer special ad packages, and earn commissions. The ad rates that stations can charge depend on audience measurements by independent researchers such as Arbitron. Promotions departments handle on-site DJ events at shopping malls, car dealers, and outdoor concerts; community partnerships for charitable causes; and radio listener contests.

TELEVISION

Holding a U.S. television station license has been called the closest thing to having the legal right to print money. Despite increasing competition in recent years, the television business continues to be very lucrative. According to Nielsen Media Research, of all advertising dollars spent in the United States in 2009, local television stations received 16 percent, network television 23 percent, and cable 23 percent. These ad revenue figures compare to 15 percent for magazines, eight percent for newspapers, seven percent for Internet, and four percent for radio.

There are about 1,600 over-the-air broadcast television stations licensed by the FCC, of which 400 are noncommercial public stations. Almost all are owned by station groups. More than 60 percent of U.S. viewers get their local over-the-air stations via cable. Nearly all stations are affiliated with one or more programming networks, all owned by global media conglomerates: NBC (General Electric), Fox (News Corporation), CBS (CBS Corporation), ABC (Disney), and CW (Time Warner). Some major market stations, such as WBZ in Boston and KNBC in Los Angeles, are network-owned and -operated (O&Os). Some stations also affiliate with cable programmers such as Fox News, CNN, ESPN, and MTV. In addition to network programming, many television stations also carry syndicated shows, including five-day-a-week shows, such as *Oprah*, *Jerry Springer*, *Entertainment Tonight*, and *Wheel of Fortune*.

Nielsen Media Research divides the lower 48 states of the United States into 210 media markets or population centers. In 2009, the top three markets in television households were New York City (seven million television households), Los Angeles (five million), and Chicago (three million), while Glendive, Montana, ranked last with 3,940 television households. Audience ratings are important because they determine how much stations can charge for their advertising. A program's audience rating is the percentage of all television households. Its audience share is the percentage of television households watching television at the time.

The concept of audience measurement has been complicated by multiple-television households and viewing over the Internet. Nielsen has "people meters" for family members to register their viewing. Arbitron, the leading radio ratings company, has introduced a wireless people-meter in 48 markets that will measure all media consumption, including television viewing.

U.S. public television is structured similarly to public radio. The Public Broadcasting Service, or PBS, originally got most of its operating funds from a federal government organization, the Corporation for Public Broadcasting. However, in recent years, it has had to rely more on fees collected from more than 300 "member" local public stations, which in turn ask viewers and corporations for donations. Much of public-television programming is produced by major public stations, such as WETA in Washington, D.C. (*PBS News Hour*), WNET in New York City (*Sesame Street*), and WGBH in Boston (*NOVA*, *Frontline*).

In 2010, the U.S. cable industry reported 62 million subscribers. The top multiple-system cable television operator, or MSO, is Comcast with 24 million subscribers, followed by Time Warner (13 million), and Cox Communications (five million).

Nearly all cable companies operate as monopolies or duopolies (*i.e.*, only two companies) franchised by local governments. Subscription packages have basic and premium tiers, and digital cable operators offer free and fee-based video on demand. Cable has two-thirds of the home television market. The other third is split among

DirecTV (18 million subscribers) and Dish Network (14 million subscribers), and telephone companies such as Verizon, which provides video and broadband Internet over high-speed fiber-optic lines.

High-definition television was introduced in the United States in 1998 and slowly gained popularity. By the time standard-definition broadcasting was terminated in 2009, more than half of U.S. households had high definition televisions, with cable systems providing a converted signal for remaining standard televisions.

The most viewed advertising supported cable networks in 2009 were USA (NBC Universal), TNT (Turner/Time Warner), and Fox News Channel (News Corporation). The top sports network, ESPN (Disney), ranked sixth. Although CNN pioneered the concept of a 24-hour all-news cable channel, it has been overtaken by Fox News, which many observers believe reports news with a conservative slant, as the mostly widely viewed cable news channel. MSNBC moved into second place in 2009 when it decided to feature liberal commentators.

Commercial television stations are divided into news, advertising, and operations departments. The editorial face of a local television station is its news personalities, supported by a cadre of producers, editors, technicians, and online news editors. The advertising department houses a sales force, video production unit for commercials, graphic designers and animators, and station Web master. Engineers in the operations department maintain the daily feed, verification of ads broadcast, technology acquisition and maintenance, and the transmitter and tower. The station manager's office handles reception and marketing, including auxiliary enterprises such as publication of a station magazine. Most television stations subscribe to the Radio and Television News Directors Association Code of Ethics (www.rtnda.org), which calls on broadcast journalists to serve the public trust, seek truth fairly and impartially, have integrity, maintain independence, and be accountable for their actions.

Technology changes rapidly in the broadcasting industry, forcing workers to update their skills continually. Television news applicants should be able to shoot and edit their own news packages with high definition cameras, wireless microphones, and lights and reflectors, as well as perform word-perfect "stand-ups" and post text and video to the Web. This multitasking approach has been nicknamed "backpack journalism."

The job seeker's video portfolio is critical, especially for production and on-air news work. Your writing for television should be more conversational than print and use pictures to tell your story. News directors and production managers look through hundreds of portfolios at a time, so put your best work first. Online portfolios with embedded video clips are now commonplace. Many stations also have opportunities for people with Web-authoring and social-networking skills. A great way to acquire these skills and to build out your portfolio while learning is to volunteer at your college television station or community cable access channel.

NEWSPAPERS

During the current period of restructuring in the newspaper industry, falling circulations and mounting revenue losses make job prospects look bleak. However, the strongest newspapers are finding ways to adapt to new technologies to deliver valuable news and information content to their readers. Newspaper reporters and editors are retooling their journalism skills for the new media. Newspapers continue to be the best source for detailed, factual information, often leading other media to the news stories of the day.

Most newspapers stress local news coverage, a reflection of the importance of local government in the U.S. democracy, which depends on a free, independent press to serve as watchdog. Despite the constitutional significance of local reportage, out-of-town newspaper chains own almost all dailies. According to the Pew Research Center's Project for Excellence in Journalism, the largest chains in terms of number of daily newspapers owned in 2010 were GateHouse Media (98), which owns newspapers primarily in small to mid-sized communities, Community Newspapers Holding (91), which also primarily focuses on small communities and local news, and Gannett (85), which owns newspapers in many large and mid-sized cities as well as the national daily *USA Today.*

In terms of weekday circulation, the Gannett chain led with nearly 7 million, with MediaNews Group (2.6 million) and McClatchy Company (2.5 million) distant runners-up.

Only three dailies are printed for the national market: the *Wall Street Journal*, *The New York Times*, and *USA Today*. A fourth national paper, the *Christian Science Monitor*, ceased daily print editions in 2009 and became a weekly coupled with an online edition. According to the Audit Bureau of Circulations, dailies nationwide lost 10 percent of circulation during 2009 to 44.5 million daily readers, while Internet readership of national newspapers increased to more than 72 million per month, making newspapers more widely read than ever before.

Most newspapers have slashed staffs and cut back on pages, which in turn accelerated the industry's circulation decline by reducing the quality of newspapers. The flipside of the newspaper print circulation decline is the sudden rise in online news readership. Pew reported the monthly number of viewers of the top online news companies in 2010: Yahoo! (34 million), General Electric (32 million), Gannett (26 million), and AOL (24 million). However, revenues from online editions have not made up what print editions have lost in classified advertising to Monster, Google, and CraigsList. In nine years, print classified advertising revenues for the industry fell from a peak of $19.6 billion in 2000 to $6 billion in 2009, a 70 percent decline. Total ad revenue, including display ads and store inserts, fell from $48 billion to $25 billion in the same period.

In covering a story, reporters attend events, investigate leads and news tips, rewrite releases, check with contacts at the police department and city hall, look at documents, research online, observe events at the scene, and interview people. They take notes on paper pads or laptop computers, and shoot photographs. Newspaper reporters also must prepare materials for the online version of their newspapers. This often means taking pictures and shooting video for posting on the Web. At any location with Internet access, they organize the material, determine the focus or emphasis, write their main stories and sidebars, and edit accompanying video material. All these materials are then turned over to editors.

Some publications use teams of reporters instead of assigning each reporter one specific topic, allowing each reporter to cover a greater variety of stories. News teams might include reporters, editors, graphic artists, and photographers working together to complete a story.

General-assignment reporters are assigned to report and write about what ever the top news of the day might be, such as accidents, political rallies, visits of celebrities, or business closings. Large newspapers can afford to assign reporters to gather news about specific topics, such as crime or education. Some reporters specialize in fields such as health, politics, foreign affairs, sports, theater, consumer affairs, social events, science, business, or religion. Investigative reporters cover stories that might take many days or weeks of information-gathering. Large newspapers have photojournalists on staff, who usually also have graphic-design responsibilities. The largest might also have their own editorial cartoonist, supplemented by cartoons purchased from syndicates.

Within newspapers, there are several types of editors who handle a reporter's stories. The executive editor oversees assistant editors and generally has the final say about what stories are published and how they are covered. Assistant editors have responsibility for particular subjects, such as local news, international news, feature stories, or sports. The managing editor usually is responsible for the daily operation of the news department. Assignment editors determine which reporters will cover a given story.

Copy editors mostly review and edit a reporter's copy for accuracy, content, grammar, and style. Copy editors are expected to use page-layout computer applications such as Adobe InDesign or QuarkXPress.

Online editors manage the look of their newspapers' Web editions. In smaller organizations—such as small dailies or weeklies—a single editor might do everything or share responsibility with only a few other people. Executive and managing editors typically do all hiring, plan budgets, and negotiate contracts with freelance writers, sometimes called "stringers."

The American Society of Newspaper Editors estimates that newsroom jobs fell from 55,000 to roughly 40,000 jobs between 2007 and 2009, a 27 percent reduction. When newspapers begin hiring again, they will be looking for journalists who are multimedia-literate.

Journalists should be curious people and have a "nose for the news." They should love words and literature, and know grammar. Working within proper journalistic writing style, they should develop their own writing "voice" that makes their work stand out. They should be skilled storytellers, because news at its heart must be a story that conveys the facts in a way that is relevant and interesting to the reader.

Perhaps most importantly, journalists should be persons of integrity who hold their influence on the public as a sacred trust. The Society of Professional Journalists' code of ethics (www.spj.org/ethicscode.asp) expresses journalists' obligation with four simple but profound directives: seek truth and report it; minimize harm; act independently; and be accountable.

Most people start their careers at smaller newspapers and work their way up. For example, Pulitzer Prize winning journalist David Halberstam got his first newspaper job at the *Daily Times Leader* in Westpoint, Mississippi. From there, he went to the Nashville *Tennessean* and then to *The New York Times*. Working for a small paper can give a young, "cub" reporter the opportunity to cover all aspects of the news. They take photographs, write head-

lines, lay out pages, edit wire-service stories, and write editorials. Some also solicit advertisements, sell subscriptions, and perform general office work.

Students can gain practical experience on their school or college newspaper, as a stringer or freelancer for the local paper, and through internships. These experiences will help to build your writing, photography, and design portfolios. Newspapers are always looking for opportunities to increase diversity in their staffs, so minorities are encouraged to apply.

DOCUMENTARY FILM AND VIDEO

A "golden era" might be unfolding for documentaries and other genres of nonfiction film, as filmmakers are finding more venues for their creations—theatres, DVDs, television, and the Internet. The cost of producing and distributing a documentary has dropped dramatically, which has opened doors for many aspiring documentary-makers.

Aspiring documentarians often get production experience in television news, cable stations, or independent film production companies. Though internships usually are unpaid and often involve considerable grunt work (getting coffee, hauling equipment, and driving cars) and long hours to meet impending deadlines, interns learn firsthand how professionals carry out their craft. Award-winning documentary filmmaker Josh Blinder has noted that interning at film production companies provides a more diversified experience than at television stations, which are more compartmentalized. A production assistants is a "jack-of-all-trades," learning about every creative and technical aspect of filmmaking and video production—scripting, storyboarding to camerawork, lighting, sound design, editing, animation, and distribution.

Because of advances in digital technology, most films now are shot, edited, and distributed digitally, and the distinction between film and video is fast disappearing. In fact, often when someone says "film," they usually mean digital. Videographers have become expert at arranging lighting, and applying digital filters to video to achieve a "film look," which is less crisp and more atmospheric than digital video. Even most high-end features shot on motion-picture film are transferred to digital for editing in Avid Media Composer, Apple Final Cut Pro, or Adobe Premiere Pro, all of which have a similar non-linear graphical interface. Experienced digital video editors are always in high demand.

Tim Curran is a documentary maker and producer for MTV's *The Real World*. He offers this advice for those interested in the field: "Documentary making is still show biz, and making it in show biz requires a thick skin and huge amounts of patience and persistence." Documentary filmmakers need to wear many hats, including that of researcher, scriptwriter, director, videographer, interviewer, editor, and Web master. Documentary filmmakers agree that you cannot learn the craft out of a book. The only way to learn is by doing. There are few barriers to entering the field. All you need is a camera, non-linear editing system, and an idea, and you can start making your own documentaries.

JOB-HUNTING TOOLS

Regardless of the career path, a job-hunter's basic tools are the cover letter, résumé, and portfolio. For communication careers, a portfolio Web site also is essential.

A good résumé identifies the employment objective, highlights your skills and knowledge, gives your experience directly related to the job applied for (jobs, internships, and volunteer activities), and provides phone numbers and e-mail accounts of your previous employment supervisors who will give you good references. When applying for a job through the mail, you should customize your résumé for that specific job. If possible, keep the résumé to one page. To provide additional information to the reader, give the address of your portfolio Web site.

A good cover letter should connect you to the employer. Highlight any personal contacts you have with the organization. Your letter should show that you have some understanding of the employer's business and operation, based on your research of the employer's Web site and from personal contacts. Your letter should discuss your skills, knowledge, experience, creativity, and energy that you can offer to the organization. It also should specify when you are available to start. Above all, your cover letter should communicate your positive attitude and enthusiasm for the organization.

A portfolio reveals your thinking and imagination. It clearly shows what you can do for an employer by showing what you have done for others:

- If you are a writer, your portfolio should have samples of your published writing for various genres and audiences, accompanied by awards and commendations if possible.

- If you are an aspiring art director, your portfolio should demonstrate your ability to design and to create.

- Web designers and film or video producers should provide color screenshots of their productions.

- If you seek a public relations career, your portfolio should include news releases, publicity pieces, and campaigns to provide evidence of your writing ability and marketing sense.

- Advertising specialists should present copywriting, ad layouts, storyboards, and media plans in their portfolios.

- Radio producers should provide program transcripts, promotions, and ad copy. If possible, include a disc or USB drive in both Windows and Mac format with additional materials, including samples of your motion media work.

With the many easy-to-use blogging sites on the World Wide Web, such as blogger.com or wordpress.com, you do not need Web-authoring skills in order to create a portfolio Web site.

Portfolio Web sites have many advantages for the communications job-hunter and employer. They can include everything in the job hunter's portfolio and more. They can be updated with the latest personal information and portfolio pieces. They can present audio, video, and motion material. You can even present a personal greeting in a video recording of yourself. The expense of producing multiple copies of a physical portfolio is eliminated. Perhaps most importantly, your portfolio Web site will show the employer that you are in tune with the latest communications technologies.

A college student, not so long ago, went to a Baltimore advertising firm to apply for an internship. The head of the firm asked a few background questions and explained the operations of the advertising firm. Then he asked the student a question: "Would you do this job for nothing?"

The student was baffled by the question and did not respond.

The head of the agency then looked at the student and said with a smile, "Find yourself a job in communications that you would be willing to do for nothing and then figure out a way to make it pay."

CONCLUSION

In the dynamic, fast-paced world of professional media, the one constant is change. Companies are bought and sold, new technologies and technical standards are introduced and old ones die out, new regulations are imposed, competitors rise and fall in the global market, and audience tastes change. As magazines, advertising, book publishing, public relations, radio, television, newspapers, and documentaries respond to these changes, there will be many employment and advancement opportunities for persons equipped with the right skills, knowledge, and attitude to deal not just with today, but with the future as well.

Media professionals such as Jennie Buckner, Anthony Moor, Mark Bowden, Jeanette Perez, Josh Blinder, and Tim Curran all recommend diversifying your skills and experience as much as possible to be prepared for unexpected opportunities. In a competitive, converged media world, new employees are expected to be more versatile and more productive than the workers they replace. The old, narrowly defined media jobs rapidly are disappearing and being replaced by new, hybrid positions requiring diverse skills addressing multiple audiences. Nearly every communications job calls for proficiency in the use and creation of online media. Every other field of study, every science, profession, business, or avocation, sooner or later needs to communicate its special interests to society. A career in communications puts people where the action is.

THE ANGRIEST MAN IN TELEVISION

by Mark Bowden

How David Simon's disappointment with the industry that let him down made The Wire the greatest show on television—and why his searing vision shouldn't be confused with reality

Behold the Hack, the veteran newsman, wise beyond his years, a man who's seen it all, twice. He's honest, knowing, cynical, his occasional bitterness leavened with humor. He's a friend to the little scam, and a scourge of the big one. Experience has acquainted him with suffering and stupidity, venality and vice. His anger is softened by the sure knowledge of his own futility. And now behold David Simon, the mind behind the brilliant HBO series *The Wire*. A gruff fireplug of a man, balding and big-featured, he speaks with an earthy, almost theatrical bluntness, and his blue-collar crust belies his comfortable suburban upbringing. He's for all the world the quintessential Hack, down to his ink-stained fingertips—the kind of old newshound who will remind you that a "journalist" is a dead reporter. But Simon takes the cliché one step further; he's an old newsman who feels betrayed by newspapers themselves.

Read the discussion about David Simon

IN MATTHEW YGLESIAS'S BLOG

Also see

WHAT DAVID SIMON HIMSELF HAD TO SAY

about this discussion.

For all his success and accomplishment, he's an angry man, driven in part by lovingly nurtured grudges against those he feels have slighted him, underestimated him, or betrayed some public trust.

High on this list is his old employer *The Baltimore Sun*—or more precisely, the editors and corporate owners who have (in his view) spent the past two decades eviscerating a great American newspaper. In a better world—one where papers still had owners and editors who were smart, socially committed, honest, and brave—Simon

READING NOTES

_____

_____

_____

_____

_____

probably would never have left *The Sun* to pursue a Hollywood career. His father, a frustrated newsman, took him to see Ben Hecht's and Charles MacArthur's classic newspaper farce, *The Front Page*, when he was a boy in Washington, D.C., and Simon was smitten. He landed a job as a *Sun* reporter just out of the University of Maryland in the early 1980s, and as he tells it, if the newspaper, the industry, and America had lived up to his expectations, he would probably still be documenting the underside of his adopted city one byline at a time. But *The Sun* let David Simon down.

So he has done something that many reporters only dream about. He has created his own Baltimore. With the help of his chief collaborator, Ed Burns, a former Baltimore cop and schoolteacher; a stable of novelists and playwrights with a feel for urban drama (including George Pelecanos, Richard Price, and Dennis Lehane); a huge cast of master actors; and a small army of film professionals shooting on location—in the city's blighted row-house neighborhoods and housing projects, in City Hall, nightclubs, police headquarters, in the suburbs, the snazzy Inner Harbor, the working docks—he has, over four seasons, conjured the city onscreen with a verisimilitude that's astonishing. Marylanders scrutinize the plot for its allusions to real people and real events. Parallels with recent local political history abound, and the details of life in housing projects and on street corners seem spookily authentic. (A New York City narcotics detective who loves the show told me a few years ago that street gangs in Brooklyn were watching it to learn tactics for avoiding cell-phone intercepts.)

Despite the show's dark portrait of "Body-more, Murdaland," local officialdom has embraced *The Wire*, giving Simon and his cast and crew free rein, opening up municipal buildings and cordoning off outdoor spaces. Many prominent citizens, including former Baltimore Mayor Kurt Schmoke and former Maryland Governor Robert Ehrlich, have made cameo appearances. The dress, manners, and colorful language of the show's cast, which is largely African American, are painstakingly authentic, down to the uniquely slurred consonants and nasal vowel sounds of the local dialect, Balmerese. *The Wire* seems so real that I find myself, a Baltimore native, looking for the show's characters when I pass through their familiar haunts.

The show hasn't been a big commercial success. It's never attracted a viewership to rival that of an HBO tent-pole series, like *The Sopranos* or even the short-lived *Deadwood*. It isn't seen as a template for future TV dramas, primarily because its form more or less demands that each season be watched from the beginning. Whereas each episode of *The Sopranos* advanced certain overarching plot points but was essentially self-contained, anyone who tries to plumb the complexities of *The Wire* by tuning in at mid-season is likely to be lost. If the standard Hollywood feature is the film equivalent of a short story, each season of Simon's show is a 12- or 13-chapter novel.

Some years ago, Tom Wolfe called on novelists to abandon the cul-de-sac of modern "literary" fiction, which he saw as self-absorbed, thumb sucking gamesmanship, and instead to revive social realism, to take up as a subject the colossal, astonishing, and terrible pageant of contemporary America. I doubt he imagined that one of the best responses to this call would be a TV program, but the boxed sets blend nicely on a bookshelf with the great novels of American history.

As *The Wire* unveiled its fourth season in 2006, Jacob Weisberg of *Slate*, in a much-cited column, called it "the best TV show ever broadcast in America." *The New York Times*, in an editorial (not a review, mind you) called the show Dickensian. I agree with both assessments. "*Wire*-world," as Simon calls it, does for turn-of-the millennium Baltimore what Dickens's *Bleak House* does for mid-19th-century London. Dickens takes the byzantine bureaucracy of the law and the petty corruptions of the legal profession, borrows from the neighborhoods, manners, dress, and

READING NOTES

_____

_____

_____

_____

_____

_____

language of the Chancery courts and the Holborn district, and builds from them a world that breathes. Similarly, *The Wire* creates a vision of official Baltimore as a heavy, self-justified bureaucracy, gripped by its own byzantine logic and criminally unconcerned about the lives of ordinary people, who enter it at their own risk. One of the clever early conceits of the show was to juxtapose the organizational problems of the city police department with those of the powerful drug gang controlling trafficking in the city's west-side slums. The heads of both organizations, official and criminal, wrestle with similar management and personnel issues, and resolve them with similarly cold self-interest. In both the department and the gang, the powerful exploit the weak, and within the ranks those who exhibit dedication, talent, and loyalty are usually punished for their efforts.

There are heroes in *The Wire*, but they're flawed and battered. The show's most exceptional police officers, detectives Jimmy McNulty and Lester Freamon, find their initiative and talent punished at almost every turn. Their determination to do good, original work disturbs the department's upper echelons, where people are heavily invested in maintaining the status quo and in advancing their own careers. The clash repeatedly lands both of them in hot water—or cold water; at the end of the first season, the seasick-prone McNulty is banished to the city's marine unit. What success the two attain against Baltimore's most powerful criminals is partial, compromised, and achieved despite stubborn and often creative official resistance.

One measure of the complexity of Simon's vision is that the powerful obstructionists in *The Wire* aren't simply evil people, the way they might have been in a standard Hollywood movie. While some are just inept or corrupt, most are smart and ambitious, sometimes even interested in doing good, but concerned first and foremost with their next promotion or a bigger paycheck. They are fiercely territorial, to a degree that interferes with real police work. In the premiere episode, the very idea of a separate squad to target the leadership of the city's powerful drug gangs—which one would assume to be a high law-enforcement priority—is opposed by the police department. It's imposed on the commissioner by order of a local judge, who's outraged when a witness at a murder trial in his courtroom fearfully recants her testimony on the stand. To spite the judge, the commissioner staffs the unit with castoffs from various police divisions. Some of the castoffs are so alcoholic or corrupt they're useless, but some, like the lesbian detective Shakima Greggs, or the patient, wise Freamon, or the ballsy, streetwise McNulty, are castoffs precisely because of their ability. In Simon's world, excellence is a ticket out the door.

In one of the show's most interesting set pieces, a remarkable police major, "Bunny" Colvin, frustrated by the absurdity of the city's useless drug war, conducts a novel experiment. Without the knowledge of his superiors, he effectively legalizes drugs in West Baltimore, creating a mini-Amsterdam, dubbed "Hamsterdam," where all of the corner dealers are allowed to set up shop. By consolidating drug dealing, which he knows he cannot stop anyway, Colvin eliminates the daily turf battles that drive up the murder rates and dramatically improves life in most of his district. Calm returns to terrorized neighborhoods, and his patrolmen, freed from their cars and the endless pursuit of drug-dealing corner boys, return to real police work, walking beats, getting to know the people they serve. The sharp drop in his district crime stats shocks the department's leadership and makes Colvin's peers jealous—and suspicious. They assume he's cooking the books.

Again, it's a tribute to the depth of Simon's imagination that this experiment isn't presented as a cure-all. He doesn't minimize the moral compromise inherent in Hamsterdam. Many addicts see their severe health problems worsen, and the drug-dealing zone becomes a haven for vice of all kinds. Decent people in the community are horrified by the officially sanctioned criminality and the tolerance of destructive addiction.

READING NOTES

The experiment ends ignobly when news of the unauthorized experiment reaches the ears of a *Sun* reporter. City Hall reacts to the story with predictable horror, scurrying and spinning to escape blame. Colvin loses his job, and the city goes back to the old war, which is useless but politically acceptable.

Story lines like these reflect the truth about Baltimore; Mayor Schmoke's own promising political career crashed and burned some years ago when he had the temerity to suggest a less punitive approach to the city's drug problem. But they don't reflect the complete truth: like Dickens's London, Simon's Baltimore is a richly imagined caricature of its real-life counterpart, not a carbon copy. And precisely because the Baltimore in *The Wire* seems so real, down to the finest details, the show constitutes an interesting study in the difference between journalism and fiction. Simon's first book, *Homicide*, was a critically acclaimed work of nonfiction, from which some of the themes, characters, and even stories of *The Wire* are drawn. (It was also the basis for the 1990s NBC show *Homicide: Life on the Street*.) Which raises the question—if your subject is the real world, why deal in fiction?

The answer has something to do with Simon's own passions and his deeply held political beliefs. "I *am* someone who's very angry with the political structure," he said in a long 2006 interview with *Slate*. "The show is written in a 21st-century city-state that is incredibly bureaucratic, and in which a legal pursuit of an unenforceable prohibition [the war on drugs] has created great absurdity." To Simon, *The Wire* is about "the very simple idea that, in this postmodern world of ours, human beings—all of us—are worth less. We're worth less every day, despite the fact that some of us are achieving more and more. It's the triumph of capitalism. Whether you're a corner boy in West Baltimore, or a cop who knows his beat, or an Eastern European brought here for sex, your life is worth less. It's the triumph of capitalism over human value. This country has embraced the idea that this is a viable domestic policy. It is. It's viable for the few. But I don't live in Westwood, L.A., or on the Upper West Side of New York. I live in Baltimore."

This is a message—a searing attack on the excesses of Big Capitalism—that rarely finds its way into prime-time entertainment on national TV. It's audacious. But it's also relentlessly ... well, *bleak*.

FROM THE ARCHIVES

"THE CODE OF THE STREETS"

(May 1994)
In this essay in urban anthropology a social scientist takes us inside a world most of us only glimpse in grisly headlines By Elijah Anderson

INTERVIEWS: "STREET LIFE"

(August 28, 1999)
Elijah Anderson talks about his book, *Code of the Street*, and the importance of looking honestly at life in the inner city

"I am struck by how dark the show is," says Elijah Anderson, the Yale sociologist whose classic works *Code of the Streets, Streetwise*, and *A Place on the Corner* document black inner-city life with noted clarity and sympathy. Anderson would be the last person to gloss over the severe problems of the urban poor, but in *The Wire* he sees "a bottom-line cynicism" that is at odds with his own perception of real life. "The show is very good," he says. "It resonates. It is powerful in its depiction of the codes of the streets, but it is an exaggeration. I get frustrated watching it, because it gives such a powerful appearance of reality, but it always seems to leave something important out. What they have left out are the decent people. Even in the worst drug-infested projects, there are many, many God-fearing, churchgoing, brave people who set themselves against the gangs and the addicts, often with remarkable heroism."

READING NOTES

_____

_____

_____

_____

_____

This bleakness is Simon's stamp on the show, and it suggests that his political passions ultimately trump his commitment to accuracy or evenhandedness. The imagination, values, and convictions of a writer play a big part in even the most accurate nonfiction, of course. Telling a true story well demands that the reporter achieve his own understanding of the events and people described, and arriving at that point can mean shading reality, even if only unconsciously. We view the world from where we sit. Truman Capote, in his nonfiction classic, *In Cold Blood*, finds a clue to the motives of the murderers, Perry Smith and Dick Hickock, in unrequited or unconscious homosexual desire. Norman Mailer's preoccupation with mystical themes gives the senseless killer Gary Gilmore a romantic aura in *The Executioner's Song*. In *The Right Stuff*, Tom Wolfe's fascination with masculinity and social status allows him to cast the early space program as a prolonged reprise of ancient single-combat rituals. In each case, the author's unique perspective gives a "true" story a starkly original shape.

But the more passionate your convictions, the harder it is to resist tampering with the contradictions and stubborn messiness of real life. Every reporter knows the sensation of having a story "ruined" by some new and surprising piece of information. Just when you think you have the thing figured out, you learn something that shatters your carefully wrought vision. Being surprised is the essence of good reporting. But it's also the moment when a dishonest writer is tempted to fudge, for the sake of commercial success—and a more honest writer like Simon, whose passion is political and personal, is tempted to shift his energies to fiction.

Which is precisely what he's done. Simon is the reporter who knows enough about Baltimore to have his story all figured out, but instead of risking the coherence of his vision by doing what reporters do, heading back out day after day to observe, to ask more questions, to take more notes, he has stopped report-

ing and started inventing. He says, *I have figured this thing out.* He offers up his undisturbed vision, leaving out the things that don't fit, adding things that emphasize its fundamentals, and then using the trappings of realism to dress it up and bring it to life onscreen.

The essential difference between writing nonfiction and writing fiction is that the artist owns his vision, while the journalist can never really claim one, or at least not a complete one—because the real world is infinitely complex and ever changing. Art frees you from the infuriating unfinishedness of the real world. For this reason, the very clarity of well-wrought fiction can sometimes make it *feel* more real than reality. As a film producer once told me, "It's important not to let the facts get in the way of the truth."

Fiction can explain things that journalism cannot. It allows you to enter the lives and motivations of characters with far more intimacy than is typically possible in nonfiction. In the case of *The Wire*, fiction allows you to wander around inside a violent, criminal subculture, and inside an entrenched official bureaucracy, in a way that most reporters can only dream about. And it frees you from concerns about libel and cruelty. It frees you to be unfair.

In a session before a live audience in Baltimore last April, for a local storytelling series called The Stoop, Simon was asked to speak on a topic labeled "My Nemesis." He began by reciting, by name, some of the people he holds grudges against, going all the way back to grade school. He was being humorous, and the audience was laughing, but anyone who knows him knows that his monologue was, like his fiction, slightly overstated for effect, but basically the truth. "I keep these names, I treasure them," he said:

I will confess to you now that anything I have ever accomplished as a writer, as somebody doing TV, as anything I have ever done in life down to, like, cleaning up my room, has been accomplished because I was going to show people that they were fucked up and

READING NOTES

_____

_____

_____

_____

_____

wrong and that I was the fucking center of the universe, and the sooner they got hip to that, the happier they would all be ... That's what's going on in my head.

This vindictive streak, this desire to show people how wrong they are, is tempered somewhat by Simon's sense of humor and his appreciation for complexity, and by the vision of his many skillful collaborators. But in the show's final season, which debuts in January, Simon will revisit the part of Baltimore that's closest to his heart, *The Sun*. The season, more than any other before it, will reflect his personal experience. Given his long memory and his inclination to settle old scores, the difference between fiction and fact will be of particular interest to his former colleagues.

The newspaper's management rightly viewed Simon's intentions with trepidation, but given that City Hall and the governor's mansion embraced his jaundiced vision, how could the Fourth Estate refuse to open its doors? So *The Sun* has allowed the show to use its name and even build an exact replica of its newsroom so that Simon and his company can flesh out their story line with greater authenticity. It isn't going to be a comfortable ride, because Simon is apparently set to exorcise some personal demons. His vision of Baltimore was shaped largely by his work as a crime reporter, and it seems likely that his anger about capitalism and the devaluation of human life is rooted in his unhappy experience at *The Sun*.

A famous quote from the great Sun Papers columnist H. L. Mencken is reprinted in large type on the wall of the spacious lobby in the newspaper's building on Calvert Street. It reads:

... as I look back over a misspent life, I find myself more and more convinced that I had more fun doing news reporting than in any other enterprise. It is really the life of kings.

It was that promise, that "life of kings," that animated Simon and many other reporters who started in the business 20 years ago.

"I love this place," Simon told the Stoop audience last April, speaking of his frame of mind at age 22, when he was starting his career as a *Sun* reporter:

This is the place of H. L. Mencken, of Frank Kent, of William Manchester. It's like you can touch things that you can be proud of. I just have to do good work for its own sake ... I'm basically happy, and it's like the least ambitious I am in my life. Until ... it gets sold out of town. And these guys come in from Philly. The white guys from Philly. And I say that with all the contempt you can muster for the phrase *white guys*. Soulless motherfuckers. Everything that Malcolm X said in that book before he got converted back to humanity—no, no, he was right in the first place. These guys were so without humanity. And it was the kind of journalism— how do I describe bad journalism? It's not that it's lazy, it's that whenever they hear the word *Pulitzer*, they become tumescent. They become engorged ... All they wanted to do was win prizes ... I watched them single-handedly destroy *The Sun*.

The "white guys" Simon so viciously abused in this talk (and not for the first time) were William Marimow and John Carroll, notable newspapermen who are my friends; Marimow was a longtime colleague of mine at *The Philadelphia Inquirer*. He eventually left *The Sun* in conflict over newsroom cutbacks with its corporate owners (originally the Times-Mirror Corporation, which was absorbed by the Tribune Company in 2000) and went on to head the news division of National Public Radio. Last year, Marimow returned to helm *The Inquirer*, a newspaper where he had earlier won two Pulitzer Prizes for reporting. Carroll became editor in chief of the *Los Angeles Times*, resigned defending the newsroom there, and is now at Harvard University. Both have impeccable reputations in their field, and I hold them both in high esteem. Simon hates them.

He hates them in part because they were agents of change at *The Sun*, the institution he loved, initiating a process familiar in newsrooms all over the country.

READING NOTES

_____

_____

_____

_____

_____

Just as the efforts of great detectives like McNulty and Freamon are neither valued nor supported by their bosses, many superb reporters and editors at *The Sun*, and with them the paper's higher mission, were betrayed by the corporate pursuit of profit margins. Marimow and Carroll were for a time agents of that process, an unpleasant role that many fine newspaper editors have found themselves in during the past decade. Yet to Simon they are all the more culpable because they didn't publicly object to a talent drain that he felt devastated the newsroom. There's nothing unique about the situation. The sad story is familiar to newspaper people all over the country. (I watched it happen at *The Inquirer*, where Knight Ridder threw just about everyone and everything of value overboard before bailing out of journalism altogether.)

Some of us chalk up this trend to market forces, to the evolution of information technology, to television, radio, and the Internet. At the long-since-departed *Baltimore News-American*, where I worked before being hired at *The Inquirer*, we used to joke that people didn't read our newspaper, they *played* it. The paper was full of number and word games, along with sports scores, racetrack results, TV listings, comics, want ads, and advertisements with clippable coupons. One by one, these multifarious reasons why people used to buy newspapers have been cherry-picked by newer media; that includes the paper's most basic offering—breaking news, whose headlines are now available on most cell phones. Declining circulation means declining advertising, which means declining revenues, so corporate managers face a tougher and tougher challenge maintaining the high profit margins that attracted investors 30 years ago. These are just facts, and different people and organizations have handled them with different measures of grace and understanding.

But to Simon, this complex process became personal, boiling down to corporate greed and the "soulless-ness" of Marimow and Carroll. It's an honest opinion, but arguably unfair, flavored by personal bitterness and animosity. (Simon told a writer from *American Journalism Review* that he was angered by the paper's unwillingness to grant him a raise after he returned from a leave of absence in 1995—he was writing *The Corner*—and he took a buyout six months later.) Given his vindictive strain, his talent for character and drama, and the national TV show at his disposal, such an opinion is also a combustible one.

I should note here that it isn't hard to join Simon's enemies list; I did it myself while writing this essay. I first contacted Simon several years ago, as a fan of his show and as a screenwriter and aspiring producer interested in learning more about him and how he'd created it. He was friendly and helpful, and I remain grateful. Then in 2006 after the fourth season of *The Wire* had aired, I decided to write a tribute to Simon and his show. I contacted him by e-mail to see about renewing our conversation on different terms, and he consented. He asked me to avoid writing about his personal life, and I agreed. I was determined, as well, to avoid discussing his dispute with Marimow and Carroll, since I liked and admired both parties, and was disinclined to choose sides.

When I discovered, after my last conversation with Simon, that the final season of the show would be based on his experiences at *The Sun*, I felt compelled to describe the dispute, but I resolved to characterize it without *entering* it. To avoid exploiting anything that had passed informally between us on the subject, I relied on Simon's ample public commentary to explain his feelings, and then, realizing that the essay had strayed in an unanticipated direction, showed him an early draft to solicit correction and criticism. I got it. The draft provoked a series of angry, long-winded accusations, which would have remained private had he not taken his complaints to *The Atlantic's* editor, in an angry letter impugning my motives in contacting him originally, and characterizing all our interactions as my attempt to win his confidence in

READING NOTES

_____

_____

_____

_____

_____

order to skewer him on behalf of my friends. I could see myself morphing into a character in his show.

Simon has already given Marimow's name to a character in *The Wire*, a repellent police-department toady who, in the hilarious words of the show's Sergeant Jay Landsman, "doesn't cast off talent lightly, he heaves it away with great force." But this was just a minor swipe: the final season of *The Wire* will offer Simon the chance to take on his old enemies from *The Sun* directly. An article that appeared in the October 2000 issue of *Brill's Content* hinted at the tack he may take and went to the core of what he says are his objections to the pair. It featured Simon, then five years removed from the paper and well into his enormously successful second career, making the case that a widely respected *Sun* reporter, protected by Carroll and Marimow, was making up stories and distorting the truth in a hell-bent effort to turn a series on lead-paint poisoning into a competitive Pulitzer submission. Simon felt the editors purposefully ignored the misgivings of some of the newspaper's veteran reporters in an effort to bolster their new star. To the editors, it was a case of an aggressive reporter who had made a few mistakes in pursuit of an important story. To Simon, it was an example of all that was wrong with the remade newspaper, and a reminder of the clash over journalistic values that had led him to quit in the first place. In his mind, *The Sun* had also abandoned its mission to really cover Baltimore, and was now fiddling while the city burned. Instead of exploring the root causes of the city's intractable problems—drug abuse and the government's unenforceable "war" against it, racism, poverty, rampant Big Capitalism, etc.—the newspaper was engaged in a largely self-congratulatory crusade to right a minor wrong.

Sure enough, one of the upcoming season's story lines deals with a newspaper's muckraking campaign on homelessness. It's likely been crafted to represent Simon's take on a typical Carroll-Marimow project: motivated less by a sincere desire for social reform than by a zeal for Pulitzer Prizes. (The paper did, incidentally, win three Pulitzers under the editors' guidance. Normally, in the newspaper world, this is considered a triumph, but for Simon it just adds bitter spice to an already bad dish.) And whereas the *Brill's* reporter who wrote the story was painstakingly evenhanded, Simon's fictional version of events will carry no such journalistic burden.

Apart from the distress this causes the real people behind his sometimes thinly veiled depictions, there's nothing necessarily wrong with this. It's how an artist shapes a fictional drama out of his own experience. Simon is entitled to his take on things, entitled to exploit his memory and experience, his anger and sense of betrayal, just as he exploited his cynicism and political outrage about official Baltimore in the show's first four seasons. Indeed, given the richness and power of his vision in *The Wire*, we ought to be grateful for his unforgiving nature. The kind of reporting he felt could no longer be done at *The Sun* he has brought to the screen. But his fiction shouldn't be mistaken for fact. It reflects, as much as anything, Simon's own prejudices.

In my decades in newsrooms, I encountered my share of hard-core skeptics like Simon, but those resembling the stereotypical Hack were the exceptions. It is true that the more true stories you tell, the more acquainted you are with suffering, stupidity, venality, and vice. But you're also more acquainted with selflessness, courage, and decency. Old reporters and editors are softened by knowledge and experience. If anything, they become less inclined to suspect or condemn. They encounter incompetence more often than evil, and they see that very few people who screw up do so in ways that are indefensible. After years of drumming up the other side of the story, old reporters are likely to grow less angry and opinionated, not more.

In that sense only, David Simon may be truer to the stereotype than the stereotype is true.

READING NOTES

_____

_____

_____

_____

_____

Chapter 14

New Voices and Opportunities

"There is so much media now with the Internet and people, and [it is] so easy and so cheap to start a newspaper or start a magazine, there are just millions of voices and people want to be heard."

—RUPERT MURDOCH

In the *Back to the Future* movie trilogy, the wise scientist and time traveler Dr. Emmet Brown, tells his young protégé and friend, Marty McFly, "The future is what you make it." This certainly applies to the media and the communication industries. The Internet revolution has enabled people from different backgrounds and with different passions to carve out new and exciting careers. From blogging to Facebook to posting videos on YouTube, people have been able to attract audiences, create community, influence politics, build markets, and express themselves in dynamic and creative ways.

Along with opening the door to completely new channels of communication and new forms of communication, the Internet has sparked a reorganization of the established media industries as well. In advertising, there are new jobs, such as "director of search engine optimization." In public relations, people manage relationships to different publics through social networks. And in journalism, in many newspaper organizations, the person who was once the editor-in-chief is now known as the "director of content."

While the Internet has had a tremendous impact on traditional media, including newspapers, magazines, and television, and not always for the better, it has also created many new possibilities in those media industries. The continuing improvement in technology has opened doors for writers, filmmakers, and musicians in many ways. Many concepts and ideas that first start on the Internet eventually find their way into more traditional media.

For example, Julie Powell first started to blog about her effort to cook every recipe in Julia Child's cookbook *Mastering the Art of French Cooking* within a year to combine her love of food and cooking with her desire to be a writer. Powell later turned the blog into a book and also wrote a memoir about the experience. Ultimately, the books served as the foundation for the 2009 movie *Julie and Julia* starring Meryl Streep and Amy Adams. Interestingly, Powell's big break came when there was a report about her blog in *The New York Times*. In 2010, the Twitter feed called Sh*tMyDadSays.com inspired a book and a network television series.

This chapter's will

- examine the emerging possibilities in communications, and
- showcase the career paths of people entering the media industries today.

Since books, magazines, and newspapers emerged as viable business opportunities more than 300 years ago, there have been many different avenues open to pursue a career in a media industry. The most traditional road to a media career was through an apprenticeship, which can be seen as a more elaborate form of internship, followed by entrepreneurial effort. One way or another, a person would wrangle a low-paid or unpaid job at a media organization and then try to advance internally or start a business in the field.

Perhaps the most famous apprentice in the history of U.S. journalism was Benjamin Franklin. Franklin, who later signed the Declaration of Independence and served as the U.S. representative to France during the Revolutionary War, securing critical help for the colonists, started his career as an apprentice in the print shop of his brother James, where he was put to work setting type and writing pamphlets. The 12-hour days working in the shop were grueling. When Ben was 15 years old, James set up the first ongoing newspaper in the United States, the *New England Courant*, and Ben began to submit articles under the pen name Silence Dogood, a fictional widow he invented. Eventually, unable to bear James's harsh treatment, Ben made his way to Philadelphia, where once again he found work as an apprentice in a print shop.

Eventually, Franklin established his own shop, and in 1729, he purchased and began to publish the newspaper the *Pennsylvania Gazette*, to which he also contributed articles. In 1734, he founded *Poor Richard's Almanac*. Eventually, Franklin became one of the most prominent printers and journalists in the United States.

Apprenticeship was the foundation for professional education through the 1880s. Not only journalists but also doctors, lawyers, teachers, and other professionals were largely trained through apprenticeships. Apprenticeships and internships were considered a viable, even preferred, way to enter the field. As late as the 1950s or 1960s, one of the best ways to get a job as a reporter at *The New York Times* was first to serve as the *Time's* campus correspondent at Columbia University or the City College of New York, and then get a job as a copyboy, running articles from the reporter to the editor and then to the production staff. Among the most notable journalists at the *Times* who took that route was Max Frankel, a Pulitzer Prize—winning reporter who later served as executive editor from 1986 to 1994, as well as A.M. Rosenthal, who served as executive editor of the *Times* from 1977 to 1988.

The apprenticeship route was available in other professions as well. Michael Eisner, the former CEO of the Walt Disney Company, television personality Regis Philbin, and the ABC News journalist Ted Koppel all got their start in the page program at NBC, a one-year training program in which participants learn about careers in broadcasting and entertainment as well as act as studio tour guides and ushers for audiences.

As media operations became more complex in the late 1800s and early 1900s, college-level programs were initiated to train professionals entering the media industries. The first program in journalism education was initiated in 1869 by Robert E. Lee, the former commander-in-chief of the Confederate Army in the Civil War, and president of what is now called Washington and Lee University, as part of a mandate to expand the college's "practical" departments. The first school of journalism was opened at the University of Missouri in 1908, and the Columbia University Graduate School of Journalism opened its doors in 1912.

Even with the widespread development of journalism education, it was not until the 1980s that a bachelor's or master's degree in journalism provided a better way to enter the field than finding a low-level job somewhere and working up the ladder.

Entry into advertising and public relations followed a similar path. As professional advertising was first developing in the mid- to late 1800s, many of the early practitioners had their roots in business, often in sales. In public relations, many of the first practitioners were former journalists. In the 1920s, advertising courses began to be offered at New York University and elsewhere. By 1928, graduates of the program at New York University had formed their own organization called the Association of New York University Men in Advertising.

The rise of university programs to train professionals for the media industry paralleled the general rise of professional education at the university level. By the mid-1900s, to practice medicine, to practice law, or even to teach, a person had to attend an accredited program, pass a test, and receive an appropriate license. With the right to speech protected by the First Amendment, journalists and other media professionals will never have to be licensed. Still, professional associations such as the Public Relations Society of America offer voluntary certification programs to ensure an appropriate level of professionalism. Nonetheless, increasingly, students find that coursework and experience with campus media give them a decided advantage for entering the media professions.

An important aspect of pre-professional education at the university level is the availability of internships. Internships are the modern incarnation of apprenticeships. College students get to learn on the job as well as study the skills they need in an entry-level position in a media company.

JOB OPPORTUNITIES

As could be imagined for complex industries and activities, all media organizations and companies have many different job opportunities. In general,

particularly in the older industries, the jobs fall into one of two categories—creative jobs that are focused on producing content for distribution, and business-oriented positions that are responsible for ensuring that a specific organization attracts clients or customers and runs efficiently. Finally, there are certain positions that serve as a bridge between the creative and business sides of the organization. The people who hold those positions often have the most authority in a particular company. For example, in both newspapers and magazines, the publisher is responsible for both the creative and business aspects of a publication, and consequently has the most authority.

Sales is one of the most important aspects of any media industry. In print, there are two kinds of sales activities. The first is circulation—attracting people to subscribe to the publication. The circulation department also ensures that people who have subscribed receive their newspapers or magazine when they are expected. The second type of sales is advertising sales—selling space in the publication to companies who want to advertise their goods or services. For media that do not charge for their content—broadcast television, the Internet, free magazines (often called controlled-circulation magazines) and free newspapers—companies must rely on ad revenues entirely, so the advertising staff is extremely important.

In print an advertising staff generally is assigned to one or a couple of magazines or newspapers, depending on the size of the publication. In broadcasting, the advertising sales are managed by staff associated with the entire station or television network and not necessarily affiliated with a specific television program. On the Internet, like in the early days of magazines, much of the advertising is handled through syndicates and brokers, or, in keeping with the technology itself, through self-service transactions. Google represents a multibillion-dollar advertising platform in which much of the sales consists of companies selecting key terms that generate text-based advertisements next to search results. If somebody clicks on the ad, Google gets paid.

The advertising staff in most media companies operates as follows. The entry-level position might be an assistant to an ad sales representative or a position as a sales representative either for a geographic area or a product category. For example, a sales representative for a magazine directed at women might have a specific territory—the northeast United States, perhaps—or a product category—perhaps skin care.

The next step might be to expand the geographic territory covered or be allowed to represent more (or more significant) product categories. Ultimately, however, people on this track will begin to manage other sales representatives. Those assignments are usually on a regional basis. Eventually, a person can become the national sales manager or director of advertising, with direct responsibility for the entire sales staff, and then perhaps the publisher.

"Sales" for advertising and public relations agencies work a little differently. In these settings, the goal is to attract new customers. Sometimes, sales is the responsibility of account managers, whose primary mission is to facilitate communication between the client and the creative side of the agency. An agency also might have a dedicated sales team responsible for signing new clients, with account managers responsible for managing the relationships.

While there are many interesting and fulfilling jobs on the business side of media companies, many people are more attracted to the content-creation side of the business. On a newspaper, the entry-level position is generally a reporter or a copy editor. A reporter eventually will be promoted to be an assistant editor or associate editor responsible for reporting on a specific area, such as sports news, business news, city news, or national news. The top position in the editorial line for newspapers is often called simply the "editor" or the "editor-in-chief."

Magazines have the same structure, except the entry-level position is often staff writer or assistant editor, and the subeditors are responsible for copyediting as well as supervising the content in the magazine. In addition to editorial content, magazines also are generally filled with photographs and illustrations. They have creative and unusual page layouts, and often use a wide variety of fonts. The person who oversees the visual look of a magazine is called the "art director."

The creative structure in broadcast is a little more complicated than for print publications because some people work "in front of the camera" and others work "behind the camera." In broadcast news, reporters and news anchors work in front of the cameras. They are supported by writers, video editors, camera operators, and sound technicians. For longer and more involved pieces or shows, a producer will be responsible either for putting a specific story together or for putting the whole show together. In a show such as the television news magazine *60 Minutes*, a producer will actually do the bulk of the background reporting and line up the interviews for the reporter or correspondent to conduct. The producer will then be primarily responsible to work with the reporter to shape the final piece.

Entry-level positions in broadcast journalism include working on the assignment desk, which assigns stories to different reporters and tracks their progress through the day. Also, on talk and interview shows, a "booker or scheduler" will be responsible for getting sources to agree to appear on the camera. In small media markets, there is still the possibility that even someone just entering the field could get a job on-camera as a reporter. However, getting a job behind the scenes, perhaps as an associate producer helping with the nuts and bolts of putting a show or segment together, is more likely.

In advertising agencies, the creative team usually consists of a copywriter and an art director. They collaborate to ensure that the words and the images in an advertisement work with each other to create the maximum amount of impact. In public relations agencies, most of the creative production involves writing press releases and developing press kits.

Advertising and public relations agencies, however, also include an array of support services. For example, a public relations agency will survey the media to see where a company has been mentioned and assess the impact of what has been said; it will help the client develop its public relations strategy through research and other mechanisms. The agency reaches out to the media to set up interviews for the officials of its clients with the appropriate media, and to prep those officials as to how to interact effectively with the press. Public relations agencies often plan events and will even intercede with communities of interest and serve as the client's representative, particularly when the organization must interact with a governmental body.

In the past, when the lines between different media industries were drawn fairly sharply, there was not much overlap in career opportunities, with the exception being that print journalists often moved over to public relations. Public relations practitioners rarely moved into journalism. Television reporters rarely became print reporters, and print reporters very infrequently moved to broadcast. Advertising by and large was isolated from the other media industries. That has changed in recent years and the boundaries separating the different industries have been blurred.

NEW POSITIONS

The Internet and media convergence have had a dramatic impact on media jobs and careers as well as other aspects of communication. Perhaps the most dramatic impact is in journalism. For people entering the field, the distinction between print reporter and broadcast journalist, and between people being "in front of the camera" or "behind the camera," has been obliterated. An increasingly common entry-level position in journalism now is called a "backpack" journalist. A backpack journalist is supposed to be able to report, write for the Web, shoot video, edit that video, and post it to appropriate Internet sites. In short, a backpack journalist has to be able to perform virtually every aspect of producing a story in print and for broadcasting.

Backpack journalist is only one of the new kinds of titles associated with Internet-based media. Among the new job classifications in journalism are community producer, online producer, and interactive producer. The responsibilities of the community producer, for example, are to focus and manage social interaction through blogs, Wikis, and other social media. The online producer primarily posts news to a Web site. A Web developer creates applications for the Web site, while a Web designer works on the look and feel of the Web site. There are also job titles such as Web reporter, Web journalist, and multimedia journalist. "Director of content" and "chief content officer" are two of the new job titles given to people who are in charge of developing content for a media organization.

Clearly, all these job functions are also appropriate for advertising, public relations, and virtually every media organization. There are other new job titles associated with advertising and public relations agencies, including "director of search engine optimization," "new media specialist," "content analyst," and "interactive specialist." What most of the new jobs have in common is that they require people to combine and understand the underlying process and techniques associated with the area with which they are associated—people working in journalism have to understand the techniques of journalism—with some technological sophistication. People entering the field have to learn what to do and to master the technical skills to get it done. Because the rate of technical changes is rapid, there is high demand for people with cutting-edge skills and for people who can learn and adapt quickly.

NEW VOICES

The revolution in communication triggered by the Internet has opened up new career paths and new career directions. The following snapshots illustrate the different ways people have capitalized on these new opportunities.

In the First Person: Chris Capellini

I graduated from Loyola College in Maryland in 1999 with a BA in Communications with an advertising concentration and minors in studio art and business. In addition to the core, major, and minor requirements, I focused my course schedule on graphic and digital design, culminating in an independent study senior year on multimedia design.

After graduating I worked at a small advertising agency in Manhattan, formerly Chinnici Direct, now Company C (a division of Kershenbaum Bond Senecal + Partners). I spent nine years there, reaching the level of art supervisor before leaving in May of 2008 to join ESPN as an associate art director for digital media.

During my time at Company C, I worked on a variety of client accounts including Chase, John Deere, Capital One, Virgin Atlantic Airways, MetLife, Fidelity, Cablevision, Barnes & Noble, and Bloomberg News Radio. My main responsibilities included conceptual work, print, and digital design. By the time I left the agency I had become the lead digital designer, working on digital campaigns for all of our clients and leading the redesign of metlifebank.com.

At ESPN my primary focus is the user experience, interface, and visual design across all the digital properties. I am a member of the design department's senior staff and help manage the day-to-day activities of the department as well as provide insight into the future direction of the group and digital media as a whole. When I first started, my main focus was to help lead the redesign of espn.com, which went live at the beginning of 2009. Since then, I've taken on the role of lead designer for Premium Products, SportsNation, Member Services, and ESPN3.com. I occasionally take on freelance projects when time allows. I hope to one day open my own design shop.

Markos Moulitsas Zúñiga

Moulitsas founded the *Daily Kos*, a blog and aggregator of political news, in May 2002 and created a buzz by approaching political communications in a new and innovative way. Besides the traditional role of news organization, Moulitsas's Web site is a community and center for political activism. The *Daily Kos* attracts large audiences, as well as an impressive cast of contributors, including then-Senator Barack Obama, Nancy Pelosi, the speaker of the U.S. House of Representatives, and Harry Reid, the majority leader of the U.S. Senate.

Moulitsas also has attracted contributions from thousands of Americans who make up the political mainstream and has successfully created an electronic "town-hall meeting" that invites all of the public to participate. One critic estimated that during the 2008 election, the *Daily Kos* had an estimated 3.7 million readers every week. That is more than the combined readership of the top ten political opinion magazines.

In an interview, Moulitsas discussed how the *Daily Kos* differs from the print media. "*Daily Kos* offers community, which is something the traditional media don't offer. Really, I don't see us in competition, so I don't see a gap to be bridged."

John Lapp, executive director of the Democratic Party's Congressional Campaign Committee, sees Moulitsas as creating a new political model that uses communications to revolutionize the way politics is done. Moulitsas has created a "signal event in political history, like the Kennedy—Nixon debates, in how it gets people involved," he said.

Moulitsas's biggest test as a communicator came in April 2004, when he decided to post articles about Blackwater USA, a private armed security firm that was providing protection to nonmilitary personnel in Iraq. Moulitsas wrote about Blackwater personnel shooting and killing Iraqi civilians. Moulitsas saw the Blackwater guards as mercenaries. The Iraq War was still popular at the time, and his articles prompted political groups to pull their advertising or remove their links.

An Army veteran, Moulitsas stood tough, saying, "Let the people see what war is like. This isn't an Xbox game. There are real repercussions to Bush's folly. That said, I feel nothing over the death of mercenaries. They aren't in Iraq because of orders, or because they are there trying to help the people make Iraq a better place. They are there to wage war for profit. Screw them."

In the First Person: Keith Thomas

I graduated from Loyola College in Maryland in 1994 as a political science major. From there, I went directly to Brandeis University for my master's degree in politics, with the idea that this was to be my first step in route to a Ph.D. After graduate school I decided to "take a detour" by doing a year of service in the now defunct Marianist Voluntary Service Communities (MVSC). Service in the MVSC took me to Cincinnati, Ohio, where I worked for People Working Cooperatively (PWC). PWC is a non-profit home repair organization dedicated to providing emergency and critical home repair and weatherization services that allow low-income homeowners to continue living safely in their own homes. I worked in several departments in PWC, learned a lot, and got to know some wonderful people.

Following my time in Cincinnati, I returned to Maryland where I did a number of things until another itch to broaden horizons took me to Buenos Aires, Argentina. For my first four years in Buenos Aires, I taught business English for a number of institutes, and also dabbled in freelance writing. Since 2005 I have worked in the marketing department of IT Convergence, a global Oracle services provider that maintains a very large offshore office in Buenos Aires. My role there has grown from working as the marketing communications writer to my current position as marketing communications analyst, where I focus on planning campaigns and lead generation. I also teach political science on a part-time basis at Universidad Austral.

Brian Stelter

Brian Stelter developed a widely followed blog while attending Towson University, a regional university located about eight miles from Baltimore, Maryland. When he was only 21 years old, Stelter saw a large hole in coverage of the cable-television industry. In early 2003, when the war in Iraq began, Stelter decided to create a blog to track cable-news coverage of the invasion. He registered the blog name CableNewser.com and launched the site on January 1, 2004. Almost immediately, CableNewser attracted an audience of television executives, anchors, producers, and viewers. As a news junkie, he wrote about the good, the bad, and the ugly of Fox News, CNN, and MSNBC. The site started as a critique of the networks, but became more of a newsfeed of ratings, rumors, and reviews.

Stelter initially did not disclose that he was a college student out of concern that no one would take him seriously. After a year of writing the cable-news blog, Stelter started corresponding with a reporter for *The New York Times* and revealed his "day job" as a college freshman. Few could imagine that network presidents, media executives, producers, and publicists would religiously read a blog with a URL ending with towson.edu. Those who praised his blog included Brian Williams, anchor of *NBC Nightly News*, and Jonathan Klein, president of CNN's domestic operations.

One reward for his outstanding blog was an invitation to the White House Correspondents' Dinner as a guest of MSNBC. "He was quite a celebrity," said Jeremy Gaines, a spokesman for MSNBC. "Literally two tables over was George Clooney, and at our table was [Stelter] and people were waiting in line to see him."

In 2004, Stelter formed a partnership with MediaBistro, which operates a Web site that covers all aspects of creating and distributing content. He expanded his "beat" to include network news operations, such as ABC, NBC, and CBS, renaming his blog "TVNewser." In May 2007, only a few days from graduation, Stelter met with five *New York Times* editors, including Deputy Managing Editor Jon Landman. The interview resulted in a job with the *Times*. "It was time to stop reporting on reporters and start *being* a reporter," Stelter said in an interview.

In the First Person: Megan Sapnar Ankerson

I graduated from Loyola College in Maryland in 1996 with a BA in Communication. Although I originally planned to work in advertising (my specialization) after college, I found myself much more interested in learning about this new communications medium, the World Wide Web. Since the Internet was still very new to the advertising world at this time, I decided to postpone an advertising career to learn as much as I could about the Internet.

A friend suggested that I contact my former professor Dr. Elliot King, who had done a lot of Internet-related work. Dr. King taught me the basics and invited me to become his teaching assistant for Loyola's new "Web publishing" course. This opportunity helped me learn Web production skills quickly, while also introducing me to some of the bigger questions surrounding the cultural impact of new media technologies. I realized that studying new media was as important to me as producing it, so I pursued a Masters degree at Georgetown University in Communication, Culture, and Technology while continuing to both teach at Loyola and work as a Web designer.

In 2003, I decided to go back to graduate school for a Ph.D. in Media and Cultural Studies at the University of Wisconsin-Madison. My dissertation examines the cultural production of the commercial Web during the dot-com boom, a topic inspired by my own early experiences teaching and working in new media. I am now an Assistant Professor in Communication Studies at the University of Michigan, where my research interests include Web history, visual culture, software studies, and digital archiving. In the future, I plan on turning my dissertation project into a book, and I hope to contribute to archival efforts in preserving the digital visual culture of the early Web.

Susan Harris

Susan Harris is one of the country's most popular garden writers. A resident of Takoma Park, Maryland, just outside of Washington, D.C., Harris had a strong interest in gardening and decided she needed to know more on the subject. That desire would result in Harris's being certified as a Master Gardener and earning a reputation as a great gardening coach. *The New York Times* and CBS would feature her in stories about personal coaches.

About that time, Harris started developing an interest in writing about gardening, although she did not have a writing background. First, she took the traditional route, contacting local papers about writing a gardening column. After some initial rejections, she landed a column with an alternative monthly newspaper. With help from local writers, Harris polished her writing style and developed her talent for writing. Harris then started looking at the possibilities the Internet offered. However, she discovered that the type of writing that worked well in her print columns was not successful in a blog. What looked good in print seemed flat and dull when posted on a Web site. Undeterred, Harris retooled her writing style for an online presence. This meant "adding a personal element, more active voice, and not sounding overly 'scientific,'" she told an interview.

The more vivid approach to writing was even more successful in reflecting Harris's passion for gardening. She soon drew large audiences that appreciated her fresh, organic approach to gardening that emphasized, among other things, using native local plants and rejecting heavy use of pesticides and chemicals.

She launched several blogs that catered to different audiences and gardening needs: a gardening coach blog, a Web site for the D.C. Urban Gardeners, and another Web site, "Regional Garden Gurus," which provided information and resources to promote regional gardening education online.

Harris would later win an award for "Best Organic Blog" from an international competition. The blog included hundreds articles covering gardens and gardening, and the occasional off-topic excursion.

When three nationally recognized writers—Elizabeth Licata, Michele Owens, and Amy Stewart—decided to launch a national gardening Web site, they invited Harris to join them. The four writers' blog, *GardenRant*, has a national following and has won many awards for Web sites, such as Best Garden Blog, Most Innovative Garden Blog, and Best Written Blog, from a jury of their peers.

Harris's success with the Internet also has resulted in success in the print media, where she is writing for several of the leading gardening publications, such as *Fine Gardening*. Harris also used her connection with the Internet to create a series of videos on sustainable gardening. Harris also works with numerous environmental and gardening groups to promote more Earth-friendly practices, such as better land use. Harris was contacted in November 2008 by Michelle Obama's office and volunteered to pull together "suggestions" for changes to the White House grounds. The resulting proposal then morphed into the media campaign "Green the Grounds," which encourages sustainable landscaping practices at the White House and official residences of U.S. governors and mayors.

In the First Person: Tina (Lariviere) Capellini

I graduated from Loyola College in Maryland in 1999 where I majored in communications with an advertising concentration and a minor in Business. Aside from the core curriculum, I took classes in graphic design, HTML development, marketing, statistics, and accounting. After graduating, I had a year-long paid internship with a business incubator in California named Net Effect Technologies. During this year, I designed and coded Web sites for the companies they were supporting, such as chemIndustry.com, kidstation.com, softrade.com, and floorsavers.com.

When the internship was over I got a job at Pavlika Chinnici Direct, an advertising agency in New York City, where I designed credit cards and print material for Chase Manhattan Bank, and worked on pitches for companies such as Mini Cooper and Brummel & Brown. When approached with an opportunity to enter into a career in magazine publishing, I left Pavlika Chinnici Direct to work for Unisphere Media. My job included working on monthly magazines designing layouts, web sites, and email newsletters. I am currently self-employed. I have freelanced for companies such as Gevalia Kaffe (Kraft), Focus Financial Partners, Virgin Atlantic Airways, Pearson Education, ALM, Revivogen, and Knowledge Delivery Systems. In the future I would like to get back into the magazine publishing world whether it is online or print.

Lisa Lillien, also known as "Hungry Girl"

Lillien writes a food blog from the reader's point of view. Her original approach to writing about food has attracted thousands of readers who follow her blogs, e-mail messages, and books. As she tells her audience: "I'm not a nutritionist, I'm just hungry."

Much of her appeal lies in the fact that she does not preach to her readers, but instead empathizes with them. As she says about herself, "I'm just an average female, struggling with the same food issues most females struggle with every day. I try the latest fad diets, chomp on new fat free foods & diet products, and yes, I too order everything on the side. I consider myself a foodologist ... not because I have some kind of fancy degree, but because I am obsessed with food, how wonderful it is, and how much of it will make it impossible for me to fit into my pants. Food is my passion and it has been my lifelong obsession."

On her Web site, Lillien approaches diets and food as one would pursue any other news beat, sharing her information with her public. "Because I obsess over food, I learn about it, read about it, research it, and dream about it. Nothing gives me a thrill like discovering a new low-cal snack or assembling a no-fat pizza. Over the years my food obsession has caused me to accumulate approximately a zillion diet and food tips, and because I am not only hungry, but also very nice, I want to share them with you."

In a typical day, Lillien will test a variety of food dishes, evaluating them from the viewpoint of someone wanting to eat something that is delicious but also healthy and low calorie. Her relentless pursuit of better ways of eating has resulted in more than a million subscribers to her *Hungry Girl* Web site. Her first book, *Hungry Girl: Recipes and Survival Strategies for Guilt-Free Eating in the Real World*, sold more than 600,000 copies.

In her writing, Lillien will attack an issue with the zeal of an investigative reporter. One continuing issue in her blogs has been nutrition labels. Lillien wants the Food and Drug Administration to enforce more honest reporting of calories and nutrients. Her chief complaint is that the labels understate calories by using unrealistic portion sizes.

For Lillien, *Hungry Girl* is light-years from her first job in communication: editor-in-chief for *Tutti Frutti*, a *Tiger Beat* kind of teen celebrity magazine. She later moved into television, working as executive producer for TV Land Online and director of convergence development at Nickelodeon Online.

Hungry Girl started when Lillien drove forty miles to have her favorite low-fat pastries tested at a lab. They were not low-fat at all. "People lie," she says. "Whether or not it's malicious, there's a lot of mislabeled stuff out there." The experience would lead to her launching *Hungry Girl*.

Once *Hungry Girl* was launched, it quickly built a following. "We've never spent one penny to advertise it," says Lillien, who adds that she chose an e-mail blast because she wanted people to want it, to sign up for it, to pass it along. One reason for Lillien's large following has been her code of ethics. She does not accept payment in exchange for a review or mention in her daily e-mail. She also accepts advertising dollars only from products she personally uses.

Lillien understands that her credibility is absolutely crucial to her success. If she compromised her standards, it would kill her efforts. "People would see right through that," she says. "That would water down the power of the brand."

In the First Person: Mike Memoli

As a communication major and political science minor from day one, my studies at Loyola College in Maryland pointed me in the right direction for a career as a political reporter. My course selection in the department—from Empirical Rhetoric and Journalism I to the capstone seminars—honed the skills I rely on to this day. My experience in the department's converged media study abroad program and extracurricular work as editor of *The Greyhound* newspaper also proved to be valuable.

Upon graduating in 2004, I entered a Washington-based political journalism internship program, which led to a full time position with *The Hotline*, a daily political newsletter. After three years I joined NBC's team of political reporters covering the 2008 presidential campaign, a post that took me all over the country following candidates right up to the historic election. For more than a year now, I've covered the White House and national politics for *Real Clear Politics*.

The media landscape is constantly changing, which is one reason I find it's an exciting time to be a reporter. In the near future it is my hope to stay in the political mix, while also continuing to train myself in the developing social/new media craft.

Joshua Micah Marshall

Marshall launched *Talking Points Memo* (*TPM*) in 2000, which to some looks like a prototype for the news Web site of the future. Marshall had a doctorate from Brown University in history, but the academic world did not excite him as much as writing about politics. The Internet was in its infancy, and Marshall started designing Web sites for law firms and then launched a Web site on Internet law.

His knowledge about the Internet led to a career as a freelance journalist who specialized in articles about free speech and the Web. In turn, he was hired as an editor for a liberal political magazine, the *American Prospect*. However, he often fought his editors over the direction of the magazine and its political viewpoint. About the same time, bloggers started to appear on the Internet. To Marshall, this was a godsend. "I really liked what seemed to me to be the freedom of expression of this genre of writing," Marshall told the *Columbia Journalism Review*. "And, obviously, given the issues that I had with the *Prospect*, that appealed to me a lot." Marshall left the magazine and launched *TPM*.

The new Web site had its first major news scoop when Marshall publicized remarks by then—Senate Majority Leader Trent Lott of Mississippi that praised Strom Thurmond's 1948 presidential run as a segregationist. The following uproar would cause Lott to resign his leadership position in the Senate. By the end of 2004, Marshall found himself one of a handful of what *The New York Times Magazine* dubbed "elite bloggers" who earned enough money to make blogging a full-time occupation.

In 2007, Marshall investigated a story that would result in *TPM's* becoming the first blog to win the George Polk Award for Legal Reporting, one of the most coveted journalism honors. Marshall would use time-tested investigative techniques combined with the possibilities of the Internet to expose a national scandal. It began when a *TPM* reader noticed that the U.S. Attorney for the Eastern District of Arkansas was being replaced with a former Karl Rove adviser. Marshall discovered that U.S. Attorney Carol Lam in San Diego was also being asked to resign. Lam had successfully prosecuted Republican Randall "Duke" Cunningham, a member of the U.S. House of Representatives, on bribery charges and reportedly was conducting an ongoing criminal investigation into a congressional scandal of historic proportions.

"I was stunned by it," Marshall told the *Financial Times*. "Normally, in a case like that, the prosecutor would be untouchable," Marshall said. The mainstream media largely ignored the matter. By the time *The New York Times* reported on Lam's firing, *TPM* had posted 15 articles on the story.

With bulldog tenacity, Marshall stayed with the story until it was disclosed to the public that President George W. Bush had fired an unprecedented seven U.S. Attorneys. Although there was nothing illegal in Bush's actions, reports raised serious questions that the seven were removed for political reasons—including some who were fired for refusing to initiate investigations against Democrats running for reelection. Never before had the White House injected such political interference into the work of the U.S. Attorneys.

The mainstream media realized that Marshall and *TPM* had uncovered a major news story that had huge ripple effects—including the resignation of then—Attorney General Alberto Gonzales.

Marshall describes *TPM* as a "hybrid" approach to news-reporting that combines traditional news-gathering techniques with a heavy reliance on readers for tips on possible stories. Marshall calls his audience "my first line of surveillance," adding that he constantly receives solid leads from the public. At the same time, Marshall and his staff of 12 full-time journalists constantly watch the news for potential stories. If a tip seems promising, the *TPM* staff will check out its reliability in what Marshall calls a "collaborative" process. Marshall and his staff also will analyze stories from numerous news sources to create a fresh look for an important news story. For example, in the case of the U.S. Attorneys, *TPM* reviewed many local articles about federal prosecutors being forced from office and drew a national picture for readers.

Marshall sees advantages in having *TPM* online as opposed to being in print. "We have kind of broken free of the model of discrete articles that have a beginning and end. Instead, there are an ongoing series of dispatches." In addition to pursuing tips from its readers, *Talking Points Memo* has been known to give them assignments, such as wading through virtual piles of documents released by the administration.

Nan Aron, president of the Alliance of Justice, a liberal legal-affairs group in Washington, D.C., explained the value of *TPM*: "There are certain stories like the U.S. attorneys that might never have seen the light of day had *TPM* not pursued it in the way that they had." Aron added, "We now count on *TPM* and other blogs to do the investigative work that reporters used to do."

In the First Person: Cara Weigand

During my junior year at Loyola College in Maryland, I realized it was a good time to start to take my major, Communications with a focus in journalism, more seriously and get an internship to find out what I really enjoyed doing on a daily basis. I applied to a number of businesses in the communications field. When I received the public relations internship with IMRE, I knew little about what I was getting into as I had only taken one public relations class and had mostly journalism credits.

Two weeks into the internship, I realized that the topics I learned in PR 101 covered the majority of what can be learned about PR out of a textbook. I also learned that I actually enjoyed PR more than I realized and that it would be a career I could see myself doing.

My internship immediately proved itself invaluable and transformed from something to simply throw on my résumé to the experience that taught me about myself—what I liked, strengths, and weaknesses—and solidified the importance of work ethic and initiative. After graduation in 2008, I pursued a year working abroad, which I quickly learned wasn't the best opportunity for me at the time. I wound up back at home with little savings and found myself drowning among the millions of other recent grads in the job search. I got a job waiting tables and began networking with contacts from Loyola, family, friends, and of course, internships.

Thankfully the experience I gained at IMRE gave me the connections I needed to earn a job with the company two months after I returned from Europe. I started as an assistant account executive working with a variety of clients in IMRE's Home & Building category including Target, John Deere, and DEWALT. A year and half later,

I am an account executive working with those same clients and more, and I am still as passionate about my work as I was the day I started. I think that stems from the fact that I not only like the work, but I like the clients. I've always enjoyed design, architecture, and building, and working with clients in these industries is a natural interest of mine. IMRE also has established a Sustainability Practice that focuses on clients tied to various eco-conscious and sustainable initiatives, which is another passion of mine.

Not only am I interested in the client base, but I also do a variety of work on a daily basis—it's never slow or monotonous, and it's not just writing press releases. Every week I get to reach back to my journalism roots as I write blog posts for IMRE's HomeIntel blog, and on a daily basis I am building relationships with media and industry influencers. In between I am following blogs and news looking for new trends and products, and soaking up everything I can to become an expert in the home, building, and sustainability landscapes. I have not stopped learning since the day I started at IMRE, whether it's about the business of public relations or the latest technology in cloud computing or power tools.

Most importantly I feel like I still have room to grow. I approach every day with a new set of near-term goals, and a constant set of long-term goals. I am determined to keeping moving and not become sedentary or stuck. In my current position I have options and the big goals never seem too far out of reach.

Mike Tidwell

Tidwell is an example of someone with a print journalism background who creates communication, both electronic and print, that matters. In Tidwell's case, his cause is saving the Earth from environmental harm. Tidwell, a travel writer, knew nothing about the environmental perils facing the Louisiana Bayou when he went there to write an article on Cajun culture. Sent on assignment by the *Washington Post*, Tidwell's concept was to hitchhike among the shrimp boats to get to know the local community. However, he quickly saw that something was going terribly wrong with the land.

While talking to the Cajun locals, he heard stories of swampland ruined by environmental damage and usable land being submerged underwater by poor land planning. Tidwell took his experiences and wrote in 2003 a breakthrough book, *Bayou Farewell*, which recounted how government efforts to protect urban areas of Louisiana caused great harm to the state's Gulf region and set the stage for incredible damage that occurred when Hurricane Katrina hit the state in 2005.

In the wake of Katrina, people started reading Tidwell's book, discovering that the destruction of the Bayou actually helped set the stage for the devastation caused by Katrina. Since Katrina, Tidwell has become a voice for the environment, using all forms of media to reach audiences. While he uses traditional print to write about environmental concerns, he also makes use of the Internet and video to show how environmental issues affect all Americans in every part of the country.

Tidwell is a sought-after speaker on environmental issues. Tidwell created the Chesapeake Climate Action Network, a grassroots nonprofit organization dedicated to raising awareness about the impacts and solutions associated with global warming in Maryland, Virginia, and Washington, D.C. He also has written a book about the aftermath of Katrina.

Tidwell has also produced a documentary film that reveals how global warming has harmed a unique fishing village in Maryland: *We Are All Smith Islanders*. The film depicts the dangers of global warming to a small Maryland community that relied on the Chesapeake Bay, only to see their livelihood destroyed when pollution killed the Bay.

He further hosts a nationally syndicated radio show, *Earthbeat*, which features groundbreaking global-warming news and interviews live from the nation's capital. In 2003, Tidwell received the Audubon Naturalist Society's prestigious Conservation Award.

Public relations in the future will probably model itself after the efforts of individuals such as Tidwell. This multimedia approach to public relations means that organizations with something to say do not have to rely on the traditional media to be heard. If newspapers and television will not provide a forum, there are plenty of opportunities for reaching the public, such as voicing opinions on the Internet, whether it is a blog or a video posted on YouTube.

In the First Person: Ashley Bertrand

I graduated from Loyola College in Maryland in 2005 with a degree in Communications with a focus in advertising, and a minor in Marketing. In addition to the communications courses offered on campus, I decided to take an internship at a Baltimore agency called gkv communications, Maryland's largest marketing communications firm serving local, regional, national, and international clients in travel and tourism, consumer goods, financial services, high tech, B2B, entertainment, hospitality, state government, health care, education, multi-outlet retailers, the food industry, and in biotechnology. This experience fostered an interest in account management. As a result, my goal after college was to gain an entry level position in this field.

Shortly after graduation, I was hired as an account coordinator for gkv in their social marketing division, gkv REACH. Social marketing was something I had only read about in textbooks, but my passion for it grew quickly as I discovered that I found marketing for a cause to be something special and important. In addition to traditional services like radio, TV, print, and interactive, I work with clients to create community outreach programs and grassroots-style promotions. I have worked on and created campaigns for a variety of clients including those related to state government, health care, smoking cessation, universities, and a professional sports team.

As I continued to grow within the division, I took on additional roles for new business projects and managed several teams of outreach staff. Five years later you can still find me with gkv REACH, where I am now a senior account manager. In the future, I hope to continue my growth in the field of social marketing, while finding ways to influence others' lives for the better.

CONCLUSION

Communications and the media industries are in a transition. This has opened up exciting new career possibilities, both in established fields, such as advertising, public relations, and journalism, and in new fields related to the Internet, such as Web development and social media management. In fact, a revolutionary new media landscape is forming, and professionals entering the field over the next few years will play critical roles in creating and cultivating it.

To thrive in the new environment will be challenging. People entering a career in the media industries will have to have to be able to think broadly about the way communication and media operate in society. They will have to understand the social impact of media on politics, entertainment, and the marketplace, and in building community. They will need the technical skills to be able to create and distribute appropriate content for the media as well as understand the characteristics and criteria of what constitutes great content for different channels of communication. Finally, people entering the media field over the next several years will need the enthusiasm and courage to take advantages of the opportunities they will encounter.

The free flow of information is the greatest force for democracy in the world and plays a significant role in cultural development as well. The media environment is getting more global and more local at the same time. A blog might be read by millions of people worldwide or by a handful of local followers. Either way, the blog's content can be very meaningful. Moreover, with communication technology changing at breakneck speed, new possibilities for communication professionals are constantly emerging.

In the final analysis, communication is the quintessential human activity. It is the basis for society. As such, communication professionals play essential roles in shaping global society today and into the foreseeable future.

Index